# The Great Famine

AT THE GATE OF A WORKHOUSE. 1846.

# The Great Famine

## STUDIES IN IRISH HISTORY 1845–52

EDITORS

### R. DUDLEY EDWARDS

*Professor of Modern Irish History, University College, Dublin*

### T. DESMOND WILLIAMS

*Professor of Modern History, University College, Dublin*

WITH A NEW INTRODUCTION
AND BIBLIOGRAPHY BY

### CORMAC Ó GRÁDA

*Associate Professor of Economics, University College, Dublin*

THE LILLIPUT PRESS

MCMXCIV

First published in 1956 by
BROWNE AND NOLAN LTD

This edition published in 1994 by
THE LILLIPUT PRESS LTD
4 Rosemount Terrace, Arbour Hill,
Dublin 7, Ireland.

A CIP record for this
title is available from
The British Library.

ISBN 0 946640 94 7

Cover design by Jarlath Hayes
Printed in Dublin by
ßetaprint

# Acknowledgements

THE Editors wish to express their sincere gratitude to the Director and staff of the National Library of Ireland for their willing help and for the facilities they provided and to the Trustees of the Library for giving permission to publish many of the illustrations included in this volume. The Editors would also like to express their thanks to Professor J. H. Delargy, Director of the Irish Folklore Commission, who initially suggested the project of writing a history of the Great Famine, and to the staff of the Irish Folklore Commission for their willing help.

The Editors take this opportunity of thanking the Government of Ireland for the generous financial grant which has made possible the publication of this volume.

The Editors also wish to acknowledge the services of Professor T. W. Moody and the late Professor J. F. O'Doherty who, for a period, acted as editors of the work. To Dr K. H. Connell a special word of thanks is due for reading and commenting on the manuscript.

The Editors finally have pleasure in acknowledging their indebtedness to Mrs. Maureen Wall, Miss Joyce Padbury and Dr K. B. Nowlan for their constant and patient assistance in the preparation of this volume.

# Foreword

It is difficult to know how many men and women died in
Ireland in the famine years between 1845 and 1852. Perhaps
all that matters is the certainty that many, very many died. The
Great Famine was not the first nor the last period of acute distress
in Irish history. The Great Famine may be seen as but a period
of greater misery in a prolonged age of suffering, but it has left
an enduring mark on the folk memory because of its duration
and severity. The famine is seen as the source of many woes,
the symbol of the exploitation of a whole nation by its oppressors.
If only because of its importance in the shaping of Irish national
thought, the famine deserves examination. But it was much
more than a mere symbol. The economic and social influences
of the famine were considerable ; many of the most persistent
trends in modern Irish life emerge with the famine, while the years
of distress also saw the end of a phase in the agitation for national
self-government. In Irish social and political history the famine
was very much of a watershed. The Ireland on the other side
of those dark days is a difficult world for us to understand, the
Ireland that emerged we recognise as one with problems akin
to our own.

In the year 1848, Charles Gavan Duffy, the Young Irelander,
full of anger and mortification could cry out that the famine was
nothing less than, ' a fearful murder committed on the mass of
the people'. That indictment has come down to us alive and
compelling in the writings of John Mitchel. This famine, which
saw the destruction of the cottier class and forced some 3,000,000
people to live on charity in the year 1847, was something which
went to the very basis of Irish society. It is easy to say, at a
distance of a century, that men like Mitchel and Gavan Duffy
wrote in an exaggerated way about the famine and that it was
quite absurd for P. A. Sillard, the biographer of John Mitchel,
to compare a respectable whig administrator, like Lord Clarendon,
with the stern Elizabethan Lord Mountjoy, who destroyed the

vii

very crops of his enemies. These accusations may be exaggerated, but their influence on Irish thought and the sincerity with which they were made can hardly be doubted.

In the existing commentaries on the famine period, it is possible to detect two trends of thought related but yet distinct. On the one hand, we find that the more actively the writer was interested in political nationalism, the more determined he appeared to place full personal responsibility on the British government and its agents for what happened in Ireland. So it was with Gavan Duffy and later with Arthur Griffith, who could say that the British government deliberately used 'the pretext of the failure of the potato crop to reduce the Celtic population by famine and exile'. In contrast to this approach, we find the heirs of Fintan Lalor less willing to see in the Great Famine a conscious conspiracy against the nation. For them the disaster has a more organic, less deliberate origin. It was the social system rather than government which was at fault. James Connolly, in his acute analysis of Irish society, could declare : 'No man who accepts capitalist society and the laws thereof can logically find fault with the statesmen of England for their acts in that awful period'. But whether Connolly's important reservations be accepted or not, the famine, as a social phenomenon, as a testing time for the nineteenth-century state is entitled to the closest study by the modern historian. The political commentator, the ballad singer and the unknown maker of folk-tales have all spoken about the Great Famine, but is there more to be said ?

The Great Famine was a challenge to its age ; an age which saw the rapid expansion of British industry and wealth and the temporary triumph of liberal concepts in economic and political affairs. The state, in the eighteen-forties, was in the curious position of having shed the trappings of the old mercantilist world without fully realising the extent of the demands which the new era with its great cities and vast populations would eventually make on the legislature. The timidity and remoteness of the administrators in the eighteen-forties may irritate the modern observer who unhesitatingly accepts the moral responsibility of the state to intervene in economic affairs in a time of crisis. But it needs patience to realise that what is obvious and uncontroversial today was dark and confused a century ago to many persons of good will. The study of the administration of relief, by Mr T. P. O'Neill, and of the medical aspects of the disaster, by Sir William P. MacArthur, show how seriously some cabinet ministers were troubled by the famine and yet, despite that anxiety, how inadequate were the measures adopted. In earlier famines men had died unnoticed by their rulers, but the new humanitarianism of the nineteenth century gradually forced upon reluctant minds a more delicate appreciation of the sufferings of others.

The tide of hunger and death burst through the forms of the science of political economy and the whig administration of Lord John Russell was compelled to depart so far from its principles as to permit the free distribution of food to the starving population in the summer of 1847. This belated emancipation, although it partly checked the course of the famine, was nevertheless not sufficiently strong to induce men to sweep away those conditions which made famine possible in Ireland. The victory was a modest one, for the laws of political economy had only been broken with the utmost reluctance. Almost as sinners against the accepted truths of political science, did the British government undertake the formidable task of supervising the distribution of food to a starving nation.

The nineteenth century throughout Europe was a time of heart searching on the subject of agrarian society. It was a heart searching that mirrored the strange conflict between enlightened romanticism and the new and harsh liberal economics. In Prussia, in the Baltic lands, in central Germany and in Russia, the agrarian issue was at the core of the social evolution of that century. In sharp contrast, however, to the Irish pattern of development, reform, in say the Baltic lands, took place within a society which had preserved to a considerable extent a sense of personal responsibility in the relations between landlord and tenant. Racial and cultural tensions did exist in many areas besides Ireland, but the extent to which tenant and landlord were separated from each other could scarcely be paralleled elsewhere in Europe. In Ireland the legal implications of land-ownership had been divorced from the moral duties of a proprietor to his dependents, while land was too often a mere investment, or an encumbered burden which yielded but a reluctant income to its owner. The divorce in culture between landlord and tenant in Ireland was probably as great as that between the Lettish peasant and his German overlord, but in Ireland there were no relics of an outmoded feudalism to shelter the people from the harsh winds of tyranny.

A reform of the Irish social system was essential, if any advance were to be made towards political or economic stability. This was quite obvious to statesmen like Peel and Russell, but what was not so clear to them was how reform could actually be accomplished without that social revolution they could never bring themselves to accept. The Irish problem was much more than one of finding the most effective means of expropriating the Irish landlords. The task of reform was one of great complexity and could only have been carried through with self-lessness, great daring and imagination. Above all, it demanded a deep understanding of the needs and aspirations of a poor, hungry rural people crowded into an underdeveloped island. The spiritual atmosphere of mid-nineteenth-century England was still that of the raw childhood of the industrial revolution tinged with a little of that new security which came with the consolidation of Britain's industrial might. The factory and health legislation testified to a broadening of outlook, but the will to reform had no great strength and the logic of English social development provided no clear or popular argument in favour of radical experiment in Ireland.

The buoyancy of the British economy was not to be found in the undercapitalised Irish rural economy, which had so developed as to ensure that a minimum amount of wealth returned to the land as productive capital investment. It is idle to speculate on the question of whether Ireland on the eve of the famine was or was not overpopulated, since no generalised picture can possibly do justice to the wide contrasts in conditions and opportunities within the country. Within the structure of the society that did exist, however, far too many people were doomed to spend their lives in very great poverty. Possibly a policy directed at giving security of tenure to the tenant farmers alone would not have sufficed, for the problem of the cottiers and landless labourers would have remained. In practice, however, no serious attempt was even made to take the initial step of protecting the tenant farmers. Throughout the famine years, the British parliament proved singularly indifferent to the issue of Irish land reform and no ministry was willing to make it a major political objective.

The legislative measures adopted, in the mid-nineteenth century, display therefore certain distinctive features. Above all they were timid and extremely limited in scope. Dr O. Mac-Donagh, in his study of emigration policy, shows how the British government hesitated and in the end failed to adopt a constructive emigration policy which might have protected the Irish emigrant from some of the hardships he had to endure in seeking a new life overseas. So it was too with land reform, public works schemes and even fiscal reform. The conventions of the day proved stronger than even the best intentions.

In folklore and political writings, the failure of the British government to act in a generous manner is quite understandably seen in a sinister light, but the private papers and the labours of genuinely good men tell an additional story. There was no conspiracy to destroy the Irish nation. The scale of the actual outlay to meet the famine and the expansion in the public relief system are in themselves impressive evidence that the state was by no means always indifferent to Irish needs. But the way in which Irish social problems so frequently overshadowed all else in the correspondence of statesmen, testifies in a still more striking manner to the extent to which the British government was pre-occupied with the famine and distress in Ireland. In the case of a man like Sir Robert Peel, we can trace over the years preceding the Great Famine a growing awareness of the need for change in Ireland, while in the case of Lord John Russell, as Dr K. B. Nowlan points out in his study of the political background to the famine, there developed a strong conviction that only a radical reform of the land system could really restore tranquillity to the country.

Modern research on the administrative and political backgrounds to the Great Famine reveals more clearly the limitations of men in office who were unwilling to rise or incapable of rising effect-ively above the economic conventions of their day and struggling with no outstanding success against a disaster that had its roots deep in Irish history. The disaster originated in that ordering of human affairs which condemned so many to a life-long de-pendence on a single crop. The potato economy, the primitive state of Irish agriculture and the bad relations between landlord and tenant were but different expressions of the same evil, poverty. The Great Famine began when the distribution of the product of the Irish soil ceased to bear any relation to the needs of the occupier and the requirements of a healthy system of agriculture. The dire events of 1846 and 1847 do not stand in isolation and no remedies however well intentioned which treated that crisis as an isolated phenomenon could possibly in a short time solve the long-term causes of Irish distress. The actual catastrophe of famine was a short-term phenomenon, but the evictions and large-scale emigration continued long afterwards. It was only slowly, in the second half of the nineteenth century, thanks to Gladstone's imaginative policy and the land agitation in Ireland, that the British government came to grips with the existing land system, one of the major causes of chronic distress in Ireland.

Political life in Ireland before the famine, as Dr R. B. McDowell shows in his study of the Ireland of the period, was not characterised by any noticeable concentration on agrarian issues. The demand for the repeal of the Act of Union with Great Britain encompassed all, for repeal was seen as the touchstone which would rid the land of the many evils with which it was afflicted. It is possible, therefore, to see the famine as one of the factors which forced men to look beyond the political structure to the economic realities. In Ireland, under the impact of the disaster, there developed a new interest in tenant-right. By 1847 the cry for tenant-right had become almost as loud as the demand for the repeal of the Union. The crisis and the quickening of the demand for tenant-right, however, brought with them no heroic phase in Irish political life and for a long time no leader emerged to replace Daniel O'Connell. Indeed, despite the new interest in the land question no really satisfactory balance between political and economic ends was achieved during the famine years. Mitchel and Fintan Lalor sought such a synthesis, but their efforts went unrewarded, as the history of the eighteen-fifties and sixties testifies.

No class in Irish society really succeeded in escaping from the hardships which the Great Famine brought with it. The dramatic decline in the total population between the census of 1841 and that of 1851 is one illustration of the impact of the famine. But the internal shifts in the structure of the rural population, as Dr E. R. R. Green indicates, are perhaps even more significant. The labouring class almost disappeared and the consolidation of landholdings which followed in the wake of the famine signalised too the passing of the small holder. These changes and the opportunity to emigrate which the famine helped to create gave to the population structure of Ireland a character which outlasted the nineteenth century.

British ministers, conscious of the many deficiencies in the Irish social system, were sometimes apt to blame the Irish landlords for their inactivity during the famine. The evidence all goes to show that while the administrators believed the state was doing much to help the stricken population, the landlords, with some exceptions, were prepared to do comparatively little on their own initiative. There developed consequently for a time in Britain a curiously hostile attitude towards that very class which represented traditionally the British interest in Ireland. In the years 1846 and 1847 the attack on the landlords' position reached its greatest intensity, and there is no doubt that, in the main, the Irish and British criticisms of the landowners were well grounded. But the famine which swept away so many small farmers did little good for the landlords. Heavily encumbered estates needed only a final blow to cripple them, and many a landlord suffered much in the years of shortage and depression. It was no accident that the famine era saw the enactment of the first encumbered estates measure, for by bringing to an end those conditions which enabled the old social structure to survive for so long, the Great Famine prepared the way for those developments which in the end marked the passing of the Irish landlord.

The Great Famine begins to emerge, then, as something too monstrous and too impersonal to be the mere product of individual ill-will or the fiendish outcome of a well-planned conspiracy. Had the successive failures of the potato crop come earlier or later in the century, they might have had very different consequences, but coming as they did in the middle of the century, they were met in a way previous generations would have regarded as humane, but which we must regard as quite inadequate. The excessive tenderness of the administration where private property rights were involved may strike us as unreal, just as it struck some contemporaries, like the Catholic hierarchy in 1847, but it may be remembered that this same elaborate respect for private property was very potent in hampering reform in Britain. The famine problems were approached from the limited viewpoints here described because the state in that era had a different view of its

positive responsibilities to the community ; but that historical
conclusion must never be allowed to obscure another equally
important one, namely, that in the mid-nineteenth century the
rulers of Britain lost an opportunity to carry through a programme
of reform which might well have influenced the future course
of Anglo-Irish relations.  The Great Famine in its own cruel
fashion opened the way for reform.  It was not accompanied
or followed by any determined effort to reconstruct Irish society
on a more just and equitable basis.  Instead of passing laws, the
statesmen of the day deemed it wiser to confine their schemes
for Ireland to the safe speculations of their private correspondence.

There had, of course, been a considerable measure of emigration
from Ireland before the famine, but the half-century that followed
the potato failure saw the foundation of great overseas colonies
of Irish emigrants ; a development which introduced a new and
potent factor into Anglo-Irish relations.  Dr R. J. McHugh's
picture of what the countryman thought about the famine makes
it clear that there was no disharmony between the folk memory
and the writings of the political commentators.  These new
Irish colonists, not unnaturally, remembered the ignominy of the
soup-kitchen, the police-guarded barns and the futile road works.
They could not know or sympathise with men who, within the
limits of contemporary English opinion, tried to curb the excesses
of famine.  The disaster, therefore, which saw the destruction
of one Ireland helped to create another Ireland which was not
confined within the shores of one small island, for the North
American Irish in particular were destined to make a remarkable
contribution to the shaping of modern Irish history.

The traditional interpretation of the Great Famine is fundamental
to an understanding of the character of Irish society in the second
half of the nineteenth century and later.  But if modern research
cannot substantiate the traditional in all its forms, something
surely more sobering emerges which is, perhaps, of greater value
towards an appreciation of the problems that beset all mankind,
both the governors and the governed in every generation.  If
man, the prisoner of time, acts in conformity with the conventions
of society into which he is born, it is difficult to judge him with
an irrevocable harshness.  So it is with the men of the famine era.
Human limitations and timidity dominate the story of the Great
Famine, but of great and deliberately imposed evil in high positions

of responsibility there is little evidence. The really great evil lay in the totality of that social order which made such a famine possible and which could tolerate, to the extent it did, the sufferings and hardship caused by the failure of the potato crop.

In the ultimate analysis, the picture that emerges from modern research has much in common with James Connolly's sketch in *Labour in Irish History*. We may reject his attempt to force the picture into a doctrinaire frame, but we must recognise with him that the evil spirit of the Great Famine was the history of Anglo-Irish relations in the very widest sense over a long period.

.    .    .    .    .    .    .    .    .    .    .

This present collection of studies is a co-operative undertaking by a group of specialists in the period. It does not claim to be a definitive history of the Great Famine but rather a contribution towards such a history. The volume has, therefore, been so arranged as to give in its introductory chapters, dealing with Ireland on the eve of the famine and the agriculture of the period, a concise general account of Irish society in the first half of the nineteenth century. In the chapter on the political background a close study is made of the developments which took place in Irish life during the famine years and of the influence of the food crisis on the relations between Great Britain and Ireland. The manner in which relief was organised and distributed is considered in detail. The beginnings of the great emigration overseas are rather fully examined while the medical problems of the famine and the famine in folklore are discussed in the concluding chapters.

The aspects of the Great Famine which are not dealt with in these pages are obvious enough. A study of the changes in the population structure during and after the famine is a task yet to be undertaken. Before such a study can be made in a satisfactory manner more preliminary research in the form of local surveys will have to be done on such fundamental questions as marriage patterns and the size of farm holdings in the century before the famine. Again, no attempt has been made to discuss at any length the long-term implications of the Great Famine. The editors would have liked to include such an assessment but were precluded from doing so through the dearth of specialised studies in Irish economic history in the late nineteenth and early twentieth centuries. To have awaited the time when such an authoritative survey could be made would have involved an even greater delay in the publication of this volume.

The editors appreciate the services done by pioneers, like the Rev. John O'Rourke, in the history of the famine. The writers of these studies hope that their work will encourage others to examine further the history of a calamity which brought with it so many unexpected consequences for Ireland, Britain and the new worlds of America and Australia.

17 APRIL 1956,                                             R. D. E.
    UNIVERSITY COLLEGE,                 T. D. W.
        DUBLIN.

# Introduction to the New Edition

The tradition of history-writing in Ireland is an ancient one. Much of the associated output, it is true, would not pass muster for objectivity or scholarship today, but modern controversies about 'revisionism' have their precedents in Keating's barbs at Stanyhurst or Madden's defence of the United Irishmen. A century or so ago, the works of Froude and Lecky vied for readers with the more populist accounts of Barry O'Brien or Michael Davitt. Half a century later, with the foundation of the Irish Historical Society and *Irish Historical Studies*, the scene had been set for a new, professionalized Irish history. The revolution inaugurated by a group of young Irish academics had just begun, though it had yet to bear fruit in published research. A lecture delivered in May 1943 by youthful Professor Theo Moody of the Department of Modern History, Trinity College, Dublin to fellow-members of the Irish Historical Society will illustrate the point. Moody's lecture on 'things to be done in [nineteenth-century] Irish history' is now available only in summary form, but reading that summary today highlights the poverty of scholarly research on that period of Irish history. Moody noted the lack of even a satisfactory general outline of modern Irish history, and referred those interested to the *Oxford History of England*. For a general bibliography, he recommended appendices to the *Cambridge Modern History*. The few specialist works on Irish history that Moody considered worth mentioning – George O'Brien's *Economic History of Ireland from the Union to the Famine* (1921), John O'Donovan's *Economic History of Live Stock in Ireland* (1940), Nicholas Mansergh's *Ireland in the Age of Reform and Revolution* (1940), and the works on land tenure by Elizabeth Hooker (1938) and N.D. Palmer (1940) – would be considered dated by most historians today.[1]

Against such competition, *The Great Famine: Studies in Irish History* wins by an Irish mile. Whatever about the evergreen charms of Mansergh, few refer to Hooker or O'Donovan nowadays, and hardly anybody believes O'Brien anymore; by contrast, most of the contributions to *The Great Famine* are still frequently consulted and cited in the literature. The book confronted an important if distressing subject with unprecedented academic rigour, and overall its contents have worn very well indeed. It certainly deserves to be welcomed by a new generation of readers in this inexpensive format.

This classic work of Irish history is one with an interesting history of its own. Most of its authors have since become household names in Irish history-writing. For three of them, their researches on aspects of the Great Irish Famine marked the beginning of distinguished careers as historians. And for all seven authors and both editors, *The Great Famine* was to bulk large in their lives for many years before it reached the bookshops in early 1957. Indeed, there is a link between Theo Moody's lecture to the Irish Historical Society in 1943 and this book, because only a few months after his lecture Moody was appointed – or appointed himself – co-director of the project that would end up, much later, as *The Great Famine*.

This book has a history rich in its implications for the development of Irish historiography in the 1940s and 1950s – and since. The idea of an authoritative study of the Great Famine goes back to early in 1944, when An Taoiseach, Éamon de Valera, proposed that the centenary of the Famine be commemorated with a monograph by 'a trained historian whose name is already favourably known'. The government, unreasonably perhaps, wanted the task completed by 1945 or 1946. In return, it promised the prospective author a fee and a subsidy towards publication. The quest for an expert led to negotiations with the recently-formed Irish Committee of Historical Sciences. Perhaps because there was no obvious candidate, perhaps because the Committee wanted to control the project itself, the ICHS quickly converted the proposal into one of the earliest exercises of cooperative history-writing in Ireland (of which the massive *New History of Ireland* is the best-known example).[2] In some respects, the experiment did not bode well for the approach. Both Professor Robert Dudley Edwards of the Department of Modern Irish History, University College, Dublin and Professor Moody, the key figures at the outset, were formidable men in their very different ways. Neither would then be deemed an expert on the Great Famine – or indeed on the nineteenth century. Yet Moody was already supervising nineteenth-century Ph.D. theses by Hugh Shearman and Rodney Green, and was about to devote himself to the history of Queen's University, Belfast and to Michael Davitt. Both he and Edwards wrote on Thomas Davis and Young Ireland in 1945.

During 1944 Edwards and Moody attempted to capture the Famine project for their planned 'general scheme for the production of historical works', mainly because the government did not want to subsidize the ICHS's non-Irish publisher (Faber & Faber). As a second-best alternative, they undertook to find a local publisher, and to set a number of graduate students to work on a selected list of topics for inclusion in a separate book. It was left to Thomas P. O'Neill, then preparing for his master's degree in University College, Dublin, to propose appropriate topics. Dudley Edwards accordingly promised de Valera's secretary 'separate contributions dealing with the events, medical history, relief (including poor law amendment), emigration, population, agriculture, the people, political implications, the place of the famine in Irish history... a book of approximately 1000 pages... in print in 1946'.[3] Specialist chapters based on masters' dissertations would form the core of the book, but these would be supplemented by contributions from the editors and a few others. For its part the government committed £1500, a very substantial sum of money in those days when professors were paid £700–£800 a year. The agreement between Edwards, on behalf of the ICHS, and Maurice Moynihan, de Valera's secretary (and also Edwards' friend and neighbour!), led to the present volume of just half the promised size and over a dozen years late. The intervening years produced instances of procrastination, wrangles between the editors and civil servants about finance, the mislaying of copy and references, the revising of plans, changes of personnel, and abortive negotations with various publishers.

Moody soon resigned from the project. His replacement, Rev. Professor John Francis O'Doherty, was given 'full responsibilities for the final revision of the work' by the ICHS in January 1947. Father O'Doherty, by all accounts a kind and gentle man, had recently relinquished his chair in ecclesiastical history in Maynooth in difficult circumstances to become a curate in Omagh. He was a curious choice for editor, and seems to have left no mark on the book.[4] Progress on the project was interrupted in 1946–8 by the Foyle Fisheries court case (which involved Moody, Dudley Edwards and other historians as expert witnesses) and by intrigues concerning the plan to create a School of Irish History within the Dublin Institute of Advanced Studies. T.D. Williams[5] replaced O'Doherty in 1949; 29 years old and held in awe by men and women much older, Williams had just been appointed to the chair of Modern History in UCD.

Both the long gestation of *The Great Famine* and its ultimate form are a curious commentary on the writing of Irish history in the 1940s and 1950s. Flawed planning and personality clashes were an important part of the story, which is told in greater detail elsewhere.[6] Between 1946 and 1950 the project lay virtually dormant, but the ICHS and the editors were prodded into productive action in 1950–1 by queries from civil service officials. The core of the book was submitted to the publishers, Browne & Nolan, in December 1954. Much to the annoyance of the editors, *The Great Famine* missed the Christmas market of 1956, reaching the bookshops on 18 January 1957.

It was widely reviewed, thanks in part to Desmond Williams's influence, and the reviews were favourable. The initial print run of two thousand copies virtually sold out within two years. De Valera, then in opposition, received a complimentary copy. He thanked the editors, though it is reported that when it was read for him – he was virtually blind by that stage – he did not much care for the book. His greater enthusiasm for 'amateur historian' Cecil Woodham-Smith's *The Great Hunger* (1962) tells its own tale. Still the world-wide and enduring success of that more evocative study also points to an opportunity lost by professional Irish historians. If Cecil Woodham-Smith was too melodramatic or 'emotive' on occasion – and Roy Foster in an unkind moment has accused her of being a 'zealous convert'[7] – one cannot occasionally escape the feeling when tackling Edwards and Williams of reading 'a narrative as dry and as cold as a Blue Book'.[8] And yet, though some of the contributors to *The Great Famine* did not share de Valera's liking for *The Great Hunger*, the two studies nicely complement each other. *The Great Famine* may lack the narrative account and descriptive 'feel' so usefully provided by Woodham-Smith, but it is more scholarly, more dispassionate, and more analytical. It is also worth pointing out that three of those involved in the Edwards-Williams project, R.B. McDowell, T.P. O'Neill, and Edwards himself, helped Woodham-Smith in her work, and became firm friends with her.

As its curious sub-title indicates, *The Great Famine: Studies in Irish History* never pretended to be the definitive, narrative account envisaged by de Valera in 1944. Half a century later, that account is still awaited. But the ICHS's own early plans were frustrated in several respects. The eventual list of contributors met one of the aspirations of Moody and Edwards – an ecumenical combination of the best talents available, North and South. But the authors responsible for 'economics' (James Meenan), and 'the place of the famine in Irish history' (the editors themselves), never delivered their texts, and the draft of a contribution by Brian Osborne on English public opinion was rejected after the 'implied condemnation' of Moody.[9] Editorial hopes that other scholars such as Kenneth Connell of Queen's University, Belfast, and R.C. Geary of the Central Statistics Office would provide chapters never came to fruition either. Perhaps this explains the administrative-historic focus of *The Great Famine*. The core chapters – by Kevin Nowlan, Oliver MacDonagh, Thomas P. O'Neill, and William McArthur – tackle the tragedy largely from the standpoint of the bureaucrat and the legislator. Nor did Edwards and Williams, as editors, ever confront several other important aspects of the Famine's history – the parts played by the churches and the gombeenman, the 'low' politics of moral economy and agrarian unrest, the working of food markets, landlord behaviour, the concept of the Famine as 'watershed', general economic conditions in the United Kingdom during the crisis, the short- and long-term social and economic consequences, the Famine in literature, the Famine in comparative European perspective, to name a few. Since the volume's publication, the researches of Austin Bourke, Raymond Crotty, Mary Daly, James Donnelly, Liam Kennedy, Joel Mokyr, Peter Solar, and Peter Gray, among others – always building on *The Great Famine* – have plugged some of the gaps. But curiously, perhaps, there is very little of the work included here which has been superceded by them. The sections on the pre-famine economy have dated most, though even they can still be read with benefit. In defence of the editors and the contributors to *The Great Famine*, the raw state of Irish historiography in their heyday must again be stressed. As noted above, very few scholarly monographs had been published on the economic and social history of nineteenth-century Ireland before 1944 (or even by 1957), and on the Famine itself little worthwhile had been published since the accounts of Canon John O'Rourke (1874) and W.P. O'Brien (1896).

Inevitably, the contributions to *The Great Famine* bear some of the methodological hallmarks (and a few of the scars) of the 1940s and 1950s. Some of the authors relied mainly on official printed sources and contemporary newspapers, rather than on the 'private' evidence of estate records, parish registers, emigrant letters, folklore, and popular literature. But that accusation cannot be made against O'Neill, Nowlan, or MacDonagh, and the bias is partly accounted for by the more difficult research conditions the authors faced. In the 1940s the National Library's collection of catalogued manuscripts was only a fraction of that available to scholars today; thousands of manuscripts lay in large wooden boxes with their lids screwed down. Only in the early 1950s did nineteenth-century estate records become widely accessible.[10] The hundred-year rule applied to Famine documents in the State Paper Office, and Irish parishes registers had yet to be microfilmed. Research in London was virtually impossible at a time when some of the authors were at work – in 1945–6.

Another hallmark of the book was the tendency of most authors to shy away from quantitative generalizations or descriptions. The useful map by Thomas P. O'Neill describing the dependence on soup-kitchens by poor law union (p. 242) gives a hint of what might have been done in this respect. Contributors largely ignored the easily available agricultural statistics and failed to exploit quantitative information in the Poor Inquiry or Devon Commission. They emitted conflicting signals on the crucial issue of excess mortality, and offered little information on prices, wages, or agricultural yields. Yet despite such limitations, the book contains a great deal of lasting value. For example, O'Neill's essay on public relief policy has provided a framework for several other researchers to follow. Kevin Nowlan on politics, Oliver MacDonagh on emigration, and Sir William MacArthur on medical aspects of the Famine produced excellent and enduring contributions. O'Neill and MacDonagh, young post-graduate students at University College, Dublin in the mid-1940s, based their chapters on master's dissertations which were commissioned as part of the ICHS project. The dissertations, completed in 1946, were transformed into what would become Chapters IV and VI below in 1950–2. MacDonagh would build on insights gained during his research into the legislation to protect ocean-going passengers during the Famine for his interpretation of nineteenth-century public policy, while O'Neill would become Ireland's acknowledged Famine expert. Kevin Nowlan (Chapter III) was recruited later than MacDonagh and O'Neill, and his able and confident contribution on the political background is largely based on a masters' dissertation completed in 1950. These three chapters provide a foretaste of the quality of scholarship that would emanate later from these academic 'young Turks'. Previous analyses of the Famine, notably those by Canon John O'Rourke (1875) and George O'Brien (1921), had relied largely on the printed word; MacDonagh, Nowlan, and O'Neill were the first to exploit archival material. With them, truly, Famine research came of age.

Sir William MacArthur (Chapter V) was already an established scholar when recruited by the ICHS to write on the medical history of the famine. Belfast-born MacArthur (1884–1964), an enthusiast for the Irish language and former head of the British Army Medical Services, had recently published a paper on 'Famines in Britain and Ireland'.[11] He was one of the first to produce a finished text. Some years later one of the editors, Desmond Williams, mislaid MacArthur's footnotes, and as a result the excellent chapter on medical history appeared virtually without references (see below, p. 469). Williams allegedly attempted to *plámás* the aggrieved MacArthur by claiming that the words of such a fine historian might stand on their own – which turned out to be correct![12]

Chapter VII by non-historian Roger McHugh on folk memories of the tragedy was largely based on replies to an ambitious questionnaire circulated by the Irish Folklore Commission in 1945. That questionnaire, largely devised by Thomas P. O'Neill, yielded almost four thousand pages of evidence from all over the island.[13] McHugh's contribution, also largely completed in the mid-1940s, is the most vivid and evocative in the book. Highly original in the methodological sense, at least by Irish standards, it prompted Dudley Edwards to note in his diary: '[John] Mitchel's popularity is explainable not because he was merely defiant. It was because he correctly interpreted the feeling of the people'. My own analysis of some of the material convinces me that a critical reading of the folklore evidence would return a more equivocal verdict on popular feeling, but the comment raises the question why Irish historians since – with a few exceptions such as Ken Connell – have been so reluctant to invoke such evidence. The case for folklore and oral history as complements to conventional documentary sources finds ample support in the material presented by McHugh. R.B. McDowell's introductory chapter on the economy on the eve of the Famine is wide-ranging and elegant, even if one of the editors privately believed its 'effort to speak well for government and landlords… [is] a little obvious'.[14] Today's readers may judge for themselves! Chapter II on agriculture by the late Rodney Green was shorter and less thorough than the rest, possibly, as Ken Connell reportedly thought, 'because he [Green] was not interested'.[15] Like MacArthur's and McHugh's chapters, Green's was finished in the first phase of the project.

The final outcome was very much a product of University College, Dublin in its Earlsfort Terrace heyday. Both editors and four of the contributors either worked or had served their time there; Browne & Nolan the publishers also had close connections with UCD. For Dudley Edwards, in whose office some of the contributions lay for many years after their arrival in 1946 or 1947, the project was a recurring preoccupation. But without the commitment and the enthusiasm of his colleagues his Kevin Nowlan, Joyce Padbury, and Maureen Wall (*née* McGeehin),[16] the book almost certainly would never seen the light of day.

In the end, despite repeated resolutions to set aside the necessary time to write what was variously described as an historiographical introduction and an epilogue, neither editor contributed a word to the body of the book, nor did they exercise much editorial control on the individual authors. There were plans to issue a companion volume of source documents but they too were dropped. The brief but broad-ranging and thoughtful introduction that did materialize was 'ghosted' by Kevin Nowlan at Desmond Williams's request.[17] The bibliography owes a good deal to that produced by T.P. O'Neill for his MA thesis,[18] and Joyce Padbury, then an associate of the Department of Modern History, contributed the index. That the index was limited to a list of names and places was the editors' decision, not hers. Overall, it must be said that Edwards and Williams performed their editorial duties in a rather lackadaisical manner; Williams, in particular, had too many other fish to fry in the latter stages of the book's gestation. Yet, despite all this, *The Great Famine*, greater than its parts, is a pioneering and an enduring work.

For an early (and friendly) reviewer, the late Professor Leland Lyons, the book proved how 'the Great Famine was a logical consequence of a vicious system of land-holding, a pitifully backward agriculture, and a social structure which invited disaster'.[19] That reading captured an important, if hidden, message of this book, viz. that populist understanding and nationalist propaganda, fed on the *saeva indignatio* of John Mitchel and Archbishop John MacHale of Tuam, had greatly underestimated the deep-seated social and economic reasons for the disaster. The point needed to be made. Moreover, subsequent research in Irish economic and social history has confirmed many of the findings and speculations of *The Great Famine*. Yet that research would also temper the implication of Lyons' apologetic claim that the Famine was somehow inevitable and that *all* the mortality was unavoidable. Dudley Edwards agonized repeatedly over this issue in his private diaries, though his worries failed to influence the content of the book. For Edwards, the fear of sanitized, 'dehydrated history' was very real. *The Great Famine* largely eschewed accounts of the suffering, the cruelty, and the callousness (on all sides) that marked the late 1840s. No doubt, the contributors were reacting to the melodramatic discourse of populist-nationalist accounts. Yet now, over three decades later, the conundrum glossed over by Edwards & Williams remains: 'though the English may not have actually caused [the famine], it was never possible to explain why the richest and most powerful empire in the world was unable to avert its worst consequences'.[20]

The unhappy history of *The Great Famine*'s long gestation must not spoil the pleasure and benefit to be obtained from reading the final product. The book itself achieved a great deal, and with it, nineteenth-century Irish history reached a new level of professionalism. The delays endured by *The Great Famine* reflected the shifting preoccupations and responsibilities of those involved, and it would be quite unfair to blame those delays on the sensitive nature of the topic. Yet they symbolized the reluctance of Irish historians to confront the horror of that tragic event in the 1940s and 1950s. Ironically, Moody's previously-mentioned shopping-list of 'things to be done in [nineteenth-century] Irish history' included topics such as the 'history of the agricultural labourers and of the urban working class... Ireland's contribution to science, her place in the main political and intellectual movements of contemporary Europe, and Irish expansion overseas', but it had failed to mention the Famine.[21] And between its foundation in 1938 and 1956 *Irish Historical Studies* yielded only two articles on Famine-related topics, both by contributors to this volume. Even in the 1960s those who, like Raymond Crotty (an economist) and Austin Bourke (a meteorologist), wrote on the Great Famine, ploughed a lonely furrow.[22] Professional historians rather frowned on Austin Bourke's research at first, and his doctorate was awarded by the Department of Dairy Science in University College, Cork! Only with the blooming of Irish economic and social history and the increasing interest of outside or foreign-trained scholars in the subject in the 1970s and 1980s has the neglect begun to be made good. Now, all of a sudden, the Famine has become a popular topic for researchers. But there remains plenty to be done. I have appended a bibliography as an indication of what has been accomplished in the interim. Perhaps it will help others contemplating work on the some aspect of the Famine.

As we have seen, *The Great Famine: Studies in Irish History* was a delayed reaction to the Great Famine's centenary. The imminence of that catastrophe's sesquicentennial can be expected to generate more overdue interest in the topic. A research network has been formed in Dublin, several interdisciplinary conferences and workshops are being discussed or planned farther afield, the Strokestown Famine Museum has opened its doors, and there is even talk of new, collaborative volumes! But in the meantime, the classic contributions that follow have provided many of the essential building blocks.

CORMAC Ó GRÁDA

## NOTES

1    T.W. Moody, 'Things to be Done in Irish History, VI: Nineteenth Century', *Bulletin of the Irish Committee of Historical Sciences*, No. 28 (December 1943), pp. 1–2. To be fair to the late George O'Brien, he never claimed much for his works in economic history, freely admitting that he wrote them as a passport to a position in UCD.

2    The *History of the Church of Ireland from the Earliest Times to the Present Day* (Oxford 1993), edited by W.A. Phillips (also of Trinity College), can claim to be the first such exercise.

3    National Archives, D/T S. 13605 (9 September 1944).

4    'Tenth Report of the ICHS', *Irish Historical Studies*, 6 (1948–9), p. 67.

5    See James McGuire's astute assessment of Williams in *IHS*, 26 (1988), pp. 3–7.

6    Cormac Ó Gráda, 'Making History in Ireland in the 1940s and 1950s: The Saga of *The Great Famine*', *The Irish Review*, no. 12 (1992), pp. 87–107.

7    Roy Foster, 'We Are All Revisionists Now', *The Irish Review*, no. 1 (1986), p. 3. Modern specialists on the Famine are by no means so dismissive of Woodham-Smith's achievement. See, for example, Peter Gray, '*Punch* and the Famine', *History Ireland*, vol. 1(2) (1993); James S. Donnelly, 'The Famine and its Interpreters, Old and New', *History Ireland*, vol. 1(3) (1993).

8    *The Freeman's Journal*, 27 May 1876 (criticizing a review in *The Spectator* of Canon John O'Rourke's *History of the Great Irish Famine of 1847* (Dublin 1874)).

9    R.D. Edwards' academic diary, 23 December 1954. So far I have been unable to trace Brian Osborne. The topic suggests that Edwards may have meant the late Brian Inglis, though Inglis assured me shortly before his death that neither Williams nor Edwards had ever asked him to contribute.

10    Professor T.P. O'Neill reminds me that in those days the Irish Manuscripts Commission was not interested in nineteenth-century material, and that access to estate records in private hands was not easily obtained by graduate students from solicitors and family representatives – 'apart altogether from the travel and maintenance costs which few postgraduate students could afford' (T.P. O'Neill to author, 6 June 1991).

11    In the *Journal of the British Archaeological Association*, 3rd ser., 9 (1944), pp. 66–71.

12    MacArthur's contribution relies heavily on two works by William Wilde: his 'Report on the Epidemic Fever in Ireland', *The Dublin Quarterly Journal of Medical Science*, VII (1849), pp. 64–126, 340–404; VIII (1849), pp. 1–86, 270–339, and his contribution to the 1851 census report. Margaret Crawford tells me that most of the missing references would be to these sources. MacArthur, lionized by the Irish historical establishment, was given every facility in his researches in Dublin. The State Papers Office temporarily moved some files for him from Dublin Castle to the National Library.

13    The replies are now compiled in Vols 1068–75 and 1136 of the Irish Folklore Commission's archive. McHugh's system of references (pp. 494–8) is thereby superceded. Cathal Póirtéir of RTÉ is currently preparing a series of radio programmes and two monographs, one in Irish and one in English, containing selections of this and other Great Famine material in the archive.

14    R. Dudley Edwards' academic diary, 22 December 1954.

15    Ibid., 29 October 1952.

16    See Tom Dunne's tribute to Maureen Wall (*née* McGeehin) in G. O'Brien (ed.),

*Catholic Ireland in the Eighteenth Century: The Collected Essays of Maureen Wall* (Dublin 1989).

17  J.J. Lee (*Ireland 1912–1985: Politics and Society* [Cambridge 1989], p. 590) credits Williams and Edwards with this 'short, brilliant' piece.

18  T.P. O'Neill, 'The Organisation and Administration of Relief During the Great Famine' (MA dissertation, NUI 1946), pp. 276–343.

19  F.S.L. Lyons, 'The Great Famine: History and Tradition', *The Irish Times*, 11 January 1957.

20  A.T.Q. Stewart, 'The Irish Century in Perspective', *The Irish Times*, 16 March 1991.

21  Moody, 'Things to be Done'.

22  R.D. Crotty, *Irish Agricultural Production* (Cork 1966); A. Bourke, *The Visitation of God? The Potato and the Great Famine* (Dublin 1993); Bourke's book is a compilation of his published and unpublished work.

# Contents

# Illustrations

# IRELAND ON THE EVE OF THE FAMINE
## By R. B. McDowell.

## UNION IS STRENGTH.

*John Bull.*—"HERE ARE A FEW THINGS TO GO ON WITH, BROTHER, AND I'LL SOON PUT YOU IN A
WAY TO EARN YOUR OWN LIVING."

*Punch,* 1846.

CHAPTER I

# Ireland on the Eve of the Famine

## I. POPULATION AND RURAL LIFE

IN the summer of 1798, just a fortnight before the Irish rebellion received a decisive check at the battle of Vinegar Hill, an English country clergyman completed an essay on the prospects of human improvement, the conclusions of which, he admitted, cast a melancholy hue over human life.[1] More than a mere chronological coincidence connected his speculations with the savage conflict which was being fought to a finish on the other side of the Irish Sea. To Malthus one of the fundamental factors underlying the social development of any community was the inevitable pressure of population on the means of subsistence. In Ireland from the close of the eighteenth century all social and political problems had to be considered in the shadow of the fact that a high proportion of a rapidly growing population lived (or indeed in some areas occasionally sank) below a low subsistence level. Poverty provided a sombre and menacing background to Irish politics ; and poverty and population were decidedly connected.

That by 1845 the population of Ireland had increased and was increasing there is no doubt whatever. But any attempt to discuss the rate of, or the reasons for this increase is seriously handicapped by deficiencies in the statistical material at our disposal. For the numbers of the Irish population in the seventeenth and eighteenth centuries all we have are estimates, which range from earnest computations based on imperfect materials to wild and biased guesses. The first official census (1811) was incomplete, those of 1821 and 1831 were carried out by methods which render them of dubious value, and it was not until 1841 (in apt accordance with

3

an ominous Old Testament instance) that an Irish census was
taken on well-planned, thorough, and accurate lines. Thus it is
impossible to measure and describe with precision the steps by
which the catastrophe was approached. We know that the population of Ireland in 1841 was just over 8,000,000. If we take at
their face value the under-estimates of eighteenth-century Irish
population experts (which would give us a population in 1780
of 2,500,000) the rate of increase between 1780 and 1841—twice
that of Great Britain—is fantastic. But if we accept the corrected
figures arrived at by the most recent worker in the field, which
give an Irish population of 5,000,000 in 1780, the rate of increase
still remains impressive.[2] Even on the basis of these revised
figures the Irish population was probably increasing at a rate
nearly equal to that of Great Britain, which of course was enjoying a period of unprecedented industrial expansion. And it
must also be taken into account that the Irish population steadily
rose in spite of a continuous drain from emigration. From before
the end of the eighteenth century Irish emigrants were moving
eastwards to Great Britain, westwards to North America, and
southwards to Australia. By the end of the eighteenth century
there were substantial Irish working-class colonies in London, and
Irish labour was regularly employed on the farms of eastern
Scotland. The rapid industrialisation of Great Britain in the early
nineteenth century provided a multitudinous and miscellaneous
variety of openings for Irish labour and cheap and fast transport
between the islands. By 1841 there were over 400,000 people
of Irish birth resident in Great Britain, most of them being settled
in London, Manchester, Liverpool and Glasgow.

At first Irish immigrants were usually employed in work of
' the roughest, coarsest and most repulsive description',[3] and
often their standard of life was on a par with or inferior to the
poorest. But presumably they were usually better off than at
home, and in many cases they rose in the economic scale as time
went on. The early nineteenth century also saw the beginning
of a great age of expansion and exploitation in the United States
and the British colonies. In Canada there were considerable
Irish settlements, a substantial proportion of the emigrants from
the United Kingdom to Australia in the forties were Irish, and the
emigration to the United States, which began to assume substantial proportions after Waterloo, averaged between 1840 and

1845 thirty-seven thousand persons per annum. A large number of the emigrants, it may be noted, went from the Protestant areas in the north where in the twenties and thirties industrial depression replaced landlord oppression as a propulsive force.[4]

Contemporaries attributed this steady increase in the Irish population to a variety of factors. It was said that Irish farmers welcomed large families which would support them in their old age. One anonymous pamphleteer declared that the recruiting bounties lavishly distributed during the long war with France had been in fact bounties on population.[5] Newenham, considering the problem at the beginning of the century, mentions the two causes to which the increase was usually later attributed, viz. 'plenty of food and frequency of marriage' (powerfully seconded, he adds, by a highly salubrious climate). Also, he points out, the ugly checks of plague, famine and war, had exercised little influence in Ireland over a long period.[6] Returning to the positive causes, it is indubitable that the Irish marriage rate was high and that Irish men and women married at a comparatively early age. In 1841 though the fertility rate was a moderate one, the high marriage rate naturally resulted in what by modern figures is an astoundingly high birth rate of thirty per thousand of the population.

Given a scrap of land the Irish peasant could throw up a cabin to shelter his family and grow the potatoes which formed their staple diet. Now the Irish land system permitted a man to obtain with delusive ease the basis of a meagre and uncomfortable life. The easy-going and unenterprising methods on which most Irish estates were managed, the desire for quick returns during the great war at the beginning of the nineteenth century, the wish of the Irish farmer to secure labour without bothering about money wages, and the anxiety of many landlords to increase their political prestige and pull by multiplying freeholders on their estates, encouraged sub-division. The peasant continually asserted his right to provide portions for his daughters and careers for his younger sons by chopping up his farm. As a largish farmer, who deplored the practice on economic grounds, put it, 'A parent must provide for his children in some way, and he cannot send them all the way to America'.[7] And charity or cupidity frequently induced an occupying tenant to allow some houseless person, who offered him a tempting rent for a place on which to

erect a hut and plant a few potatoes, to share his holding.  Landlords who tried to check the process found farms broken up
before they knew what was happening and were in any case ' not
asked upon that subject between the fathers and their children',[8]
with the result that there was ' scarcely one profitable acre in
Ireland but is subject to a graduated scale of proprietors each
being on a previous profit rent'.[9]  Admittedly by the forties
sub-division was being deplored on all sides.  Rents were harder
to collect when after the Napoleonic wars came to an end the
price of wheat fell, the disfranchisement of the forty-shilling
freeholders destroyed the political motive for sub-division, and
the economic and social respectability of the comparatively large
holding was frequently emphasised by the prevalent school of
agricultural experts.

But it was hard to eradicate the consequences of a long period
of thoughtless selfishness and lazy generosity.  In many instances
the efforts of landlords to check sub-division were evaded ; and
moreover on the majority of estates it was not a question of
arresting a process but rather of reversing it.  If (as was generally
thought) agricultural improvement depended on the consolidation of farms and clearing of plots, it implied evictions.  And
this, in a country where the population was growing and industry
languishing, meant for the evicted hopeless and hungry beggary.
There was an alternative to emigration.  Frequently it was urged
that Ireland's surplus population could be provided with an
economic existence if the quantity of land under cultivation was
increased, and the reports of the commission on the practicality
of draining and cultivating the Irish bogs which appeared between
1810 and 1814 were frequently referred to.  But it may be observed
that these reports dealt with the problem largely from the
engineering point of view, and were rather guarded concerning
the probable productivity of the land which might be recovered.
Also, it could be argued, if existing tendencies continued, reclamation would be only a temporary palliative.  In the event, owing
to the prevailing pessimism, the solution was never tested properly,
for the inertia of the majority of the Irish landlords was seconded
by the reluctance of capitalists to speculate in Irish agricultural
improvements.

If the most productive use was to be made of the soil, it was
clear that Irish rural economy required to be drastically reorgan-

ised.  And only two forces, the state or the Irish landowners, could be expected to undertake the task.  The former was inhibited partly by lack of the requisite machinery and knowledge, and partly by respect for the dominant *laissez-faire* outlook which assumed that if the state intervened in economic affairs it would probably blunder badly and certainly interrupt the healthy and harmonious play of natural forces.  On two occasions after the Union the legislature ventured tentatively to improve the law affecting the relations of landlord and tenant in Ireland.  In 1816 an act was passed to amend the law respecting the recovery of small tenements.  In accordance with the ideals of contemporary legal reformers it provided a cheap and quick procedure for determining suits respecting tenure.  As its critics pointed out it facilitated evictions.  The sub-letting acts of 1826 and 1831 which penalised the tenant who indulged in unsanctioned sub-letting were also strongly criticised for weighting the scales unfairly in favour of the head landlord.  In any case the evidence produced before the Devon commission suggests that these two latter acts were very ineffective.  Probably some of the best work done by the state during this period was the collection, through parliamentary and royal commissions, of a mass of information about Irish conditions.  But before much of this clinical material could be effectually used the catastrophe occurred.

As for the Irish landed interest, it is quite clear why as a body it was deficient in the drive necessary for the achievement of an economic revolution.  It would be a mistake to regard Irish rural society as a solid pyramid, with clearly defined layers—landlords, tenant farmers and labourers.  The huge transfers of land carried out after the savage wars of the sixteenth and seventeenth centuries, the lazy creation of long-term intermediate interests (often consisting of thousands of acres) the readiness of large-scale farmers to rent land from several landlords, the hungry zeal with which the poorer peasants sought for land from their better-off neighbours, the readiness of the farmers to install their labourers as cottier tenants, created a confusing variety of legal and personal claims on the soil.  If the term landlord is restricted to those who held in fee, then the land of Ireland was held by a comparatively small group ; if it is taken in a wider sense to include all who derived part of their livelihood from letting land, then it would be a hyperbolic approximation to the truth to say that Ireland could

be described as a nation of landlords. Thus the Irish landed
interest was composed of a numerous collection of persons con-
trolling the soil through a multiplicity of forms. There was a
world of difference between wealthy landlords such as Lord
Palmerston, Lord Headley or Lord Farnham, managing their
estates with benevolent if aloof intelligence, and the pauperised
descendants of some early eighteenth-century grantees in Mayo.
The former gave premiums for building, supplied standardised
plans for cottages, laid out roads, organised draining operations,
erected limekilns, employed agricultural experts and tried to check
sub-letting. The latter were to be found in 1840 clinging to their
estates, with incomes eaten away by settlements, living like the
poorest farmers, but scorning to bring up their children to any
sort of business, and screwing out of their miserable tenants in
addition to rack-rents, butter, eggs and fish.[10]

It would be as futile as it is tempting to try to sum up the
behaviour of such a large and heterogeneous class in a few generalisations. But it can be safely said that the Irish landlords on the
whole seem to have been regarded by their contemporaries as
goodnatured, unenterprising and spendthrift. Over most of
the country a vigorous, planning landlord was a rarity, and
witnesses before the Devon commission not infrequently describe
local landlords as ' indulgent' (a term carrying a savour of
ineffectiveness). It is easy to understand why many landlords
must have found it hard to be improving or even indulgent.
War prices at the beginning of the century had encouraged the
conspicuous consumption and extravagant pleasures characteristic
of a proud landed class. And as Bishop Doyle said, ' when the
peace came many gentlemen had establishments which could not
easily be cut down for we all know how painful it is for a man to
descend from a certain rank in life to another below it'.[11] Estates
were burdened with settlements, debts and mortgages, and in
the years immediately succeeding the famine many Irish landowners were to stagger into the encumbered estates court
weighted down by special charges which amounted often to ten
times their rental.[12]

But the strength of the landowners' position in a country where
industry was languishing and population growing is demonstrated
by the conditions on which land was held by all but the largest
or most fortunate tenants. Rents, fixed by competitive proposals

from the prospective tenants rather than on a valuation of the land, tended to be high. Naturally, many tenants found themselves unable or unwilling to pay the rent so fixed, and every year a number of ejections took place and distresses were levied—the latter being a wasteful and embittering way of recovering arrears by a seizure of the tenant's crops and possessions. Legally it was usually easy to get rid of a tenant, for the great bulk of the occupying tenants held at will, which in practice meant on a yearly tenancy, so that insecurity—with its inevitable concomitants, inertia, improvidence and untidiness—was a distressing feature of Irish peasant life. Finally the question of improvements was usually ignored in the agreement between landlord and tenant, with the result that if the latter of necessity undertook them, he had no claim to compensation at the termination of his tenancy. Admittedly there were scattered through the country improving landlords who encouraged their tenants to build and drain by grants of money and materials and remissions. Moreover in Ulster where landlord and tenant had been partners in the great plantation undertaking, it was not only customary for the latter to be left undisturbed on his holding so long as he fulfilled his contract, but he had the right to sell his good-will, and so could recuperate himself for any improvements he might have made.[13] Custom in time hardened into a system which in the tenacious opinion of the countryside had a binding force at least as strong as that of more formally sanctioned law. Any violation of it was rapidly penalised by agrarian direct action, and an experienced observer was sure that if the Ulster landlords attempted to destroy tenant-right there was not ' sufficient force at the disposal of the Horse Guards to keep the peace of the province'.[14]

If one looks at the Irish agricultural system as a whole, it is clear that it was bound to produce muddles, misunderstandings, harsh dealings and savage reprisals. Irish agriculture was backward judged by English standards, yet an improving tenant unprotected by contract almost invited unfair treatment, and an active landlord was likely to take steps, such as evicting tenants and consolidating farms, which would arouse intense hostility. If one predominant note can be detected in the two thousand pages or so of evidence delivered before the Devon commission, it is embittered frustration ; and each type of witness was quick to see the motes in the eyes of the other classes connected with the

system.   As one level-headed farmer put it, ' It is just like harnes-
sing horses ;  if they are badly handled they will not pull well—
and the people all seem to be badly harnessed.   It seems to me to
commence with the landlords, it then reaches the middle-men
and goes down to the humblest man in society ;  they seem to be
all going wrong '! [15]

## II. INDUSTRIES AND COMMUNICATIONS

The ramshackle, ill-balanced Irish agricultural system not only
failed to provide a satisfactory and productive economic existence
for the majority of those engaged in it, but in addition it exercised
a crippling effect on Irish industrial development.   Not only did
the badly rewarded peasantry constitute a poor market for Irish
manufactures, but in many instances the agricultural labourer,
finding his services unwanted for about half the year, in desperation
took to weaving and, by providing a flow of desperate and semi-
skilled recruits for the textile industries, depressed wages and
standards.   Finally in the case of the linen and cotton industries
the uncertainty of agricultural tenure over most of the country
was a vital factor in halting the growth of the textile manufactures.   In Ulster the small farmer, guaranteed security of tenure
and other advantages by local custom, was able to accumulate
the capital required for domestic spinning and weaving and to
devote himself to mastering marketing and manufacturing techniques.   From early in the nineteenth century the well-established
and prosperous linen manufacture of Ulster was moving slowly
from the domestic to the factory stage.   Outside Ulster attempts
to establish the linen and cotton industry had for the most part
failed catastrophically.   Factories, built before markets had been
found, collapsed.   And the peasantry lacked the economic stamina
required to combine domestic manufactures (except for home
consumption) with farming.[1]

In other respects Irish manufacturers were handicapped by
adverse circumstances during the early decades of the nineteenth
century.   For the greater part of the previous century the more
important Irish industries had been the victims of imperial mer-
cantilism, but in the eighties and nineties the Irish parliament
energetically encouraged them with bounties, subsidies and tariffs.

And Irish manufacturers, able to command comparatively cheap labour, the raw materials available in an agricultural country and easily accessible water power, could look forward to the future with confident expectation.   Two factors which could scarcely have been foreseen, the Union and the industrial revolution, changed the situation about the beginning of the new century. The latter meant an intensification of British competition ;   the former the disappearance of the possibility of resisting it by protective duties.   What might have happened if Ireland had retained parliamentary independence, if the Irish parliament had taken drastic steps to protect Irish manufactures (presumably at the expense of the home agricultural interest), and if these manufactures had been able to absorb the surplus rural population, offers an interesting problem in hypothetical economic history. Unfortunately, history rarely permits the controlled experiment, and we can merely trace the dreary story of what actually occurred.

In the new age of coal and iron Ireland with comparatively scanty exploitable mineral deposits was bound to be at a disadvantage.   Writing at the beginning of the nineteenth century, Wakefield declared that though there were inexhaustible veins of iron to be found in Ireland, ' taking a comprehensive view ' he was convinced that the iron industry was lost to Ireland for want of fuel.[2] Half-way through the century his gloomy prognostications were shown to be sound.   For though Ireland was said to possess no fewer than six coalfields, of which the Munster one covering portions of Clare, Limerick, Kerry and Cork was considered to be ' the most extensive in the British empire', they were unfortunately of more significance to the geologist than to the economist.   In the late thirties collieries were functioning at only five places in Ireland. Their output amounted only to about 150,000 tons of coal and culm a year, about two-thirds of it coming from the Kilkenny group of collieries where a few hundred men were employed. Other forms of mining and quarrying were carried on at about thirty places.   These enterprises, the great majority of which were minute concerns, included half a dozen lead and half a score of copper mines.   Of the latter the two most important were the mines at Allihies (co. Cork) and Ballymurtha (co. Wicklow), employing 1,500 and 700 men respectively.   The bulk of the ore mined at both places seems to have been exported to Great Britain. At Arigna there was the only Irish iron mines.   At the beginning of the century their story was a melancholy one. Quarrels and failure characterised their financial history while a labour dispute had culminated in the murder of a manager. By 1845 these mines were producing comparatively little.[3]

The Irish textile industries just before the famine present a series of contrasts. Silk, after a long struggle, was almost dead, and wool which had been declining seemed to have stabilised itself at a low level, cotton after a period of feverish expansion had fallen into an intensifying depression from which it was never to emerge, and the securely established linen industry, while undergoing painful changes in organisation, was at the opening of an age of expansion and success.

The silk industry lingered on only in Dublin, where about four hundred weavers, mostly engaged in the poplin manufacture, worked up to fifteen hours a day, and earned about twelve shillings a week. The decay of the trade since the eighteenth century was attributed partly to French and English competition and partly to what employers considered the tyrannous control exercised by the workers' combination, which resisted by intimidation and violence any attempt to alter wage rates or the customs of the trade.[4]

The Irish woollen industry had suffered severely during most of the eighteenth century from British restrictive measures. Later it found its home market severely limited. Among the peasantry in the early nineteenth century the women spun the wool and the local weaver who still flourished in the late thirties, in out-of-the-way areas at least 'where shop cloth has not been introduced', made up 'job webs of coarse frieze blankets, sheeting, shirtings and bandle linens for the use of the peasantry'.[5] Still, for the first couple of decades of the century, the Irish manufacturer had at least protection from British competition. Though, if the view of a keen free-trader is accepted, this was a bane in disguise. Protection, he argued, 'paralysed' the Irish industry, due regard was not paid to economy, wages were kept at an artificial level, and the manufacturers indulged in shocking jobbery over the valuable army and militia clothing contract which they regarded as vested right.[6] In any case a few years after the duties on imported cloth disappeared came the slump of 1825. The British manufacturers, left with large stocks on hand, threw them on the Irish market at ruinous prices. The weaker Irish woollen firms collapsed and went out of business. At the end of the thirties the production of Irish woollen goods was half what it had been twenty years before and it was estimated that three-quarters of the frieze worn by the Irish peasantry was imported. In towns such as Birr, Carrickfergus, Maryborough or Rathdrum with its flannel hall closed since 1830, the woollen industry was dead or rapidly declining. The Irish manufacture of woollen cloth on a commercial scale was in fact confined to the Dublin area. At Balbriggan, and in Dublin itself, a few comparatively small firms were gathering together the woollen weavers—an unlucky class—according to harsh critics, demoralised by irregular employment.[7]

The cotton industry had been introduced into Ireland towards the close of the eighteenth century and naturally enough gravitated towards the north, where it could draw on the reservoirs of capital and skill built up by the long-established and flourishing linen trade, which for a short period at the beginning of the new century it seemed destined to supersede. It easily survived the disappearance of protection in the early twenties but was badly hit by a slump due to over-production in the thirties. Its recovery was retarded by the growing competition of finer quality cloth from England and in the north of Ireland capital began to move back to the linen industry where Ulster products were less subject to competition. That the depression of the middle thirties marked the beginning of the decline of the Irish cotton industry was clear, at least to the far-sighted, at the end of the decade. By 1838 there were only six cotton mills in Belfast, several of the others having recently been turned over to flax spinning. By 1841 there were only three.[8] Strangely enough in the early forties the largest cotton mill in Ireland, the Mayfield mill owned by the Malcolmsons, was not in Ulster but at Portlaw in county Waterford. It employed about 1,200 hands, and the proprietors, a great Quaker family, were benevolent employers, who provided good ventilation in the mills, studied the health of their employees scientifically, and had set up schools, a library and newsrooms.[9] Another Quaker cotton factory was flourishing at Mountmellick ; in the late thirties a Scotsman, attracted by cheap labour, had started a cotton shawl factory at Limerick ; and at Stratford, where Wakefield at the beginning of the century had found a colony of 300 Presbyterian cotton weavers from Paisley with their library and benefit society, a tourist was delighted about 1840 to find the

dullness and monotony of the Wicklow landscape agreeably
relieved by the tall chimneys of a cotton factory.[10] For the rest
the industry had almost vanished from the south.  The corduroy
trade of Bandon which at one time employed nearly two thousand
handloom weavers had been swept out of existence in a few years
by English power-loom competition.  At Collon, the cotton
industry established by Foster, which had employed thirteen
hundred looms at the opening of the century, had by the thirties
entirely ceased.  With the exception of a few isolated points in
the south which have been mentioned, the cotton manufacture
by the beginning of the forties was almost confined to Antrim
and north Down, 'the small manufacturers scattered over the
other parts of the kingdom being precluded from competing with
the concentrated capital and skill of Belfast'.[11]  Most of the weavers
were also small farmers, and according to their critics were incompetent at both occupations.  In the halcyon days of the industry
they had been relatively prosperous, a man being able to earn over
a pound a week, and a somewhat severe observer had commented
sharply on 'the dressy appearance' of the young female weavers
of the Ards, who it was painful to observe spent so much of their
earnings in adorning their persons in a manner unsuited to their
station in life.  But in the late thirties and early forties the situation
was darkening ; wages had fallen badly and the northern handloom cotton weavers were entering on their long and hungry
struggle against technological progress.[12]

By the forties the lines on which the Irish linen industry was
going to develop were definitely discernible, though the process
would be brutally painful for those who were reluctant to con-
form.  The industry was becoming concentrated both in its
organisation and geographically.  All over Ireland outside Ulster
the linen manufacture had vanished or was in decline, and spinning
at least was now a factory process.  In the south, where Dingle,
Bantry and Killarney had once been thriving industrial centres
the trade was also extinct.  In the west, in Sligo and Mayo, it was
of little importance.  In Drogheda the position about 1840 was
tragic.  The wealthy manufacturers finding themselves undersold
by English and Scottish firms had emigrated north, and the
condition of the handloom weavers, left to fight a hopeless
battle, was appalling.  Their wages were the lowest in the trade,
their cabins 'fearful specimens of what habit will enable a human

being to endure'. Rents were high and 'damp and dirt reigned undisturbed in the weavers' quarter of Drogheda'.[13]

In Ulster the handloom weavers were holding their own, but their economic status was changing. An observer, taking a broad and rather premature view about 1840, summed up the position by saying that 'the advantages of concentrated capital, and ingenuity and enterprise over the isolated efforts of the lowly and industrious rural weaver' were 'day by day transplanting the loom from the cabin of the cottier to the factory or weaving shop of the manufacturer'. In fact, though an attempt was made to use power-looms in Ulster in the twenties, weaving had scarcely yet become a factory occupation. Several Belfast manufacturers had set up weaving factories, dubbed 'lock-ups' by the weavers who loathed the strictness and regularity imposed on them. But even in these factories the work was done by hand. Up to 1845 the most notable change in the structure of the industry was the slow elimination of the independent countryman, who combined the manufacture and marketing of cotton in a small way with farming on a modest scale. His place was being taken by cottiers or even cottagers without land working up material for big manufacturers, many of whom employed several hundred, or even over a thousand weavers. And the peasant households—engaged in the linen industry—with the weaver owning his loom and having the help of his family in subsidiary processes were scattered thickly through Antrim, Down, Armagh and Londonderry. Thus, though the linen handloom weaver was generally speaking definitely better off than the mass of the rural population, wages were not high enough to make it economic to introduce power weaving. The famine and the consequent emigration were to force wages up, and so lead in the later forties and the early fifties to linen weaving becoming a factory process.[14]

Spinning had of course become a factory industry decades earlier. About 1825 the process known as wet-spinning was introduced and the first spinning factory equipped with steam power built in Belfast. Requiring coal, the spinning factories naturally clustered round the port and by 1841 there were no fewer than twenty-five in Belfast. During the second quarter of the nineteenth century, the city which had for generations been a bustling trading centre was becoming industrialised, and 'at once the Manchester and the Liverpool of Ireland', to quote the proud

but on the whole justifiable boast of its inhabitants.[15]   Yet during
the early nineteenth century the port could only be reached ' by
a channel meandering through the extensive slobs in so tortuous
a manner as to be extremely difficult of navigation, and so badly
lighted that steamers sailing at night had to send down boats
beforehand to hang up lanterns upon beacons'.   The growth of
industry naturally promoted the development of the port, and
from the year of Waterloo the question of improving the channel
was under consideration.   Owing to legal technicalities, the many
interests involved—the harbour corporation, ship-owners, property
owners, the lords of the treasury and the lords of the soil, and the
differing opinions of engineering experts of the status of Rennie,
Telford and Cubitt—things moved exceedingly slowly.   But in
1830 a new harbour authority with wide powers was set up and
in the year of Queen Victoria's accession it started to work on an
extensive scale.   Since the commissioners of public works were
reluctant to advance the funds required, the board boldly issued
bonds, and between 1839 and 1851 it expended half a million in
purchasing property on either bank, constructing docks and quays,
and cutting the Victoria Channel, opened in 1842.   On the land
reclaimed as a result of these operations there was to be found
in the fifties the greatest of the Belfast shipyards.   But from the
end of the eighteenth century Belfast was a leading Irish shipbuilding centre, and as early as 1838 the Belfast yards had turned
out their first iron ship and amongst the numerous wooden ships
they constructed about the same time was one for the eastern
trade—the aptly named *Hindoo*.[16]

The Irish communications system, like so many other aspects
of Irish life, was characterised by grandiose planning, shrewd
improvisation, an impressive degree of achievement, state intervention and jobbery.   From the end of the eighteenth century
visitors had been agreeably surprised by the Irish roads.[17]   Their
fine condition was largely due to two factors.   In a poor country
there was comparatively little heavy traffic to tear up their surfaces, yet nevertheless plenty of money had been expended on
them.   Most Irish roads were built and maintained by the grand
juries, and since (until the middle thirties) road contracts offered
the most profitable pickings to those engaged in county government, presentments for purposes of this kind were eagerly sought
and usually easily secured.   But as, even in the eighteenth century,

some results had to be shown for the expenditure of public money, though the system might be defective both economically and ethically, many fine roads were built. In 1845 at the end of the coaching age there radiated from Dublin no fewer than thirty coach routes and on these together with the nine that radiated from Drogheda there ran weekly outwards and inwards over two hundred coaches. The main coach roads, running for the most part from Dublin, were supplemented by the two great canals in the midlands and in the south and west by the service of outside cars run by Bianconi, an enterprising Italian, who beginning as a pedlar and carrier—by thrift, initiative and a quick grasp of human nature—had built up a vast enterprise. The 'bians', carrying their passengers precariously perched back to back, exposed to wind and weather, probably offered the *ne plus ultra* in travelling discomfort. But they covered routes on which no other commercial vehicle would venture and served the purposes of a gregarious community whose readiness to endure the pains of travel astonished the contemporary tourist.

But roads and canals were being rapidly outmoded by the railway, and in regard to railway building Ireland lagged sadly behind the rest of the British Isles, having in 1845 only about seventy miles to Great Britain's two thousand.[18] This was made up of three short strips, Dublin to Kingstown, Dublin to Drogheda and Belfast to Portadown. The situation was obviously unsatisfactory, and in 1836 the government appointed three highly competent civil servants to consider the future of Irish railway development. This commission went about its work deliberately and after a couple of years produced a scheme for a scientifically planned system which would have presented an impressive contrast with the piecemeal haphazard building which was going on in England. And it recommended that if private capital was not forthcoming in sufficient quantities to complete the scheme, the state should advance the money to private persons or local authorities who were willing to carry out the work on the lines laid down by the commission. The report was naturally greeted with a chorus of criticism by the directors of prospective lines such as the Dublin–Drogheda and the Great Munster and Leinster Railways whose plans conflicted with the schemes laid down by the commission—though the critics were swift to seize on the suggestion that public money might be advanced for railway building and to suggest that it might be entrusted to themselves. As for the government, it was naturally startled by the magnitude of the scheme devised by its own nominees. Spring-Rice, the chancellor of the exchequer, himself an Irishman and an improving landlord, writing to the chief secretary, declared, ' If you have any hope of reconciling the Irish at once to a centralisation of railways which will put down local jobbing, that will deprive attorneys of fees on private bills, engineers of their cost of surveys and country gentlemen of their expected composition and that in addition to energy to counter these difficulties you can devise and reconcile Ireland to a general local tax to provide for 6,000,000 then there is somewhat of a probability that parliament will adopt the railway project'. In any case Spring-Rice only hesitatingly admitted that the construction of railways in Ireland might prove an exception to the general rule that ' if private capital cannot be profitably applied . . . public capital derived from the taxation of individuals ought not to be applied'. And when he brought the matter before the cabinet in November 1838 he declared that to suggest to parliament that so great an outlay should be met from the imperial exchequer would be to invite defeat.[19] However, a month later he was more hopeful about his colleagues' attitude and in March when the house was in committee Viscount Morpeth, after taking some trouble to show that ' the course which is perfectly consistent with true political economy' might not be the same in Ireland as in England, announced that the government proposed to empower the board of works to construct a line from Dublin to Cork, the capital required being secured from exchequer bills. The proposal was subjected to considerable criticism, particularly from Sir Robert Peel, the leader of the conservative opposition, who basing his case on the orthodox arguments of the liberal economists, described it as an insult to Irish enterprise. In the end the government, which was struggling with a multiplicity of difficulties, dropped the measure.[20] Nevertheless each of the three Irish railways during the next few years received substantial loans from the public works loan commissioners—advances amounting in all to nearly three hundred thousand pounds—though the application of the Ulster capitalists for assistance for the Belfast–Portadown railway was at first characterised by the indignant chancellor of the exchequer as something very like fraud.[21]

### III. CENTRAL AND LOCAL GOVERNMENT

Irish economic and social life during the first forty years of the nineteenth century was obviously in an unhealthy condition. Still during this period something was accomplished for the community by legislative and administrative action. The machinery of government, both at the centre and locally, was rendered more efficient, an effective police force was built up, a bold attempt was made to provide a system of universal elementary education and efforts, culminating in the poor law of 1838, were made to cope with the problem of destitution.

The act of union, though of momentous political significance, affected only slightly the Irish administrative machine. Opponents and supporters of the measure implied in their speeches that a substantial degree of administrative unification was about to take place. But the act itself made no provision for this—except in the clauses foreshadowing at a probably distant date the fusion of the British and Irish exchequers. Inertia, the undeniable existence of local problems and the strength of local official vested interests prevented the legislative union being immediately followed by a wholesale amalgamation of British and Irish departments. When the lords and commons departed from Dublin the civil servants remained. But the next forty years saw considerable changes. From the beginning of the nineteenth century there were persistent efforts in parliament to secure an inexpensive and efficient civil service. As early as 1804 a commission of enquiry into the Irish revenue departments was appointed and in its first report it catalogued a long list of offices as superfluous.[1] In 1817 and 1824 a number of Irish offices ranging from the surveyor general of crown lands and the accountant general to the board of the master of the revels were abolished.[2] Along with abolition went amalgamation. In 1816 the separate consolidated funds of Great Britain and Ireland were replaced by a single United Kingdom fund. This involved the amalgamation of the exchequers, the commissioners of the treasury and the commissioners of the national debt of the two countries.[3] Naturally enough, the unification of the British and Irish boards of customs and excise, stamp boards and commissioners for auditing the public accounts rapidly followed. Lastly in 1831 the British and Irish post offices were united.[4]

## JUSTICE TO IRELAND.

"She gave them some Broth without any Bread,
Then whipp'd them all Round, and sent them to Bed."

*Punch*, 1846.

But the vigorous reformers on both sides of the house, whose views in the end usually prevailed in parliament, were not content with retrenchment and reorganisation. The Irish problem was continually being brought to their attention by frequent debates on emergency legislation and the annual discussion of the Catholic claims. Irish ills demanded new remedies, and a remedy often meant a new government department. So between 1820 and 1845 several boards were set up to supervise or control widely differing aspects of Irish life, while during the same period newly created United Kingdom departments began to function in Ireland.

The government services operating in Ireland by the beginning of the forties can be divided into two classes.[5] There were those which were merely branch offices of a London department. The treasury for instance had no fewer than three satellite offices operating in Dublin—the paymaster of the civil services, the excise office (with a staff working throughout the country) and the stamp office. In addition, it was strongly represented on the commission for the drainage of lands and controlled the commission for improvement of the Shannon.[6] Moreover several Irish departments had to submit their salary scales for treasury approval. The board of trade had one small Irish offshoot, the joint stock companies registry office, the Irish quit-rent office worked under the direction of the commissioners for woods and forests,[7] and the poor law and the postal services were operated from London, though there were comparatively large subordinate offices in Dublin. Secondly there were a number of departments concerned solely with Irish affairs, of which the most important were the chief secretary's office, the commissioners of national education, the board of education, the ecclesiastical commission, the board of charitable donations, the board of public works, and the general survey and valuation. These departments reported to the lord lieutenant who nominated the senior members of their staffs. But the commissions, which were statutory bodies, enjoyed a large degree of autonomy.

In spite of the multiplicity of government offices in Dublin the number of civil servants employed was by modern standards small. One of the larger departments, the chief secretary's office, which was responsible for law and order managed with a staff of about sixteen clerks. Even the post office had only eighty clerks

in its Dublin office and several of the public boards were satisfied
with a clerk or two. Ireland was fortunate in the quality of many
of its early nineteenth-century officials, men of the highest ability
such as Drummond, Shaw Kennedy, Thomas Kennedy, Griffith,
and Burgoyne, finding in an ill-adjusted country an outlet for
their organising powers. And it may be added that amongst their
subordinates in the early forties were Anthony Trollope in the post
office and Robert Ball, the distinguished naturalist and zoologist,
in the chief secretary's department. The former managed to
secure promotion, hunting, and material for his novels, the latter
was officially ill-fated. First he was refused promotion because
he was working so well as to be indispensable ; later though his
duties were faithfully performed, he was retired on the grounds
that ' he devoted too much attention to scientific pursuits '.[8]

The supreme direction of Irish affairs was shared by three
ministers, the lord lieutenant, the chief secretary, and the secretary
of state for home affairs. Theoretically the chief secretary was
the viceroy's principal subordinate, while the viceroy himself was
responsible to the home secretary. But since the Union the chief
secretary had grown in importance until by the forties he overshadowed his nominal superior. The chief secretary had several
advantages over the viceroy. A promising junior minister, frequently quite young by official standards, he spent the parliamentary session in London handling Irish affairs in the commons,
while the lord lieutenant, who had usually clearly reached or even
passed the culmination of his career, was condemned to glorious
isolation in Dublin. As for the relative capacities of the holders
of the two offices, they are indicated by the fact that four of the
chief secretaries between the Union and 1846 ultimately became
prime ministers, while of the viceroys the most outstanding were
Wellesley a ' failed ' premier, and the able but erratic Normanby.
Nevertheless the viceroy, with his status, formal powers, and real
control over patronage, could not be ignored, and Lamb when
chief secretary under the imperious Wellesley tactfully requested
the home secretary not to ask his opinion through official channels
since there was ' no such thing as an original public correspondence
between the chief secretary to the lord lieutenant and the secretary
of state. Everything the chief secretary writes is commanded
and directed by the lord lieutenant. Some jealousy has already
been excited upon this point and I am afraid of more '.[9] The short

terms of office generally enjoyed by lords lieutenant and chief
secretaries during the first half of the nineteenth century must
have been a factor in checking the development of friction between
them ; also several of the strongest secretaries had accommodating
viceroys. Arthur Wellesley was in office under the easy-going
Richmond ; Peel's viceroys were Richmond, Whitworth and
Talbot. Stanley and Morpeth worked with viceroys whose views
on Irish problems coincided closely with their own. On the other
hand Wellesley and Goulburn, who were appointed simultaneously
to satisfy conflicting groups, naturally were frequently in disagreement. And when Peel became prime minister for the second
time in 1841 he appointed De Grey, a self-assured, inexperienced,
great nobleman with ultra-Protestant connections, lord lieutenant,
and Eliot, a hesitant, intelligent, moderate chief secretary. De Grey
promptly started to shower ecclesiastical patronage on the opponents of the national education scheme which the conservative
government had decided to continue. Eliot complained about not
being consulted, pointing out that he was ' more or less responsible
for every act of the government, and no one likes to be responsible
for acts which he does not altogether approve '. De Grey for his
part made it quite clear that he felt himself saddled with a timid
secretary whose opinion was valueless. Peel strove to soothe the
irritated Eliot by emphasising that the undoubted difficulties of
his post, ' the legislative authority of the secretary balanced against
the executive authority of the lord lieutenant ; the indefinite
nature of the relation they stand towards each other ' made it ' a
most invaluable preparatory course for higher duties '. Graham,
the home secretary, testily informed De Grey that difficulties
between himself and Eliot, if submitted in an understandable
form, could always be laid by the home secretary before the
cabinet which could pronounce a final decision. But he made it
quite clear that he disliked being pestered by his Irish colleagues.
Privately he speculated hopefully on the possibilities of Eliot
being removed from Ireland to Canada or the house of lords.
Relations between De Grey and Eliot became so strained at the
end of their first year in office that Peel was driven to considering
the abolition of the viceroyalty.[10] Three years later Eliot himself
suggested that his own office might be abolished. Its duties he
thought could be performed by the home secretary, and it would
be more satisfactory to have the minister for Irish affairs in the

cabinet. Curiously enough in May 1844 about the time he made
this suggestion, Eliot was compelled to defend the existing arrangements against the attacks of Joseph Hume, the member for
Aberdeen and the most pertinacious advocate for retrenchment
in the house. Hume, who had raised the question on previous occasions, urged that the offices of lord lieutenant and chief secretary
should both be abolished since their duties could perfectly well
be performed in London, mainly by the home secretary.[11]

The continuous turbulence which distinguished Irish political
life until the end of the sixteenth century prevented the parish
which plays so vigorous a part in English local government developing administrative functions. And when in the seventeenth
century an English legal framework was being imposed on the
country it seems to have been assumed that only a larger unit,
the county, could cope successfully with the problems of local
government in an unsettled community.[12] So from early in the
century onwards parliament thrust on the grand jury, which like
its English prototype was chosen by the high sheriff and was
supposed to comprise a selection of the leading landowners of the
county, a wide range of administrative functions. The Irish grand
jury was responsible for the construction and repair of all roads,
bridges and public buildings in the county, the support of hospitals,
asylums and dispensaries and the payment of the police. At the
assizes it not only considered bills of indictment, but also ' presented ' (i.e. voted) large sums to be raised from the county, for
these purposes. In 1840 grand jury presentments amounted to
the substantial amount of £120,000.

In the early nineteenth century the whole system was subjected
to continual and vehement criticism. Not only did it flagrantly
violate the principle that there should be no taxation without
representation, but it was alleged that the grand juries, unrepresentative and irresponsible bodies, frequently misused their powers.
Roads, it was declared, often described curves inexplicable by the
ordinary rules of civil engineering when approaching the gate of
a grand juror, contracts were too readily granted to a grand juror's
dependants, and, it was asserted, encumbered estates had been
freed through the owners sitting on the grand jury. Defenders
of the system pointed out that the grand jury had no control

whatever over a large portion of the county expenditure, a number of presentments being obligatory, so that the members were in the unpleasant position of being automatically compelled to impose taxation. They dwelt too on the devoted and unrewarded public service rendered by many grand jurors and on the importance and value of the work accomplished. But while it was argued that many of the charges levelled against the system were grossly exaggerated, it had to be admitted that the grand juries had not time to perform their duties properly. They were compelled during a few days in the midst of all the bustle and business of the assizes to levy an indefinite amount of money for an innumerable variety of purposes. It was impossible for the jury to give more than a few minutes to each presentment, and the business was only got through because each juryman was prepared to trust his fellows' opinion on the needs of their localities.

Several leading Irish M.P.s, including Wyse and O'Connell, advocated transferring county administration from the grand juries to popularly elected county boards. The government however shrank from so drastic a step, which would not in any case have guaranteed economical administration. But beginning with the act of 1817, a series of measures, culminating in the great consolidating statute of 1836, were passed, extending into the local sphere the venerated constitutional principle of checks and balances. There was instituted in each barony a special sessions, composed of the justices of the peace and a number of cess-payers selected from the highest cess-payers of the area, to deal with local presentments. And a county presentments sessions, composed of all the magistrates of the county together with some of the highest ratepayers from each barony, handled public works for the county at large. The grand jury was placed in a position analogous to that of the nineteenth-century house of lords in relation to money bills. It could reject but not alter the original presentments. All public works were contracted for and carried out according to a strict and precise statutory procedure. The county officials, the secretary to the grand jury, the county treasurer, the clerks of the crown and peace, the county surveyors, had their salaries and duties fixed. And in 1826 there was begun a valuation of the country on scientific lines which was to form the basis of an equitable system of rating.

The rules and regulations of the reform era were successful

in eliminating waste and graft from Irish county affairs. After 1840 the principal and indeed only serious weakness in Irish local government in the rural areas was its failure to arouse much enthusiasm or interest. The bulk of the ratepayers had no say whatever in the choice of the local governing bodies, and the members of the presentment sessions, nominated and confined largely to routine duties, often showed little interest in their work. The system was characterised by a reasonable degree of efficiency and a definite lack of enthusiasm. One of the most striking features in the history of Irish local government during the early nineteenth century was the control over county affairs acquired by the central government. The valuation survey was carried out by the government though the counties paid for it. The police from 1836 were completely controlled by the crown. On the request of the ratepayers the government could order works to be undertaken which the grand jury had refused to sanction. The government appointed not only the clerks of the crown but also the county surveyors. Inspectors nominated by the lord lieutenant visited the county asylums and gaols and fixed the scale of the allowances in the latter.

Turning to urban government there were, in 1800, one hundred and seventeen parliamentary boroughs.[13] Eighteen of them did not possess a corporation. Of the ninety-nine corporations which existed at the time of the Union thirty-six disappeared with their only *raison d'être*—the right to return members to parliament. There remained sixty-three places, ranging from Dublin and Cork, with populations of over 100,000, to villages such as Castlemartyr or Inistioge, all of which were nominally governed by municipal corporations. Of these corporations thirty-six did practically nothing,[14] and the other twenty-seven comparatively little—usually inefficiently. Each corporation was composed of a governing body, together in some cases with freemen. Except in the case of Dublin the members of the governing bodies held office for life, and in nearly every case they were self-elected. Where they were not, matters were so arranged that the governing body exercised considerable influence over the elections. The electors—where there were elections—were the freemen, and the freemen were usually admitted by the governing body. Though Catholics had been eligible for membership since 1793, the corporations were in 1834, with one exception, exclusively Protestant bodies. Except

in a few towns the corporate revenues were small, having suffered
from mismanagement and fraud, and frequently a considerable
proportion was absorbed by the salaries of their higher officers.
Though most of the corporations had a staff of decoratively
designated and poorly paid officials—serjeants at mace, chamber-
lains and water-bailiffs, they performed few useful functions.
Some of them struggled hard to collect tolls, keep up a market,
maintain a public pump, keep a clock going, repair the streets,
prosecute vagrants or distribute a little in charity. And in a
number of places the corporation was able to provide an easily
accessible court of summary jurisdiction and record. In a few of
the smaller boroughs the presence, in the background, of an energetic and public-spirited patron stimulated the corporation to
action, and in most of the larger towns the corporations if unrepresentative and irresponsible were moderately active and tried
to perform the essential urban administrative functions. But in
several instances the legislature had had to create other bodies
to perform some of the corporation's duties. By an act of 1828
it was possible for any borough, in which light, water, cleansing
and paving were not provided, to secure a body of commissioners
elected by the five-pound ratepayers with powers to provide these
services and to levy a rate. By 1840 at least twenty towns had
taken advantage of this act, and set up modern functional, democratic authorities to supplement their ancient corporations.

Antiquated, inefficient, cliquish and riddled with petty jobbery,
the Irish corporations were definitely unfit to survive in a reforming age. Three years after the passing of the great reform bill the
English municipalities were reformed and commissioners were
appointed to report on the Irish ones. Their carefully planned
and detailed survey of the heterogeneous and absurd collection of
administrative bodies that mismanaged Irish municipal affairs
rendered the defence of the Irish corporations impossible. And
when Morpeth introduced in 1836 a measure modelled on the
English municipal reform act the staunchest tories did not attempt
to advocate openly the preservation of the existing Irish corporations. Instead the conservatives immediately produced what may
be described not unfairly as an obvious opposition alternative to
the government's proposal. Determined to limit as much as
possible the powers which would inevitably fall into the hands of
' an Irish faction ' (i.e. their political opponents), they suggested

that in place of municipal bodies of the new English type the largest Irish towns should be granted merely boards of commissioners with strictly defined duties, of the type set up under the act of 1828. On three successive occasions the government's bill was defeated by delaying tactics in the lords. But in 1840, as a result of a compromise, in which the financial interests of the Irish establishment were weighted against municipal democracy, it was passed. All the old corporations were abolished. The ten towns with the greatest populations were given new, severely functional governing bodies (mayor, aldermen and councillors) elected by the ten-pound occupiers, and these bodies were empowered to raise rates, attend to the paving, watching and lighting of their boroughs and generally make rules for the good government of the borough. Their bye-laws could be disallowed by the lord lieutenant, who was also empowered to nominate the sheriffs in the county boroughs. Any town with a population of over 3,000 might be incorporated by the queen in council on the petition of a majority of the ratepayers. Actually only one town (Wexford, incorporated 1845) was added to the original ten during the next ten years. The other boroughs were encouraged to adopt the act of 1828. If they failed to do so the property of the defunct corporations was entrusted either to elected municipal commissioners or to the local poor law guardians.

The creation of a well-disciplined national police force, organised on semi-military lines and directly controlled by the central government, was a slow process with overlapping stages, jealously watched by the Irish country gentry, who abhorred the arbitrary tendencies inherent in centralisation almost as much as they disliked the destruction of local patronage. By legislation passed at the close of the eighteenth century the lord lieutenant was empowered to appoint a head constable in each barony, the sub-constables being nominated by the grand jury.[15] The baronial police force so created was later steadily brought under tighter government control. The lord lieutenant was empowered to dismiss constables, to issue equipment, to move members of the force from one district to another, and (in 1822) to appoint four provincial inspectors general with power to issue rules for the constabulary forces in their areas.[16] In 1814 the baronial police was supplemented and stiffened by the peace preservation force, the first ' peelers '. In districts which were ' in a state of disturbance and

. . . required an extraordinary establishment of police ' the lord lieutenant could appoint a chief police magistrate with the powers of a justice of the peace, having a special corps of constables under his command.[17]   A number of these special magistrates were appointed and they and their ' rough and ready boys '[18] carried on a conflict with lawlessness which at times developed into an adventurous guerrilla war.   In 1833 the peace preservation force, which was mainly concentrated in a few counties, numbered about a thousand.   The baronial police force, distributed over the whole country, numbered about seven thousand.[19]   In addition to these two forces there was the revenue police, a creation of private enterprise.   Early in the century it was customary for revenue officers engaged in the perilous duty of ' still hunting ' which involved ' proceeding into very remote and wild parts ' to secure the assistance of small military detachments.   The military authorities about 1817 forbade the practice, on the grounds that it was bad for discipline.   Thereupon active gaugers organised bands of their own, ' men caught up and hired and arms put into their hands, mere countrymen ', ' every man almost, married with a tribe of children, they were wretchedly lodged and miserably clothed '. The undisciplined proceedings of these revenue irregulars aroused more hostility than their naturally unpopular if essential duties warranted.[20]   Lastly there was the Dublin police which had been the subject of frequent legislation from the early eighteenth century.   As a result of a long series of enactments Dublin in 1835 possessed a police establishment comprising four divisional police courts and a number of constables.   It was administratively top-heavy, exceedingly costly, and notoriously inefficient.   The day patrol for the whole city amounted to a few score constables, and the night watch was made up of feeble and decrepit old men, clothed in rough great-coats which served to cover the deficiencies of the rest of their clothes, whom an experienced magistrate refused to parade in daylight since he knew their appearance would only excite ridicule.[21]

In the middle thirties the government took energetic and extensive measures to give the country a police force which would both effectively cope with crime and rapidly respond to the orders of the Irish executive.   Morpeth's police act of 1836 amalgamated the county police and the peace preservation force.   An inspector general was appointed, empowered to ' provide one uniform system of rules and regulations for the Irish police establishment'. Gradations of rank based on those used in the army were introduced, the men were clothed in a plain, workmanlike rifleman's uniform and it was declared that recruits were to be 'of sound constitution, able to read and write and of a good character for honesty, fidelity and activity'. In 1839 a depot for training recruits was set up in Dublin and a reserve created which could swiftly be sent to any part of Ireland.[22] In 1845 the force which numbered 9,000[23] had been brought to a high pitch of efficiency, and, possibly owing to the fact that when 'the Irish people are persuaded that a man is doing a duty which is a legitimate duty the greatest possible allowance is made for him',[24] the force was apparently not unpopular. In the same year as Morpeth introduced his police bill he took steps to give Dublin an efficient force under the immediate authority of the chief secretary. Two commissioners were appointed, some trained officers were imported from England, and in 1844 the Dublin metropolitan police numbered eleven hundred. In the same year William Brereton was placed in command of the revenue force, which he rapidly reformed, selecting his officers carefully, requiring recruits to be of respectable character, and establishing a depot in which they were trained on military lines, 'for luckily the movement of light infantry was discovered to be applicable to still hunting '—the police advancing in extended action when tracking down the still, then falling into a closed square when carrying off offenders. In the early fifties the force numbered about one thousand, a third of it being stationed in the north-west corner of Ireland.

## IV. SICKNESS AND POVERTY

In the prevalent attitude to the poor at the beginning of the nineteenth century severity (bordering on contempt) was incongruously blended with compassion. Economic theory, newly systematised, declared with adolescent confidence that the intricate series of relationships between supply and demand which secured the maximum satisfaction of human wants, was so delicately poised, that any interference with it would have untold and probably disastrous consequences. In any case there was no reason to interfere, for the regularly working mechanism automatically assured every able-bodied individual of his due reward. On the other hand rationalism, evangelicalism and humanitarianism had bred anxiety to relieve suffering and a distaste for brutality. Caution therefore, not callousness, marked the age's approach to social problems. The traditional objects of human pity : the young, the infirm, the aged, economically speaking *hors de combat*, must be aided. But no one who was capable of economic exertion was to be permitted to shirk playing his part in the productive process. The most important piece of social legislation enacted by the Irish parliament in the eighteenth century, the act empowering counties to erect houses of industry, is solidly based on these ideas. A clear division is made between the deserving poor and the rest. The helpless poor, ' reduced to that state by sickness or misfortune', were to be badged and authorized to beg, or to be cared for in the houses. But ' disorderly persons', 'strolling vagrants capable of labour' were to be conditioned to honest toil by imprisonment and hard labour.[1] The scheme was certainly comprehensive. But as its execution was entrusted to local bodies of administrative amateurs, unsupervised and undirected by any central authority, it was initiated in only a few areas. Most counties ignored the act. Only nine adopted it to a limited extent.

Less ambitious but more successful were the attempts to provide for the sick poor, which were begun in the early nineteenth century. Three different types of institution were founded, dispensaries where the poor could receive free medical advice and medicine, infirmaries for serious cases and fever hospitals.[2] In 1805 it was enacted that if a dispensary was set up voluntarily, the grand jury could annually make a grant equal to the amounts subscribed. As a result dispensaries multiplied. By 1833 there were 450, twelve years later there were 632—only 20 short of the total which it was estimated would meet the country's needs. Unfortunately their distribution was not ideal, Connacht the poorest province having only thirteen per cent. of the total number. But this was inevitable in the case of institutions established by private enterprise. Dispensaries apparently were sometimes opened because the subscribers wanted to secure—partly of course at the expense of the rates—the presence of a competent medical man in the neighbourhood to attend to themselves.

As a class the dispensary doctors were not well paid. The

average income from a dispensary was only seventy-one pounds
per annum at a time when, according to Stokes the celebrated
Trinity professor, a dispensary doctor ran greater risks than a
soldier on active service.[3] Naturally the dispensaries were highly
popular though the cantankerous grumbled at the quality and
lack of variety in the medicine supplied. Dispensary doctors
themselves frequently pointed out that medicine alone was not
sufficient to ensure health, their view being bluntly stated by a
beggar who remarked that poor creatures often went to a dispensary doctor ' when a bellyful of victuals would do them more
good than salts '.[4]

Behind the dispensaries were the county infirmaries, in 1843
thirty-four in number. These ' receptacles for the infirm and
diseased' (as they were described in one of the acts relating to
them) varied in size, containing from thirty to seventy beds. On
the whole they were well conducted, and the policy of the Queen's
County infirmary—never to refuse a patient urgently requiring
attention even if the institution was full to capacity (after all
children could be put two in a bed or sheds erected)—at least
shows a determined good nature.[5]

The fever hospitals were a direct result of the prolonged and
widespread epidemic of 1816–18, which coincided with the immediate post-war depression. Sympathy and selfish fear (for, as the
statute book candidly declared, fever among the poor menaced
the health and prosperity of the whole community) both demanded
prompt and positive relief measures. And in 1818 committees in
every county were empowered to build fever hospitals ' as plain,
as durable and at as moderate expense as may be '. By 1830 over
forty had been opened, fifteen years later there were just over a
hundred, and only three counties had failed to erect at least one.
At first they were distrusted, it being said that a poor man attacked
by fever was as likely to recover under a hedge as in a fever
hospital. And a description of conditions in a Limerick fever
hospital during a typhus epidemic between 1816 and 1819, with
patients lying three in a bed in an intolerably hot room—shows
that the popular notion was not altogether absurd. But by 1843
it was thought that the poor had lost their prejudices against going
into a fever hospital.[6]

Finally, during the early nineteenth century, an attempt had
been made to provide for the most helpless class in the country.

At the beginning of the century the only accommodation for the lunatic poor was a few miserable cells, mere kennels attached to the houses of industry. Three parliamentary committees considered the problem, and in 1810 a grant was made for the construction of the Richmond asylum in Dublin. When it was opened five years later the governors, adopting the humane methods advocated by Pinel, dispensed with the usual chains, fetters and handcuffs for treating the insane. By a series of important measures passed between 1817 and 1827 the central government was empowered to erect ten large district asylums, each serving several counties. These in 1840 were well managed institutions employing humane methods of treatment. Their principal defect was that by then they had become seriously overcrowded so that not only were pauper lunatics being confined in gaols, but the poor law commissioners had proposed lodging them in the new workhouses, where the accommodation for the insane was both inadequate and out-of-date. In 1842 a parliamentary commission commented sharply both on the overcrowding and on the remedies employed. As a result the government took comparatively prompt steps to enlarge the asylums and to construct a special institution for the reception of criminal lunatics.[7]

If Irish medical relief at the beginning of the forties was of a limited and often crude kind, contemporaries could congratulate themselves on what had been achieved since the beginning of the century. The laws of supply and demand had in this instance at least worked, and the Irish poor enjoyed better medical services than their fellows in wealthier and healthier countries. The working of the same laws was shown on a smaller scale in Dublin, where at the beginning of the century there were only eleven hospitals. During the next forty years private enterprise guided by zealous medical men and aided in some instances by government grants had almost trebled the number, and by 1845 there were fully thirty public hospitals in Dublin. Of these twenty-one were specialist institutions, including four lunatic asylums, six maternity and four fever hospitals. If these hospitals were a response to the needs of a city in which an enormous mass of poverty was concentrated, the Dublin tradition of medical training was to a great extent the most important bye-product of their work. In 1784 the Dublin college of surgeons was incorporated.

It developed rapidly into a teaching and examining body, and though its licentiates were naturally surgical specialists they were trained and tested in other branches of medicine.[8] In 1785, possibly stimulated by the surgeons' enterprise, the well-established college of physicians in collaboration with the board of Trinity college took measures to broaden the range and raise the standards of the medical course in Dublin university. Corporate bodies are uneasy yoke-fellows and long negotiations and several acts of parliament were required before the university medical school was placed on a satisfactory footing. But by 1810 it had five chairs and a newly built clinical hospital. During the next forty years an amazing galaxy of medical talent clustered round the Trinity college school. In 1813 James Macartney, the greatest anatomist of his day was appointed university professor of anatomy and surgery. Often distracted by academic squabbles, he insisted on regular attendance at lectures, raised the standard of examinations, and, for the first time in a British or Irish university, introduced lectures on pathology.[9] His colleague Whitley Stokes (professor of physic 1830–45), theologian, social worker, economist and politician, was the founder of a remarkable medical dynasty. His son and immediate successor William Stokes, a pioneer in the use of the stethescope, in alliance with Robert James Graves (professor of the institutes of medicine 1826–7) strove to introduce systematic methods of clinical instruction. They emphasised that a medical student must not merely ' as it is quaintly enough termed *walk* the hospitals ', but must ' anxiously cultivate the habit of making accurate observations '. Though Graves' name is usually associated with a form of goitre (Graves' disease) he also paid special attention to the epidemics which ravaged Ireland, claiming as his epitaph the phrase which summed up his treatment : ' he fed fever '. His older contemporary Colles, whose name is also permanently preserved in medical terminology by ' Colles's fracture ' taught at the college of surgeons for over thirty years until shortly before his death in 1843. Macartney, Stokes, Graves and Colles were ably seconded by a number of first-class if less eminent physicians, including Crampton a bon-vivant and one of the most daring surgeons of his day, Wilde the eye-specialist and statistician, Carmichael who declared his reputation rested on three legs—syphilis, scrofula and cancer—and Jacob and Maunsell, keen medical politicians, unrestrained in ferocity when fighting for professional reform in the *Dublin Medical Press* which they edited. One sign of the vitality of the Dublin medical world was the comparatively large number of medical journals which appeared there during the first half of the century, the Dublin *Journal of Medical and Chemical Science* claiming indeed to be the first successful Irish periodical since the Union. Another sign was the existence of several private medical schools, organised by small groups of medical men who relied on their reputations to attract pupils, whose products could qualify at the examinations held by the college of surgeons.[10]

Until the end of the thirties sickness was the only form of distress for which anything approaching adequate relief was available in Ireland. One of the most striking differences between England and Ireland was the absence in the latter of any equivalent to the Elizabethan poor law. When this great collection of palliatives was being systematised in England, Ireland, disunited and distracted by civic commotions, was scarcely in a position to devise scientific measures of social security. Commonplace poverty was easily overlooked amongst the hideous miseries of endemic civil war, and when later, during the placid eighteenth century, the Irish parliament had time to attend to the condition of the poor it was content to rely on less comprehensive expedients. In England parochial charity might be unsympathetic and stinted, but at least it assured the aged, the young, the permanently infirm and the unemployed, of a subsistence. In Ireland these unhappy categories were unprotected by any national scheme. Admittedly a number of agencies ministered to their needs. But they were badly distributed, unco-ordinated, and often ill-supported, and their united efforts were puny compared with the vast sum total of misery they were striving to alleviate.

The houses of industry, of which there were twelve in 1836, have already been referred to. The Dublin house, with its large modern buildings and separate departments, was an impressive and efficient institution. The Belfast poorhouse admitted only the aged and the young. It was managed with 'admirable economy', the inmates being fed at an average cost of $2\frac{1}{2}d$. each per day. They were quiet and orderly (except a few old people whom no precautions could keep from drinking), perhaps because they were kept busy—most of the work of the house, repairs, gardening, washing and coffin-making being done by the inmates. Each of the other houses contained a heterogeneous, closely packed collection of both sexes, the able-bodied, the sick, lunatics, idiots and in some places children. In spite of the name little or no work seems to have been performed in these houses, with the result that by the early thirties the Ennis establishment was said to be 'approaching, if it has not already touched the dangerous point, when the cunning, lying idler will exert all his ingenuity to get into it or to keep in it when he ought to be turned out to make room for a proper object'. And at Cork 'a host of drones' (according to the governors) were only driven away when discipline was tightened up and the rations cut down.[11]

Up to 1838 the government attempted to cope with Irish distress mainly along two lines, by encouraging local health services and by subsidising public works. During the eighteenth century the Irish parliament, aware of the requirements of an economically backward country, eager to assert its right over any surplus in the Irish exchequer, and responsive to local lobbying, had with growing generosity made large grants towards the improvement of communications, and the development of the textile industries. After the Union this tradition persisted and the imperial parliament for many years voted considerable sums in the shape of loans or grants for the construction of harbours and post roads, and canals, the erection of bridewells, gaols and workhouses, the building of churches and the widening of the Dublin streets.[12]

The primary object of these measures was not of course the provision of work for the Irish poor, though that was an important consequence of their operation, but in 1817 the government, striving to cope with the post-war depression, set up a comparatively large loan fund from which advances might be made, to individuals or corporate bodies 'interested in any works of a public nature which might afford employment for the labouring classes'. By further legislation these facilities were extended, and between 1817 and 1830 well over a million was advanced for fisheries, roads, mines and public buildings.

In 1831 the duty of supervising loans and grants for public works was entrusted to the newly constituted board of works, and between then and 1845 that body advanced loans and grants amounting to well over a million.[13] The board was under the presidency of Burgoyne, a scientific soldier with a fine Peninsula record for courage and capability, and had definite views which it expressed with pungency in its annual reports.[14] As far as possible the execution of projects on which public money was being spent should be carried out under the supervision of a responsible government department. The claims of landowners for compensation should be scrutinised strictly, for as soon as the public purse was opened the most exorbitant demands were made. In selecting from the multitude of schemes pressed on the government, those which conferred an immediate and exclusive advantage should be carefully distinguished from others of greater utility whose benefits would be diffused throughout the community. The former would almost certainly be pushed with greater importunity, the latter were to be preferred. The board deplored the blind refusal of many local bodies to realise that the cost of productive public works would to a great extent be recovered by the locality. And it regretted the way in which grand juries when planning public works neglected the poor, uninfluential, out of the way parts of the country. The board emphasised that it was bad policy to put off the Irish labourer with insufficient remuneration. There was some truth in the accusation that the Irish peasant was often a listless worker. But the reason was obvious. He was so burdened with arrears of rent that any extra exertion on his part merely profited his landlord. The board, as an employer, paid 'task wages' (i.e. piece-work) and the results were most satisfactory. Though the board was convinced that public works should not be begun solely with the aim of giving employment, it considered that when 'well designed projects capable of effecting permanent improvements could be made auxiliary to such a desirable object the result was most satisfactory'. And it was delighted when in 1842 'by a happy coincidence' it was able to start works in Kerry and Connemara just at a time when the population was suffering from severe privations, and that by the arrangements thus made 'employment was so diffused as to give every family a portion of its advantage'. Another and more significant fact afforded the board considerable satisfaction. The planned network of roads which it had built in the undeveloped districts had opened them up with the results which might have been expected—the methods of cultivation had been improved, primitive implements abandoned and far greater respect paid to law and order.

Public works and the houses of industry, the state's methods

of coping with distress, were supplemented by various forms of
private action, mendicity societies, almshouses, church collections,
endowments—which supplied small doles of food or money—
and of course the charity of the poor towards one another.  The
almshouses which existed in a dozen Irish towns contained only
a few inmates, and the charitable funds though fairly numerous
were pitifully small.  The most prominent and active charitable
organisations were the mendicity societies, which aimed at driving
the beggar off the streets by both making it difficult for him to
ply his trade and at the same time presenting him with a hard
alternative means of livelihood.  Of these societies the Belfast
house of industry founded in 1800 claimed to be the oldest, while
the Dublin Association was the most publicised.  The Belfast
society owed its success to ' its zealous, intelligent and benevolent
conductors, who administered relief not under a blind and heed-
less impulse of benevolence, but . . . with a degree of harshness
which sometimes goes against their better feelings '.  While its
beadles took up beggars and clapped them in ' a miserable vault ',
the society granted rations of meal, potatoes, and soup to six
hundred poor families (to whom a strict means test was applied),
employed destitute men and women on stone breaking and spinning and distributed daily to the poor and destitute as much hard
bread as they could eat.  The Dublin Association, which was
founded in 1818 when the streets of the city were filled by crowds
of ' clamorous beggars ', exhibiting misery and decrepitude in a
variety of forms and frequently carrying about on their persons
and garments the seeds of contagious disease, gave to all who
applied two square meals a day (made up partly of the broken
meat its carts collected).  Those who were incapable of work
were given a few pence a week, while the able-bodied were
employed in spinning, breaking stones, bruising oats and picking
oakum.  The other Irish mendicity societies, most of which were
in the north, usually merely distributed food or money.  The
mendicity societies' charity may have been hard, but their supporters were keenly conscious that they alone were carrying a
burden which ought to have been shared by their less public-
spirited neighbours.  Occasionally they were driven to suggest
that a general rate should be levied for the poor, and at one time
when the Dublin Association was badly in need of support its
members threatened to close the institution, turning the beggars

out on to the street to howl before the houses of the non-subscribers.[15]

The efforts of the mendicity societies and the total intake of all the houses of industry could only affect comparatively small zones. Over most of the country there was no public provision whatever for the aged, the permanently disabled, or the unemployed. The aged were looked after by their children, quartered themselves on charitable neighbours, or drifted over the countryside begging. The able-bodied unemployed—a category to which most labourers belonged for some months at least of every year—lived on their potato plots, bought food on credit from shopkeepers and hucksters, reduced their consumption, starved, or begged. If Ireland had been a prosperous country, with a progressive and balanced economy, or at the worst a contented one, then the deplorable deficiencies in its social services might have been disregarded or at least endured. But from the beginning of the nineteenth century it was painfully obvious that Ireland was destined to be the great distressed area of the United Kingdom. Within three months of the Union coming into effect parliament was asked to enact emergency legislation for the preservation of order. And if in the highly charged war-atmosphere of the immediate post-Union years, Irish disturbances could be attributed to agitators or enemy agents, later, with the United Kingdom at peace and Irish agriculture sustaining the full force of the post-war depression, it was quite obvious they were deep rooted in agrarian distress. Unfortunately during the period between the Union and the Famine, Catholic emancipation and repeal almost monopolised public attention and threw their shadow over the consideration of every other subject. Although the general situation justified Sheridan's comment, that to concentrate on the Catholic question while ignoring social problems was like 'dressing or decorating the topmasts of a ship when there are ten feet of water in the hold',[16] it must be admitted that religious disabilities and the constitutional situation had economic repercussions, and controversialists when discussing them did not hesitate to conscript economic arguments to support their case. But as long as these two great debating questions occupied the stage, Ireland's problems were usually found to be considered in political or theological terms. Nevertheless from the beginning of the nineteenth century there was a constant flow of comment on Ireland's

economic conditions and prospects. Four parliamentary committees and two important royal commissions surveyed the state
of the Irish poor, English tourists took advantage of the improvement in communications between the islands and discovered a
part of the United Kingdom, and there was a constant flow of
pamphlets either pressing a specific panacea or recommending an
ambitious programme of reforms. Nearly all this remedial literature is strongly marked by two features—a realistic and gloomy
appreciation of existing circumstances, and an abounding optimism
concerning the acceptability and value of the plans advocated.

This wide and sometimes arid expanse of print was ably sum-
marised by the poor law commissioners of 1833 when ponderously
narrating the difficulties which had confronted them. ' On every
side,' they wrote, ' we were assailed by the theories of those who
were born or had long resided in the country. One party
attributed all the poverty and wretchedness of the country to an
asserted extreme use of ardent spirits, and proposed a system for
repressing illicit distillation, for preventing smuggling and for
substituting beer and coffee. Another party found the cause in
the combination amongst workmen, and proposed rigorous laws
against trades unions. Others again were equally confident that
the reclamation of the bogs and waste lands was the only practicable remedy. A fourth party declared the existing connection
between landlord and tenant to be the root of all the evil ; pawn-
broking, redundant population, absence of capital, peculiar religious tenets and religious differences, political excitement, want of
education, the maladministration of justice, the state of prison
discipline, want of manufactures and of inland navigation, with a
variety of other circumstances, were each supported by their
various advocates, with earnestness and ability, as being either alone
or jointly with some other, the primary cause of all the evils of
society ; and loan funds, emigration, the repression of political
excitement, the introduction of manufactures, and the extension of
inland navigation were accordingly proposed, each as the principal
means by which the improvement of Ireland could be promoted.'[17]

It need hardly be emphasised that the effect of each project on
the standard of living of the Irish poor would be limited and often
indirect and distant. Also it is noticeable that in this eclectic and
lengthy list of remedies there is one striking and significant omission, nothing is said about an Irish poor law based on the English

model. This however is scarcely surprising, since one of the main contentions of the report was that such a measure was thoroughly unsuited to Irish conditions. In taking this line the commission of 1833 was merely following precedent. Three parliamentary committees had already issued tremulous warnings against the introduction of the English poor law system into Ireland.[18] But the very phrases used in these reports reflect an uneasy awareness that such a measure might be as inevitable as it was undesirable. Most of the other schemes for the relief of Irish distress would take time to implement, while a poor law though only an unsatisfactory palliative would have immediate and direct results. Admittedly the beginning of the nineteenth century was an inopportune period to consider copying the English system of poor law relief. With its principles obscured by war-time innovations, and discredited by maladministration and extravagance, it was a target for continual criticism. Nevertheless, as was often pointed out in discussions on the subject, ' the abuse of a thing did not take away the lawful use of it ', and between 1825 and 1837 no fewer than seven Irish poor law bills were introduced into the house of commons by private members. These ranged from modest proposals empowering the Irish vestries to raise a rate for the relief of the helpless poor, to Poulett Scrope's comprehensive measure of 1835 which attempted to set up elaborate machinery—locally elected authorities and a central board—for relieving the destitute and employing the able-bodied workless on the construction of canals, road-making and other public projects. According to Scrope, only two parties opposed a poor law for Ireland, a section of the Irish landlords and a section of political economists. The reason for the hostility of the former was simple. They did not want to pay rates which it was asserted might rise to confiscatory levels and make the rich landlords paupers on their own estates. The economists' opposition was based on more general and theoretical arguments. The introduction of a poor law into Ireland, they declared, would convert charity into a legal obligation, encourage the indefinite growth of a servile population, tax production for the benefit of the idle, fatally weaken the spirit of prudence and industry, and finally lead to the poor ' becoming co-proprietors of the soil ' and all classes being confounded on a dead level, leaving ' none at liberty and leisure to sound the depths of science or cultivate the field

of knowledge '.[19]   The *Edinburgh Review* which in a glittering
article slashed out on the subject, declared that a poor law for
Ireland could safely be introduced into Ireland only if there was
in Ireland a superabundance of good principle, and of sound sense,
of thoughtfulness for the wants of tomorrow, of careful providence—if there was a horror of all jobbery, and an acknowledged
purity in dealing with the public money, and a love and respect
for the law and its pure administration.[20]   Advocates of a poor law
for Ireland retorted by emphasising the proverbial and unparalleled poverty of the country, ' the atmosphere of misery ' which
Musgrave, who introduced the bill in 1836, declared he felt whenever he returned home,[21] and the danger that the Irish poor
unemployed and unprovided for at home would pour across the
Channel, forcing down by their hungry competition the standard
of living of the English labourer and driving up the rates.   It was
fallacious to assume that a poor law would diminish capital in
Ireland.   Rather by promoting peace and security it would encourage investment, while landowners, stimulated by the pressure
of a poor rate, would probably find some more profitable way of
employing the paupers on their estates.   As for the argument that
the absence of a poor law stimulated charity, the *Quarterly* suggested that the sight of a large proportion of the population being
kept in a state of poverty for the sake of encouraging the generous
feelings of their slightly happier neighbours was worthy of
inclusion in *Gulliver's Travels*.[22]   In any case the organ of economic
radicalism pointed out the landlord was already taxed by his
having to maintain an army of mendicants and had so much less
left for rent.   Admittedly the beggar by his badgering probably
raised more than any rate-collector could, but then the workhouse
system would probably be cheaper.[23]

Lord Grey's government, finding Ireland its most intractable
and urgent problem, in September 1833 appointed a strong commission with wide terms of reference to inquire into the condition
of the Irish poor and suggest remedial measures.   The commission
which ultimately numbered twelve, included the two archbishops
of Dublin, the active-minded Whately and the mild Murray,
Vignoles, the placid and shrewd dean of the Chapel Royal,
Carlile, a Scotsman, an educationalist, and vehement Protestant
controversialist, three English poor law experts, Bicheno,
a sharp-minded barrister who had published a wordy work

on Ireland, Wrightson ' an old-fashioned whig ' and Corrie, a
Birmingham Unitarian, who was one of the early supporters of
the British Association, three Irish country gentlemen, More
O'Ferrall, Napier, a reforming landlord, and the methodical Hort,
father of the famous theologian, a young Catholic whig, Lord
Killeen, and Anthony Blake, the chief remembrancer, a leading
Catholic layman, noted for his wide and intimate knowledge of
Irish affairs, tact and unobtrusively exerted influence on govern-
ment policy.

The commissioners began by appointing a number of sub-
commissioners who visited institutions, toured the country and
collected a mass of statistics relating to the standard of living
of the peasantry and the existing methods of relief. In a number
of parishes throughout the country, the sub-commissioners
assembled a heterogeneous group of the inhabitants and encouraged
them to state their views on social conditions in their neighbourhood. Their voluble replies, recorded verbatim, resulted in a
volume of half a million words. The commission's report based
on a gigantic accumulation of detailed evidence finally appeared
in the spring of 1836, and though diffuse and ill-arranged was
a bold and constructive document.[24] Accepting the widely
held opinion that in Ireland the problem was not ' to make
the able-bodied look for employment but to find it profitable
for the many who seek it ', the commissioners advocated the
appointment of a board which would promote ' a comprehensive
scheme of national improvement '. The board, which was to be
financed partly by local taxation and partly by grants from the
exchequer, was to improve communications, carry on reclama-
tions and drainage on a large scale, replace insanitary cabins by
decent cottages, and further schemes of agricultural education.
A special administrative court of review was to decide ' promptly
and justly ' all legal questions arising out of the board's operations.
The commission also recommended that the fiscal powers of the
grand juries should be transferred to elected county boards, that
the leasing powers of tenants for life should be enlarged (their
exercise being supervised by the board of improvements), that
local loan funds should be established for the poor, that the state
should buy out the tithe owners (making a handsome profit on
the transaction), that the licensing laws should be tightened up
(dram shops being closed on Sundays) and that emigration which

the commission regarded as a temporary 'essential auxiliary to a course of amelioration', should be properly organised. Emigration depots were to be set up from which vagrants were to be transported as free labourers, and where poor persons desiring to emigrate would be granted the cost of their passage and the means of settling themselves in a British colony.

On the most topical question they had to tackle the commissioners had decided if muddled views. They were convinced that 'out-door employment' (i.e. the allowance system) would demoralise the peasantry and swallow the rental of the country. As for the new English poor law system based on the workhouse it was 'not at all suited to Ireland', firstly because distress was so widespread that accommodation would have to be provided for well over two million people, and secondly because the Irish poor would refuse to resort to the workhouses. Having thus, in the opening section of the report, pronounced decisively against relief for the able-bodied in either of the usual forms, the commissioners later adumbrated a plan for reorganising and supplementing the existing methods of coping with distress. Elected boards of guardians in each district were to levy a poor rate and take measures to provide for the insane, the sick and infirm poor, the aged, helpless widows with young children, the families of the sick poor and cases of casual distress. In fact, torn between fear and good nature, the commissioners ended by producing a confused and ill-defined compromise. Cornewall Lewis, an able and assiduous young whig civil servant, who had some experience of Irish conditions, immediately pointed out that the commission had blundered badly by excluding the able-bodied from relief and at the same time admitting a number of other categories some of which might be stretched to include able-bodied persons. The first decision was unfair, the latter invited fraud on a large scale.

Taken as a whole, however, the report was bold and positive and was destined to win the unstinted admiration of a subsequent royal commission seventy years after publication. But any government might well have been daunted by a document whose eclectic recommendations could only have been implemented by forcing several highly controversial measures through parliament. And though Whately was confident that it was impossible for so variegated a body of commissioners 'as different from each other in the modes of their education, and in their subsequent habits of life, as any men could be', to concur 'in any *one* erroneous notion ',[25] the whole conception of extensive, energetic and prolonged intervention by the state in economic life was utterly alien to the prevalent trends in economic thought.

Cornewall Lewis in the extensive memorandum, which at the request of the government he wrote on the report, dismissed summarily most of the commission's development plans, ' the scheme of the government managing everything for individuals is very captivating and plausible at first sight, but it invariably ends by producing lethargy and helplessness in the people '. If they attempted to perform the part of a capitalist, ' of managing private property by a public authority ', it would lead either to nothing whatever being done because of bureaucratic caution and legalism or endless frauds and jobbing ' which would assume so many and subtle forms, as to elude the most keen-sighted and upright public officers, even if we were justified in expecting that these qualifications would be universally found among the persons who would be employed in laying out public money upon the properties of Irish landlords '. Nassau Senior, the government's other economic consultant, was also shocked by the powers which were to be given to the board of improvement which he was sure would be abused. The suggestion that the board should assist landlords to improve lands already under cultivation would obviously lead to endless expenditure.[26]

Though Senior and Lewis belonged generally speaking to the same school of economic thought, they differed sharply on one practicable issue when dealing with the Irish problem. Senior was firmly set against relieving the able-bodied through a system supported by public money. The standard of living of the poor in Ireland was so low that any provision made by the state would be superior. Lewis on the contrary (as might be expected from his background—his father Frankland Lewis being the chairman of the new English poor law commission) was an eager advocate for the extension of the English system to Ireland. The workhouse test of ' less eligibility' could, he was confident, function there in spite of the low standard of comfort, for ' the *forced labour,* the *discipline*, the *separation*, and the *confinement* will be sufficient checks against unfounded applications for relief '. He argued that increased agricultural productivity and a decent standard of living for the bulk of the Irish peasantry depended on holdings being consolidated and the labourer being paid his wages in cash instead of being fobbed off with a minute potato patch. But he was aware that it was almost impossible under existing conditions to induce the Irish cottiers to relax their tenacious grip on the few acres which lay between them and starvation. And the Irish peasantry could employ in self-defence a powerful if ugly weapon, ' the whiteboy code of terrorism '. But if the poor were guaranteed by law a minimum subsistence when destitute, the Irish landlords (whom Lewis contemptuously tolerates as performing rather badly necessary economic functions), relieved from the pressure of public opinion, could go ahead and manage their estates on progressive lines.

After penning his memorandum on the lines just indicated, Lewis was confident that he had made ' a complete smash '[27] of the poor law commission's report. And the direction in which the government was tending was clearly shown a couple of months later, when at the beginning of the recess, George Nicholls was instructed to visit Ireland and enquire into the question of poor relief. Stolid, public-spirited and full of administrative energy and self-assurance, he spent six weeks in Ireland travelling round by the approved tourist route. Within another six weeks he produced a short, readable report, in which having surveyed Ireland's problem from the standpoint of a poor law expert, he unhesitatingly recommended the extension to that country of the system he had done so much to initiate in England. Though, as he was careful to point out, he did not expect his poor law policy to work miracles, the consequences he predicted are astounding enough. If the poor law was introduced measures could be taken against mendicity. It would enable the country to pass quietly through the transition period, from the existing situation where the peasant paid in labour the rent of a small plot to the time when he would be a daily wage earner. It would break the Irish vicious circle in which want of capital produced unemployment, and lack of work led to turbulence and insecurity which discouraged the investment of capital in Irish agriculture. In short, the general development of the country and the elevation of the great mass of the Irish people ' appear to be all the more or less contingent on the enactment of a soundly devised poor law '.

There was Nicholls emphasised only one problem with which a proper law could not cope—a general famine. This was a contingency 'altogether above the powers of a poor law to provide for'. The workhouses could not hold the people who would demand food, and the expectation of outdoor relief would only 'lessen the inducements to a provident economising of their means of support on the part of the people' by a timely resort to which the occurrence of actual famine may be averted. Moreover if there was an actual deficiency, 'to assess the ratepayers in order to enable the non-ratepayers to continue their ordinary consumption would only be to shift the suffering'. Finally the problem seemed rather academic. 'As the habits, intelligence and forethought of the people improve with the increase of wealth and the progress of education' it was highly unlikely that any considerable proportion of the Irish poor would suffer from famine.[28]

Nicholls reported in November 1836, and in the following spring the government (Melbourne lamenting that his Irish colleagues could not think of anything better) introduced an Irish poor relief bill which finally received the royal assent in the July of the following year. Ireland was to be divided into a number of unions, each with its workhouse and board of guardians. The boards were to be composed of *ex-officio* and elected guardians in the ratio of one to three, the former being local justices of the peace, the latter chosen by the ratepayers. This introduced a considerable measure of democracy into local affairs, since the poor rate was to be paid by the occupier who could then deduct from his rent half the poundage rate he had paid. Several regulations however ensured that numbers would be balanced by property. Occupiers rated at under five pounds could arrange with their landlord that he should pay the rate, and the large ratepayers were allowed extra votes in accordance with the value of their property. Direction, control and drive were to be supplied by the English poor law commission whose jurisdiction was extended to Ireland. The English commissioners were empowered to issue orders covering all aspects of poor law administration, to take evidence on oath, to form unions, to arrange for the election of guardians, to fix the salaries of the union officials, and if necessary remove them, to build workhouses, inspect hospitals maintained by the grand jury, and even supersede unsatisfactory or inefficient boards of guardians by its own officials. Care was taken to prevent the moral stamina of the Irish poor being undermined by the new system. No right to relief was granted and all relief was to be administered within the workhouse. The relief could be declared a loan and recovered from the recipient. It may be added that the natural affections and economy were made to coincide. The family (i.e. parents, and children under fifteen) being treated as a unit, parents were responsible for maintenance of children, and children could be sued for relief given to parents.

As the parliamentary debates on the bill were conducted with an unusual and agreeable absence of party feeling, they rather meandered, while many of those taking part fumbled honestly with the problem instead of delivering a clear-cut exposition of a partisan case. In the commons O'Connell, after some hesitation came out definitely against the bill on the grounds that it ' would tend to diminish self-reliance, to paralyse industry, to decrease economy and above all to damp and extinguish the generous feelings of nature towards parents, children, relations and friends ', and he was supported by a curious medley of members drawn from almost all quarters of the house. In the lords by incongruous chance the opposition was led by Lyndhurst, O'Connell's much abused *bête noire*, who on the second reading delivered an early but vigorous attack on the principle of delegated legislation. The bill, he complained, was a series of blanks to be filled in at pleasure by the officials in Somerset House. Throughout these discussions the opponents of the bill were badly handicapped by their unwillingness or inability to produce an alternative. Public works were only tentatively and timidly referred to, for the rest opponents of the bill fastened with gusto on the many points of detail which they considered defective, emphasised the arbitrary powers of the commissioners, and prophesied that Ireland would be ruined by a system of relief which would probably swallow half the rental of the country.[29]

Within a fortnight of the bill receiving the royal assent steps were taken to implement it.[30] Nicholls, who had drafted it, watched over its progress, and when necessary, ' put spirit into the members of the government ', was appointed resident commissioner in Ireland. But though he was detached from his colleagues at Somerset House, the poor law commission's indivisibility was preserved—in form by its seal being kept in London, in fact by a constant interchange of minutes between London and Dublin. To assist him Nicholls had at first eight sub-commissioners—four experienced English officials and four Irishmen. The latter were John William Handcock, William Clements, a younger son of the earl of Leitrim, who had served in the army and was later to sit in parliament as member for county Leitrim, Denis Phelan, a medical man who had written on the question of poor relief, and John O'Donoghue, a young barrister of pronounced liberal opinions, in later years editor of the *Freeman's Journal*. The first secretary to the commissions in Dublin was William Stanley, that *rara avis*, an Irish utilitarian who had pronounced love of country to be ' a mere illusory excitement '—national boundaries often obstructing economic and social progress—and called for far-reaching political reform.

During the next five years or so the commission accomplished the gigantic administrative task of installing and starting the new administrative machinery in Ireland, and the system can be studied in detail in their annual reports, well drafted, readable documents, at times almost oozing complacency. By July 1841 Ireland had been divided into 130 unions, each with its limits defined, its electoral divisions fixed, its valuation almost completed, its board of guardians beginning to function, and in fourteen instances with its workhouses open. Shortly after Nicholls arrived in Ireland it was discovered that the poor law commission had not been empowered to delegate its duty of constructing workhouses to the obvious agency, the board of works. Nothing daunted the commission appointed its own architect, Wilkinson, who had had considerable experience in building workhouses in Wales, and who promptly produced a plan which could be easily adjusted to any size of house.[31] His workhouses, built in rough stone in what was usually described as a Tudor style, still form a formidable feature of many Irish towns. Wilkinson considered that his gabled roofs, elevated chimneys, and mullioned windows gave ' a pleasing and picturesque appearance ' and he ventured to say that if a few trees were planted round the house, ' that the whole may be an ornament rather than the reverse to the neighbourhood '. In three unions however the guardians, agreeing in matters of taste with Lord Palmerston, demanded and obtained ' Italian details and proportions ' in the windows and overhanging roofs. Under Wilkinson's general supervision the work was carried out rapidly by local contractors, and in spite of the Irish weather, combinations amongst the labourers (which the commission always

met by threatening to suspend building) and the untrustworthiness
in a few instances of the contractors, operations were almost completed by 1842, when 122 workhouses were ready. Admittedly
in spite of the commission's emphasis on economy, the total cost
in the end exceeded the first estimate of £1,000,000 by £145,000.
Again the speed with which this large-scale, government directed
building programme was rushed through produced the inevitable
crop of blunders and negligences. The poor relief act in the clauses
relating to the erection of workhouses had provided an excellent
basis for an almost interminable series of squabbles. While the
commission was to buy the sites and erect and furnish the houses,
the boards of guardians had to foot the bills. Naturally the
guardians, debarred from calling the tune, felt fully entitled to
criticise the commission's performance. And a monotonous
anthology of acrimony might be compiled from their correspondence with the commission over the condition of the houses when
they were handed over. Walls were damp, roofs dripped, gates
failed to fit, floors stank, drainage was inadequate, in one institution the bell was cracked, in another the kitchen boilers were the
wrong size, in a third the architect had failed to make proper
provision for the horses and carriages of guardians attending a
board meeting. In addition to this plethora of complaints on
points of detail, there was a widely repeated allegation that the
commission had in many instances sanctioned grossly extravagant
expenditure. Nicholls, who had returned to sit on the board in
London in 1842, offered to go back to Ireland to enquire into the
whole question. Reasonably enough, Graham, the home secretary, discouraged him, pointing out that 'your visitation of the
workhouses would not be regarded a satisfactory inspection, since
it is your own work which is to be revised, your own measures
which must come under examination'. Instead, Nash's old pupil
Pennethorne, the London town planner, was sent over to investigate. He produced a thorough and level-headed report to the
effect that the commission had attempted to carry out operations
on a large scale, in a hurry with an inadequate staff. As a result
sites had been chosen without expert advice being taken, a number
of items of expense had been overlooked in the original estimates,
and in many cases, particularly in connection with fittings and
furnishings, the tenders accepted had been too high. Nicholls at
once pointed out that if this report was accepted by the govern-

ment and presented to parliament, the guardians would certainly resent being asked to pay the expenses which should not have been incurred.[32]

The condition of the workhouses was not the only subject on which the two newly created administrative organs, the poor law commissioners, efficient, well-meaning, and rather rigid bureaucrats, and the local boards of guardians, self-assertive and public-spirited, clashed. When the Cork board tried to raise a rate to pay for the emigration of paupers chargeable to the union at large, the commissioners sharply reminded it that section 51, the section of the poor relief act relating to emigration, only empowered them to provide assistance for paupers chargeable on a definite electoral division.[33] When the Limerick board tried to secure power to remove its clerk, the commissioners declared that this was not in accordance with the spirit of the act, and when the board went on strike, compelled it to resume work by initiating proceedings in the queen's bench.[34] When several boards decided to take steps to reserve a portion of the workhouses for fever patients, the commissioners vetoed their schemes, telling them that they ought to construct proper fever hospitals attached to the workhouses. Probably the commission was right, but of course their direction implied expense and delay. The Balrothery guardians who wished to give the paupers some extra food on Easter Sunday, and the Lurgan board who wanted to buy a little tobacco for the pauper who whitewashed the wards, and the Ballyshannon guardians who employed a dirty, unshaven porter—who they declared was a hard-working creature, known as the king of the beggars—were all sharply rebuked by the commissioners.[35]

On one issue the commission was compelled to beat a definite if dignified retreat. Shortly after the first boards of guardians were elected, it tried to damp their enthusiasm for unsuitable forms of activity by issuing an order excluding the press from board meetings. Acknowledging the need for a check on the work of elected bodies, the order pointed out that the poor law commission could be trusted to provide it. If the press was admitted ' a desire for popularity would be awakened . . . prejudices would be excited, passions would be inflamed, personalities would arise, and the most respectable members of the board . . . would be borne down by clamour or wearied by lengthy discussion, if not finally compelled to abandon their post '. The Cork board obeyed this persuasive admonition for a short time and then started to admit reporters again on the ground that members were supplying partial reports to the press. On being informed that the law officers of the crown had decided that the order excluding reporters was legal and should be acted on, the board did not receive the opinion with that deference which ought to be paid to an opinion proceeding from such high legal authority. Other boards followed Cork's example and the poor law commissioners reiterating their reason for considering that reporters should be excluded withdrew their order.[36]

The attitude of the commissioners clearly reflects their conception of their functions. They were not merely departmental officials engaged in guaranteeing the indigent Irishman from starvation, but warriors in a great administrative crusade. The poor law system, they were convinced, was bound to play a mighty part in inaugurating a new era in public life, when the prevalence of official impartiality, efficiency, economy and standardised and scientific methods of administration would raise the moral tone of the whole community. In the meantime the respectable as guardians, and the poor as paupers, were to be taught by experience the practical expression of the most recent and soundest political theory. The methods by which the guardians were inspired and disciplined have been mentioned. As for the paupers their lives were ordered by a series of detailed memoranda and letters of instruction issued by the commission. On arrival at a workhouse the pauper was to be cleaned and classified, and thereafter his life, governed by the regular ringing of the workhouse bell, would be spent in ' irksome employment ' calculated ' to awaken or increase a dislike to remain in the workhouse '.[37] Meals were to be eaten in silence, so that ' order and decorum ' should prevail. Paupers were not to be allowed spirits or alcohol. Bad language, malingering, waste, idleness or disobedience were to be punished by confinement or reduced rations.[38] The regular dietary finally recommended by the commission was not extravagantly sumptuous. Generally speaking there were to be two meals a day in the house, breakfast consisting of seven ounces of oatmeal and dinner consisting of three and a half pounds of potatoes, with each meal a pint of buttermilk being served. In those parts of Ireland (mainly in the north) where the labourer was accustomed to three meals a day, the guardians were allowed to serve three in the

house, and in the cities where the poor eat ' animal food ' it might
be placed on the workhouse dietary.  It might be added that in
the former instance there was to be little or no increase in the
amount of food served, and in the latter ' animal food ' meant
soup.[39]  To find an ordinary dietary inferior to the usual fare of
the Irish labourer was found to be difficult, indeed almost impossible, and the commissioners were compelled to rely on ' regularity,
orderliness, strict enforcement of cleanliness, constant occupation,
the preservation of decency and decorum, and the exclusion of
all irregular habits and tempting excitements' to keep all but the
genuinely destitute out of the house.[40]  Finding suitable work for
the destitute proved more difficult, and the poor law commissioners failed to devise any original occupations for the Irish
pauper.  The able-bodied were employed in performing the
duties of the house.  When there was nothing more to do the
men were kept busy stone-breaking, the women knitting.  The
aged and infirm, if fit, were set to work picking oakum, spinning,
or knitting, the children were either instructed by ' tutors ' in the
house or sent to the nearest national school.  As the system aimed
at teaching the last mentioned to earn their own living, the girls
were prepared for domestic service by being taught sewing and
employed in household duties, and some of the boys were taught
carpentry, tailoring or shoe-making.  But the commissioners early
recognised the difficulty of giving adequate industrial training in
the workhouse, as well as the problem of finding suitable openings
for the workhouse-bred lads in a country suffering from chronic
unemployment.[41]  They were compelled to admit that the best
that could be done was ' to send the youth forth imbued with the
habits of industry and with his frame braced and strengthened
and inured to laborious exertion and with his temper and mental
faculties duly cultivated, and above all, with a sense of religious
duty deeply impressed upon his mind '.

For years emigration had been advocated as a solution for
Ireland's economic problems, but the poor law reformers were
afraid of doing anything which might weaken the pauper's self-
reliance, and the section of the poor relief act of 1838 relating to
emigration merely provided a complicated procedure through
which the ratepayers could impose additional taxation on themselves for the purpose of assisting emigration from the locality.
The Cork board of guardians in their first year of office selected

a number of paupers (most of whom were the old stock of the
Cork house of industry) as potential emigrants. It then approached
the government for a grant. The commissioners of colonial land
and emigration, to whom the matter was referred, sent a crushing
reply in which they pointed out that if they acceded to the Cork
request they would be overwhelmed with demands from all over
the British Isles, that they had only a small fund at their disposal
from which emigration could be assisted, and that habitual paupers
were not likely to prove enterprising emigrants. Thrown back on
their own resources the Cork guardians attempted to assist emigration out of the rates, received another official rebuke, started
again and finally let the matter drop.[42] The Belfast guardians also
attempted in 1842 to levy a rate to assist emigration. But the
ratepayers of the three electoral divisions concerned refused permission on the grounds that to send emigrants to Canada in winter was
to offer them the prospect of 'a cold grave and snowy winding-
sheet'.[43] The poor law commissioners seem to have been greatly
impressed by the 'judicious and instructive' reply of the commissioners of colonial lands to the Cork guardians. Nevertheless
in 1843 they simplified the procedure for aiding emigration. But
the guardians displayed little eagerness to use their new powers,
and few paupers were assisted to leave Ireland before 1846.

The poor law commissioners' continuous insistence on the precise
observance of the act of 1838 and their directives, along with what
their critics considered their dictatorial and domineering tone,
helped to make themselves and the system thoroughly unpopular.
The Irish landowners objected to being lectured almost as much
as they disliked being taxed. And they had, in their self-appointed
champion O'Connell, a vigorous critic of the whole system.
There was for a short time also some opposition amongst the
poorer ratepayers, and over a fairly large area it seemed as if a
rate war was to succeed the tithe war. In about twenty unions
the rate-collectors had to receive police support and even occasionally military backing. But the amending act of 1843 relieved the
smaller ratepayers of the duty of paying directly ; by 1844 the
commission could congratulate itself that only eight per cent of
the rates were uncollected, and the disturbances which were never
serious had died down by the beginning of 1845.

About the close of 1845 the poor law commissioners might
reasonably have considered stock-taking. The system had been

working for five years, and though the crisis which was to strain
it to breaking-point was hidden, the commission saw a fearsome
enough ordeal ahead in the shape of a parliamentary enquiry.
To begin with, they could have congratulated themselves that
they had succeeded in the face of widespread criticism and hostility
in getting the new poor law machinery going in every union.
Secondly, they could point to a substantial mass of poverty
relieved. Admittedly though the workhouses had not been
anything like filled to capacity, there were complaints that beggars
were almost as numerous and troublesome as before. To the
first of these criticisms the supporters of the new system could
reply that at least the prophecy that the workhouses would be
swamped had not come true, and to the second that, with
workhouses available, the public was to blame.

### V. THE STATE AND EDUCATION

Another aspect of Irish life in which the state was slowly
entering the field was education. Before 1830 the efforts of the
state to promote education in Ireland had been unfortunate.
Statutes of the Tudor period reinforced by later legislation had
instituted on paper a complete system of national education. But
the state left to the clergy of the establishment the task of founding
and maintaining the parish schools, and since through the disturbed
and dismal sixteenth and seventeenth centuries the discipline of
the established church was often enforced with difficulty and the
clergy were on the whole poor and often non-resident, the parish
schools did not exist in any number, and in any case were regarded
by Catholics as instruments of protestantisation. During the
eighteenth and early nineteenth centuries the state gave financial
assistance to other less ambitious attempts to educate the Irish poor.
The Incorporated Society for Promoting English Protestant Schools
in Ireland, founded in 1733, received large subsidies for many
years. Eagerly supported by those who desired to secure the
Protestant ascendancy by protestantising, civilising and anglicising
(the three terms were often treated as nearly synonymous) the
Irish peasantry, it established about fifty boarding schools. But
its affairs were ill-managed by committees of languid, education-
ally inexpert amateurs, and its schools, staffed by incompetent
and unscrupulous teachers, developed many of the worst features

associated with eighteenth-century jobbery and nineteenth-century institutionalised charity. The founders of the Irish Society for Discountenancing Vice, panic-stricken by the French revolution, hoped to check infidelity by improving the morals of the rich by exhortation and the minds of the poor by education. They made grants to elementary schools open free of charge to those who could not afford to pay, on condition that the schools were under the complete control of the Protestant clergy, that the masters and mistresses belonged to the established church, that the Scriptures were read by all children, and that those belonging to the Church of Ireland were taught the catechism. About 1825, the society which had over 200 schools was receiving about £7,000 a year from the state. Lastly there was the Society for Promoting the Education of the Poor of Ireland (usually known as the Kildare-place Society) which attempted to secure wider support by being less rigidly Anglican. The society which adopted up-to-date methods of training teachers and produced intelligent spelling and reading books enjoyed for some years a substantial grant from the state. After a little over ten years its work became involved in a controversial storm of the first magnitude. It was asserted by O'Connell and several Catholic bishops that the rule respecting the reading of the Scriptures without note or comment made it impossible for Catholics to co-operate with the society. In any case the fact that the society was largely managed by evangelically-minded Protestants would naturally make it suspect in the eyes of Catholics. Finally in 1831 the state grant to the society ceased.

In addition to the schoolmasters and mistresses employed by the societies subsidised by the government, numerous other teachers differing widely in accomplishments and qualifications earned a living by imparting knowledge to the peasantry. Most of them had school-houses of a kind, but a few were literally ' hedge ' schoolmasters. Some professed to give a grammar school education, most at least taught the three Rs. In many places the parish priest appointed and at times raised funds for a village schoolmaster, and catechetical instruction often provided a basis for further education.

But in spite of all these efforts to satisfy a widespread and eager desire for knowledge, the need for educational reform was continually being urged from the end of the eighteenth century.

The early nineteenth century was an age which put its trust in instructed reason, and in a country where every attempt at social and economic reform involved coping with baffling and interminable complications, education, whose workings were so imperceptible and unmeasurable, was often talked of as comparatively easily produced *deus ex machina*. The state-subsidised societies had inadequate resources and for theological reasons were distasteful to the majority of the population. The popular schoolmasters were frequently criticised, partly on educational grounds—some of them probably were pretentious and poorly educated—and partly because these educational irregulars, it was believed, frequently inculcated dangerous ideas on political and social questions. As in France, the village schoolmaster could be the centre of criticism directed against the squire and parson. Finally (and the bewildering variety of educational organisations as well as the continuous controversy over their methods may obscure this most essential fact) a high proportion of the population in many counties was illiterate.[1]

The commission on Irish education appointed by the whigs in 1806 in its final report declared that what was needed was 'a systematic and uniform plan of instruction'. It recommended the creation of a board which would receive an annual parliamentary grant. The board would set up 'supplementary schools', train teachers and provide books. And it hoped that the ministers of each denomination would give religious instruction to the children belonging to their own faith. The commission of 1825 also recommended that the state should provide schools of 'general instruction' where the children, united for all other subjects, would receive separate religious instruction.[2]

The frequently expressed belief that better educational facilities were required in Ireland ; the demand that the state should intervene and provide them ; and the resentment of the Catholics at the way in which the private societies under Protestant control were being used to make converts ; all, in October 1831, persuaded Stanley, the first chief secretary of the reforming era, to issue a manifesto in the grand whig manner, in the shape of a letter addressed to the duke of Leinster. He invited the duke to act as chairman of a board composed of individuals representing the different denominations. On his acceptance it was agreed the government would place a sum of money at the disposal of the board to assist local schools, and that in those schools children of different persuasions would receive combined 'literary and moral' and separate religious instruction.  The board laid down that if it approved of a local application it would give a grant covering two-thirds of the cost of building the school and would supply it with books at the reduced price and pay a gratuity to the teachers.  In return the applicants for a grant were to guarantee to keep the building in repair, to pay part of the teacher's salary, and to purchase the books produced by the board.  The local applicants could appoint and dismiss their teacher, but the persons appointed should receive the approval of the board, and once the board's model school was functioning only persons who had passed through it were to be appointed to posts in the national schools. Finally the board was to sanction all books used in the schools, and through its inspectors to see that a reasonable standard of efficiency was maintained.

On the delicate subject of religion the board struggled to be fair, but a zealous flank in each of three major Irish denominations was strongly hostile to the scheme as it stood.  A large number of the Church of Ireland clergy, including nearly all the bishops, supported the Church Education Society whose aim was to assist schools under the supervision of the parochial clergy in which all the teachers would be members of the establishment, where scriptural instruction would be included in general education, and the Church of Ireland children be taught the catechism.  The synod of Ulster at first would have nothing to do with a system which many Presbyterians contended rendered the board supreme over the church in matters which pertained to the latter.  However the board made some concessions and by the early forties the Presbyterians were accepting grants for schools under their patronage.  The majority of the Catholic hierarchy were in favour of accepting grants from the board, but they made in 1840 a strong and unsuccessful effort to secure modifications in the scheme which would strengthen their influence over the education of children belonging to their church.  John MacHale, archbishop of Tuam, firmly opposed the introduction of the system into his province.

In spite of the powerful interests ranged against it and the controversies which raged over its work during the thirties and forties the board achieved a fair measure of success.  By 1838 a

training college for teachers had been established in Dublin where
elementary lectures were given in English, history, geography,
political economy, natural history, mathematics, the elements of
logic and rhetoric, and the art of teaching and conducting schools.
The object of this comprehensive programme was to enable the
teachers ' to aid in forming the minds of the children and directing
their power of reading into beneficial channels '.   To do this the
board pointed out that the teacher must know 'much more than
is expressed in the lessons themselves ', or else he not only would
be unable to explain them but would undoubtedly find himself
in the humiliating position of being unable to answer ' the
innumerable questions that will be put to him as soon as the understanding of his pupils begins to be exercised on any subject '.   In
addition the teachers in training were given every evening talks
on agriculture and on Saturdays were taken to a farm where they
saw ' theory reduced to practice '.   Agricultural instruction was
also given at the district model schools which will be referred to
in a moment, for the board was convinced that the reason why
the Belgian smallholders lived in comparative comfort while
those in Ireland were steeped in misery, was that the former
understood good husbandry, while the latter did not.   By 1845
the board was pleased to be able to say that there were five agricultural model schools in operation and another five proposed ;
in addition seven of the ordinary national schools had land attached
and gave agricultural instruction.   Five years or so after the
national education scheme came into operation Ireland was divided
into twenty-five school districts (later raised to thirty-two) in each
of which there was to be a model school, the superintendent of
which inspected and reported to the board on the schools in his
district.   Teachers were to be classified in three grades, and the
superintendents were to hold examinations from time to time
' with a view of raising meritorious teachers to a higher class or
of depressing others who may have conducted themselves improperly ' or who had mismanaged their schools.   Fixed salaries
were attached to each class and the board in 1840 in almost
aggressively emphatic terms announced that no application for
an increase would be entertained.   The board's conception of
how the teacher should conduct himself is shown in a series of
practical rules which it issued in 1844.   Teachers were to promote
by precept and example ' cleanliness, neatness and decency ' and

to impress upon their pupils the great rule of regularity and order
'a time and a place for everything, and everything in its proper
place'. They were to treat their pupils with kindness combined
with firmness, and to keep the register, report book, and class
lists accurately and neatly, to study the board's school-books and
teach out of them.

By 1845 the national board had schools containing 432,000
pupils. The board's approach to the problem of Irish education
(amply revealed in its reports) has sometimes a slightly absurd
air. But its patent pleasure in its own bustling activities, its naïve
self-satisfaction on most matters, and its delicate balancing on
religious issues, must not obscure the fact that in a country where
so much was futile and faulty the national board accomplished
an enduring piece of work. The national teacher became a stock
character in rural society and the schools helped to mould the
Irish mind for a century.

With the other stages of Irish education the government had
as yet comparatively little to do. Education above the primary
level was to a great extent left to fend for itself. Still even in this
sphere of Irish life there was a degree of state control and direction.
Three types of grammar schools were supervised by the state,
diocesan schools which were built by the grand juries and partially
maintained by the clergy, the royal schools, founded and well
endowed in the seventeenth century, and about a dozen grammar
schools of private foundation.[3] All these schools which prepared
boys for the university and whose curriculum was therefore
classical and mathematical were theoretically open to all denominations, but their head masters (who in the case of the diocesan and
royal schools were appointed by the lord lieutenant) invariably
belonged to the established church and were usually clergymen.
In spite of their founders' intentions the schools admitted only a
small proportion of free pupils, the royal schools in particular
being regarded 'as schools for the sons of gentlemen who preferred them to private schools as more respectable and not designed
for all classes'. In 1813 a board composed of *ex-officio* and
nominated members with a small staff was set up to supervise these
schools, and during the next forty years it showed considerable
zeal in tracking down endowments, arranging for their proper use
and in managing the school estates on efficient and progressive
lines. Admittedly the commission's reports rather confirm the

opinion of its critics that it was so absorbed in administrative and financial duties that it tended to underrate ' the functions connected with the intellectual management of the schools '. Nevertheless the commissioners required reports from headmasters, occasionally—sometimes unexpectedly—visited schools, tried to encourage the study of history and to discourage the use of corporal punishment, and gave small grants for school libraries. Educational planners led by Wyse, believing that ' to a well educated middle class the state must be mainly indebted for its intellectual and moral progress ', called for a state-organised system of well-equipped county academies in which classical and commercial instruction would be combined. But although this scheme was propounded in 1838, by 1845 nothing had been done, and the Irish Catholic middle class tackled their own educational problems during the next thirty years. In addition to the schools which have been mentioned. there was a bewildering variety of institutions for secondary education. There were Erasmus Smith schools, Quaker schools, Christian Brothers' schools (which offered something in advance of an elementary education) the Royal Belfast Institution and the Belfast Academy (both of which reflected the go-ahead atmosphere of the north) and a miscellaneous variety of schools which yearly drew parents' attention to their moderate charges, home comforts and the academic successes and social standing of their pupils.

With university education the Irish government was only slightly concerned, though by 1845 the demand for changes in this field, which were bound to involve state intervention, was growing in strength and was about to be met in accordance with Peel's policy of killing repeal by kindness. But though successive governments over the next seventy years were to produce and partly implement a variety of complex solutions for the Irish university question, the position in 1845 was still exceedingly simple, if highly unsatisfactory. There was only one Irish university, in Dublin, with one college, Trinity. Constitutionally it was an abbreviated Cambridge, with the university machinery supported entirely by the single college. In 1845 its staff of fellows and professors numbered about fifty and there were about fifteen hundred students on its books. As an educational institution it had a highly respectable record. Its dons unlike their English equivalents had never enjoyed an era of academic slackness, all its staff worked either as administrators or teachers, the teaching methods were effective, the courses had been kept up to date and examinations were frequently held, seriously conducted and keenly contested. The university's critics dwelt not on constitutional faults nor educational deficiencies, but on the fact that fellowships and scholarships could be held only by members of the Church of Ireland. The position corresponded with that in the English universities, and by the same logic which supported the establishment could be defended. Obviously it bore hardly on the bulk of the population, and in 1845 Heron Caulfield, having been successful in the scholarship examination, made a gallant attempt, based on a highly ingenious (and, as it seemed, rather disingenuous) interpretation of the statutes, to compel the board to elect him. After a hard tussle, first before the visitors and then in the courts, he failed. The abolition of tests in the older universities was still a generation away, but the government was to take steps just before the famine to remedy the situation, while leaving vested interests undisturbed, by the creation of additional facilities for higher education in Ireland.

### VI. THE CHURCHES

In the decades preceding the famine economic and social issues received, as has been seen, a considerable degree of attention. But the two subjects which loomed largest were religion and politics, and these, it need hardly be said, were frequently found to be entangled. It would be almost impossible to overrate the part played by religious or sectarian feeling in Irish life during the early nineteenth century. Inter-denominational controversy was continuous, the output of polemical theological pamphlets was prodigious and most of the outstanding figures of the period displayed intense confessional loyalty. Some of the political issues of the period such as those concerning the temporalities of the establishment were directly related to the readjustment of the sectarian balance which slowly followed emancipation, and the discussion on many others became sooner or later impregnated with *odium theologicum*. For instance an inquiry into the public health services included a careful consideration of the influence of a doctor's religious opinions on his professional career. An inquiry into the working of the poor law spent some time trying to discover if the religious opinions of paupers in the South Dublin Union had been interfered with, and a house of lords committee on law and order badgered witnesses about the proportion of Catholics to Protestants in the Dublin police until an experienced official exclaimed that ' the fact is the Roman Catholic policemen in Dublin get their heads broken as fast as the Protestants. . . . A policeman gets well beaten without reference to religion '.[1]

The tense bitterness which invaded so many spheres of Irish life in the early nineteenth century was the result of the general course of Irish religious history since the reformation. At the beginning of the sixteenth century the Irish state—if one can apply the term to the shadowy lordship of Ireland—was abnormally weak, and the country as a whole, content with its traditional, rich and archaic cultural pattern, to a great extent isolated from the renaissance world. From about the middle of the century the invigorated and protestantised Tudor state and the forces of the Catholic revival ran a close race for the control of Ireland. The result was a species of draw, for by the time the state had extended its masterful rule to every corner of the island, Catholicism had secured the religious allegiance of the majority of the people. But though during the seventeenth and eighteenth centuries the economic balance was rudely shifted in favour of Protestantism, the Catholics on the whole clung tenaciously to their faith. As a result in the early nineteenth century, when the attempt to convert Irish Catholics by political pressure had been abandoned as both immoral and futile, a highly anomalous situation had been created. The Church of Ireland, the ecclesiastical body which had been receiving the patronage of the state for centuries, was designed to cater for the religious needs of the whole population. It held whatever religious endowments survived from medieval times, it was supported by tithe, a tax levied on landholders in general, and it enjoyed a variety of privileges—representation in the house of lords, and control of the ecclesiastical courts and of the governing body of the only Irish university. But its adherents numbered only eleven per cent of the population. At least eighty per cent of the inhabitants of Ireland were Catholics, and about eight per cent were Protestant dissenters—for the most part Presbyterians. The Presbyterians were concentrated in Ulster, about fifty per cent of them residing in the dioceses of Down, Connor and Dromore (the counties of Antrim and Down). The members of the

Church of Ireland were somewhat more evenly distributed, but even so fifty per cent were in the seven northern dioceses. The Catholics predominated in every province. In Ulster they formed over sixty-two per cent of the population, in Leinster eighty-five per cent, and in Munster and Connacht ninety-five and ninety-six per cent respectively. And in only a limited area in the north east (the diocese of Down, Connor and Dromore) did they amount to less than fifty per cent of the total population.[2]

But statistics alone would give an incomplete picture. Each denomination was thoroughly lop-sided in its social composition. Nearly all the Irish peers, the bulk of the landed gentry, many of the great commercial families and the majority of the professional classes belonged to the establishment. Naturally enough many of the outstanding leaders in Irish political and social life were amongst its devoted adherents. In three provinces the great mass of the peasantry, a large proportion of the shopkeepers and businessmen, and a still small and struggling, but a growing section of the professional class, were Catholic. In the fourth province, Ulster, the same general social balance prevailed, but it was complicated by the presence of a comparatively large Presbyterian community. Though the gentry of the north, even when of Presbyterian origin, agreed with that travelled theologian Charles II on the social deficiencies of Presbyterianism, there were large numbers of Presbyterian farmers, and Presbyterians predominated in the social and professional life of Belfast. The comparatively close and unhappy coincidence between social and sectarian divisions embittered nearly every Irish political dispute during the early nineteenth century. Communal strife and political and economic warfare, snobbery and theology were inextricably mingled.

In the high eighteenth century the attitude of the state to religion in Ireland, if harsh, was clear-cut (and except in one instance which will be referred to in a moment) consistent. It maintained an establishment to which the spiritual interests of the community were committed. The existence of dissenters was reluctantly recognised, and it was considered (by members of the establishment) that they should be grateful for any degree of toleration. But political pragmatism kept breaking through the theoretical crust. When the adherents of the establishment were outnumbered by eight to one more persuasive if less orthodox instruments, for the inculcation of loyalty and good manners, had to be found, and by 1840 both the Catholics and the Presbyterians were receiving subsidies from the state. In the case of the latter this went back to the close of the seventeenth century, when the Presbyterian clergy—who never forgot that their community in Ireland was an offshoot of the church established in Scotland—received an annual grant from the crown. This grant which had grown by degrees was greatly increased at the Union, when it was arranged that the state would pay a large proportion of each Presbyterian minister's stipend. In 1845 about £35,000 was being paid to the Presbyterian clergy. The arrangement was a rather one-sided one, for in return for this substantial subvention the state had demanded no concessions. At the beginning of the century, however, the government probably hoped to win the grateful and expectant support of the Presbyterian clergy. But in 1813 the synod of Ulster (the representative body of the largest of the Presbyterian bodies) passed a resolution in favour of Catholic emancipation, and some years later in face of the government's obvious disapproval the synod decided definitely to elect a professor of divinity for the Belfast academical institution, one of the members demanding what right has an individual calling himself Lord Castlereagh 'to obtrude himself on our deliberations'.[3] The *regium donum* did not deprive Irish Presbyterianism of its radical strain and it was the play of social and economic forces which in time aligned Irish Presbyterians in a body in support of the Union settlement.

Before the eighteenth century was out even the Catholics were receiving aid from the state. The French revolution paralysed simultaneously the system by which a supply of trained clergy was secured for Ireland and for the moment made Catholicism almost popular in English conservative circles. Burke, who had long advocated the cause of his Catholic fellow-countrymen, vehemently urged the government to form an alliance with the Irish Catholics in defence of Christian and conservative principles. The characteristic caution of the Irish hierarchy and the strongly Protestant tone of the Irish administration would of course have had to be overcome if his policy was to be successful. However a step was made along the path so eloquently indicated by Burke when the administration made an effort to provide for the training of the Irish priesthood at home, by sanctioning and financing the foundation of a large seminary at Maynooth. As in the case of the Presbyterians no explicit concessions were demanded and little or nothing was obtained, for the Irish priesthood remained completely independent of government control, and the interference of the state with their education was limited to partly paying for it.

Maynooth was a symbol of the securely rooted strength of Irish Catholicism. Its students came from all over Ireland, and its staff—after the death or retirement of the first professors, *émigré* Frenchmen, often puzzled or annoyed by Irish horseplay— were all Irishmen.[4] Since by 1845 half the bishops (including three of the four archbishops) and nearly half the parish priests had been educated there, its influence on Irish clerical life was immense and immeasurable. By the middle of the nineteenth century the bulk of the Irish Catholic clergy were home-bred with all-important consequences on their political outlook.

To the logically minded—or indeed to the merely staunch upholder of the establishment—the concurrent encouragement by the state of competing, if quite different, forms of dissent, was disturbing enough. But the course of events which followed Catholic emancipation in 1829 filled keen churchmen with alarm and despondency. Catholic emancipation had been followed by the tithe war—a general strike of tithe-payers over large areas in the south and west. If some of the established clergy decided to refrain from attempting to collect their incomes by force, others were determined to defend the rights of their church. An embittering conflict followed. Many incumbents found themselves reduced to penury, and though violence was more often threatened than employed it was said to be impossible for a Protestant clergyman in the south to insure his life.[5] Each party saw the problem as a moral issue. Supporters of the establishment argued that tithe was a property held by long prescriptive right and applied to the most righteous of public purposes, the proclamation of religious truth. The majority of the tithe-payers saw no reason why they should support a church which could render them no spiritual assistance and which, moreover, they believed to be engaged in propagating heresy and error.

In 1838 the question was settled (after several years had been spent in debating the disposal of a hypothetical surplus) by converting the tithe into a rent-charge equal to three-quarters of the old charge, payable by the person entitled to ' the first state of inheritance ', i.e. the landlord.[6]  Four years earlier the whigs, mildly anti-clerical in outlook, anxious to conciliate public opinion in Ireland, moderately zealous for administrative reform and not averse from tampering with a tory interest, passed the Irish church temporalities act, a step towards redistributing on rational lines the revenue of the establishment.  Though keen churchmen denounced the whigs' ecclesiastical policy as merely legalised sacrilegious spoliation, the church benefited from its machinery being improved and its unpopularity being diminished.

The church temporalities act provided that the Church of Ireland should be composed of twelve dioceses, governed by two archbishops and ten bishops ; but in 1845 there were still fourteen dioceses the intentions of parliament being temporarily baulked by the survival of the bishops of Clogher and Kildare, the latter having received a mitre a few years after the beginning of the century. Birth and scholarship were both well represented on the bench. No fewer than seven of the bishops were peers' sons (two indeed later inheriting the family title) and Leslie of Kilmore was not only the son of a baronet but a cousin of the duke of Wellington. The outstanding figure in this group was fittingly the primate, John George Beresford.  As an ecclesiastical politician, he was continually reduced to futile expostulation, but he managed to conduct a long rear-guard action, with the bearing of a prelate of the *ancien régime*, and he employed his immense wealth with discerning and magnificent munificence.  Four of the bishops held reputable positions in the academic world, the most outstanding figure amongst them being Whately, archbishop of Dublin.  Whately who had arrived from Oxford in 1831 was one of the most energetic, talented and intelligent men in Ireland. But his rather self-conscious aloofness from local prejudices was unlikely to be popular, and his pugnacious common sense possibly generated more heat than light.

In the fourteen dioceses there were about eight hundred beneficed clergy, assisted by about eight hundred curates.[7]  And since they were distributed on the general principle that the establishment was the national church, rather than in relation to denominational requirements, they were to be found in every corner of Ireland.  Admittedly in the three southern provinces the Church of Ireland rector even when his jurisdiction extended over a large area usually had a comparatively small flock—there were even parishes without a lay Protestant—but this did not render him by contemporary standards superfluous. An influential section of opinion considered that the clergy of the establishment were a valuable substitute for the absentee landlords.[8] And in many cases the clergy, who were frequently of landed stock, dispensed charity and advice and were in the commission of the peace for the county. Their success in fulfilling this complex role varied, one county Donegal rector remarking, apropos his relations with his Catholic parishioners, ' there is nothing that I could not make them do but they will not pay tithe '.[9]

The clergy of the establishment were frequently taunted with being rich and non-resident, but though there was an element of truth in both these charges tendencies were at work which were soon to render them almost baseless. At the beginning of the century non-residence was fairly widely prevalent and was sometimes excused as arising from pluralism, the unfortunate but inevitable result of a number of poor livings. By the forties however the rising standards of clerical conduct and the activities of zealous bishops and of the ecclesiastical commission in amalgamating small livings and providing parsonages were rendering clerical non-residence difficult to excuse and highly discreditable. Clerical incomes in the establishment varied greatly. To state that the average income of a beneficed clergyman in 1836 was £375 would give a most imperfect picture of the situation, since, as might be expected in the case of such an ancient corporation, its revenues were distributed in a traditional and erratic fashion. But the small group of prize winners in what Sidney Smith termed the lottery of ecclesiastical life were far outnumbered by the holders of blanks. Or, to state the position in a more concrete form, there were in 1830 about sixty incumbents with over £1,000 per annum, and about two hundred and forty with less than a tenth of that income. And just over half of the total number of incumbents had less than £300 per annum. It need scarcely be added that the curates were much worse off. They formed an ecclesiastical proletariat with an average stipend of £75. It may be added that from the thirties the general trend of ecclesiastical incomes as a result of the legislation which has been mentioned was downward.

But if the clergy of the establishment as a body enjoyed incomes lower than their critics implied, though perhaps no higher than they deserved, they were nevertheless the best paid clerical body in Ireland. The Catholic parish priests (of which there were in 1845 over a thousand) had incomes, derived from the contributions of their flocks and dues on baptisms, marriages and funerals, ranging from £100 to £400, and the average income of a parish priest, £300, was considerably lower than that of a Church of Ireland rector. Besides out of this the former had to pay his curate or curates. As for the Irish Catholic bishop he derived his income merely from holding a parish or two, and from a small contribution from each of his parish priests. But probably the poorest body of clergy were the Presbyterians (who usually were married men). Even when the *regium donum* is taken into account their incomes rarely exceeded £300 and were generally about £200 per annum, and the wife of one Presbyterian divine was reduced to arranging for a local draper to purchase at a fixed annual sum the funeral scarves presented to her husband.[10]

Turning to those aspects of church life which elude statistical analysis, a great and perceptible change had occurred in the ethos of Irish Protestantism about the beginning of the nineteenth century. Eighteenth-century Irish Protestantism, with its sober piety, rational faith, restraint and ethical emphasis, seemed to many doctrinally deficient and spiritually lifeless. Towards the end of the century the evangelical movement began to gain ground in both Great Britain and Ireland. Evangelicals dwelt vehemently on the saving necessity of fully apprehending Christian dogma, and though they quarrelled almost equally vehemently over many points of systematised theology they agreed in having an earnest and intimate concern for the individual soul, in stressing the vital importance of a warmly felt realisation of God's purpose and in proclaiming the need to learn His will through the humble searching of the scriptures.

The origins of this movement which affected both the established church and the Presbyterian dissenters were manifold and obscure. Wesley on his frequent visits to Ireland met with much sympathy, and it was not until 1816 that his Irish followers after great soul searching decided to receive the sacrament at the hands of their own ministers. At the turn of the century there were in Trinity college 'praying students', 'serious lads', who received encouragement from at least two of the fellows, Stopford and Walker. And the latter, a strong Calvinist of rigid if eccentric righteousness, after preaching for some years at Bethseda, the centre of Dublin evangelicalism,[11] renounced his fellowship, left the Church of Ireland, and placed himself at the head of the Walkerites, a small sect, soon torn by dissension.

Walker was not alone in exemplifying the earnest and energetic individualism of Irish Protestantism. Kelly, the celebrated hymn writer and founder of the Kellyites, and Hutchinson, Parnell and Darby, the founders of the Plymouth brethren, were all Irishmen. Many evangelicals however continued to work in the church and though they never formed the sole element in the establishment, their unsparing activity, literary productiveness, strong if amiable cliquishness, and the organising ability which helped them to control so many church societies enabled them to influence enormously the outlook of the average Irish Protestant and to stamp on the Church of Ireland many of its characteristic features.

While the established church was able to shed its extreme evangelicals quietly, and digest the rest, Presbyterianism went through violent convulsions, and as a result the theological liberalism which had long predominated in Presbyterian circles was discredited in the popular mind and displaced from its position of supremacy. Irish Presbyterianism at the beginning of the century was divided into three bodies, the synod of Ulster (with its unorthodox appendage, the presbytery of Antrim), the secession synod, and the reformed presbytery (popularly known as the Covenanters). The two latter had been formed by the missionary labours of preachers from the Presbyterian churches of Scotland who about the middle of the eighteenth century travelled through the north of Ireland denouncing the ministers of the synod of Ulster for being heretical and slack. Though their attacks were over-vehement the outlook of the synod's clergy was infected or influenced by the fashionable Scottish philosophy and moderatism. In the early twenties the reaction against this set in on both sides of the channel, and evangelicalism began to assert itself among the ministers of the synod of Ulster. Henry Cooke far from departing into schism took as his slogan ' we must put down Arianism or Arianism will put down us ', and started a ferocious but skilfully directed campaign to reduce to a strict conformity the ministers of the synod. And in spite of the opposition of the equally eloquent Montgomery, after a series of dialectical displays marked by erudition, vehement sincerity, personalities and histrionics, the synod of Ulster decided in 1830 to impose conditions on its clergy which a small minority were unable to accept. Logically the next step was union with the severely orthodox secession synod, and this followed in 1840. The outstanding figure in the new church was naturally Cooke, and though he met with occasional setbacks, he never ceased emphatically to enunciate his policy for Irish Presbyterianism—a militant alliance with the establishment for the defence and propagation of evangelical Protestantism.[12]

Though many Irish evangelicals were self-sacrificing, sincere and benevolent, and although the movement exercised a most beneficial effect on church life in Ireland, in the political field its consequences were less happy, Irish Protestants from the battle of the Boyne had tended during the eighteenth century to rely largely on economic pressure to weaken Catholicism. But the evangelicals felt an urgent sense of personal responsibility for their Catholic fellow-countrymen's salvation. And during the early nineteenth century vigorous efforts were made by preaching and distributing bibles to convert Irish Catholics to Protestantism.

However it was an unfortunate time to choose for these activities, since crusading Protestantism found itself confronted by resurgent Catholicism. From about 1800 Irish Catholicism had been emerging from a catacomb existence. During the eighteenth century, though the church had preserved its diocesan and parochial organisation and continued to function, immense material losses had been sustained, and the first half of the nineteenth century was naturally a great era of ecclesiastical reconstruction. New parish churches, large barnlike structures, replaced the small eighteenth century chapels, cathedrals were begun in several dioceses, the parochial clergy increased in less than half a century by about fifty per cent, Catholic schools multiplied and three great orders, the Irish Sisters of Charity, the Irish Sisters of Mercy and the Christian Brothers were founded.

## VII.. THE POLITICAL SCENE

For at least twenty years before the famine, Irish politics were dominated by the burly figure and boisterous oratory of Daniel O'Connell.[1] From the beginning of the nineteenth century he had

## HEIGHT OF IMPUDENCE.

*Irishman to John Bull.*—"SPARE A THRIFLE, YER HONOUR, FOR A POOR IRISH LAD TO BUY A BIT OF — ———
A BLUNDERBUSS WITH."

*Punch*, 1846.

been prominent amongst Irish Catholic politicians, and during the twenties by a rare combination of organising ability, debating power, and advertising talent, he had turned the Catholic association into an enormous popular pressure group, commanding a large revenue, and marshalling the Catholic masses in a great law-abiding but menacing association. The achievement of emancipation though it greatly raised his prestige, at least amongst his Irish supporters, did not leave him in the awkward position of a politician who having completed his programme is in doubt where to go next. His political creed was basically a mixture of Catholicism and nationalism, so closely blended, that though his genial good nature and realistic appreciation of the requirements of the situation made him strive to obtain Protestant co-operation, he frequently seems to have identified the Irish nation with Irish Catholicism. Proud, his critics would say to an excessive degree, of Ireland's distinctive characteristics, he naturally hankered after political independence. He had grown up during the heyday of Grattan's parliament, Grattan always remained his political hero, and his first appearance in Irish politics had been at a meeting of Dublin Catholics to protest against the Union. Therefore it was not surprising that as soon as Catholic emancipation was disposed of he should begin to tackle the question of repeal. Probably he scarcely realised what a herculean task he was undertaking. A thorough optimist he seems to have been fascinated by his own technical ability in organising political agitation, and to have convinced himself that there was no obstacle he could not overcome. He does not seem to have realised the advantages the Catholic cause had over that of repeal. By about 1825 the ground had been prepared for emancipation by a long series of parliamentary debates, nearly all the first-class brains of British politics were on the Catholic side, in Ireland the Catholic body was solidly in favour of its own emancipation and a considerable number of Protestants either considered the disabilities unfair or felt there was no point in clinging to an untenable position. In the case of the Union the balance of forces was very different. English opinion was almost unanimously in favour of maintaining the settlement of 1801, many Irish Catholics were content enough with it, and the mass of Irish Protestants, including most of the liberals of the north were fervent unionists. If moral force was to be O'Connell's weapon, the terrain was definitely unsuited to its employment.

By a curious but easily understandable course of events the question was not put seriously to the test during the decade which followed emancipation. Scarcely had emancipation been granted than the struggle for parliamentary reform began, and O'Connell, abandoning his incipient attempts to organise a repeal movement, threw himself into the battle for the bill. Political rigorists might sneer at this semi-*volte face* (in fact only the tories, who taunted the ministry with their new allies, resented it), but O'Connell was strictly practical—better a reformed than an unreformed parliament. Immediately after reform had been won, O'Connell broke with the whigs mainly on their failure to deal adequately with the tithe question and their readiness to resort to coercion, but before the repeal movement could gather impetus one of the most dramatic reversals of fortune in British political history occurred. The Melbourne ministry was compelled to resign, and, though, after six months they returned to office, their huge if heterogeneous majority had melted in the general election of 1835. Again O'Connell was faced with the radical's dilemma—to adhere obstinately to his programme and probably thereby open the way to power for the conservatives, or to support a moderately liberal government moving too slowly for his liking. O'Connell again did not hesitate, and putting repeal into cold-storage for some years, he backed the tottering liberal administration of Lord Melbourne while it continued the constructive legislative labours of Lord Grey's administration. As he said himself—'I may be blamed by some for supporting the present administration instead of looking for the repeal, but in the first place the cry for repeal would only give increased strength to the vile Orange faction who are violently anti-repealer. . . . In the next place I want to realise as much good for Ireland as I can'. And finally he thought that as opinion was hardening against the house of lords there was the distinct possibility that that barrier to repeal might be weakened.[2] His decision it can be argued was a sound one. On the whole Ireland benefited from the whigs being in office between 1835 and 1841. Tithe was commuted and reduced, the municipal corporations were reformed, the machinery of county government was improved, the police were reorganised, poor relief was instituted, and the national board's educational system built up. Admittedly from O'Connell's standpoint, some of these measures were open to criticism. Tithe reform did not go far enough. And the poor law and the national education system were by no means adapted to Irish conditions. But the whigs were certainly well-intentioned, and the defects and deficiencies in their legislative programme were outweighed, in O'Connell's opinion, by their eagerness to win by sympathetic administrative action the good-will of the Irish public. Conservative magistrates were rebuked, liberals received a large share of official appointments, and when the landlords of county Tipperary demanded emergency legislation they were reminded by Thomas Drummond, the under-secretary, that 'property had its duties as well as its rights'.[3] In fact by 1837 O'Connell was able to speak of ' the great experiment we are making to ascertain whether or no Ireland can be well and justly governed by an imperial legislature or whether we shall be driven to look for the restoration of our own parliament'.[4]

But the experimental period was a relatively short one. From about 1837 onwards it became steadily clearer that the swing of the political pendulum in Great Britain, combined with bad luck and administrative incapacity, was bound within a short time to lead to a whig defeat, and by 1838 O'Connell foreseeing ' the dismal prospect' of ' the insolent tories' being again in power,[5] began to gear up the agitation machinery and in 1840 he founded the National Repeal Association.[6]

The general election of 1841 fulfilled his most dismal apprehensions, for the conservatives secured in the United Kingdom a majority of about seventy. Even in Ireland from O'Connell's point of view things did not go too well. The Irish electoral system in 1841 was a rather complex one. The whigs when framing the Irish reform bill of 1832 had attempted simultaneously to introduce a rational and uniform electoral system, to treat with respect existing rights and to lodge political power in the hands of the respectable and responsible middle classes. The result was a multiplicity of franchises, amounting to eleven in the county constituencies, nineteen in the counties of cities and towns, and seven in the boroughs. But in spite of the multitudinous forms of franchise there were remarkably few voters, the Irish electorate totalling only 100,000, distributed amongst constituencies varying in size from Dublin with over 20,000 voters and Belfast and Cork with over 4,000 apiece to about a dozen petty boroughs with less than 500 electors. As for the county constituencies the majority had less than 2,000 voters.[7] In these circumstances it was easy for an experienced party manager from a close inspection of the registers to be almost certain of the result before the polling began, and consequently it is scarcely surprising that in the general election of 1841 over two-thirds of the seats were uncontested. In the contested constituencies, with prolonged and open voting, party passion often turned the polling into a riot. At Cork the nominations were carried out amidst ' tumult, yelling, whistling, cheering and breaking of forms '. Dundalk was in possession of the mob the night following the poll, and a tory newspaper declared the gentlemen who stood by Bruen in Carlow worthy to be compared to the soldiers of Waterloo.[8] Throughout Ireland there were complaints of intimidation and corruption. The conservatives denounced the Catholic clergy for coercing their flocks, the liberals accused landlords of bullying their tenants. On the whole the conservatives improved their position capturing Carlow and unseating O'Connell in Dublin, but they won only forty seats (including the two university ones), and more than half the conservative M.Ps. came from Ulster, the tories holding twenty-four of the twenty-nine Ulster seats. The remaining sixty-five Irish members were distributed under a variety of labels, which reflect the diversity of anti-conservative or progressive opinion, whig, liberal, reformer, radical and repealer. Repeal was mentioned only occasionally during the struggle, and the repeal members numbered only eighteen, the smallest following that O'Connell had had since 1832. Though the liberals had done reasonably well in Ireland, in the United Kingdom as a whole they had suffered a severe defeat, and when Melbourne met parliament in August 1841 he had to resign, and was replaced by Peel. To O'Connell his course was now simple, the time had come ' for the perfect organisation of the repeal agitation ', and, cheered by the belief that a great radical movement was gathering force in England, and that Peel had given himself ' a brain blow ' by his income tax plan, he started to build up the National Repeal Association, until with its weekly meetings in Dublin, local branches and repeal wardens, repeal rent pouring in to the tune of several hundred pounds a week, committees and reports on different aspects of Irish administrative and economic life and repeal reading rooms in every country town, it had become a most formidable political organisation. And the foundation of the *Nation* in October 1842 provided the movement with what it had hitherto lacked, a newspaper which combined a wide circulation with good literary and intellectual standards.[9]

The year 1843 was marked by a number of great open-air meetings in the south of Ireland, at which O'Connell addressed tens of thousands, and which displayed the strength of public opinion behind him in its most visibly impressive form. O'Connell was in splendid form, delivering a series of racy and eloquent speeches prophesying speedy success and packed with promises. Once Irishmen were managing their own affairs, he declared, manhood suffrage and the ballot would be introduced, poor rates would be abolished, the tithe charge used for poor relief, taxation reduced, Irish industries protected, the tenant farmer would be given security of tenure (landlords being compelled to grant twenty-one-year leases), a fair rent and compensation for improvements, and steps would be taken to break up some estates and sell them in small lots.[10]

After the enormous and enthusiastic mass meetings any further step short of complete success would have seemed an anti-climax. Fortunately for O'Connell, just at the point where the futility of his methods was likely to be demonstrated, the government intervened and saved his face. At the end of 1843 the cabinet which was seriously alarmed by O'Connell's movement since they were by no means confident it would remain a peaceable one,[11] banned the last of the great meetings which, with O'Connell's proclivity for mixing martial allusions and moral force, was to be held at Clontarf, where eight hundred years before the Norse had been driven into the sea. A few days after the meeting, O'Connell and seven of his leading associates were charged with conspiring to alter the constitution by force. The legal proceedings afforded O'Connell a first-rate theatre for the display of his talents, and were marked by protracted displays of eloquence and forensic fencing. The outcome was a glorious and surprising victory. Having been found guilty by a solidly Protestant, and probably conservative jury (carefully selected by a strenuous use of the crown's right to challenge and possibly by less legal methods), he and his friends appealed to the house of lords, which by a majority of one quashed the sentence. It was O'Connell's last great triumph, for the initiative in Irish politics was passing into other hands. Early in 1844 the government began a bold attempt to conciliate at least a powerful section of Irish opinion by a constructive policy,

and about the same time the younger and more extreme of
O'Connell's followers began to criticise his attitude and outlook
publicly and by degrees to challenge his leadership.

Peel had almost a political lifetime's experience of Irish affairs.
He had begun his official career as chief secretary, holding the
post for six years.  Later he had been eight years at the home office.
Competent, industrious, cold, upright, at times sharply severe in
his judgments, Peel combined frequently expressed distaste for the
jobbery or good-natured slackness of Irish public life, with a
genuine if businesslike concern for the condition of the country
and its inhabitants.  Graham, the home secretary, and his chief
confidant on Irish matters, was in character and politics a less
impressive replica of his chief.  The first two years of Peel's
administration were devoted to carrying out extensive changes
in English financial and commercial policy and the cabinet's
approach to Irish affairs, if well intentioned, was not particularly
striking.  A determined effort on the part of the Irish tories to
undermine the whig national education scheme, by obtaining
from a friendly government a separate grant for exclusively
Protestant schools, was defeated in the house of commons by the
government, the cabinet deciding that such a grant would ultimately mean separate grants all round and lead to separate secular
education.  Also Peel and Graham deplored, what the latter termed,
' off-hand legal flourishes ' on the part of the Irish government.
For instance Graham emphasised that the right of the crown to
challenge jurors should be exercised with discretion, and when the
Irish lord chancellor—greater as a chancery lawyer than a politician—dismissed justices of the peace for being repealers, Peel
reminded him that conditions in Ireland 'make it a matter of
grave consideration what particular thing should be done, at
what time it should be done, and in what mode '.[12]  And when
the duke of Wellington in the summer of 1843, considering that
Ireland was ' no longer in a social state ', advocated the formation
of a local force which in practice would be exclusively Protestant
Peel and Graham turned the suggestion down.[13]  From time to
time Peel expressed his wish that a proportion of official posts
should be granted to suitable Catholics.  He deplored the Dublin
Castle doctrine ' that you cannot conciliate your enemies, therefore you give everything to the most zealous of your friends ',
as tending to produce an administration of an exclusive kind.

The implications of emancipation, he argued, would have to be accepted. If they were, he was confident that an influential though numerically small section of the Catholic body would be induced to co-operate with the government.[14]

While the state trials were in progress the leading members of the cabinet discussed the first principles that should govern their Irish policy. Peel pointed out that mere force was not a permanent remedy for the social evils of Ireland and that it was impossible to govern Ireland by constitutional means, preserving for instance trial by jury, unless they could detach from the repeal ranks a considerable proportion of the respectable and influential Catholics. Something, he felt, must be done, and he did not despair ' of weaning from the cause of repeal the great body of wealthy and intelligent Roman Catholics, by the steady manifestation of a desire to act with impartiality and to do that which is just', and thus break up the ' sullen and formidable confederacy against British connection '.[15] Graham reflected the prime minister's views strongly diluted with pessimism. He was of course for maintaining the Union and the Protestant church. ' But while we are inexorable on these two points we ought to stretch out the hand of fellowship on every other, even hoping against hope, and endeavouring by patronage and every persuasive means to soften animosities and to amalgamate the two nations.' Failure he thought would be catastrophic, ' for if Ireland be not reconciled to Great Britain she will destroy us, by opening a breach in our defences through which our foreign enemies ultimately may triumph '. For killing repeal by kindness Graham suggested several measures. A commission to consider the relations between landlord and tenant and, if it were possible, ' a grant even on a liberal scale ' to the Catholic bishops and clergy. To this latter measure however he saw three objections. The Catholic clergy would repudiate a provision from the state, the British public would be opposed to it, and the Irish Protestants would certainly resent contributing to any fund required for the purpose.[16] Stanley, the colonial secretary, who for a few exciting years had been a whig chief secretary, saw another method by which a hold on the affections or control over the training of the Catholic priesthood might be secured : an increased grant to Maynooth. Peel supported this suggestion in a powerful memorandum in which he argued, as he later did in the commons, that the principle of assisting the college had been admitted since its foundation, but the existing meagre grant being insufficient the state ' got no credit for indulgence or liberality ', and a priesthood was sent out ' embittered rather than conciliated by the aid granted by the state for their education, and connected by family ties, from the character of the institution with the lower classes of society rather than with the aristocracy or gentry '.[17] The prime minister was also prepared to provide educational facilities for the Catholic laity by providing provincial academies.[18]

The first step in the new departure in Irish policy was taken towards the end of 1843 by the appointment of the Devon commission to investigate the relations of landlord and tenant in Ireland. It reported early in 1845, and though its recommendations were timid, at least it collected a vast amount of evidence, giving an almost photographic survey of Irish agricultural life just before the famine. As a result of the report the government late in the session of 1845 introduced into the lords a bill giving Irish tenants the right to compensation for three sorts of improvements, building, draining and fencing, and establishing an elaborate machinery by which improvement commissioners, appointed by the government, would sanction and value improvements, and arbitrate in disputes between landlord and tenant. In moving the second reading of the bill Stanley emphasised that Irish agriculture required capital, and that the only way to induce the tenant to invest in his holding was to give him security for his investment. The bill was strongly opposed by those who disapproved of state intervention between a landlord and his tenantry and of bureaucratic regulation of economic life—'Act of parliament improvement' it was declared ' put an end to all improvement '. The bill secured a second reading by a small majority. Then Stanley admitted it had to be extensively amended, and announced it would be dropped for the session.[19]

In 1844 the government introduced and carried the charitable bequests act, which set up a new board for the management of charitable bequests, of which at least five members must, and a majority might be, Catholics.[20] The bill was vehemently attacked by O'Connell who argued on somewhat flimsy grounds, that it threatened to subject the church to state control. The cabinet regarded the bill as not only a concession to Catholic feeling but as a means of creating a body with which the government could negotiate on matters relating to the Catholic community, and Peel was scarcely displeased to see that the controversy over the bill in Ireland had led to ' a schism in the Roman Catholic body, produced by no low intrigues, no specious promises not likely to be realised, but by a reasonable and conciliatory proposal for the carrying out of the act '.[21] For a moment it seemed as if the government had overreached itself, since O'Connell's denunciations of the bill were so strong that it seemed doubtful if three Catholic prelates could be found to accept seats on the board ; the bishop of Killaloe retracted his acceptance and the archbishop of Dublin wavered. In the end however the two primates and the bishop of Down and Connor were prevailed on to join the board, and the chief secretary rejoiced that a great step had been taken towards dissolving existing party bonds in Ireland, and making the distinction between the parties political and not religious—which incidentally would weaken O'Connell.

In the following session, that of 1845, the last before the famine, two important Irish educational measures were brought before the house. Each of them involved decisions on matters of profound principle, each was debated vigorously in parliament and out of doors. The first measure, increasing the grant to Maynooth from £9,000 to £26,000, was indignantly opposed by unbending tories, who frowned on the state assisting dissenters, radicals who disapproved of the subsidising by the state of theological teaching, and fervent or bigoted Protestants who detested popery. But the prime minister, reflecting he had with him 'all the youth, talent, and real influence from public station in the house ',[22] persevered and carried the bill by large majorities. The second measure was the academical educational bill, which set up three colleges, at Belfast, Cork, and Galway, for the higher education of the Irish middle classes. A capital endowment of £100,000 and an annual income of £21,000 equally divided between the three colleges was provided. The government were to make appointments and supervise expenditure in the colleges, and the thorny problem of adjusting denominational claims was met or avoided by the decision that there should be no official religious instruction in the colleges. This aroused many members' misgivings but was justified by Sir Robert Peel as being the only possible solution under Irish conditions.

The other factor which complicated Irish politics in the year or so preceding the famine was, as has been said, the rise of a new generation of repealers. During the thirties O'Connell had been by far the most outstanding figure amongst the advanced Irish liberals, and with his old associates, such as Wyse and Sheil, shaping their careers on their own lines, he had conducted his campaigns with the help of minor politicians who were his acquiescent admirers. But when he began his last great drive for repeal in 1840 a number of gifted and enthusiastic younger men joined the movement. In 1842, three of them—Davis, Dillon and Duffy—founded the *Nation*, an ably edited weekly. The history of Irish journalism over the previous forty years was littered with the wrecks of literary periodicals, but the *Nation* by following the example of the *Examiner* and supplying its readers with news, comment, essays, poetry and criticism, managed to combine strict adherence to principle, high literary standards, and a large circulation. Though the contributors did not systematically formulate their views, they approached the many Irish problems which they discussed in their weekly articles from firmly grounded common assumptions. Their ideals were similar to those which animated nationalists all over Europe in the romantic era, and traces of them can be found in the speeches of O'Connell and Grattan. Now however the importance of cultivating a self-conscious, active sense of nationality amongst Irishmen was urged with astonishing vehemence and clarity. 'Nationality meant,' the *Nation* once explained, 'the application of all the forces of the country to improve its physical comfort, enlarge its powers and ennoble its soul. It means to a nation what prudence and great desires mean to an individual and can only be secured to the one as to the other, by self-respect, self-rule and self-reliance . . . In seeking nationality the Irish seek to get the whole means of Ireland at the disposal of those who know and love them best.'[23] Thus a vast number of activities were to be mobilised with the aim of enriching the nation's life, and were themselves to be stimulated by a sense of national purpose. And Davis called for the development of Ireland's economic potentialities, the devoted and detailed study of Irish history which would ' give a pedigree to nationhood ', for Irish novels, for ballads in the vein popularised by Scott and Macaulay, and for historical painting on a scale which would have gratified Benjamin Haydon.[24] Irish institutions were to be scrutinised and judged by the value of their contribution to the nation's life, and Irishmen were to prepare themselves for national service by submitting to a severe self-imposed educational discipline.  In a country where differences of religion and historic tradition provided the basis for bitter political and sectarian conflict, the writers in the *Nation* preached a generous and comprehensive nationalism.  They looked forward to the time when the races of Ireland would ' become harmonious, and related with intimacy sufficient for combined and single-minded action without any race losing its special propensities or its hereditary powers '.[25] It was this attitude which inspired Davis to strive both for the production of biographies of the great Anglo-Irish heroes, Curran, Grattan and Flood, and for the revival of the Irish language.

It is scarcely surprising that differences of opinion between O'Connell and his able and ardent young followers arose, though the rift, which it could be argued was to exist in different forms in Irish politics for the rest of the century, widened slowly and almost imperceptibly.  Partly of course it was a matter of temperament and personal relationships.  The leaders of the *Nation* group were young, thoughtful, outspoken men, much of an age, closely knit by social ties, with the severe intellectual and moral standards which frequently accompany political inexperience.  O'Connell, though genial and kindly, was inclined to be overbearing, particularly in the associations he founded.  Then, his public statements, usually delivered to admiring audiences, were often only too obviously the productions of a busy man, being repetitive and diffuse, with jocularity, cheerful or vulgar, according to one's taste, serving at times for argument.  Also as Duffy rather naïvely puts it, ' O'Connell was deficient in a disposition essential to a leader, he did not foster conspicuous merit among his adherents by recognising and applauding it '.[26]  Then there were differences of outlook.  While sharing a common enthusiasm for Ireland O'Connell and the *Nation* group were inclined to stress different aspects of the national tradition.  O'Connell, though a convinced believer in religious liberty, was a fervent Catholic, and was inclined to emphasise the fact that Ireland was a predominantly Catholic country. The young men continually deplored ' sectarianism '.  The two attitudes were not irreconcilable, but implied a different approach to certain problems.  Again, O'Connell abhorred violence in politics, and sincerely believed that if public opinion was properly organised, it would attain its objectives.

He never tired of denouncing the use of force, and he continually recalled his victory in 1829. At first the *Nation* ostensibly agreed with him, and Davis in a private letter written in 1842 gave reasons for believing that English public opinion might be convinced of the justice of repeal. But incidentally in this letter he refers to the possibility that ' sterner counsels ' might prevail. And the *Nation* while it had leaders exhorting the people to strive by peaceful and constitutional means to attain repeal, also printed a continual stream of poems whose emotional appeal was all to romantic militarism. In fact, unlike O'Connell, the young men did not consider the use of force as in itself immoral—indeed they implied that in some circumstances it might be ennobling.

For some time these differences of outlook were hidden and only sedulous searching can detect the symptoms of the later breach. The young men admired many of O'Connell's qualities ; they appreciated the prestige of his name, and the *Nation* fully reported his speeches, frequently underlining his arguments and treating him as the unchallenged head of the repeal movement. Still there were signs of a divergence in outlook. The *Nation* asked for the amendment of the poor law which O'Connell desired to repeal and the *Pilot*, O'Connell's organ, sneered at the new paper. In March 1843 Davis, in a private letter, described O'Connell's *Memoirs of the Irish Nation* as ' miserable in style' and some months later O'Connell referred to the ' poor, rhyming dullness of the *Nation* '. Also he was said to be crotchety about justice having been done to Sheil over the Catholic Association in an article in the *Nation*.[27] These reciprocal literary criticisms were the prelude to more serious disagreements. For some years Sharman Crawford, a leading northern liberal, had been urging that the solution of the Anglo-Irish problem lay in the adoption of a federal scheme rather than in the simple repeal of the union advocated by O'Connell. When O'Connell was in prison a number of leading Irish liberals began to play with this idea which offered an attractive compromise to moderate men, and Davis in October 1844 went north to discuss the matter with some of the local liberals. Suddenly O'Connell issued one of his long commentaries on the political situation in the form of a letter to the Repeal Association. After repeating a long string of arguments, which he was accustomed to employ to show that if repeal were won the Irish Protestant had nothing to fear from his Catholic fellow-country-

men, he ended by declaring his immediate preference for the
federal plan, on the grounds that besides giving the Irish parliament 'full and perfect local authority' it gave Ireland influence
in imperial concerns.  It might be said that O'Connell scarcely
grasped a rather ill-defined matter, for both the plan he forwarded
to O'Brien about this time and the scheme published by Crawford
in the following month reserved important financial powers to
the imperial legislature.  In any case his decision was abruptly
challenged, for Duffy in a letter to the Nation warned O'Connell
that federalism was inferior to repeal, and that to adopt it would
destroy the moral influence as well as the raison d'être of the Repeal
Association.  Davis for his part was annoyed at O'Connell's
precipitance and indirectly requested him to remain quiet for a
while.  The anti-unionist press for a week or so discussed the
alternative policies, with the wordiness which frequently character-
ises the consideration of abstract political issues, and on the whole
tended to pronounce against federalism.  Just a fortnight after his
first letter O'Connell produced a second in which, after a technical
discussion of the position of Grattan's parliament, he proposed that
the whole question of federalism or simple repeal be postponed.
And the Nation hastened to paper over the crack which was appearing by an article headed 'Cordiality and Conciliation' in which it
explained that O'Connell obviously agreed with its point of view.
Though the federalists who believed that O'Connell had been
trying to humbug them were left with a grievance, O'Connell
had avoided committing himself, and the young men had differed
with him deferentially. But though the clash within the repeal
movement had been oblique rather than head on, it was nevertheless a real one.[28]

The second breach which occurred just before the famine was
much more spectacular and involved a fundamental question of
principle, though as often happens in political controversy the
main issue was overlaid by matters of detail.  The Nation greeted
Peel's college bill with qualified approval.  Of 'the two great
principles of the bill—mixed education and government nomination' it stated in a leader 'we are resolved for the first as we are
against the second'.  Its objections to the government appointing
professors were the obvious ones.  On the religious issue the
Nation argued that separate education was a preparation for mutual
animosity, and it was reluctant to admit that even in history and

philosophy common instruction would not be possible. O'Connell on the other hand from the outset condemned the whole scheme sharply, and indicated that he preferred separate education at the university level for each of the three main Irish denominations. The Catholic bishops issued a careful statement, accepting the scheme with qualifications. They insisted that a fair proportion of the professors should be Catholics approved by their bishops, that the professors should be appointed by the trustees which should include the Catholic bishops of the province in which the college concerned was situated, that Catholics should not attend lectures on history, philosophy, geology or anatomy unless given by a Catholic professor, and that there should be a Catholic chaplain to look after the Catholic undergraduates. Both O'Connell and the defenders of the college argued that this statement favoured their view, and after a highly emotional debate in the association the matter was dropped.[29] But harsh words had passed, and though the death of Davis in September imposed a temporary truce, within a couple of weeks hostilities had recommenced, and the *Pilot* announced that a new journal called ' Old Ireland ', ' a name associated in the public mind with those political tactics which had been consecrated by success ' was about to be founded, on the same day as it announced the appearance of the potato blight.[30]

CHAPTER II

# AGRICULTURE
## By E. R. R. Green.

THE CAUSES OF EMIGRATION FROM IRELAND.

*The Lady's Newspaper,* 1849.

# CHAPTER II

# Agriculture

## I.  INTRODUCTION

ACCORDING to the census of 1841, out of a population of a little over 8,000,000 in Ireland, 5,500,000 or 66 per cent were dependent on agriculture.  But the striking feature of the Irish economy was not so much this dependence on agriculture as the tiny size of the individual units of production.  Forty-five per cent of those over an acre in size were reported to be under five acres and only 7 per cent more than thirty acres.

Geographically, the chief contrast in Ireland is between a relatively fertile east and a relatively infertile west.  This contrast is increased by the proximity of the east to British markets and influences.  Perhaps the most remarkable fact shown by the 1841 census was the dense agricultural population and the very small holdings of the west.  In Connacht, which possessed 43 per cent of the 6,000,000 acres of uncultivated land in the country, 78 per cent of the population was dependent on agriculture and 64 per cent of the holdings over one acre were under five acres in size.  By contrast, only 37 per cent of the holdings in Leinster fell into this category.

In the population figures the same pattern emerges.  There were 217 people to the square mile of arable land in Ireland as a whole.  Connacht, with 386 people to the square mile of arable, was more densely populated than either Munster or Leinster.  Ulster was the most densely populated province with 406 people to the square mile of arable, but there only 61 per cent of families were dependent on agriculture.  The most thickly populated county in Ireland was in Ulster—Armagh, with 511 people to the square mile of arable.  But second place was taken by Mayo, one of the most remote and infertile counties in the country, with 475 people to the square mile. Of six other counties with population densities of more than 400 to the square mile of arable, five were in Ulster and the sixth was Kerry, the poorest of the Munster counties in natural resources. Meath and Kildare with 201 and 187 people to the square mile respectively were the most thinly populated counties in Ireland.[1] It follows that in Ireland density of population and size of holdings bore little relation to the fertility of the soil. The great mass of Irish cultivators, in fact, were subsistence farmers, often forced to find that subsistence in the least generous soils.

It is not very surprising that agricultural output per head of the population was low in Ireland. England, a country of capitalist farms with proportionately only half as many people engaged in agriculture, produced twice as much per head. Little more than a quarter of all the families in England were engaged in agriculture, yet there were 2.06 acres of cultivable land per head of the population while Ireland had 2.08 acres per head.[2] A French economist, writing in the fifties, reckoned that the gross yield per hectare was the same in Ireland as in France, also a land of family farms. But in France there were only sixty people to every 100 hectares while in Ireland there were a hundred people. Divided among the population, the agricultural yield gave 100 francs per head in Ireland compared with 140 in France and 200 in Britain.[3] To contemporaries arguing from such a comparison between rural population and agricultural output, Ireland seemed the living proof of the inefficiency of small-scale farming.

During the eighteenth century the traditional bias of Irish agriculture towards grazing had shifted to tillage, making it easier for the expanding population to obtain land on which to raise their potatoes. As good mercantilists, Irish politicians had been concerned by the small quantity of grain raised in the country. Ireland's position in the empire made effective action difficult, although the granting of bounties on the transport of corn to Dublin had some success in encouraging tillage. After the Irish parliament achieved its independence in 1783, a comprehensive corn law on the English model was enacted. Foster's corn law of 1784 gave bounties of 3s. 4d. a barrel on the export of wheat until the home price exceeded 27s. a barrel and 1s. 5d a barrel on oats, while the home price was no more than 10s. A duty of

10s. a barrel was laid on imported wheat when the home price was under 30s. Export duties were also granted and import duties levied on flour, meal, barley, rye, and peas. The long war with France proved a far more powerful encouragement to tillage than any legislation could have been. Finally, under the pressure of wartime conditions the protected English market was opened to Irish grain in 1806. As a result, the price of wheat in the Dublin market rose 61 per cent and oats 59 per cent between 1791–5 and 1811–15.[4]

The subdivision produced by wartime tillage-farming was ultimately the responsibility of the Irish land system. By the beginning of the eighteenth century the land of Ireland had passed into the possession of a small class of Protestant landowners. Their property was based on a wholesale confiscation of Catholic estates, so they always felt some degree of insecurity in a Catholic country. As a result, they regarded their estates as sources of revenue rather than long-term investments. Unlike his English counterpart, the Irish landlord sank little capital in his estates in the form of buildings, fences, and drainage or in compensation for improvements. Many of the landlords were absentees who cared little for their tenants and judged agents only by their ability to forward rents. Other estates were let on long leases to middlemen who had no other motive than their own pecuniary gain in dealing with tenants. There were few landlords who did not take advantage of the competition for land to exact rack rents which left the tenant with only the barest subsistence. By holding out penalisation rather than reward for industry, the system left the cultivator without any hope of betterment. The low standard of living and the hopelessness bred by the land system were as much responsible for reckless subdivision as the fruitfulness of the potato which made life possible on such tiny holdings.

During the war, landlords acquiesced in subdivision because in the short run it meant bigger rent receipts. Contemporaries thought that the extension of the 40s. freehold franchise to Catholics in 1793 was also an important cause. Although the act gave the tenant a political importance which he had not had before, there were few contested elections, and at no time was the poll very heavy. At the most, the franchise represented the relaxation of still another restraint on subdivision.

Less attention has been paid to the opportunity which the

possession of a lease gave for subdivision.  While the lack of
security of tenure was one of the worst features of the Irish land
system, all leaseholders, no matter how small their holdings,
tended to subdivide either for profit or to provide for their
children.  Lord Monteagle voiced the general opinion of his
class when he told Nassau Senior that 'the Irish tenant is not to
be trusted with a lease.  His instinct is while he is alive to sublet
the land, in order to have an income without trouble, and on his
death to divide it among his children.'[5]

By 1841, subdivision had gone so far that nearly half of the
holdings of more than one acre were officially reported as under
five acres.  It would not be unreasonable to take such a holding
as a typical Irish farm.  Peter Mohun was the tenant of 3½ Irish
acres on the Shirley estate in Monaghan.  He had his land under
half an acre of wheat, half a rood of oats, a rood of clover, and
3½ roods of potatoes.  His 1½ acres of pasture was never broken
up, but cut for hay and a cow grazed on the rest.  He had two or
three pigs, and his wife kept fowl.  His annual expenses amounted
to over £8.  The rent had recently been raised from £3 19s. 11d.
to £5 19s. 9d., the cess was 3s. 3d. a year, the rent of bog was
4s. 6d. plus 6d. for a ticket for permission to cut turf.  He had to
take extra land on which to grow potatoes at £2 a rood.    A
brother had a horse and ploughed for him ; no money was asked
for this, but some return had to be made, usually in help at a busy
time.  But for this, ploughing would have cost another 12s. 6d.
or 15s.  Mohun wove for his own family, bought oats and made
meal, and in his younger days had made a 'little store' at the
loom and by mowing in summer.  The picture is grim, yet Peter
Mohun was 'the best man that can pay the rent in the townland'. [6]

The final stage of subdivision was represented by holdings of
no more than one acre on which all the work was done by spade
and the only crop was potatoes.  It was estimated that there were
some 65,000 of these in 1845.[7]  The absence of a farm labouring
class, paid in money wages, was made good principally by these
cottier tenants.  While there was no great difference economically
between cottiers and very small tenants, socially and tenurially
they were quite distinct.

Cottier tenure was essentially under-tenancy and customarily
involved labourer status.  The cottier system was also distinguished
by the substitution to a large extent of labour services for money

rents. If he had regular employment, this often meant that the cottier might be better off than many a small farmer.[8] The cottier tenant paid a rent of £1 10s. to £2 a year for his house and garden and proportionately for any land he might hold in addition. It was the land rather than the dwelling that was valuable. The cottier houses were wretched, run up by the farmers or the labourers themselves and kept in the worst possible state of repair. The annual rent often represented a profit of 50 per cent on the original outlay. Generally a small patch of garden for potatoes or cabbage went with the house. Turf and permission to keep a pig were almost always included.

In more prosperous days the cottier had been able to take sufficient grazing for a cow, a practice that by the thirties survived in counties Antrim, Down, Tyrone, and Londonderry and was becoming rare even there. This was known as a wet cot-take or tack, while ordinary cottier tenancy was called a dry cot-take. Near Omagh, for instance, a full or wet tack cost at least £7 per year, but carried with it a cow's grass, half an Irish acre of good corn land, land for sowing five gallons of flax, ten Irish perches of manured land for potatoes, bog for two days' cutting of turf, and several days' work of a horse to draw turf and manure.[9] The cottier's garden patch rarely grew enough potatoes to provide for his family, his pig, and his fowl. As he usually had more manure than he needed for his garden, his employer-landlord was glad to give him land on which to grow potatoes and even to make it ready for the crop.

This simple accommodation between farmer and labourer was not quite the same as the conacre system, where the agreement was between strangers and a competitive money rent had to be paid. The system of taking land in conacre became of major importance with the rapid advance of subdivision. Conacre letting consists in selling the use of a portion of land for one or more crops. Both the tenant who let his land in conacre and the middleman aimed at making a profit out of their holdings without actually working the land themselves, but in the case of conacre no relation of landlord and tenant arose. The use of the land was essential and the valuable old leas and manured ground offered in conacre had perforce to be taken. The land was generally manured and made ready for the seed before letting. Whoever took it provided the seed and all subsequent labour. The poor

THE FAILURE OF THE POTATO CROP.

*Pictorial Times*, 1846

quality of the Irish farmer's leas often made it necessary for him to take meadows in conacre to provide himself with enough hay. Taking land in conacre on which to grow flax or oats was more in the nature of a speculation. Servant men and the like sometimes took conacre and held over the crop until a scarcity when they sold on credit at exorbitant prices. The old lea ground which was broken up for conacre generally belonged to needy farmers. Conacre rents ranged from £4 for the worst land manured with lime to as much as £10 or £12 per acre in the neighbourhood of towns.

The cottier who had potato ground from his employer was much better off than small tenants who had to take conacre where they could find it and usually pay a money rent. The whole business was a speculation in food itself, for if the conacre failed the only escape from starvation was begging on the roads. The landlord, on his side, had no hope of recovering the promised rent in the event of a failure of the crop. Conacre provided the labouring classes with food independently of the fluctuating markets. By furnishing a ready source of food supply, it undoubtedly encouraged subdivision, early marriage, and large families.[10]

Money wages were regularly paid only by the gentry and they alone gave steady employment. The farmers usually gave food to labourers whenever they employed them with a corresponding reduction in wages. Wages rose in harvest time and at the potato digging, particularly if the season were a late one, and were reduced from November 1 to May 1. Over most of the country wages ranged between 4d. and 10d. a day. The lowest rate was paid for winter work, with food provided ; the highest about a gentleman's place where the labourer had to feed himself, but where he was guaranteed steady employment. On the east coast in Leinster and Ulster as much as 1s. per day was paid. In Leinster, 2s. or even 2s. 6d. per day was paid at harvest time, but usually only to migratory labourers ; 1s. or 1s. 6d was as much as the local labourer might expect. In Munster and Connacht harvest wages were no more than 10d. or 1s. per day.[11] By 1844 the Devon Commission found that daily wages were as high as 1s. only in Antrim, Armagh, Down, and Londonderry. In Carlow, Fermanagh, and Tyrone 10d. a day was paid. In Connacht, Clare, Kerry, West Cork, and Longford wages were only 6*d*. to 8*d*., and elsewhere in the country daily wages were from 8*d*. and 10*d*. Tipperary seems to have been suffering particularly badly from unemployment by 1844, wages there having sunk as low as 6*d*. to 8*d*. a day.

The annual income of the labourer even in reasonably steady employment was small, ranging from £8 to £16, made up of the wages he earned and the sale of his pig, eggs, and poultry. The pig was the great standby of the Irish cottier. Fed on the surplus potatoes from his garden and conacre patch, it provided cash for the rent and the few necessities he needed to buy. A sty was sometimes hollowed out of a bank and roughly thatched for the animal, but generally it was kept in the house with the cottier and his family.[12] Apart from his rent and other outgoings, the cottier needed money to buy food between the end of the old potatoes and the time for digging the new crop. Distress occurred every year according to the length of time which elapsed before the new crop was ready. The lumper potato, the usual food of the cottier, was popularly supposed to go bad after Garlick Sunday, the first in August, and the new lumpers were not ready until mid-September or October. During these weeks the poor had no resource but to buy potatoes and meal, often from the local usurer on exorbitant credit terms.

The Irish labourer could not hope for steady employment even at these low wages. Around 1835 probably not more than a third of the labourers had permanent employment. Even as near Dublin as Balrothery only 200 labourers out of a total of 600 had steady employment, and in thinly populated Kildare it was reckoned that a quarter of the labourers were out of work for four months in the year. All over the country it was the same; in the barony of East Maryborough in Queen's county only 366 labourers out of 913 had constant employment; in one parish, in Clare, only 80 labourers out of 347 had steady employment, and in another, 100 out of 556.[13]

While population continued to grow, the necessity for farm labourers was declining. Falling prices forced farmers to do more of their own work, the bigger farmers were turning away from tillage, and improved methods such as the drilling of potatoes reduced the number of men needed.

Unemployment was worst in the towns, for there those who were virtually unemployable concentrated. The poor inquiry commissioners said that the suburbs of Kells in co. Meath, for example, contained ' the greatest misery' which they had ' ever seen in any country'. They described what they had seen as follows :

> Cabins of single rooms are there frequently occupied by a large family, with sometimes a widow or an old man lodging with them, or occupied altogether by several widows, or by one or more, and one or two old men, and all (pigs included) sleeping in the different corners of the room.  The families are those of labourers, who generally get but very little employment ;  and the old men and widows subsist chiefly by begging, except those who are wholly or in part supported by their children, who give them all that they can spare of the wages they earn at service. . . .  A number of these cabins are situated in little courts at the back of the main row of cabins which form the front of the street or road. These courts are seldom more than six or seven feet wide, and that space, which forms the only passage or entrance to the cabins, is usually blocked up with the heaps of manure made by the pigs, and with the rubbish and filth thrown out of the houses at the very doors.[14]

The bogs similarly had become the resort of the evicted and the unemployed, many of them having become complete villages. The squatters lived in huts of sods until they had succeeded in clearing themselves a piece of ground and building a cabin.  The building of a road through a bog was the signal for the appearance of squatters.  Weld gives an example of this on the bog roads between Roscommon and Lanesborough around 1832 :

> Their first efforts are directed to the formation of a small hut, chiefly composed of the dry upper sods of the bog, and these served both for the walls and the roof, . . .  The little potato garden which is laid out, the first year, near the hovel, is commonly very rough, and the produce inconsiderable ; but with each succeeding year it wears gradually a better appearance, and yields more, as ashes and manure are spread upon it.  The patch of oats comes next, and willow fences are made round the enclosures.[15]

In contrast to the otherwise thinly populated county of Kildare, for example, was the town of Kilcock and the adjoining bog, which ' have an immense population and nothing can equal the wretchedness of the poor '.[16]

## II.  TILLAGE

In discussing the history of tillage in Ireland before the great famine, a very broad distinction can be made between grain raised by the plough as a cash crop and potatoes raised by the spade as a subsistence crop.  Between 1847 and 1851, with the exception of Limerick, the counties where most wheat was grown lay east of a line connecting west Louth and west Cork, so that it is possible again to distinguish on a geographical basis between the corn-growing eastern half of the country and the potato-raising west.

The era of wheat growing in Ireland falls between the passage of Foster's act and the repeal of the corn laws.  During those years the farmers depended upon wheat as their cash crop wherever it could be grown.  As late as 1836, it was reported that in Kildare ' the small tenants principally strive to make their rent of wheat '. For that reason they had been particularly badly hit by the low prices of the thirties.  Even in Ulster, ' wheat, where the land will produce it, is their chief dependence '.[1]  When the first agricultural returns were made in 1847, there were 743,871 acres under wheat with an estimated produce of nearly 3,000,000 quarters.  Of the area under crops and pasture in Louth and Waterford, over an eighth was under wheat, and in Kilkenny, Tipperary and Dublin the proportion was a fifth.[2]

The inland carriage bounties had originally led to the building of the flour mills which played a decisive part in establishing wheat growing.[3]  For example, the building of the Rock mills on the Funcheon in co. Cork resulted in the three adjacent baronies, ' formerly an open grazing country ', becoming ' enclosed, tilled, and almost as full of inhabitants as the lands along the sea coast '.[4] Arthur Young was told that the building of the flour mills at Crumlin in co. Antrim in 1765 had more than doubled the tillage of the surrounding district.[5]  The building of a large flour mill near Killarney began ' the era of tillage ' in Kerry.[6]

Foster's corn law succeeded in its immediate purpose ;  within twelve years, more corn, meal, and flour were sent out of Ireland than had been exported in the entire period from 1700 to 1784. War prices encouraged the Irish farmer to continue growing wheat.  Curwen, travelling through the north in 1813, observed the great increase in wheat growing and the fact that Derry had become a corn exporting town.[7] Galway developed an export trade in wheat during the war. The first flour mill there was built about 1780 and by 1820 there were twenty-three mills in the city and twelve in the county.[8]

The flour mills in the wheat growing areas were often very large. In 1834, an English traveller described Tipperary as 'one great granary' and compared the mills around Clonmel to 'the great factories, which we find in the English manufacturing towns districts, and employ almost as many persons'.[9] A flour mill at Drogheda had cost £20,000, and the machinery was driven by a 50 h.p. steam engine. Another flour mill near Trim ground 40,000 barrels a year. The mills built by Lord Caledon in Tyrone milled 9,000 tons of wheat per year in the thirties, in a district where scarcely an acre of wheat had been grown at the beginning of the century.[10]

Irish exports of wheat and flour to Britain rose steadily until about 1838. The quality of Irish wheat improved, too, and by the thirties the difference in price between English and Irish wheat had fallen from 15s. or 16s. per quarter to 4s. or 6s. English seed had been substituted for the 'old Irish wheat' grown at the beginning of the century. When Irish wheat was kiln dried with coke, as in fact most of it was, the difference in weight between the best Irish and the best English wheat did not amount to more than a pound per bushel.[11] The coming of the steamship helped the Irish milling trade, as previously there had been the danger of flour heating on a long voyage.

Wheat and flour imported into Great Britain from Ireland, 1800–42.[12]

| | | | |
|---|---|---|---|
| 1800 | 749 qrs | 1825 | 396,018 qrs |
| 1805 | 84,087 ,, | 1830 | 529,717 ,, |
| 1810 | 126,388 ,, | 1835 | 661,776 ,, |
| 1815 | 189,544 ,, | 1840 | 174,439 ,, |
| 1820 | 403,407 ,, | | |

The methods by which wheat was grown were not progressive ; as late as 1840 it was still common to fallow for wheat. The first ploughing was postponed as long as possible to allow the cattle to graze the grass and weeds. In three or four weeks the land was ploughed again and then cross ploughed some time before the crop was sown. These ploughings with long intervals between only gave weeds an opportunity to grow and provided no proper fallow at all.

Nothing, perhaps, improved so much in Irish agriculture in the early nineteenth century as ploughing, almost entirely as the result of the introduction of wooden ploughs on the Scottish model and later of two-horse iron ploughs. The new implements meant an immense saving in labour, both of horses and men. The Irish wooden plough had been very unsatisfactory. A team of four to six horses was required to draw it ; men were needed to drive the horses, to hold the plough in the ground by pressing on the beam, and to turn back the furrows by spade in the wake of the plough. With such an implement, it was impossible to plough straight, to plough hills laterally, or to plough deeply enough. Its only virtue was its cheapness—it cost no more than 10s. to 15s.[13]

In the best wheat districts the seed was sown broadcast and ploughed under in ridges on the fallows. Wheat was usually trenched in Ireland, especially on leas. Trenching made up for the deficiencies in drainage and ploughing and the lack of harrows and rollers. The land was formed into ridges about four feet wide with trenches about a foot wide between them. The seed was sown broadcast and covered up with earth from the trenches. The smaller farmer often put in his whole crop with spade and shovel, but the earth in the trenches might be loosened by running the plough between the ridges. Sowing wheat after potatoes became more common every year, the seed being ploughed under and rolled in the spring. The corn was cut by the sickle, four or five reapers to each ridge. One reaper cut a passage along the furrow and the others each cut an eighteen-inch swathe. A woman followed each pair of reapers and bound the sheaves.[14]

The grain was threshed and hurried to market as soon as possible, for the farmer usually was in urgent need of the money to pay the rent. The general introduction of threshing machines in Meath was said to be mainly due to the necessity for realising the value of the grain as quickly as possible. By the thirties, machines made in Dublin were to be had from £30 to £35.[15]

Oats were grown in much the same way as wheat. The ground was harrowed before sowing and the seed covered with soil from the furrows by shovel. When the crop was cut, it was left ' on the ledge ' for two or three days at great risk of ruin by weather,

but the oats were so weed-infested that if they had been stooked
straight away there would have been danger of heating. The
farmers made their stacks small and without foundations with
the result that the grain suffered from damp.[16] A variety known
as potato oats was the most common seed. An English corn
merchant, indeed, giving evidence before a parliamentary inquiry,
spoke as if they were the only Irish variety. Black oats, an inferior
variety with a great quantity of hull and offal when threshed,
were widely grown in mountainous parts.[17] That oats, like wheat,
were a rent-paying crop is shown by the steady increase of exports
to Britain.

Oats and oatmeal imported into Great Britain from Ireland,
1800–42.[18]

| 1800 | 2,411 qrs | 1825 | 1,629,856 qrs |
|------|-----------|------|---------------|
| 1805 | 203,202 „ | 1830 | 1,471,252 „ |
| 1810 | 492,741 „ | 1835 | 1,822,767 „ |
| 1815 | 597,537 „ | 1840 | 2,037,835 „ |
| 1820 | 916,251 „ | | |

With over 75,000 tons, Waterford was the chief corn exporting
Irish town in 1835. Galway was second with nearly 60,000 tons.
Limerick took third place with 49,000 tons, and Cork was fourth
with over 36,000.[19]

Potatoes were grown by primitive methods which belonged
to a pioneering stage of agriculture. It was the spade and the
potato which had brought much of the land under cultivation
since the introduction of the crop at the end of the sixteenth
century. The land was trenched in much the same way as for
wheat or oats. The beds were anything from two feet to six
feet wide, according to the wetness of the land, and the intervening trenches were about a foot wide and two feet deep. The
sets were laid on the surface of the ground or on the sod in grassland and earthed up from the trenches. After the shoots appeared
the crop was again moulded up from the trenches. This method
enabled a crop to be taken from the wettest land, for the trenches
provided a complete system of drainage as well as making it
possible to cultivate steep hillsides where a plough could not be
used.[20]

It was very common to pare and burn land for potatoes, even
fine old pasture ; another clear indication of the pioneer character

of much of Irish agriculture. Burnbate and the setting of potatoes on the grass sod were presumably reclaiming methods in origin, but were now used to save manure. By the latter method the fine land of the Golden Vale in Limerick would produce two crops of potatoes without manure, the second often better than the first. Special implements were used for ' scrawing ' the ground before burning, such as the ' grassaun ' of Kerry. In 1835 a parliamentary committee was told that ' a fifth of the arable of Connacht was at that time burning or covered with ashes '.[21] Nine-tenths of the potatoes in co. Galway were planted on burned ground in 1807. A dry spring in that county always meant abundant crops of potatoes, as there was no difficulty in burning the land.[22]

In Clare the land was pared and burned for the first crop of potatoes and manured with about six or eight tons of seaweed to the acre or with sea-sand for the second crop. Sand was carried twenty to thirty miles inland and was as useful as lime in bringing new land into cultivation. The lazy beds in this county were about six feet wide, the intervening trenches varying in width from one and a half to three feet according to the depth of the soil. In Iveragh in Kerry, the system was to spread seaweed, cover it thinly with earth from the trenches, spread sand, set the seed potatoes, and then cover them with soil from the trenches. The lazy beds in the Tralee district were six to nine feet wide, and there the manure was laid on the grass sod and the seed earthed up from the trenches. For the second crop the ground was dug deep enough to get through the unbroken sod on which the first crop had been grown. Holes were made in the soil into which the seed was dropped by a dibble, or ' stiveen ' as it was called in the west. This was a pointed stick, shod with iron, with a cross piece inserted at the side for the foot.[23] In Waterford, the land was ploughed for the first crop of potatoes, the ridges levelled by the spade, the seed dibbled in, and earthed up with soil from the furrows. When the plants were above the ground, between four and eight tons of lime to the statute acre were spread, and the potatoes earthed up a second time. This was the ' general Irish mode of culture on old, rich, arable ley ' as late as 1839.[24]

Drilling potatoes was far more economical in labour, gave a better yield, and was the obvious method once the farmers were provided with the improved ploughs. It was reckoned that six

men and two horses were sufficient to sow an acre of potatoes
in drills and that thirty men were necessary to set them in the old
lazy beds.  Drill cultivation was spreading in the better farming
districts, particularly in Leinster, where in co. Wicklow it was
already universal by 1812.  Farmers found that it paid them to
put manure out on land that they let in conacre, drill it in and
leave the tenant with only the seed to drop, as it left the land
cleaner than the old spade tillage.[25]

The chief varieties of potatoes grown in Ireland at this time
were the black potato, the Irish apple, the kidney potato, the
red potato, lumpers, and cups.  The black potato was grown as
early as 1730 and under various names was known all over the
country.  The apple was a white potato, first heard of in 1770,
and an excellent variety which brought prices of twenty to
twenty-five per cent more than other potatoes.  Kidney potatoes
were also known as ' bangers ' and ' red nebs ', of which the
Wicklow banger was a well-known early variety.  They do not
seem to have been grown much after about 1820.  Cups were
used for the table by all who could afford them, but the lumper,
a coarse, prolific potato, was the food of the great majority.
There is no mention of it before 1808, but lumpers rapidly came
into use as they were ' more productive from a little manure than
any other kind '.[26] A song exulting in the downfall of the wartime profiteers in 1815, says :

> Our gentry who fed upon turtle and wine
> Must now on wet lumpers and salt herring dine.[27]

Many of these old varieties failed to survive the potato blight.

The potato will grow on land which is too poor for grain and
not of much value for grazing.  As a result, by burning and
liming, spade cultivation was extended far into the bogs and up
the mountains.  Curwen makes the observation that ' by counting
the ascending range of cabins [on a mountainside], a tolerably
correct computation might be formed of the generations from
its first settlement '.[28]

Twenty to thirty-acre farmers were ' yearly enclosing and
bringing new pieces into tillage ' on the mountains of the Cork–
Limerick borders in the thirties.  They pared and burned the
sod, limed for the first crop of potatoes, manured for the second,
and followed with two crops of oats.  The grass that grew after

this course of crops was naturally poor for some years. If the
land remained wet, which was not unusual, the fields soon became
full of rushes and poor grasses.

In the Kerry mountains the necessity of growing potatoes
forced the farmers to bring new land into tillage every year.
Near Kenmare they half burned the surface the first year, limed
the ground at the rate of twenty-five barrels to the acre, and laid
on manure as well, raising a crop of potatoes in lazy beds. The
second year they changed the trenches and laid on a small quantity
of manure for a second crop of potatoes. The third year they
had a good crop of oats and the fourth year very good natural
grass.

The chief capital outlay in enclosing new land was making
fences, which also provided the only drainage, and making roads.
The landlords were often willing to do this. Much waste was
brought under cultivation by tenants who were allowed to hold
the land rent free until they had brought it into a productive
state, when they were given the alternative of giving up the
holding or paying a rent. Farmers, too, generally planted cottiers
on the worst land on their holdings which they had to reclaim for
their potatoes.[29]

### III.   GRAZING AND DAIRY-FARMING

There was a strong social prejudice among Irishmen against
tillage. A Kildare land agent told a parliamentary inquiry that
' according as they get wealthy I consider that they give up
tillage '.[1]   The wealthiest Irish farmers were the graziers of
Limerick, Tipperary, Roscommon, and Meath who would not
have deigned to turn a sod with the plough. The English green
crop rotation and house feeding system had made little progress
in Ireland. Indeed, nature fought against it by providing grass
all the year round. Pasture and tillage were kept strictly separate
in Ireland. The pastures were neglected—the dry land covered
with heath, thistles and briars and the lowlands swampy and
full of rushes. In Galway an abatement of rent was given for
these swampy lands where the cattle could feed only in dry weather
or during hard frosts. Most graziers seemed ' to have an aversion
to draining land '.[2]

Typical of the graziers were those who gave evidence before

the Devon Commission, such as R. W. Reynell of Killynan, Westmeath, who occupied about 3,000 statute acres in that county and in Meath, only 150 of which were in tillage; Patrick O'Connor of Dundermot in Roscommon who held about 2,500 acres with about forty acres in tillage ('only what I want for my own use,' as he said); and the Garnetts, father and son, who occupied 1,300 acres in Meath.[3]   Grazier farms in Roscommon were between 300 and 1,000 Irish acres, many of them at least in part freehold, and brought their owners between £1,500 and £5,000 a year. Weld gives an interesting picture of these Roscommon ranches about 1830 :

> The cattle are allowed to take an extensive range; it is believed that they thrive in proportion to this liberty, and vast herds may be observed together, spread over the hills, where scarcely a tree or even a bush is to be seen   Habitations are few . . . Yet often mounting upon some of the bleak and dreary hills, where an extensive prospect is opened for miles around, many a spacious and solid mansion may be observed in the distance, sheltered and surrounded with its woods and plantations.[4]

Hely Dutton tells a story of a Connacht grazier who, when asked if he wished to see a farm in Burren in Clare before he offered a rent for it, answered : 'Not I by G—— ; I did not see it these thirty years, and probably never will'.[5]   The main business of the Irish grazier was buying and selling. He was a speculator in cattle rather than a farmer.

The livestock industry was based on a regional division between rearing and fattening, meat production and dairying, with an internal trade linking up the various districts. Milch cows were most numerous in the Munster counties, Kilkenny, and the north-western counties. The more numerous the stock of milch cows the less food there is for other stock which must be sold off at an early age. On the other hand, districts with milch cattle had surplus milk for pig-feeding.

A wedge consisting of the Leinster counties, except Kilkenny, but including Galway and Roscommon in Connacht, utilised their grasslands to rear calves and stores from the adjoining counties. This midland plain had dense herds of dry cattle and sheep and drew its stock largely from dairying areas to north and south which concentrated on butter making and pig raising. The base of this grassland triangle rests on the east coast adjoining Britain which made it easy to extend the cattle trade across the channel. The agricultural revolution in Britain had made it more profitable for the farmer there to fatten imported Irish stores with green crops than to breed his own stock.

The cattle acts which prohibited the import of Irish live cattle into England were part of the mercantile system formulated at the Restoration. The result was the development of an Irish provision trade which lasted until after the peace of 1815, although free trade in cattle was restored in 1776. Geographically, Ireland was ideally situated to develop a trade in provisions to the West Indian colonies, France, and Spain and in the victualling of ships. The provision trade never recovered from the post-war depression brought about by the end of the lucrative army and navy contracts. The years 1815 to 1819 were described as having 'swept off' all the big Connacht graziers.[6] High wartime prices in Britain had led to the neglect of the West Indian and Newfoundland market which was finally lost when the ending of the old mercantile system in the twenties threw open these colonies to the United States exporter. The coming of the steamship and the railway made the transition to the export of live cattle easier and the numbers sent out of the country rose rapidly.

Ballinasloe fair was the great centre where the graziers of the midland counties bought in store cattle from the west and it was one of the biggest sheep and cattle fairs in the world.[7]

The Leinster grazier bought his cattle at Ballinasloe in October. These cattle stayed out all winter, sheltered only by the high hedges of the grazing farms and given hay at night. In spring they were turned out to get 'the early bite' in fields which had been left ungrazed for that purpose and were ready for Dublin market in June. A new stock was bought in May and sold fat in December. Sheep alternated on the grass with the cattle to eat up what they had left.[8]

There had been steady improvement in the breed of Irish cattle. The long-horned cattle developed by Robert Bakewell at Dishley in the mid-eighteenth century had been brought to Ireland almost as soon as they became known in England. David Low, writing in 1842, described them as still the 'prevailing race' of the country. They were the general stock of the Limerick dairymen. The cow was described as ' a capital milker, but its frame and carcass are not so heavy, or so roomy, or broad, as the English kinds '. In Waterford it was crossed with half-bred English bulls by the dairy farmers.[9] Cross-breeding was becoming the practice of the farmers everywhere and the favourite cross was the shorthorn.

The Leicester breed were not good milkers and a dual-purpose beast was considered essential for Ireland. This was found in the short-horned Durham cattle, said to have been first introduced into Ireland by Sir Robert Bateson of Belvoir Park near Belfast. As early as 1813, Commissioner Wynne had shorthorn cattle at Rathmines, co. Dublin. One Wicklow farmer told the poor inquiry commissioners that he had seen over 500 half- or thoroughbred Durham cattle at a recent fair, all of which were purchased by English dealers at high prices.[10] The native breed of mountain cattle, the Kerry, had been almost lost through crossing with long-horns, and as far back as 1800 was said to be extinct except around Bantry Bay. It was from these cattle that Lord Hawarden's agent, Dexter, produced the breed which bears his name.[11]

There was more specialisation in dairying in the south than among the northern small farmers. Throughout the south cows were let to dairymen in return for an annual rent per cow, paid partly in money and partly in kind. In 1835, a Limerick farmer with 370 acres was paid a rent of 1½ cwts of butter and 40s. ' horn money ' for each cow which he provided for a dairy. He estimated that a cow brought him £7 10s. by this system every year. ' Horn money ' was a share of the sum made by the dairyman on the calves which he fed and the pigs which he fattened with skimmed milk.[12] Another method was to give the land and cows to the management of a dairyman who in return for two collops of grazing undertook to give 1¼ cwts of first quality butter, a guinea ' horn money ' for each cow, and a fat pig weighing 2 cwts for each twenty cows. Anything that he made beyond this was his own. Meadow was attached to every dairy for winter food which the dairyman was obliged to save himself. In addition, the dairymen often kept about a rood of cabbage for pig-feeding. The cabbage was boiled, chopped up, and mixed with sour milk.

The dairy cows in Iveragh were universally of the Kerry breed, producing no more than 60 to 70 lbs of butter per annum. There was so little ground which would raise hay that during winter

cows were kept on potatoes and unthreshed oat straw.[13] The
farmers of the Golden Vale ploughed no more of their rich
pastures than was necessary to feed the population. Even the
milch cows were kept out at night in winter to feed on the
luxuriant grass.

The dairy system was disappearing in Carlow, Kilkenny, and
Waterford early in the nineteenth century. In Waterford, twenty
cow dairies were the most common and the cattle were housed
in winter if sufficient outbuildings existed. The yield of butter
in Carlow was about 1½ cwts per cow, and in this county dairies
of twenty to fifty cows were the common size. Carlow butter
was shipped to Dublin by canal, where it was regarded as the
best quality in Ireland.[14]

The quality of Irish butter generally was maintained by the
strict regulation of the trade rather than by the producer, as the
butter was not produced under good conditions. The poor
inquiry commissioners 'scarcely found any dairy tolerably
clean, and properly situated, fitted up, and ventilated, among the
large farmers' and the small farmers rarely had any dairy at all.[15]

Every Ulster small farmer had a cow or two and produced
small quantities of poor quality butter. This butter was sent to
market in small tubs and eventually found its way to the ports of
Sligo, Londonderry, Coleraine, and Belfast. Newry exported
the butter collected in the markets as far west as Enniskillen.[16]
Butter was the most valuable of Irish agricultural exports, amounting to over a quarter of the total of £11,000,000 in 1835.[17]

Some progress was made in sheep breeding, mainly by crossing
the native varieties with Bakewell's Leicester sheep. By the
thirties the Irish-Leicester cross was the usual breed in Leinster.
Robert St. George of Balief Castle, Kilkenny, was the pioneer.
In partnership with Astley of Odston, he imported sheep from
the best breeders of the New Leicesters. The extent of his business
may be indicated by the fact that in one season he let thirty rams
for £1,744. The result of his work was revolutionary—the new
breed of sheep were ready for market at two years old instead of
four, and it was now possible to compete with the English breeder.[18]
The export of sheep from Ireland only began in 1797.

The South Down sheep, another favourite cross, were first
introduced in 1801 by Wynn of Sligo, the vice-president of the
Farming Society of Ireland. Symes of Ballyarthur introduced

South Downs into Wicklow in 1805, where they were successfully crossed with the local breed. The marquis of Sligo brought South Down sheep to Mayo about the same date.[19]

Native breeds of mountain sheep were also found, especially in Kerry and Down. The mountain sheep, except in Wicklow, were sheared twice a year or simply had part of their wool cut off whenever some was wanted to spin. They were either left to wander over the mountain where they died from want and disease in large numbers, or were coupled together and left to pick up what they could.[20] Wild and half-starved, the nimble mountain sheep were a scourge to crops. The graziers, too, were careless of their flocks. As late as 1831 sheep were frequently blinded by thistles in Roscommon, but as they were the perquisite of the herds who burned them and sold the ashes, the thistles continued to flourish without interference.[21]

Roscommon was the most important sheep breeding county in Ireland. Galway, Clare, Limerick, and Tipperary were also sheep counties. The Leinster graziers bought in ewes at Ballinasloe in autumn, sold the lambs at Dublin in June or July and the ewes in November. At Ballinasloe fair, 60,000 to 80,000 sheep were generally exhibited.

Although the Irish producer had no market for his surplus potatoes in a country where everyone produced his own requirements, they became an important source of income when turned into pork. The pig paid the small tenant's rent and was almost the cottier's sole source of money income. It was during this period that the pig established his connection with the Irishman in the imagination of the outside world. The animal lived about the house, was fed on scraps, and often was housed in the cabin so that he naturally became very domesticated. Travellers described him as ' the chief person in the household ' and ' the national pet '.[22]

The old Irish pig was tall, long-legged, high-backed, and bony and remarkable for its huge, heavy ears. These pigs were slow to fatten and produced poor quality pork. Their place was being taken by a breed nearly always described as ' thick,' and by 1840 or so, the original Irish pigs had been confined to Connacht, except where pigs were bought from Connacht drovers.[23]

In 1835 the largest export of live pigs, 94,343, was from Drogheda, followed by Cork and Waterford with about 75,000

each.   In official returns provisions included butter and beef as
well as pork, bacon, and hams, but it was certainly pig products
which made Belfast, with 17,011 tons, the second largest provision
exporting town in 1835.[24]   Belfast's reputation for curing, which
had once been as good as that of Limerick, was lost by the inferior
breed of pigs kept in Ulster.   Limerick built up its great reputation
in the curing trade in the twenties after Russell and Matterson
began to cure the first Limerick hams.[25]

Swine, pork, bacon, and hams imported into Great Britain
from Ireland.[26]

|      | Swine   | Pork             | Bacon and Hams   |
|------|---------|------------------|------------------|
| 1815 | 127,570 | 105,766  barrels | 213,569  cwts    |
| 1820 | 99,107  | 105,973     ,,   | 260,549     ,,   |
| 1825 | 65,919  | 883,783     ,,   | 361,139     ,,   |
| 1835 | 376,191 | —                | 379,111     ,,   |

IV.   THE WESTERN SEABOARD

Western counties, such as Donegal, Mayo, and Kerry, where
there was the most complete dependence on the potato and where
subdivision had been carried to the greatest extremes, constituted
the core of the Irish agricultural problem.[1]   Because of their
remoteness, primitive methods of agriculture and ancient forms
of social organisation continued to survive in such areas.
    Much land in the west was held by a system of joint tenure
or tenure in common known as rundale.   The origin of the
system is obscure.   Whether it was a product of the tillage
movement and the pressure of population or a survival of an
early Irish agricultural system cannot be said with certainty.   A
return of 1845 estimated that there were almost two million acres
of land in the country held in common or by joint tenancy.   It
would be a mistake to regard this as evidence that such an extent
of land was being farmed by the rundale system, as much of it is
probably made up of mountain grazing.   Nor can it be automatically assumed that all tenants who held their land jointly
farmed under the rundale system.   The typical rundale farmers
lived in villages which are clearly to be seen on the maps of the

first edition of the ordnance survey. A rundale village and the
land attached to it was usually coterminous with a townland.[2]

Each man had his holding of arable land scattered among those
of his neighbours, perhaps in as many as thirty or forty pieces.
In Erris, lots were cast every three years after the course of cropping
was completed, and a general change round took place. The
strips of arable were divided by stone marks and balks about a
foot wide which were left unploughed.[3] Meadow was divided
up in the same way ; it was recorded in 1824 that ' one sometimes
sees patches of meadow divided by stones into as many shares
as there are tenants on the farm ; and the grass is perhaps trodden
down, or the season lost, before all the disputes that arise upon
this division can be adjusted '.[4] Grazing was held in common,
the basic unit being the ' sum ' or ' collop ', a land measure of use
rather than of area. The ' sum ' was reckoned variously, sometimes as the quantity of grass necessary to support a horse, a cow,
two yearling heifers, or six to eight sheep.

A man's holding both of arable and pasture was in proportion
to the share of the rent which he paid. Only one or two persons
took the townland from the landlord and were held responsible
for the rent. The village was ruled by an elder who collected and
paid the rent, apportioned taxes like the county cess, settled
quarrels, and generally guided the work of the community.
Rundale has strong resemblances to the open-field systems of
England and the continent, but contemporaries were inclined to
regard it as another landlord expedient for drawing rent without
investing capital. There is no doubt that a number of joint
tenants were able to pay a rent that a single occupier would have
found quite beyond his means.[5]

The landlords found that nothing produced such rapid subdivision as a partnership lease. The townland was originally
taken by only three or four persons, but within twenty years
there would be ten or twenty families. This finally resulted in
the grazing being divided into units smaller than the cow's grass
or ' sum ', such as the ' foot ', a quarter cow's grass, and even the
' cleet ', which was half a ' foot '.[6] The confusion in the dispersed
tillage holdings as a result of subdivision almost defied attempts
to carry on ; an example is quoted of a half-acre field held by
twenty-six different people. As a result, when partnership leases
fell in, they were not renewed.

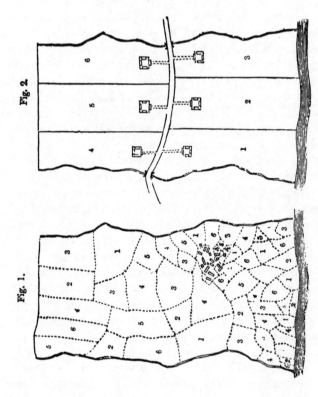

**Fig. 1.**

**Fig. 2**

THE CONSOLIDATION OF RUNDALE HOLDINGS (Fig. 1)
INTO COMPACT FARMS (Fig. 2).

Hall, *Ireland*, vol. iii.

Until about 1815 rundale seems to have been very widespread, but by 1845 Mayo was the only county where it remained the predominant form of tenure. In the poor law unions of Ballina, Swinford, and Westport alone, 364,603 acres were held in common or joint tenancy. Although no acreage was given for the union of Castlebar the 'greater part' was said to be held in common. Joint tenancy was also the prevalent tenure in the unions of Dunfanaghy, Letterkenny, and Milford in Donegal, of Gort and Scariff in south Galway and Clare, of Skibbereen and Kanturk in Cork, and of Kenmare in Kerry.[7]

There are several descriptions of rundale villages from which an idea can be formed of what they were like. Sir Charles Coote described a village called Blackstaff in Farney which was broken up about 1798. The village was 'composed of about two hundred miserable cabbins, and its site was in the centre of five hundred acres of a great range of bog, heath, and immense rock'. The inhabitants met on a particular day every year to choose a 'chief magistrate'; apparently the owner of the 'largest potatoe garden was sure to be elected mayor'. His fees were paid in whiskey, but Coote acknowledges that 'so implicit an obedience was paid to his decisions, that the neighbouring magistrates had never any trouble from this quarter'. After the inhabitants had been placed in holdings of their own and the old village pulled down, 'they yet frequently visit its dear remains, and on the ruins of Blackstaff, they still celebrate their ancient sports and pastimes'.[8]

T. C. Foster who was sent to Ireland by *The Times* in August, 1845, described Menlow, an unusually large rundale four miles from Galway, whose 2,000 inhabitants lived by keeping cows to supply the city with milk. 'As this is the largest village I ever saw,' he writes, 'so it is the poorest, the worst built, the most strangely irregular, and the most completely without head or centre, or market or church, or school, of any village I ever was in. It is an overgrown democracy. No man is better or richer than his neighbour in it.'[9]

When Lord George Hill bought the Gweedore property in Donegal in 1838, it was entirely under the rundale system. Only 700 of the 3,000 inhabitants paid rent. The tenants kept their cattle in one end of their dwelling houses. They grew enough corn to pay the rent which ranged from 3s. to 30s. a year. Five or six sheep were kept whose wool supplied them with clothing.

The women knitted socks, the sale of which brought in enough money to buy tobacco or pay the county cess.

Closely associated with rundale was the system of booleying (buailteachas) or transhumance. The young people went up with cattle on the mountains for the summer months and made butter which they brought back on their return. As Lord George Hill describes it, the practice seems to have existed in a very fully developed form in the Gweedore district :

> It often happens that a man has *three* dwellings—one in the mountains, another upon the shore, and the third upon an island, he and his family, flitting from one to another of these habitations, as the various and peculiar herbage of each is thought to be beneficial to the cattle, which are supposed, at times, to have a disease requiring a change of pasture, whilst in reality they only want more food.[10]

There were many criticisms levelled at the rundale system, most of them similar to those which were made of the English open-field villages in the eighteenth century. For instance, the cattle were brought down from the mountains on a fixed day and turned into the arable, so that crops which had not been removed by that time were ruined. Work could not begin in spring until after the day when the cattle had again been taken to the mountain. Growing green crops on the unenclosed tillage was impossible, as they would inevitably be eaten by the mountain sheep. There was no advantage to the individual in reclaiming land from the waste as it would be divided up among all the tenants in proportion to their rent after one crop. The problems of mearings and rights of way were an eternal source of litigation. Yet when the farms were 'striped' and the people scattered in isolated houses much of their social life and community sense was lost. Dutton, writing of Galway in 1824, sensed this when he wrote :

> Though latterly in most cases ruinous to the tenants of this county, yet it tends to encourage such strong attachments, generally strengthened by intermarriages, that though they may have some bickerings with each other, they will, *right or wrong*, keep their companions ; this is frequently the source of much disturbance at fairs or any other public meeting.[11]

Road building played a large part in breaking up rundale villages. For example, when a new road was built in Iveragh ' the old inhabitants of the hill left their cabins and built new ones along the new road sides. The same has taken place with every other new road that has been made '. Writing of Erris, the Devon commissioners said : ' Until such works are accomplished, the village system, so prejudicial to individual industry, cannot be broken up '.

In 1822 the policy of giving parliamentary grants for road-making was adopted, as a result of the success which had met such a policy in the Highlands of Scotland. These roads gave the people access to a market for their produce, made possible the transport of lime for the reclamation of new land, and checked illicit whiskey distilling. Before the coming of the roads potatoes were grown for food and barley for distilling. The people could hardly have been expected to carry grain in 3 cwt lots on horseback to a market many miles distant where they would be forced to sell at whatever price was offered.

Towns like Belmullet, Clifden, and Roundstone in the west owe their existence to the making of the roads. After the main road was made through Erris, the export of corn from Belmullet rose from 80 tons to 1,600 tons annually within twenty years. Cars were still a rarity in three Kerry baronies as late as 1834. Between that date and 1845, 233 miles of road were made in the county, 140 of them by the board of works at a cost of £123,000. The county surveyor wrote that as a result, ' every horse has now his car instead of his baskets '.

The work of individual landlords had also made changes. Lord George Hill built a corn mill, a store, and kiln at Bunbeg on his Gweedore property, providing an alternative market to the illicit poteen still for the first time. Goods were sold in the adjoining shop at the same prices as in Letterkenny, twenty-six miles away. The holdings were consolidated, not without strong objections from the tenants, and new houses built. The tenants were forgiven their arrears of rent. On the Headley estate at Glenbegh in Kerry roads were made, rundale broken up, rents reduced, and arrears permitted to be paid in labour. £5,000 of arrears were taken in embanking 500 acres of land from the sea. The land there had all been held on the rundale system and the rents paid by the sale of butter, or rather by money borrowed at high rates of interest from the butter merchants who came round in the spring.[12]

Seasonal migration had become a common solution of the problem of paying rents on the tiny holdings of the barren western mountains and coasts. The men poured out in increasing numbers every year to seek work as harvesters. The tillage movement of the late eighteenth century had first brought the 'spalpeen' to seek work at harvest time. His wife and children often set out with him to beg potatoes and meal from house to house until their own crop was ready.

It had not been long until harvesters began to cross over to Britain, where extra hands were welcome on the big farms. This movement had reached considerable dimensions by 1841 when the number of harvesters going to Great Britain was 57,651. Connacht as a whole provided 25,118 or 43.5 per cent of the total migrants, the great majority of whom embarked at Dublin or Drogheda, and landed at Liverpool. The heaviest seasonal migration was from co. Mayo where over a third of the population went to work as harvesters. The total of harvest workers from Ulster was 19,312, the majority from the counties of Donegal and Londonderry. Over half of them travelled from the port of Derry to Scotland. 7,477 embarked at Belfast and 1,740 at Warrenpoint.

Only 1,817 went from Munster to the English harvest as there was plenty of work for them in their own province or in Leinster. Even as far north as Dungarvan the farmers relied on the assistance of Kerry labourers in bringing in the harvest. In Limerick, small farmers' sons and labourers came down from the mountains to work at the harvest when they had their own potatoes set in June and stayed until after the potato harvest. Single men from the Cork and Kerry mountains went to work as harvesters for 8d. a day and their food rather than work at home for the same wages without food.[13]

The seasonal migrant was able to bring back at least £3 from England. The sum could be raised to £5 if he went in time for haymaking. The tenants on Lord Westmeath's estate on the Mayo-Galway border paid their rent in one lump sum for the year with their English earnings. Others went to earn enough to pay their conacre rents.[14]

### V.  SUGGESTED REMEDIES

Contemporaries were well aware of the economic and social ills which afflicted Ireland.  The government's concern is perpetuated by a vast bulk of evidence taken down by commissions and select committees and of reports which they prepared.  The English bias in favour of large-scale capitalist farming and the belief that the natural economy of Ireland was grazing led easily to the assumption that over-population was the whole problem. It was a view which encouraged a policy of drift.  Those who held it asked only that the fact should be recognised and the surplus population got rid of, perhaps by state-sponsored emigration.

The contention that the country suffered from under-production rather than over-population was not often heard outside Ireland. If the problem was one of unemployment, something might yet be done.  Men who had to live in the country could not accept with the detachment of English economists the inevitable disaster implied in the over-population theory.  Too many, unfortunately, who took this point of view destroyed their case by exaggerations of the fertility of the country and of the numbers of people which it could support.  Almost without exception they saw the solution of the problem in an extension of the arable area through the reclamation of waste land.

The most important advocate of waste land reclamation was John Pitt Kennedy, an engineer officer and land-agent.  He acted as secretary to the Devon commission and his theories are most easily to be found in the digest which he prepared of the findings of that body.  He took as his base the calculation of Richard Griffith, the valuation commissioner, that there were over one and a quarter million acres in the country which could be brought under cultivation and another 2,330,000 which might be drained for coarse meadow or made fit for grazing by sheep and young cattle.  Kennedy claimed that this land would provide eight-acre holdings for 192,368 families and enlarge the holdings of another 133,720 families to the same acreage, thereby permanently reducing the number of labourers in the market by 500,000.[1]

The fundamental criticism of Kennedy and the other advocates of reclamation is that their premises were those of the peasant himself—that all that was wrong in the country was a shortage of land. Even if it were possible to reclaim a large area of waste land, no consideration was given to the problem of whether such marginal land could continue to be farmed indefinitely. The fact was also overlooked that state-sponsored reclamation of waste land would undoubtedly have acted as a spur to population increase, intensifying the population problem still further within a very short time.[2]

The most practical proposals for dealing with the problem of Irish agriculture were made by William Blacker, an Armagh land agent. He aimed at intensifying the cultivation of the land already in use rather than extending the arable area. His was the soundest approach to the problem, for by increasing the income of the individual farmer it would lead to a higher standard of living, the absence of which had been largely responsible for subdivision and the growth of population outstripping the demand for labour.

Blacker started out with the orthodox Irish assumption that ' a pauper population must be *employed* or it becomes *dangerous*, and when they cannot get work, they must get *land* '.[3] Having accepted the necessity for subdivision, he set out to prove that its effects could be countered by the introduction of green crops and house-feeding on the small holdings. He believed that the agricultural output of Ireland could thus be increased threefold. Essentially what he was trying to show was that the English tillage revolution could be carried out equally well on small farms as on big ones.

Before publishing his schemes, Blacker had already put them into practice with considerable success on the large properties which he managed in co. Armagh. The first step had been the employment of an agricultural instructor from Scotland, entrusted with the task of persuading the tenants to adopt a proper rotation instead of exhausting the land with successive corn crops. Realising that the tenant could not be expected to risk his very food by using his scanty supply of manure to grow a green crop instead of potatoes, Blacker had given a loan of sufficient lime for the first crop. The tenants were given clover and vetch seed on six months' credit if they undertook to sow the former with their first grain crop and the latter instead of a second grain crop. By intensive agriculture these small farmers were able to obtain heavier yields than were common even in England—8 to 10 tons of potatoes, 16 to 18 cwts of wheat and 17 to 19 cwts of oats to the acre. By the new system tenants of 2½ and 5 acres were able to keep cows for the first time.[4]

The government were also interested in reclamation. A commission appointed in 1809 carried out a survey of the Irish bogs which took five years to complete and cost over £50,000. Select committees of 1819, 1823, and 1830 urged that work should be begun on the basis of the 1814 report of the bogs inquiry.[5] The Irish board of public works was established in 1831, concentrating the functions of five existing bodies. A works programme had been very successful in opening up the Scottish Highlands. A select committee on the state of the poor had urged this example as worthy of imitation in Ireland in 1830. Fisheries and inland navigation were under the control of the new board, and it had a large grant for the construction of roads, bridges, small harbours, and piers.[6] The reports of the select committee on public works of 1835 urged that ' very extensive operations for reclaiming waste lands ' was an essential task of the board of public works. It was claimed that large numbers of cottiers would be induced to abandon their holdings by reclamation works. The result would be to increase the amount of arable land available, to diminish agrarian crime, and to break up ' densely populated cottier settlements '.[7]

In spite of all exhortations from official and non-official sources, the government made only one small-scale experiment in the reclamation of waste land. The scheme was begun in 1833 on the crown lands at King Williamstown near Kanturk. A road was made from Kanturk to Tralee, a village built, a model farm of 300 acres laid out, and the land divided into small holdings on which suitable buildings were erected. A lime quarry was opened and a kiln built. The tenants who were settled on the unreclaimed mountain were provided with lime, but one visitor claimed that they paid a conacre rent of £6 an acre and brought the land into cultivation by two crops of potatoes in the same way as reclaiming tenants elsewhere. Every effort was made to establish an improved agriculture by building up a stock of dairy cattle, green crop cultivation and a proper rotation. Caird, writing after the Famine, condemns the experiment and incidently the schemes of the whole waste land school :

The success of the scheme was thus totally based on the potato ; and the scheme seems rather to have been intended to show how many people could be kept alive by the cultivation of waste land, than to exhibit an example of *an improvement in the condition of the people* resulting from the reclamation of land.[8]

The government was more ready to provide facilities for agricultural education, and a scheme of instruction under the auspices of the national board was undertaken. A model farm was set up at Glasnevin in 1838, where student teachers would be trained to give instruction in agriculture in the national schools. It was intended to create a system of twenty-five district model agricultural schools and that the national schools should each have a patch of land on which practical instruction could be given. John Pitt Kennedy, who had been an ardent advocate of the inclusion of practical agriculture in the national school system, was appointed first superintendent of the scheme. He resigned in 1839 when the government refused to act on certain of his suggestions.[9]

The work of agricultural societies is also of an educational nature, and government money was forthcoming for the support of such bodies. Inevitably they were inaugurated and supported by the gentry and were primarily interested in stock-breeding. The most important had been the Farming Society of Ireland, founded by the marquis of Sligo and John Foster. The society laid down as its aims the improvement of breed in cattle, the raising of farming standards by the employment of itinerant instructors, and the encouragement of the use of improved implements. A factory had been set up in Dublin under their auspices for the manufacture and sale of agricultural implements. The society had secured a government grant of £5,000 per annum. Shows were held at the great Ballinasloe fair.

The Royal Dublin Society tacitly agreed to confine itself to research, the original purpose of its foundation, until the Farming Society came to an end in 1828. On the initiative of Lord Downshire, a 'committee of agriculture and planting' was formed and shows of livestock held in the society's yard.[10] The Agricultural Improvement Society of Ireland was founded in 1841 at a time when the Royal Dublin Society had many difficulties to face. The chief aims of the new society were to co-ordinate the efforts of local agricultural societies and to hold an annual show, always in some different centre in each of the four provinces in succession if possible. The society was given a charter, received considerable official support, and did succeed in establishing a sort of federation of county agricultural societies. Twenty existing societies became affiliated at once. The number then rose to a peak of 110 in 1845 and thereafter declined.[11]

The work done by the agricultural societies in improving stock and introducing new breeds was of real importance in providing a model for Irish farming. Long term capital investment such as this is not lightly to be criticised. But the mass of Irish small farmers were too poor and ignorant to benefit from the type of education provided by agricultural schools and societies. The agriculturist employed by the landlord, with the landlord's coercive power behind him, held out the most hope, so long as he did actually go among the tenants and not spend his time in experiments in stock breeding and growing new crops.

Responsibility in Ireland still lay with the landlords; there were few as yet to suggest that the solution of her agrarian problems should be undertaken by the state. The *ancien regime* was still accepted in Ireland, the landlord still secure in his position if only he could do something to avert approaching calamity. The Great Famine had to come before John Stuart Mill could declare that the existing land system was 'the very foundation of the economical evils of Ireland' and assert that it was 'absolutely incompatible with a prosperous condition of the labouring classes'.[12] The state of affairs which had been largely created by the landlords, however, had passed beyond their control.

The whole economic structure of Irish agriculture rested ultimately on the potato. High rents without any investment and farming without any monetary return depended on the continued productivity of this plant. The crops of corn the farmer raised by a primitive rotation of white crops and potatoes were turned into cash which was almost entirely absorbed by rent. As there was not enough money left to pay the wages of labour, payment in kind by permitting the use of land and a dwelling were substituted. The conacre system also enabled the farmer to shift some of his burden of competitive rent on to the shoulders of the cottier class.

That dependence on the potato was the real danger, much more so even than dense population, is shown by the contrast between Connacht and Ulster. Subdivision had been carried even further in Ulster than in the west. In Mayo there were $2\frac{3}{4}$ acres of arable land per head of the population and in Galway $3\frac{1}{2}$ acres. There were only $1\frac{1}{4}$ acres of arable land per head of the rural population in co. Armagh and $1\frac{1}{2}$ acres in co. Down.[13] Although the land was not so fertile as in the south nor the standard of farming very high, yet Ulster was undoubtedly the most prosperous and economically the most secure part of the country. Subdivision, therefore, was not necessarily disastrous so long as there was a balanced economy such as existed in this province.[14]

The proportion of the population of Ireland dependent on the potato had increased steadily, not only under the pressure of an ever-growing population but by high rents, fluctuating prices, the collapse of the domestic system of industry, the gradual decline of tillage among big farmers, and the adoption of improved methods and implements, all of which reduced employment. It had become obvious that the physical survival of the cottiers and large numbers of the farmers depended on the potato crop. The poor were eating more and more of the best yielding but worst quality lumper potatoes. The weeks between the end of the old potatoes and the digging of the new ones annually rehearsed in miniature what would take place in the event of a failure of the potato crop. After the 1822 famine, a government enquiry noted that people whose only possession was a potato plot were helpless in the event of a failure. Their conclusions are worth quoting in full :

There was no want of food of another description for the support of human life. On the contrary, the crops of grain had been far from deficient, and the prices of corn and of oatmeal were very moderate . . . those districts in the south and west presented the remarkable example of possessing a surplus of food whilst the inhabitants were suffering from actual want. . . . The calamity of 1822 may therefore be said to have proceeded less from the want of food itself, than from the want of adequate means for purchasing it ; or in other words from the want of profitable employment.[15]

## VI. THE FAMINE AND AFTER

The potato blight made its appearance in the late autumn of 1845. Only certain districts were affected, and the early potatoes, representing about a sixth of the total crop, had already been dug and escaped completely. Partial failures like this had happened before, and there was no undue alarm. Next year came complete disaster. By the first week in August potato crops everywhere were ruined. The marquis of Lansdowne, speaking in the house of lords in January, 1847, estimated the loss at nine to ten million tons, the equivalent of the produce of one and one-half million acres of potatoes.[1] The ravages of the blight were not nearly so widespread or severe in 1847. Most of the potatoes which should have been kept for seed had been eaten, however, and the country was so demoralised that only a fraction of the usual acreage of potatoes had been planted.

In the autumn of 1847 the government, wishing to know what food supplies there were in the country, made the first annual collection of agricultural statistics.[2] The agricultural returns are not of great value for the famine itself, as they do not begin until the worst was over. These figures do make it possible to fix the disaster in proper perspective.

There were only 284,116 acres under potatoes in the country in 1847 ; these produced slightly over two million tons. There are no earlier crop returns to measure these figures against. Statistics of agricultural holdings and livestock were collected at the time of the 1841 census. Using them as a basis for reckoning the amount of potatoes consumed as human and animal food, it has been estimated that there were two and a half million acres devoted to potatoes in 1841.[3]

The result appears in the reduction in the number of agricultural holdings. The 1841 census made no return of holdings of one acre or under, but a drop of 59 per cent in the number of holdings over one and not more than five acres shows how severely the cottier and small-holder class had been hit.

| Holdings | 1841 | 1847 | Difference |
|---|---|---|---|
| Not exceeding one acre . | — | 73,016 | — |
| 1–5 acres . . . | 310,375 | 139,041 | 173,334 |
| 5–15 „ . . . | 252,778 | 269,534 | 16,756 |

| | | | |
|---|---|---|---|
| 15–30 „ . . . | 79,338 | 164,337 | 84,999 |
| Above 30 acres . . | 48,623 | 157,097 | 108,474 |

Pigs and poultry, which like people were dependent on potatoes for food, were greatly reduced in number after 1841. The number of pigs had fallen from about one and a half million in 1841 to 622,459 in 1847 and of poultry from eight and a half million to under six million.[4] The position is reflected in the export figures for pigs :

| | |
|---|---|
| 1846 | 480,827 |
| 1847 | 106,407 |
| 1848 | 110,787 |
| 1851 | 68,053[5] |

In 1841 there had been 1,863,116 head of cattle in the country, and in 1847 this had risen by over 7 per cent to 2,591,415. The increase in cattle was entirely on holdings of over fifteen acres. On the smaller holdings the numbers had decreased by 432,003. This shows that the very small tillage farm was already ceasing to be typical and the small mixed farm was taking its place. A similar, but not so marked change was taking place in the case of sheep. There was an increase of 80,358 head on the 1841 figure of 2,106,189. This had taken place only on the holdings over thirty acres in extent ; a total decrease of 519,948 head having taken place on the smaller holdings.[6] Cattle exports had steadily increased, and sheep, a large proportion of which had been in the hands of small-holders, also show a jump in exports during the famine :

| Year | Cattle | Sheep |
|---|---|---|
| 1846 | 186,483 | 259,257 |
| 1847 | 189,960 | 324,179 |
| 1848 | 196,042 | 255,682 |
| 1849 | 201,811 | 241,061[7] |

The danger of sheep stealing by the starving and desperate was in part responsible for owners disposing of their sheep. Consolidation of farms is also reflected in the reduced numbers of horses in the country.

Another year of distress and disappointment came in 1848. The season was cold and wet and crops were bad. Confidence had been returning and the people had made great efforts, many selling their only cow to buy seed potatoes, of which the supply had been more plentiful than had been expected.[8] The potato acreage had been raised from 284,116 acres to 742,899 acres but only yielded 30 barrels per acre compared with 57 barrels in 1847. As a result of reduced sowings, bad weather, and the fact that in 1847 white crops had been in the ratio of 4.5 acres to one acre of preparation crop, the total produce of grain was down by 673,488 tons. The yield of oats fell from 8.4 barrels to 7.6 barrels. A table of percentages under the various crops on farms of each class will best illustrate the effect of this poor harvest.

| Farm | Wheat | Oats | Potatoes | Turnips | Meadow and Clover |
|---|---|---|---|---|---|
| Under 1 acre | 6·98 | 26·54 | 37·60 | 4·44 | 4·08 |
| 1– 5 acres | 9·90 | 41·07 | 23·24 | 4·10 | 9·83 |
| 5–15 ,, | 9·26 | 45·46 | 17·95 | 4·20 | 12·98 |
| 15–30 ,, | 10·10 | 42·71 | 15·84 | 4·49 | 17·30 |
| Above 30 acres | 12·29 | 32·34 | 11·95 | 5·57 | 29·51[9] |

The disastrous year of 1848 overwhelmed many of the small farmers who had survived the potato failure. The effects were seen in the 1849 statistics which show that while the decline in holdings under fifteen acres was not so rapid, those between fifteen and thirty acres were decreasing in numbers more sharply than in 1848. A table of the percentage alterations in the number of holdings and the value of stock on them between 1847 and 1848 illustrates how the capital of the small farmer was dwindling.

| Farm | Alteration per cent Holdings, 1847–8 | Alteration per cent Value of Stock, 1847–8[10] |
|---|---|---|
| Under 1 acre . | −30 | −26 |
| 1– 5 acres . | −20 | −13 |
| 5–15 ,, . | −11 | − 4 |
| 15–30 ,, . | − 3 | + 5 |
| Above 30 acres . | + ·03 | + 5 |

The 1849 harvest saw an increase of nearly 2 per cent in the produce of the crops, and although the acreage under potatoes was down by 86,841 acres, the crop produced over four million tons, about 12 per cent more than in 1848. The extent of the potato crop increased in an interesting group of counties which form a compact area in the north and west. These were Antrim, Donegal, Fermanagh, Londonderry, Tyrone, and Sligo. The area remained about the same in Mayo and Roscommon. In all other counties, except Wexford, traditionally a tillage area, the potato acreage had been reduced. The extent of corn crops also increased in the northern and western counties of Tyrone, Mayo, Roscommon, Cavan, Longford, and Sligo as well as in Wexford and Cork. It is clear that the pre-famine economy was making a strong attempt to revive in Ulster and Connacht.

The value of livestock in the hands of cottiers actually showed an increase of £37,459 in 1849, still another sign that the effects of the famine were wearing off. The greatest reduction in value of stock was among the farmers of five to fifteen acres (£158,075). Fifteen to thirty acre farmers had £21,739 worth of livestock less than in 1848, although the value of cattle and pigs on such holdings had increased. The value of stock on holdings over thirty acres had increased by nearly £400,000.[11]

The decrease in the number of holdings in 1850 was less than half of what it had been the previous year. The area under crops showed an increase of 214,544 acres or 3·8 per cent on the 1849 area. This increase was made up of green crops, as white crops had been reduced by 24,868 acres. The value of livestock on holdings over thirty acres had risen by no less than £1½ million. There were decreases on all holdings under thirty acres, the greatest being on those between five and fifteen acres.[12]

The 1851 statistics provide an opportunity for reviewing the changes made by the ten eventful years since 1841. The figures make it possible to place the changes in population alongside those in agriculture. There had been a loss of about a quarter of the population, three-quarters of which is accounted for by emigration to North America. Those who remained actually succeeded in extending the area under cultivation by 1,338,281 acres, an expansion moreover which had been continuous in every county in Ireland except Limerick since 1847. There could hardly be more conclusive proof of the under-employment that characterised pre-famine agriculture. In 1851 half of the holdings in Ireland were over fifteen acres instead of a fifth as in 1841. The contrasts will be best shown by a table :

| Holdings | | 1841 | Per cent | 1851 | Per cent |
|---|---|---|---|---|---|
| Above 1 acre–5 acres | . | 310,436 | 44·9 | 88,083 | 15·5 |
| 5–15 acres | . . . | 252,799 | 36·6 | 191,854 | 33·6 |
| 15–30 acres | . . . | 79,342 | 11·5 | 141,311 | 24·8 |
| Above 30 acres | . . | 48,625 | 7·0 | 149,090 | 26·1 |

In 1851 statistics also give more detailed figures for holdings of over thirty acres which show that almost half of these ranged between thirty and fifty acres.

Consolidation had brought a better balanced farming, which is shown in the ratio between white and preparation crops, 2·3 acres to one in 1851 as against 4·6 acres to one in 1847. The bigger family farm, too, concentrated more on cattle. There were now 2,967,461 cattle in the country, an increase of 1,104,345 on the 1841 figure. The total increase in value was about £6½ million, but on holdings over fifteen acres the increase in value had doubled. The value of stock in the country rose from £21 million in 1841 to over £27½ million in 1851.[13]

Tillage made a determined effort to regain its old place in the agricultural economy, and the struggle was finally determined in favour of grazing only by the bad seasons in the early sixties. Oats, for instance, reached their maximum extent in 1852, and potatoes as late as 1859. Tillage as a whole, however, reached its greatest extent in 1851 and thereafter declined. The four counties of Donegal, Mayo, Galway, and Clare, representing between them five million acres of the poorest land in the country, continued to increase their cropped area in 1852. The causes which had produced the famine had never been eradicated on the western seaboard, an area later to be accorded special treatment as the 'congested districts'. Antrim, Londonderry, Tyrone, and King's county also showed increasing areas under crop.[14] The balance between industry and agriculture in Ulster preserved the old social framework more completely.

The counties which showed the greatest increase of land under crop between 1847 and 1851 were admittedly those hardest hit by the famine, but they were also those where the conditions which produced the famine survived longest. Mayo increased the area under crops by 37·2 per cent in these six years, Leitrim by 34·5 per cent, Roscommon by 25·6 per cent, Sligo by 23·6 per cent, and Kerry by 22·4 per cent. Mayo had suffered terribly ;

in 1848 the county showed no signs of recovery when the rest of the country was making a great effort to get under way again. At that time the country between Crossmolina and Killala was described as ' for the most part unoccupied and, except near the residence of a proprietor, shows no signs of cultivation '.[15]

The strong tendency of tillage to recover and possibly even increase after the famine is obscured by the drastic reduction in the acreage under wheat. Yields were poor and the price slumped from 37s. 5d. to 21s. 9d. between 1846 and 1851, while the repeal of the corn laws had removed the protected British market. The result was that there was an almost continuous decline in the acreage under wheat after 1847.[16]

The famine had much the same effect on Irish agriculture as American competition had on British and European farming over twenty years later. In both cases the emphasis in agricultural production shifted from cereals to livestock and livestock products. By 1852 the modern pattern of Irish agriculture was already clear despite the survival of pre-famine conditions on the western seaboard. The small family farm had emerged out of the ruin of the potato blight. The reduced population had not only maintained but actually increased the area under cultivation. The hay, potatoes, and oats which were raised were not sold directly off the farm, but in the form of livestock. This is mainly the explanation of the 38 per cent increase in the value of stock on Irish farms between 1841 and 1852.[17] The structure which emerged from the disaster of 1847 was strong enough to survive the great agricultural depression and to bring a struggle for land reform to a victorious conclusion.

YOUNG IRELAND IN BUSINESS FOR HIMSELF.

*Punch,* 1846.

# THE POLITICAL BACKGROUND
By Kevin B. Nowlan.

# CHAPTER III

# The Political Background

## I. INTRODUCTION

THE purpose of this study is to examine the manner in which the great famine, which accompanied the successive failures of the potato crop in the mid-nineteenth century, influenced the course of political development in Ireland.

The great famine demonstrated the grave structural weakness of rural Ireland, but the extent of the disaster and the problems it created inevitably influenced the character of political thought and action. The years of famine saw, then, a quickening of the pace of political development and change and witnessed the destruction of the old repeal movement, of that approach to national issues which was so peculiarly the product of Daniel O'Connell's genius, and so much in contrast to subsequent expressions of Irish nationalism. The destruction of the repeal movement makes the years before 1848 seem strangely remote, a remoteness that is emphasised by the way in which men, in the succeeding decade, turned away from purely political nationalism to concentrate their attention on agrarian grievances.

Though the year 1845 lacked the tension of 1843, the calm was superficial and somewhat deceptive. In Britain, the tories, under Peel's remarkable leadership, seemed destined to pursue, in security, a course of cautious reform. But these very reforms provoked criticism, and the watchfulness of the agricultural protectionists could be paralleled in another sphere by the hostility of many towards Peel's Irish policy, and the reluctance of parliament to sanction even the most modest measure for Irish land reform. In Ireland, the very hopelessness of the situation was both O'Connell's strength and his weakness. In demonstrating the power of the depressed peasant population, O'Connell had introduced a novel element into political life, but the very nature of that achievement made peculiar demands. O'Connell could not afford to abandon the fundamental factor of popular agitation ; if he did his movement was destined to face political stagnation. He had to retain his grip on the popular imagination and yet he had, if violent revolution were to be avoided, to reconcile as far as possible, his mode of political action with the conventions of the British parliamentary system.

O'Connell showed himself a 'realist' in his handling of political problems, he was prepared to put repeal aside, as he did under the Melbourne ministry, when he considered he could win concessions to strengthen the Irish position. It is difficult to form a clear impression of what O'Connell conceived nationalism to be, just as it is difficult to assess the exact implications of what he meant by repeal, but it does seem reasonable to conclude that he was not so much concerned with nationalism, as an end in itself, as with the advancement of the spiritual and material well-being of his people. He saw in legislative independence allied to religious freedom potent forces in the regeneration of Ireland. Such an attitude was well enough attuned to the needs of a country which was socially prostrate, but it was in ill accord with much that characterised nineteenth-century nationalism, and could not really satisfy the Young Irelanders with their belief in an all-embracing nationalism which could never be made the subject of compromise.

Since Peel's defeat of the 'monster meeting' agitation in 1843, repeal had made but little progress, and the disputes between O'Connell and his critics over federalism, 'mixed' education, and co-operation with the whigs, only emphasised the dangerous under-currents of dissatisfaction within the Loyal National Repeal Association. Peel, as much as the whigs, was anxious to see moderate reform in Ireland, as the increased Maynooth grant and the land bills of 1845 and 1846 testify, but the past precluded any contact between Peel and O'Connell. The latter in his difficulties could only look to Lord John Russell and the whigs and hope for their speedy return to power.

Purely political considerations, therefore, tended to be dominant in Ireland in 1845-6, but the famine deaths, the breakdown of the relief schemes, the indifference of so many landlords to the sufferings of the people, introduced a new factor into the dark story of nineteenth-century Ireland, a factor which had considerable influence on the course of political affairs. Not merely did social questions, like tenant-right, come to assume a greater importance, but there emerged an interpretation of the great famine itself which had a profound emotional effect on the men of 1848, and which has found its way into the common fund of Irish nationalism. It is the belief that utter indifference, if not real antipathy towards the Irish people, marked the conduct of the government of the United Kingdom during the famine years.

The history of the great famine does not sustain a charge of deliberate cruelty and malice against those governing, but it is a chastening story of how fashions in social and economic ideas and human limitations can combine to increase the sufferings of people, and drive brave men to acts of seemingly hopeless defiance.

## II. THE COMING OF THE BLIGHT

The potato blight came in the autumn of 1845. Reports of its presence were received from the south-eastern counties and from county Louth as early as the opening weeks of September, but a considerable measure of uncertainty prevailed as to the true extent of the calamity.[1] The potato losses were by no means uniform, even within the same county, and this patchwork character of the failure made the task of forming a just estimate of the position most difficult.[2] The official returns indicate that by the close of October the blight had established itself firmly in, at least, eleven counties, yet between November and January, there was evidence of a decline in the virulence of the disease in counties as far apart as Fermanagh and Cork.[3]

Though the partial failure of the potato crop was regarded in Ireland as but another demonstration of the painful weakness of the national economy, this failure was seen, in Britain, as a problem which brought into question the whole future of agricultural protection.

By the autumn of 1845, Sir Robert Peel appears to have been satisfied that the restrictions on the importation of foodstuffs, as well as the remaining tariffs on manufactured goods, had little to recommend them in practice. Peel had felt compelled to move further and further away from the rigid protectionist stand long adopted by his party, but the final decision to abandon agricultural protection could only be taken by a conservative minister at the cost of serious division within the ranks of his own supporters. A national crisis might justify and make more palatable the logic of Peel's arguments, but the British landed interest proved unwilling to be silenced by the threat of a food crisis in Ireland.[4] The fate of the Irish potato crop was, nevertheless, a critical factor in Peel's plans. From the outset, therefore, he gave his attention to the task of ascertaining the true position in Ireland. The constabulary were instructed to report on the state of the crop and, as an additional precaution, a scientific commission was set up to investigate the nature of the disease and to suggest possible remedies.[5] Any measure that might complicate his position was, however, avoided. Peel firmly rejected the lord lieutenant's suggestion that the export of potatoes should be prohibited and insisted that it would be most improper to advance state funds for relief works while resisting the duty free importation of badly needed food.[6] The protracted cabinet discussions on protection had the inevitable effect of delaying any formal declaration of the government's policy. The opinion was widespread that Peel would fail in his efforts to hold a ministry together, and this opinion seemed well founded when Peel, unable to overcome the protectionist opposition led by Stanley, offered his resignation at the beginning of December. But Russell encountered difficulties in reconciling conflicting claims to office among his own supporters while some of the more conservative members of his party hesitated to commit themselves to full free trade. In the circumstance, Russell made it clear that he would not undertake to form a government without explicit assurances of support from Peel. These were not forthcoming, and Peel was recalled to form the government which was to carry the repeal of the corn laws at the cost of conservative unity.[7]

The early reports of the potato blight had produced few striking indications of alarm in Ireland. It was only slowly, almost imperceptibly, that what proved to be the famine came to occupy anything like a central place in Irish politics. Except for the half-hearted espousal of the anti-corn law cause, very largely a gesture to English reformist opinion, and the demand for the closing of the ports, the remedies put forward by nationalists were simply the economic medicines they had long prescribed as cures for the ills of the country. The potato failure they regarded, quite correctly, as a social evil that owed its real importance to the poverty of the people and the bankrupt condition of Irish agricultural society. Despite the absence of tension, the dramatic developments in Britain and the painful slowness of the government in adopting a definite relief policy had political repercussions in Ireland. O'Connell was quick to stress the inevitability of the return of the whigs to power and the futility of expecting any constructive measures from Peel, while the Irish tory opposition to Peel became increasingly vocal and now had a common grievance to share with the English protectionists.

The first important symptom of public unrest was when the Dublin corporation, on October 21, set up a special committee to enquire into the causes of the potato blight. O'Connell, whose influence in the corporation was considerable, proved to be the guiding force behind the committee, which was subsequently expanded to represent the liberal elements among the citizens generally. On O'Connell's proposal, it was decided to send a deputation to the lord lieutenant to stress the necessity of placing restrictions on brewing and distilling and on the export of food stuffs.[8]

This decision to force the issue, by seeking a declaration from Heytesbury, placed the lord lieutenant in a rather difficult position. It was obviously the time for some reassuring statement, but he had been instructed by Sir James Graham to do no more than promise to refer whatever the deputation might have to say to London.[9] Even had he wished to do so, Heytesbury had not the information to exceed Graham's directive, and his reception of the deputation was cold, guarded and unsatisfactory.[10] Beyond stressing the government's awareness of what was happening in Ireland, and its anxiety to help, he had nothing to say.

The deputation returned to the city dissatisfied, and O'Connell made good use of the situation to turn what had been a mere *ad hoc* committee into a permanent body, to be subsequently known as the Mansion House committee. O'Connell was well aware of the rumours current regarding the differences within the conservative party. If he were to profit by the change in Peel's fortunes, it was essential that his repealers should not occupy too isolated a position. So, while O'Connell denounced in bitter terms the slowness of the administration to adopt relief measures, in almost the same breath, he was at pains to stress that politics should be excluded from the Mansion House committee.[11] The committee, in practice, was essentially liberal and reformist in character, and so provided a convenient meeting place for whig and repealer—another modest demonstration that practical results could be achieved by co-operation between the two.

The Mansion House committee was not, however, destined to achieve any great political significance. It served as a useful clearing-house for information relating to the spread of the potato blight and as an agency for counteracting the protectionist denials of a serious food crisis in Ireland. Its opportunities for political action were limited. By December, it was only too evident that Peel was determined to act on the assumption that there was a danger of a famine in Ireland, while O'Connell had openly indicated the terms on which he was prepared to co-operate with the whigs, and his demands were far from exacting.

O'Connell clearly counted on an early election, and the triumphant return of the whigs to power. This possibility and the onset of the food crisis had the effect of reinforcing O'Connell's realistic approach. ' If I had only the alternative of keeping the people alive or giving up the repeal, I would give up the repeal . . .' he declared, though he was careful enough to add that the whigs had not pressed him to make any such choice.[12] O'Connell, in the critical weeks that marked the close of 1845, went so far as to argue that a conservative government would mean famine and that in consequence a reasonable understanding with the whigs was essential, if Peel's baneful influence were to be eliminated.

The possibility of an alliance with the whigs seemed to offer an escape from the political deadlock of 1845. An understanding between O'Connell and his lifelong opponent, Peel, was impossible, and the famine danger only intensified rather than diminished the suspicion between them. It was easy for his critics to deplore O'Connell's renewed association with the whigs, but the weakness of his parliamentary following and the failure of 1843 left him in a far from promising position. In association with the whigs, O'Connell might exercise some influence, isolated he was lost. A franchise reform had to come before O'Connell could be assured of a reasonably large parliamentary following. From Peel he could expect little in this respect, from the whigs he might reasonably hope for some concessions. It was hardly surprising, in the circumstances, that O'Connell, in outlining the conditions for co-operation with the whigs, should have placed particular stress on the importance of franchise reform and the need for improvement in the structure of municipal government in Ireland.[13] Except on the issue of the repeal of the act of union, O'Connell was confident that he could make some progress with Lord John Russell.[14]

The dominant theme in political discussions, in the winter of 1845–6, was this question of O'Connell's future relations with the whigs. The problem was almost as old as the repeal movement itself, and co-operation with English politicians not pledged to repeal had led to more than one passage of arms between O'Connell and his followers. Feargus O'Connor disliked it, and Archbishop John MacHale, of Tuam, had consistently remonstrated with O'Connell on the subject.[15] Now, to the threat of a possible whig alliance the Young Irelanders responded by urging frank defiance towards the tories and studied aloofness towards the whigs.[16] But while the Young Irelanders could stress the need for independence of English parties, they were unable to offer any practical alternative to O'Connell's design. The exigencies of the moment, the likelihood of a food crisis and the imminent downfall of Peel all strengthened O'Connell's hand, especially when it seemed that the radical free traders were about to secure a triumphant victory.[17]

Though Gavan Duffy suggests that disagreement within the Repeal Association, in 1845–6, extended beyond the question of co-operation with the whigs, to the issue of what should be done to avert a famine, there is little evidence to sustain such a view.[18] In fact, there appears to have been widespread agreement within the repeal movement on the need for public works and embargoes on the export of foodstuffs. O'Connell had been early in advocating the closing of the ports, and to contrast the Nation's policy on this matter with that put forward by O'Connell seems artificial in the extreme.[19]

If the issue of what was to happen when the whigs took office, rather than the problem of the potato failure, held the centre of the stage within the repeal movement, outside it the alleged treachery of Peel profoundly disturbed Irish landlord opinion. The Irish landlord's position was not an easy one ; he could expect little support or goodwill from the impoverished and

exploited tenant farmers and he received but scant sympathy from
the whigs and English radicals. The protectionists in parliament
could embarrass Peel, but they could do little to help their Irish
conservative allies at Westminster, who indeed did not speak
with a united voice.[20] Some nine Irish tories were castigated by
the *Dublin Evening Mail*, the Orange journal, for supporting
Peel, and on the basis of an analysis made after the general election
of 1847, there were 15 supporters of Peel returned for Irish constituencies and some 25 protectionists.[21]

Just as the possibility of the whigs returning to power had
increased the tension within the Repeal Association, so also the
break-up of Peel's party released or weakened the bonds which
had secured the body of Irish landlord opinion to English conservatism. The crisis did not destroy their conservatism, but it
turned many of them temporarily adrift and introduced yet
another disturbing factor into the uncertain political scene of
1846. In the coming struggle within the repeal movement, the
efforts to win the support of discontented and often frightened
landlord opinion were to result in futile attempts to devise some
formula which would attract the conservatives to one or other
of the rival repeal groups.

Peel's task was a difficult one when he came to face parliament,
in February 1846. His majority, if one were to exist, depended
on the goodwill of the whigs, while the protectionists were both
strong and determined. To neutralise his enemies as far as possible,
Peel resolved to proceed with three questions which he regarded
as inter-related and forming a compact whole, namely, the
substantial repeal of the corn laws, famine prevention measures
for Ireland and a coercion bill to ensure the preservation of public
order in Ireland.

As early as December 1845, Peel had pressed the Irish government to transmit the draft of a coercion bill, for he feared that a
food shortage would have the effect of provoking still more
formidable displays of unrest in rural areas. In fact, however,
the famine years were to prove conspicuous for their tranquillity
rather than their turbulence.[22] Peel hoped to integrate Irish and
British needs, to make the Irish coercion bill a logical concomitant
of the other measures he intended to propose. Throughout the
protracted debates of 1846, he constantly insisted that the state
of Ireland and the success of his earlier tariff reforms justified in

themselves the virtual abolition of agricultural protection, but that relief measures would be of little value if lawlessness prevailed in Ireland.[23]

The protectionist resistance to the repeal of the corn laws was strong and unrelenting. The whigs, embarrassed at having to support a measure not their own, were very largely silent, while the Irish liberal and repeal members displayed but slight interest in any parliamentary measure except the coercion bill. This bill, introduced into the house of lords on February 20, was by no means a unique measure, but its provisions were undoubtedly severe. There had been a sizeable increase in the incidents of agrarian unrest, the source of which the government readily acknowledged was the unsatisfactory relations between landlords and tenants. The bill was partly a confession that no immediate improvement could be expected in Ireland and partly an admission of the inability of the government to rule Britain and Ireland according to the same basic laws.[24] Under the Protection of Life (Ireland) Bill, additional police could be drafted into proclaimed areas, a rigid curfew could be imposed, and collective fines levied to compensate victims of outrages. The provision that aroused most dissatisfaction, however, was that providing the punishment of fifteen years transportation for breach of the curfew. In the lords the bill encountered but little opposition. In the commons it was otherwise.

In contrast to the indifference displayed by the Irish repeal members towards the actual relief measures, the coercion bill seemed to galvanise the Repeal Association into a new activity. The strongest weapon the Irish members had was their ability to impede the passage of the corn importation bill by prolonging the debate on the coercion bill and thereby intensifying the general feeling of uncertainty. The obstructionist tactics of the Irish appealed to neither Peel nor Russell. If Peel hoped to carry the coercion bill on the back of the corn law measure, he was fated to disappointment, while the whigs and radicals knew only too well the importance of pushing the corn importation bill through with a minimum loss of time.[25] Russell agreed to a first reading of the coercion bill, but the repealers firmly resisted any compromise arrangement to allow the corn laws to be disposed of first, for with the corn laws out of the way, Peel would be in a far stronger position to press the coercion measure through the house.[26]

Throughout March and April, the Irish maintained their pressure on the whigs and radicals and in the course of the negotiations it seemed, just for a moment, that the repealers might forget their tepid enthusiasm for the anti-corn law cause and vote with the protectionists. O'Connell made his position quite clear when he stressed that, so far as he was concerned, the corn laws were but a subsidiary issue in his political schemes.[27]

Even more significant was Smith O'Brien's reaction to the manner in which his country was being used in the corn law debate. As a nationalist, he felt that Irish interests were being forgotten, and so to bring the interminable debates to an end and to take Irish affairs out of the realm of party controversy, he suddenly made a direct personal appeal to Bentinck, the protectionist leader, asking him to consent to a temporary suspension of the corn laws until the famine crisis had past.[28] Coming as it did so soon after O'Connell's strictures on the radicals, this proposition gave rise to much speculation. There seems, however, no reason to doubt that Smith O'Brien acted on his own initiative without consulting the other Irish leaders.[29] Though Bentinck assured the house of his willingness to meet O'Brien's request, the matter did not arouse much interest.[30] It was a proposition that could please neither whig nor tory, while O'Connell showed no disposition to encourage Smith O'Brien in his impulsive though understandable gesture.[31]

With the Irish liberals uneasy and rebellious, Russell might well have found himself in an unpleasant position, but circumstances favoured him. On 25 May, Russell deemed the corn bill safe enough to oppose the second reading of the coercion bill, which he denounced as a harsh and oppressive measure.[32] The protectionists, bent on revenge, resolved to join with the whigs and the Irish repealers to oppose the bill, on the rather ingenious plea that if Peel really considered the Irish situation dangerous, he should have sacrificed the corn law bill to the coercion measure.[33] On 25 June, the free trade measure was passed by a house of lords unprepared for a struggle, and on the same day, the government was defeated in the commons on the second reading of the protection of life bill by the substantial majority of 73 votes.[34]

These closely interwoven debates on corn and coercion are important because they determined the precise setting in which the social problems of Ireland were considered. In the tense, acrimonious months between February and June, there was little objective or enlightening discussion. The very fact of the potato failure became little more than a side issue in a dispute which bore but slightly on fundamental Irish needs. Yet the relief measures adopted to meet the short term problem created by the first failure of the potato crop were to prove reasonably successful within their limited field.

In linking Irish relief with an essentially English question, Peel may have deserved much of the criticism directed against him by the protectionists, yet it must be admitted that his government showed reasonable promptness, despite the distractions of the corn law debate, in introducing relief measures. Already in November a relief commission had been constituted, while the Public Works (Ireland) Bill was introduced on 23 January and three other measures, the County Works Presentments (Ireland) Bill, the Drainage (Ireland) Bill and the Fishery Piers and Harbour (Ireland) Bill were introduced in the succeeding weeks. The general scheme envisaged by these measures was to provide relief, partly from local sources and partly from the imperial exchequer. From the outset, there was a distinct refusal, on the part of the British government, to accept the principle that the distress caused by the potato failure should be met completely from the resources of the whole United Kingdom. The unfortunate assumption was that the relief of famine victims was something closely analogous to the relief of casual paupers under the poor law code.[35]

The Irish reaction to Peel's relief measures was to be critical of their narrow scope and the lack of generosity in the matter of imperial grants.[36] In nationalist circles, it was felt that the whole taxable resources of Ireland should have been employed as a distinct unit, but apart from such general criticism it is difficult to distinguish any really fundamental objections to the scheme put forward by the government to meet the first season of famine.[37] O'Connell still sought an absentee tax, but though Peel could not agree to this, there was a remarkable degree of unanimity between men so divergent in outlook as O'Connell, Peel and Smith O'Brien in urging the Irish landlords to do their duty.[38]

Apart from the purely emergency legislation to meet the potato failure, Peel had, however, little to offer to Ireland in the way of remedial legislation. He had carried through his modest schemes

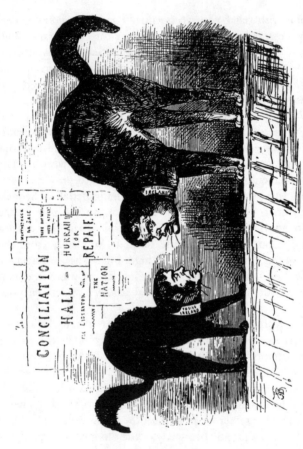

THE KILKENNY CATS; OR, OLD AND YOUNG IRELAND "COMING TO THE SCRATCH."

"Oh, leave them alone,
They'll fight to the bone,
And leave naught but their tails behind 'em."

*Punch*, 1846.

to placate Catholic opinion in 1844 and 1845, but there was no indication that he was prepared, in 1846, to go further and deal with the critical problem of the relations between landlord and tenant in a just and comprehensive way. The failure of Peel to face the Irish land question instead of agrarian outrage was just as conspicuous in his approach to Ireland in 1846 as it had been in the previous year.[39] A tenant compensation bill was introduced, but it was little better than the much criticised bill Lord Stanley had brought forward in 1845. A tenant could only secure compensation, for improvements he had made in his holding, on the determination of his tenancy, and since no security of tenure was to be given to the tenant, he would still remain at the mercy of the arbitrary decisions of his landlord. This feeble bill made its appearance late in the session and, amid the distractions of the time, received but scant consideration.[40] When Russell came into office the measure was dropped, but nothing better took its place.[41]

Despite the obvious defects in his policy, Peel showed foresight, at least, in the handling of the Irish food question. Though he deliberately strove to keep state intervention at a minimum, he did not make the foolish mistake of assuming that private traders could meet the demand for food as his successors did.[42] The importation of Indian corn on the government's account and the sale of the meal, through the local relief committees, at a moderate price did much to check any attempt to exploit the market in the spring and summer of 1846.[43] Despite food riots, in the month of April, the indications all are that the relief measures fulfilled their immediate purpose in preventing exceptional hardship during the traditionally 'hungry months' of the summer.[44] Even the *Nation* admitted that the government had done its best within the framework of the existing social structure.[45]

The food shortage remained in the background throughout the summer of 1846, but if expedients had neutralised, for the moment, the challenge of famine, Peel went out of office without having accomplished anything to make the people better able to meet the misfortune that lay ahead of them.

## I. The Political Crisis

The hair-splitting debates of July, 1846, in the Repeal Association marked the culmination of a long process which reached back to the failure of the monster meeting campaign to shake Peel's resolution to oppose the repeal of the act of union. The disputes and recriminations revealed the difficulty of reaching a working arrangement between a man like O'Connell, who placed so much emphasis on the importance of immediate and practical reforms, and a group who saw in nationalism an absolute ideal which could in no wise be compromised. The famine was to prove a serious complicating factor in weakening the political effectiveness of the repeal movement, but it was not the famine nor the threat of famine that was really fundamental to the political crisis of the summer and autumn of 1846.

The disputes over federalism and the colleges' bill drew men's attention to the real issues at stake between O'Connell and his critics. It became increasingly obvious that the *Nation* group were unwilling to trust O'Connell in any negotiations with non-repealers, and were, further, resolved to build up an independent, partially Protestant force in the Association to counteract the O'Connell family influence which they felt was too clerical and opportunist in character.[1] It is difficult to see how a fatal clash could have been avoided. O'Connell was quite aware of the novel threat to his hitherto undisputed word in the association, while an understanding of some kind between the repealers and the whigs seemed essential to O'Connell if he were to exercise any effective influence on state policy.[2]

It was easy for O'Connell's critics to deplore any understanding with the whigs, but such an attitude, in itself, did not suggest any obvious method of bringing Irish grievances forward in a forceful manner. If, however, the critics were not in a particularly strong position, O'Connell seems to have approached the whig alliance with considerable reserve, for, as he confessed to Smith O'Brien, parliament was not particularly well disposed towards passing 'any measure really efficacious for Ireland'.[3] The prospects were not encouraging, even had the movement gone forward united, for the Repeal Association had exhausted its armoury, and party manoeuvres alone remained.

Though the Young Irelanders frankly regarded expulsion from the Association as something to be avoided, the manner in which O'Connell succeeded in silencing them was well adapted to the end he had in mind. They objected strongly to allowing Sheil to be returned unopposed for Dungarvan as a gesture of goodwill towards the whigs, and their opposition on this point was just the kind of embarrassment O'Connell was anxious to be rid of.[4] The abortive prosecution of Gavan Duffy, the editor of the *Nation*, for sedition, provided O'Connell with an ideal opportunity to propose that the Association, as a precaution, should sever all connections with newspapers and reassert in very definite terms its complete reliance on peaceful and legal methods alone.[5] The opponents of O'Connell rose to this well-designed bait, and while the protracted discussions of July show how deeply concerned the Young Irelanders were with abstract principles, the debates had, for O'Connell, the satisfactory outcome of clearly determining the limits of orthodox repeal views.[6] Withdrawal was the Young Irelanders' only alternative to submission, and though a final breach with O'Connell was hardly contemplated at first, the decision of men like Thomas Francis Meagher to take no further part in the proceedings of the Association marked the end of nominal unity within the repeal movement.[7]

The secession had come about for political reasons, and right through the remaining years of the repeal movement's history, the division remained essentially political in character. To contemporaries the secession was seen as a victory for O'Connell, while the church leaders, when they spoke, made it evident that their sympathies were with O'Connell, and that support counted for much. As *The Times* put it, ' Old Ireland has beaten its young rival. The priests have done it '.[8]

The rapid failure of the potato crop, for a second time, in the autumn of 1846, had a most disturbing influence on the political calculations of O'Connell and his critics. It quickly became apparent that little beyond promises and inadequate expedients could be expected from the whigs. By early December, O'Connell found himself in the unhappy position of having to denounce in bitter terms the meagreness of the measures adopted by the government. The folly of division within the repeal ranks seemed only too evident, and the public demand for reunion began to assume significant proportions, especially in the larger towns.[9]

After the formal breach with the Repeal Association, the Young Irelanders, at first, were quite content to accept a suggestion made by Smith O'Brien and contribute articles to a special section in the *Nation*, devoted to the instruction of 'their fellow countrymen in that intellectual and moral discipline that best fits men for freedom'.[10] The pressure to organise, to appear in public, came from outside the inner councils of the Young Irelanders.[11] In Dublin, and in other urban centres, from September onwards, rising food prices and unemployment caused much discontent among the artisan class, but it was not until October that this discontent began to assume a definite form, which was critical of the policy being pursued by the Repeal Association.[12] From Cork demands came for re-union, but it was in Dublin that the opposition assumed its most formidable aspect, when the majority of the repeal wardens, the key-men in the repeal organisation, adopted a remonstrance protesting against not only the peace resolutions but the whig alliance as well.[13] These developments were a real challenge to the Young Irelanders, and though some like Smith O'Brien were inclined to hang back and merely watch the proceedings in Dublin, others, like Richard O'Gorman and Thomas Francis Meagher, realised the danger of inaction.[14] The danger was, as O'Gorman observed, that O'Connell, annoyed with the paucity of the relief measures, might take up more vigorously the national cause, while they stood by and did nothing but write newspaper articles.[15]

In the circumstances, it was not surprising that several of the leaders of the Young Ireland group took part in a meeting organised by the Dublin remonstrants, on December 2. The meeting was well supported by working men and it agreed to take such measures as were necessary to re-commence the repeal agitation and to hold yet another public meeting early in January.[16] This December meeting provoked an immediate reaction in Conciliation Hall. On December 7, not only did O'Connell denounce the whigs for their failure to cope with the famine, but he declared that the time had come for all sections of the community, regardless of social differences, to join together and save the nation from utter disaster. So far as the repeal movement was concerned, for unity's sake, he was prepared to let a representative committee go into the whole question of the peace resolutions.[17] This friendly gesture on O'Connell's part was well timed. No matter what the outcome of the negotiations might be, the fact would remain that the great Liberator had acted in a magnanimous manner towards his critics.[18]

A conference was arranged between O'Connell and the secessionists, but it proved a failure. The Young Irelanders viewed O'Connell's offer with mixed feelings. Some, like John Dillon, felt that every effort should be made to get back into the Association, while Smith O'Brien flatly refused to discuss the peace resolutions and did not attend the conference.[19] At the meeting, O'Connell indicated that, while he was quite prepared to confine the peace resolutions to Anglo-Irish relations alone, and not regard them as being of universal validity, the question would, nevertheless, have to be considered first. Then, if they reached agreement, such issues as the whig alliance could be discussed when the Young Irelanders returned to the Repeal Association.[20] Such a course the Young Irelanders refused to adopt and by demanding a capitulation, when some compromise might have been secured, they let O'Connell win whatever credit there was to be gained.[21] Never again, in 1846–7, did the opposition to the Repeal Association assume so threatening a form as it did in November and December. Through indecision and bad tactics the Young Irelanders lost a valuable chance of winning and retaining popular goodwill.

The year ended with the repeal movement still divided and unprepared to meet the problems created by a full-scale famine. The secessionists, after much hesitation, finally decided to launch, early in January, a new political movement, the Irish Confederation, with a rather reluctant Smith O'Brien at its head.[22] In the towns they could count on some support, elsewhere, the only friends they could hope to win were from among the landed class. This was an expectation which was not to be fulfilled.[23] O'Connell, for his part, found himself in the unhappy position of having to denounce those very politicians, whose advent to power, just a few months previously, he had acclaimed in such warm terms. Instead of an era of generous measures for Ireland, there only came a time of inadequate expedients and pauper relief.

## II. The Social Crisis

Lord John Russell's return to office had been initially received with satisfaction in Ireland. O'Connell, despite privately expressed fears, hoped to gain concessions from the whigs, while the repeal press, excepting the *Nation*, welcomed the formation of the new administration.[24] Russell's ministry, however, assumed office under distinctly unfavourable circumstances. Peel was the acknowledged and victorious champion of the anti-corn law cause, a fact which robbed the new government of a certain measure of public prestige in Britain. Again, Russell's supporters were in a minority in the commons, and the survival of the government was dependent on the continuance of hostilities between the two sections of the conservative party. Prudence demanded of the government a legislative programme which involved no very startling or controversial measures.[25] Russell was by no means free to act as he pleased. He had to watch carefully his majority in both houses, a situation which only strengthened his natural caution and hesitancy.

Little progress was made with Irish affairs in the first month of the new administration, but Russell's statement in the house of commons, on July 18, is of importance since it does indicate the general character of the whigs' Irish policy. Like Peel, Russell readily acknowledged the need for remedial legislation, having a long term rather than an immediate effect on the Irish social system. He promised a landlord and tenant bill to take the place of the unwieldy measure introduced by his predecessors. The franchise was to be so adjusted as to put England and Ireland on a basis of equality and something was to be done to encourage the cultivation of waste lands.[26] These cautious proposals avoided such controversial topics as the extension of the Ulster tenant-right to the whole country or the penalising of absentee landlords. Again, Russell's refusal to continue the temporary relief measures, after August 15, was an early indication of that parsimony which was to characterise the whole approach of the Russell administration to the Irish famine.[27]

As early as May, 1846, reports had been received of the re-appearance of the blight, and by mid-July the general opinion in Ireland was that the disease was gaining a foothold even in areas where it had not been very noticeable the previous year.[28] Though some hardship had been caused by the partial failure of 1845, the most serious consequence of the first failure was that it deprived the cottiers and small farmers of whatever reserves of food they might have accumulated.[29]   Seed potatoes were in short supply, since the stock had been used for food, with the result that the total acreage under potatoes declined by some 250,000 acres. Even had the crop not been destroyed, 1846–7 would have been a difficult year for the people.[30]   Without reserves of healthy potatoes, they were already defenceless when the blight struck again.

At the beginning of August, Russell laid down the principles on which his government intended to act during the months of famine.   It could not become an established practice for the state to supply the people with food at uneconomic prices.   It was contrary to the real interests of the community to do so as 'trade would be disturbed . . . supplies which are brought to us by the natural operations of commerce would be suspended . . . the inter-mediate traders . . . would have their business entirely deranged'. The feeding of the people was therefore to be regarded primarily as a matter for private enterprise, though the state might have to dis-tribute food in very remote areas.   The sovereign economic law of supply and demand would solve the Irish food problem, or so Russell thought.  If the business of getting food to the people was to be left to the private traders, the financing of public works was to be defrayed not by absolute grants from the treasury, but by loans to be repaid in the form of a rate.[31]   Fortified by the conventional orthodoxy of these views, Russell made the Poor Employment (Ireland) Act the foundation of his Irish relief policy.

Though Russell was not altogether blind to the danger of a potato failure, his comments later in the year suggest that he, in common with other observers, both British and Irish, seriously under-estimated the extent of the failure and the complexity of the administrative problems it involved.   From the outset, the Russell administration worked on the assumption that a well-organised retail trade in foodstuffs was established in Ireland, when, in fact, such a trade could hardly be said to exist outside the towns.  The notion that the provision trade could cope with the problem reveals that disconcerting remoteness from reality in official circles which made its appearance only too often during the critical months of the famine.[32]

It is important, however, to stress that the rigid doctrinaire principles laid down by Russell did not provoke, at once, an unfavourable reaction in Ireland, except among those who were not prepared to work with the whigs.   O'Connell expressed his confidence that the government's measures, if energetically applied, should prove sufficient to meet the emergency, and the influential *Freeman's Journal* agreed with him.[33]   It was hardly surprising, therefore, that the Poor Employment (Ireland) Bill passed virtually undebated through parliament.   It aroused but scant attention in Ireland, and having been read a second time in the commons on August 18, was read a third time on the 22nd of the same month.[34]   The struggle between Old and Young Ireland still held the stage, and it was not until the famine had become a reality that men began to grow really alarmed.   But though the bill was passed silently into law, it was destined to become the centre of controversy and bitterness and to fail singularly to mitigate the sufferings of the people.

The complete destruction of the potato crop made the disaster a national one, yet the government, fearful of tampering with economic laws and convinced that the Irish landlords were not doing their duty, endeavoured through the poor employment act —better known as the labour rate act—to put famine relief on a strictly local basis, and compel the landlords in each area to bear a substantial share of the burden.   The intention of compelling the landlord to do his duty—by either providing employment, or paying for the support of the people through the labour rate— was praiseworthy had it been accompanied by a policy that would have checked speculation in foodstuffs.   But, unfortunately, no such policy was adopted, except in a few rather remote districts.

About the middle of September, the first serious attacks on the labour rate act were voiced.   The various baronial and county sessions had been called to recommend relief schemes to the board of works.   These schemes had to be of a public nature benefiting no particular individual, but presumably of value to the community as a whole.   This, in practice, meant that the loans raised under the act were to be expended on unnecessarily elaborate road works or in the completion of schemes commenced under the earlier relief measures.   The landlords, in the sessions, showed themselves willing enough to vote relief schemes, but the realisation that these costly undertakings would be largely unproductive in character caused widespread dissatisfaction.[35] The demand was, at once, raised for productive works, which in effect meant the improvement of private estates to increase the output of agricultural produce.[36] The demand was not an unreasonable one, for one of the worst problems of Irish society was the undercapitalised condition of agriculture. If the land were to be taxed, it seemed but natural that the money so raised should be expended in such a way as actually to improve the productivity of the soil. It is significant, too, that this protest was taken up by repealers of both camps, and the demand for productive works became one of the principal ties linking the landed class with the nationalists during the critical months of 1846-7.[37]

The plea for state advances to aid agricultural improvements, rather than unproductive works, was by no means confined to repealers and disgruntled country gentlemen. Both Lords Monteagle and Devon were active in urging the need for productive works, and Monteagle carried on a correspondence with members of the administration on the question, which is of considerable value in helping us to understand the official point of view.[38] Russell clung to the contention that the support of the Irish poor must remain primarily a charge on Irish property, and could not be regarded as an imperial burden, an attitude which Wood, the chancellor of the exchequer, fully endorsed. The attitude of the ministers was considerably strengthened by the fact that the civil servants charged with the administration of relief were firmly opposed to any extension of the scope of state intervention in what they deemed to be private commercial matters. The whole temper of the age was unresponsive to bureaucratic interference, and Charles Trevelyan of the treasury summed up the official point of view when he observed that ' for the government to undertake by its own direct agency the detailed drainage and improvement of the whole country, is a task for which the nature and functions of government are totally unsuited '.[39]

It was quite natural, therefore, for the government to look upon the landlords as the culprits, when the relief system began to break down. Men, like Russell and Trevelyan, saw the government as a great humanitarian force doing all it could for a suffering people, while the gentry hung back and failed to fulfil their obligations.[40] Though Russell and his chancellor of the exchequer,

Charles Wood, judged the Irish landlords severely, the Irish land owners were not without some influence in the whig councils. Lord Bessborough, the lord lieutenant, was an Irish proprietor, while the marquis of Lansdowne, the lord president, proved a stout champion of their interests.[41]

Bessborough and the Irish under-secretary, Thomas Redington, were quick to press the need for some relaxation of the provisions of the labour rate act, in order to assist private improvement schemes, on the ground that Irish agriculture was very short of capital.[42] Russell and Wood firmly resisted the request, at first, but in the end they permitted the advances to be made, but on such terms as drastically curtailed the value of the concession.[43] The new rules, made public in a circular letter from the chief secretary, Labouchere, had, however, the immediate effect of helping to ease the political tension in Ireland and preventing a public rift between the London and Dublin administrations, which the cabinet was, naturally, anxious to avoid.[44] The Irish question, nevertheless, continued to disturb the relations between the members of the government, with the result that the only policy Russell could afford to press was one which gave the minimum offence to any interest, but which proved quite inadequate for the needs of Ireland.

Russell, rightly, conceived the famine to be a period of transition in the social history of Ireland, but there, in effect, he stopped.[45] He chided Wood for regarding the potato failure as no extraordinary calamity, yet he was unable or unwilling to assert sufficient authority in his cabinet to silence the advocates of parsimony and established interests.[46] Before a determined assault by Lansdowne, Russell abandoned a plan to extend the income tax to Ireland, as a means of raising additional revenue for Irish needs, while Lansdowne's and Clanricarde's objections to permanent provision being made for outdoor relief prevailed over Bessborough's more generous proposals.[47]

It was easy for Lord John Russell to deplore the delinquencies of the Irish landlords, just as it is comparatively easy for us to detect the weak points in a relief system based on the labour rate act and uncontrolled food prices. Yet it is essential to realise that Lord John Russell and his colleagues were not animated by ill-will or hatred towards the Irish people. The whigs had long realised the need for reform in Ireland, but the task demanded braver hearts than could be found in the ranks of the aristocratic whigs of the mid-nineteenth century. They should, perhaps, have risen above the economic prejudices and beliefs of their day, but they did not, and the unfortunate consequence was that much unnecessary suffering was inflicted on the poor of Ireland during the long months of 1846–7. Russell believed in the need for some measure of justice for the Irish tenant farmer, yet between his expressed intentions and his practical achievements there lay a tragic gap.[48]

The British government's food policy resulted in the people being left to the tender mercy of a relatively small number of traders and speculators, who did not hesitate to exploit the plight of the peasantry.[49] Yet, even the relief committees, in receipt of government aid, were directed not to undersell the merchants, but rather to follow the general movement of prices.[50] The grain harvest, of the previous year, had been an indifferent one throughout Europe, and this dearth resulted in exceptionally heavy buying in 1846–7.[51] At the end of August, wheat sold for 50s. 4d. per quarter, in London, but by February 6 1847, the price had risen to 76s. 4d. per quarter in the same market.[52] With other foodstuffs showing similar advances and with the speculators active, it is hardly surprising that those entrusted with the task of administering the relief system began to lose confidence in it.[53]

Despite the inadequacy of the government's measures, they remained the chief resource of the people. The numbers employed on state-aided schemes rose quickly to the maximum figure of 734,792 in March 1847.[54] Indeed, the very scale of the works and the fact that a money wage, however small, was paid, gave rise to the criticism that the relief schemes were drawing labour away from normal agricultural tasks.[55] The public works scheme was too cumbersome and too open to abuse, and it did not always reach the weakest and most distressed sections of the community, but the famine did not wait for public servants to discover their mistakes.[56] The reports of privation and deaths from starvation increased in number, while the mortality rates from the workhouses told a terrible story.[57] In April 1847, the weekly death rate in the workhouses had reached 25 per thousand inmates, compared with 8 per thousand, in the last week in August, when the revised relief system had time to demonstrate its good effect.[58]

The government, reluctantly enough, came to the conclusion that the public works could not meet the disaster.[59] This decision, in practice, involved the abandonment of the labour rate act, which Russell had so confidently brought forward, in the autumn, as the most judicious means of averting famine in Ireland. The reversal of policy took the form of permitting the free distribution of food to the needy, as a temporary measure in the spring and summer of 1847. This step, undoubtedly, helped to check the worst evils of the famine, but it came too late to save the people from a winter of hunger and death.[60] The soup kitchens warded off starvation, but that was all.

The state, in the mid-nineteenth century, was struggling to adjust itself to the demands of a new world, which was anxious to throw off the bonds of state paternalism and yet was slowly becoming conscious of the social obligations of the community to its members. Russell, then, had to reach a compromise between economic theories and the social reality, but it was a compromise that could satisfy few and it left behind it a bitter legacy. It was out of the suffering of 1846–7 and its aftermath, that a new, harsh and implacable hostility towards the British government found its way into the thought of Young Ireland, and that of many nationalists in later generations.

### IV. THE IRISH PARTY

The failure of the government to halt the progress of distress, in the winter of 1846–7, inevitably disturbed the earlier confidence moderate repealers had displayed in the new government. From September onwards, uneasiness spread throughout all classes and infected the repeal movement too. In a letter to the Association, in mid-September, Daniel O'Connell put forward the suggestion that a permanent council representative of all interests should be established to induce the government to take effective measures to save the country from ruin.[1] This suggestion was endorsed by the *Nation*, and received sympathetic consideration even in landed circles, for, as we shall see, the conviction was gaining strength among many landlords, that the time had come to fight back and stem the rising tide of taxation imposed to meet the cost of the unpopular public works.[2]

The solicitude shown by the O'Connells towards the landed

class was an attitude shared by all sections of the repeal party at this time. If the landlords were alarmed and needed allies, so did the rival factions in the repeal movement.[3] Even Young Irelanders, like John Mitchel, who were later to adopt a decidedly radical attitude, could urge the landlords to place themselves at the head of a united people.[4] It was the British government rather than the Irish nationalists who were most anxious to fix responsibility for the distressed condition of the country on the Irish landlords. The year 1847 was, however, to see a weakening of this early enthusiasm to conciliate the landed class, but with the landlords isolated and sullen, the opportunity to woo them seemed too good to be missed.[5] For the moment, their faults could be treated with some indulgence.

The landlords showed signs of restlessness as early as October, and tentative efforts were made to organise a meeting of landed proprietors in Dublin, but it was not until December that a coherent organisation finally emerged, under the name of ' The Reproductive Works Committee ', a title which emphasised its essentially economic character.[6] It was, however, supported by men of every party. Not merely did Daniel O'Connell and his son John subscribe to its principles, but so did the tory Frederick Shaw, the member for Dublin, and the liberal Robert Kane.[7] Controversial issues were excluded from the committee, which set about organising a great meeting of the landed gentry and members of parliament for early in the new year. The atmosphere was a promising one for nationalists. The committee was not merely well received by repeal and tory press alike, but there was a strong consensus of opinion that soon the landlords would turn in their anger to repeal.[8] How widespread or genuine such a feeling was, in the confused and difficult days of December–January, it is impossible to say, but there can be no doubt that landlord opinion was profoundly disturbed by the political upheaval in Britain and the social collapse at home.[9]

True to its promise, the Reproductive Works Committee arranged a meeting of peers, members of parliament and gentry, in Dublin, on January 14, which proved a remarkable expression of public opinion. Meeting as it did on the eve of the re-assembly of parliament, it seemed to demonstrate in a dramatic way that, under the stress of famine, a new sense of national unity was about to reveal itself. In point of fact, however, the January meeting marked the only effective phase in the attempt to bring all sections of the nation together. Thereafter they tended to drift apart once more.[10]

The Dublin meeting was attended by such great proprietors as the marquises of Ormonde and Sligo, and the earl of Erne as well as some 26 members of parliament drawn from all parties and a large number of gentry and professional men. The resolutions and the speeches reflected the fleeting mood of compromise and goodwill. The government's policy of depending on private enterprise to supply the people with food was deplored and any excessive tenderness for the laws of political economy condemned. The famine, they considered, to be an ' imperial calamity', and so, in consequence, all public works should be regarded as a burden on the imperial exchequer alone. The proposals adopted for the permanent improvement of the country were distinctly cautious in tone, but they are of importance in that they show how far a representative group of landlords was prepared to go at this juncture. If the proposals are modest in scope, they nevertheless do suggest that the assembled proprietors were willing to recognise the need for concession, if rural society were to be saved from utter disintegration.

It was agreed that a permanent relief system should do more than merely relieve pauper distress. If their country were to be taxed for the support of the poor, there should, in fact, be some return in the form of capital works such as land reclamation. More important than their attack on the existing poor law, was their recognition of a tenant's right to reasonable compensation for agricultural improvements. Though the meeting was careful to avoid any detailed proposals on the subject, the landlords' gesture to the tenants was seen as a welcome indication of a new spirit of co-operation.[11] This impression was further confirmed by the willingness with which 83 peers and members of parliament pledged themselves to act in concert as an Irish parliamentary party and to bring before parliament the measures recommended by the Dublin meeting. It seemed that the often projected Irish party had at last come into being. By May, however, the Irish party had become the subject of little more than idle recriminations, while even at the time of the January meeting the lord lieutenant doubted the determination of the members of parliament to act as an independent group.[12]

The deliberations of the Dublin meeting and the decision to found the Irish party were well received in repeal circles, and not least by the Young Irelanders, who were ever anxious to make good their numerical weakness by winning recruits from the conservative ranks.[13]   With all immediate hopes of a settlement with O'Connell dashed, the Young Irelanders, on January 13, held the first meeting of their Irish Confederation—in the same week as that in which the landlords met.[14]   The decision to found the Confederation was a hurried one, and the confederates had no clearly formulated programme, but there could be little doubt as to their ultimate aim.   In the full tide of romantic nationalism, they saw the nation as something superior to mere class interests, and the claims of nationality as a force which in a quite undefined way could resolve conflicting interests.   At the first meeting of the Confederation, Thomas Francis Meagher was at pains to emphasise that their cause was not that of democracy or sect, but Ireland.   In their speeches, John Mitchel and Gavan Duffy, too, showed themselves just as anxious as Smith O'Brien to induce the landlords to reform their ways and embrace repeal.[15]

Repeal was the touchstone which would transform the nation, and the Young Irelanders were loath to let other issues obscure their objective, but in the bitter months ahead, it proved difficult to cling to the view that nationalism could in itself resolve the conflicting interests of landlord and peasant.   For the moment, however, it seemed that the Irish were, at last, able to formulate their demands on parliament with a fair measure of agreement between themselves, and their position was hardly weakened by Lord John Russell's virtual admission, when parliament met in January, that his relief measures had proved a failure.

As early as the end of September, the question of recalling parliament for November had been raised.[16]   Russell feared that any serious modification of the labour rate act would need parliamentary sanction.[17]   But ultimately the promise of an indemnity act to cover any possible irregularities that might result from sanctioning some productive works satisfied Dublin, and the proposal for an early meeting of parliament was dropped.[18]   This meant that during the most critical months of the famine winter parliament was not sitting.   Whether a November session would have made much difference is, however, doubtful.   Both

Bessborough and Lansdowne felt that a meeting before Christmas would only provoke needless debate and controversy over untried measures, while Russell feared that parliament, in any event, would not be disposed to sanction large advances for Irish purposes.[19]   Again, it was not until the end of the year that the necessity for extending the soup-kitchen system as the best means of helping the starving poor, was belatedly accepted.[20]   In October 1846, Russell could write, ' It must be thoroughly understood that we cannot feed the people ', but nine months later over 3,000,000 persons were in receipt of free food rations daily.[21] Even in parliament, when it met in January, Russell defended the theoretical soundness of an employment policy based on the labour rate act, though he could not deny that the act had failed in its primary task of protecting those least able to look after themselves.[22]

The relief policy, as presented to parliament, contemplated the gradual abandonment of the public works and their replacement by the free distribution of food through the agency of the local relief committees.[23]   This arrangement, it was emphasised, was only a temporary one to carry the people through the spring and summer.   Then it was hoped, with the introduction of a revised poor law, the whole burden of relief should become a charge on the distressed localities alone ;  a far from encouraging prospect for a hard-pressed people.

In contrast to the strictly emergency measures and his bleak proposals on the subject of a permanent poor law, Russell outlined to parliament a series of long-term measures which were not without merit and might well have constituted the basis for really constructive legislation.   Land drainage, he promised, would be given greater attention, the law was to be revised to enable renewable leaseholds to be converted into freeholds while, most striking of all, £1,000,000 was to be made available for the reclamation of waste land in Ireland, and compulsion would be employed, if necessary, to secure the land from unco-operative landlords.   The reclaimed land was to be sold or let to small farmers and, as a final gesture, Russell assured the house that the government was giving every consideration to the difficult questions of compensation for tenants' improvements and the sale of heavily encumbered estates.[24]

The contrast between the relief measures to be introduced at once, and the promised remedial legislation, did not escape notice in Ireland, where, indeed, the legislative scheme as a whole was received with considerable reserve.[25] Russell's attitude suggested a certain unwillingness to come to grips at once with the fundamental realities of the Irish situation, and from a purely political point of view his reluctance was understandable. Any legislation involving the ownership of landed property was bound to provoke suspicion and possibly strong opposition in the lords and it might well disturb Russell's uncertain majority in the commons. Under strong pressure from a really united Irish representation, parliament and the government might have been jolted into activity but, as it proved in practice, the really worthwhile measures in the government's programme were quietly dropped on one pretext or another. The contrast between the promises of the Russell ministry and its achievements was the measure of the failure of the Irish parliamentary party, which proved too weak to survive the struggle that centred round Russell's final and least attractive measure, the Poor Relief (Ireland) Bill, and the storm provoked by Bentinck's Irish railway scheme.

The English protectionists, although they had argued against the likelihood of famine, in 1846, showed themselves less bound by economic conventions in their approach to the general problems of Irish relief than either Peel or Russell. The protectionists had little reason to feel grateful towards contemporary economic theory, while the obvious failure of the government's Irish policy and the emergence of the Irish party, gave the opposition in parliament an excellent opportunity to disturb the political balance at the beginning of 1847. The government's doctrinaire measures were criticised as utterly inadequate to meet a national disaster, and Bentinck, the protectionist leader in the commons, went over to the offensive by proposing an ambitious railway development scheme for Ireland.[26]

Whatever may have been the defects in Bentinck's railways bill, it could not be said to err through lack of generosity. Some £16,000,000 were to be advanced through the treasury to finance railway development in Ireland, the loans being repaid by the companies over a period of not less than thirty years.[27] This measure, which had the approval of Hudson, the great English railway promoter, was well received in Dublin, for it represented the kind of capital investment that had long been advocated in

Ireland.[28]  With tories and Young Irelanders alike expressing
their approval it was hardly surprising that the Irish parliamentary
party should have voted Bentinck their unanimous approval
when he addressed them on February 2.[29]  Bentinck was,
however, destined to disappointment if he expected sustained
support from the Irish party.

Bentinck was at pains to stress the non-controversial character
of his bill when introducing it, but since the whole principle of the
measure involved a direct criticism of the government's relief
and financial policy, Russell could not permit it to go unchallenged.[30]  The prime minister made it clear to the Irish
liberal and repeal members that if the bill were given a second
reading, the ministry would be forced to resign.[31]  This decision
put the Irish members in a most difficult position.  Bentinck
might well, and did, expect them to abide by their resolution of
February 2, but the repeal members, though dissatisfied with the
whigs, were not particularly happy at the prospect, however
remote, of the return of the tories to power, coupled with the
inevitable alienation of whig goodwill.[32]  Hurried efforts were
made to avoid the evil hour of decision, by securing a postpone-
ment of the second reading, but the principals, Russell and
Bentinck, were determined to reach a speedy and decisive conclusion, so that the efforts of the Irish party were quite in vain.[33]
The weakness of the party was not to be hidden by miserable
expedients.

The nature of the contest tended to obscure the merits of the
bill.  The Irish conservative enemies of Peel supported Bentinck
with spirit, but those repealers, who spoke, for the most part
merely expressed a rather anaemic support for the principle of the
measure.  Gone was the fine enthusiasm with which they had
greeted it, while Peel, for his part, though he might privately
criticise the government's handling of the famine, revealed himself
as a valuable ally of the ministry, denouncing strongly state
intervention in commercial matters on the scale envisaged by
Bentinck and his friends.[34]

In the circumstances, the bill could have but one fate.  It was
defeated on the second reading by 332 votes to 118.[35]  It was
much more than a defeat for the English protectionists, for it
was a disastrous setback for the Irish party.  Of the 70 Irish
members who voted on February 16, only 37 actually supported

the motion, or as the *Nation* put it, 'thirty-seven only acted as they spoke . . . thirty-three voted against Ireland for the whigs . . . many stayed away'.[36] The repeal members must bear some of the responsibility for the voting debacle. Seventeen of them, it is true, supported Bentinck, but five abstained and six openly supported the government.[37]

The Irish party might possibly have survived the railway bill crisis, but the revised poor law killed it. The landowners were willing to bear part of the cost of employment schemes which would, directly or indirectly, increase the value of their estates, but they looked askance on a permanent poor law which would merely expand the scope and increase the cost of the poor law system and bring with it no real economic advantages. The conservatives, therefore, firmly opposed the introduction to Ireland of a system of outdoor assistance similar to that in operation in England. Public relief, apart from the temporary measures to meet the famine, they insisted, would have to be given within the walls of the workhouse.[38]

The government's Poor Relief (Ireland) Bill was a rather unimportant piece of administrative reform, except for one innovation. It permitted, what the landlords disliked, outdoor relief. The conditions governing the granting of outdoor relief in the bill were aimed at keeping it within narrow limits. It could only be granted to the aged and sick and, in very exceptional circumstances, to the ablebodied poor. The government made it clear that once the emergency measures were wound up in the autumn of 1847, Irish destitution would have to be met by a local poor rate ; a singularly unattractive prospect when it was recalled that even in the years before 1845, the poor rate had been regarded as an intolerable burden by landlords and tenants alike.[39]

The Irish poor law of 1838 had never been particularly popular with any section in Ireland, least of all with O'Connell, or really successful in relieving a distress which was too widespread and too symptomatic of a fundamental weakness in the economy to be remedied by any mere pauper relief scheme. There was little reason to believe that the new bill would involve a radical improvement, but the very fact that it involved some change placed the popular representatives in parliament in a difficult position. They could find little cause for satisfaction in the measure, yet they could not afford to let the bill, however weak, be endangered by

the tory opposition.   Both sections of the Irish party were dissatisfied with the bill, but for different reasons.

The conservative section fought the bill with determination,
denouncing it as ' confiscation commencing by revolution '—
meaning that taxation would drive the landed class out of
existence.[40]   In contrast, John O'Connell did not hesitate to
assert that the existing misery of the people silenced any objections
he might otherwise have had to the bill, and his father appears
to have been in agreement with him.[41]

In these circumstances, the poor law rapidly became a critical
and fatal question for the Irish party, and of the 105 Irish members
of both houses who subscribed to a resolution attacking the bill,
only 4 were repealers.[42]   This indication of dissent was followed
by the abstention of John O'Connell and his followers from the
meetings of the party, though Smith O'Brien clung to the hope
that it might still achieve some good.[43]   The landlords' agitation
against the poor law had a further and rather paradoxical result,
it enabled the government to demonstrate its goodwill towards
the Irish landed class.

Though radicals, like Roebuck and Scrope, might thunder
against the Irish landlords, the government still had a healthy
respect for the rights of property and the interests of the landowners.[44]   The bitter taste of the new poor law was sweetened
by the acceptance of a conservative amendment, requiring the
surrender by an applicant for relief of his holding of land, if it
exceeded a quarter of an acre in extent.   This amendment was
frankly expected to facilitate the removal of the famine-stricken
smallholders and it in fact proved a convenient aid in the clearances
of 1847–8.[45]   The poor relief measure became law, but little else
of Russell's ambitious scheme found its way to the statute roll.

Little attention is usually devoted to the Irish party interlude,
but we think it of importance in helping to form a true picture
of the structure of Irish political life at a critical period in the
famine, and indeed, in the history of Irish nationalism.[46]   As a
conception it expressed well the type of organisation the middle-
class nationalists hoped would lead the landowners to accept the
repeal creed.   It represented the one possible mode of canalising
Irish political influence in a period of social chaos and though it
failed quickly, the idea behind it did not die with it.   The
difficulties to be overcome were many.   It was impossible to

disguise for long the fact that the interests of the landowners and the tenants were not the same in the mid-nineteenth century, just as it was difficult to ignore the fact that any lasting political settlement had to involve the overthrow of that political ascendancy which it had taken centuries to create.

The collapse of the Irish party marked, too, the end of any really serious effort to compel Russell to honour the promises he had made at the beginning of the session. Russell's Destitute Poor (Ireland) Act, better known as the soup-kitchen act, fulfilled its modest role of tiding the people over the months of acute shortage, but no grand scheme took shape to raise the standard of living of the stricken multitude. The ambitious £1,000,000 waste-land measure which Russell had outlined, at the beginning of the session, was abandoned on the plea that its compulsory clauses were bound to prove unacceptable to the house of lords, while the pressure of other business was offered as an excuse for not attempting to deal with the long delayed question of compensation to tenants for agricultural improvements.[47] As some compensation, however, for abandoning the waste land bill, the government agreed to permit the treasury to advance £620,000 by way of loans for railway development and £40,000 for harbour works, but these concessions alone could not hide the inadequacy of the government's Irish policy.[48] Russell's retreat was followed by no concerted onslaught from the Irish benches. The repealers might fret, but they proved unable or unwilling to bring home to parliament the true urgency and tragedy of the position in Ireland.

The desperate plight of the people and the feebleness of the government's measures should have stirred the repeal party into purposeful activity, but they did not. The Repeal Association was in a rather unfortunate situation in the early months of 1847. Its leader was dying and that in itself gave rise to a feeling of uncertainty about the whole future of the movement.[49] Perhaps even more important, the famine had disorganised that disciplined public opinion which played so large a part in O'Connell's plans and he was now quite beyond the task of rallying an apathetic and dispirited people. By the beginning of March, the weekly repeal rent, a useful guide to the prosperity and mood of the country, had fallen to the miserable sum of £18. 11s. 5d.[50] Without funds or a spirited population to back it, the association could only cling to the whig connection.

From the autumn of 1846 onwards, Daniel O'Connell and his son John had given the government the benefit of their advice, and in a cold, distant way the authorities were grateful, but Russell was emphatic in his directions to the chief secretary, on the question of rewarding the docile repealers with public employment. 'I do not see myself', he wrote, 'that much is given to O'Connell, but at all events I myself prefer non-repealers to repealers'.[51] Not quite in full opposition and yet not really trusted by the whig government, the official repeal movement was destined to play out its existence in an atmosphere of futile indecision.[52]

The Young Irelanders, too, had their difficulties. They persisted in stressing the all embracing character of their movement. It was open to rich and poor alike, and they undoubtedly hoped to make progress with those elements who were repelled by the methods employed by O'Connell. Though the Young Irelanders clung fiercely to their objective of national independence, they never seemed able or, perhaps, had never the opportunity, in the short lifetime of their confederation, to clarify their methods and give definition to their secondary aims. In the winter of 1846–7, it seemed possible that many landlords might seek refuge in repeal, but the Young Irelanders' efforts to win their support proved fruitless.[53] The Irish party was a failure, yet the Young Irelanders were primarily responsible for organising a successor to it, the Irish Council, which had a brief and unpromising life.[54] The majority of the confederate leaders proved unwilling to depart from their belief in a comprehensive nationalism which did not recognise social revolution as a means of achieving a political end, but a minority could not avoid making the experiment of appealing directly to the peasant population. Though the name of O'Connell stood like a solid wall between them and the people, they hoped through tenant-right to escape from the frustrating situation of being cut off from their last source of support, the famine-stricken multitude.

It was hardly surprising that political life was so feeble in the spring and early summer of 1847. The efforts to rally the Irish political forces had failed, and the country was in a state of acute social disruption. By June 5 some 2,729,684 persons were estimated to be in receipt of food rations issued by the relief authorities ; by July that number had jumped to 3,020,712, and even allowing for fraud and waste this number gives a fearful impression of the extent of destitution among a population of some 8,000,000 souls.[55] The disruptive effect of the famine could be seen in almost every department of national life, attendance at the schools dropped sharply in 1847, while the agricultural returns for that year show that the destruction of the smallest class of farmer, holding from 1 to 5 acres, had got quickly under way.[56] The famine was bound to have a deep emotional and enduring influence, but it was an influence that only slowly matured through the months of darkness. The surface developments were conventional enough, only hints were dropped of what was taking form slowly in the minds of those who dwelt upon the wider implications of the potato failure.

Companions in misfortune, the two sections of the repeal movement tended to come together once more, and dally with the idea of reunion. John O'Connell as early as March 29 in an extremely conciliatory speech had urged that steps should be taken to heal the division, while Gavan Duffy and Dillon were alive to the value of unity to the Young Irelanders, though Smith O'Brien, despite the disappointments he had suffered, maintained an attitude of hostility towards any concession of principle to O'Connell.[57] The negotiations of May 1847, between the two camps of repealers, were brief and unsatisfactory. They began badly. Smith O'Brien would have no truck with a whig alliance which John O'Connell had to admit in the preliminary correspondence had been largely a failure, while in his turn John O'Connell could hardly have been expected to concede, at that juncture, the confederate demand that the Repeal Association be dissolved and a new organisation be set up in its place.[58] This was a solution which would prove more acceptable in 1848, but while John O'Connell was prepared to agree that no repealer should take office under a government not pledged to repeal the act of union, to have accepted the demand for the dissolution of the Repeal Association would have been to recognise the confederates as the victors in a struggle where there were no victors at all. On the plea of the absence of his father, who was nearing his death, John O'Connell brought the negotiations to a close.[59]

The atmosphere of impotence in the face of disaster characterised Irish political life in the summer of 1847. Though the negotiations for reunion had failed, both the Confederation and the Repeal

THE FUNERAL PROCESSION OF DANIEL O'CONNELL PASSING HIS
HOUSE IN MERRION SQUARE, DUBLIN.

*Illustrated London News, 1847.*

Association were at one in calling upon the Irish members of parliament to withdraw from Westminster, and meet as a council of national distress in Dublin.[60] But apart from the Irish council, which endeavoured unsuccessfully to revive the spirit of the Irish party, nothing concrete emerged from these calls to action.[61] In the midst of all these disappointments and failures, Daniel O'Connell died, leaving behind him no leader of sufficient stature to meet the challenge and the problems of a period of social turmoil. It is idle to dwell upon the question of O'Connell's mental decay. The evidence is uncertain and he was old ; suffice is to say that, as late as the summer of 1846, O'Connell was still skilful enough to drive the Young Irelanders out of an organisation they were reluctant to leave, but the famine and the terrible issues it involved proved too great a task for a man who had lived long, and fought at times nobly. His death made but little difference to the Ireland of 1847, but he left to the Repeal Association the legacy of a name. The expedient—the whig alliance, which he had hoped would tide Ireland over the difficult years, had failed, but with whigs, tories and confederates he had to face in Ireland a hopeless inheritance of misgovernment and oppression that could not be remedied by the means men considered reasonable and moderate in the mid-nineteenth century.

In the midst of the tribulations of 1847, the general election of the summer came as a rather incongruous interlude. The activity it provoked and its results were somehow rather remote from the facts of the situation—the feverish activity at the hustings in Ireland was belied by the general apathy of the people, while the results suggested that repeal possessed a strength which, in reality, it did not have. The general election did not come as a surprise. The break-up of the conventional English parties in 1846 made an election inevitable and it produced few unexpected results. Russell was returned to power, but his government still needed the passive goodwill of the Peelites and radicals to survive.[62] With some 453 members of free trade sympathies against 202 protectionists, Russell's position was reasonably safe, provided he avoided dangerous innovations ; a situation which suited his policy well enough.[63] The circumstances clearly demanded a resolute and disciplined Irish representation, but the election of 1847 signally failed to provide such a group.

The general election was a triumph, numerically speaking, for the Repeal Association, which showed more spirit and life than might have been expected in the circumstances.[64] In contrast, the Young Irelanders exercised comparatively little influence. Regarded as having hastened the death of the Liberator, they could do little more than endeavour to persuade candidates to pledge themselves against place-hunting.[65] However, only two successful repeal candidates were prepared to profess full agreement with the Irish Confederation. One was Smith O'Brien, the other, a curious Tasmanian protege of his, Chisholm Anstey, who was returned for Youghal, but abandoned repeal in 1848.[66] John O'Connell, however, firmly rejected the Young Irelanders' pledge against place-hunting, because it would give the Orange connection a virtual monopoly of office, though he had to admit that no English party was prepared to embark on a radical policy in Ireland.[67] John O'Connell was in an even more difficult position than the Young Irelanders, for if they had no clear plan of action, the Repeal Association had tried one plan and it had failed. Petty concessions, in the matter of public offices, were all John O'Connell could expect and all he got.

On the surface, all the formalities of a well-fought election were preserved. The whigs were successfully opposed in five constituencies by repealers.[68] The attorney-general for Ireland was defeated and even Sheil was challenged in Dungarvan. In all, 39 repeal members were elected though the allegiance of some of them was rather doubtful.[69] The weakness of the party, however, could not be disguised. They made no progress in the entrenched tory constituencies of the north, while the failure of the majority of the repeal members to remain free of whig influences undermined their effectiveness as an opposition. It seems, nevertheless, that the influx of nominal repealers into the association, on the eve of the election, was not as great as Gavan Duffy suggests.[70] Some 19 of the repealers returned had sat in the previous parliament, while of the others, not all newcomers to repeal, 14 were listed as supporters of repeal even by the *Nation* newspaper.[71]

If there was little coherence or form about the repeal movement, in the summer of 1847, the speeches of the election period do, at least, demonstrate that men of all sections of the movement were becoming increasingly conscious of those social issues which had been brought so forcibly before their attention during the previous twelve months. The conventional political issues were stressed, but the demand for tenant-right, of security for the peasant faced with eviction, became a popular cry with nationalists. The *Freeman's Journal*, the principal organ of moderate repeal opinion, insisted that, ' tenant-right should be elevated into an election test '.[72] Though few were prepared to press this demand to anything like its logical conclusion, the increased interest in the plight of the small farmers was, perhaps, the most significant development in 1847, for it pointed to a new approach to Irish nationalism.

## V. TENANT-RIGHT AND REPEAL

The major social question, which faced Ireland in the mid-nineteenth century, was the future of agricultural society, and it was a problem which expressed itself most acutely in the unsatisfactory relations between landlord and tenant. The proceedings of the Devon commission, and the unsuccessful land bills of Lord Stanley, in 1845, and Lord Lincoln, in 1846, revealed a genuine recognition by those in authority of the need to mitigate some of the evils of insecurity of tenure. The failure, however, of both Peel and Russell to devise really practical reforms emphasised how powerful a grip the doctrine of the inviolability of property rights still had on men's minds.[1]

The agrarian issue constituted, then, the hard core of the Irish nation's material grievances, though usually economic and social problems tended to be regarded as subordinate to the over-riding interests of repeal itself. This gave a certain lack of cohesion to the nationalist approach to the land question. Daniel O'Connell did not envisage a social revolution, but rather sought with spasmodic enthusiasm for some modification of the existing land system. He frequently spoke of tenant-right, which to him meant compensation for improvements and the compulsory granting of leases to the tenants for periods of 21 or 31 years.[2] O'Connell was anxious to see, not the expropriation of the landowners, but a system that would ensure a measure of security and continuity of possession to the occupying tenant.[3] Convenience and common sense demanded some revision of the Irish land system, and O'Connell did not go much further in his analysis of the question.

If strictly practical social questions alone were at stake between Old and Young Ireland, there would have been no reason for the secession. We have already examined the close identity of outlook on famine relief among all repealers, and the same harmony of views prevailed on the land question until the summer of 1847. The Young Irelanders had long been careful to stress the view that the landlords and tenants were not enemies, but natural partners, who should co-operate or perish.[4] They were preoccupied with the task of inducing the landlords to embrace nationalism, and if at times a note of warning was sounded, the over-riding desire was to achieve harmonious co-operation between the classes.[5] The establishment of a peasant proprietary was contemplated as an ideal for the future, but it could only come through landlord goodwill.[6]

The circumstances favoured an increased interest in agrarian questions in 1847. The government failed to fulfil its promise to introduce a landlord and tenant bill. Instead, it had facilitated land clearances through the ' quarter acre clause ' in the new poor law measure. With commendable tenacity Sharman Crawford had, year after year, endeavoured to secure adequate legislative protection for the tenant's claim to compensation for worthwhile improvements, but neither the government nor the Irish party showed themselves responsive to his efforts.[7] The silence of the Irish landlords, in parliament, and the fear that, in the end, some meagre compensation measure would be offered as a legal substitute for tenant-right, encouraged a feeling of uneasiness in Ulster, where the farmers had most to lose through any weakening of their customary rights and where, as the evidence given to the Devon commission testified, some landlords were not slow in seeking to check and curtail the tenants' claims.[8]

In Cork a tenant-right league was established in February 1847, the organisers urging the importance of getting up similar associations throughout the country.[9] Efforts were made to organise the farmers in Wexford, and in the north the movement rapidly became strong and influential. Meetings were held at Coleraine and Derry, and the legal recognition of tenant-right was demanded, not merely for Ulster, but for the rest of the country as well.[10]

This recognition of the common economic interest of the farmers of the north and south anticipated to some extent the ideas which were to animate the great tenant-right movement of the eighteen-fifties, but the repeal movement and all it implied had to be swept away before a purely social agitation could emerge on a nation-wide basis. Though the tenant-right agitation lay in the future, the widespread interest in the claims of the impoverished peasantry was, nevertheless, of considerable significance ; it made all the more attractive the proposition that the repeal agitation should be linked with an arresting campaign to win land reform that would rouse the people from their torpor.[11]

Tenant-right was then a popular topic, in 1847, though its meanings were many. To John O'Connell, as to many other tenant-righters, it meant a virtual ownership of the land, once the tenant paid his rent, and in this he seems to have gone further than his father. To Sharman Crawford, it meant a more circumscribed right, but for all it symbolised an escape from the perils of insecurity of tenure and the sentence of eviction.[12]

It was against this background that James Fintan Lalor entered into communication with the Young Irelanders. Lalor had long meditated on the problem of landlord and tenant in Ireland, while his father's part in the anti-tithe agitation, no doubt, helped to concentrate the vigorous mind of this physically frail man on the question of the abstract and practical validity of the existing social order in rural Ireland.[13] Fintan Lalor's entry into political life was sudden. He had watched the repeal movement closely, but though he was by no means in full agreement with any section, he felt most attracted to the Young Irelanders, and accordingly to them he turned early in 1847.[14] Fintan Lalor in his letters to Gavan Duffy, at this time, did not spare the confederates in his analysis of their defects and he showed an acute realisation of the weakness of the Confederation on the crucial question of a plan of campaign.[15]

Lalor's outspoken criticism was, at first, welcomed by Gavan Duffy, who saw in it a means of stimulating the new movement, but soon it became evident that while Gavan Duffy admitted the strength and vitality of Lalor's writing, he felt most uneasy about Lalor's opinions, urging that the methods he suggested were ' a very bold and clever mistake '.[16] If Gavan Duffy grew sceptical, the fascination of Lalor's theories was not easily shaken off by other Young Irelanders, for they slowly gained a firm grip on the thought of men like Mitchel, Devin Reilly, and to a great extent Michael Doheny.[17]

Lalor's analysis of the Irish land system and of the role of the land agitation in a national movement is, perhaps, best developed in his early letters to the *Nation*, before he became involved in the disputes and the activities of the succeeding months. Lalor recognised private ownership in land to almost the same extent as it was recognised by English law. It was rather in his views on the origins and moral implications of land ownership that he departed from the accepted legal propositions. For Lalor, the title to land derived not from the crown but from the people. As in English law, he accepted the principle that there could be no absolute ownership in land, the ultimate proprietor, however, being not the crown but the community. The landholder could only justify his position, so long as he acted in harmony with the needs of the people as a whole.[18]

Turning to the immediate position in Ireland, Fintan Lalor argued that the famine and the collapse of the social fabric represented ' a dissolution of the social system . . . a clear original right returns and reverts to the people—the right of establishing and entering into a new social arrangement'. The people could confer new titles to the land of Ireland, but only to those who were prepared to meet the demands of the rural population for security of tenure.[19] With society, as he conceived it, in a state of dissolution, the time had obviously come to link the demand for political independence with the even more pressing demand for economic security.[20]

Though Lalor never fully clarified the question of the relative importance that should be attached to political and agrarian ends, his bold policy of linking political nationalism with agrarian grievances, nevertheless, had a direct influence on his contemporaries, especially John Mitchel. The popular influence of Lalor during his lifetime was slight, but he most certainly had a direct effect on those who helped to shape and form the pattern and philosophy of Irish nationalism.[21]

The first eight months of 1847 may be regarded as a period of fairly rapid transition in Irish political thought under the impact of a social upheaval. As we have seen, all sections of the nationalist movement became more and more concerned with economic issues, though their rate of progress was far from uniform. Policies remained fluid and undetermined. In the Repeal Association the enthusiasm for tenant-right was carried over into the troubled months of the autumn, with John O'Connell stressing that tenant-right was as essential to the well-being of the nation as repeal itself.[22] O'Connell was careful to add a proviso, which no moderate Young Irelander could object to, namely—that there was an essential harmony of interests between landlord and tenants, a harmony which would become only too evident if good sense prevailed.[23] Rejecting a struggle between the classes, John O'Connell saw in the formation of a council, representative of all interests, the best means of compelling parliament to deal with Irish problems.[24] The idea of an Irish party still had its attractions.

While John O'Connell insisted on the need for co-operation between the various sections of the community, the leaders of the Irish Confederation were closely associated with the foundation of the Irish council, in the early summer of 1847, which aimed, with indifferent success, at bringing men of property, but enlightened views, together.[25] The council attracted some of those who had been active in connection with the great January meeting of landlords, but beyond hinting at what might be done if men would only combine for the good of the country, it proved powerless to achieve any serious results.[26]

The Young Irelanders' task was complicated by two rather obstinate problems, namely, the obvious unwillingness of the vast majority of the conservatives to commit themselves either to repeal or moderate land reform, and the continuance of famine conditions. There were brief, alarmist rumours that Protestant opinion was on the point of turning to nationalism, but the mass conversion never took place.[27] Instead, there were the disheartening incidents, like the failure of the Irish council to adopt a firm resolution in favour of tenant-right.[28] The social scene, too, made a mockery of the plans for co-operation between the classes. By the autumn of 1847, the poor were more destitute than ever, with yet another blighted and sadly reduced potato crop as their only means of support, unless public aid were again to be given to them.[29] The prospect was not a pleasant one, and a less ardent spirit than John Mitchel's might well have been forced to draw the same drastic conclusions as he did.

Mitchel had long hoped that, through the Confederation, the landlords would be gently led to nationalism and land reform, and, as late as the summer of 1847, he was still prepared to give

them another chance to redeem themselves.[30]   It, however,
needed little to complete his conversion to Lalor's point of view
that an agrarian agitation was essential to the triumph of
nationalism.[31]   This was the conversion Gavan Duffy earnestly
strove to avert.[32]

The efforts to achieve a union of all interests reached a sorry
anti-climax in November.   John O'Connell's activities resulted
in a much publicised meeting of Irish members of parliament at
the beginning of the month.[33]   The conference was, of course,
held under the aegis of the Repeal Association, a fact which did
not particularly please the Irish council, as it too was busy arranging
for an independent meeting of its own.   The upshot of the lack
of co-operation between the two organisations was that the
meetings almost clashed, and less was achieved than might
reasonably have been expected from one well ordered and well
supported meeting.[34]   Though John O'Connell had the consola-
tion of securing the goodwill of Smith O'Brien for his meeting,
he failed utterly in his attempts to attract tory opinion.[35]   Of
the 33 members of parliament who attended the council, all, but
the two or three whigs, were repealers.[36]   Ignored by the conservatives, and the bulk of the Irish whig connection, it went into
private session from which it never emerged.

The near farce of the national council was re-enacted two days
later in the Irish council's meeting of peers and commoners.   It,
too, achieved nothing, but its proceedings indicate clearly enough
that membership or non-membership of the Repeal Association
no longer indicated the deepest division in the nationalist camp.
The meeting was planned as a repetition of the January meeting
of landlords, to stress yet again the need for union if the crisis
created by the famine were not to be perpetuated in national
bankruptcy.   In practice, however, the meeting was but a faint
shadow of the January conference.   Only two peers, both with
repeal sympathies, attended ; for the rest, the meagre attendance
was made up of Young Irelanders, the few liberal enthusiasts
from the Irish council, and a handful of repeal members of parliament—including John O'Connell.[37]

The inevitable resolutions relating to relief works and the
encouragement of industries were adopted, but the agrarian
question speedily became the crucial and fatal issue before the
meeting.   A report on the relations between landlord and

tenant submitted by the Irish council studiously avoided tenant-right and confined itself strictly to some rather limited proposals to compensate tenants for substantial improvements to their holdings.[38] Smith O'Brien set the tone of moderate repeal opinion when he declared that the non-controversial recommendations of the Irish council were the wisest and most encouraging in the circumstances, though personally he was inclined to favour wider concessions to the tenantry.[39]

The question of tenant-right was long and thoroughly debated, each speaker interpreting it to suit his purposes best, but from the protracted debate there emerged the fact that John Mitchel had little time for temperate compromises on the land issue, even though he did not yet speak in openly revolutionary terms. Tenant-right he urged should be proclaimed the law and custom of Ireland without delay—without waiting for parliamentary action of any kind, for the paramount right of the people was superior to legislative action ; a natural enough conclusion to draw from Lalor's principles. Tenant-right for Mitchel was not something which arose from the industry and applications of a tenant, as Smith O'Brien or Sharman Crawford contended, but an absolute property right in the tenant to sell ' the bare tenancy or occupancy ' of the farm. The tenant, in fact, would have a full ownership in the land, subject to a rent charge which could not be arbitrarily raised.[40]

This challenging thesis was rejected and opposed, not only by Smith O'Brien, but by Gavan Duffy's close supporter D'Arcy McGee, while Michael Doheny, who seconded Mitchel's amendments at the meeting, stressed the lack of unity within the Irish Confederation on the land issue. By a narrow margin of two votes, Mitchel's amendments were defeated. The defeat in itself, in an unrepresentative gathering did not signify much, but the utter futility of the proceedings was not lost on the radical wing of the Confederation. If the newspapers regarded the proceedings as inconclusive, Mitchel saw in them another demonstration of the indifference, if not the hostility, of the land-owners to the aspirations of the nation.[41] He had taken another step forward, a step the bulk of his colleagues were unprepared to take.

The structure, then, of Irish politics from the late autumn of 1847 assumed a rather complex pattern under the pressure of the economic and social upheaval. It was no longer easy to differentiate along reasonably logical lines between confederates and O'Connellites, but it did become increasingly obvious that repeal was being divided between moderate and radical, with the question of agrarian agitation as the critical issue between them. Both the supporters of Gavan Duffy and the followers of John O'Connell were determined to make use of the agrarian issue, but to keep it subordinate to the old demand for repeal. Members of the radical tail of the movement may have differed among themselves as to how the agrarian agitation was to be integrated with repeal, but both Mitchel and Fintan Lalor were in agreement on the importance of pressing forward with the agrarian struggle regardless of the feelings of the landed class.[42]

The unity of the repeal movement was hardly furthered by Gavan Duffy's persistent efforts to have the aims and policy of the Confederation clarified. On Gavan Duffy's suggestion the task of drafting a programme was entrusted to Smith O'Brien, who appears to have presented a statement towards the end of September.[43] This document was subsequently published in the *Nation,* but it satisfied neither Gavan Duffy nor Mitchel.[44] This was hardly surprising, for Smith O'Brien was content simply to urge the necessity of harmonious co-operation between all classes in returning courageous and independent members to parliament.[45] This was little better than stating, as Mitchel put it, ' the mode of bringing up the public mind to a state of preparedness,' but it did not give a rational answer to ' practical but timid people who asked how we mean to repeal the union '.[46]

Gavan Duffy, rather than Smith O'Brien, remained the driving force in this effort to stabilise confederate policy. He urged Smith O'Brien to secure recruits, like Sharman Crawford, from among the ranks of liberally minded landlords, and to secure such supporters he was prepared to follow the example set by Daniel O'Connell, in 1843–4, and admit them not as pledged repealers but as federalists.[47] Under pressure from the radical wing, it seemed that the story of secession was to be repeated yet again within the repeal movement.

The task of drafting a policy for the Confederation was, ultimately, entrusted to a committee which included both Gavan Duffy and Mitchel, but this committee marked the end rather than the beginning of the attempt to devise an agreed policy.[48]

Gavan Duffy persisted in his demand for a programme based essentially on constitutional action and political education—a limited plan which was to prove less and less attractive to Mitchel and the few who agreed with him.[49]

Famine, destitution and death added a sharpness to the arguments of men like Mitchel, but these grim burdens weighed heavily on the thoughts of others too, and helped to create an attitude towards the famine which lent point to much that the radicals had to say.

### VI. KINDNESS AND COERCION

The cost of combating the famine was enormous and unprecedented in its period. We are sometimes apt to overlook the scale of the outlay between 1845 and 1848, but contemporaries were not so unmindful. By the end of 1848, it was estimated that some £7,918,400 had been expended on famine relief, or if certain items, like drainage schemes were included, £9,536,000.[1] Of these sums, about £3,635,000 had originally been advanced as loans, and though the government accepted the principle of imperial responsibility, in 1853, for the outstanding balance, it did seem, in 1847, that Ireland would have to bear a heavy burden of debt and also meet the cost of current relief at a time when the potato crop had again failed.[2] It was hardly surprising that resistance to the payment of rates became a serious source of unrest in the rural areas. It was an expression of the deeply felt dissatisfaction of the people.[3]

In November and again in December, the aid of the military had to be sought to protect the rate collectors, while popular pressure was often brought to bear on farmers to deter them from meeting the rate demands.[4] This resistance to the poor rate was directed against the rather impersonal force of the state, but popular discontent took another form, too, which was directed against the landlords.

Rent and rates were equally burdensome and equally difficult to meet, while the provisions of the poor law encouraged a clearance policy on estates subdivided between pauperised tenants. Landlords were responsible directly for the full rate on occupied properties with a valuation of less than £4, so that they had a direct financial interest in ejecting tenants from the small marginal holdings.[5] The landlords, like the tenants, were fighting for survival, but they had the advantage of being supported by the law and the rate of eviction from small holdings continued at a disturbing level throughout 1847–8.[6]    This unfortunate deterioration in the relations between landowner and peasant naturally gave an immediate significance to the tenant-right movement, but more than that, the attempts to secure rents, the seizure of stock, and the exportation from the country of agricultural produce, helped to provide the necessary material for those who were coming to regard the famine as something artificial, prolonged unnecessarily by the policy of the British government and the selfishness of the Irish landed class.[7].

    As early as the month of August the question of food exports was raised, in the Irish Confederation, by Fr. John Kenyon, Mitchel's friend, and one of the few active supporters of the Confederation among the Catholic clergy.  He contended that British exploitation had resulted in the export of crops from an impoverished country, ' year after year our plentiful harvests of golden grain, more than sufficient—even since the potato blight— to support and support well our entire population—are seen to disappear off the face of the land '.[8]  Mitchel took this argument a step further when he suggested that if an impartial examination were made of the mutual indebtedness of the two countries, it would be found that Britain was, on the balance, very much Ireland's debtor.  He, therefore, pleaded that since Ireland was experiencing a famine, she was under no obligation to repay the advances made by the government to meet the emergency— which in effect meant that the food earmarked for export should be kept in the country.[9]  It was but a short step from this position to argue that as the landlords had shown an uncompromising and stubborn resistance to the needs of the people, the landlords' excessive demands, like the government's poor rate, should be resisted.  For those who agreed with Mitchel it became increasingly obvious that the country was involved in nothing less than a war of property against poverty.[10]  Mitchel's strictures, at this period, were, however, mild compared with the attack launched on the exportation of food, by his disciple, Thomas Devin Reilly.  In an open letter to the Irish council, Reilly put forward a thesis which later John Mitchel elaborated in words that have left an enduring impression on the memory of the nation.  Reilly contended, in unqualified terms, that the object of all official schemes was nothing less than the extermination of the Irish people, the purpose of the poor relief system being to ensure that a people 'which once numbered nine millions may be checked in its growth and coolly, gradually murdered'.[11] From being a visitation of Providence, the famine was becoming the greatest act of vengeance ever perpetrated against the Irish nation by its enemies, internal and external.[12]

Men like Mitchel and Reilly expressed the sense of dissatisfaction in its most extreme and aggressive form, but the feeling of grievance was widespread, and deep-rooted. Mitchel and those who followed him may have given greater precision to one approach to the famine, but they drew to a considerable extent on a common fund, bred of suffering and disappointment. The resistance, spasmodic but widespread, to the payment of rates and rent left little doubt as to the attitude of a famine-tried people, but the dissatisfaction took more coherent shape as well. In the Repeal Association, for all the emphasis it placed on the need for peaceful action, the iniquity of the existing relationship between landlord and tenant was coupled with the injustice of exporting food from a country suffering such great privation.[13] The Catholic hierarchy, too, led by the outspoken John MacHale, archbishop of Tuam, presented a strongly-worded memorial to the lord lieutenant deploring the fact that 'the sacred and indefeasible rights of life are forgotten amidst the incessant re-clamations of the subordinate rights of property'. For the bishops, the seizure of the peasants' crops and the harsh treatment of the evicted tenants were all signs of the grave defects in the existing land system.[14] Repealers of all shades of opinion, tenant-right advocates and landlords with reformist views were all conscious of the injustices inherent in the existing land system, but the material difficulties to be overcome made reform appear almost an utopian ideal.[15]

The Irish landlords were coming to be regarded very much as the villains of the piece, as the class which, ignoring the common feelings of humanity, took refuge behind the might of the imperial government. But though the landlords, as a group, displayed no particular generosity, their economic position was by no means enviable. They had to bear a heavy burden of taxation, while their lands were often encumbered with mortgages and onerous rent-charges.[16] The accumulated problems of the Irish rural

economy demanded a comprehensive solution, and whatever
were the faults of the Irish landowners, they alone and unaided
could hardly have found, even if willing, such a solution in the
midst of a social crisis.

Lord John Russell, despite his orthodox economic principles,
had to admit his conviction that only security of tenure could
really pacify Ireland.[17] Fixity of tenure, however, was not the
simple mode of escape it might at first appear. It could not, in
itself, solve the problems of the small farmers holding between one
and five acres of land, a class which had been reduced to dire need
by the famine, while security for the tenant farmers could mean
but little to the labourers, themselves usually the sub-tenants of
the farmers and compelled to pay exorbitant rents.[18] Fixity of
tenure would, however, have helped in the task of undoing the
results of past injustice and mismanagement, yet even a modest
measure of land reform was not forthcoming. Russell appreciated
the value of security of tenure but, once again, an unbridgeable
gap separated his private thoughts from what he was prepared
to risk as a party politician. The most his government could
offer, in 1847–8, was a trivial measure to allow dispossessed tenants
some compensation for improvements, but even this limited
proposal was not destined to become law.[19] Instead of facing
the hazardous task of reform in Ireland, men of all parties in the
imperial parliament, were content to prop up the existing social
structure with hastily devised expedients, such as the crime and
outrage bill. When reform came in the late nineteenth century,
it came much too late for men to overlook what went before.

Lord Clarendon, on the death of Lord Bessborough, in May
1847, was appointed lord lieutenant. He undertook the commission to govern Ireland with some misgivings. ' The real difficulty ',
he complained to his friend Henry Reeve, of The Times, ' lies with
the people themselves. They are always in the mud . . . their
idleness and helplessness can hardly be believed '.[20] Clarendon
was an able, slightly cynical man with a wide knowledge of
diplomacy and his letters dealing with Irish affairs are both vivid
and revealing. While he did not subscribe to the grim view of
the chancellor of the exchequer, that there was no escape for
Ireland save ' through a purgatory of misery and starvation ',
he nevertheless realised that no matter what the government did
for the people, ' we shall be equally blamed for keeping them

alive or letting them die, and we have only to select between the censure of the economists or the philanthropists . . .'.[21] Two matters, however, quickly attracted his attention, the task of lessening the hostility of so many of the Catholic clergy to the government, and secondly the problem of how to repress the growing disorder provoked by the attempts to collect rents and rates. For Clarendon both of these problems were closely related to one another.[22] Clarendon worked hard to gain the confidence of the bishops, and, as we shall see, these efforts to win the goodwill of the church provoked much uneasiness in nationalist circles and were stoutly resisted by MacHale, who did not take much trouble to hide his suspicion of the new lord lieutenant.[23]

The task of suppressing disorder was one which Clarendon felt should be approached in a determined manner, much too determined, it proved, for the London government.[24] Clarendon considered that if a serious emergency arose the simplest and best procedure would be for parliament to suspend, for a time, the habeas corpus act, and he made it quite clear that a limited police measure would be of no use to him.[25] Until the feared emergency came, he would, however, be satisfied with new legislation to regulate the licensing of arms and to impose collective fines for agrarian outrages.[26] All these demands put Russell in a difficult position, especially as Clarendon hinted that he would not carry on the government of Ireland without adequate precautions being taken.[27] Russell had helped to drive Peel from office, ostensibly over an Irish coercion bill, but now he was being asked to go perhaps even further than Peel. Faced with Clarendon's virtual ultimatum, the government sought a compromise and asked parliament to pass the Crime and Outrage (Ireland) Bill. It was, compared with Peel's bill of 1846, a relatively moderate measure enabling the lord lieutenant to proclaim disturbed areas and to draft into such areas additional police. As a further precaution, the carrying of unlicensed arms was prohibited in the proclaimed areas on penalty of two years' imprisonment, and the constabulary were empowered to search for such arms.[28]

Clarendon was not particularly cheered by the bill, but was prepared to accept it as a token demonstration of official firmness, while the vast majority of the members of parliament not only welcomed the bill, but in many cases complained that it did not go far enough.[29] Russell had little to fear from parliament, for apart from this modest police measure and a promise of a tenant compensation bill, his Irish policy, controversial or otherwise, was conspicuous by its absence, and tory protectionists and Peelites alike were well content that this should be so.[30]

When parliament met, on November 23, it did so under the shadow of a major commercial crisis, which reached its climax in October. The general food shortage in western Europe, in 1846-7, had resulted in sharp competition in the American and Russian grain markets, with the inevitable rise not merely in grain prices but in the prices of a wide range of other commodities as well. These developments involved a decided pressure on Britain's financial reserves, while the efforts of the railway promoters to secure additional capital tied up considerable sums in dubious and speculative undertakings. Discount rates and grain prices were both high, in the summer of 1847, but August brought a very sudden reversal in price trends. In May, London wheat prices were as high as 115s. per cwt, but by mid-September the average price had fallen to 49s. 6d. This rapid fall helped to pull down the unsteady superstructure erected on grain speculation, and over-investment in railway schemes. The crisis was largely financial rather than industrial in character, and the Bank of England succeeded in riding the storm with its credit intact. But though the crisis passed quickly enough, it left behind it a feeling of insecurity and a distaste for economic experiment which was hardly conducive to courageous action in relation to the social ills of Ireland.[31]  Britain's economic difficulties rather than Irish affairs held the centre of the stage, and the fumbling repeal opposition did little to force the urgent needs of Ireland on the attention of parliament.

The first clear indication of the repeal party's weakness in parliament was to be seen in its approach to the government's new coercion bill. The bill, in itself, could hardly have provoked much criticism had it been accompanied by any positive measures, but its introduction did afford an opportunity to emphasise the dissatisfaction felt in Ireland with the essentially negative approach of parliament to the needs of the country. A disciplined, sustained opposition to the bill might have achieved something, but it was precisely such an opposition which was missing. The burden of the Irish resistance was borne by John O'Connell, Smith O'Brien and three or four others, but from the rest of the repeal party they received but indifferent support.[32]  Although it was estimated, after the general election, that some 39 repealers were returned to parliament, only 20 members could be found to vote against the motion for leave to introduce the bill, and of these three were radicals representing English constituencies.[33]  Only 19 votes were cast against the second reading, while only 14 members voted against the government on the third reading.[34] With such a trivial opposition to contend with, it was hardly surprising that the bill sped swiftly through both houses, in striking contrast to the stubborn resistance offered to Peel's measure, in 1846.  The bill was first introduced on November 29, and on December 20 the royal assent was given to it.[35]  Lacking discipline, firm leadership, and a vigorous popular agitation with clear objectives to back it, the repeal party in parliament had all but disintegrated.  It only needed the absurdity of Feargus O'Connor's resolution on the repeal of the union to make a tragic position slightly farcical.

The relations between the chartist movement and repeal had never been particularly cordial, and the Young Irelanders as much as the friends of O'Connell were anxious to dissociate themselves from the violence, at least of speech, which characterised chartism. The chartist emphasis on class was alien to the orthodox repeal approach to political action, yet on practical questions like franchise reform, repealers and chartists shared common aspirations.  Again, the personal histories of some chartist leaders, like Feargus O'Connor and his critic, James Bronterre O'Brien, forged a living link between chartism and Ireland.  O'Connor first sat in parliament as a supporter of Daniel O'Connell, and though he found O'Connell's leadership too firm and too moderate and so turned to English radicalism, he did not lose interest in the Irish repeal campaign.[36]  Somewhat unexpectedly returned to parliament, in 1847, he lost no time in putting himself forward as a lone champion of repeal and a critic of John O'Connell's handling of Irish interests.[37]

It may well have been that O'Connor, who did not under-estimate his own rather wayward abilities, aspired to the leadership of the repeal movement, hoping to oust John O'Connell by a show of daring and courage.  But whatever were his motives, there can be no doubt of his strong hostility towards O'Connell.[38] In the debate on the crime and outrage bill, he launched a bitter attack on O'Connell's speech, describing it as weak and humble in character.[39] The onslaught on O'Connell was followed by his resolution on the act of union. He demanded the setting up of a select committee of the house to report on the means by which the union was accomplished, its effects on both Britain and Ireland and the probable consequences of its continuation.[40] In introducing this resolution O'Connor apparently acted on his own initiative, without consultation with the Irish members.[41] In a house, constituted as was that of 1847, this direct attack on the union was destined to prove a failure, unless it was O'Connor's intention to stress something which was only too obvious ; the firm opposition of the major English parties to any change in Ireland's constitutional position. The repeal members made a half-hearted attempt to support O'Connor, but the debate rapidly degenerated into near flippancy, with the home secretary indulgently trying to protect the closing repeal speakers from constant interruptions.[42] O'Connor's resolution met a not unexpected end, when it was defeated with only 23 votes cast in its favour and 255 against it.[43]

The repeated failures of the repeal party in parliament had their repercussions in Ireland, where the weakness and lack of harmony among the repeal members seemed to symbolise the inadequacy of a purely parliamentary campaign.[44] To the belief that the landlords and government had abandoned the people to their fate was added the conviction that a parliamentary campaign would only lead to further measures of repression, like the crime and outrage act.[45]

This growing impatience with the failure of parliament to cope with the problems of Ireland made the task of devising an agreed policy for the Irish Confederation most difficult. Mitchel's views had hardened into a conviction that liberals and tories alike had failed to save the people from hunger and the exactions of the landlords. For him, therefore, only one course remained : the people should enforce tenant-right, keep their arms and pay no poor rate.[46] Such an argument neither Smith O'Brien nor Gavan Duffy could accept, and the inevitable consequence was Mitchel's break with the *Nation* newspaper and his withdrawal, along with Devin Reilly, from the committee on policy.[47]

It is not necessary to examine in any great detail the complex manoeuvres of the last weeks of 1847, in the Confederation, but it is essential to stress that though the differences between the main protagonists were clear, Mitchel and Reilly only expressed in an extreme form a widespread feeling of dissatisfaction. Though men like Meagher, Richard O'Gorman and Doheny were unwilling to follow Mitchel, nevertheless it is possible to detect a note of uneasiness in their reaction to the handling of the situation by Gavan Duffy and those closest to him. Gavan Duffy, for example, was by no means anxious to encourage too determined an opposition to the crime and outrage bill, lest the gentry be further estranged, but both Meagher and O'Gorman felt that undue consideration for the interests of the landlords might well result in the loss of such popular sympathy as the Confederation had secured.[48] Again, the charge of dictatorship was made against Gavan Duffy for his treatment of Mitchel.[49] Yet, whatever misgivings they may have felt, the majority of the confederate leaders felt constrained to take their stand with Gavan Duffy and Smith O'Brien when the test came.[50]

The Confederation, in February 1848, adopted, on Smith O'Brien's advice, a series of resolutions which effectively enunciated a policy based primarily on a parliamentary campaign, and which specifically dissociated the movement from the methods dear to Mitchel ; resistance to the exactions of the landlords and refusal to pay the poor rates.[51] Despite the rejection of Mitchel's approach to political action, the Confederation remained to some extent divided and Mitchel had active sympathisers among the rank and file of the Dublin confederates.[52] Because they could not accept Mitchel's drastic proposals, it did not follow that the other Young Irelanders viewed with any complacency the plight of the peasant population. Smith O'Brien, perhaps, best expressed the growing sense of apprehension when he declared that the famine was not so much the outcome of an 'inevitable doom', as the result of the 'stolid incapacity of British misgovernment'.[53] The moderate Young Irelanders rejected Mitchel and Lalor, but with troubled spirits they could only pursue a course of action which seemed destined to achieve but little. Such popular feeling as survived still remained loyal to the Repeal Association and the O'Connell name. The machinery of agitation was there, but there was little on which the agitators could work.

If political issues were primarily responsible for the initial secession within the repeal movement, there can be but little doubt that the hardship produced by the famine was the irritant which now led to this fresh division within the ranks of the secessionists themselves.  From the point of view of the development of Irish political thought and the discipline of political action, the second secession, if it may be so called, was in some ways more significant than the first.  It was the expression of a new approach to Irish political problems.  It took, perhaps, a narrower view of nationalism than its critics could accept, but it realised the latent possibilities of the economic grievances of the rural population.  It was, however, something more than a mere technique of agitation, for the logic of this 'new departure' assumed a criminal neglect of duty, on the part of both government and landowners, a deep-rooted antipathy to the people of Ireland.  Such a criminal conspiracy against a nation could only have the effect of releasing the people from their obligations to those who wished them nothing but evil.[54]  Mitchel and Fintan Lalor may have disagreed, to some extent, as to the precise mode of procedure to be followed in enlisting the aid of the rural population, but both were convinced of the need for a radical change in the existing political and social structure which they saw as a closely integrated whole opposed to the interests of the exploited and impoverished people.[55]

Mitchel and his supporters did not contemplate revolution at the close of 1847, they were quite aware of the weakness of the Confederation and the apathy of the people, but they were developing a thesis which was to colour men's reactions to the great famine for long, because the sentiments they expressed found an echo, however faint, in many hearts in a land where distress abounded.[56]

It is easy to appreciate how this interpretation of the history of the famine took root.  The export of grain and other foodstuffs, during the height of the crisis, had aroused much adverse comment, especially as these exports took place against a background of declining stocks in the hands of the small farmers.[57]  The provisions of the new poor law, the ejectments that followed in the wake of starvation and the obvious reluctance of the government to embark on a policy of comprehensive reforms, all contributed still further to the creation of a picture in some men's minds in which stark black and white alone predominated.

### VII. THE MONTHS OF REVOLUTION

Circumstances, in the opening weeks of 1848, seemed auspicious for yet another attempt to bring the Confederation and the Repeal Association together. The Confederation was divided and had made but slight progress outside the cities, while the Association still lay in the shadow of the unsuccessful whig alliance. The disputes within the Confederation had, however, made it clear that the moderate section of the Young Irelanders were by no means ardent revolutionaries. Mitchel and his friends did not withdraw completely from the Confederation, but their newly founded newspaper, the *United Irishman,* rather than the affairs of the Confederation, absorbed their attention.[1] The moderates had triumphed and this was not lost on John O'Connell, who for all his limitations as a national leader, showed himself an astute and competent politician.

Perhaps even more important as an inducement to close the ranks of repeal was the appearance of a new threat to the independence of the Catholic church. The Repeal Association was closely identified, in the minds of the people, with the vindication not only of their political liberties, but of their religious position as well. In gratitude to the O'Connell family, the vast majority of the clergy gave their allegiance to the Association, a fact which naturally made that organisation particularly sensitive to any attack on the independence of the church.[2]

Freedom of worship was secure, but the church, the greatest single force in the country, had no clearly defined legal place in the affairs of the state. The relations between the Catholic church and the government was a problem that had long exercised Peel's mind, and it was not surprising that the whigs, in their turn, should have endeavoured to stabilise their position in Ireland through a settlement with Rome.[3]

The relations between the British government and the church, in the winter of 1847-8, were rather delicate. If Palmerston's Italian policy, aimed at minimising conservative and especially French influence, in Italy, was to succeed, papal goodwill was essential, while in Ireland the outspoken comments of the hierarchy on the government's famine relief measures indicated the importance of the church as a potentially formidable critic of state policy.[4] The church was jealous of her reputation as an

independent force, and it was believed, especially by Dr John
MacHale, of Tuam, that Lord Minto's diplomatic mission in Italy,
if successful, could only weaken the position of the church in
Ireland, by establishing an official connection between London
and Rome. From the government's point of view, the time was
opportune for an agreement with the Holy See. The 'Godless
Colleges' issue remained unsettled, while the open association of
many Catholic clergy with the demands for tenant-right had led
to bitter attacks on them as the instigators of agrarian unrest.[5]
Lord Clarendon was particularly perturbed by the activities of
the priests and felt that the Pope should send a confidential agent
to Ireland to ascertain the true position.[6]

It is hardly surprising that the publication, early in 1848, of a new
papal rescript on the political activities of the clergy had a most
disturbing effect in Ireland.[7] The influential Irish clerics in
Rome, led by Dr Paul Cullen, had endeavoured to counter Lord
Minto's representations, but they were unable to prevent the
transmission of the rescript to Dr Crolly, the Irish primate.[8]
The rescript was mildly and cautiously worded, but there could
be no doubt as to its general intention. The Congregation of
Propaganda, it declared, could not believe that the Irish clergy
condoned murder, but to prevent any false allegations, it urged
the primate to admonish the clergy to attend to spiritual affairs
alone, and in no wise involve themselves in secular matters.[9]
The rescript represented not the first fruits, but the sole result of
intense British pressure in Rome.[10] In Ireland the reaction was
sharp, for even Dr Murray, the archbishop of Dublin, who was
prepared to co-operate with the government, was quite alarmed
by the activities of Minto and Petre, the unofficial British agent
in Rome.[11] On the whole, however, Clarendon appears to
have been satisfied that the rescript constituted a welcome
rebuff to MacHale and his party.[12]

That Rome should have taken such action added greater urgency
to the efforts to secure unity within the repeal movement. John
O'Connell applied himself with no little energy to the task and
his enthusiasm may have been further strengthened by the
fact that his opposition to the coercion bill had resulted in a distinct
coolness between him and the administration.[13]

A much milder tone was adopted towards the moderate Young
Irelanders. Gavan Duffy was described by John O'Connell as ' a

decided moral force and " patient courage " man ', while on the
occasion of his visit to Limerick, at the end of 1847, O'Connell did
not hesitate to urge the importance of unity.[14]  These conciliatory
gestures were, on the whole, well received in confederate circles,
but though negotiations for reunion followed, they broke down
at two points.  The Young Irelanders considered that the only
satisfactory arrangement would be for both organisations to be
dissolved and a new one established in their place.  O'Connell,
understandably enough, would not agree to this proposal, though
it was the course finally adopted in the weeks before the abortive
revolution.[15]  The second point at issue was closely related to
the first.  The confederates felt that the discipline of the organisation should be strengthened to exclude place-begging, and so
bring to an end any future reliance on whig favours.[16]  John
O'Connell, however, remained firm in his resolution that the
Young Irelanders would have to return to the existing Association
just as it stood.[17]

The failure of the negotiations could not disguise the fact that
there was a widespread desire for some measure of unity within
the repeal movement.  The Association and the Confederation
were companions in adversity, destined, it seemed, to pursue an
unrewarding course of parliamentary agitation, while Mitchel, in
isolation, wrote words which could bear little fruit in an utterly
prostrate country.[18]

It was but natural that the overthrow of the French monarchy,
in February 1848, should have caused a profound sensation in
Ireland.  In every land where the emergence of the new political
and national forces was opposed by authority, the events in Paris
were seized upon as proof that militant liberalism not only lived,
but was now triumphant in the homeland of revolution.  The
French revolution, of February 1848, captured men's imaginations,
because it was almost bloodless.  The order and good feeling it
engendered were symbolic of a willing co-operation between
all classes of society.[19]

In Ireland, especially in the month of March, hopes ran high
that the British government, faced with a hostile and revolutionary
France at the head of the liberated nations of Europe, would soon
have to capitulate to a united Irish demand for the repeal of the
act of union.[20]  The mounting chartist agitation suggested, too,
that allies would not be lacking among the discontented people

of Britain.[21] Such an approach, however, overestimated the missionary ardour of revolutionary France, and the strength of chartist influence in Britain.[22] But with sturdy republicans, like Ledru Rollin and Louis Blanc, in the ascendant, for the moment, in France, there seemed little reason to doubt the firmness of purpose of the new France.

John O'Connell, who was in Paris at the time of the revolution, at once wrote to Ledru Rollin describing the events in Paris as, ' the really sublime spectacle presented to the world '.[23] With equal promptness the Young Irelanders responded to the events on the continent. Smith O'Brien wrote to Lord Cloncurry urging that the time had come for repeal unity and a joint address by both organisations in favour of repeal.[24] Almost overnight a more spirited tone was to be detected in the speeches of men like Gavan Duffy and Dillon, the former even hinting that stronger methods might have to be resorted to than those contemplated a few weeks previously.[25] The revolutionaries of Paris seemed to provide the kind of coercive power which was lacking in Ireland. Cheered by the success of a peaceful revolution the Irish repealers believed they had, at last, found an escape from the humiliating weakness of the famine years.

In Ireland, there was almost a conscious cultivation of the language and spirit of the February revolution. An O'Connellite newspaper, like the *Pilot*, could urge the people to emulate the ' most glorious revolution recorded and consecrated in history ', while the *Nation* was of the opinion that the Old Irelanders, of Dublin, were ' animated by the same noble spirit of fraternity and forgiveness ' as the Young Irelanders.[26] Ledru Rollin's warm reply to John O'Connell's message and Lamartine's manifesto to the great powers seemed to fulfil the most sanguine expectations of Irish nationalists and gave an additional impetus to the sudden revival of political life in the country.[27]

This new enthusiasm found most dramatic expression in the arrangements made to send fraternal delegations to France. In Dublin, the fragile cordiality between Old and Young Irelanders resulted in the setting up of a committee, which included not only moderates, but John Mitchel and his friends. The primary object of the committee was to organise a public demonstration of solidarity with France. The committee, had it survived long enough, might well have become a most useful link between the various groups. In practice, however, jealousies and long-harboured suspicions effectively precluded the committee from assuming a really satisfactory role.[28]

Almost from the outset, the committee lost favour with John O'Connell, who became alarmed at the radical tone adopted by Mitchel—for Mitchel did not hesitate to tell the committee that they should not be over zealous to keep within the law.[29] Alarm at Mitchel's inflammatory outbursts was, however, by no means confined to John O'Connell and his followers, for the moderate Young Irelanders, too, were most reluctant to be left alone on a committee with Mitchel.[30] Determined efforts were made by Gavan Duffy to secure O'Connell's support, but the negotiations which took place made it clear that the Association would only take part in the demonstration, if it were given a dominant place on the organising committee.[31]

The public meeting, strongly supported by the Dublin artisans, was ultimately held on March 20, without the co-operation of John O'Connell, but it did not prove, as some conservatives feared, the beginning of revolution.[32] Its achievements were slight : it asked the French people to consider Ireland's sufferings, voted a fraternal address to be conveyed to Paris by a delegation, and finally asked the Queen to restore self-government to Ireland.[33]

The proceedings at the Dublin demonstration, and at other similar meetings about this time, illustrate well the curiously confused state of mind then prevailing in Ireland. While John O'Connell indulged in timid praise of revolution, the Young Irelanders embarked on an even more uncertain course, seeking to avoid the extremes of Mitchel's republicanism, on the one hand, and the excessive caution of the Repeal Association on the other.

The Confederation adopted an address of its own to the people of France, and as a deliberate gesture to the new democratic spirit, included a working man in the delegation which was to go to Paris.[34] Thomas Francis Meagher renounced those errors which had led him to suspect the untutored democracy, and the Young Irelanders, who had once scorned the English chartists, now appeared side by side with them at meetings in the north of England.[35] Yet, when Mitchel returned to the council of the Confederation, there was an uneasy feeling in moderate circles that his demand, for a repetition of what happened in Paris, might

end in utter disaster for the middle classes.[36]   Again, on March 22,
Mitchel, Meagher and Smith O'Brien found themselves charged
with sedition, but if the government viewed all three as potential
revolutionaries, Smith O'Brien was quite resentful that his opinions
should have been confused with those held by John Mitchel.[37]
To add a final element of complexity to the scene, as soon as the
news of the arrests for sedition became known, John O'Connell
and his brother Maurice, promptly offered their services as bailsmen,
to enable Smith O'Brien and Meagher to proceed on their mission
to Paris ;  a gesture which touched Smith O'Brien.[38]

By deciding to send a mission to Paris, the confederates and
the committee responsible for the Dublin demonstration intended
to emphasise the deep emotional link between nationalist Ireland
and revolutionary France, but in so doing they made Anglo-
Irish relations an element of some importance in the diplomatic
negotiations between the United Kingdom and the French
republic.   The British government may have thought lightly
enough of repeal activities in March 1848, but they were watchful,
as the prosecutions for sedition testify.[39]   Not merely were
more troops sent to Ireland, but, on the diplomatic level, determined
and successful efforts were made to neutralise French influence on
Ireland.[40]

It was fortunate for British diplomacy that Lamartine, as foreign
minister of the republic, recognised the value of British goodwill
for the survival of revolutionary France.   France, under the leadership of a man like Ledru Rollin, might have embarked on a warlike
course, but Lamartine was quick to realise that it was wiser to have
the one great parliamentary power in Europe as a friend than a foe,
especially as the overthrow of Louis Philippe was received with
little regret in England, where Palmerston, the foreign secretary,
and the whigs generally, regarded the house of Orleans as a rival
rather than a potential ally in continental affairs.[41]  Palmerston,
who respected Lamartine's qualities, was well content to accept
revolutionary France, provided the republic did not meddle in
the internal affairs of other states, particularly Britain.[42]   The
British government, for the moment, however, suspended
judgment on the new France, by declining to give the republic
more than informal recognition.   Without allies, Lamartine
gladly accepted any indication of British approval, and so, in
practice, set himself against any effective assistance to Ireland.

Though Lamartine had, at times, to use brave words in public, to placate the more extreme republicans, in private, he made it clear that he could never consider Irish nationality 'in any other sense except as identical with English nationality'.[43] This piece of temporising inevitably involved him in difficulties. At the height of the political tension in March, he received a deputation from the Irish residents in Paris. The reception was a public one and took place at a time when the socialists and radicals were particularly distrustful of his conduct of foreign policy. Lamartine in an effort to justify himself may have overstepped the bounds of diplomatic caution in his eulogy of Ireland and Daniel O'Connell, for whom he entertained a deep respect, but what particularly provoked British annoyance was the report that he had accepted an Irish flag from the deputation, as a symbol of French sympathy with Irish nationalism.[44]

The British government's reaction was immediate and sharp. Lord Normanby, the British representative, demanded a full explanation of the incident, and though Lamartine denied receiving any flag, Normanby warned him that unless the newspaper reports were officially contradicted, the consquences might well be unfortunate for the relations between the two powers.[45] Lamartine did not hesitate to meet the British demand, and in a public message assured the British government that France recognised no other national flag except that of the United Kingdom. In receiving the deputation, Lamartine added, he merely wished to express his sympathy with the cause of religious and political reform in Ireland.[46] Lamartine's virtual surrender augured ill for the success of the mission on its way from Ireland, for the British government did not hesitate to follow up this initial success by issuing direct warnings of what would happen in the event of any member of the provisional government making public observations on the affairs of the United Kingdom.[47] Before Smith O'Brien and his companions arrived in Paris, on March 26, the ground had been thoroughly prepared by Palmerston and Normanby.

Lamartine, after his last experience, was not particularly anxious to receive the Irish on behalf of the government, but rather than risk the indiscretions of a jacobin, like Ledru Rollin, he decided to undertake the task himself.[48] Before he received the Irish mission in public, Lamartine took the precaution of outlining his remarks to Normanby, and, in addition, it seems, made it clear to Smith O'Brien, privately, that no support or encouragement could be expected from France for Irish national aspirations.[49]

True to his undertaking, Lamartine, when he received the Irish addresses, on April 3, made it abundantly clear that the French government would not encourage any interference in the internal politics of the United Kingdom.  He was friendly and polite, but it was evident that Irish nationalists would have to go their way unsustained by French assistance.[50]  Small wonder that Palmerston asked Normanby to thank Lamartine for so loyally fulfilling the promise he had made.[51]

In contrast to Lamartine's reserve, the Irish were given a colourful and warm reception in the revolutionary clubs, while Ledru Rollin, the minister for the interior, who had long cherished an interest in Irish nationalism, seems to have assured Smith O'Brien of his personal sympathy.[52]  Faced, however, with the firm refusal of the government to interest itself in Irish grievances, the daring utterances in the clubs were of little value.[53]

Though efforts were made to minimise the effect of Lamartine's formal declarations, there can be but little doubt that the reception given to the Irish mission fell short of what it had expected.[54] It is, perhaps, significant that in the speeches and discussions from this time, less and less attention was paid to France, for, as Mitchel put it, ' we are well pleased that M. Lamartine has let us know distinctly we must rely on ourselves '.[55]

The failure of the mission to France did not, however, cause any real change in the general character of developments in Ireland.  Among the Young Irelanders more and more emphasis was placed on the importance of an armed and watchful national guard, while the confederate clubs began to adopt a distinctly military role.[56]  In the Repeal Association, too, despite John O'Connell's influence, a more truculent tone could be detected. Many members of the.Association were to be found fraternising with the confederates in the clubs, while J. N. Dunne, a prominent Dublin supporter of the Association, declared that if the government persisted in its threat to the constitutional rights of the country, the people would be fully justified in taking to the barricades.[57]

Gavan Duffy's ' Creed of the *Nation* ', published shortly after the enactment of the new treason-felony bill, probably best sums up the position of the majority of the Young Irelanders at this time. Though the famine had become for Gavan Duffy 'a fearful murder committed on the mass of the people', he still clung to the conviction that independence could best be won by a union of all classes, for 'nationality is broad, comprehensive, and universal'.[58] Gavan Duffy's statement was a courageous one. He did not hesitate to advise an ultimate recourse to arms should negotiations fail, but in practice it was to prove extremely difficult to work for a negotiated settlement and yet continue to think in terms of a revolutionary upheaval. When the testing time came, it was only too evident that the repealers were in no position to present an ultimatum in terms of a surrender by the government or revolution.

The martial tone of the speeches and declarations were hardly calculated to reassure the more conservative elements in the community, yet side by side with such demonstrations of political impatience could be found a new attempt to draw the conservatives and Protestants into repeal. The majority of repealers, confederates and followers of John O'Connell alike, still viewed with distaste Mitchel's republicanism and social radicalism, and consequently saw in any indication of interest in nationalism among conservatives a most welcome sign.[59] With the assistance of A. R. Stritch, of the Repeal Association, and Samuel Ferguson, a conservative convert to repeal, a new attempt was made, in confederate circles, to interest the Protestant middle-class in repeal. But though this attempt did result in the formation of the short-lived Protestant Repeal Association, nothing substantial was achieved. The prevailing temper among Irish Protestants was hardly conducive to the success of such an experiment, while the government was, at last, beginning to show signs that in an emergency it would not abandon the ascendancy.[60]

The whig government was far from anxious to take repressive action in Ireland, but this reluctance was in the end overborne by the growing panic among the members of the Irish administration, especially Clarendon. The lord lieutenant, at the beginning of the new year, showed himself well enough satisfied with the measures which had already been taken to preserve public order, but he did not disguise the fact that socially, Ireland was in a most unstable condition, and that little was needed to provoke unrest.[61]  Sensitive to the possible dangers in Ireland, Clarendon's reaction to the developments which followed the Paris revolution were sharp enough.  He was quick to report on the enthusiasm with which the revolution was greeted in Ireland, and again urged the need for remedial legislation to counter any possible resurgence of political agitation.[62]  On the balance, the authorities in London and Dublin felt, that, for the moment, a policy of watchful inaction was the wisest.  Sir George Grey, the home secretary, considered that it would be better not to prosecute the editors of the extremist newspapers unless success was assured, while Russell vacillated between indifference to the threat of agitation and alarm at the tone of the Nation and the United Irishman.[63]

For the administration, as for the repealers, the first critical move was the decision to hold, in Dublin on March 20, the demonstration in favour of Franco-Irish friendship.  To meet any possible emergency, the lord lieutenant worked out a careful time-table.  If the meeting resulted in violence, then he intended to have Mitchel and Gavan Duffy immediately arrested, but if the day passed off quietly, he intended waiting a little longer before bringing a sedition charge against the agitators.[64]

While the Dublin demonstration proved, as we have seen, something of an anti-climax, the prosecutions of Meagher, Smith O'Brien and Mitchel, which followed, had hardly the good effect the government had expected.[65]  Clarendon soon admitted that the prosecutions had not a tranquillising influence on the country, while the task of proving the illegality of the mooted national guard quite eluded the skill of his legal advisers.[66]  By the end of March, the lord lieutenant was apprehensive, and he felt ' cruelly embarrassed by the almost total absence of law for repressing sedition or checking revolutionary preparations '.[67]

The renewed demands from Clarendon for further legal sanctions against the agitators placed the whig cabinet in a rather difficult position.  They had already, with some reluctance, gone a certain distance with repressive measures, but could they, with any confidence, introduce novel and more repressive laws ?  The internal position in Britain was far from satisfactory, and if parliament were asked to accept a scheme of emergency legislation the Irish members might well resort to delaying tactics.[68]  The British government was prepared to make available to Clarendon as many troops as he needed, but troops alone could not restore peace in Ireland.[69]

With characteristic indecision, the Russell administration failed to reach any clear agreement on Irish policy. Clarendon did not believe the government could carry a suspension of habeas corpus in the face of Irish opposition, while the home secretary was convinced that it would be most impolitic even to attempt to do so.[70] Russell, however, believed that the bitter medicine of coercion might be successfully sweetened. In a frank cabinet memorandum, he suggested that restrictions should be placed on the landlords' power of eviction and he proposed that more money be made available for public works. As a further gesture of good-will, Russell considered that some reasonably generous provision should be made for the endowment of the Catholic church. If some such measures were introduced, he believed that the government could safely ask parliament to suspend habeas corpus for one year as a temporary security measure.[71] In the absence of extreme provocation, both Earl Grey and Charles Wood were averse to suspending the constitutional safeguards, while Palmerston and Lansdowne, themselves Irish landlords, counselled great caution in any attempt to tamper with the landowners' legal rights.[72]

The British government was, therefore, in the unhappy position of not knowing really what to do in Ireland, at a time when the chartist menace in Britain was growing rapidly. A possible mode of escape was, however, suggested by Lord Campbell, a former Irish lord chancellor and the future lord chancellor of England. The essence of the proposal was that since it was undesirable to proceed in Ireland under an antiquated and harsh treason law, a new statutory offence of treason-felony should be created.[73] The government gladly accepted Campbell's suggestion and embodied his proposals in the Crown and Government Security Bill. This measure, which extended to Great Britain as well as Ireland, provided that the capital offence of compassing and designing to levy war against the sovereign could be dealt with as an ordinary felony and so be punished by transportation instead of death. In an important provision the offence was extended to include all persons who should promote treasonable designs ' by open and advised speaking '.[74] This new bill, however, did not altogether satisfy the lord lieutenant,

who realised only too well that the nationalist political clubs
would have to be suppressed before the position in Ireland could
be regarded as secure.[75]

Faint-hearted the government had shown itself on the critical
issue of social legislation, and the same faint-heartedness marked
even its coercive measures. The government refused to insert
clauses in the bill to suppress rifle clubs and prevent the manufacture and sale of pikes, and the lord lieutenant was given the
comfortless advice that he should rely on the common law and
the coercion act passed in the previous session.[76]

The government had hesitated to introduce a strong coercion
bill lest it should encounter too sustained an opposition, but in
this they overestimated the strength of the Irish resistance. The
debate, on the Crown and Government Security Bill, provided
Smith O'Brien, fresh from Paris, with an opportunity to make a
defiant speech, but Smith O'Brien alone spoke in angry terms.[77]
Like John O'Connell, the other nationalist members remained
content with formal protests, while Chisholm Anstey, the only
confederate in the house apart from Smith O'Brien, not merely
voted for the bill, but actually spoke in its favour, for repeal was
only a passing phase in Anstey's rather curious career.[78] Fearful
of chartists in England and nationalists in Ireland, parliament
willingly passed the treason-felony bill. Introduced on April 7,
it received the royal assent fifteen days later.[79]

It seemed for a brief period that the stiffening of the government's
attitude had strengthened its position in Ireland. John O'Connell
felt constrained to subscribe to a declaration of loyalty, drawn
up by the Irish conservative members of parliament, denouncing
agitation—an address which he later admitted was slavish in
character, while the lord lieutenant could observe with satisfaction
that 'the steam goes down here every day'.[80]

From the nationalist point of view, the political scene was far
from encouraging at the end of April. O'Connell's unhappy
attempt to interest the commons in repeal proved a complete
failure, while even his private approaches to Russell, seeking
among other things an abandonment of the prosecutions, were
met with a sharp rebuff.[81] Then again, in the more radical wing
of the repeal movement a new and rather unpleasant dispute
developed which resulted in the final withdrawal of Mitchel from
the Confederation.

The immediate cause of the trouble was a personal incident involving Smith O'Brien and Mitchel. To prevent any misunderstanding as to his views, Smith O'Brien declined to attend the same public meetings as Mitchel, an arrangement Mitchel accepted. However, through no real fault on Mitchel's part, they were both present at a meeting in honour of the 'prosecuted patriots' in Limerick, on April 29.[82] Limerick was a curious commentary on the state of the public mind at the time. Smith O'Brien was respected in Limerick, but the populace looked upon Mitchel as nothing more than a vilifier of the name of the dead Liberator. The mob, without much compunction, broke up the meeting, and Smith O'Brien, who was slightly injured, retired in mortification, disgusted both with the mob and what he considered to be a breach of faith on Mitchel's part. The upshot of the whole affair was that Mitchel left the Confederation, though he made it quite clear that more fundamental issues were involved than the Limerick incident, for unlike Smith O'Brien, Mitchel believed that the time for conciliating the landlords had long passed.[83]

News of what happened at Limerick was received with obvious satisfaction by the lord lieutenant, who came to the conclusion that now was the time to put a final end to a troublesome and potentially dangerous agitation. The repeal movement was disunited but he was afraid that with the distress the 'hungry months' of the summer would bring, the agitators might yet secure widespread support among the peasantry.[84] Even before the long delayed sedition trials took place, Clarendon had decided as an 'experiment', to prosecute Mitchel under the new treason-felony act.[85]

The acquittal of Smith O'Brien and Meagher on the sedition charges did not surprise the government, but the trial of Mitchel was seen in a much more serious light. In both London and Dublin it was rashly hoped that Mitchel's conviction and transportation would really frighten the agitators into silence.[86]

The outcome of the trial, which opened on May 26, had hardly ever been in doubt, and neither Mitchel nor his counsel attempted to deny that he advocated civil war in his newspaper, the *United Irishman*.[87] The severity of the sentence, fourteen years' transportation, came as an even greater challenge than his arrest, but he was removed from Ireland without any disturbance of the

peace.   Meetings of protest alone were held, denouncing the
packing of the jury and the speakers included both confederates
and supporters of John O'Connell.[88]

Because of their followers' lack of military training and arms,
the confederate council decided not to undertake an armed rescue
of Mitchel from prison.[89]  The confederate leaders had probably
no alternative but to accept the situation and do nothing, though
Mitchel was far from satisfied with this inactivity.  The feeble
resistance to the transportation of Mitchel was, however, no
more than an expression of that general spirit of indecision which
characterised the activities of the repeal movement in 1848.[90]

Mitchel's trial marked the culmination of a remarkable individual
agitation.  His conversion to a belief in an agrarian struggle had
been gradual, but though he drew on Fintan Lalor's original
thought, he made his own special contribution to the development
of Irish nationalism by linking this agrarian struggle with a militant
republicanism.   Mitchel overestimated the warlike spirit of the
countryside and the natural discipline of a famine exhausted
population, but it must always be remembered that he regarded
famine deaths as battle losses, and that he saw in armed revolution
a far more worthy form of combat than death by starvation.[91]

The Mitchel trial had, however, one positive result, it gave
an added urgency to the efforts to unite the repeal movement.  On
May 29, John O'Connell announced, in Conciliation Hall, that
he had met Smith O'Brien that same day, and while no detailed
plans for reunion were made, the principle of active co-operation
had been agreed upon.[92]  By June 3 or 4, the provisional agreement for reunion had been accepted by both parties, and it was
decided that the two existing organisations, the Repeal Association
and the Confederation, should be dissolved, and be replaced by
a new association, the short lived Irish League.  The confederate
clubs, the nucleus of a national guard, were for legal reasons to be
separate from the League, though in practice it was intended that
they should act in close connection with the new organisation.[93]
For the moment it seemed that nothing stood in the way of a
successful reunion of the nationalist forces, but the repeal movement, in 1848, remained true to its unhappy history.  Unexpected
difficulties arose, for which John O'Connell was not altogether
to blame, difficulties that both delayed the formation of the League
and deprived it of the prestige value of the O'Connell name.

Gavan Duffy's handling of the situation was hardly the most tactful. Proposing that the Confederation should adjourn indefinitely, once the preliminary agreement was finally adopted, he described that agreement as a victory for the Confederation, since he believed the League would provide a convenient means of introducing the armed clubs into areas where the Confederation had made little progress.[94] John O'Connell could hardly be expected to react favourably to such a description of the agreement, and so he resorted to a variety of expedients to avoid a final dissolution of the Repeal Association.[95]

O'Connell's position was by no means an easy one. The financial position of the Association was so bad that he had to confess that, even were the Association not dissolved, it could hardly survive much longer.[96] Within the Association, too, John O'Connell had to face a new danger in the form of a growing body of critics who resented his efforts to hinder the formation of the League.[97] Despite the obstacles in his way, O'Connell nevertheless succeeded in delaying the foundation of the League. On the plea that Daniel O'Connell's old organisation should not be swept away until the provincial repealers had been consulted, the final decision to wind up the Association was postponed for two weeks.[98] This move made the task of concluding a speedy and satisfactory settlement more difficult, since it afforded John O'Connell an opportunity to rally his supporters, and to raise the old cry that the organised repeal movement should be kept free of illegal activities.

The appeal to the members showed how divided opinion within the Association had become. There were strong indications that if O'Connell did not give way, there would follow another secession, and, indeed, the upshot of the discussions was such a secession and the final break-up of the Repeal Association.[99] Out-voted on the peace pledge demand which he put forward, and convinced that the Repeal Association's days were numbered, John O'Connell finally declared that he would no longer resist the foundation of the Irish League, though he could never join it.[100] The damage was, however, done and the Irish League, though it was supported by some of O'Connell's most influential followers, came too late to achieve anything of importance.

With the Repeal Association for all practical purposes defunct, and the Confederation dissolved, the Irish League became, apart from the clubs, the sole repeal organisation. The elimination of the older associations did not resolve the problem which had long perplexed the nationalist leaders ; how to reconcile revolutionary language and activities with a constitutional agitation. Smith O'Brien and John Dillon clung to the hope of winning the landlords' support, at the very time when the clubs were arming and the radical press was filled with inflammatory articles directed against both the government and the landed ascendancy.[101] Apart from the activities in the clubs, more discreet discussions took place among the Young Irelanders, with the object of making preparations for a possible revolution later in the year, but these deliberations failed to win Smith O'Brien's approval and it seems he would have nothing to do with them.[102] With Smith O'Brien suspicious of revolution and men like Doheny and Fintan Lalor profoundly dissatisfied with the new experiments in constitutional agitation, it appeared that repeal unity was to remain as elusive as ever.[103]

The problem of reconciling the growing incompatibilities within the nationalist movement did not long remain a practical one, as the British government decided, again rather reluctantly, to make another attempt to silence agitation in Ireland. The lord lieutenant's easy optimism, of early May, gave way to a nervous anxiety in June, for the trial of Mitchel instead of discouraging the repealers had only helped those who sought to unite the nationalist forces. The clubs, in particular, worried the government. Legally it was difficult to deal with them, though their quasi-military character was quite obvious. Grey, the home secretary, considered that the only effective way to suppress the clubs was by suspending habeas corpus, and imprisoning the organisers, though he did not think, even in June, that the government would be justified in proposing such a drastic course.[104]

While Clarendon did not, at first, press for a suspension of habeas corpus, his fear of a revolution in autumn, or even earlier, grew stronger.[105] For the lord lieutenant, the clubs were the root of the evil, and by the middle of July he was quite convinced that only the most energetic measures could prevent rebellion.[106] In contrast to the tense, anxious letters from Dublin, the cabinet, in London, continued to press the lord lieutenant to apply the existing law and not to seek any extraordinary powers, but Clarendon remained adamant and in the end triumphed over the liberal inclinations of the cabinet.[107] Though the lord lieutenant may have exaggerated the dangers of insurrection, yet the possibility of an autumn revolution was something even Russell could not afford to ignore.[108]

On July 22, Lord John Russell obtained leave to introduce a bill suspending habeas corpus until 1 March 1849.[109] The ease with which this drastic measure passed, almost undebated, through all its stages, in one day, revealed the weakness, indeed the utter collapse of the repeal party in the house of commons. Only eight members could be found to oppose the government's original motion, and three days after it was introduced the bill had received the royal assent.[110] It was unfortunately easier to pass legislation of this kind than to undertake the long delayed task of removing the grave evils of the Irish land system.

The suspension of the constitutional guarantees made a humiliating submission or a premature revolt inevitable, for the authorities left the nationalists little time to resolve their differences or to organise their scattered and ill-prepared supporters. On July 21, Dublin city and county were proclaimed under the 1847 coercion act, while the final blow came, on July 26, with a second proclamation which declared that membership of a political club would be regarded as a sufficient reason for arresting any person following the suspension of habeas corpus.[111]

As a last desperate measure to provide the clubs with some sort of a central authority, the representatives of the Dublin clubs set up a council of five, but this move proved of no value, since the council never met.[112] The suspension act scattered the leaders throughout the country and the confused and abortive attempt at rebellion, which followed, marked not only the end of Young Ireland, but the extinction of the great movement founded by Daniel O'Connell to secure a simple repeal of the act of union.

### VIII. CONCLUSION

The repeal movement had begun its course as a political undertaking to undo the act of union. By the time that movement disintegrated in 1848 its character had been changed in certain ways, that is if we think of repeal as a whole and disregard for the moment the distinctions between the factions.

Before 1847–8, social reform, the amelioration of the lot of the poor was to have taken place within the tight limits of an idealised society of the years before 1800. With men like Fintan Lalor and John Mitchel reform became a question involving a radical criticism of society. This social radicalism owed its shaping, its severe colour, its urgency to the famine which brought more than 3,000,000 people to seek public aid in the spring and summer of 1847. When Fintan Lalor wrote 'I never recognised the land-owners as an element or as part and portion of the people' or Rev. John Kenyon said 'year after year our plentiful harvests of golden grain, more than sufficient even since the potato blight, to support and support well our entire population, are seen to disappear off the face of the land' they simply unveiled the forces which worked upon their thoughts. The famine which dis-organised and impoverished the O'Connellite repeal movement made a direct issue of something which had hitherto been an indirect issue ; the question of Irish agrarian reform.

A Fintan Lalor may have recognised this more acutely than more powerfully placed men. But he was not unique. Lord John Russell's cure for Irish woes was not Fintan Lalor's but he could not avoid speculating on the need for land reform and social change. Repeal candidates in the general election of 1847, land-lords and nationalists in session together in January 1847, and a treasury apologist, like Trevelyan, in his *Irish crisis* were all faced with the same unavoidable question by the Irish famine, namely what was to be the future structure of rural society in Ireland ?

The February revolution of 1848 in Paris appeared to offer Irish nationalists an escape from the difficulties which beset them at the close of 1847. In 1847 it seemed that unless nationalists were prepared for something like a class struggle, the way ahead was obscure and discouraging. Few were prepared for that struggle yet the famine had left nationalists hurt, angry and increasingly conscious of the social issues, of the apparent clash between the interests of the Irish people and their rulers. The French revolution of 1848, with its curious mingling of political and social aspirations was attractive. But it did not solve for most Irish nationalists the question of what was the place of the landlord, the man most obviously to be affected to his detriment, in any new, reformed social order in Ireland.

For most repealers and liberal reformers, the vague tenant-right formula had been the key to a new social balance, but it was a solution which could only come through compromise and with time, if the goodwill of the landed class was to be secured. Even in the most critical days of 1848, the Young Ireland leaders for the most part clung to the hope that they could somehow induce the landlords to support the cause of Irish nationalism. The years 1847–8 were transitional in a very particular way. Political actions had become deeply influenced by a play of forces of a different order. The famine had brought to the forefront the social factors. There was an awareness of this new development, but there was a tendency among Irish repealers and conservatives alike to go on arguing in terms derived from the political situation before 1845–6. This contributed much to the indecision and lack of purpose which characterised the activities of the politically conscious elements in Ireland in 1847–8.

The revolutionary gesture of 1848 helped to clear the position. The political approach was tried and it failed under both O'Connell and the Young Irelanders. Even one of its most determined advocates, Gavan Duffy, admitted, not long after his release from prison in 1849, that 'we cannot go back to the Irish League at this moment. It was the birth of warm hope and deep labour and to revive it now would be as fruitless as growing corn in December'. The consequence of that experience, of that apposition of famine to political agitation was that the land problem became, for a time at least, the central one.

The tenant-right agitation, which was given a formal organisation in the Irish Tenant League of 1850, seemed to offer the possibility of bringing with it a new phase in constitutional political action. From one aspect it might even appear that the great famine had, in the end, focused attention on the land issue and that a united nation would force the English whigs to make those reforms Lord John Russell had felt to be necessary even in 1847. But the tenant-right movement which brought Ulster Presbyterians and southern Catholics together had no purpose beyond the tenant-right question; a question notorious for its lack of definition.

In 1850–1, the landlord was still a power in Ireland. The encumbered estate legislation, and the poor rates may have hurt him, but the pattern of legislation from the 1847 poor law to the coercion measures had shown that the community of interests between the government and the Irish landed classes was strong,

despite the political differences and the complications arising from
local peculiarities and problems.  Landlords might have changed
but landlordism survived the famine.  The forces which might
have challenged landlordism between 1850 and 1860 were not in
harmony and full understanding one with the other.  The disturbing effect of the ecclesiastical titles controversy and the
dissolvent effect of the Aberdeen coalition on the tenant-right
movement, between 1852 and 1855, are pointers to the internal
weakness of the tenant-righters' position at a critical time.

The famine had presented the Irish social problem in all its
urgency ; that was to the reformer's advantage.  But time and
indifference were against him in the eighteen-fifties and the landed
influence on the British government remained a strong one.  The
eighteen-fifties were to prove a time of lost opportunity to British
governments and Irish opposition alike in the matter of Irish land.
The appalling urgency of the famine had passed but the fundamental problems survived into the second half of the nineteenth
century.

Political action remained weak in the post-famine years.  In
character it was primarily constitutional, but among those who
gathered around the dying Fintan Lalor and took part in the
armed demonstrations of September 1849, were men who
continued to think in revolutionary terms.  Under Lalor's influence
the social factor was at first strong, but revolutionary nationalism
was destined to take another course at a time when the tenant-
right agitation had come into disrepute.  The importance of such
early associates of Lalor's as John O'Leary and Thomas Clarke
Luby in the history of fenianism is considerable, but their impact
on the Ireland of 1849–50 was slight.

In those years which followed the fall of repeal, it seemed for
a time that the new force, land reform, the outcome of the famine
and of the widely-felt insecurity on the land, was to mould a new
kind of political pattern in Ireland.  That expectation was not
fulfilled in the eighteen-fifties.  The successful advance of land
reform was to await a different time and different men.

# THE ORGANISATION AND ADMINISTRATION OF RELIEF, 1845–52

By Thomas P. O'Neill.

i. Introduction

ii. Sir Robert Peel's relief scheme, 1845–6

iii. Relief by public works, 1846–7

iv. The soup-kitchens, 1847

v. Poor law relief, 1847–52

vi. Conclusion

FAMINE IN IRELAND ; SEARCHING FOR POTATOES.

*Illustrated London News,* 1847.

# The Organisation and Administration of Relief, 1845-1852

## I. INTRODUCTION

POVERTY and destitution were widespread in Ireland in the first half of the nineteenth century. For a great number no margin of safety above bare subsistence level existed. Early in 1846 it was estimated that almost one half of the population was dependent on the potato[1] and a partial failure of that crop was sufficient to reduce families to starvation. Despite the prevailing poverty there was no poor law system in the country until 1838. A statute passed in that year divided the country into poor law unions and provided for the election of a board of guardians and the erection of a workhouse in each union. Ireland, unlike England which had a system dating from Tudor times, was looked on as an unspoiled field where a poor law in complete accord with prevailing economic theory could be introduced. As a result a rigid system was imposed which in no circumstances allowed assistance to be given to any but those who became inmates of the workhouses. Residence in the workhouse was made ' as disagreeable as was consistent with health' lest anyone should desire to depend on public assistance. The French traveller, Gustave de Beaumont, said of the system, ' With one hand they offered the poor an alms, with the other they opened a prison'.

The system was in operation in practically all parts of Ireland by 1843, but it lacked elasticity and was incapable of dealing with a major crisis. There was accommodation in the workhouses for little more than 100,000 people and this was the maximum that would be assisted in any way under the scheme.

In the harvests of the early 1840's a hitherto unknown disease made its appearance among the potato crops, first in North America and later in Europe.  The danger of such a visitation to the Irish crop was noted but serious apprehensions were not raised until early in September 1845 when the disease was noticed in Waterford and Wexford.  It quickly spread to other counties.  Causes, scientific and otherwise, were suggested in the newspapers for this threat to the staple food of the Irish people.  A number blamed the government grant to the Catholic college of Maynooth for rousing the divine anger, while others blamed the fairies of Downpatrick for filching the potatoes.  The suggested cures were as diverse and, in most cases, quite unscientific, though one person did suggest that copper sulphate killed the fungus which caused the decay.

Within a week of the appearance of the disease the government took steps to collect accurate information regarding its progress. On September 16 the constabulary were directed to report weekly on local potato crops and to estimate the extent of the loss.  The earliest reports suggested that, as the crop was unusually heavy, the loss would be compensated for by the increased yield.  On October 16, however, a bad state of decay was reported from seventeen counties.  A few days later two scientists, John Lindley and Lyon Playfair, were sent to Ireland.  They were associated with Robert Kane on a commission set up by the lord lieutenant to suggest means of preserving potatoes which were sound when dug, of using diseased potatoes and of procuring seed for the coming year.

This commission was unsuccessful in suggesting means to prevent the spread of the blight.  The members misunderstood the cause of the decay and blamed dampness rather than a fungus, and so they were fundamentally astray in their proposals.  The prime minister, Sir Robert Peel, offered to provide free any chemical which they thought would end the disease, but they considered that since dampness was the cause, properly ventilated storage pits were the cure.  Instructions on the building of such pits were circulated by the thousand but they were of no avail. Potatoes, which were sound when pitted, were found when uncovered to have reached an advanced stage of decay.  The most successful method of preserving the potatoes was found to be that adopted by some people of leaving them in the ground, undug, until they were required for use. Regarding uses to which diseased potatoes could be put, the commission proposed that they be pulped and the diseased parts washed away. The residue could be used to make bread. The cost of machines for pulping was too great, however, to make the suggestion practical for the poor. After less than a month the commission prepared a final report which recapitulated the views expressed in their interim report. They had failed to stay the progress of the disease.[2]

Private individuals were not satisfied that the government was taking sufficient precautions and on October 31 a committee was formed at the Mansion House in Dublin to examine the extent of the loss and to propose remedies. The government's enquiries had been kept secret and it was feared that no preparations were being made to meet the danger of famine. On November 3, Lord Heytesbury, the lord lieutenant, received a deputation from the Mansion House committee which suggested the closing of distilleries, the prohibition of food exports, the establishment of food depots throughout the country and the provision of employment. The lord lieutenant, as yet unaware of the decisions of the cabinet on these questions, replied non-committally giving assurances of the government's interest and concern.[3]

The reaction of the public press to Heytesbury's reply was indignant. The *Freeman's Journal*, in a leading article, denounced it.

> They may starve ! Such in spirit, if not in words, was the reply given yesterday by the English Viceroy, to the memorial of the deputation, which . . . prayed that the food of this kingdom be preserved, lest the people thereof perish.[4]

From October 13, however, Peel had been in correspondence with the secretary of state for home affairs, Sir James Graham, and had announced that he had no confidence in the prohibition of exports as a remedy. He was already toying with the idea of using the potato failure as an excuse to cover a reversal of policy in relation to the duties on the importation of corn.[5] Hitherto agriculture had the benefit of protective duties and Peel had been elected to uphold them. Lord John Russell and the whigs were publicly committed as being in favour of free trade.

Exportation of food was prohibited by several European countries at this time as they feared a general scarcity[6] and there was a general clamour for similar action in Ireland.[7]

Potatoes were purchased by the Dutch at Cork in October and it appeared that something might be done to prevent their export when, at the end of the month, the lord lieutenant asked the customs officials at Dublin and Cork for statistics for shipments of food.[8]  Nothing was done, however, partly because it was deemed unwise to retain such a perishable commodity.[9]  Potatoes shipped from Ireland to Belgium, though sound on leaving port, were quite rotten on arrival and several cartloads exported from Derry to Antwerp had to be thrown into the Scheldt.[10]

Peel decided in favour of repealing the corn laws and immediately made the Irish potato failure a matter of political contention. Many English opponents of the repeal denied the existence or danger of any scarcity in Ireland.   As the blight had not appeared in every district and, in some areas, had attacked the crops in only occasional fields, it was possible to produce evidence of good crops from even the worst districts.   These denials of the danger to the staple food held up the work of relief and impeded the collection of subscriptions.   While Peel decided on repealing the corn laws ostensibly to meet the situation he nevertheless did not depend on this alone to avert starvation.

## II. SIR ROBERT PEEL'S RELIEF SCHEME, 1845–1846

The conflicting reports of the extent and effects of the potato disease in Ireland in the late autumn of 1845 complicated the problem facing Sir Robert Peel's administration.   In taking steps to meet the situation, the prime minister had no accurate estimate of the possible food deficiency to be expected.   A crisis was imminent but its dimensions were unknown.   It was realised that the existing poor law system could not meet the impending disaster.   That system was in operation in all but four poor law unions but relief, under the 1838 act, could be given only to inmates of workhouses.   The accommodation in these institutions was limited and could not meet the demands of the hundreds of thousands of persons likely to be destitute because of the potato failure.   The government considered the provision in the poor law which prohibited the granting of relief outside the workhouses fundamental.   To make the system capable of meeting a general scarcity it would have been necessary to change, perhaps only temporarily, the principle but it was feared that any change might become permanent.[1] Instead it was decided that a temporary scheme of relief parallel with, but distinct from, the existing system should be established. The new plan was to be based on local efforts and central aid was to be auxiliary to district committees.[2] On November 1, Peel proposed to his cabinet the establishment of a relief commission for Ireland to act as the central authority in relation to the scheme.

The members of the commission were nominated on November 18 and represented the various government departments in Ireland which were expected to co-operate in the tasks to be undertaken. Sir Randolph I. Routh, of the commissariat branch of the army, Colonel Duncan McGregor, police commissioner, Sir James Dombrain, of the coastguard service, Edward B. Twistleton, a poor law commissioner, and Theobald McKenna, assistant under-secretary, were members. Dr Robert Kane was added so that there would be a Catholic member[3] and the Right Hon. Edward Lucas was appointed chairman but resigned after a few months and was replaced by Routh who was the most active member. The first meeting of the commission was held on November 20 with Captain John Pitt Kennedy as secretary.[4]

The commission, as its first task, made arrangements to receive and store a supply of Indian corn and meal from the United States. This had been ordered, early in November, by Peel and Henry Goulburn, chancellor of the exchequer, on behalf of the government, at a cost of £100,000. In doing this they anticipated the sanction of the lords of the treasury.[5] The commission detailed commissary officers to find storage space in Cork for this food. Strict secrecy was maintained regarding the transaction and no inkling of the government's purchase reached the newspapers for a fortnight after the arrival of the food in Cork in the end of January 1846.[6] The commission also collected information regarding the stocks of biscuits and alternative provisions in the army stores, in England and Ireland.[7] Information was collected from all parts of the country regarding the progress of the potato disease. Reports were sought from the constabulary, resident magistrates and poor law guardians. They were tabulated and formed the basis for calculations as to the expected extent of the resulting shortage of food and the date at which the scarcity would be felt. These were reported to the lord lieutenant and to the prime minister.[8]

Towards the end of January formal and detailed instructions regarding the work of the commission were issued by Charles Edward Trevelyan, assistant secretary of the treasury, on behalf of the lords of the treasury. Trevelyan was a well-meaning but officious civil servant with whig sympathies. He was caricatured by Anthony Trollope, in *The Three Clerks,* as Sir Gregory Hardlines who ' wore on his forehead a broad phyllactory stamped with the mark of Crown property '. The treasury instructions clearly stated to Routh

> that the chief responsible authority in Ireland is the Lord Lieutenant, and that you are to obey any directions which His Excellency may at any time think necessary to give, even if they should differ from the instructions with which you have been furnished from this office.[9]

Despite this clear definition of authority, officials of the treasury in April did interfere, and, in an honest desire to check expenditure, caused difficulties for the lord lieutenant which were resolved only by the decisive action of Sir James Graham, the home secretary. In the course of correspondence with Heytesbury he remarked on the attitude of the treasury officials, of whom Trevelyan appears to have been the most important.[10]

> Your arrangements in Ireland should not be thwarted or impeded by this undercurrent, which appears to be stronger than the force of any instructions that I can issue. The provoking thing is that those who thwart are not responsible, while those whose directions are set aside will be held accountable for any disaster which may ensue.

By the end of April he had overcome the difficulties and he informed Heytesbury that he should act boldly on his own discretion.

' This calamity,' he wrote, ' cannot be adequately met in any other way. The case does not admit of the long delay of regular official correspondence '.[11]

In the first few months the commission sat on at least three days each week and occasionally even on six days. Meetings were usually held at 11 a.m. and lasted for two or three hours. On February 23, on the suggestion of Sir James Graham, Routh, Kane and Twistleton were appointed as a committee to meet daily and deal with current matters. Meetings of the full commission were then held only on Tuesdays. The committee meetings were also held in the mornings and lasted at least two hours. The major duties undertaken by the smaller body were the implementation of decisions of the commission and the application of their principles to specific areas from which complaints were received.[12]

Early in February the commission undertook the establishment of food depots with commissariat officers in charge of each. The sites were chosen mainly because of their accessibility by water which facilitated distribution from Cork harbour. Stores were established in the west at Limerick, Kilrush, Galway, Westport and Sligo. Depots at Waterford, Clonmel, Dublin and Dundalk were to supply the south and east, while Banagher, Athy, Tullamore and Longford were chosen as distribution centres for the midlands. These stores were, as the occasion arose, to provide food for distressed areas from the stocks available. Rumour exaggerated greatly the extent of the government imports, so that in March it was stated that the depots held sufficient to feed 4,000,000 persons daily for four months. In fact, had the stocks been used continuously, they would have provided food for but one quarter of that number for a fortnight.[13] The purpose of the imports was not to replace private traders but rather to control them. Monopolists were not to be allowed to corner markets and raise prices. As Sir James Graham explained on behalf of the government:

> We believed that under the judicious management of this supply the markets would be so regulated as to prevent an exorbitant price for native produce.[14]

Sales began at the depots in Cork, Clonmel and Longford on March 28, and by June 1 all the stores were opened. During June and July the Limerick depot sold 500 tons of Indian meal per week while in Cork 600 tons were sold weekly. Private traders were not supplied from the depots and local relief committees were allowed to purchase only when prices in their district were rising.[15]

In addition to building up the central organisation of the temporary relief scheme, the commission was instructed to stimulate, direct and support the efforts of local landowners to provide against the distress in each district. Instructions for local committees were drafted by Routh and passed unanimously by the commission on 16 February 1846. They were then submitted to the treasury and the lord lieutenant, and were passed finally within a fortnight. Financial aid was given to the local committees by the commission on the warrant of the lord lieutenant, who was advised by the committee of the commission as to the amount of the grant. In some distressed areas, however, committees were not formed or had insufficient funds to purchase food and the commission arranged for the opening of sub-depots by the coastguards and police in such places. Seventy-six sub-depots were opened by coastguards along the south and west coasts of Ireland and twenty-nine others, mainly inland in Connacht and Munster, were operated by the police.[16] These stores were supplied from the nearest depot of the relief commission and the officers in charge were ordered by the commission not to sell to retailers but only to the poor. Their instructions envisaged the possibility of difficulties arising in payments on employment schemes and allowed the coastguards and constabulary to issue food in lieu of wages on the certificate of a superintendent of works. This, however, did not arise and their actual duty was limited to sales.[17]

A strong prejudice among the people against Indian meal had to be overcome by the commission. In some parts of the country it became known as ' Peel's brimstone ' but by mixing a quarter of oatmeal in the ration with three quarters Indian meal the objections were abated if not removed. The total ration sold at the government stores to individual purchasers was two pounds of the mixture.[18]

As early as November 1845 the lord lieutenant suggested the organisation of local committees to meet the apprehended scarcity.[19] It was not until February, however, that the relief commission published rules for such committees whose main initial tasks were to raise subscriptions and encourage employment. Committees were formed throughout the country in March and April and by 10 August 1846, there were 648 of those bodies. The only counties in which there were no committees were Armagh, Derry, Fermanagh and Tyrone.[20] In some places they had been formed at meetings for a whole barony which laid down territorial divisions, usually Catholic parishes, for each committee. In other areas civil districts or parishes of the established church were adopted as the unit so that occasionally disputed portions lay between two committees and got assistance from neither. As a general rule the committee which had received subscriptions from the proprietors of the unwanted district eventually agreed to accept the responsibility.[21]

The personnel of the committees included county officials, poor law guardians and clergymen of all persuasions. In some cases local farmers were admitted to membership so as to stimulate their liberality and in a few cases all who contributed £1 automatically became members of the committee. When this resulted in the committee being too unwieldy a small working body was usually appointed while the nominal committee exercised but slight supervision.[22] Some few landlords refused to contribute to the local collections and, frequently, where several middlemen intervened between the working tenant farmer and the original owner, the absentees shirked their responsibilities. The relief commission instructed committees to publish their subscription lists so as to discourage default by landowners, and the names of non-subscribing landlords were sent privately to Dublin Castle. The relief commission, on the warrant of the lord lieutenant, gave grants to the local funds in proportion to the money subscribed locally. Contributions from persons abroad or from societies were not taken into account in estimating the size of the grant.

During the spring and early summer the donation was usually equal to two thirds of the local contributions, though in areas which were most affected by the potato blight sums equal to those subscribed were granted. In July and August almost all the grants were equal to the contributions. In all, 484 committees were given grants totalling £70,545 10s. 0d. during this year and more than £100,000 was subscribed by local persons to committees which forwarded returns to the lord lieutenant.[23]

Committees receiving grants were bound by regulations drawn up by the relief commission. In particular they were prohibited from giving food gratuitously unless the local workhouse was full and then, only to persons incapable of working. They were also ordered to sell food at cost price. In practice the first regulation was ignored and committees gave free food on their own initiative, even though workhouses were not full, to families whose removal to the workhouse would have caused hardship which would not be offset by the supposed advantage. Temporary inability to work due to sickness was usually considered by committees as meriting assistance without imposing the workhouse rule. Free food was also frequently given when there was a delay in starting public works and committees in county Limerick distributed food gratis to small farmers who were tilling their own land so as to give them a chance to sow the crops for the coming season.[24]

A task of work was required of applicants for relief capable of working and various works were initiated. In Inch, co. Tipperary, spinning and weaving of frieze was carried on by women under the direction of the committee and street paving and local improvements were made in various places by the committees. These tasks were, however, mainly intended only to tide over the period of distress before the commencement of public works, for the government had also taken steps to create employment as the funds of local committees were usually too limited to provide employment over a prolonged period.[25]

The provision of employment during periods of scarcity has long been an accepted method adopted by governments to relieve distress. To economists of the mid-nineteenth century this alone should have been sufficient to meet any food crisis, for the provision of ready money for the purchasers of food should have been sufficient to attract the food. A commissary officer of the inauspicious name of Edward Pine Coffin objected to the importation of food by Peel's government and maintained that the provision of public employment was the limit of the government's duties.[26] Sir Robert Peel did not accept these economic doctrines but he did start public works to give the people the money to purchase food as an integral part of his relief system.

The social economy of the Irish labourer made the operation of an organised relief system difficult because before the famine many labourers were not paid wages in cash. In many areas the farmer balanced the labourer's earnings against the rent of a piece of potato ground. There was seldom any cash transaction involved and money was a measure of value rather than a medium of exchange. The labourer lived on the produce of the potato plot and the system was in reality one of barter in which the exchange medium was the potato. The failure of the potato crop undermined this economic structure for the existing rate of wages was purely nominal and if paid by the farmer weekly in cash would not have sufficed to purchase food.

It was sufficient to meet the rent of a piece of ground but insufficient to purchase the amount of food produced by that plot.

Many farmers, on the failure of the potato, increased the rate of wages and remitted the conacre debt for the labourer's allotment and paid regularly in cash. Some farmers in north Cork, however, took legal action against labourers who took land and who contracted ' to work against the rent ' at a certain rate per day and who refused to work unless paid in money. These farmers were unsuccessful but the fact that the farmers as a body were the creditors of the labourers created a problem. If the labourer continued in his ordinary employment he would generally be working for an employer who might set off the conacre debt against a claim for wages.[27]

To meet the consequent unemployment, the government initiated public employment schemes. That works of a reproductive nature were envisaged by Peel's administration is clear from the bills which he presented to parliament in January 1846 for facilitating the development of harbours and the erection of piers and for amending the existing drainage legislation. The main work, however, was carried out under two statutes which laid down procedure for undertaking road improvements. Under one of these the board of works controlled the relief work ; one half of the cost was to be charged to the consolidated fund and the other half was to be repaid to the government in the county cess by the local landowners over a number of years. The total cost of the works under the other statute was repayable to the government which gave no grant but advanced a loan to the full amount. In this case the work was controlled locally and carried out by contractors.[28]

Employment on the board of works schemes was given to holders of tickets issued by the local committees among whose duties was the compilation of townland lists of families with remarks on the circumstances of each. The tickets were distributed at committee meetings to those considered unable to provide food for their families and they were an authority to the superintendent of the works to employ the person to whom they were granted. Contractors on the locally controlled public works were not prohibited from employing labourers who were not destitute but the schemes were always in necessitous areas and so helped to create a demand for labour. In many cases local relief committees took the contracts for works of this type and, of course, employed only those in need.[29]

In principle it was accepted that wages on the public schemes should be less than the ordinary rate of wages in the district. The local works supervisor made the ultimate decision on what that really was—a difficult task when it is understood that the wage rates of farm labourers were purely nominal and that the actual payment for labour was the portion of potato ground. The board of works officials made attempts to estimate the actual value of the exchange between the farmer and the labourer and paid less than it but more than the nominal local wage. The usual rate of pay was about 10*d.* per day and, though this was supposed to be lower than the value the labourers received from farmers, it was attractive enough to cause the spring work to be neglected. Part of the reason was the fear of labourers to work for a farmer who might set off a conacre debt against his wages. There was also the fear that, if they deserted the public works to take temporary employment from farmers who offered wages in cash, the labourers would not be re-employed by the supervisor when their services were no longer required by the farmers.[30]

As many labourers before the famine received no wages, one of the difficulties of the pay clerks on the public employment schemes was the shortage of currency to pay those employed. Special arrangements had to be made to issue more silver in the south and west of Ireland. Despite this, there were occasional delays of as much as three weeks in the paying of the wages and this left the poor at the mercy of dealers from whom they bought food on credit at exorbitant prices. This happened in a few isolated areas in Mayo and Leitrim, but it was a foreshadowing of the chaos which was to overtake the country in the following winter.[31]

The largest number of persons employed under the schemes controlled by the board of works in this season was 97,617. In the week ending on August 8 1846 these schemes were in operation in every county in Ireland except Derry, Tyrone, Fermanagh, Armagh and Down. A total of £476,748 6*s.* 6*d.* was expended, one half being a government loan and the remainder a free grant. The government gave loans totalling £130,000 for the works carried out by local contractors, and £9,915 was expended on the erection of piers and harbours in Donegal, Louth, Galway and Wicklow, of which £6,483 6*s.* 8*d.* was a grant. If these gave employment in the same ratio to the amount expended as the schemes controlled by the board of works they must have employed practically 30,000 persons. The local committees also gave some employment so that it is probable that under the various agencies organised by Peel's government about 140,000 persons were employed at one time. If each person thus employed had four dependents about 700,000 individuals were sustained by the schemes.[32]

As only six weeks remained before the new harvest, no immediate change in the principles of the relief schemes was made by the new prime minister, Lord John Russell, or the whig government which came into office on the defeat of Peel's administration on 29 June 1846. The new chancellor of the exchequer, Charles Wood, however, issued instructions on July 21 which indicated an acceptance of the advice of those treasury officials who, some months previously, had tried to thwart the lord lieutenant and home secretary in relation to Irish relief. A new rule limited the power of the local committees of issuing tickets for employment on the public works and the local board of works inspectors were ordered to employ only ' those who are proved to have no other means of subsistence '.[33] A rigid interpretation of the terms of this instruction would have entailed untold hardship as destitution is difficult to prove, but the rule was too late to affect the relief schemes of this season. In another matter, too, Wood showed a rigidity which alienated Lord Monteagle a whig politician and an Irish landlord. Wood ordered the gradual closing of all the public works from August 8 irrespective of whether they were completed or not. Monteagle denounced this as a breach of faith with the taxpayers as they would be saddled with the total cost of completing the schemes. The controversy became purely academic, however, as the new harvest brought the grim news of an almost total failure of the potato crop and it was impossible at any stage to discontinue the works completely.[34]

The activities of the relief commission were concluded, however, on August 15. It had spent £105,256 8s. 8d. in the United States for Indian meal, and £45,923 0s. 1d. in Great Britain for Indian meal and some oatmeal in Ireland was purchased for £6,544. The total expense, including freight, kiln-drying and grinding, amounted to £185,000, of which £135,000 was recovered from sales, so that the cost to the exchequer was £50,000.[35] Between the grants to relief committees, public works and to the relief commission, the government during this season expended £365,000 in grants and provided also £368,000 in loans to meet the scarcity.

The principles adopted by Peel's government to meet the distress were successful. Isaac Butt wrote a year later :

This timely precaution [of introducing Indian meal] and the subsequent judicious distribution of this store had the effect of bringing the people through the winter that closed the year 1845 without exposing them to any very severe privations. . . . However men may differ as to the merits of Sir Robert Peel as a politician, whatever estimate may be formed of his measures, it is impossible to deny that for the limited distress that existed consequent on the partial failure of the potato crop of 1845, provision was made with the most consummate skill—at least with the most complete success. Uninfluenced by party representations, the minister had evidently accurately informed himself of the nature of the calamity, and clearly foresaw its extent.[36]

If success is the yardstick of judgment in this matter, Peel's measures certainly merit praise. He showed an initiative unusual in that era of *laissez faire* and undertook tasks at variance with current economic theory. The entry of the government into the market was a spectacular example of this and it gave him an effective means of price control so as to defeat monopolists. The public works were not all centralised under the bureaucratic control of the board of works, and the government undertook the payment for the distress to a large extent by grants. It is true that the failure of the potato was partial and that the food exported during the first year of the potato blight would have been sufficient to feed the people had exportation been prohibited. It is also true, as witnesses of the most varied political opinions testify,[37] that he did not let people die of starvation. He allowed the Irish scarcity to become a political question by linking it with the repeal of the corn laws, but he did not allow the consequent controversy to affect his relief measures. The *Freeman's Journal,* which cannot be accused of favouring Peel, said :

The limited distress which Sir Robert Peel was called upon to meet, he provided for fairly and fully. No man died of famine during his administration, and it is a boast of which he might well be proud. Widen the circle of destitution in 1845 and it could be effectually encountered by the proper extension of the same policy.[38]

This perhaps overestimates Peel's powers but it is ample testimony to his success.

### III. RELIEF BY PUBLIC WORKS, 1846-7

On 14 July 1846, Sir Randolph Routh reported to Trevelyan that the potato disease had reappeared[1] and five weeks later the prime minister informed the house of commons :

> I am sorry to be obliged to state that . . . the prospect of the potato crop this year is even more distressing than last year—that the disease has appeared earlier and its ravages are more extensive.[2]

The full danger of a total failure of the crops was not, however, appreciated and the government thought that harvest work and the surviving potatoes would be sufficient to allow a respite of some months. This period was intended as breathing space to allow a review of the schemes of the previous year and to prepare for the eventual scarcity which it was hoped would not be felt until late in the season. Trevelyan was instructed to prepare a memorandum on Peel's system for the information of the cabinet.[3] It was submitted on August 1 and was the basis of the plan proposed to parliament by Lord John Russell a fortnight later. The major duty of the government was to provide employment, according to the prime minister. The provision of food and the organisation of local committees were subordinate.[4]

Trevelyan maintained that ' the supply of the home market may safely be left to the foresight of private merchants ' and that any purchases which the government made should be made in the home market so as to encourage the importers. With this Russell was in agreement.

> We do not propose [he said] to interfere with the regular mode by which Indian corn and other kinds of grain may be brought into the country.[5]

The chancellor of the exchequer was even more emphatic when he told the house of commons—

> It was not the intention at all to import food for the use of the people of Ireland. In fact many merchants had declared that they would not import food at all if it were the intention of the government to do so, and unless the government would give such an assurance.[6]

The government had apparently surrendered to the threats of the merchants and were not interfering with importation of food. In a letter to Thomas Matthew Ray, Daniel O'Connell denounced this—

> Unhappily [he said] in the present state of the country it will not be sufficient to procure employment for the people. The great difficulty is the procuring sufficient food—food is already at a famine price and the leaving in the hands of the mercantile men the supplying [of] food as a commercial speculation will necessarily keep it at famine price. The intervention of government is therefore absolutely necessary. Such intervention is surrounded with great difficulties, and will impose an enormous additional burthen upon the government—it must, however, be done or the people will starve.[7]

Apart from the decision on not competing with importers, both Trevelyan and Russell realised that over a large part of the country there were no traders and that commissariat officers would have to act in place of retailers. Trevelyan in his memorandum of August 1 suggested that depots should be established only along the west coast and that even there the stores should sell food only when all other sources of supply failed.[8] Accordingly a pledge was given that the government would not open depots east of the Shannon or on the north, east or south coasts from Derry to Cork. In December, Routh protested to Trevelyan that the commissariat should be prepared to meet scarcity in the eastern portion of Ireland.

> In a great calamity [he said] we cannot be found wanting. The relief must be forthcoming. We could not fall back on our pledge.[9]

Two days later, on Christmas Eve, Trevelyan informed Routh that the chancellor of the exchequer was firmly resolved to allow no deviation from the pledge. This he amplified in a later letter :

> The chancellor of the exchequer will on no account permit you to undertake to provide food for any portion of the eastern district of Ireland. . . . No exigency, however pressing, is to induce you to furnish supplies of food for any districts except those for which we have already undertaken.[10]

The reason advanced by Trevelyan for this rule was that the commissariat stocks were insufficient to meet even the demands of the western district. The government despite its announced intentions had been forced to purchase Indian corn abroad to supply the depots in the west, and by mid-December had succeeded in importing a total of but 4,800 tons.[11] The previous July, Commissary-General Hewetson had suggested to Trevelyan that since blight had already reappeared, a stock of 4,500 tons of Indian meal should be purchased at once.[12] This warning had been ignored and purchases began too late in the season to ensure the arrival of sufficient quantities before Christmas. In the meantime Routh had represented to Trevelyan :

> The country is abundantly supplied with wheat and oats, the prices are most encouraging for sale, but nevertheless for payment of rent they are exported to Liverpool and Scotland, and the people, deprived of this resource, call out on the government for Indian corn, which requires time for its importation.[13]

He denounced this exportation as ' a most serious evil '[14] but he was ordered by Trevelyan not to countenance in any way the idea of prohibiting export.[15] Thus the stock of food in the country, which could have bridged the gap until the new year, was allowed to be exported.

The administration of the government food depots, which were confined this season to a corner of West Cork, Kerry, Donegal and counties west of the Shannon, was carried out by commissariat officers who were recalled from the British colonies for this task.[16] No relief commission was established and the officers were under the direction of Routh. Even in the west the depots had a much more restricted scope than in the previous year. They were not allowed to open while there were any supplies of food in the neighbourhood.[17] Though numerous deaths by starvation occurred at Skibbereen between November 5 and December 21,[18] the local depot did not open until after December 7,[19] and no general permission to commence sales in all stores was issued by the treasury until December 28.[20] Rigid rules were also laid down by the treasury governing the price of food sold at these stores. In the first instance Trevelyan favoured adding 30 per cent to the actual cost price so as not to undercut local retailers. Routh, however, maintained that 15 per cent should be sufficient profit as, because of the scarcity, the trade was a ready cash one with a quick turn-over. Ultimately the ruling factor was the average market price at the nearest towns.[21]   Indian meal which had cost the government less than £13 per ton was sold at the depots at £19 in the end of December.[22]

The duties of the commissariat department also included the control of the local committees.  Routh drafted rules for these bodies and submitted them to Trevelyan.  The country was divided into nine districts and an inspecting officer was appointed to supervise the committees in each area.  This control was exercised in all parts of Ireland and was not confined to the west.  The inspectors were ex-officio members of local committees and had authority to examine the finances and proceedings of these bodies. They were particularly charged to see that the committees exercised care in preparing lists of persons needing employment on the public works.[23]

In the previous season the exertion of local proprietors and others had been availed of by the government through committees scattered throughout the country.  In his memorandum to the government on August 1, Trevelyan recommended the continuance of such bodies though he suggested that the rules could perhaps be improved.  Modified rules, however, were not agreed between the lord lieutenant, the treasury and the prime minister till two months later.[24]  The lieutenants of counties were instructed to lay down the limits of the jurisdiction of the new committees so as to avoid the anomalies of the previous season.  More important was the rule governing membership of the new committees.  The lieutenants of counties had discretion to add to the persons laid down in the regulations (magistrates, principal clergymen, chairmen of poor law unions and police and coastguard officers) but rarely did so.[25]  The result was that many active members of the previous committees were not re-appointed.  The secretary of the Fermoy committee was excluded under the new rules[26] but probably the greatest mis-take was the exclusion of Catholic curates.  'Without them,' wrote Lord Monteagle from Limerick, 'and here they are labouring like tigers for us, working day and night, we could not move a stroke'. They were particularly conversant with the circumstances of the people and were in a position to prepare employment lists and to assess the urgency of the need of each family.  They also had youth and enthusiasm while those whose offices entitled them to committee membership were usually senior men.[27]

The funds of the committees were, as in the previous year, derived from subscriptions aided by government donations. In the new rules the amount of government grant which was to be paid by Sir Randolph Routh, on the authority of the lord lieutenant and chief secretary, was limited to one half of the total local subscriptions. In the middle of December, when faced with widespread famine, the treasury authorised Routh to give grants equal to the subscription and a fortnight later authorised grants in aid of contributions from abroad.[28] The local subscriptions collected up to 6 March 1847 totalled £112,114 7s. 9d. and government grants amounting to £104,004 16s. 0d. were given to the committees.[29]

The main task of the relief committees, besides preparing lists of those needing employment, was the provision of food. In the instructions issued at the end of September this food was to be sold and no provision was made to allow gratuitous relief to the infirm.[30] In the regulations laid down for the inspecting officers the principles governing the committees' duties were more clearly stated. They were prohibited from selling food below the price prevailing in the neighbouring market towns and were actually to add to that price the cost of conveying the food from the market to the committees' stores. Free food was to be distributed only to the infirm and unemployable and not at all while any room was available in the local workhouse.[31]

Because of the success of the Society of Friends in meeting distress by establishing soup kitchens, Routh, at the end of the year, encouraged relief committees to undertake the system. Many did so, particularly in Munster and Donegal. The commissariat office issued a pamphlet containing recipes for cheap food and suggestions for organising the system.[32] The regulations regarding the sale of food were, however, not relaxed and the system was unable to meet the conditions which prevailed in the closing months of 1846.

The provision of employment was considered to be the most important task of the government. Lord John Russell thought that if the people were able to purchase food, the normal channels of trade would supply it. In his memorandum, Trevelyan proposed that, to prevent waste, all the public works should, this season, be controlled by the board of works and that the expense ' should fall entirely on the persons possessed of property in the distressed district '. Trevelyan suggested that the works should be unproductive so as to impose limits on the applications for employment schemes.[33] These proposals were embodied in a statute passed in August 1846 and the board of works was re-organised and a relief scheme section established under Richard Griffith and Captain Thomas Larcom.[34]

The effect of the reorganisation of the public employment system was to centralise control and this caused delay in undertaking works under the new act. Presentment sessions could be held only when called by the lord lieutenant. This did not occur until the condition of a locality became critical. The proposed schemes had then to be examined by officials of the board of works before being transmitted to the treasury for sanction. This entailed untold delay with the result that distress was frequently far advanced before works were opened. This made the work of the board officials difficult and from the beginning the central office was harassed by the vast numbers to be employed. Despite the protests of the lord lieutenant, the new works were not in operation until October.[35]

The labourers were mainly paid by task work which it was thought would ensure that the maximum amount of work would be done. The rate of wages was fixed so as to enable the moderate worker to earn 10d. to 1s. per day and a good labourer, who exerted himself, from 1s. 4d. to 1s. 6d. This, however, was not satisfactory as the most destitute labourers were frequently too weak to earn even 10d. daily and a large number were not provided with implements and so could earn less than half of the minimum set as a standard by the board. At Cong the inspecting officer reported that seventy-five men were employed and had between them but two wheelbarrows, two crowbars, and a wooden lever. Those who had these tools could earn up to 10d. but the others earned only $3\frac{1}{2}d.$ or 4d. daily. The rate of wages in general was found to be insufficient and each week families fasted for from twenty-four to thirty-six hours until next pay-day. Under this system labourers gradually became weaker and those who, at first, were able to earn over 1s. daily were later able to earn only 6d. at the same work and at the same rate of pay. Ultimately, because of the inequality of the return labourers were able to give, payment by task had to be abandoned.[36]

Delays in paying wages seriously impaired the efficacy of the schemes. Payclerks were not always trustworthy and zealous and, though the lord lieutenant ordered the regular weekly payment of wages and appointed an inspector of payclerks, to enforce it, payment continued to be in arrears in many places. Local committees and individuals occasionally advanced money to payclerks when funds failed to arrive to pay the labourers. Difficulties were then sometimes raised regarding reimbursing the loan. To avoid delaying payments till the value of task work was calculated a subsistence allowance was paid weekly. This was roughly three-quarters of what was actually earned and the balance was paid later when the work was measured. Delays were never completely eliminated and in some areas payments were on occasion five weeks in arrears. Denis McKennedy of Caharagh, co. Cork, who died on October 24 on the roadside, was employed by the board of works up to the day of his death and was owed wages for a fortnight. The jury brought in a verdict that he ' died of starvation due to the gross negligence of the board of works '.[37]

Occasionally advantage was taken by payclerks themselves of the delay in issuing money. When such a delay occurred unscrupulous payclerks advanced meal to the labourers and when the cash arrived they reimbursed themselves with handsome profit. Having once got into debt the labourers had to continue to purchase meal from the clerk. Traders more frequently took advantage of the labourers in this fashion. Once a family went into debt they fell victims to village usurers and gombeen men. Each week's pay went to pay off the debt and the food for the ensuing week had to be obtained on credit, frequently at exorbitant prices. Skibbereen had a population in 1841 of 4,715 persons and in the three winter months of 1846-7 forty thousand pawn tickets were issued in the town. Benevolent landlords occasionally attempted to rescue their tenants from the clutches of traders into whose debt they had fallen by advancing sufficient money to clear their commitments, but the majority took no action and the famine gave a great harvest to pawnbrokers and unscrupulous merchants.[38]

The dependence of families on regular wages raised the problems also of what should be done during bad weather. It was foreseen from an early stage that the people would have to be paid or fed but the government failed to give any decision on the matter. The question became serious during January and February 1847, but despite the pressure of enquiries for a direction in the matter from

local officials, no decision was announced.  The officials had to
decide what to do themselves and there was a great diminution in
the numbers employed in the second week of February.  In most
areas, however, the works continued and it was quite common to
see even women working on the roads among snowdrifts.  The
weekly pay packet was so important that within the family the
needs of the wage earner took precedence over all other claims on
the available food supply even to the denial of sustenance to the sick
and famished members.  Women and girls worked with the men,
too, digging, wheeling barrows, carrying loads of earth and breaking stones, sometimes carrying helpless children on their backs.[39]

Many people objected to the type of works undertaken.  In
general they consisted in the building and repairing of roads.
While the policy of the government was not simply to provide
works irrespective of their utility, it became necessary as the useful
roads were completed to build others less useful.  The inability
to supervise properly the selection of schemes meant that many
almost useless schemes were undertaken.  The final abandonment of
works left a number of incompleted roads as monuments to the
futile attempts of the government to meet the crisis.  Lord Devon
and Lord Monteagle led an agitation against the limitation of
schemes to road works and succeeded in impressing the lord lieutenant with the advisability of changing government policy and
allowing more reproductive employment.  He sent the under
secretary, Thomas N. Redington, to England to persuade Lord
John Russell of the necessity for this and also advised Monteagle to
write to Trevelyan to impress him with the same view.  He
admitted to Monteagle that, unless Trevelyan could be won over
to his policy, Sir Charles Wood, the chancellor of the exchequer,
would not sanction any change.  It is quite clear that the assistant
secretary of the treasury was considered more important than the
responsible minister and that Wood was ruled by the officials in
Whitehall.[40]

After six weeks, the agitation met with some success and a change
of policy was announced in a letter of the chief secretary, Henry
Labouchere, on October 5.  The lord lieutenant had taken on
himself the responsibility for making this change but the procedure
laid down was so complicated that the effect was negligible in
starting reproductive works.  Under the letter, the sum needed for
the employment of the poor was to be assessed at presentment

sessions in each barony. The proportion chargeable on each electoral division according to the poor law valuation was then ascertained. Presentments could then be made for useful works in any electoral division which so desired, up to the amount of its assessment. In the case of drainage an undertaking had to be given by the proprietor whose land was to be drained that the charge would be levied exclusively from the lands to be improved. Though works under the letter were carried out in most of the counties, they formed but a small proportion of the total works. It was difficult to get unanimous agreement among the proprietors of any electoral division for reproductive work, and a single dissentient had the power of veto. The delay in reaching a decision on the drainage question also had an effect in keeping down the number of reproductive schemes, as baronies which in September proposed roadworks were not allowed to reconsider them in the light of Labouchere's letter. In all, only 5 per cent of the cost of employment schemes was spent on drainage and less than one in forty of the labourers employed were engaged on these works.[41]

The main significance of the controversy is that it shows the lack of unity between the lord lieutenant and the treasury, and the lack of initiative on the part of the chancellor of the exchequer. The latter blamed the Irish administration for the shortcomings of the relief schemes, while Bessborough insisted that the treasury was at fault. The prime minister maintained a vacillating neutrality between the two departments and displayed his inability to cope with the situation.[42]

Another form of reproductive employment which was proposed was the building of railways. The government, however, objected to this as the building of earthworks was the only part of the schemes which would give employment to unskilled workers and two-thirds of the cost would be expended on rails and equipment. After the change of policy in relation to drainage, certain railway schemes were allowed, but so hedged round by qualifications that the Waterford and Limerick Railway Company alone succeeded in eliminating all the obstacles after a long delay. Lord George Bentinck introduced a bill in parliament envisaging a comprehensive state-aided railway building scheme to provide employment in Ireland in February 1847, but it was defeated. The one really reproductive project pushed forward by the government took the form of aid to fisheries by the establishment of fish curing stations on the south and west coasts, and by selling fishing tackle. Even this was on a limited scale and was simply supplementary to the work of the Society of Friends.[43]

The numbers employed rose steadily from 26,000 in the beginning of October. By November 21 over a quarter of a million persons were engaged on the public schemes and in March 1847 the number reached 714,390. Of these, roughly one in fifty were women and one in twelve were boys. In Clare, more than one-fifth of the population was employed by the board of works. In some areas, because of the number of children employed, the national schools had to be closed. To maintain this number of employees the board of works became the centre of a colossal organisation. About 12,000 subordinate officials had to be supervised and the board received thousands of letters daily. Under the stress of the demands, the officials were unable to cope with the problem and the result was scenes of horror in all parts of the country.[44]   The board of works, however, deserves great credit for the manner in which it dealt with the tasks imposed on it. These were impossible, but it is doubtful if any department of state could have done more. In a matter of months employment was found for up to three-quarters of a million people. The deficiencies in the schemes were due to government policy rather than to departmental lethargy.

Deaths became quite commonplace during that winter. Schull and Skibbereen in Cork became a byword because of the weekly descriptions of conditions there which appeared in the *Illustrated London News*.[45]   Some instances from letters of visitors to the distressed areas give a clearer picture than any generalisations.

At a poor nailor's cabin ; his wife some time dead ; two children on a miserable bed, some scanty covering thrown over them, but destitute of clothes ; one of them so weak from want of food, as to raise himself with difficulty for the purpose of shewing his emaciated limbs. A labourer, with his wife and two children, sitting round a bit of fire ; a younger child lying dead in its cradle, much emaciated from the insufficiency, as it was supposed, of maternal nourishment, the poor woman herself suffering from want ; and the family unable to provide a coffin for the deceased. At Aghadown the police informed us that the night before, while on patrol, they were attracted to a cottage by an unsteady light ; on proceeding to ascertain the cause, they found a father and son were lying dead whilst the survivors, being unable to purchase even a candle, were endeavouring to keep up a light with straw pulled from the thatch.[46]

One person wrote from this area of Skibbereen in February 1847 :

I have got a coffin with movable sides constructed, to convey the bodies to the churchyard, in calico bags prepared, in which the remains are wrapped up. I have just sent this to bring the remains of a poor creature to the grave, who having being turned out of the only shelter she had—a miserable hut—perished the night before last in a quarry, she was found with some flax around her, lying dead.[47]

From Arranmore, co. Donegal, a visitor wrote :

Many . . . rushed out of their cabins imploring me to visit their relatives—told me that every day people fell down exhausted working on the roads and were carried home. I saw men and women trying to work, and also girls and boys, from the age of twelve years. . . . It would be useless to enumerate particular instances of distress as all had some tale of woe. . . . The magistrate informed me that he believed it was not uncommon for mothers, both on the island and the main, in addition to the infant at the breast, also to try and afford the same nourishment to one or two of their other children up to three and four years of age.[48]

At Louisburgh, in Mayo, between ten and twenty deaths daily were reported during January 1847. Coffinless burials, bodies uninterred, corpses with but a handful of straw for a shroud, the quick and the dead lying side by side in the same bed, such were the daily reports in the newspapers in the early months of 1847. Verdicts at inquests of ' death by starvation ' were commonplace despite the efforts of the board of works to prevent the juries from reaching such conclusions. Ultimately, magistrates decided that they could not find time to hold inquests. At Lismore, co. Waterford, a jury added a rider to the conventional verdict stating that ' death was caused through the negligence of the government in not sending food into the country in due time '. In Galway, in one

instance the jury agreed that as Lord John Russell and Sir Randolph
Routh had combined to starve the Irish people by not taking
adequate steps to meet the crisis they were both guilty of wilful
murder.[49]

The failure of the system of relief by public works was gradually
made clear to the government, and a new scheme was introduced
during the spring of 1847. The numerous deaths by starvation
and the fact that labourers deserted agricultural employment in
favour of roadwork were factors in bringing about the change.
It was decided to reduce the numbers employed by twenty per
cent on March 20 and the schemes were to be completely shut down
by May 1. Though this strict rule of thumb reduction could not
be adhered to and those employed were paid off more slowly than
originally planned, the cessation of works left many projects
unfinished and even coach roads were left in a dangerous condition.
The total cost of the relief works was £4,848,235 2s. 6d. all of
which was to be paid out of local rates.[50]

Criticism of the schemes has centred largely on their unproductive character, and it has been suggested that all the famine
works were useless. The improvement of road communications,
however, was as important a part of economic development as
railway building, but the limitation of this type of work meant that
many useless and ill-considered projects were commenced and quite
a number of them were left unfinished. While schemes of local
development, particularly the improvement of waste lands, should
have been started, it must be remembered that any such schemes
could not, during the winter of 1846 and 1847, have added to the
stocks of food in the country. Their effect would have been felt
in subsequent years and the millions of pounds which were waste-
fully expended would have been diverted to increasing the production of the country. Having decided to make the cost a local
burden, the government should have seen to it that the capital was
not wasted. The opportunity to improve the country was lost,
however, and the effect was to increase the demands on already
heavily mortgaged property by leaving a heavy debt to be repaid
out of rates. It is true, of course, that it is simpler to provide work
on roads in cases of urgency. Accurate surveying was a first
essential for a proper drainage system. It was, however, over-
burdening the landowners to make them liable for the costs of
useless works.

IV.  THE SOUP-KITCHENS, 1847

In the middle of January 1847, Trevelyan wrote to Colonel H. D. Jones of the board of works :

> It is feared that we have arrived at a very important crisis of our operations, and I am desired to request an early expression of your confidential opinion on the subject of it.  The tide of distress has for some time past been steadily rising and appears now to have completely overflowed the barriers we endeavoured to oppose to it. . . . The question I have to ask you therefore is whether the time has not arrived for having recourse in a direct and effectual manner to what we have been aiming to arrive at by many indirect means, namely, the out-door relief of every destitute person.[1]

Quite obviously, Trevelyan was thinking of relieving the board of works of the burden which had been placed upon it and, in doing so, was influenced by the success of the private associations which had established food centres.

The accounts of the scenes throughout Ireland in the winter of 1846 caused the formation of relief associations which collected funds from all parts of the world.  One of the first in the field was the Central Relief Committee of the Society of Friends, which was founded early in November.  This body received, in the succeeding months, subscriptions and food from abroad, mainly from the United States, to a total value of about £200,000.  The method of relief adopted by the committee was mainly the establishment of soup kitchens.  William Edward Forster, who came to Ireland to assist his fellow-Quakers in their relief work, had previously adopted the system to help the poor in Norwich and Quakers in Cork city operated soup kitchens with success from the beginning of November.[2]

In the initial stages, Routh was opposed to committees selling cooked food, as it increased the dependence of the poor.  He suggested that it was preferable to teach the poor to prepare their food and to supply them with the ingredients.[3]  Faced with the success of the committee of the Society of Friends and the rising tide of starvation in early December 1846, he decided to have resort to the soup kitchens.  He instructed his officers to establish them and on December 30 he wrote to Trevelyan :

THE CORK SOCIETY OF FRIEND'S SOUP HOUSE.

*Illustrated London News*, 1847.

The soup system promises to be a great resource and I am endeavouring to turn the views of the Committees to it. It will have a double effect of feeding the people at a lower price and economising our meal.[4]

The extension of this system, to replace the employment schemes, was undertaken by the government in January 1847. This meant a reversal of previous policy in regard to poor relief in Ireland and it was decided that a temporary act to establish soup kitchens should be passed so as to bridge the period until the harvest of 1847. Permanent legislation amending the Irish poor law could be passed during the spring and summer and allow the new poor law system to operate from September 1847. It was generally felt that the famine could no longer be dealt with as a temporary feature of Irish poverty but that the regular poor law system should be equipped to meet it.[5] The new temporary measure was introduced in the house of commons on January 25 and became law on February 26.[6]

At the end of January, Sir George Grey informed the lord lieutenant that he should forthwith establish a commission to superintend the new scheme. Sir John Burgoyne was selected as chairman and was granted leave of absence from his duties as inspector of fortifications in Ireland. Edward T. B. Twistleton, Harry D. Jones, Duncan McGregor and Sir Randolph Routh, representing respectively the poor law commissioners, the board of works, the constabulary and the commissariat, were appointed members as well as Thomas N. Redington, under secretary to the lord lieutenant.[7] Officials who were working with the commissariat department relief were transferred to the commission and inspecting officers were chosen from those employed by the board of works and the commissariat.[8]

The duties of the commission included the preparation of instructions for the local committees and the inspecting officers, but their most important function was the supervision of the provision of funds for the local bodies. The sources for these funds were expected to be local poor rates, subscriptions and government donations. The commission was authorised to advance loans to be repaid out of the rates and to give grants equal to the subscriptions and rates. In cases of extreme urgency, authority was given to the commission to give even larger donations to meet pressing claims of want and destitution.[9]

It was arranged that according as the relief committees were reorganised under the new rules, their correspondence was answered by the commission instead of by Routh.[10]  Thus there was a gradual transfer of duties from the commissariat to the commission.  The commissariat, however, continued to supervise the import of food for the depots in the west.  The principle of not supplying the markets in the eastern half of Ireland was adhered to, though a depot was opened at Enniskillen.  There was, however, no change from the principles adopted by the depots in the preceding months. In its early months the new commission spent much time drafting rules for the new committees and by April 10 had distributed fourteen tons of paper in regulations, forms and instructions.[11]

As the finances of the new scheme depended on the poor rate, the local organisation had to be changed from parochial divisions to poor law units. This entailed the reconstruction of the committees for the third time.  In each poor law union a finance committee of from two to four persons was appointed by the lord lieutenant to supervise the expenditure of the local committees. These latter were formed in district electoral divisions throughout the country.  Sometimes two districts were united under one committee but the accounts of each area were kept distinct.[12]

On March 4, the lord lieutenant issued an order specifying who should be members of the district committees.  Residents in relief districts, such as justices, archbishops and bishops, and persons with a local interest such as the principal clergyman any part of whose parish was in the district, the chairman of the board of guardians, justices holding land in the area, and the highest ratepayers.  The parish clergy and justices of the peace were allowed to appoint deputies subject to the lord lieutenant's approval.[13]

The district committees were to draw up lists of persons requiring assistance, dividing them into four categories : (1) destitute helpless persons, (2) destitute able-bodied persons not holding land, (3) destitute able-bodied persons holding small portions of land, and (4) the able-bodied employed at wages insufficient for their support at the current high price of food.  All except those in receipt of insufficient wages were entitled to gratuitous relief while the others were to be allowed to purchase the cheapest types of food, but not at less than cost price as there was to be no relief in aid of wages. The holders of land were to get gratuitous assistance on condition that they cultivated their lands.  Estimates of the cost of feeding the people in the ensuing fortnight were prepared and submitted to the finance committee which checked them. The inspecting officer then signed the estimates and sent them to the relief commission in Dublin. On the recommendation of the commission the lord lieutenant issued a warrant to the boards of guardians to pay the estimated sum from the poor rates to the local committees.[14]

This network of red tape caused great delay in the operation of the scheme and failure to comply with all the regulations held up food supplies. The re-organisation of the committees was slow and the public works scheme had to be prolonged in many areas. No matter what distress existed between the closing of these schemes and the introduction of the new plan, the commission sanctioned no payments to committees until the estimates were submitted and passed by the finance committees. The inspecting officers occasionally caused unnecessary delay by departing from instructions and excluding Catholics from the new bodies. The bishop of Meath, Dr John Cantwell, and the Catholic clergy of Mullingar, were allowed to serve on the local committee only after appealing to the under-secretary. In general, those who had been most energetic on the earlier committees had by the spring of 1847 tired of the onus placed on them, and failed to attend regularly. It was not surprising that voluntary members of committees did not attend to the task of form filling which seemed so remote from directly providing food.[15]

Gradually, the new committees were organised. Of the 2,049 electoral divisions in the country, 1,248 had come under the new scheme by May 15 and in the following two months a further 600 accepted the rules. Relief committees under the soup kitchen act were established in every poor law union in Ireland except three, during the summer of 1847. Those three were Antrim, Belfast and Newtownards.[16] They issued ration cards stating the amount of food to which each applicant was entitled and they had to enforce all the rules laid down by the relief commission in relation to the distribution of free food. Personal cleanliness was insisted on and since no family, of which one person was employed, was allowed soup gratis, committees saw that all the able-bodied members of a family were present at the soup kitchen before food was issued. The inadequacy of wages made this regulation futile, for the person in employment was able to purchase less food for his family than was received free by those unemployed. This caused the numbers on the relief lists to increase. Some farmers dismissed their employees and engaged them only at odd times so as to enable them to get on the lists. Committee members and even poor law guardians put themselves on the lists and the numbers receiving daily rations in some districts exceeded the total population according to the 1841 census.[17]

Though a number of committees were liberal in issuing ration cards, others were strict. Ratepayers called meetings to force committees to reduce the numbers being assisted. An amendment which was being discussed in Westminster in the debates on the new poor law scheme for Ireland—' the Gregory clause '—excluding from relief those who held more than one quarter acre of land, was thought by many committees to apply to the soup kitchen act, and they accordingly refused assistance to those holding more than a rood of land. Landlords in some instances actually enforced this false interpretation so as to clear their estates. Applicants for relief who owned a horse or a cow, or, in some instances, even a donkey, were excluded from the relief lists in some areas, but in May the relief commissioners decided that owners of animals were entitled to relief if there was a prospect of their being able to support themselves through this property later.[18] In general, the decisions of committees excluding persons from relief were not interfered with by the government, though numerous appeals were made to the lord lieutenant and chief secretary. In one instance an army pensioner from Newbliss, co. Monaghan, was asked, when he made such an appeal, why his eldest son aged fourteen did not enlist in the army.[19]

The government in the spring of 1847, because of the spread of dysentery, typhus and other epidemic diseases, established a board of health and the relief commission sought the advice of the board on the ration of food to be given by the committees. One pound of meal, or a cooked ration made from that quantity of raw meal, was deemed sufficient daily for each person over nine years of age, while younger children were to be given one-half of the adult ration. Some committees refused to give the amount recommended by the health authorities but this was checked by the inspectors of the relief commission.[20]

In May, the board of health recommended to the commissioners that all rations should be cooked before being issued, as a number of people had no means of cooking the food and were eating raw meal.

There was strong opposition to the cooked food in many places and many committees remained adamant against introducing the system until forced to do so by the relief inspectors.[21]

The period of changing from the earlier scheme of relief to the new system was one of great privation which was relieved mainly by the charitable activities of private associations. The Central Relief Committee of the Society of Friends and the British Relief Association were the most important of these bodies, but there were many smaller societies which helped to bridge the gap. The Society of Friends proposed to help districts which suffered badly during this interval, if the relief commission would undertake half of the expense, but the commission declined. Nevertheless the Friends, with their limited resources which they gathered by appeals to the United States of America and to their English co-religionists, gave great assistance. The British Relief Association agents throughout the country helped local committees to purchase boilers and encouraged them in their efforts to introduce the new scheme. Their agent in north Connacht gave prizes to the relief committees which put the scheme into operation soonest.[22] Once the new plan of relief was in operation, the British Relief Association curtailed its activities, but the Quakers continued to be very active throughout the summer months and gave grants of from £3,000 to £7,000 weekly to assist the poor.

The system extended gradually throughout the country. In May, 777,884 daily rations were issued free by local committees, while almost 50,000 persons bought rations. On June 5, 2,729,684 persons received rations and of these 107,000 were purchasers. This number continued to rise, and by the middle of August over 3,000,000 persons received food at the government soup kitchens each day.[23] The total amount advanced by the relief commissioners was £1,724,631. These loans were to be repaid in full from the current local rates as the lords of the treasury did not wish to extend the period of repayment lest anticipating the rates would make the local support of the poor in the succeeding years more difficult. Scarcely any of the loans were repaid, however, during the progress of the relief scheme except small sums from Baltinglass, Dundalk and Dunshaughlin.[24]

The success of the soup kitchens depended largely on the continued charity of individuals. Many landowners, though greatly impoverished by the inability of their tenants to pay their

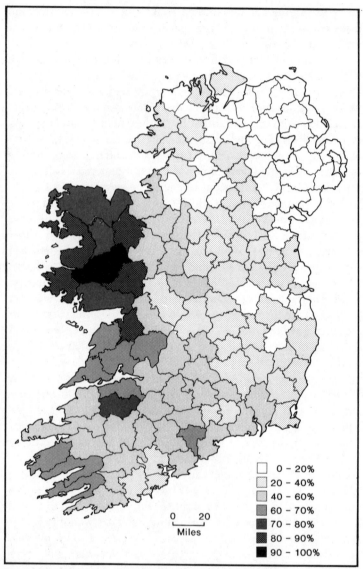

| | |
|---|---|
| ☐ | 0 – 20% |
| ⬚ | 20 – 40% |
| ▨ | 40 – 60% |
| ▩ | 60 – 70% |
| ▦ | 70 – 80% |
| ▧ | 80 – 90% |
| ■ | 90 – 100% |

0    20
Miles

Percentage of the Population on Food Rations in July 1847

FIGURE 1.

*Map showing the numbers receiving rations in each poor law union in Ireland in July 1847 as a percentage of the population in the 1841 census.*

rents, assisted them in every possible way and denied themselves all luxuries during the crisis. On them fell the burden of work on local committees, as well as the duty of subscribing to the funds of the local bodies. They were frequently poor law guardians, and large estates sometimes extended into several relief districts and multiplied the calls on the owner's time and income. The non-residence of many landowners made the position of the resident landlords more difficult ; though they supported the tenants on their own estates they were still liable for assessment for the maintenance of the poor of the estates of absentee neighbours. Many landlords acted as local almoners, wrote petitions to benevolent societies and met daily many persons begging for assistance. As one Quaker visitor wrote from Belmullet in May 1847 :

> I would greatly prefer being a donor to being a distributor of relief. It is much easier for a man to put his hand into his purse, than to labour from morning to night in filling out stirabout to crowds of half-clad, hungry people sinking with weakness and fever. Between today and yesterday, I saw the corpses of a girl, a man and an old woman who died of hunger. This day I saw a woman sinking into a faint, while I was giving out relief at Pullathomas to some peculiarly wretched families. I saw thousands today of the most miserable people I have ever seen. . . . It is difficult for any but an eye-witness to form a correct idea of the position of the handful of persons in this miserable country who are properly qualified for the distribution of grants. Placed in the midst of a starving and mendicant population, whom . . . they are unable to supply with enough even to support nature, they are liable to continual charges of unfairness, partiality, indifference or want of judgement. It should be remembered that those who thus labour for the poor do so at a great sacrifice of time and trouble, and are in continual danger of being attacked by the pestilence which rages around them.[25]

The danger from disease was indeed the greatest trial which all who assisted the poor had to suffer. Though the soup-kitchen scheme did gradually, as it extended, meet the problem of starvation in the summer of 1847, fever had got a grip of the population and endangered the lives of all who came in contact with it. Though

death by starvation decreased during this period, the actual death
rate from disease increased.

The success of the soup-kitchen scheme was helped by the fact
that cargoes of food began to arrive in quantity from February
onwards. In the months after the harvest of 1846 there had been
slight imports while Irish corn was exported. The government
refused to interfere but, nevertheless, the exports were smaller
than in normal years. With the new year, the balance of trade was
in the opposite direction and during the ten months from 1 September 1846 to 1 July 1847 wheat imports were five times as great
as the exports. The import of Indian corn and meal was three
times as large as the total Irish export of cereals. Oats was the major
item exported in large quantities but the amount exported was not
as large as the total imports of wheat. It is anomalous, however,
that there should have been any food exported while people in the
country died of starvation. The prohibition of export would not,
of itself, have solved the problem but the food in the country
after the harvest would have been sufficient to tide the people
over the months which elapsed before importation on a large scale
could take place. The British government was subject to too many
political forces to take such a step. Committed in England to a
free trade policy, Russell was unable, even if he willed it, to take
the step of cutting off the Irish harvest of grain from the English
market. He, and his advisers, were also cognisant of the danger
of causing a shortage of food in England by supplying the needs
of Ireland.[26]

The quantities, in tons, of cereals imported and exported
between 1 September 1846 and 1 July 1847 were :

|              | Exports | Imports |              | Exports | Imports |
|--------------|---------|---------|--------------|---------|---------|
|              |         |         | Wheatmeal    |         |         |
| Wheat        | 18,169  | 96,495  | and flour    | 12,743  | 62,843  |
| Barley       | 8,990   | 24,698  | Barleymeal   | —       | 2,575   |
| Oats         | 102,938 | 8,353   | Oatmeal      | 7,814   | 3,377   |
| Indian Corn  | —       | 391,505 | Indianmeal   | —       | 37,935  |

### V. POOR LAW RELIEF, 1847–52

The temporary relief measures of Peel and Russell in 1846
and 1847 did not replace the poor law system during those years.
Despite the fact that it was difficult to collect rates, many applicants
for assistance were accommodated in the workhouses. In

September 1846, Lord John Russell advised the lord lieutenant, Lord Bessborough, to make more use of the poor law relief facilities than had been made in the previous season.[1] As a result, the workhouses became seriously overcrowded in the following winter when the public works scheme failed. On 23 January 1847, there were 108,487 persons in the Irish workhouses which had been built to accommodate 100,480.[2] This overcrowding was mainly felt in the establishments in the south and west of the country and ninety-three of the one hundred and thirty workhouses contained more inmates than they were built to contain.[3] Kanturk workhouse originally erected with a maximum capacity of 800 had 1,653 inmates and was probably the worst example of overcrowding, but in practically all the workhouses there was overcrowding in some sections.[4] The policy pursued under the soup-kitchen act of allowing local committees to refuse assistance to the poor until the institutions were full helped to keep them crowded throughout the summer of 1847.

To alleviate the overcrowding, boards of guardians were encouraged to erect temporary sheds for the poor or to hire local buildings suitable for conversion into an auxiliary workhouse.[5] Such expedients, though helping to relieve congestion, created new problems for there was an insufficient stock of bedding. A Quaker visitor to one workhouse described the scene :

> In the bedrooms we entered there was not a mattress of any kind to be seen ; the floors were strewed with a little dirty straw, and the poor creatures were thus *littered* down as close together as might be, in order to get the largest possible number under one miserable rug—in some cases six children, for blankets we did not see. . . . In a corner of one of the day rooms, with nothing but a little dirty straw between the damp stone floor, and a rug to cover him, lay a poor old man, whose emaciated form and sunken, death-like features told that his sufferings were near a close.[6]

A government inspector sent to Lurgan workhouse in February 1847 by the board of health found, in one section of the building, but 76 cubic feet allowed to each inmate and that as many as four persons shared a bed. The inspector reported that

> the supply of clothes was quite inadequate, and that it had hence become necessary to use the linen of some of those who had died

of fever and dysentery, without time having been afforded to
have it washed and dried ; and that, from the same cause, damp
beds had in many instances been made use of.[7]

A permanent change in the Irish poor law system was made by an
act passed in June 1847.[8]  It was planned that the temporary system
of relief should be replaced and that the poor law should be made
pliable enough to allow of its meeting extraordinary periods of
poverty.   Hitherto the supervision of the Irish poor law had
rested in the British poor law commissioners who delegated their
authority to assistants.   In August 1847 a separate commission was
established for Ireland, and Edward Twistleton, an English poor law
commissioner who had been sent to Ireland in November 1845, was
appointed chief commissioner.   With him were associated the chief
and the under secretaries, Sir William M. Somerville and T. N.
Redington, and in them was vested the control of the whole poor
law organisation in Ireland.   Subject to the sanction of the lord
lieutenant, they issued rules for the operation of the relief system.[9]
In 1849, Twistleton resigned and was replaced by Alfred Power,
who had previously been an assistant commissioner.[10]
    The administrative units for poor relief were poor law unions.
Under the 1838 act the unions varied in size and those in the west
were usually the largest.   As a result, some districts were as much
as forty miles from the nearest workhouse.   The new commission
found it necessary to have the union boundaries reorganised and in
1848 the number of unions was increased from 130 to 163.[11]   To
supervise these, the commissioners were empowered to appoint
inspectors.   Ten persons were appointed in permanent posts but,
because of the continuation of the distress after the harvest of 1847,
it was found necessary to nominate temporary inspectors.   The
persons selected for these positions in 1847 had been inspecting
officers under the temporary relief schemes.   These officers
examined the accounts and administration of the unions, and
reported incompetence and maladministration to the commission.
They also kept the commissioners informed of the conditions and
prospects of their districts.[12]   At the end of 1848, the commissioners
instituted enquiries through the inspectors on the pawning of
clothes,[13] and these officials also assisted in the organisation of a
British Relief Association scheme for feeding school-children in
the most distressed poor law unions from west Cork to Donegal.

In March 1848, over 200,000 children were receiving food under this scheme.[14] Normally, each inspector had charge of a single union, but in a few instances controlled two districts.[15]

Local control over the poor law was exercised by boards of guardians. The commission in Dublin decided what number of elected guardians should be on each board, and laid down a property qualification ranging from £10 to £30 for candidates for election. The electors were the ratepayers and they had votes in proportion to the rateable valuation of their property. The elections were annual and took place in March. Justices of the peace were *ex officio* guardians but, under the 1847 act, these were not allowed to exceed the number of elected guardians. Nevertheless, the result of the system was to ensure that landlords had a majority on practically all the boards.[16] There were usually two meetings of each board of guardians weekly. At one the general business of the union was attended to, and at the other the poor were admitted to relief. The *ex officio* members were more active at the first meeting, while those elected took greater interest in the actual granting of assistance.[17] These were sometimes subject to external influence and occasionally succeeded in establishing claims to relief for themselves.[18]

When boards of guardians were incompetent or neglected their duties, the commission was empowered to dissolve them and appoint paid vice-guardians. Remissness in striking a rate, taking proceedings against defaulters or attendance at meetings were usually followed by a notice of dissolution.[19] The vice-guardians were unpopular but efficient and succeeded in putting affairs in order. These paid officials were occasionally in charge of as many as three unions at the same time.[20] Between August 1847 and March 1848, thirty-three boards were dissolved and replaced by vice-guardians. A further six boards were suspended in the following twelve months. Thus, through most of 1848 and 1849, about one-quarter of the unions in Ireland, mainly in the west, were administered by paid officials.[21]

The finances of the boards of guardians were derived from local rates on property. The burden of the rates was shared equally between the landlords and the tenants on property of £4 or more rateable valuation. In the smaller holdings the tenants were exempt and the landlord had to pay the full rates.[22] Collectors were appointed by the guardians, subject to the approval of the commission, and they received a poundage on their receipts. They had the power of distraint on goods on rateable property and were most unpopular.[23]   One collector in Fermanagh was murdered and it became extremely difficult to induce persons to undertake the duties.  In Castlebar, 2s. 6d. in the pound had to be given before any-one would fill the post.[24]   Collectors were frequently very harsh in their treatment of ratepayers.  They seized far in excess of the rates due and at Feakle, co. Limerick, ratepayers whose property was distrained actually died of starvation.[25]   In general, the financial position of the boards was in a perilous state from 1846 to 1849. Guardians' cheques were dishonoured and contractors refused to supply food or clothing to workhouses.  In Castlerea while the rate collector was distraining for rates, the sheriff was seizing in the workhouse for the debts of the union.[26]

The government, through the poor law commissioners, had to give assistance from 1847 to 1849 to the distressed unions to keep the relief system in operation.[27]   The British Relief Association, after the harvest of 1848, also helped in this way and gave grants totalling £145,253 in the following nine months.[28]   In May 1849, an act was passed to allow the poor law commission to levy a rate of 6d. in the pound on all rateable property in Ireland to assist the insolvent unions in the west.  In 1850, a levy of 2d. in the pound was made and the income from these levies, £409,468, placed the poorer unions in a stronger financial position.[29]   The treasury in 1850 also advanced loans totalling £300,000 to liquidate the debts of many unions.  The rate-in-aid clearly showed the attitude of the government to Ireland.  If the political union of 1800 were complete, the rate-in-aid should have been levied not on Ireland alone but on England, Scotland and Wales as well.  The justice of objections to making each locality responsible for its own poor was admitted by the levy on wealthier unions in Ireland.  This was a departure from the principles laid down by Lord John Russell's administration but the logical conclusion of levying on Britain was not accepted.

Under the earlier poor law, the person who examined applications for relief and acted as liaison officer between the guardians and the poor was the warden.  He was a part-time official but under the reform of 1847 he was replaced by a full-time relieving officer in each union.  These received salaries ranging between £30 and £40 per annum and had to give security for the performance of their duties.[30]   They attended meetings of the boards of guardians and received applications for assistance. In urgent cases they were authorised to give provisional orders for admission to the workhouse or to allow outdoor relief temporarily. Normally, however, they had to submit reports on applications to the boards of guardians who gave the ultimate decision on the assistance to be given.[31] Their powers, particularly of allowing provisional relief, were very salutary but a few of them exercised this discretion in their own favour and were guilty of embezzling money and diverting food to their own use.[32]

The most important change in the principles underlying poor relief in Ireland brought about by the 1847 act was the recognition of the right of the destitute to support. Under the original statute of 1838, the guardians were allowed to support the poor but the 1847 amendment laid it down ' that the guardians of the poor of every union in Ireland shall make provision for the due relief of all . . . destitute poor persons '.[33] This brought the Irish system into closer conformity with the English scheme, but a legal title to relief did not provide food to the starving, and made little real difference to the treatment of the poor.

Of great immediate importance was the amendment which allowed, under certain conditions, the granting of relief to the poor not resident in workhouses. These establishments continued to be seriously overcrowded in the years after 1847. The peak was reached in 1849 when 932,284 persons were maintained for some period in the workhouses. In the meantime, too, accommodation was extended. In March 1847 the maximum number of inmates which the workhouses could contain at one time was 114,129, but four years later this total had been raised to 308,885.

The routine discipline in the poorhouses was severe. Smoking, drinking of intoxicants, card-playing or games of chance were prohibited. Visitors were allowed in some places only on one day a week, and then saw the inmates in the presence of the master, matron or porter.[34] The dietaries were bad and in practically all areas compared unfavourably with those of the nearest gaol. There were normally but two meals daily, and the poor frequently committed crimes to get transferred to gaol.[35] The inmates were provided with employment, mainly stonebreaking for the men and spinning, sewing and knitting for the women. In some places even the women were made break stones and in December 1848 the picking of coir was introduced as a task suitable for the poor.[36]

Young girls found sufficient employment in domestic duties in the institutions and boys were sometimes assigned to stonebreaking.[37] In 1849, boards of guardians were allowed to purchase farms not exceeding twenty-five acres to provide agricultural training for boys under sixteen years of age. Adults were not allowed to work on these farms as the poor law commissioners felt that it would make residence in the workhouse less irksome for them if they were allowed to work outside the enclosure.[38]

Most of the workhouses had schools attached to them, but the education imparted was usually of the lowest standard. The schoolmaster at Lowtherstown admitted that 'he was no great hand at writing' and there seems reasonable doubt as to his ability at reading and arithmetic. Of one workhouse school, visitors wrote :

> We found about eighty boys and sixty or seventy girls in the schoolrooms, but there was no paid schoolmaster or mistress, and no books whatever ; and a poor miserable looking man on one side, and a bare-footed woman on the other, each whip in hand, were endeavouring to keep their squalid charge in order.[39]

Despite rules governing religious observance and the appointment of chaplains, cases of immorality in the workhouses were common. This was partly due to the disorganisation caused by overcrowding, which made impossible the enforcement of regulations regarding segregation of the sexes. In Ballinrobe a boy of sixteen years of age shared a ward with four adult females.[40] Cases of immorality between porters, female attendants and the poor were frequent, and Dr John Derry, Catholic bishop of Clonfert diocese, said that to his knowledge one woman with an adolescent daughter refused to go to a workhouse because of the moral dangers involved.[41]

The prison-like discipline and the treatment of the poor like criminals gave the workhouse system an unpopular character which lasted through succeeding generations. The poor were allowed to leave the workhouse on giving three hours' notice to the master provided that no person left without taking his dependents.[42] In one instance at least, a man who left Loughrea, because of the prohibition of smoking, died of starvation within ten days,[43] and others preferred death to entering these institutions.[44] Admission to a workhouse did not, of itself, guarantee against death, for the overcrowded conditions caused great danger from fever, which was rampant. The death rate was highest in April 1847, when one-fortieth of the inmates in Irish workhouses died in one week.[45] After this, there was a fairly steady decline, though in June 1848 five carpenters were daily employed in Scariff workhouse making coffins.[46] By 1850 the death rate had been reduced to normal proportions though at the time an outbreak of ophthalmia was widespread in the workhouses.[47]

Under the provisions of the poor law amendment act of 1847, boards of guardians were allowed to give assistance outside the workhouse to destitute persons who were permanently disabled by old age, infirmity or bodily or mental defect. Those permanently deprived of the means of earning a subsistence by reason of severe illness or serious accident, and poor widows with two or more legitimate dependent children, were also eligible. Others could be assisted only in the workhouse unless the poor law commissioners issued an order extending the classes to whom outdoor aid could be given. Before such an order was issued for any poor law union it had to be shown that adequate relief could not be provided by the workhouse and a special meeting of the board of guardians had to be convened to request the commission to grant the extension.[48] The orders issued generally allowed only slight increases in the classes eligible for home assistance. Widows with one child were first allowed and later able-bodied men with dependent families, according as the need arose in various unions.[49] In Ballinasloe all classes except unmarried men qualified, and in Ballinrobe the right was extended to everybody.[50] This right was also allowed in areas where there was an outbreak of contagious disease in the work-houses.[51] During the last few months of 1847 and the whole of 1848, an extension of the classes receiving outdoor relief was sanctioned in seventy of the one hundred and thirty Irish poor law unions.

Work was provided for the able-bodied on outdoor relief, mainly breaking stones,[52] and labourers were divided into three classes according to their health and to the amount of stones they were expected to break daily.[53] Eight hours work was the minimum required and overseers on each working party called a roll at 8 a.m. 1 p.m. and 5 p.m. In inclement weather the roll was called but no work was done.[54] These overseers issued tickets for rations to the workers who were to be supplied, according to the act, with food only.[55] The commissioners ruled that this food should be issued cooked but this was never fully carried out because workers could not carry cooked food long distances to their dependents and keep it edible. In May 1849 in only two of the thirty-one unions which employed labourers outside the workhouse was cooked food alone issued. In six others some cooked and some uncooked food was given. In twenty-three unions all food issued was raw.[56] The food issued was not in proportion to the work done, as married men received rations for themselves and their families while single men got sufficient only for themselves.[57] The usual amounts given were one pound of Indian meal to an adult and a half-pound to a child under twelve years of age.

Parsimonious guardians and vice-guardians kept the rations as low as possible, and despite the recommendations of the board of health that one pound twelve ounces of meal be given to each adult, the amounts were not increased.[58] Several instances occurred of persons receiving rations dying of starvation.[59] In some areas the least excuse was sufficient to enable guardians or officials to strike the poor off the relief lists. The vice-guardians at Ennistymon took this step with those who were injudicious enough to look healthy.[60] In one instance a magistrate had to intervene to prevent a woman from being removed from the relief lists because it came to light at the inquest on her starved brother that she gave a few spoonfuls of her ration to his children.[61]

The horrors of the winter of 1846 to 1847 were re-enacted in the two winters which followed. Persons refused relief for one reason or another were later found dead from starvation, or else, demented, attempted suicide.[62] Burials without coffins were again common. Horse and ass flesh was eaten in counties Galway and Roscommon.[63] Dogs fed on the corpses of the dead and the dogs, in turn, were eaten by the starving people.[64] Crime increased under the stress of hunger. Girls were driven to prostitution[65] and attacks on property were frequent. Ships off the west coast were plundered by fishermen who went as far as ten miles from the coast to board the ships.[66] In defence of one sheep stealer, a resident magistrate gave sworn testimony that the man's wife was so deranged with hunger that she had eaten the flesh off the legs of one of her own children dead with fever.[67]

Evictions added greatly to the distress during these years and they were stimulated by the poor law system. Landlords were liable for all the rates on holdings and cabins of less than £4 valuation, and many preferred to have the cabins eliminated than to have to pay the rates. Even if in cases of distress a landlord remitted the tenant's rent, he was still liable for that tenant's poor rates. To avoid the rates, the cabin had to be pulled down.[68] The 1847 amendment of the poor law included a notorious provision, inserted at the suggestion of William Gregory, M.P. for Dublin city, known as the ' quarter acre clause ' which increased the number of evictions. In March 1847, *The Times* had advocated such a clause which excluded from relief all who held more than one rood of ground.[69] It was foreseen that this would result in great hardship[70] and landlord guardians operated the system so as to clear the smallholders from their estates. Between November 1847 and the following June one thousand houses were levelled in Kilrush union and six thousand notices to quit were served on tenants.[71]

In some areas the boards of guardians insisted on applying the workhouse test to all applicants for relief. They insisted that the family enter the workhouse for a period and then they would be put on the outdoor relief lists and allowed to go home. In the meantime, advantage was taken of their absence to have their cabins levelled. Occasionally, having succeeded in getting the family out of their house, the guardians withdrew the assistance which they had granted.[72] Many of the poor clung to their holdings despite the utmost privations, and even suffered death rather than relinquish their homes. This was partly due to the fact that some landlords, to clear their estates, helped tenants to emigrate. If they left their tenancy to obtain relief, the landlord had no further interest in paying their passage to America or Australia.[73] In May 1848, the poor law commissioners authorised boards of guardians to give some assistance to the families of men who refused to give up their holdings, but the landlords on the boards strongly opposed this ruling and in many places refused to act on it.[74]

Opinions varied on the effect of the Gregory clause. Aubrey de Vere, the philanthropic poet, believed that it was useful, though it had operated harshly,[75] while Catholic clergy protested several times against it.[76] Two parliamentary committees, one of the lords and the other of the commons, sat during the first half of 1849 to inquire into the operation of the Irish poor law. The lords committee suggested that the quarter acre clause be clarified,[77]

while the commons committee thought that the poor law commission should be given power to suspend it.[78]  The clause was not
modified, however, until 1862, when holders of more than one
rood of land were allowed relief but only within the workhouse.[79]

An indication of the length of the continuance of famine
conditions may be found in the numbers on outdoor relief.  Despite
their eagerness to end the system the poor law commissioners
had to allow extensions of outdoor relief until October 1849.
The maximum number receiving aid outside the workhouses under
the poor law was reached in July 1848 when 833,889 persons were
on the relief lists.  Twelve months later there was a slight decrease
to 784,367.  The increase in workhouse accommodation and the
gradual improvement of conditions caused a great reduction in 1850
when the maximum number assisted was 148,909.  By 1851 this
had fallen to 19,979 and in the following years seldom exceeded
4,000 persons.  The decrease was much slower in west Munster
than in Connacht, so that on 23 February 1850, while the total
numbers on outdoor relief was 148,909, over 100,000 of these were
in Munster and less than 20,000 in Connacht.[80]

The effect on the consolidation of estates during the famine was
probably the most important aspect of the poor laws.  In 1841
there were 573,153 holdings greater than one acre and less than
fifteen acres.  A decade later this number was reduced to 279,937.
By far the greatest amount of reduction took place in the holdings
of between one and five acres.  In 1841 there were 310,375 such
tenancies whereas in 1851 there were but 88,083.  Smallholders,
who before the famine had the social status of farmers, were
practically wiped out.  Many had emigrated or died, but many
more were reduced to the ranks of day labourers and helped to
swell the figures of holdings of under one acre which increased
between 1841 and 1851.[81]


## VI.  CONCLUSION

The failure of the government to cope with famine conditions
was reflected in the census report of 1851.  In 1847, 6,058 deaths
were attributed to starvation, and between 1846 and 1851 the
number of recorded hunger victims was 21,770.  Hundreds of
thousands died from fever, dysentery and other famine diseases.

While in these cases starvation was not the immediate cause of death, it was frequently a contributory factor. It was calculated that the natural increase between 1841 and 1851 should have resulted in a population of over 9,000,000. Actually the census returns showed that the population in 1851 was but 6,552,385 persons. This was two millions less than the estimated population in 1845. Emigration accounted for just over one million of the loss but the rest was due to deaths.[1]

In September 1846, Trevelyan wrote to Stephen Spring-Rice :

> The poorest and most ignorant Irish peasant must, I think, by this time, have become sensible of the advantage of belonging to a powerful community like that of the United Kingdom, the establishments and pecuniary resources of which are at all times ready to be employed for his benefit. At any rate, the repeal of the union will not be seriously demanded while so large a proportion of the Irish people are receiving union wages and eating union meal.[2]

Less than a year passed before a bewildered Lord Palmerston wrote to Lord John Russell regarding the results of a general election :

> I see that almost all the Irish elections have gone in favour of repeal candidates ; and this just after two or three millions of Irish have been saved from famine and pestilence by money which if the union had not existed, their own parliament would never have been able to raise. This is not natural.[3]

Perhaps it was natural that the Irish who survived should remember those who died and that they felt that the resources of the British empire were not used for the benefit of Ireland.

Most of the money expended by the governments in Ireland for relief was to be repaid. The total cost of the wasteful public works of autumn 1846, almost £4,500,000, was to be repaid, but one half of this was remitted in 1848.[4] Debts arising out of the soup kitchen scheme totalled almost £1,000,000. These were to be repaid in various ways, some immediately out of poor rates and others over periods ranging from ten to twenty years, out of county cess. In 1850 these were consolidated into a single debt. Previously, of the £8,111,941 expended by the treasury for famine relief, over £500,000 had been repaid, and a further

£3,722,255 was to be repaid over a period of forty years with interest at 3½ per cent.[5] Because of the continued poverty in Ireland, even these repayments could not be made, and further postponements had to be allowed.[6] In 1853, in his first budget speech, William Ewart Gladstone announced that the debt would be completely remitted and that instead duties on spirits would be imposed and income tax would be extended to Ireland.[7]

This was not well received in Ireland. The newspapers were practically unanimous in their condemnation of the change which was received as a boon only in those areas which had the largest rate of repayment under the annuities acts, and the least liabilities under the income tax scheme. Those who benefited most from the change were the new landowners who, under the encumbered estates act, had purchased farms cheaply because of the famine debts and now had some of these debts removed.[8]

Any comparison between the policies of Peel and Russell is made difficult by the difference in the extent of the problem faced by each. The potato disease in 1845 did not, as in the following year, wipe out the whole crop. Scarcity was not felt, in that first season, until the spring, and the problem facing Peel was much less than that which his successor had to meet. There are, however, points of contrast between the policies pursued. Peel brought food into the country and helped to control prices in all parts of it by judicious sales in areas where prices tended to rise. To keep prices down he allowed food to be sold at less than cost price at government depots. Russell, on the other hand, closed depots in the east of Ireland and supplied food only in the west. Even there the price was pinned to what was being charged locally, though the market might have been cornered by a monopolist. From the beginning, too, Peel's administration paid one half of the cost of relief works out of central funds, whereas Russell made the total cost a local one and remitted the repayments only when it became impossible to collect them. Peel and Sir James Graham were more independent of the economic theories of the time than were Russell and the whigs,[9] but if faced with the greater problem, it is impossible to say that Peel would have been any more successful.

Both parties suffered from the fact that they ruled Ireland from Westminster. They were committed to a free trade policy and dared not interfere with the food which was exported from Ireland.

Russell was particularly cognisant of the danger of creating shortage nearest his own door, and wrote to the duke of Leinster, ' Any attempt to feed one class of the United Kingdom by the Government would, if successful, starve another part '.[10] The extent of the exports has frequently been exaggerated, but it was anomalous that any food should have been exported while the people starved. A prohibition of export was probably essential in the autumn of 1846 to bridge the period until food could be imported from America. Neither party could, however, cut off Irish supplies from England after repealing the corn laws to provide cheaper food. The fetish of free trade had tied their hands. Such a policy, too, of prohibiting food exports from Ireland would have raised great problems. If exportation had not been allowed, the government would have had to ensure that the corn was not held back by farmers or speculators but reached the open market. Generous financial aid too would have been needed, so that the poor could buy the food. So simple an expedient as closing the ports would not have solved these problems and neither would it have provided a full year's supply of food for the population.

The adoption of a *laissez-faire* policy in nineteenth-century England often concealed an admission that a problem was insoluble or that it must be endured because nobody could think of a method of solving it.[11] The Irish crisis was allowed to develop because no English party saw a solution in the generation after the Napoleonic wars. The population increased but the country's resources were not improved to keep pace in production. The famine came to cut a Gordian knot of disparity between production and population by reducing the latter. Indicative of the *laissez-faire* approach to the question was Trevelyan's letter to Lord Monteagle in October 1846 :

> This [problem] being altogether beyond the power of man, the cure had been applied by the direct stroke of an all-wise Providence in a manner as unexpected and as unthought of as it is likely to be effectual.[12]

It was effectual only in reducing the population but not in increasing production in the country.

In his account of the famine, written in 1848, Trevelyan maintained that the government adopted a policy ' to stimulate the industry of the people, to augment the productive powers of the soil, and to promote the establishment of new industrial occupations so as to cause the land once more to support its population, and to substitute a higher standard of subsistence, and a higher tone of popular character, for those which prevailed before '.[13]

Yet herein lies the greatest failure of the administration, for Trevelyan's assertion is no more than wishful thinking. Ireland's debts were increased but the famine brought no stimulus to old industries and did not develop new ones. The government relief schemes had no long term purpose and even in their immediate aim were not particularly successful.

Far greater foresight was shown by charitable organisations, particularly the Quakers, in their relief efforts. Much of their charity had, perforce, to be directed to immediate relief of the starving, but, nevertheless, attention was directed to improving fishing methods and establishing clothing manufacturing. When the extreme distress of early 1847 had passed, the Quakers purchased and operated a demonstration farm in county Galway to improve agriculture.[14]

Individual efforts, or even those of associations, made little impression on the economic structure of Ireland, yet the sacrifices made on behalf of the starving people were inspiring. When every visitor to a cabin risked death from fever, the heroism of those who undertook the distribution of food for the Central Relief Committee or the British Relief Association, or countless smaller societies, was admirable. Resident landlords and their families, clergymen of all persuasions, doctors and innumerable others played a noble part. That these efforts should have been marred by the missionary zeal of a minority of clergymen, mainly of the established church, who sought to use the hunger of the poor to purchase souls has had a regrettable influence in wiping out the memory of private charity. This attempt on the Catholic religion was confined mainly to Connemara, west Kerry and a district on the Tipperary-Limerick border. It met with limited and very temporary success, but it served to undermine the goodwill which the charity of the single-minded had engendered. Because of the religious purpose of a few, the people distrusted all charity.[15]

The government officials, too, throughout the country ran serious risks and many died of fever contracted in the discharge of their duties, while others had to retire because of ill-health. They were seriously overworked, but gallantly endeavoured to bring the best possible result from the schemes laid down for them by the government. Trevelyan, at the treasury, despite the faults in the plans he evolved, worked unceasingly while Routh, in particular, in Dublin spent twelve or fourteen hours daily organising and administering the relief operations. He was an able but rather unimaginative administrator who was willing to accept and operate all Trevelyan's orders as if they were his own. That the plans were a failure was not his fault.

Edmund Burke, in his *Thoughts and details on scarcity,* had propounded the view that, in periods of food shortage, government should not interfere with trade. This was the principle which motivated Lord John Russell's ministry in dealing with Ireland ; but Burke had gone on to state that if the calamity was so great as to threaten actual famine, the poor should not be abandoned to the flinty heart and gripping hand of base self-interest but passed into charity beyond the rules of commerce. The British government treated the Irish crisis as if it came within the definition of ' scarcity ' rather than ' famine '. In all official correspondence and speeches, the more euphemistic term ' distress ' is used, instead of ' famine ', and the policy followed was that laid down for a minor rather than a major crisis.[16]

In spite of the loss of life, Trevelyan could still, in 1848, refer to the famine as ' local distress '.[17] He had emerged from the crisis without any greater understanding of how to deal with a similar situation than he had in 1845.

> There is only one way [he said] in which the relief of the destitute ever has been, or ever will be, conducted consistently with the general welfare, and that is by *making it a local charge.*[18]

Sir Charles was later to spend many years in the Indian service and recurring famines in Behar, Madras and Bengal may have caused him to revise his opinions, for, a famine code was developed which admitted the responsibility of the state in saving life. Neither the duty nor the cost could be passed on to local proprietors.[19] Had such a code been formulated before 1845, the Irish famine might have been more capably countered.

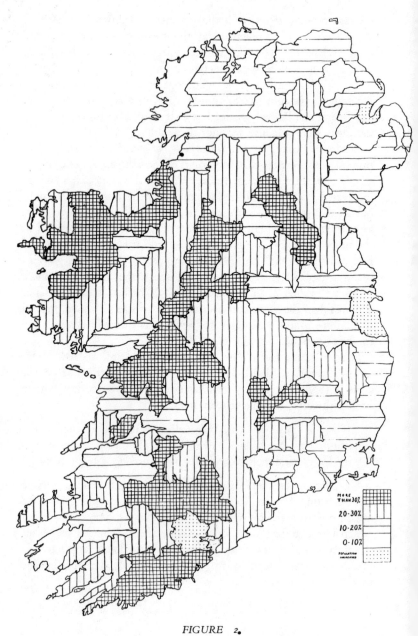

MORE
THAN 30%

20-30%

10-20%

0-10%

POPULATION
INCREASED

FIGURE 2.

*Map showing percentage decline in population, 1841 to 1851.*

# MEDICAL HISTORY OF THE FAMINE
By Sir William P. MacArthur.

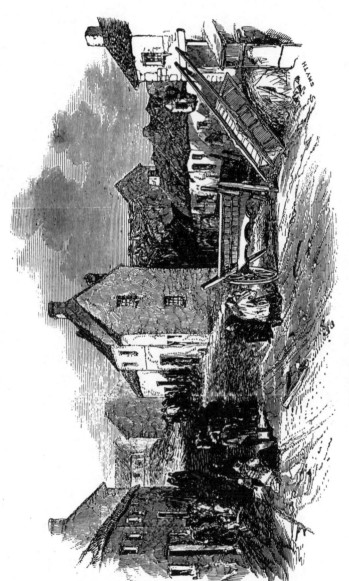

FAMINE FUNERAL, SKIBBEREEN.

*Illustrated London News*, 1847.

# CHAPTER V

# Medical History of the Famine

## I. INTRODUCTION

OVER a period of many centuries recurring famines were the lot of European countries, sometimes limited in their range, sometimes so widespread that men declared that the hand of God was lifted against the people of Christendom. In early Ireland, famine conditions seem to have resulted mainly from loss of animal stock, due to prolonged bad weather and to heavy outbreaks of epizootic disease. Thus, a great mortality of cattle is recorded in Ireland in A.D. 699 and 700, with an accompanying famine so terrible ' that man would eat man '. With this came a famine pestilence, as would be surmised even if it were not recorded. To cite a later example : the very severe winter of 1115 caused great destruction of cattle ' whereof grew great dearth throughout Ireland '. The famine brought in its train the usual pestilence which raged ' so that it desolated churches and strongholds and districts, and spread throughout Ireland and oversea and caused destruction to an inconceivable degree '.[1]

During the same period England suffered in a similar way, but as economic and social standards improved, there was no longer a large proportion of the population living at such a level that a poor harvest could precipitate a general famine. Local shortages with outbreaks of fever occurred, but widespread famines and famine fevers like those of 1087, 1196, 1258 and 1315, came to an end. Moreover, English wars after the Norman conquest involved mainly the nobles and their levies ; there were no great invading armies to spread destruction and famine far and wide. Even the civil war between king and parliament left the general life of the countryside but little disturbed.

It was otherwise in Ireland.  Here from the Norman invasion onwards, wars of conquest, internal turbulence, confiscations, and penal enactments combined to check a similar economic advance ; and finally, over-population called on the soil to bear a burden beyond its capacity.  As late as the middle of the nineteenth century large numbers of the Irish peasantry lived in a deplorable state of poverty, weighed down by rents that competition had forced to a level far above the value of the holdings.  Not even in favourable years could the small-holders accumulate reserves of money, stock, or food sufficient to carry them through the lean years that were sure to follow.  Apart from local shortages of food, more or less severe, dreadful famines broke out, for example, in 1739, 1800, 1816 and 1845, involving the whole country in their disastrous effects.  The predisposing causes of these calamities were constant, but the exciting cause was not always the same.  That of 1816 resulted from prolonged cold and wet weather so that the unripened potatoes rotted in the ground, and the corn was still green when winter began ; the distress was heightened by the unemployment and agricultural depression which followed the temporary prosperity associated with the Napoleonic war.  On the other hand, the cause of the famine of 1845–50 was a fungus disease of the potato due to *Phytophthora infestans* which appears in the form of black spots on the leaves, with, on the under surface, a whitish mould containing the spores.  These are conveyed to other plants by wind, rain and insects.  The fungus is checked by dry weather, but flourishes in profusion when the weather is warm and damp.  The resulting catastrophe can be pictured when it is remembered that the potato was almost the sole food of about one-third of the population, and a main article of diet of a much larger number.  Three classes who depended on the potato for their existence were : occupiers of cabins with small holdings of from one to five acres ; cottiers living on the land of farmers for whom they worked, occupying a cabin with a small plot of ground of from one rood to a half or one acre ; and labourers who had no fixed employment and no land, living in hovels and hiring yearly a scrap of land from some farmer.

On the heels of every famine, however provoked, there came an epidemic of fever which broke out with such regularity that its advent was confidently predicted when the famine began. This close association was expressed in the dictum ' No famine,

no fever ', so vigorously proclaimed by Corrigan. Here ' fever '
did not refer to localised outbreaks or sporadic cases of infection—
these were everyday possibilities—but to a great and rising tide
of pestilence which engulfed the whole country. The prevalent
famine fevers were typhus fever and relapsing fever, and as both
are conveyed by the same agent, the common louse of man, they
were often present together though in differing proportions.

## II. GENERAL DESCRIPTION OF THE DISEASES WHICH BECAME WIDELY EPIDEMIC IN THE FAMINE

Hereafter follows a general description of the diseases—typhus,
relapsing fever, dysentery and scurvy—which became widely
epidemic in 1845–50, intended to give the non-medical reader
some information of their cause, symptoms and course ; and
where helpful, of their earlier history. In the succeeding section,
there is a further account of these diseases as they were actually
experienced during the famine. The only exception to the plan
of description under two heads, as just explained, is famine dropsy.
All that it is neccesary to say of this condition is for convenience
given complete in the second of the two sections.

The causative organisms of typhus are minute bodies which
constitute a species of the group *Rickettsia,* named after Ricketts
who discovered them, and who later died of typhus accidentally
contracted. They show as short rods or dots, measuring about
$\frac{1}{50,000}$ of an inch. Typhus is essentially a disease of the small
blood vessels which are extensively damaged as a result of the
invasion of *Rickettsia*. Those of the brain and the skin are
particularly liable to attack, which explains the delirium and
stupor so prominent a feature of typhus, and the development
of the characteristic spotted rash. The *Rickettsia* swallowed by
the louse with the patient's blood invade the cells which line
the insect's intestine. They multiply inside these cells which
therefore become enormously distended and ultimately burst ;
the organisms thus set free pass out of the intestine with the
insect's faeces, and if meanwhile it has transferred itself to another
host, the *Rickettsia* penetrate the skin, often being inoculated by
scratching, and thus cause infection. Sometimes the invaded
intestinal cells are ruptured by pressure if the louse is crushed

as in the act of scratching. The onset of the attack is less abrupt than in relapsing fever ; the subject shivers and complains of headache and aching pains. The congested face, bloodshot eyes, muscular twitchings, and the stupid mental state give the patient the appearance of drunkenness. About the fifth day the rash comes out, the symptoms are then intensified and the earlier delirium deepens into stupor. In cases of ordinary severity the fever lasts for about 14 days, and may end by a crisis, but less regular and dramatic than that in relapsing fever. Relapse and jaundice are not features of the disease. Although in some outbreaks of relapsing fever the death rate has exceeded seventy per cent, as a rule typhus is a more fatal disease, and in the epidemics of the famine years its death rate in general was three or four times higher than that of relapsing fever ; this difference alone may suffice to indicate which of the two was in greater evidence in any place.

The dusky hue of the skin in typhus suggested the name still heard, at least in Donegal, *fiabhras dubh* (black fever), in contrast to *fiabhras buidhe* (yellow fever) a name for relapsing fever not yet altogether forgotten. So current at one time was the term *fiabhras dubh* that it was used as a malediction by the evil minded, and a true story in this connection is recorded of the famine fever of 1816. A lady refused to listen to a strolling beggar-woman who was importuning her for alms. As she turned away, the beggar cursed her loudly, calling on the ' black fever ' to strike her down. By some coincidence, that same evening the lady sickened with virulent typhus, and died after about a week's illness. Her husband also developed the disease, and died a few days after his wife. All this to the infinite terror and dismay of the superstitious, and no doubt to the profit of the tribe of strolling beggars. In a medical report of 1849, a doctor cited this sequence in support of his belief that an attack of typhus might be induced by a severe mental shock.

The name ' typhus ' (*tuphos,* mist), to describe the clouded mental state, was introduced only in the middle of the 18th century. Other names in earlier use were, spotted fever, gaol fever, camp fever, malignant or putrid fever, etc., and the disease was once included in the term ' ague ', as in *Macbeth* where it stands for famine fever. Writing of Ireland in the Cromwellian wars, Gerard Boate described typhus, under the name ' the malignant feaver', as one of the two reigning diseases of Ireland, dysentery being the other. He says that the malignant fevers are 'vulgarly [popularly] in Ireland called Irish agues, because that at all times they are so common in Ireland as well among the inhabitants [permanent settlers] and the natives, as among those who are newly come thither from other countries'. The 'Irish ague' that paralysed Cromwell's army in Ireland in the winter of 1649 was typhus.

Relapsing fever is due to a spirochaete, a thread-like spiral organism about forty times longer than that of typhus. After being swallowed by the louse, the spirochaetes multiply in the substance of the insect's body—not in the intestinal cells like *Rickettsia*—and are extruded in large numbers on to the host's skin if the insect is crushed or damaged. Infection takes place commonly through the skin. Spirochaetes are found in large numbers in the patient's blood during the fever stage but in the intervals are sparse or absent, and reappear when a relapse takes place. The onset is more sudden than in typhus, and is often accompanied by a violent rigor and severe gastric symptoms— sickness and vomiting—whence the name 'gastric fever' often used during the famine. The fever lasts for several days, most commonly five, and ends by a sharp crisis with profuse sweating and exhaustion. After an interval of about seven days a relapse occurs, and several such may follow before the attack finally ends. In some epidemics jaundice is very common, hence as already mentioned, the once popular name 'yellow fever'. It must be understood that relapsing fever has no connection with yellow fever of the tropics, a mosquito-borne disease.

The earliest example of the name 'relapsing fever' quoted in the *Oxford English dictionary* is dated 1865, but it was in use in Ireland before that date. Dr H. Kennedy (Dublin), writing in 1849, says: 'The relapsing fever varied somewhat in its characters . . .' Dr Reid (Belfast) writes in the same year:

The term synocha has long been used in connection with fever . . . but it has appeared to me desirable to associate it with some word which would form a title as descriptive of it as maculated [spotted] typhus is of another species. I have, therefore, prefixed to it the word Relapsing, which indicates with precision the disease it is applied to.

The equivalent 'relapse fever' was in general use during this epidemic.

In Europe, epidemic typhus and relapsing fever being spread by the same means have always tended to occur together ; and before laboratory diagnosis became possible they were often confused. None the less they may be distinguished in old accounts of famine fevers if there is any mention of sharp crises, relapses, or jaundice, on one hand ; and of rashes, or outstanding brain symptoms, on the other. Clearly one of Hippocrates' clinical descriptions refers to relapsing fever, and it seems certain that the 'yellow pestilence' of the sixth century was this disease. There is clear evidence of relapsing fever occurring along with typhus in the English civil war. Under the name of 'intermittent fever' it is recorded in Ireland, e.g. in 1728 and 1729 when it was epidemic in Dublin, and described as accompanied by 'some of the petechial kind' [typhus]. Rutty the Quaker physician of Dublin gives a clear identification of relapsing fever in the famine which began in 1739 :

> It seems also not unworthy of notice that through the three summer months [June, July and August of 1741] there was frequently here and there a fever altogether without the malignity attending the former [typhus], of six or seven days duration, terminating in a critical sweat, as did the other also frequently, but in this the patients were subject to a relapse, even to a third or fourth time, and yet recovered.

In spite of this, during the famine of 1846 some doctors argued that typhus and relapsing fever are no more than clinical variants of the same infection, pointing out that a patient's illness might begin as 'spotted typhus' and later assume the characters of 'relapse fever', or *vice versa* ; and that in two patients removed together from the same house and even from the same bed, the attack might follow a 'spotted typhus' course in the one and a 'relapsing' course in the other. It is known now that such vagaries are due to the co-existence of both diseases.

Dysentery of the bacillary variety has always been a constant attendant on famine and on war. The disease is caused by one or other of a group of bacilli, transmitted like those of typhoid fever by food, fingers, and flies. After being swallowed they multiply and produce inflammation and ulceration in the intestinal wall, sometimes so intense as to end in gangrene. The bowel discharges swarm with these bacilli and are highly infectious. Bowel colic, painful and exhausting straining, violent diarrhoea with passage of blood, constitute the typical picture. An attack cannot develop except through the agency of the specific bacillus, but anything causing an intestinal upset, unsuitable food for example, predisposes to infection. Dysentery is intensified in virulence by famine and by other exhausting diseases occurring along with it.

The infection has been known in Ireland since ancient times. Thus under the name of *ruith fola* ('bloody flux') it is recorded as widely epidemic in A.D. 763; a king of Connacht died of it in 767. *Teidm tregait* and *pláigh bhuindech* are among the other names used for it in the annals. In the past, no army subjected to the privations of a protracted campaign in Europe could escape the twin plagues of typhus and dysentery; and Gerard Boate writing in a time of war, says that ' the looseness ' (dysentery) is so general in Ireland that the English inhabitants ' have given it the name of the country-disease '—a term used by Cromwell in his despatches from Ireland in commenting on his losses from sickness. Boate gives a warning that if those attacked with ' the looseness ' do not check it ' they do commonly after some days get the bleeding with it . . . and at last it useth to turn to the bloody flux'.

Two non-infectious conditions arising from food deficiencies were rife among the hunger-stricken—scurvy and famine dropsy. Scurvy is caused by lack of vitamin C, contained in fresh vegetables and fruit. In normal times scurvy was absent from Ireland, an eloquent testimony to the anti-scorbutic properties of the potato. Dr Curran (Dublin) writing on this point in 1847 says :

> Millions of peasants in the centre and west of Ireland have lived for years exclusively on potatoes . . . yet scurvy was unknown in Ireland until within a very recent period.

The disease gives rise to spongy swellings and ulceration of the gums, with eventual loss of teeth. Haemorrhagic blotches appear in the skin—the ' purpura ' so often recorded in the famine—and in advanced cases there are massive effusions of blood into the muscles and under the skin, causing tension and great pain. The legs may be completely black up to the middle of the thigh ; it

was such discolourations that gave rise to a colloquial name for
scurvy, *cos dhubh* (black leg).  There are also painful effusions
around and into the joints.


### III.  CHARACTERS OF THE EPIDEMIC DISEASES

The famine did not begin everywhere at once.  Potato blight
showed itself in 1845, but was limited in its distribution so that
there was severe want in some localities, and abundant food
in others.  The summer of 1846 was damp and of ' unprecedented
heat ' ; the blight broke out once more, this time with the greatest
virulence, and swept over the country.  One day the fields were
covered with a luxuriant growth ; a few days later the leaves
and stalks were black and dead, and the food of a whole countryside had vanished.  The price of potatoes rose from two shillings
a hundredweight to seven shillings, and later to twelve shillings
when obtainable at all.  The people had not the means to obtain
grain food as substitute, and famine conditions became almost
universal through the country though much worse in some parts
than in others.  Epizootic disease broke out, *Scamhach*, i.e. pleuro-
pneumonia of cattle.  When the famine began many farmers
of the more comfortable class sold their cattle, sheep and fowls,
fearing that these would be raided by mobs of the starving
peasantry, a short-sighted measure that later recoiled on their
own heads, and aggravated the general misery.  By the winter of
1846–47 the food position had become desperate, and widespread
starvation reigned.

Even in good years there was always an undercurrent of ' our
old endemic fourteen-day maculated typhus ' in the poorest
parts of the country and towns, though very variable in severity
and extent from year to year.  The following extract from a
report by Dr Lynch (Loughrea) illustrates the situation in one
of the bad endemic centres :

> Previously to the breaking out of the epidemic in 1843–4
> [mainly relapsing fever] there was nothing remarkable in the
> sanitary conditions of the district.  During the preceding five
> years maculated typhus, terminating on the eleventh or twelfth
> day, and seldom followed by relapse, was more or less prevalent,
> and varied remarkably in severity in different years.  In the

year 1840 the type of fever was very bad indeed, and many of the gentry and middle classes were cut off by it. With the exception of that year fever assumed for many years in this district the features of typhus melior [milder], and was fatal in the proportion of about one in six amongst the better, and one in fifteen amongst the lower classes ; but during the year 1846, most of the cases assumed the worst form of typhus, and few were rescued.

From which it is instructive to see that in such localities the continuing presence of typhus, even if of a less severe type, was considered ' nothing remarkable'. Of the country town of Tullamore, for example, Dr Ridley reports that the numerous small lanes of the town are very dirty, and the removal of nuisances totally neglected. The number of poor is very large and there is always existing a vast amount of fever out of proportion to the extent of the population.

The advent and extension of famine and the consequent deterioration in the sanitary standards of the afflicted people provided a fertile soil ready to receive the seeds of fever. Those exhausted by hunger and struggling to keep body and soul together by what they could find of dock leaves and nettles or an odd handful of raw meal, were not likely to trouble greatly about personal cleanliness, even had they the strength to fetch water or firing to heat it. Such of their clothing as had any market value had been sold to passing pedlars, and the rags that were left they wore night and day, huddling together for warmth. The neighbours crowded into any cabin where a fire was burning, or where some food had been obtained which might be shared or bartered. The lack of cleanliness, the unchanged clothing and the crowding together, provided conditions ideal for lice to multiply and spread rapidly. (The rate at which louse-infestation ran through the occupants of dug-outs and billets in the first World War came as a revelation to those who witnessed it, and here the victims of the insect invasion had not been reduced by hunger to a state of indifference and despair.) In such circumstances an initial case or two of fever could serve to infect a whole district. In general, the worse the famine in any part, the more intense the fever, and crowds of starving people forsook their homes and took to the road, thus carrying disease with them wherever they went. To the voluntary migrants were added others evicted for rent default, turned adrift 'to find a living where no living is to be found'. Undoubtedly this was the most active means by which fever was conveyed from infected areas to those previously healthy, a fact so generally recognised that the epidemic was often called the 'road-fever'. Many of these wayfarers were incubating fever when they left their homes, and later developed the disease in a frank form. Others, still more dangerous, had it of too mild a type to be prostrated by it, though equally infectious—'I saw many pass through the fever while they were literally walking about'. Convalescents, too, carried infection in one way or another.

Writing of conditions in Trim and Kilcooley, Dr Lamprey describes these districts as among the wealthiest in Ireland. The people were comfortably circumstanced and engaged mainly in grazing pursuits. Hence the failure of the potato crop—moreover not complete in the locality—did not result in starvation. Notwithstanding these special advantages, disease became very prevalent. Dr Lamprey's report continues :

> By far the chief agent in propagating it (perhaps the origin of the epidemic is due to the same cause) was the constant practice that the people of the western and more stricken counties had of migrating towards the eastern parts of the island. These poor creatures, obliged from their poverty to sleep in the open air, in ditches and other wretched places, carried the fever, at that time more prevalent in the west, in their own persons, and, mixing with the people attending markets or fairs, for the purpose of begging, imparted the disease to them. I have often observed whole families belonging to distant counties lying in fever on the roadside.

These wretched migrants swarmed into the poorer parts of the towns, they congregated around the charity soup-kitchens and relief depots ; and wherever they went they served as centres for disseminating infection.

A steady increase in fever can be traced in many places before the storm broke. In the week ending 7 December 1844, there was a total of 362 cases of fever in the workhouses ; in the corresponding week of 1845, the number was 526 ; and in 1846, it had reached 1,738. Over the same period the number of work-houses having fever patients increased from 32 to 71 in a total of 130. In Abbeyleix (Queen's county), for instance, Dr Swan places the onset of the epidemic at about September 1846, and says that by the autumn and winter of that year the district was overwhelmed with it ; but he points out that for about 18 months previously fever had been gradually becoming more prevalent there.

The epidemic developed and spread in this irregular and sporadic fashion, as the following examples show, until nearly the whole country was engulfed. In co. Kilkenny fever was rampant as early as the summer of 1845. In Cork it broke out early in 1846, and reached its height in the following year. Some parts of co. Galway were attacked in the spring of 1846, and others in the autumn of that year or the following spring. In co. Roscommon disease became widespread at the end of 1846 or early in 1847 ; similarly in co. Sligo. The Navan district was heavily involved in June 1847, but fever of the relapsing variety had been ' pretty generally epidemic ' there in 1845. The counties of Wicklow, Longford and Louth escaped serious invasion until the early part of 1847. In Dublin the epidemic was described as beginning with the year 1847 or a few weeks earlier. Fever in Belfast began to spread in September 1846. Tyrone was attacked in December 1846, and Derry in the spring of 1847. In co. Down fever appeared generally in the early spring of 1847, but the Hillsborough district escaped fever until the middle of June, after which date ' it prevailed greatly '. It is interesting that in Wexford fever broke out in two distressed areas—Arthurstown and Killan—in April 1847, but in the rest of this county where there was little actual starvation, disease did not appear generally for more than another year. The remote northern parts of co. Leitrim escaped until the middle of 1847, and the western islands of Inisbofin and Inishark until the middle of 1848, by which time the epidemic was virtually over in some parts of the country.

The sole extensive district to escape famine fever was that of Warrenpoint-Rostrevor (co. Down). Local medical opinion ascribed this freedom to the fact that, because of the amount of employment given by the wealthy and numerous gentry, want was seldom or never known there. Other parts of Ireland, however, equally favoured in this way suffered heavily from imported fever. The most likely explanation of this peculiar immunity is that the district lies off the direct route to the larger towns which were the goal of the hosts of starving migrants. It is significant that the same locality also escaped the famine fever of 1816–18.

The granting of requisitions by the board of health for the provision of temporary hospitals indicates the dates at which the epidemic was recognised as having got out of hand. Requisitions for the larger towns were granted as follows : Dublin, 4 May 1847 ; Waterford, 5 May 1847 ; Cork, 17 May 1847 ; Limerick, 24 May 1847 ; Galway, 29 May 1847 ; Belfast, 13 November 1847.

Typical of the rise of the epidemic in other towns is Dr Callanan's graphic and moving story of Cork :

What has been called the epidemic fever of 1847 in truth commenced in this locality, and, as I am informed, in many others, early in 1846, as is abundantly proved by workhouse and other returns throughout the district. From the commencement of 1847, however, *Fate* opened her book in good earnest here, and the full tide of death flowed on everywhere around us. During the first six months of that dark period *one-third* of the daily population of our streets consisted of shadows and spectres, the impersonations of disease and famine, crowding in from the rural districts, and stalking along to the general doom—the grave—which appeared to await them at the distance of a few steps or a few short hours.

By the end of 1846, parts of that county had been reduced to the direst straits of hunger and fever as is shown in the following extract from a letter dated December 17, addressed to the great duke of Wellington by Mr N. M. Cummins, a justice of the peace :

Having for many years been intimately connected with the western portion of the county of Cork, and possessing some small property there, I thought it right, personally, to investigate the truth of the several lamentable accounts which had reached me of the appalling state of misery to which that part of the country was reduced . . . Being aware that I should have to witness scenes of frightful hunger, I provided myself with as much bread as five men could carry, and on reaching the spot I was surprised to find the wretched hamlet deserted. I entered some of the hovels to ascertain the cause, and the scenes that presented themselves were such as no tongue or pen can convey the slightest idea of. In the first, six famished and ghastly skeletons, to all appearance dead, were huddled in a corner on some filthy straw, their sole covering what seemed a ragged horse-cloth and their wretched legs hanging about, naked above the knees. I approached in horror, and found by a low moaning they were alive, they were in fever—four children, a woman, and what once had been a man. It is impossible to go through the details, suffice to say, that in a few minutes I was surrounded by at least 200 of such phantoms, such frightful spectres as no words can describe. By far the greater number were delirious either from famine or from fever. Their demoniac yells are still ringing in my ears, and their horrible images are fixed upon my brain . . . the same morning the police opened a house on the adjoining lands, which was observed shut for many days, and two frozen corpses were found lying upon the mud floor *half devoured by the rats.* A mother, herself in fever, was seen the same day to drag out the corpse of her child, a girl about twelve, perfectly naked ; and leave it half covered with stones. In another house . . . the dispensary doctor found seven wretches lying, unable to move, under the same cloak—one had been dead for many hours but the others were unable to move either themselves or the corpse. To what purpose should I multiply such cases ? If these be not sufficient, neither would they hear who have the power to send relief and do not, even ' though one came from the dead '.

As has been explained, the famine fever was made up of two distinct species of disease, typhus and relapsing fever. The former had always existed in the more depressed and congested parts of the country and in the poorer parts of the towns. As the famine grew, the existing centres of typhus extended their range until few places escaped its ravages. The features of the disease were familiar to every doctor in Ireland—' the fever natural to this climate '. Relapsing fever, however, was not so generally disseminated in normal times, and some doctors did not recognise the disease when it reached their areas, and reported that ' it differed widely from the ordinary fevers of the country ', and ' presented symptoms of a new and extraordinary nature '. When the invasion of relapsing fever took place, the pre-existing typhus was often outdistanced by the new disease, for it was the general experience that in similar surroundings relapsing fever was diss-eminated much more rapidly than typhus, and ran through whole families in a few days. The delicate legs and antennae of lice are easily broken off, and the exuding fluid swarms with spirochaetes ; these organisms are readily transferred to others, as by the fingers, and can cause infection by penetrating the skin or the eye. In hospitals the disease has often been contracted by careless handling of blood taken from infected persons for the purpose of diagnostic examination. Bleeding from the nose was a common complication of relapsing fever in the famine epidemic, sometimes so profuse that it could be controlled only by plugging the nostrils where they enter the throat. There were also extensive haemorrhages from other sites, due to associated scurvy. In such cases the patient's bed and its surroundings must have been saturated with blood, and in the primitive conditions existing in the crowded cabins where the other occupants were the only attendants on the sick, they could not have escaped contamination with blood, potentially infective by way of the skin or the eye.

The following particulars are given to indicate the proportional distribution of typhus and relapsing fever in certain localities which are representative of many others. In Nenagh (Tipperary), two-thirds of the cases were relapsing fever, and one-third typhus ; in Kilmallock (Limerick) nine cases out of every ten were relapsing fever : in Kinsale (Cork), of one group of 250 cases, 240 were relapsing fever ; in Kilkenny, nineteen-twentieths of the inmates of the workhouse who developed fever were attacked by the relapsing form ; in Dublin, relapsing fever preponderated, and typhus was rare ' comparatively speaking '. On the other hand, in some areas the epidemic fever was mainly or entirely typhus. Thus from Monaghan it was reported : ' The spotting was universal—it was present in every case ' ; from Strangford (co. Down) ; ' Relapse, *contrary to what so generally took place in many other districts, did not occur in a single instance* ' ; from Lowtherstown (Fermanagh) : ' Relapses were seldom seen ' ; in Tullamore (King's county), five out of every seven cases of fever were typhus ; and in Dromore (Tyrone), four out of every five ; in Oranmore

(Galway) where in May 1847, three-quarters of the population were ill, only typhus is mentioned. Again, in some districts the species of the prevailing fever was subject to change ; for example, in Ballygar (Galway) where the epidemic began in 1846, typhus appeared first ; in 1847 relapsing fever was much in evidence and spread rapidly ; and in 1848 typhus again became ascendant ; in the Ballinrobe area, the epidemic was solely typhus until late 1847 when relapsing fever broke out, and thereafter both diseases continued together. In the hospitals of Cork city the numbers of cases of typhus and of relapsing fever appear to have been about equal ; in Belfast the proportion was about three of the former to two of the latter. It must be understood, however, that the figures recorded in those times are often no more than rough approximations. It was beyond the power of country doctors to keep track of the multitude of sick, and even in the capital it is recorded :

> All who had to go amongst the poor at their own houses were well aware that vast numbers remained there, who either could not be accommodated in hospital, or who never thought of applying. It was quite common to find three, four or even five ill, in a house where application had been made but for one.

In their reports, many doctors were careful to distinguish ' maculated, or spotted, typhus ' from ' relapse fever ' ; the latter disease appears under many names—' the short fever ', ' gastric fever ', and ' gastro-purpuric fever ', the last term being suggested by the onset of scorbutic symptoms which, through the general unfamiliarity with scurvy, were thought to be part of the febrile infection. Jaundice commonly complicated the relapsing fever especially in severe attacks when the whole body might assume a deep orange-brown hue ; such cases were frequently labelled ' jaundice fever ' and ' yellow fever '. In other instances the terminology used is ambiguous and puzzling, and if characteristic symptoms are omitted from the account, it is impossible to say what disease is implied. For example, one doctor records that four per cent. of his fever cases were spotted typhus, and 18 per cent yellow fever ; his confused terminology makes the remaining 78 per cent unidentifiable with any degree of certainty. Lastly, a few doctors maintained that relapsing fever and typhus are no more than symptomatic variations of the same infection, and so made no attempt to distinguish the two.

The term ' famine fever ' was used in several senses, most commonly as a generic name embracing both the species of fever that accompanied the famine—as it is in this present account. It was sometimes applied exclusively to relapsing fever, especially by those who saw the disease in the famine for the first time, and by others because of the ' insatiable ' desire for food that followed close on the crisis—' they had the hunger in their hearts '. Again, it was used for a lingering type of low fever met with in the starving, without rashes and not defined by periods, stages, or crises, and terminating in death from inanition alone. ' It required no medical treatment for its cure, as recovery took place on administering proper nutriment '. One doctor, who practised in one of the more favoured districts which suffered little from famine, reported that his cases were mostly relapsing fever with some typhus, and that because of the absence of starvation there was none of the famine fever common elsewhere.

The subject of the relative prevalence of typhus and relapsing fever cannot be left without discussing the strangely unequal distribution in the different social classes, which was reported from all over the country as it had been similarly reported in earlier famines. In the better classes, relapsing fever was almost unknown, whereas typhus was contracted by many doctors and clergy from their attendance on the sick, and by members of the gentry who were infected ' in crowded assemblies either while presiding as magistrates in petty session courts, sitting on relief committees, or attending as jurors in assize towns, in which places they necessarily came into contact with large assemblies of the poor ' ; as well as through setting up relief depots in their houses or grounds, thus attracting crowds of the destitute—' from this circumstance . . . many excellent individuals have fallen victims . . . to their zeal and extraordinary efforts to alleviate the overwhelming distress with which they were surrounded '.

Another class difference commonly stressed is that among the better classes of society a fever patient did not infect others of the household, whereas among the poor the disease tended to run through the whole family ; and a third to be emphasised is the constantly higher rate of mortality from fever among the better class. The following extracts from medical reports, which could be multiplied many times, bring out these points of difference:

> The number of persons who contracted the disease, whose duties brought them constantly in contact with fever patients, such as physicians, clergymen, and hospital nurses, clearly shows the contagious nature of the late epidemic. But it is equally worthy of note, that most of these persons were attacked with maculated typhus, and comparatively few with the short relapse-fever, although chiefly exposed to the contagion of the latter.

> Many of what are termed the middle classes, such as shopkeepers and small farmers, were under my care in the relapse-fever. All the cases of fever I have met with among the gentry, and they were very numerous, were instances of maculated typhus.

> The mortality was much greater among the higher classes than the poor, amounting to about forty per cent. in the former, and not more than about four per cent. in the latter.

> In Innishannon, the mortality amongst the higher and middle classes was very much greater than amongst the poor, in the ratio of about 16 to 1.

> Pure typhus without dysentery occurred in the better classes, and short fever [relapsing fever] with diarrhoea and dysentery among the poor (these complications being caused, or precipitated, by starvation).

In one district where the epidemic was pure typhus, the doctor reported :

> The mortality among the better classes was truly great, six or seven out of every ten attacked dying of it ; while, amongst the poor who got any care at all, not more than one out of every four or five attacked was carried off by it.

> It was remarked, however, that among the upper classes . . . the disease, though appearing in a very malignant form in one individual, seldom attacked the attendants or other members of the family.

> Except in three or four cases out of many hundreds of persons affected with maculated fever, whom I have attended within

the past ten years, I know of no instance where the disease was communicated among respectable families.

I have seen over thirty of the gentry attacked by severe typhus fever and in no case has a second member of the family become affected, although in no instance was there a system of separation or seclusion resorted to.

Such are the facts. It remains to suggest an explanation. The reader will remember that the organisms of typhus are contained in the faeces passed by the louse. This intestinal matter dries to a light dust which is easily diffused. Consequently it is possible for a person to become infected by this faecal dust—either through scratches etc. in the skin, through the undamaged conjunctiva of the eye or by inhalation—without having lice on his body. This mode of infection does not appear to take place in relapsing fever, for the organisms causing the disease remain within the louse and are set free only when its delicate structure is sufficiently damaged— as in scratching—to allow its body fluid to exude on to the skin. The great increase of body vermin among the starving was common knowledge, and the efforts of the better classes to avoid picking up these parasites would at the same time save them from relapsing fever, but not from typhus when conveyed by faecal dust. Persons who contracted typhus in this way, being themselves free from lice, would not transmit the disease to others. The higher rate of mortality from fever among the upper classes is explained in part by their liability to contract the more deadly typhus rather than relapsing fever ; but their death-rate from typhus was also higher than that from typhus among the poor. Age here would be an important factor. The mortality from typhus is much greater in the middle-aged and elderly than in the young, because of the strain thrown on the heart ; most of the victims among the better classes—clergy, doctors, magistrates and others set in authority—would fall into the group unfavourably placed as regards age, and so were handicapped from the start ; whereas among the poor where the whole family was liable to infection, the milder attacks usual in children and adolescents would keep the average mortality at a lower figure. In addition to this, however, it has long been observed that the natives of localities where typhus is always endemic, suffer less severely from the disease than others who have not had the same close

personal association with it. The probability is that a proportion
of the former have developed some degree of immunity either
from mild and unrecognised attacks in childhood, or by a process
of vaccination with small and non-infective doses of virus over
a considerable period, such immunity being insufficient to protect
from a subsequent heavy infection, but enough to lessen the
virulence of the attack.

Many medical men fell victim to fever. In Munster in one
year (1847) 48 died, mostly of typhus ; seven died similarly
in that year in Cavan. A sad story comes from Connacht :

Along the coast of Connemarra, for near thirty miles, where
the villages are very small and hundreds of cabins detached,
sickness and death walked hand in hand, until they nearly
depopulated the whole coast, although they had the advantage
of three medical men sent specially from the board of health, two
of whom fell victims . . . to the disease. Another criterion I will
give to judge the mortality by. During the years 1847 and
1848, four medical men died between Clifden and Galway ; three
between Oranmore and Athenry, a distance of about seven miles;
four more between Anadown and Kilmain, making in all eleven.

Of the 473 medical officers appointed by the board of health
to special fever duty, one in every thirteen died at his post.

The most informative and detailed account of the epidemic
in any one place is perhaps that given by Dr Seaton Reid for
Belfast, where the ' epidemic extended itself precisely over a
period of two years [September 1846 to September 1848], and
was one of unprecedented prevalence . . . It could not be said
that scarcity of food, or want of employment, was the *originating* cause of our epidemic here, because our working classes
were fully employed, and provisions unusually cheap till the
early part of the year 1847 '. Thus it was the old story once
more—fever conveyed by fugitives from elsewhere. These
incomers to Belfast numbered about 10,000, a figure to be added
to the then 100,000 inhabitants of the Belfast union district.

The figures of admissions to hospital, described as very nearly
correct, were : fever 13,469 (mortality, 13 per cent) ; dysentery
1,836 (mortality, 32 per cent) ; smallpox, 325 (mortality,
31 per cent). The figure for fever and that for dysentery,

Dr Reid says, should be increased by at least one-fourth to allow for those treated in their homes. Three hospitals were in operation, with, in addition, tents sufficient for 700 convalescents. In the worst week (July 1847) there were 660 admissions, and the largest number of hospital inmates on any one day, July 17, was 2,118. Under 'fever' are included typhus and relapsing fever, but the total numbers in each group are not stated; judging by the admissions given for one individual hospital, they occurred in the ratio of about three to two, with a mortality of 20 per cent, and 7 per cent respectively. Included also in the fever total are many cases of ' the ordinary continued fever of our country' i.e. typhoid, a disease which also became epidemic in Belfast. Of 4,600 fever admissions to one hospital, 970 were given this diagnosis. In these the tongue is described as being ' dry and brown ', and ' the brain a good deal involved '. The mortality was 10 per cent. This suggests typhoid of an ordinarily severe type, but it is hard to reconcile this with the short average duration which is stated as 15 to 20 days, whereas an attack of typhoid generally lasts considerably longer. An average duration of 15 to 20 days might suggest paratyphoid fever, but the dry brown tongue and delirium—given as constant signs—as well as a 10 per cent mortality, would not be in keeping with this identification. Dr Reid was clearly a precisian, and his diagnostic criteria for typhus and relapsing fever were so severe that many genuine cases of both diseases are likely to have been excluded and relegated to some other group of fever. Dr Reid noted the complications met with in the various types of fever he describes, so it is strange he says nothing of intestinal haemorrhage in the group labelled typhoid, a sudden and alarming event—occurring in about 6 per cent. of cases—which could not have been overlooked. It seems likely, therefore, that some considerable proportion of the cases were in reality atypical typhus, perhaps without a rash, or mild relapsing fever without a relapse, and the inclusion of these would lower the figure of the average duration of attack in the whole group called typhoid. It is of interest that the senior physician of Cork street fever hospital, Dublin, records that only one case of typhoid was seen there, the diagnosis being verified by post-mortem examination.

Dr Reid stresses the sudden onset of typhus, and he found almost invariably that the patient ' described himself as being

on any particular day in a state of perfect health, and on the next
to have been seized with rigor, headache, pain in the back and the
usual symptoms of fever'. 'The pulse increases very gradually
in frequency, and seldom at any time during its course exceeds
120 or 130 beats in a minute. Even after crisis it requires a few
days to subside within the healthy limit, and sometimes descends
so low as 35 or 40 beats'. 'About the fifth day an eruption
resembling measles, which is first observed on the soft white skin
in front of the shoulder-joints, and on the epigastrium, appears
on the body ; for a few days it is capable of being momentarily
removed by pressure, but becomes less so as the disease advances'.
He points out that although the rash generally lasts for the course
of the attack ' it may remain out only thirty-six or forty-eight
hours, but it is as characteristic of this species of fever as a peculiar
eruption is of either scarlatina or measles'. The duration of the
attack is ' generally fourteen days from the rigor, and the mode
of crisis either by an increased secretion of urine or gentle perspiration ; if the latter be profuse it is in general a fatal symptom '—
a point much stressed in those times. ' The brain is always more or
less involved'. The complications mentioned are bronchitis and
pneumonia, and suppuration of the parotid gland ; complicating
dysentery was comparatively rare because dysenteric patients
were isolated in a separate building. Another complication,
recorded from many parts of the country, was erysipelas. Dr Reid
describes how a patient who has had a favourable crisis ' may in
a few days be seized with a rigor and a return of febrile symptoms,
which in about three days will be followed by some redness, pain,
and swelling about one of his ears, thence extending over the whole
scalp, across the face, through the nostrils into the pharynx, and
then into the larynx, producing there one of the most fatal
complications that can occur'.

The onset of relapsing fever he describes as even more sudden
and marked than that of typhus. ' The rigor is most severe and
the pulse, within twenty-four hours after it, becomes as frequent
as 120, 130, or 140, and a day or two after may reach 150 or 160.
The headache is in general very severe, but there are not the
vertigo and ringing in the ears, with the suffused and injected eye,
that are found in maculated typhus'. ' From the commencement
there is very great irritability of the stomach, which rejects everything, and which is accompanied by very great thirst . . . Most

severe pains in all the muscles of the body are very frequently present, rendering the patient almost as helpless in bed as if he suffered
from acute rheumatism . . . A very fatal complication in this
species was jaundice'. (Dr Reid here must refer to intense
jaundice, for it was considered usual for relapsing fever patients
to show ' a yellow tinge of the skin varying from a straw-colour
to very deep jaundice'.) ' When these violent symptoms have
continued to the fifth day, the patient falls into a most profuse
perspiration, often preceded by a rigor, saturating the bed-clothes,
and in a few hours the pulse will fall from perhaps 150 or 160 to
70 or 80. No sooner has the crisis taken place than the patient
at once feels himself in the most perfect health, and is most clam-
ourous for food and permission to leave his bed '. Dr Reid made
a careful study of 385 patients with relapsing fever, and noted,
inter alia, the interval between the rigor of onset, and the first
crisis. In none did the latter appear before the third day, or later
than the ninth ; in 146 of these, it occurred on the fifth day.
The extremes of the duration of the relapse were one day, and
nine days. Besides intense jaundice, a fatal complication was
suppression of urine. Inflammation of the iris occurred occasionally, and ' in one or two instances ' blindness,[2] famine dropsy,
and scorbutic symptoms ' purpurous spots on the limbs and effusion
into the knee-joints ', very often followed. Dr Reid is emphatic
that he never saw more than one relapse in any case, contrary to
the general experience elsewhere ; nor did he see a second attack
of typhus, nor a second attack of relapsing fever, in the same person.
As evidence that the several fevers did not protect against one
another, he mentions that he recently discharged from hospital
a patient who in March 1847 had an attack of maculated typhus ;
in July of the same year an attack of relapsing fever ; and in
January 1849 an attack of typhoid.

No age was immune from relapsing fever, ' from the child
on the breast to the old man of seventy on his staff' all were
liable to attack. Typhus in the very young was much rarer.
Dr Lynch (Loughrea) a man of very great experience says, ' I
never saw an instance of maculated fever in a child under five
years, but I saw many instances of the short relapse-fever in
children under that age '.

The widespread and fatal dysentery which prevailed during
the famine was generally ascribed to bad food, and no doubt

this tended to set up an irritative diarrhoea and prepare the way for true dysentery. For example, Dr Pemberton (Ballinrobe) attributes the dysentery to eating diseased potatoes in the first place, and then to the sudden change over to Indian meal 'which they did not know how to cook; and many of them I have seen devouring it raw, from hunger, not having tasted food for some days previous to their obtaining it'. Dr Dillon (Castlebar) blames the quality of the Indian meal in this connection, 'all of which, ground in this country, contains a large proportion of the husk and skin'.

No doubt there was much confusion between famine diarrhoea and the milder forms of dysentery, and indeed these may be indistinguishable except by laboratory tests not possible at that period, but the more characteristic signs of the disease in its various degrees of severity were well recognised—the presence of blood and mucus in the faeces, the passage of blood and mucus only, and the dreaded stools consisting solely of fluid resembling water in which raw meat has been washed, a warning that gangrene of the intestine has set in. Dr Cullinan (Ennis) describes such patients as having 'twelve or twenty alvine [intestinal] evacuations in a few hours, consisting of serous bloody fluid, often without a trace of mucus or faecal matter. The fluid resembling very closely, except in colour, the rice-water evacuations in malignant cholera'. This resemblance gave rise to false alarms that Asiatic cholera had broken out. (There was no true cholera during the famine years until December 1848, when the epidemic then prevalent in Europe invaded Ireland.) Dr Purefoy (Cloughjordan) is deserving of remembrance for his determination and resource in carrying out a series of post-mortem examinations on victims of the famine. The relative part of his description of the intestine is quoted here because of its admirable clarity:

Inflammation or congestion of the mucous membrane was a frequent occurrence in the lower third of the ileum, but ulceration was rarely found, except in cases of dysentery, and then the ulcerations were chiefly seated in the mucous membrane of the rectum. In protracted cases of dysentery this membrane has been found literally honeycombed by an innumerable number of ulcers, many of them very minute, and a few as large as a four-penny piece, and so deep in some instances as to have completely laid bare the serous covering of the bowel.

The infectious nature of the disease was not generally appreciated. Some persons complained that subjects of dysentery 'which is not infectious' were being admitted to fever hospitals ; others complained that these cases were being excluded. In some hospitals, dysentery patients were isolated where this measure was possible, because of the recognised danger of infecting others. The complete lack of even the simplest of nursing facilities in the homes of the poor helped to spread the disease. Dr Lamprey (Schull) says that it was easy to know if any of the inmates in the cabins were suffering from dysentery ' as the ground in such places was usually found marked with clots of blood '.

In most parts hard hit by famine, dysentery was rampant before fever had begun to spread. Elsewhere, according to circumstances, it might precede the fever, accompany, or follow it. Although dysentery was general in Limerick, the neighbourhood of Bruff is said to have escaped this visitation completely. In Waterford city, fever broke out in October 1846, but it was not until the autumn of 1847 that ' dysentery made its appearance as an epidemic distinct from the fever . . . It presented itself in a very severe form, and was exceedingly fatal '. In Cork where dysentery had been common throughout, it is recorded that the fever ' appeared to reach its culminating point in the city in the month of July [1847], beginning to decline in August, when, in the course of a fortnight, the type was suddenly converted to dysentery '. In Dublin, epidemic dysentery appeared in November 1846 ' even before there was any change of diet, and when there was no general want abroad '—presumably imported by migrants from some of the districts which then had been affected for many months. Of the subsequent association of fever and dysentery in the Cork street fever hospital, Dublin, Dr Kennedy wrote :

> Epidemic dysentery is a serious disease in itself, but joined to fever it becomes a truly formidable affection . . . With the late fever it joined itself in every stage. I saw cases of dysentery, which had continued for some days, suddenly put on all the signs of the worst fever, and so carry the patient off. Here the fever was added to the dysentery. In other cases again, and these by far the majority, fever existed, and then dysentery supervened ; while in a third the patient would be convalescent from the fever before dysentery showed itself. No matter at what time, however, it appeared, it was a serious affection.

He makes the sound clinical point that 'extensive ulceration of the intestines existed in many cases where the discharges were those of simple diarrhoea'.

The extent and degree of scurvy in any locality indicated the severity of famine there. Before the advent of fever had confused the clinical picture, generalised scurvy was met with in two main degrees of gravity. In the more severe, the initial mouth lesions were later followed by haemorrhages ; in the other, the great majority of cases did not progress to this second stage. The following quotations—the first from Galway and the second from Mayo—illustrate these two types of the disease :

> Shortly after the potatoes had ceased to be an article of diet, purpura or acute scurvy first attacked the poor. I observed it on the mucous membrane of the mouth, in white blisters, in some running on to sloughing, and affecting the throat and tonsils.

The condition was so general that this writer reported it officially as an epidemic. He continues :

> Purpuric eruptions soon followed, being very prevalent in June and July, 1846, characterised by livid spots on the hands, face, chest, and other parts of the body, and in many attended with haemorrhage from the bowels.

The less intense form, limited as a rule to the mouth, is described as follows :

> Scurvy was very prevalent for some months before [the fever], evidenced by the purple hue of the gums, with ulceration along their upper thin margins, bleeding on the slightest touch and deep and sloughing ulcers on the inside of the fauces [throat], with intolerable fetor, which attacked both sexes indiscriminately, and the child as well as the adult, but unattended with purpuric spots, or other discolouration of the skin, in all the cases I saw, except one child, about two years of age, that had purpuric spots on its face, trunk, and extremities.

Again, in persons existing on the border-line of scurvy, the disease often became manifest for the first time during or after an attack of fever, especially relapsing fever, perhaps for the reason that in the country as a whole this was the commoner variety

among the ill fed. Further, in relapsing fever there is a haemorrhagic tendency as shown in attacks of nose bleeding and the
occasional appearance of small spots of blood in the skin.
Consequently this infection, when super-imposed on latent scurvy,
might reinforce the existing pre-disposition to haemorrhage
resulting in the onset of frank scorbutic signs. The terminology
employed in some of the reports is often confused so that it is
difficult to know what exactly the writers meant by ' purpura '.
Others, more precise, make it clear that in their usage the term
was restricted to large purple or livid patches in the skin, which
are no part of uncomplicated relapsing fever. Besides these,
there are mentioned haemorrhages from mucous surfaces, and
painful effusions into muscles and joints. The onset might be
dramatic in its suddenness. Thus in one patient convalescent
from fever and seemingly out of danger, ' haemorrhage suddenly
occurred from the nose, mouth, bladder and intestines, with
large purpuric spots over the entire skin and mucous membranes
as far as visible. It terminated fatally '.

As has been emphasised, scurvy was unknown in Ireland in
ordinary times, and so unfamiliar with the disease were some
of the doctors, practising during the famine, that they believed
its purpuric signs to be a complication or a sequel of the febrile
attack, hence the name ' gastro-purpuric fever' which they
often employed for relapsing fever. It is significant that there
is no mention of purpura occurring among well nourished
persons who contracted this disease. It is significant, too, that
its incidence in relapsing fever varied greatly in different parts,
so that it is recorded : ' purpuric spots were very common ' ;
' purpuric spots were rare ' ; ' no purpuric spots observed '—
these differences seemingly being determined by the degree of
food shortage in the several localities.

Dr Curran (Dublin) quotes a most interesting observation
from Waterford city :

> At first and until lately scurvy was mainly confined to a
> class above what could be called poor, such as shoemakers,
> carpenters, tailors etc., and their wives, who had been living
> on bread and tea, or stirabout (mostly of Indian meal) and
> milk. The destitute were exempt from it. I can really attribute
> this to nothing else but the *soup given them by the Quakers, which
> was well seasoned with vegetables.*

Famine dropsy is brought about by the lack of certain food elements which are necessary to maintain the balance of fluids in the body tissues. Throughout the famine its occurrence was evidence of extreme and prolonged want. Fever often, and dysentery sometimes, attacked those in comfortable circumstances, but famine dropsy was limited to the starved. In those not altogether reduced by foregoing scarcity, an attack of fever frequently completed the work that hunger had begun, so that many reports mention dropsy as a usual complication or sequel of fever, the condition showing itself first in the lower extremities and increasing until the unfortunate victim became water-logged. Of the parish of Schull, where at one period the deaths in a population of 18,000 numbered fifty a day, the Rev. Dr Traill[3] wrote :

> Frightful and fearful is the havock around me . . . the aged, who, with the young—neglected, perhaps, amidst the wide-spread destitution—are almost without exception swollen and ripening for the grave.

This devoted rector, who laboured unsparingly for these unhappy creatures, himself died of typhus.

It might be of assistance to the reader to state the order in which the diseases just described made their appearance, as recorded by Dr French of Ballygar dispensary, Galway : (1) scurvy, mouth signs first ; later, purpura and haemorrhages ; (2) extensive dysentery ; (3) famine dropsy ; (4) 'very fatal' typhus ; (5) relapsing fever 'fast propagated by contagion, but not so fatal'. 'As soon as the vegetable kingdom afforded a mixed diet, the general health improved, fever and bowel affections were not so frequent, and the healthy state of the district improved much' ; but in 1848, with the return of winter and spring, (6) typhus, with well-marked rashes, increased once more.

## IV.  MEDICAL ORGANISATION AND ARRANGEMENTS

To meet the apprehended danger of fever which invariably followed any prolonged scarcity of food, the Temporary Fever Act, 9 Vic., cap. 6 was passed on 24 March 1846. This empowered the lord lieutenant to appoint commissioners of health, not more than five in number, who were to serve without any salary or reward ; and to appoint medical officers at such salary as he might direct, such salaries and expenses to be paid out of the treasury. Any two commissioners in writing could require a board of guardians to set up a temporary hospital, and provide nourishment, bedding, medicines, and medical appliances, with nurses and attendants, also accommodation for a dispensary. Under the act the following commissioners were appointed to constitute the central board of health : Sir Randolph Routh,[4] Sir Robert Kane,[5] Edward Twistleton, Esq.,[6] Sir Philip Crampton,[7] and Dominick John Corrigan, Esq., M.D. [8]

The summer of 1846 passed without producing in the opinion of the board much cause for alarm—applications for their intervention had numbered only seventeen—and the act was allowed to expire on the appointed day, 31 August 1846, a lamentable act of official misjudgement. The board therefore ended its sittings on August 15, and its activities, then limited to four unions, ceased, the additional medical officers appointed by the board being discharged. It was ruled that where it was necessary to keep on a fever hospital, this could be done under the Poor Law Amendment Act, 6 and 7 Vic., cap. 92, sec. 15.

A report, dated 5 December 1846, signed by Dr Francis Baker, secretary of the board, gives their considered opinion on the situation as determined mainly by an analysis of the fever admissions to the Dublin hospitals in twelve previous years. There had been a great increase in the number admitted in 1846, but this was not considered a certain indication of the rise of fever as an epidemic malady, in as much as such fluctuations were known to occur, being brought about by states of the weather, changes of season, increase or diminished poverty and other causes. It was considered a favourable omen that petechial eruptions [typhus] were then very rare. In fairness to the board it may be stated that the fever admissions for the year 1840 were considerably higher than those for 1846, yet, as the event showed, the rise in the figure for 1840 did not herald an oncoming catastrophe. One reason why the board doubted that the increase of applicants to the fever hospitals indicated the beginning of an epidemic of fever was that the applicants were chiefly females ; whereas it had previously been the experience that at the beginning of a serious outbreak the male applicants were in a majority. The reason of this discrepancy is not clear, but most unfortunately the board attached a significance to the change in ratio which proved to be without foundation. The prevalence of diarrhoea and dysentery they attributed to a summer of unprecedented heat, followed by an autumn of unprecedented wetness. Their summing up of the situation was that the existing scarcity of food by favouring all the concurrent causes of spread of contagion, namely, crowding of poor dwellings, neglect of personal cleanliness, arising from deficient clothing and want of fuel, added to the increase of strolling mendicants, must excite an apprehension that disease, most probably fever, might spread extensively, but that appearances were rather to suggest that this development might not take place.

As the season advanced, the optimistic, if guarded, prognostications of the board of health were falsified by reports pouring in from grand juries, boards of guardians, doctors, clergy, and private persons. Thus : Erris—fever dreadful in nature has set in and daily extending, scarcely a family exempt ; Killarney—unfortunate people literally dropping in the street, hospital unfurnished ; Donaghadee and Newtownards—great prevalence of disease ; Carlingford—dysentery of alarming and malignant character ; Castlebar—the town is dead with fever ; county Cork—officers of the several workhouses attacked with fever, in many cases fatal ; Skibbereen—bodies lying unburied for six or eight days, large wages will not induce men to bury them.

In view of the many alarming developments, the lord lieutenant re-appointed the board of health in February 1847, and from this date the board continued in being until the end of the parliamentary session of 1850.

Unfortunately the hospital arrangements in Ireland were ill adapted to meet a general epidemic. The provisions then existing for the sick poor were : (1) workhouse infirmaries for ordinary cases ; (2) workhouse fever hospitals ; (3) district fever hospitals ; (4) county infirmaries ; (5) dispensaries. Of these, the county infirmaries had no accommodation for fever cases, and the treatment of such patients in workhouse infirmaries was disapproved of by the poor law commissioners as dangerous to other patients.

The Irish workhouse system was established in 1838 by the act 1 and 2 Vic., cap. 56. The country was first divided into

130 unions, and these subdivided into 2,049 electoral areas ;
extensive surveys and valuations had to be carried out, and a
workhouse built in each of the unions. The completion of the
scheme was delayed in some places by obstruction from interested
parties, which yielded only to force of law ; but by the end of
1844, 113 workhouses were open ; a year later, 122 ; and the
remaining eight opened early in 1846. Each workhouse included
an infirmary, and a fever hospital, unless provision for fever
patients already existed in the neighbourhood.

Under the existing poor law the guardians had three methods
of dealing with fever patients : removing them from the
workhouse to a fever hospital, the cost of removal and maintenance being chargeable to the rates ; renting a house for the
treatment of fever patients ; or erecting a building in the grounds
of the workhouse but separate from it. Except from a workhouse, there was no legal power to remove a fever patient to
hospital against his will.

In theory these arrangements may have seemed workable.
A government spokesman said in the house of commons on 11
February 1846 :

> With respect to the danger of approaching fever, which
> unhappily, generally follows a period of scarcity in Ireland,
> the poor law commissioners have made the most ample
> arrangements.

Actually the hospital accommodation was insufficient and
unequally distributed. The county fever hospitals were small
and poorly equipped, and their funds inadequate for the expansion
necessary to meet a sudden emergency. Large areas of the
country were unprovided for ; in Frenchpark (Roscommon),
for instance, a population of 30,000 scattered over an area of 135
square miles lacked hospital provision of any kind ; there was
no doctor within 22 miles of Erris. The experience of Doonane
fever hospital illustrates the rigidity of the system and the lack
of co-ordination at different levels of authority. This hospital
had exhausted its funds ; the guardians of the union refused to
take it over ; the poor law commissioners ' had no power ' to
help it ; and the lord lieutenant ' had no means '. The dispensaries, originally designed to provide ordinary outdoor medical
relief, were utterly incapable of coping with thousands of fever

patients lying in wretched cabins scattered over miles of country. Before the temporary fever-hospital came into operation in the Dingle dispensary district, the Society of St Vincent de Paul relieved a weekly average of 50 families suffering from fever.

There were in many instances six or seven inmates of the cabin, in fever, without bedding, all huddled together in one apartment on the damp ground . . . we purchased two tons of straw, and distributed it amongst the poor fever patients . . . they considered it the greatest luxury to procure a good bed of straw.

In Ballingarry, for example, the dispensary doctor attended 15 persons ill with fever in one small room. The medical officer of Castlerea union (Dr Tucker) in July 1846 asked permission to exceed his duty and attend the sick in dispensary districts, and asked further if he might order blankets for some of them who 'sleep on green rushes, and are only covered with rags'. He was told that he might do neither.

### V.  DISEASE IN HOSPITALS, WORKHOUSES AND GAOLS

As the famine extended, the accommodation and equipment provided in the workhouses proved totally inadequate for the numbers of applicants who clamoured for admission, yet crowds of the destitute were accepted by the officials against their better judgement, the only alternative being to leave them to starve to death outside. The increase in the workhouse population, and the terrible conditions that prevailed in these dismal abodes, are shown by an extract from a report by the clerk of Skibbereen union. On 21 November 1845, the workhouse (with accommodation for 500) contained 240 inmates ; in the infirmary, 40 ; in the fever hospital, none ; one death in that month. On 21 November 1846 : inmates, 889 ; in the infirmary, 729 ; in the fever hospital (containing 40 beds), 140. That is to say, of nearly 900 inmates occupying space intended for 500, there were only 20 who were not ill in hospital. Deaths in the month had risen from 1 to 67. The overcrowding increased still further. On 18 January (or February) 1847, 90 'miserable creatures', most of whom had barely sufficient strength to crawl to the workhouse, applied for admission. As the house was grossly overcrowded, and fever and dysentery were prevalent, the authorities considered the only safe course to be rejection.

But when dinner had been supplied to these famishing creatures and the officers came to put them out, they had to desist—such were the heartrending shrieks of the poor wretches, saying that they would lie down and die round the walls of the house. They could not drive them out into the heavy rain.

In the end, 75 of the applicants who seemed too weak to reach the town a mile distant, were admitted to the institution already crowded far beyond the danger limit. It is recorded from Cork :

The pressure from without upon the city began to be felt in October [1846], and in November and December the influx of paupers from all parts of this vast county was so overwhelming, that, to prevent them dying in the streets, the doors of the workhouse were thrown open, and in one week 500 persons were admitted, without any provision, either of space or clothing to meet so fearful an emergency. All these were suffering from famine, and the most of them from malignant dysentery or fever.

More fortunate at first than many similar institutions, Ballinrobe workhouse escaped fever until the end of February 1847, when a strolling beggar was admitted and a few days later died of typhus. The disease swept through the establishment crowded far beyond its capacity with men, women and children huddled together in the same compartment, living and sleeping in their clothes for they had neither straw to lie on, nor a blanket to cover them. Large numbers died. The physician, chaplain, master, matron, and clerk of the union were attacked with typhus simultaneously, and only two of these survived.

In such places any kind of effective isolation of the sick was impossible—convalescent wards, living space, school rooms and even stables were crowded with sick, often with more than one patient to a bed, others lying on the floor in between, and it was common for those recovering from one infectious disease to contract another. Admission to a workhouse in those conditions, too often meant for the starving only the exchange of death from hunger for death by disease. Of the 95 persons who died in the Lurgan workhouse in one week of February 1847, 52 had been free from disease when they entered that institution. In the single year, 1847, the deaths in Cork workhouse reached the appalling total of 3,329, and in March of that year, 757 of the inmates perished. In this workhouse hospital in February of that year, the space per bed, normally 800 cubic feet, was reduced to 133–350 in the adult wards ; in one children's ward the space per bed was only 80 cubic feet, and in the least crowded of these 120 cubic feet. At the same period, Fermoy workhouse with accommodation for 900 inmates, held 1,533 ; Kilmallock had 1,500 instead of 800. In the fever hospital of Armagh, there were 255 fever patients, with accommodation for only 100.

The dreadful overcrowding of the workhouses though general was not without exception. In September 1847, there is a complaint from Castlebar where fever prevails 'to a most awful pitch ', that thousands of beggars crowd the streets, yet the workhouse with provision for 600 inmates is half empty, in spite of copies of the vagrant act displayed throughout the town.

The unwillingness of many workhouse and hospital officials to harden their hearts and refuse further admissions, had disastrous consequences beyond those mentioned already, and through the heavy expenditure entailed, some of the institutions were brought to bankruptcy. To give one example. On 29 March 1847, the board of Skibbereen workhouse is reported penniless ; money is owing to the bank ; one contractor refuses to supply food as his bill for £115 is unpaid ; the master is buying food for the inmates out of his own pocket ; the treasurer has advanced £200 on private security ; £80 as an interim measure has been sent by the poor law commissioners. On March 10, the board of health had directed houses to be hired as temporary hospitals in four of the electoral districts of Skibbereen union, also plans of sheds to be erected to increase accommodation were dispatched. In reply to an appeal for a special grant to cover this expenditure the treasury replied on March 27 '. . . as to the establishment of fever hospitals in the Skibbereen union, I am directed by the lords commissioners of her majesty's treasury, for the information of the lord lieutenant, that as a bill is under the consideration of parliament intended to make more effective provision for this object through the relief committees, it appears to their lordships to be desirable that the consideration of these papers should be deferred for the present '. Presumably as a consequence of this refusal, Dr Lamprey on April 8 reported from Skibbereen that many inmates 'are expelled from the house when they appear to be ill, and wandering through the country, expire in the fields'. On April 14, the lord lieutenant ordered the dispatch of £150 (£50 by 'this night's mail') for medical relief, and approved other measures including the loan of four military hospital tents. On April 19, the board of health ordered the erection of hospital sheds in three places in Skibbereen union, each capable of holding 100 patients (according to the plans of Mr Wilkinson, architect to the poor law commissioners); the cost of each with bedsteads exclusive of bedding was £250. On April 29, the lord lieutenant approved the advance of £750 for the cost of these hospital sheds, 'Mr Wilkinson to take the necessary steps'.

Many of the gaols and their hospitals became hot-beds of disease in the same way. Large numbers of persons committed petty offences in hope of being sent to prison where at least there would be food, and the results of the consequent over-crowding of sick and healthy are almost too dreadful to contemplate. Dr Crumpe, medical officer of Tralee gaol, describes how crowds of poor starved wretches, hurried in droves to gaol for petty thefts, generally committed for the purpose of being imprisoned, were quickly carried off by the fever. From these it spread among the previously healthy prisoners who had never suffered from starvation. The hospital was speedily crowded out, in spite of appeals for additional accommodation. In 'this horrid den', those suffering from other diseases, those ill from fever, those dying and the dead from fever and dysentery, were promiscuously stretched together. Most of the attendants were ill with fever, which intensified the existing horrors.

> So insufferable was the atmosphere of the place, so morbidly fetid and laden with noxious miasma, notwithstanding constant fumigation with chloride of lime, that on the door being opened I was uniformly seized, on entering, with the most violent retching.

The mortality was enormous and, in the most exhausted and worn-down subjects, death often took place within a few hours of admission. Similar tragedies befell in other gaols; in Castlebar, 'our Roman Catholic chaplain [Rev. James MacManus, P.P.], deputy governor, deputy matron, and a turnkey, fell victims;

every hospital servant was attacked ; and from our wretched, over-crowded state, the mortality was fearful—fully 40 per cent '.

## VI. FEVER ACTS, AND TEMPORARY FEVER HOSPITALS

The Temporary Fever Act, 9 Vic., cap. 6, had proved in practice to have many defects. The advances made under it to local authorities were to be repaid by the grand jury assessment on the county ; this threw the whole expense on the occupiers and householders instead of on the more equitable taxation of the poor rates. The local boards of health, of 13 persons appointed by the lord lieutenant in each area, were practically independent ; moreover it was impossible for him to assess the suitability of those to be nominated as members. The act established the fundamental error of leaving decisions as to the necessity of relief of the sick to the opinion of interested local parties. Where a board of guardians refused to provide a hospital, it was difficult to coerce it, especially if the law courts were not in session, and the central board of health had no funds of its own to make good the deficiency.

The succeeding act, 10 Vic., cap. 7, made provision for a finance committee, and under it a relief committee for each electoral area or for several in conjunction, as might appear desirable. Further, 10 Vic., cap. 22, enabled the expenses of medical relief to be defrayed out of the funds placed at the disposal of the relief committees under 10 Vic., cap. 7, and required the relief committees to provide the necessary medical aid.

When an application was made to the board of health for a requisition to provide temporary hospital accommodation under the act, the board asked for information including the extent of epidemic disease in the district, and the number of beds considered necessary. Where accommodation was required for adjoining or neighbouring districts, the board advised the provision of one large central hospital in preference to several small ones. If in doubt, the board sent one of their medical inspectors to the district to report. In all, 576 such applications were made and, of these, 373 were granted.

Temporary hospitals were commonly established in houses rented or occasionally lent for the purpose, and in wooden sheds built to a prescribed official plan. Additional accommodation for existing hospitals was provided for by expanding into other buildings or by erecting sheds or tents. The ordnance department in Ireland held 1,528 tents of military patterns, and although all types were used in an emergency, only the hospital tents, each providing 14 beds, proved adequate for the sick. There was a further reserve of 1,900 tents in England. In practice, sheds proved more suitable than tents, and the latter provided for Cork street hospital, Dublin, were reported in March 1847 to have been put out of action by a storm ; none the less tents were retained here for more than half the duration of the epidemic, when sheds took their place. The board of health advised that tents should be reserved for country places and villages, because in towns houses or stores were available for hire, or else wooden sheds could easily be erected there. In July 1847, the ordnance board announced that they could provide no more tents for civilian use in Ireland.

Some of the temporary fever hospitals were of a large size, those at Kilmainham and Drumcondra having 990 and 600 beds, respectively. The number of days which each patient spent in these hospitals averaged 24, and the daily cost of each patient was about 10½d. [9]

The numbers of patients in temporary fever hospitals on 21 August 1847 were : Ulster, 3,064 ; Munster, 6,966 ; Leinster, 4,952 ; Connacht, 1,171. In September 1847, patients in these hospitals numbered 26,378. The expenditure to this date under 10 Vic., cap. 7, amounted to £120,000 including the erection and furnishing of fever sheds. This was authorised to be completely defrayed by the state. In relief of rates, the Government made free grants amounting to £552,992. The total number treated in temporary fever hospitals from July 1847 (when weekly returns began to be furnished regularly) to August 1850, was 579,721, with an average mortality of 10.4 per cent. In some individual hospitals the mortality rose at times to 30 per cent. It must be remembered that a large proportion of those attacked with fever, in many parts the great majority of the sufferers, did not enter hospital, and their numbers, therefore, are unknown.

VII.  ACTIVITIES OF THE BOARD OF HEALTH AND LOCAL AUTHORITIES

The board of health were generous in their appointment of medical officers additional to existing staffs, and in creating new posts.  When it was proposed to bring naval and military officers from England to help in the most fever-stricken parts, the board refused, pointing out that there was no difficulty in securing medical men of the right type who knew the country and the people.  It should be remembered in this connection that Gaelic was then the speech of some 4,000,000 of the people, and that in the western counties where disease was at its worst, the majority of the peasantry knew little or no English.  New dispensaries were established, and recalcitrant boards of guardians brought to book.  The Ballingarry guardians, who proposed to turn the wings of the workhouse into fever wards, were instructed to erect hospital sheds.  When the Galway guardians wished to delay setting up a fever hospital in Spiddal, they were told to go ahead at once.  On 21 May 1846, there were 34 cases of fever in Cavan workhouse.  The guardians had failed to provide a fever hospital as required by 9 Vic., cap. 6.  They were ordered to do so.  They refused because of the expense entailed.  By July 16, they were ready to co-operate with the board, and the treasury was appealed to for funds.  (This illustrates the weaknesses inherent in the act ; had the succeeding act been in force then, the guardians could not have obstructed, the cost of the fever hospital would have been defrayed by the local relief committee, and ultimately by the state.)  Complaints were investigated by the board's medical inspectors who took steps to ameliorate the dreadful conditions which had come about in many institutions. In February 1847, the authorities of Lurgan workhouse were told by the board that their mismanagement was adding to the misery of the destitute poor, and causing an unparalleled increase of sickness and mortality.  (It should be pointed out here that two medical officers of the hospital were then ill with fever.)  The clothing of those dead from fever had been issued without disinfection to paupers newly admitted to the workhouse.  The diet was unwholesome and insufficient, and the supply of bed-clothes quite inadequate.  They were directed to increase the accommodation by hiring a house or erecting hospital sheds— 36 military tents were later dispatched—and to make arrangements for ample dispensary relief including the issue of food and drink. In the same month Dr Richard Stephens, one of the board's inspectors, reported that Bantry workhouse was reduced to a deplorable state of filthiness and disorder. After a sworn enquiry, the physician was called on to resign, and the master and matron dismissed.

To relieve the overcrowding in the hospital of Cork workhouse (already described) where in one week of February 1847 164 patients died, the board directed that Elizabeth Fort was to be taken over, as agreed with the military ; 11 houses hired as temporary hospitals in neighbouring rural districts ; and hospital tents and sheds erected. Nine additional physicians were appointed to the hospital, paid by the treasury. A main contributory factor in causing the congestion and chaos had been the refusal of Cork fever hospital in January 1847 to accept any more patients from the workhouse, as the accommodation was fully required for the increasing fever in the city.

After a delay of some weeks [reports Dr Popham], in endeavouring to set to work the complicated machinery of the board of health, the local authorities resolved to act for themselves, and, on application, the trustees of the North Infirmary gave up their hospital [the patients were transferred to the South Infirmary], which was, I believe, the first public step made in this country for meeting the epidemic. The hospital was ready for the reception of patients on February 23, and was worked by a medical staff for three weeks before the board of health was ready to give the necessary sanction.

This additional accommodation, however, proved insufficient for the large numbers hourly applying for admission, so in March and April two other large hospitals were opened and sheds added to the Cork fever hospital ' so that in a population of 80,000 we had for several months from 700 to 800 patients under daily treatment for fever '.

A situation perhaps unique in the history of hospital administration came to a head in Hillsborough (co. Down) in June 1847. The town was served by a temporary fever hospital established at Culcavy, but for some reason which does not appear, certain persons incited by the archdeacon of Down (Rev. Robert Moorhead) set up a ' so-called fever hospital ' in several old

houses in Ballynahinch street ' nominating themselves governors ',
and ' several persons labouring under Fever ' were brought there
in carts.   The local relief committee resolved unanimously :

> That immediate measures be adopted to remove the said
> persons labouring in fever, under the directions of Dr Croker,
> and *by compulsion, if necessary,* to such fit and proper place,
> as Dr Croker shall point out ;  and, that the persons legally
> appointed officers of health, at the last Easter vestry of this
> parish, be requested to use the powers vested in them by the
> 59th George 3, Cap. 41, to ensure the attendance of the police
> on the above occasion, in order to render such assistance, as
> the said act enjoins ;  and in case of resistance to bring the
> different offenders before the proper functionaries, in order
> to their being dealt with according to law.

The archdeacon's faction then attempted to bring fever patients
into the town by force, and for a time a serious riot seemed likely
to develop ;  but the presence of two magistrates—Colonel
Hawkshaw and Hill Wilson Rowan, Esq.—with a body of police
overawed the crowd, and after denouncing the action of the
authorities, the archdeacon advised his party to withdraw peace-
fully, which they did, taking their fever patients with them.
The burden thrown on the resources of the hospitals was
increased in many ways.   When the sick were refused admission
for lack of space their friends often brought them in carts at
night, and having deposited them at the door or nearby, departed
in the hope that the hands of the staff would thus be forced.
Many claimed to be suffering from fever merely to secure food
and shelter.   Again, numbers of those worn down by starvation
were wrongly thought to be cases of fever.   In March 1847, Dr
Stephens reported to the board of health that he had seen many
such ' lying in their wretched hovels on miserable beds ' who had
been reported as fever cases.   But on examining them and
inquiring into their symptoms and history, he found generally
that they ' complained only of weakness and a feeling of sinking
about their hearts. . . .   When they find themselves in this state
they lie down in their beds such as they are, and they are at once
said to be in fever, and from this alarm and terror are spread
abroad and reaching the ears of the gentry and others the
consequences are obvious '.   No doubt the obvious consequences

referred to were the alarmist reports which irresponsible people hastened to send to the board of health without having troubled to inquire if the allegations they made had any foundation of fact. Perhaps Dr Stephens had particularly in mind a hurried journey he had undertaken to Kells, only to find that the reported outbreak of fever did not exist.

### VIII. ATTEMPTS TO LIMIT THE SPREAD OF INFECTION

In general, hospitals were satisfactorily managed, according to the standards of the time, where they escaped overcrowding either because disease in the neighbourhood was less intense, or through the resolution of the staff in rejecting applicants. The governors of the Dublin fever hospitals set themselves to combat the worst evils of overcrowding even at the cost of wholesale rejections, a step which first became necessary in September 1846 ; until that date no fever patient had been refused admission since March 1838. In July 1847, 1,285 patients were admitted, and 553 rejected. In June, there had been rejected 778, more than half of those who applied. At the end of this month, all these hospitals put together had one vacant bed. In August there was an improvement, in part due to a fall in the number of applicants, and in part to increased accommodation, so that at the end of the month 147 beds were vacant. Applicants refused admission to a hospital were entitled to receive treatment and nutriment in their homes.

It is one of the failings of human nature that evil is always more widely noised abroad than good, so it is pleasing to be able to quote reports to the effect that a fever hospital is ' airy and commodious ' ; that ' dispensary relief is sufficient ' ; that disease is ' mild and yielding to treatment ' ; that there is ' no want of hospital accommodation ' ; and that boards of guardians are anxious to co-operate with the board of health, and even to anticipate its wishes. Many localities took action under 59 Geo. 3 cap. 41 which empowered a parish vestry to appoint officers of health. Their duties included cleansing lanes, yards, courts, and closing up sewers ; ventilating and fumigating houses in which fever had appeared ; washing and purifying the clothes of the inhabitants ; and further, ' preventing the unrestrained intercourse of strolling beggars, vagabonds and idle persons '.

In Cork at a time when two out of every five hospital patients were strangers to the place, a protective guard formed under this act was posted round the city with a view to checking the influx. In April 1847, the police of Dublin asked that the mayor, church-wardens and officers of health be requested to organise a staff of able bodied and if possible well disciplined men, to be placed at the principal entrances to the city to prevent the further influx of country paupers. The fever act, 10 Vic. cap. 7, enabled the relief committees to enforce and pay for the cleansing of houses, persons, and clothing, powers which were freely used, as in Kenmare union where 5,107 cabins were whitewashed inside and out. These measures were credited with having saved 'innumerable' lives.

One instance may be quoted of the effect of control of the epidemic by hospital isolation. The islands of Inisbofin (pop. 1,600) and Inishark remained free from fever until the summer of 1848 in spite of preceding severe distress and starvation, for not only had the potato crop failed, but the fish for two years past had deserted that coast. Dr Fry, sent by the board of health, arrived in August to take charge. Relapsing fever which ' could not easily be confounded with typhus ' had then prevailed for at least two months ' and had proved very fatal '. Dr Fry continues:

> I bought up all the milk I could get, and distributed it among the sick, most of whom had nothing to drink but water, and after a few days I was enabled to allow my patients a little rice, in addition to the milk, through the generosity of the Friends' Central Committee, who, with their wonted liber-ality, forwarded me a cargo of rice, on my communicating to them the state of want and destitution in the district. A dispensary and temporary fever hospital were next fitted up, by which means the progress of the epidemic was arrested, and, finally, got under completely in three months. . . . When any one individual of a family got the fever, and was not immediately moved to hospital, in a few days every member of the family was attacked ; and, on the other hand, where separation of the sick from the healthy was attended to at once, the disease was arrested. . . . When the hospital was first opened, I had numerous enemies to encounter, and many difficulties to overcome, owing to the ' fairy doctors '[10] and

the ignorance and superstitions of the people. However, after some time, when they saw the patients whom I had in hospital recovering, and some, who could not be persuaded to come into hospital, dying, their prejudices gave way, and they began no longer to look upon me as a dangerous emissary from the Government.

In contrasting this success with the many failures to stay the epidemic in other parts, it must be remembered that in these isolated islands there were no invading hordes of fugitives to swamp the hospital with their numbers.

The transmission of fever by contagion was in general recognised by everyone, though some doctors believed that the diseases might possess some further inherent power of originating themselves in the absence of foregoing contact, so rapid was the spread especially of relapsing fever. The recorded instances of disease appearing, where seemingly there had been no contact with another case, are no doubt explained by the occurrence of infections so mild that they were overlooked, and by the conveyance of infected lice by convalescents or by persons themselves unaffected, or by transmission of infective louse faeces.

The efforts made to break the chain of contagion between the sick and the healthy accorded with the theories of the time and the circumstances of those concerned. In hospitals where the demands for admission were not excessive, or where, as in Belfast, the initial chaos was eased by expansion, the aim was that cases of typhus, relapsing fever, and dysentery, both active and convalescent, should be kept separate ; but as the agency of the louse in transmitting these two fevers was unknown, and indeed was not proved for another sixty years, many of the methods of fumigation and disinfection then in vogue in hospitals would fail in their object, though the ancillary measures of ventilation and spacing out of the sick, where these could be effectively enforced, were soundly conceived. The local relief committees were directed to impress on all assembling at the food depots the necessity of personal cleanliness, and if possible to organise public washhouses. Steps of this nature, though not specifically directed against the louse, would result in a reduction in the numbers of this vector of disease, proportionate to the thoroughness and persistence with which the procedures were carried out.

Centuries ago wise men taught, that to 'withdrive' lice 'the best is for to wasshe the [thee] oftentimes and to chaunge often-tymes clene lynen'.

At first the peasantry accepted the epidemic in a fatalistic spirit, and when one member of a household was attacked, they were resigned to see fever run through the rest of the family. But this attitude altered, and resignation was replaced by alarm. Through fear of 'road-fever' many of them abandoned their ancient custom of never denying to the poorest wayfarer whatever shelter and hospitality they had to offer ; and even neighbours who came from fever-stricken houses were driven from the door. People soon became aware of the danger of contracting fever through contact with the bodies of the dead, although the mechanism of conveyance was not understood. As a body cools after death, the lice which require bodily warmth for their existence, become for a time very active, leaving the surface of the body and coming out from their lurking places in what-ever clothing or coverings are worn. Given the opportunity of contact, the cold and hungry insects will eagerly transfer them-selves to the new host, carrying with them the organisms of disease which they have acquired. Through fear of infection the cere-monies which traditionally preceded burial were stopped. Bodies lay for days in cabins which the survivors had deserted ; and in some instances, failing any other means of disposal, the cabin was pulled down over them and set on fire. The rector of Kilcoe parish told how a small girl, refused shelter or help by every neighbour, tried to struggle to the local 'gentleman's place', a centre from which soup was distributed ; she fell exhausted in the avenue and lay there all night before she was discovered. All her family were dead and her mother and two sisters, the last to survive, had lain unburied in the house for days past, two of the bodies lying on the floor, and the other propped against the wall 'in the attitude of life'. Existing graveyards soon became 'choked up', and efforts to find new ground elsewhere provoked a public outcry, for fear of infection. The yards of workhouses were turned into burial-grounds, the graves extending to the very door. Where individual coffins could no longer be obtained, coffins with a sliding bottom, through which the corpse was dropped, were made use of, but in the worst affected parts even this device became impossible, and bodies were buried coffinless, several in one ordinary-sized grave, or in batches of thirty or more in large pits. So formidable had this problem become that the act, 10 Vic., cap. 22, empowered the relief committees to make arrangements for 'the proper and decent interment' of the dead, and to defray the cost from their funds.

Some of the peasantry adopted procedures of their own to isolate the sick. In Cappawhite (where later a temporary hospital was set up), a medical inspector of the board reported that when fever occurs in a poor family, the person affected is through fear of contagion abandoned, the door of the room or cabin is built up, and a hole made in the outward wall through which the dispensary doctor creeps to administer relief. At least in one parish of Donegal, the people tried to check the extension of fever by building rows of huts made of sods and wood (*bothógaí*), like the sheilings they occupied during cattle-grazing in the hills. Here the sick were carried on litters. Nourishment obtained from a 'soup house' (*teach brat*) in the grounds of the local landlord was passed in through the door of the huts by means of long-handled shovels, those of the sick not utterly prostrated assisting in the feeding of their helpless fellows. Within the memory of many still alive, survivors of the famine used to point out the ruins of the 'soup house' and the sites of the fever huts.

Port quarantine was imposed because of complaints from the authorities of Irish ports to the effect that passengers with fever were landing there from England. On 2 July 1847, her majesty's privy council ordered the customs commissioners to enforce that masters of all steam and sailing vessels (mail packet excepted) arriving in any port in Ireland with deck passengers from England, hoist the yellow flag and proceed to the quarantine station, to be detained there until inspected and passed by a medical officer.

### IX.  OUTBREAK OF CHOLERA

As though Ireland's cup of sorrow were not already full, cholera broke out in December 1848 ; it reached its height in May 1849, and began to decline in June. The disease was imported from England, by way of Scotland to Belfast, and had no direct connection with the famine. Epidemic cholera is spread almost entirely by contaminated water, but this means of conveyance had not then been discovered. At that time there was a division of opinion as to whether or not cholera is 'contagious'. The London board of health held that the disease cannot be passed on by contagion, on the grounds that persons coming into direct contact with cholera patients commonly escape infection. The Irish board of health decided to accept this view, and advised, therefore, that isolation of cholera patients was unnecessary. Graves challenged this decision with great vigour, and maintained that cholera can be conveyed by the infected person, though the mode of transmission, he argued, must differ in some way from that of other communicable diseases such as influenza. Many of the local health committees rejected the official pronouncement and wisely preferred to act on Graves' advice. The epidemic was severe and the mortality heavy especially in the towns. In proportion to their population, Drogheda, Galway, Belfast, Limerick, Waterford, Kilkenny, and Cork suffered most ; the rural districts escaped more lightly, and some counties entirely, as Donegal, Tyrone, Cavan and Fermanagh. According to the census figures there were 2,502 cholera deaths in 1848, 30,156 in 1849, and 1,768 in 1850. It is certain that cholera was not responsible for all these. In the account given of dysentery the confusion of one severe form of that disease with Asiatic cholera is referred to, and by 1847 over a thousand deaths had been attributed to cholera, this at a time when the disease did not exist in Ireland. The tendency to wrongful diagnosis, already in evidence in the pre-cholera period, would increase enormously with the advent of the true disease, for the outstanding objection to a diagnosis of cholera would no longer hold.

## X. END OF THE FAMINE EPIDEMICS

The potato blight did not end with the calamity of 1847, but broke out again with great virulence in 1848, and appeared once more in 1849 but with diminished fury, though sufficient to cause another serious failure of the crop. By 1850 the disease was clearly on the wane, and although the potatoes were affected in some counties, the loss was only partial and much of the crop was saved. The authorities had organised a campaign with a view to inducing the people to cultivate green vegetables, and root crops other than potatoes. 'Practical instructors' travelled through the country lecturing and distributing seed. The project had some considerable success, as in Glenties, Donegal—the county in which scurvy came to notice first—where the whole aspect of the countryside was described as having been changed by the new cultivation. Unfortunately in many parts the peasantry refused to change their traditional practices of agriculture, and each succeeding failure of the potato crop brought a continuation of hunger and distress. A welcome and beneficent change in the food situation came about by a marked fall in the price of oatmeal, which declined steadily from its peak of 25 shillings a hundred-weight in early 1847, until 1850, when it never increased beyond about ten shillings.

The diseases associated with the famine declined in the same gradual fashion, but still more slowly. In Dublin the epidemic was regarded as over in February, and in Belfast in September, of 1848 ; in which year many of the temporary fever hospitals were closed ; but fever and dysentery lingered on in many districts through 1849 and 1850, with a continuing high mortality which was attributed to the terrible privations which the sufferers had undergone. Finally, the operations of the fever acts came to an end in August 1850.

As has been explained in these pages, famine and disease were not uniform in their distribution and intensity. The west and south west of the island endured the heaviest visitation of fever, in particular, Galway, Mayo, Clare, Roscommon, Limerick city, Cork county and city, and Tipperary ; with these, one county of Leinster and one of Ulster should be included, Queen's county and Cavan, respectively. The most fortunate counties in this respect were, Antrim excluding Belfast, Down, Fermanagh, Tyrone, Dublin excluding the city, Westmeath, and Louth— that is, taking each as a whole, for in some areas of these, fever exacted a heavy tribute. The counties in which the highest proportions of the recorded deaths were attributed to dysentery were, Antrim, Kerry, Cork, Mayo, Galway, Leitrim, and Sligo.

### XI. THE CENSUS OF 1851

According to the census of 1851, deaths from fever during the famine years numbered 192,937 ; from dysentery and diarrhoea, 125,148 ; 20,402 deaths were attributed to starvation, but to this figure most of the 22,384 deaths shown as due to ' dropsy ' should be added, as no doubt the great majority of the subjects suffered from famine dropsy. Although scurvy must have contributed to much of the mortality, less than 200 deaths appear under this heading ; it is significant, however, that there was a four-fold increase in the number of deaths attributed to spitting and vomiting of blood—entries distinct from those under the heading ' consumption '. The rise shown in the deaths from ' marasmus ' (wasting) and ' infirmity, debility, and old age ' suggests that famine was largely responsible for the increase. In 99,015 cases, the cause of death was not specified. The deaths in union workhouses between 1841 and 1851 are given as 283,765, a figure probably substantially correct ; it applies mainly to the famine years, for in the early part of the decade the workhouses were only in course of construction.

At the famine period the present system of certification of deaths was not in force, so that the basis of the census tables was the returns furnished by hospitals and similar institutions, and information obtained from householders by enumerators appointed for the various districts. These latter collected their data after the famine, when parts of the country were virtually depopulated and whole villages laid waste. Many of those who had suffered most, and would have been best qualified to speak with authority, were gone, no one knew where. Thousands died in their cabins without having been seen by any doctor ; others were found dead along the roads, in ditches, in fields and in deserted houses. In explaining his inability to estimate the mortality in the Tuam district, the dispensary doctor wrote ' many people died without having applied for medical relief at all and, of those who did, many never applied a second time, or were totally lost sight of '. The following description originally written of the year 1741, was quoted by eye witnesses as equally true of 1817 and 1847 :

> The roads spread with dead and dying bodies ; mankind the colour of the docks and nettles which they fed on ; two or three, sometimes more on a car going to the grave for want of bearers to carry them, and many buried in the fields and ditches where they perished.

At the most tragic part of 1847, a Mayo road-inspector reported that he had secured the burial of 140 bodies which he found lying by the wayside. Is it to be imagined that the poor wretches who died thus, perhaps far from home, were ever identified or their deaths recorded ?  No doubt valuable figures based on first-hand knowledge were furnished both by doctors and clergy, but in the terribly devastated districts, where death had been most busy, too many of them were newcomers who had assumed office only when the worst was over.  In Clougheen, for instance, the doctor, an apothecary, and three Catholic clergy died of typhus within about ten days.  In presenting reports on the epidemic to his readers, the editor of the *Dublin Quarterly Journal of Medical Science* wrote :

> From several districts of Ireland, where the late epidemic committed fearful ravages, no reports have been received. In many cases we regret to say that this has been caused by the lamentable mortality amongst our professional brethren.

Hospital returns at their best were subject to inaccuracy, for many patients were admitted in a dying state when a diagnosis might be no more than a guess.  Large numbers had some variety of fever along with dysentery, and often scurvy or famine dropsy as well, and so did not die of one disease but from a combination of causes, and the particular heading chosen to embrace such deaths would be a matter of individual choice, and vary from hospital to hospital and from one recorder to another.  There were also gross shortcomings in the mere matter of entering up hospital books.  It was reported from one union : ' The causes of death have not been supplied, because the documents from which the desired information might in a great measure have been supplied, have been lost ' ; from another : ' Records are so imperfect and mutilated that it was quite impossible to glean from them the required information '.  The medical officer of one workhouse could find no entries of the causes of deaths prior to his appointment at the end of the summer of 1848.  In another workhouse hospital, 1,057 of the deaths were attributed to fever, but in 2,107 other fatal cases ' the diseases are not recorded in the doctor's books '.  In the books of other hospitals there are gaps of several months, owing to the death or illness of medical officers from fever ; and in the returns of the Sick Poor Institution, Dublin, for 1848, the figures for four months of the year— representing probably over 6,000 cases of disease—are missing, because of the ' almost contemporaneous ' deaths of two members of the medical staff from typhus, and the illness of three others from the same disease. Many institutions kept their books with exemplary care notwithstanding heavy handicaps, as in the north union workhouse, Dublin, where within a year one-half of the entire paid staff contracted fever, and of these more than half died. But between this high standard of performance and failure to keep any adequate records at all, there must have been many grades of clerical defect and omission which are not manifest in the census tables, though here and there this can strongly be suspected. Again, certain of the figures are puzzling. For instance, Dunfanaghy workhouse was opened in June 1845 to serve a part of Donegal which suffered heavily from famine and disease ; also a temporary fever hospital, independent of the workhouse, was set up in the same place in December of that year. Yet according to the census, the deaths from fever for the whole period of the famine numbered five in the workhouse, and 38 in the temporary fever hospital (in contrast, in Ballina workhouse 67 persons died of fever in one week). Similarly in Letterkenny workhouse, opened in March 1845—where there was no other fever hospital to affect the admission rate—the fever deaths are given as totalling 13. If these figures are correct, it must be assumed that the people of Donegal preferred to stay in their own homes, and die there.

These observations are not intended as a criticism of the compilers of that great work, the census of 1851. They faced many difficulties in gathering their figures of death and disease, and sorted and analysed them with scrupulous care and infinite patience. They themselves were well aware of the unreliability of many of the returns they dealt with, and were careful to point out some of the possible sources of error. None the less it is well to warn the reader against accepting the figures of mortality at their face value, and against basing any theory on the relative proportions of the several groups, because the possible error in each of the totals is so large that any deductions drawn from the differences between them would not only be valueless but actually misleading.

As Graves pointed out, twice as many emigrants left Ireland in 1847 as in 1846, with the inevitable result that ships were not only crowded but packed with passengers. There was hardly a single ship in which typhus did not break out, and thousands of emigrants met the fate from which they had fled. Graves mentions two emigrant ships by name : the 'Ceylon' with 257 steerage passengers had 117 deaths on the voyage, and 115 persons in fever on her arrival ; the 'Loosthank' with 349 steerage passengers had 117 deaths at sea, and only 20 passengers in all escaped fever. Within about nine months of 1847, 5,293 Irish emigrants died of typhus on the voyage to Canada ; 8,563 more were admitted to the quarantine station at Grosse Island, of whom 3,452 died—an average death rate of 40 per cent ; and of those who were taken into the marine and emigrant hospital, Quebec, or who had gone elsewhere in that city up to October 9, there died 1,041 an aggregate of 9,786 deaths in a little more than nine months among emigrants to Canada alone.

It is impossible to arrive at any accurate estimate of the total mortality in these fatal years, but there is no doubt that the deaths were far in excess of those stated in the official census, and probably reached some figure well above 500,000. Dr Curran, twice quoted in this account, died of typhus. In his obituary notice, the writer estimated that nearly a million persons had died from famine, or its consequences, up to the latter part of 1847. This is certainly an exaggeration but his estimate, if made applicable to the whole of the famine, may not be far from the truth.

### XII.   CONCLUSION

At an early stage of the war against famine and disease, the government and its agents lost the initiative by two fundamental miscalculations. Basing their forecast on previous happenings, they assumed that after the partial destruction of the potato crop in 1845, the next year would bring, if not a rich crop, at least a sufficient one, for never before had the blight in its second year of duration swept across the country with all-consuming fury. For the second error, the board of health was responsible : the misreading of portents so that the diminution in fever observed in the summer of 1846 was taken as an indication that the local outbreaks had already begun to decline. It is impossible today to dissociate oneself from after-the-event wisdom, and assess the culpability of the members of the board for their failure to discern the signs of times. They could not foretell that the scheme of relief works, which looked admirable on paper, would miscarry in practice, as the best laid schemes have a way of doing. Had it succeeded as was hoped and believed, there would have been no starving crowds to throng the roads and carry disease all over the country.  If the board had been wiser in its deductions, or if its members had included a prophet or a prophet's son, whatever preventive measures it might have proposed in order to meet the approaching epidemic, there was only one then available which could have had any immediate and far-reaching effect, namely, to provide additional hospitals to isolate all the sick as the cases arose, and so limit infection.  In view of the obstruction offered later to the board by local authorities when the epidemic was actually upon them, what would have been their response, and that of the treasury, to proposals to provide hospital beds to accommodate tens of thousands of fever cases which did not then exist, and which never might exist?  It was unfortunate that the board of health never enjoyed the confidence and full support of the medical profession.  Two of its three medical members— Crampton and Kane—would never have been appointed if the advice of any representative body had been sought.  Crampton chanced to be President of the College of Surgeons, but his long experience as surgeon to the Meath hospital was no preparation for the burden he had to share.  Kane had long ceased the practice of medicine, and, as Graves said, he was absolved of all blame for the shortcomings of the board through his uniform non-attendance at its meetings.  Corrigan, the third medical member, did not neglect his duties ; on the contrary he was attacked for doing too much, and for being in himself the whole board of health.  He was not popular with his fellows who thought him vain and self-assertive ;  his head had been turned, it was said, by his being called on to take the viceregal pulse.  But to many of his critics any stick was good enough to belabour Corrigan and the board.  He was held responsible for the outrageous daily fee of five shillings which the treasury paid for attendance at the fever hospitals, and for all the other instances of government parsimony in medical affairs. His opponents fancied that, by some magic which Corrigan did not possess, they in his place could have softened the stony heart of the treasury in London ; clearly they had never studied the peculiar quality that distinguishes the nether millstone.  Curran, an able young professor of medicine, denounced the official fee as an insult and, refusing to accept it, continued to attend fever patients gratuitously.  His lamented

death from typhus, by some process of reasoning, was laid to the
charge of the board of health.  Some of the critics were biased by
past controversies with Corrigan.  Knowing that an outbreak of
fever followed every famine with the regularity of clockwork, he
contended that hunger originated the fever.  This inference,
of course, was not correct, but he was right to this extent, that
it was the whole circumstances of famine that allowed the fever
to blaze up and spread.  One opposing party maintained that
fever was engendered by overcrowding and uncleanliness.
They were equally wrong and equally right, for these conditions
cannot generate fever, but only enable a pre-existing focus of
infection to extend its range.  In blaming the relief measures
for spreading disease by causing crowds of the destitute to congregate, they forgot, or did not choose to remember, that famine
fever had ravaged Ireland, long before anyone dreamt of poor
laws, relief acts, or government aid.  In what way nearly three
million persons could receive food gratuitously from the hands
of relief officials in one single day—besides those assisted by
private organisations, religious and lay—without causing the
recipients to gather in crowds in the process, they did not explain.
In fact, where the evils of overcrowding were at their most potent
was in the homes of the poor, and in order to remedy this, millions
of people must have been re-housed.  It does not come within
the scope of this survey to discuss the possible results if the food
shortage had been handled from its beginning with generosity,
vigour and foresight.  But once famine had the country in its
grip, fever was inevitable, and no board of health at that date, even
if given dictatorial powers and unlimited funds, could have brought
the epidemic to a speedy and dramatic end.  A century before
the famine, Lind had evolved the theory that typhus is carried
by lice, but abandoned it through misinterpreting some observations designed to test its truth, and medical opinion returned
to the belief that the disease is transmitted by noxious emanations
given off from the body of the sufferer.  It was known that typhus,
even in its most malignant form, would not spread if the subject
were thoroughly cleansed, and given fresh clothing which was
kept clean. But of all the methods of disinfection used at the famine
period with the object of counteracting the supposed bodily
emanations retained in contaminated clothing and bedding, and
rendering them infective, only two would have served to eradicate

the lice which infested these, namely, stoving in heated ovens, and boiling. Neither of them could have been chosen for use as a general measure, because of the impossibility of setting up an organisation and providing equipment on a scale sufficient to meet the needs of millions of people ; and the substitutes adopted— so far as the destruction of lice in clothing and bedding was concerned—were no more than a mere beating of the air. Today, only by wholesale treatment of a population with the new insecticides, and this compulsorily enforced by some authority with the power of military law, could epidemic typhus and relapsing fever of a like degree be stamped out effectively and with dispatch.

William Stokes, a great Irish physician whose name is still remembered in medicine, was inclined to join those who held the authorities responsible for spreading fever by assembling ' so many miserable men, women, and children ' to receive relief. None the less, looking back at the famine in after years, he wrote :

. . . If many were lost, perhaps ignorantly, let us think on the number saved. We cannot be suddenly wise. Nations, as well as individuals, must purchase experience, even though the cost be ruinous. And whatever fault we may find with the modes adopted for relief to the sufferers in the famine of 1847, we must applaud the intention, and be grateful for the efforts that were made.

CHAPTER VI


IRISH EMIGRATION TO THE UNITED STATES OF
AMERICA AND THE BRITISH COLONIES DURING
THE FAMINE

By Oliver MacDonagh.

i. Introduction

ii. Landlord-assisted emigration

iii. Government policy and state aid for emigration

iv. Assisted emigration to Australia

v. Shipping and the voyage

vi. The Irish in British North America

vii. The Irish in the United States of America

Appendix 1. The volume of overseas emigration

THE DEPARTURE OF AN IRISH EMIGRANT SHIP.

*Illustrated London News,* 1850.

# Irish Overseas Emigration during the Famine

## I. INTRODUCTION

EMIGRATION was not immediately affected by the famine. Down to 1846, the season was virtually confined to spring and early summer. Consequently, the blight which manifested itself in the autumn of 1845 could have had no influence upon the emigration of that year. Indeed, it was scarcely to be felt even in the first six months of 1846 ; and this was only to be expected, because the first failure had caused no really serious alarm, and emigration was not a matter to be decided lightly. The slight increase in numbers in these months[1] needs no unprecedented happening to explain it ; it can safely be regarded as a natural development in the movement in progress for many years.[2]

Totally different was the second, and universal, blight of July and August 1846. This had an instantaneous and unmistakable effect. For the first time in Irish history, there was a heavy autumn exodus. For the first time, thousands risked their lives upon a winter crossing, ready, it was said, to undergo any misery 'save that of remaining in Ireland '.[3] Equally significant was the fact that they embarked without sea stock,[4] for such an unprecedented omission suggested either extreme poverty or precipitate departure. Again, the evidence from the new world marks a change. The Canadian officials were astounded by so vast and reckless an immigration at the fag end of the year ; and they were in no doubt that it had sprung directly from the second blight. Almost every immigrant had confessed that it was this which had driven him away.[5] Finally, we have the

testimony of Irish observers during the winter of 1846–7.
'Nothing', Clanricarde wrote to Russell in December, 'can
effectually and immediately save the country without an extensive
emigration. And I have not met in Town, or in Country, a reflecting man who does not entertain more or less the same opinion'.[6]
Monteagle summed up the general impression by saying that the
blight had totally reversed the peasant's attitude to emigration :
what had been looked upon as banishment was now regarded as
release ;[7] and the burden of the evidence of innumerable Irish
witnesses before select committees in the spring of 1847 was
that the new passion to struggle free from the 'doomed and
starving island' was scarcely to be credited. No longer did the
traditional resistance to removal, or the length, the dangers and
the difficulty of the voyage seem to go for anything.[8] All this
can scarcely be accepted at its full face value. In the distress
and agitation of these months, there was a natural tendency to
be overwhelmed by what one saw, to place too great an emphasis
upon the outward manifestations of disturbance. Yet, by and
large, contemporaries were right in noting at least the first
stage in a profound social perturbation. At worst, their error
lay in pre-dating its complete development.

For the very first month of 1847 had brought a rush of Irish
emigrants to Liverpool : in January, 6,000 had embarked.[9]
This first wave consisted mainly of the poorest cottiers, who were
in no position to delay even a few weeks.[10] But it was immediately
followed by an outrush of smallholders of every sort. The
current comments in pamphlets and parliamentary papers, and,
more particularly, the reports and advertisements in the local
press, establish that thousands of farms were being thrown upon
the market in the south and west ;[11] that the internal transportation
systems—canal and long-car—were completely overtaxed ;[12]
that the demand on shipping rapidly outstripped the usual supply;[13]
and that epidemics of typhus and famine fever were sweeping
through the embarkation ports where hundreds of disappointed
emigrants had congregated.[14] Almost every circumstance indicated that the existing machinery could not cope with the vast
increase in numbers, or with the unprecedented disease, poverty
and improvidence of the departing. No longer was the season
confined to spring or summer ; no longer was the movement
held within a long established pattern of ports and trans-Atlantic

shipping ; no longer were decisions taken slowly and with care, or laborious months spent in preparation. On the contrary, the spring emigration bore all the marks of panic and hysteria, from the fights for contract tickets at the embarkation points to an outbreak of deliberate felonies, committed in the hope of transportation.[15] Newspapers were filled with stories of men who had not dreamed of going a few weeks before, but were now feverishly arranging their departures.[16] They proceeded from no settled calculation—' all we want ', as one group put it, ' is to get out of Ireland . . . we must be better anywhere than here '[17]—but from the impulse of the moment and the example of their neighbours.

This element of hysteria explains why the movement took especially heavy toll upon particular communities. The returns for the diocese of Elphin, for instance, show that, in many parishes, between 10% and 17% of the total Catholic population left for North America during the spring, while from others the loss was relatively small.[18] Similarly, it was said that some Galway villages lost almost one third of their people during March and April.[19] In the light of such evidence, it seems reasonable to conjecture that the prevailing want and misery had left the peasantry in an unstable condition, ready to be swept by some mass sentiment; and that, in such a situation, the sight of one neighbour after another throwing up his holding had a powerful psychological effect upon the survivors. Thus, we would find (though as yet in pockets rather than generally) something which was more a headlong scrambling from a stricken area, more a flight of refugees, than an emigration as ordinarily understood.[20]

To some extent, this is borne out by the relatively high proportion of ' snug ' farmers and urban bourgeoisie amongst the emigrants of 1847 ; for, of all classes, these were the least likely to surrender so long as hope remained. Three of the most competent observers of the time, Fr Mathew, Monsell of Limerick and John Robert Godley, believed that it was the small farmer, if not indeed the class above him, who formed the backbone of the 1847 movement ;[21] and, all through the year, newspapers drew attention to the numbers of the ' well-to-do ' amongst the current emigrants :[22] to 10 or 20 acre men who felt they could not face another season of disaster ;[23] to merchants whose businesses were ruined once the famine destroyed the bacon and provision trades ;[24] and to holders of over 20 acres, and even landed men, who were frightened by the accumulated burdens of the labour rate and the proposed system of outdoor relief.[25]  Other evidence and factors, amongst them colonial and American reports, the unsatisfactory nature of casual contemporary observations as a source for such conclusions, and the considerable extent of land-lord assisted, pauper and cottier emigration during the year, all incline us to reduce the proportion of better class emigrants to 25% or thereabouts.  But the surrender of even 50,000 of those who passed for ' well-to-do ' in famine Ireland would be sufficient to establish an ominous weakening of spirit for so early a stage in the process of disintegration ;  and therefore to reinforce the conclusion that the unsettling of society had gone far already.

When the 1847 season ended, it was found that, apart from the tens of thousands who had settled in Great Britain,[26] some 230,000 persons had emigrated to the new world and Australia. If the figures for 1846, 116,000, had caused astonishment and dismay, those for 1847 almost passed belief : so much so that popular tradition still dates the great migrations from that year. As we have seen, the tradition is not altogether wrong.  1847 was indeed a year of wonders, producing the first mass movement upon a grand scale,[27] and containing the first considerable emig-ration of the more stable classes.  The gnarled conservatism which had restrained the flood for decades was now broken, and the general morale perceptibly diminished.  Yet we must look to succeeding seasons if we are to see these revolutionary processes entire.  If 1847 has shown the peculiarities of the famine movement most spectacularly, it has also shown them incompletely. Mass emigration may still have been local rather that general ; the stable classes were not altogether, or even mostly, in despair ; and public opinion, as a whole, did not yet believe that Ireland was entirely ruined, or further large scale emigration quite inevitable.

If anything, there seemed ground for hope in the period between the harvest of 1847 and that of 1848.  After all, some 3% of the total population had emigrated in the preceding season ; and few believed that such a rate of loss could possibly be maintained. Again, grave disasters had overtaken the 1847 emigrants, about 40,000 or 20% of whom had perished at sea, or upon disembarka-tion ; and it was confidently expected that this would sober peasant

opinion considerably.[28]  As early as the autumn of that year, the
lord lieutenant had told Russell that ' owing to the accounts of
emigrant suffering that have reached this country, the emigrating
spirit has received a check'.[29]  Finally, the potato failure of 1847,
ruinous though it was, had yet been neither so widespread nor
so complete as that of 1846.  Thousands of small farmers might
have clutched even at such a straw : perhaps they should hold
on for one season more : perhaps the corner had been turned
at last.[30]  It is true that, despite the sharp fall in emigration towards
the close of 1847, there was a remarkable revival in the early
spring of 1848.[31]  But most of this activity sprang from an anxiety
to get away before the new passenger bill received the royal assent,
and the cost of passages, in consequence, increased.  When the
bill reached the statute book in March, and fares rose, albeit only
temporarily, emigration dwindled away ; and the complements
of all the late spring vessels were extraordinarily small.[32]  It is
also true that, amongst the very poorest, the desire to emigrate
seemed undiminished.[33]  The agents of a group of Sligo properties,
for instance, found their cottiers as eager to be off in 1848 as ever
they had been in 1847.[34]  But the cottiers were ruined already,
and of all classes had now the least inducement for remaining.
On the whole, therefore, the months with which we are here
concerned seem to show a suspension of the process initiated
in 1846.  Because of the rapid development of the remittance
system, and the peculiar strength of Irish family relationships
a very considerable emigration would, in any event, have followed
in the wake of 1847.  But it was not inevitable that the revolution
in sentiment and practice should have been immediately completed.
Whether or not it was to be carried through absolutely appeared
to hinge upon the outcome of the harvest following.

As this drew near, however, reluctant whispers in a few counties
grew to hopeless certainty everywhere.  The potato had failed
once more—totally and in all parts of Ireland—and the effect
was both immediate and profound.  The autumn and winter
of 1848 brought a wave of emigration which must have equalled
that of the first five months of 1847—and this time it swept on
without check right through the following season.  Panic seized
Munster once the full extent of the blight was known.[35]  Almost
overnight, the ports of the south and east became choked with
small farmers clamouring for passages at once.[36]  Throughout

the winter, tracts of land were simply left to waste, and what rural civilisation there remained seemed to fall in pieces. 'Those farmers', said the *Limerick Chronicle* in November, 'who could manage to prepare the land for tillage have not the courage to encounter a third or fourth adverse season. Such a climax of social disorganisation is without parallel'.[37] Despite the extreme slackness of the spring and summer, therefore, the total emigration for 1848 did not fall far short of 1847 in extent ; and it was now taken for granted that the next seasons would exceed in magnitude anything which had been known before. These expectations were well justified. In the years 1849 to 1852, emigration averaged well over 200,000 persons annually, and reached a climax in 1851, when all but a quarter of a million left for North America alone. So far as emigration went, then, the blight of 1848 appears to have completed the work of 1846, and finally confirmed the tendencies of 1847. When the year began, the smallholders and cottiers who still held on had already suffered three seasons of disaster, during which both capital and confidence had more or less steadily diminished. Now (we might almost say) they were placing Ireland upon final trial, and taking a fourth successive blight as lasting proof of guilt. This does not mean, of course, that anything like a majority determined on immediate departure ; but that, for the great bulk of the population, emigration had become at last a practicable course to be debated seriously, and that for hundreds of thousands the decision had become already one of timing their departure rather than one of whether they should go or stay. The course of emigration during 1849 makes it clear that some such alteration in opinion had been brought about, that some last restraining force had snapped.

As we have said, the first few months of 1849 brought no slackening in the tide from Munster.[38] On the contrary, things reached such a pitch in spring, that landlords had to coax their solvent tenants not to abandon holdings,[39] for the strange mood of reckless desperation which many observed in the departing, the feeling that come what might, 'they could not be worse off in America',[40] appears to have been almost universal. And matters were now no better in the west or north. As in 1847, there was an outbreak of felonies in Connacht with transportation as their object,[41] and, during February and March particularly, thousands of small farmers in the belt of country running north from Limerick to Mayo threw up their holdings.[42]   Similarly, there was considerable evidence of the sale of tenant-right in Ulster ;[43] and several witnesses before select committees, and northern members, testified that emigration was making dangerous inroads into the three main sections of rural society in the province : the farmers of more than 20 acres, ' the smallholders ' and the poorest cottiers.[44]

Most of the multitude of reports upon the volume of emigration during 1849 commented as well upon its quality : so much so that we may reasonably conclude that the emigrants of that year were, on the whole, of higher social standing than those of former seasons.[45]   To take one instance, Captain Larcom, whose employment at the Custom House in Dublin brought him in constant contact with the departing, believed that those of 1849 were of a most ' superior type '.[46]   Again, the medical inspectors at Liverpool reported that the bulk of the spring examinees were prosperous, and showed no signs of previous deficiency or want.[47] And with this evidence we can place the alarm expressed at home at the loss of capital and solvent farmers ;  and the mounting demand that the government interfere to check the flood.[48] All through the spring and early summer, the Irish members sustained this agitation in the commons ;[49] and in Ireland they were backed by landlords, newspapers, nationalists, priests and even permanent officials.   Almost every articulate Irishman, of whatever class, appears to have accepted Horsman's picture of the country in this year :  ' a ruined proprietary, a fugitive tenantry, a destitute people, and a desolate land '.[50]

It may well be that the real significance of such lamentation is not so much its evidence of fact.   While we cannot suppose that it was, to any material degree, illusory, we must recollect that no one could form a real estimate of the capital loss ;  and that once an outcry of this sort is raised, it is apt to be accepted uncritically by newspapers and politicians.   What is perhaps more important is that it seems to have expressed a deep mood of staleness and defeat, which had its origin in 1848, and which was to work right through the next three seasons.   The peasant who cried out, ' Let me go to the land of liberty.   Let me see no more of the titheman and the taxman ',[51] epitomised a universal weariness with struggling against hopeless odds at home.   The cumulative effects of increased taxation and repeated failures had

broken most resistance ; and there was now a final enemy, the
rate-in-aid, to take the field. Consequently, even the partial
success of the harvest of 1849 did little to reduce the feeling, or to
staunch the flow. If many of the farmer emigrants postponed
their departures till the autumn, they did so, not in the hope
that the potato would restore the old social fabric, but in the hope
that it would yield them enough to emigrate in comfort. It had
been noted in the spring that thousands of smallholders were
merely ploughing up the lea, ' evidently with the intention of
removing in the autumn ' ;[52] and when harvest came, there was
a prodigious increase in the practice of decamping which Clarendon
had previously described in these words :

> There is emigration going on but of those people only whom
> one would wish to keep—farmers with 1 or £200 in their
> pockets. They cut the corn on the Sunday, sell it on Monday
> morning, and are off to America in the evening, leaving the
> waste lands behind them and the landlords without rent.[53]

Gone completely were the fears of autumn or winter crossing
which had been so potent only four years before. Roche, a
Dublin broker, sold three times as many passages in the last
quarter of 1849, as in the corresponding period in 1847 ; and this,
he believed, was the universal experience of the trade.[54] Indeed,
it seemed that nothing could now act as a serious deterrent :[55]
neither the lateness of the season ; nor the promise of the harvest ;
nor the new restrictive legislation ; nor the news that cholera
had broken out at sea ; nor the repeated tidings of depression
and hardship coming back from both the new world and
Australia.[56] The fall and winter emigration was at least as heavy
as the previous year's, and continued without pause well into
1850. It is, above all, this indifference to other considerations
which establishes the power of the impact of 1848.

There is one last observation to be made upon the emigration
of 1849. This is the rapid growth of remittance and pauper
emigration.[57] It may seem paradoxical that the movement of
the very poorest should have got thoroughly under way in the
season of greatest middle class surrender. For an explanation
we must revert to 1846 and 1847, when it was most common
for cottiers and labourers, by a supreme individual or communal
effort, to raise enough to pay the passages of one or two members

of a family,[58] and when landlord assisted emigration was at its height. By 1849, the fruits of these emigrations were beginning to be felt upon a considerable scale. In the interval, the immigrants of 1846 and 1847 had saved sufficiently to provide passages and capital for the voyage for those who survived at home, either on the old holdings, or, much more commonly, in workhouses. The newspaper evidence suggests that this type of emigration became extensive during 1849, and continued to multiply for several years, with the net of relationships and beneficiaries spreading ever wider ; and this evidence is corroborated by the returns of the changing houses, and, to some extent, by American and colonial reports.[59]

The pattern of 1849 was followed almost exactly in the succeeding seasons.[60] There were variations : there was a minor wave of ' optimism ' in the spring of 1850 which ran a shorter, and even more uncertain, course than that of 1847-8 ; there were marked improvements in the conditions at sea as a result of the regularisation of the trade and the rapid development of restrictive legislation ; there was an extensive failure of the crop in 1851. Most curious, both government and public opinion, which had been so agitated by the movements of 1846 to 1849 and so forward with proposals either to foment or restrict the exodus, appear to have lost interest in it after 1850. But, on the whole, we can say that down to 1854 or 1855, it was the cataclysm of 1845-9 which was working itself out in emigration. Because of the force of the final disillusionment, and the prodigious extension of remittances, only a sudden and ubiquitous recovery in the entire Irish economy could have even reduced materially the emigration : and this was out of the question. Nevertheless, signs of ultimate recovery were to be seen as early as 1851. Sligo provides us with a fair illustration of how the process was to work. During the famine years, both voluntary and landlord emigration from the county had been heavy. Though small in area, it had then stood near the top of the county emigration scale. But in 1851, when there was a distinct labour shortage in the district, and wages were rising steadily,[61] it sank to the very bottom of the scale.[62] Similarly, the emigration commissioners noted, ' not without satisfaction,' a fall of 30,000 in the total emigration from Ireland in 1852. They observed that the number of ablebodied paupers in Irish workhouses had declined ; that there was a marked shortage of Irish labour in Great Britain ;[63] that the proportion of wage-earners to unemployed in Ireland was now 'considerably larger that formerly' ; and from it all they concluded that the 'surplus' of labour was already drained away from many parts.[64]

If the commissioners anticipated an immediate and heavy falling off in Irish emigration, they were mistaken. Just as the famine emigration had largely post-dated the potato blights, so also did recovery fail to take effect at once. But in the long run, their analysis was right. The whole matter can be stated briefly. Granted the existing agrarian framework, the Ireland of the early 1840's was grossly overpopulated, and now, at last, the overpopulation was reduced. A comparison of the censuses of 1841 and 1851 bears this out most spectacularly. By 1851, the total population of Ireland had declined by 20%, and the rural population by almost 25%. The cottier class had virtually disappeared. The number of holdings under one acre had dropped from 134,000 to 36,000. And with this trend and the consequent easing of the pressure upon land, there went a pronounced improvement in agriculture. In 1841, there had been 440,000 holdings of five acres or under as against 380,000 of over five acres ; in 1851, the figures were, respectively, 124,000 and 482,000. Again, the total area cultivated had increased from 13,400,000 acres to 14,800,000 ; the number of persons per square mile of this land had fallen from 355 to 231 ; and the average productivity had risen greatly. In short, the modern revolution in Irish farming had begun. Already, the supreme problem of a reasonable standard of living was well on the way to being solved, and there were yet vast emigrations to come throughout the decade.[65]

Two conclusions may be drawn from this comparison. The first is the importance of emigration in cutting the Gordian knot of overpopulation : the plain fact that more than two million persons left Ireland permanently during the decade, 1845 to 1855, speaks for itself. The second concerns the nature of the emigration. The returns suggest that the famine movement swept away a whole section of society, rather than a mere aggregation of individuals : in fact, that its basic unit was the family. Much of the contemporary evidence which we have already considered goes to support this conclusion. Whether the current emigration which contemporaries were discussing was pauper, cottier, smallholder or middle class, they generally implied that it was the family as a whole which was going, not its ' surplus members '. And this is corroborated by the age groupings of the emigrants of 1851 to 1855.[66] According to these tables, 42% of the emigrants were either under twenty years or over fifty, a proportion so extraordinarily high, by the common standards of migrations, as to reinforce considerably our general conclusion.[67]

We can now sketch in the outlines with some confidence. 1847 and 1848–9 were the most revolutionary seasons, the first showing the beginnings of mass emigration and other changes, and the second, their culmination. But the really critical years were 1846 and 1848. In both, the potato failed completely, with the second rounding off the destruction which the first had wrought. And these hammer blows struck home so surely because they were accompanied by disheartening forces of every kind : death by starvation and great physical suffering close at hand ; the protracted, seemingly endless struggle against wretched harvests, rising taxation and fixed rents ; the partial collapse of ordinary commerce, especially in cities depending on provision trades ; the pricking of the repeal bubble long before O'Connell's death ; and the humiliating outcome of the 1848 rebellion. The failure was not merely economic, not merely the long prophesied disintegration of an iniquitous, top heavy system of land tenure, which denied anything like a tolerable standard of living to more than half the entire population. It was a failure of morale as well. The mood prevailing from 1848 onwards seems to differ from the earlier terror and excitement. Wherever it is caught, it is marked by a note of doom, an air of finality, a sense that a chapter in history has come decisively to its close. This mood explains many of the peculiarities of the famine movement, not least the bitterness and sense of wrong which so many emigrants carried with them to the new world.

In all, about a million and a half people emigrated in the actual years of blight. Relatively speaking, no other population movement of the nineteenth century was on so great a scale. Even if we allow for a steady replacement by births, and ignore the extraordinarily high death rate of 1846–8, this represents a loss of almost 18% of the entire population in less than seven years. Yet, in retrospect, even so vast an emigration may seem overdue. Cobbett's comment on the English farmers in 1821, ' they hang on,

IRISH EMIGRANTS RECEIVING THE PRIEST'S BLESSING.

*Illustrated London News, 1851.*

like sailors to the masts or hull of a wreck', could have been
applied with much more force to the Irish peasants of the 1830's.
In this sense, certainly, the famine emigration may be looked
on as a population movement unnaturally postponed. But I think
it a mistake to go further, to argue that it was no more than
the pre-famine exodus writ large. No doubt, the movement of
the three decades which followed Waterloo accustomed public
opinion and politicians to the concept of emigration as a partial
solution of Ireland's economic difficulty, and spread the practice
of emigrating to many parts of the south and west where it had
hitherto been unknown.[68] But, for all that, the new context
of famine and desolation brought about a real change in essence.
Indeed, the mere novelties of size and celerity, occasioned by
its mass and infectious character, would seem sufficient to bring
it into a new category of demography. And these were but the
outward manifestations of a profound inward alteration in opinion.
One might almost say that the potato blights of 1845–9 caused a
*volte face* in the general attitude to emigration. Broadly speaking,
by relaxing the peasant's desperate hold upon his land and home,
they destroyed the psychological barrier which had forbidden
his going for so long. Something of the same sort may have
happened, under special circumstances and in particular districts
during 1815 to '45. But it was now group rather than individual,
universal rather than local. For in one sense, at least, the dreadful
seasons of 1845 to 1849 broke the back of Irish farming. I do
not mean, of course, that the tenant ceased to struggle fiercely to
maintain his holding, but that these catastrophes, following upon
decades of a hand-to-mouth existence, broke his exclusive passion
for survival at home, and forced him to recognise that there was a
*deus ex machina* at hand, a practicable, if unpalatable, alternative
to be considered. Perhaps it may be put like this : where previously
the average holder had regarded emigration as a most exceptional
course of action, something that another might consider seriously
rather than himself, he was now compelled to look upon it as a
'personal' possibility, a genuine alternative to maintaining the
struggle against such fearful odds. Some might prefer to say
simply that the famine drove the mass of Irishmen to think of
last resorts. But wherever the emphasis is placed, the brute fact
of change remains ; and once the revolution was accomplished,
large scale emigration was bound to play a major, if negative
part, in the entire Irish social system for many decades.

## II.  LANDLORD–ASSISTED EMIGRATION

For many years before the famine, landlords had realised
that assisted emigration was a simple, and, in the long run, cheap
solution to the problem of overpopulation on their estates.[1]
Most properties could not have been improved without some
clearances ; and, in any event, there was a growing desire to replace
the wasteful tillage and uncertain rents of the cottier system
by livestock and dairy farming.[2]  Unquestionably, larger holdings
would yield better returns, and two simultaneous tendencies,
the perfection of steam transport and the urbanisation of the
British population, had created a new and important market
for agricultural produce.  This movement, working with other
factors to the same end, had brought about wholesale evictions
in the 1830's and early 1840's ; and, in several cases, assisted
emigration had accompanied these clearances.  By 1846, Colonel
Wandesforde, for example, had sent out 3,000 persons from
Castlecomer, at a cost of £5 each.  His ' investment ', he believed,
paid cumulative dividends, for the emigrants formed regular
settlements (the farmers in Upper Canada, the miners in Potts-
ville, Pennsylvania), and their encouragement and remittances
induced many of the remaining tenants to join them.[3]  But
one real difficulty in the years before the famine was the reluctance
of the cottiers to leave their homes.  Gore Booth's experience
was that they preferred poverty on their own holdings to
' prosperity elsewhere ' ;[4] and a land agent told the Devon
commission that, though he had offered his tenants emigration,
' there's such a clinging to the country that they would live on
anything rather than go '.[5]  The main work of the potato blights
in regard to landlord-assisted emigration was to weaken this
prejudice considerably, and to persuade many proprietors, who
had hitherto been deterred by the expense, bother and responsibility that was involved, that the practice had to be adopted.

Landlord emigration during 1846 was unusually heavy, but,
as with voluntary emigration, it was more an extension of existing
courses than anything revolutionary.  Over 1,000 of the emigrants
to Quebec alone had been assisted.  A third of these came, as
might have been expected, from Limerick ;[6] and a fair proportion
of the remainder from Dublin, where many of the landlords
had agents who managed their removals.[7]  Few of the tenants

were sent out in parties, though one large group came from Derry Castle, in Tipperary, which Spaight of Limerick had bought in 1844.[8]  He had found the estate burdened with a ' deadweight ' of paupers, and, being himself a shipper, had set about clearing it by emigration.[9]  But this was the only large scale removal to be attempted,[10] for proprietors were loth to commit themselves to great expense.[11]  After all, the first potato failure had been partial only ;  and even when the second covered the whole country like a blanket, they still cherished a hope that government would be forced to adopt systematic emigration.[12]  Not until the beginning of March 1847 did it become quite certain that the state would take no action.[13]  Then came an amazing outburst of landlord activity.   There were reports that Miley, the Dublin shipping agent, was booking over 8,000 passages on behalf of landed men ;[14] that Lord de Vesci was undertaking extensive removals from Queen's county ;[15] and that more than 500 of Spaight's cottiers had accepted his offer of passage and provisioning to Quebec.[16]  Some of the proprietors mentioned, Ormonde, Wyndham and Spaight himself, had used emigration extensively in earlier years, but the great majority had never resorted to it before.[17]  For them, it was a most exceptional remedy, called for only by so desperate a situation.[18]

The landlord emigration of 1847 followed closely the pattern of former seasons.   Limerick and Dublin were, as usual, the centres of the movement.   During the spring and summer, Dublin sent 2,000, and Limerick 1,400 assisted emigrants to Quebec alone ;  from the other Irish ports came 2,000 more.[19]  But, however conventional in form, it was unprecedented in magnitude and wretchedness, and unusual in at least two respects :  one, that the tenants were sent out, not as a few scattered families, but in large, relatively compact groups ;  the other, that their mortality at sea was lower than that amongst ordinary emigrants.[20] As for the extent, 1847 was quite without parallel.   Well over 5,000 landlord-assisted emigrants reached Canada during the year ;[21] the New Brunswick emigration was extraordinarily heavy ;  and, very probably, the number disembarking at American ports was correspondingly increased : at any rate, the Irish evidence would suggest as much.   The great majority of the emigrants had received only their fares ;  a few, provisions as well ;  and a handful, some small gratuity upon landing.[22]  On the whole, they were much more miserable and helpless than in former years.[23]

But Irish landlords were not at all discouraged by the scandals of 1847, or the tumult of colonial recrimination which followed them.   On the contrary, it was said in 1848 that some of them were forcing emigration upon their reluctant cottiers ;[24] and though the landlord-assisted emigration of that year was smaller than the previous season's, it was still, relatively speaking, large, and as destitute as ever.[25]   Once again, Munster and the counties south of Dublin provided the lion's share of the emigration ; once again, proprietors like Spaight and Wyndham continued their systematic clearances.[26]   But the 'remedy' was spreading widely, and the example of the south and east was being followed more and more in Connacht ;[27] so much so, in fact, that, by the end of 1848, emigration had firmly established itself as the satisfactory 'humane' means of getting rid of cottiers.   The famine was only partly responsible for this advance in favour. Many, as we have seen, had been using it scientifically, year after year, to clear their lands ;[28] others, like Lord Stanley, did not adopt it on a considerable scale until the worst of the famine crisis had passed away.[29]   What was, perhaps, more important in popularising the practice was its almost universal success from the proprietors' standpoint.   If Sir John Walsh had, as he himself put it, 'very great difficulty' in persuading his poorer tenants to accept passages to Quebec, he felt that his exertions had been well repaid by the restoration of tranquillity to north Kerry.[30] Similarly, Monsell observed that many estates became quite peaceful, once the more turbulent cottiers had been removed to the ruder society of North America ;[31] and these comments are thoroughly representative of the whole.

Despite such satisfaction, however, the volume of landlord emigration fell sharply after 1850.   This was only to be expected. The pressure of population was easing almost everywhere ;  and most of the landlords, who desired, and could have afforded to assist emigration, had already undertaken it either before or during the famine years.[32]   There were still, of course, occasional large scale clearances.   In 1851, for instance, Lord Lansdowne, on his agent's advice, spent £14,000 in sending out every pauper chargeable upon his Kerry properties.[33]   But the general falling off may be estimated from the fact that, during the 1850's, the average number of landlord-assisted emigrants to land at Quebec each year was less than 500,[34] as against an annual average of over 2,000 during the famine years. Even in the period, 1846–52, landlord-assisted emigration must have been very small; it can scarcely have exceeded 50,000 in extent.[35] Yet it achieved much more than these numbers might suggest, for it set the population moving from many places where the congestion was most hopeless. Remittances were substantial evidence of success in the new world, and enabled many of the remaining tenants to pay their passages;[36] and the presence of neighbours, friends and relatives in North America, often living together in the same city, was a still more powerful encouragement to emigrate. Moreover, it appears to have left little bitterness on the surface, at any rate. Though public opinion was far from steady, there was scarcely any contemporary counterpart of the deep seated hostility and resentment which grew up later on. Even the *Freeman's Journal* once headed a description of the dispatch of Ashbrooke's tenants to America, ' Good landlords '.[37] To appreciate this interpretation of landlord-assisted emigration at its full value, it is only necessary to conjecture the furore it would have provoked, say, thirty years later. As it was, proprietors could plead that it set many districts on their feet again, and that, all things considered, the emigrants themselves had much reason to be grateful.

Such a plea involves us in the ' ethics ' of the matter. To put it over simply, perhaps, was landlord-assisted emigration justified? In this form, the question cannot be answered directly by the historian. So much depends upon the standpoint of the participants; upon whether the view taken is ' practical ' and ' realist ', the estate manager's or the political economist's; or something which undercuts these arguments completely by opening its discussion at the origins and history of ownership. But, without attempting impertinent moral judgments, we may yet go some distance in elucidation. First, we may say that even ' undertaking ' emigration sometimes involved inhuman callousness. ' Dr Donovan and Mr Swanton ', wrote the commissariat clerk of Skibbereen in 1847, ' are applying the funds sent to them for the destitute poor, in shipping wretched, naked creatures to England and Wales '.[38] Similarly, an offer of ' assisted emigration ' often meant no more than eviction and a small sum which could not possibly have

paid the fare.[39]   And again, as Peel himself wrote privately in
1849, for ' forced emigration ' and consequent disturbances,
Clare and Donegal presented many close parallels with Skye and
North Uist.[40]   For compulsion did not have to be direct and
positive.   Almost every landlord could have claimed that, in the
literal sense, his emigration scheme was quite voluntary.   When
Lansdowne's agent offered his wretched tenants free passage
and a few shillings over, he may well have been justified in saying
that ' not the slightest pressure [was] put on them to go ' ;  or
that they knew too well which side their bread was buttered on
to listen to the cries of ' extermination ' which were raised.[41]
But the nationalist or, indeed, anyone with common sense
could answer that the cottier's ' choice ' was often a complete
illusion.   There was, as the bishop of Elphin reminded Shrews-
bury, ' a vast distinction between . . . *voluntarium simpliciter* and
*voluntarium secundum quid*'.[42]   A poor tenant, ringed about by
bailiffs and destitution, unable to pay his rent and struggling to
keep his family alive, was in no position to refuse even a penniless
landing on a strange shore.   He had neither legal rights nor
bargaining power ;  and if, as sometimes happened, his landlord
treated him humanely when he sent him out, that was a simple
matter of humanity and nothing more.   For in the relationship
of Irish landlord and tenant, there was no element either of feudalism or of partnership.[43]   As often as not, a high proportion of
the people on an estate were squatters or sub-tenants ;  and Russell
voiced the general opinion of landed men upon their rights when
he said, ' you might as well propose that a landlord compensate
the rabbits for the burrows they have made '.[44]

A single instance, that of Major Mahon's Roscommon estate,
will illustrate sufficiently the average landlord's dilemma and
point of view.   In 1848, his agent said, the 2,400 people occupying
his 2,100 acres produced only one third of the food needed for
their own support.   The union workhouses could not cope with
the destitute, and both rates and rents were three years in arrears.
If the estate were to be run on business lines, a drastic clearance
seemed essential ;  and the total cost of sending the ' surplus '
to America was considerably less than the expense of maintaining
them for a single year as paupers.[45]   It was therefore determined
to offer them the choice of emigration or eviction.   The terms
of the offer, free passage and provisions, with permission to sell

or carry away stock and effects, was certainly no worse than usual ;[46] and, if the estate accounts can be believed, the sea diet was intelligently prepared and extraordinarily lavish.[47] All things considered, then, Mahon probably thought himself a generous man. He might have argued that the removal of his tenants was as necessary for their own survival as it was for the improvement of his estate,[48] and boasted that he had spent £14,000 from his private capital to achieve it.[49] It is true that, as things turned out, 25% of his emigrants died at sea, and the medical officer at Quebec reported that the survivors were the most wretched and diseased he had ever seen.[50] But, almost certainly, Mahon would have disowned all responsibility for this ; and, indeed, have failed entirely to understand those who blamed him for what occurred. Yet, within a few months of this very undertaking, Mahon was murdered, the victim, like so many of his class, of ' agrarian outrage '.[51]

It is, of course, more difficult to see the other side of the medal ; there is little material which might elucidate the attitude of the cottier who accepted emigration. But some slight evidence survives in the correspondence between the commissioners of woods and forests and their agent, arising from their decision to clear the crown lands at Ballykilcline. The estate, wrote Clarendon in 1847, ' was for years past the most mismanaged in Ireland ',[52] and many of the cottiers accepted the first offer of assisted emigration readily enough. But while the party was being got ready for departure, feeling against emigration grew steadily ; the agent complained that people were constantly changing their minds.[53] Perturbed by this report, the commissioners refused to make public their decision to compensate tenants who were unwilling to emigrate with money, lest a very large number should then refuse to go.[54] By such an exercise of ' tact ', they managed to pack off 200 persons without unseemly recriminations ;[55] but twenty-five families still clung on by one means or another. The agent now renewed his demand for a total clearance of the property, so that he might redivide it into twenty acre farms ;[56] and once the commissioners agreed to this, pathetic, half-literate petitions began to pour in from the remaining tenants. Each of them, embedded in archaic, preposterous flattery, amounted to a prayer to be allowed to die ' in the land of their forefathers and their birth '. They pleaded the ' decline '

in their families, or the delicacy of their parents, or the fact that
they had never taken a part with the ' lawless banditti ', as grounds
for refusing emigration and being allowed to retain their lands.[57]
Needless to say, no attention was paid to these petitions ; but,
though the piece of evidence is slight, it does seem to bear out
what we should have thought most probable in any case : that
many of the tenants, who accepted emigration, did so with great
reluctance ; and that landlords could, and did, bring pressure
of a questionable sort to bear upon them.  For here the crown
behaved, by and large, as any ordinary landlord would have
done.[58]

A much darker light is thrown upon the worst aspects of
landlord-assisted emigration by the scandals, charges and counter
charges of 1847.  For these, the undertakings of Palmerston and
Gore Booth, neighbours in co. Sligo, provide fair illustrations.[59]  It
must be granted, at once, that Gore Booth took his responsibilities
unusually seriously, and that he had devoted uncommon attention
to the whole question of assisted emigration.[60]  Nor was it ever
suggested that he was unpopular with his tenants.  The parish
priest of Lissadell, where he lived, paid tribute to the concern
of Sir Robert and Lady Gore Booth for their people—they were,
he said, ' deeply rooted in the affections of a grateful peasantry '—
and testified that the emigration was altogether voluntary and
well provided for.[61]  The vessels were liberally victualled ;[62] and
though the number of people whom Gore Booth sent to New
Brunswick was very great,[63] no other group of Irish immigrants
was so well cared for in the province.[64]  The masters of his
vessels, co-operating with a timber merchant whom his brother
employed in St John, got immediate employment for many of
the tenants ;  forwarded some to Fredericton and the interior ;
and fed and lodged the remainder in the city.[65]  And though the
assisted emigration from Palmerston's estate had none of these
pretentions to paternalism, the terms of passage and provisions
were comparatively good.  Indeed, Palmerston had spent considerably more *per capita* upon his tenants.[66]

If, however, either of them had felt satisfied with his undertaking,
he was soon shaken by the colonial reaction.  From the first,
Perley, the chief emigration officer at St John, demanded that
Gore Booth be publicly condemned for ' shovelling out ' the
helpless and infirm ;[67] and when the third vessel from Sligo was

on its way, he remarked that 'another infliction of paupers may be expected'.[68]   He had, of course, the satisfaction of realising his worst anticipations : very many of the passengers were a public burden from the moment they disembarked.[69]   And this feeling was altogether exceeded by the resentment which Palmerston's emigrants aroused.[70]   The first attack on Palmerston was launched as soon as his cottiers landed at St John.[71]   End, a member of the provincial assembly, examined them, and then accused the master of threatening them into silence, and Palmerston's agent of throwing old and helpless people on the colony.[72]   This was followed by a general wave of indignation when Palmerston's second vessel, the *Æolus,* arrived at the fag end of a season of miseries.   The common council of St John condemned such 'inhuman callousness';[73] and Harding, the quarantine surgeon, exclaimed that 99% of the emigrants would remain a public charge : 'who [is] so tame as would not feel indignant at the outrage ?'[74]   Still later in the season, Palmerston's third vessel reached Quebec.   This provoked the final explosion of colonial resentment.   Ferrie, the chairman of the Canadian emigration committee, led a fierce and inaccurate attack upon Irish 'landlordism' generally, and Palmerston's 'human cargoes' in particular.   To bring about such 'barbarity', he concluded, tenants had been forced to accept passages by starvation and false promises of clothes and landing money.[75]

In replying to these accusations, neither Gore Booth nor Kincaid, Palmerston's agent, made any attempt to defend the type of people they were sending out.   Gore Booth openly admitted that he had got rid of 'what might be termed bad characters';[76] and Kincaid confessed that he himself always selected 'those who were the poorest'.[77]   It is true that, in rebutting specific charges, both of them could score debating points, for the colonial attacks had been wild enough to lend colour to counter charges of credulity, exaggeration and over-reliance upon the fragmentary conversation of malcontents.[78]   But even on matters of fact, the evidence was often overwhelmingly against them ; and in many cases, the arguments they fell back upon were manifestly absurd.[79]   The truth was that, once they had confessed that those whom they sent were the least desirable of their cottiers, the only possible defence was that the emigration was essential for the survival of their estates, and that their tenants could not possibly be worse

off than they were at home.[80]  It was both absurd and disingenuous to suggest, as did Kincaid, that the emigration was to
the advantage of the colonies, or that he had the welfare of his
cottiers first in mind.[81]   Obviously, those who were unwanted
and ' surplus ' in Ireland would be unwanted and resented in
America ;[82] and, obviously, landlords were treating their tenants,
by and large, as economic ciphers :  if emigration did improve
the tenant's lot that was an incidental, if welcome, consequence.
Nevertheless, there is no general moral judgment to be passed.
Landlords stand condemned for specific acts of inhumanity,
dishonesty and irresponsibility ;  but not, in justice, for a point
of view and tangle of economic difficulty, which, in nine cases
out of ten, they had merely had the misfortune to inherit.


### III.   GOVERNMENT POLICY AND STATE AID
### FOR EMIGRATION

Almost every contemporary remedy for Irish distress envisaged
the removal of a considerable portion of the population, as the
indispensible preliminary to economic improvement.   So long
as properties remained clogged with useless dependents, the
argument ran, there was not working room to introduce new
measures ;  and since agriculture was the only possible occupation
for the population as a whole, the standard of living could
not be raised while there was still not nearly enough cultivated
land to go around.   These beliefs explain the ceaseless attraction
of the ' emigration policy '.   How tempting it was to solve the
basic problem, and clear the way for reconstruction, by a simple
transfer of millions to another continent ;  what a finality the
prospect seemed to offer.   Moreover, the single stone promised
to bring down many birds.   The ship itself would become buoyant
with the lightening ;  the question of waste lands in the colonies
would be answered ;  the flood of Irish paupers to Great Britain
would be checked ;  new markets would spring up for expanding
British industry ;  and, if it were judiciously conducted, the centre
of resistance to imperial authority might be destroyed.[1]

It was not surprising, then, that the ' policy ' should have
persisted for more than quarter of a century.[2]  Nor (since its
appeal was strongest whenever the distress became unusually
acute) was it a coincidence that it came closest to realisation

at the two junctures in the famine most favourable to such reforms, late 1846 and late 1848. For the first was the period of desperate remedies, when the full force of the disaster was recognised at last ; and the second, at once the season of deepest despair in Ireland, and the time when government was searching about for something to end expedients, and set a permanent improvement under way. Yet, even at these stages, the odds against its coming to fruition were very great. The deterrents may have been concealed, but, in reality, they were much more deeply rooted and persuasive. Some have been touched on in the preceding chapter ; others will become apparent in the course of this, the necessity for colonial approval, for example, or the technical difficulties of organising such a project, or the current attitude towards public expenditure, or the opposition of the emigration commissioners themselves. And overshadowing all was the vast voluntary movement then under way. It was clear that this was doing much to solve the worst of difficulties : could the state possibly do more within the same field ? In all probability, it was said, the subjects of any state undertaking would be either those who were too destitute to emigrate at all, or those who would sooner or later emigrate themselves. In the first case, it was easy to conjecture what the colonial outcry would have been, had the 'refuse' of Ireland reached their shores under the very aegis of the state. In the second, it was equally certain that opinion at home would be outraged by the unnecessary expenditure of public money. As the commissioners put it, 'all those who now go by their own or local resources . . . would expect to be paid for. . . . To make such a grant would evidently be unjust to the tax-payers of this country'.[3] In short there was a real danger that the existing remedy would be impaired, and that the state would assume great responsibilities and expense, only to achieve, at best, what was being done already. On balance, therefore, it seems clear that, once cooler judgement and expert knowledge could prevail, any project of the sort was bound to be rejected. But, if this were so, how are we to explain the constant recurrence of the 'policy' during 1846–9 ? I should say, by the conjunction of two factors, the successive potato blights and Grey's acceptance of the colonial office in 1846. As to the first, the continuous Irish pressure and the failure of so many other remedies caused ministers to clutch at straws, and threw the attractions of emigration into high relief. As to the second, Grey's appointment gave the cause of colonial reform the false appearance of new life. In fact, the heyday of Wakefieldism was passed by 1845 ; already, the emphasis was rather on *laissez faire* and individualism in colonial affairs. Together, these factors go far in explaining the fact that ministers could never bring themselves to abandon emigration finally, though there was, at no stage, a genuine prospect that they might take it up.

At any rate, Stanley, who was colonial secretary when blight first struck the crops in 1845, never toyed with an ambitious undertaking of this nature.[4] He had decisively rejected an opportunity for applying a grandiose scheme to Ireland, when he refused to carry out the Devon commission's recommendation of systematic emigration ;[5] and, very soon after, Gladstone succeeded him in office. Gladstone does not appear to have considered the ' emigration policy ' at all. For one thing, he had little interest in Irish matters at this time ; for another, he was still prone to accept the point of view of his permanent officials.[6] In any event, Peel's ministry fell within a year, and the free trade controversy filled the intervening months. Not that Peel himself would ever have undertaken systematic colonisation. He had once been persuaded to support Wilmot Horton's experiments from Ireland,[7] but he was disinclined for anything further of that nature. Even in the worst moments of 1846, he maintained that emigration was really irrelevant as a solution of Irish difficulties : instead, the country needed immediate remedies with immediate effects. And months later, when he was in opposition, he went out of his way to reiterate that a state planned movement would give, at best, only a partial and remote relief ; that it would call for the most laborious preparation in the colonies ; and that, no matter how extensive or well executed, it could not mitigate the current distress.[8]

But when the whigs took office a new hope for emigration opened up. It is true that Russell seemed to share Peel's point of view. ' Emigration . . . ', he told Bessborough, in November, 1846, ' could not possibly be carried on to such an extent as to be really a relief to the peasantry '.[9] But Russell was notorious for his sudden changes in attitude,[10] and his approach to both Irish and colonial affairs was generally supposed to be quite wide and sympathetic. Moreover, Earl Grey was his secretary for the colonies; and Grey, with his brother-in-law, Charles Wood, at the exchequer, and his cousin, Sir George Grey, at the home office, held a strong hand in the cabinet.[11] This seemed important, because it was generally assumed that Grey was a rigid, severe believer in systematic colonisation; a doctrinaire, in fact, ' more closely identified than any one else in the inner ring of statesmen with Wakefield's colonial reformers ';[12] and the radical position was supposed to have been finally consolidated when Grey made Hawes (once one of Durham's clever young men) his under-secretary, and persuaded Buller to accept the sinecure office of judge advocate, upon the understanding that they would work together in colonial affairs.[13] In reality, these appearances were deceptive. There is no evidence that Grey intended to work closely with the colonial reformers while he was in office; and whatever his cantankerous dogmatism, he was bound to be driven into compromises and postponements by the realities with which he had to deal.[14] As Disraeli later observed, ' the real key to Lord Grey's position is that he talked too much Wakefieldism out of office, and found, when at length Secretary of State for the Colonies, that his theoretical colonial reform was a delusion '.[15] Nor, indeed, can we find, within our own limited field, much justification for the common interpretation of Grey as a rigid doctrinaire in these affairs.[16] On the contrary, the impression one gets is of a man who was comparatively ill informed upon the very subjects he was meant to have made his own, and who was rapidly discouraged when he came to know more about them.

But, in the autumn of 1846, none of this was apparent. Instead, there seemed great promise of a ' grand experiment '; and when the second, and total, failure brought the question to the forefront, Monteagle, who was on good terms with the whigs,[17] joined with many others in pressing Grey to adopt state assisted emigration, in conjunction with the existing poor relief.[18] Grey responded coldly to the appeal : he was always wary of Irish panaceas, and anxious neither to raise wild hopes in Ireland nor to admit that he considered the country overpopulated.[19] At the same time, he determined to use this opportunity, for an experiment upon his own lines, and wrote at once to Russell in respect of Monteagle's letter, ' I hope to be able very soon to propose to you measures which I think will give much encouragement

to "systematic emigration" '.[20]  Though he disliked the Irish
heartily and feared their influence in Canada,[21] he was, in
the circumstances, disposed ' to assist them in removing some of
the present excess of population (or what they so consider) to
our colonies provided care is taken that they are well mixed
with English and Scotch '.[22]  Grey's ideal of Irish emigration was,
as we might suppose, that of a community transplanted completely to the new world, led by its parish priest, and paid by its
landlords to be off.[23]  He hoped that the government would be
charged with the expense of settlement alone ; and, consequently,
wrote to ask Monteagle whether Irish landlords would pay ten
pounds for every tenant who took advantage of the project.[24]
When Monteagle replied that very many would meet, at least,
the cost of passages for tenants and their families,[25] Grey and
Buller settled down to develop the scheme in detail.[26]  Though
the cabinet had vaguely sanctioned these activities,[27] it is difficult
to say what precisely Russell knew or thought about them.  He
was under great pressure from Ireland to adopt some measure
of the kind ;[28] and undoubtedly he himself wished to promote
poor law emigration from the western unions.[29]  On the other
hand, he had by no means freed himself from whig presupposit-
ions,[30] and his experience as colonial secretary had taught him
something of the difficulties inherent in systematic emigration.[31]
In short, at this stage (as at so many others in his career) Russell
was at the mercy of several contradictory influences ; and his
conclusion was very indecisive.  He knew, he said, that the
colonies could not absorb great masses of destitute people : there
was ' no use in sending them from starving at Skibbereen to
starving at Montreal '.  But if the commissioners could promise
to provide for them, he would draw upon the rates for
emigration.  ' We all agree ', he ended inconsequentially, ' that
emigration to do any good ought to be " systematic " '.[32]

Meanwhile, Grey's project was completed on the last day
of 1846, and handed to Elgin, the new governor-general, to
bring with him to Quebec.  It proposed that the emigrants be
formed into communities of sixty families or so, under the
direction of Catholic priests.  Each community was to have a
church, a school and the other basic social needs.  The holdings
were to be small, since it was hoped that the settlers would
ultimately buy them out ; and Elgin was authorised to make

EMIGRATION DURING THE FAMINE

advances of £50,000 to the owners of Canadian waste lands who would prepare them for village settlements. Deliberately, the plan was no more than an outline sketch, so that Elgin might have complete freedom of negotiation. Grey was by now so confident of success that he had begun to consider whether he might not pay the passages of emigrants from imperial funds, provided the state could handpick subjects for the grand experiment.[33] But he was immediately, totally and justifiably disillusioned, for the scheme was both naive and slovenly. He had paid no attention to the question of organising the emigration in Ireland, and, however tentative the proposals were meant to be, this was an inexcusable omission. For the rest, the Canadian ministers had no difficulty in showing the deficiencies. Draper, the attorney-general,[34] pointed out that there were not even sufficient holdings of suitable land ; furthermore, ' employment for daily labourers . . . requires . . . labour near to their homes ; but this involves their being placed in a township settled by resident farmers, a postulate at direct variance with the other parts of the scheme '.[35] Many were astounded to learn that Grey had been rash enough to assume full responsibility, at a cost of £60 at least for each family, for the first twelve or fifteen months after disembarkation.[36] But even before the Canadian replies arrived, the public landowning companies had shown Grey that his scheme was quite impracticable.[37] They were much too experienced to touch it : *a fortiori,* he himself wrote sadly, no individual would assume the responsibility.[38]

This was a decisive defeat for systematic colonisation. Grey's initial impetus had been checked, ignominiously, at the moment that seemed most favourable to it ; and, now, more conservative and cautionary forces could come into play. The first of these was Grey's permanent officials. They had always regarded state assisted emigration with disfavour,[39] for they were well aware (as Grey was not, at first) of the immense practical difficulties of putting any scheme of this kind into practice. In the first place, it was doubtful whether there was, in Ireland, a sufficient body of ' acceptable ' emigrants ; and, even if there were, it would have been impossible to select, prepare and send them out without a very great expenditure. Secondly, all Wakefieldism rested upon the sale of waste lands, the hundreds of millions of idle acres in the colonies. In British North America, the right to dispose of these lands belonged, not to Westminster, but to the provinces themselves ; and the provinces would certainly refuse to accept a considerable Irish emigration.[40]  Almost of equal influence in turning Grey aside was the whig conception of public economics.[41]  In this, Wood was a creature of his time, and invariably opposed spending with a fanatical determination.  As Grey wrote to Buller in 1847, ' it is mortifying to the last degree, but I . . . can do nothing to promote " systematic colonisation ", there is not a farthing to be had from the Treasury '.[42]  As we shall see, state aided emigration was to come to the front again, but it did not do so under Grey's direction ; and these forces, which would have defeated it in 1846-7 had it passed the initial stages, were still more strongly entrenched two years later.

Meanwhile, the current voluntary emigration raised grave questions.  At the close of 1846, the emigration commissioners had been warned by colonial officers that 1847 might bring unprecedented suffering ; and the situation in Ireland was sufficiently well known to all.[43]  Accordingly, they suggested to Grey that the passenger acts be consolidated and overhauled. This he refused to consider ; and, instead, accepted only a few minor alterations in the acts (those ' most urgently required ') lest any obstacle should be thrown in the way of emigration.[44] 'All that it is necessary to do . . . ', he had explained to Elgin, ' is to persevere in the system, which has now for some years been acted upon with so much advantage . . . extending the means employed in proportion to the expected increase in the number of emigrants '.[45]  Parliament would do no more than indemnify the provinces in advance by raising its grant for immigrant relief from £2,500 to £10,000 ; and Grey trusted that less than half this sum would be required.[46]  The only other precautions, which he deemed necessary, were minor increases in the corps of emigration officers ;[47] *ultra vires* directions to the agents to examine every passenger who was embarking, and put back any suspected of having fever ; and some trifling regulations.[48]

Such measures would have been useful advances in an ordinary year, but they seemed almost irrelevant in 1847.  For a time, however, the government succeeded in living in a fool's paradise. On March 15, Grey assured the lords that the Canadian facility for absorbing emigrants moved in a geometrical progression ;

that the machinery for distributing the newcomers would work as smoothly as before ; and that the season promised to be the largest and most successful ever.[49] But, by the end of April, the true situation was revealed. Many vessels had put back to Liverpool and the Irish ports were riddled with typhus.[50] It was by then, however, much too late to take effective measures ; and everybody realised that the season must end badly. Even the commissioners were reduced to the forlorn hope that the volume of emigration might be kept down by the shortage in shipping and the recent increase in fares.[51] And the tidings from the colonies soon made it certain that 1847 had been disastrous. Many thousands had died at sea ; the colonial quarantine arrangements had been altogether overwhelmed ; disease was spreading rapidly in the interior ; and the consequent discontent in British North America was, as we shall see, so dangerous that the imperial government was forced to assume full responsibility for the emigration, and to meet a bill of almost £200,000—money spent by the provinces upon relief.[52] In these circumstances, it was only too easy to overwhelm the forces of the ' left ', the Irish and the colonial reformers. He had been under the strongest pressure in the spring, Grey said, to foment Irish emigration at the state's expense ; but he had wisely refused to stimulate artificially a natural movement.[53] This was disingenuous on Grey's part ; but, as a line of argument, it seemed no more than common sense after the experience of 1847. But the other criticism, that the government should have anticipated the disasters, and taken effective measures to avert them, was considerably more difficult to meet. Grey's foolish optimism of March 15 was much too recent to have been forgotten ; and the best defence the commissioners could muster was, first, that no one could have foreseen what was to happen ; and, second, that, even had they, no prohibition would have been effective without the most elaborate administrative machinery, and fearful epidemics in the embarkation ports.[54] It was untrue to say that the disasters of 1847 were altogether unforeseen ; but the second proposition contained a partial answer to their critics, had it been developed. For all precautions depended upon machinery to enforce them rigorously ; and this could not be improvised. On the contrary, it was built up painfully and by slow experience, having to overcome the more or less steady opposition of the passenger trade, and the

occasional opposition of those whom it was meant to help.  Even
if the commissioners had possessed foreknowledge of every
happening in 1847, they had neither the statistical information
nor the administrative techniques to prevent them altogether.
This is not, however, to shield them from all blame.[55]  Without
adopting new techniques or legislation, they could still have done
much to mitigate ship fever.  They might, for instance, have
added considerably to their staff of emigration officers, or used
government transports as hospital hulks at Liverpool and Cove.
This would have involved fresh and great expense ; but all the
happenings of the year (whether in Ireland or abroad) show that,
where human lives were at stake, and administrators acted boldly,
the imperial government ultimately endorsed their undertakings.[56]

Grey had, of course, been under fire throughout the
parliamentary session.  In February, Hutt, a colonial reformer
who had once worked with Smith O'Brien for systematic
colonisation from Ireland, had recommenced the agitation for
state assisted emigration ;[57] and, later in the year, it was renewed
by Lincoln, who demanded a royal commission to investigate
the subject.[58]  The government had resisted these efforts, only
with considerable embarrassment ;  and when Monteagle raised
the matter once again, Grey (albeit with his usual disdain for
' amateurs ') agreed to set up a select committee.  He did not
believe, he said, that it would add anything to the findings of the
' able men ', who had already considered the question ; but it
would, at least, deliver the *coup de grâce* to ignorant agitation.[59]
In this, Grey was partly justified, for the committee's report
represented a sharp rebuff to the doctrinaires.  Both the passenger
acts and the conduct of the commissioners were, it said, entirely
satisfactory ;[60] and, because of the lateness of the season and the
inadequacy of the evidence before it, it refused to declare either
for or against systematic emigration, except to say that far reaching
measures should not be rashly undertaken.[61]  Some months
later, Monteagle took his revenge in the lords, in a vicious, but
well grounded, attack upon Grey's timidity and parochialism
in office, which he contrasted effectively with his daring in
opposition.  The famine, Monteagle said, had made emigration
a great imperial issue, and a matter of prime importance to
Ireland, but Grey's conduct was, at best, ' feeble and inconclusive '.[62]  Grey fell back upon the argument which he and

Russell had used *ad nauseam* since spring : ' the proper function
of a government . . . is not to supersede the efforts of individuals, but rather to judge and assist individual exertion '.[63]
The honours lay unquestionably with Monteagle ; but his triumph
in dialectics had no material result ; and the ministry repelled,
to its own satisfaction, a further succession of parliamentary
onslaughts, during the remainder of the session.

But beneath the new exterior of *laissez faire,* the pendulum
began to move back once again.   There were many reasons why
this should have happened.   As the tension of 1847 disappeared,
the imperial government recovered from its panic, and the
colonies came gradually to question their hasty discouragement
of further emigration.   Moreover, after three years of desperate
expedients and administrative living from hand to mouth, there
was one of the periodic recurrences of that feeling which Greville
had once expressed as ' in the state of the game [in Ireland] a deep
stake must be played or all will be lost '.[64]   As for the domestic
objections to new undertakings, Clarendon told Russell roundly
at the close of 1847 that, however empty the treasury, and whatever the English people threatened, Great Britain had no alternative
but to relieve Ireland : ' This country can no more get on unaided
until next harvest than it can fly into the air '.[65]   In spite of the
renunciation of 1847, therefore, the attractions of the emigration
policy were operating powerfully again.   By now, Grey had come
round to agree with Elgin that systematic colonisation in British
North America depended ultimately upon a very great demand
for immigrant labour, and had finally settled upon a scheme for
building a railroad from Halifax to Quebec.   As usual, he had
colonial objects first in view : Quebec would be open to shipping
the whole year round ; the railroad would pass through a compact
mass of land, on which the Irish labourers might settle ; and the
continual Canadian agitation for some such project would be
satisfied.   There were, however, several new difficulties which
Grey had overlooked.   In the first place, it would have been
impossible to benefit a single province in North America without
arousing the jealousy of the others ;[66] and it would have provoked
widespread indignation at home, if the government, having
rejected Bentinck's proposals, which would have done much to
relieve the situation in Ireland, was itself to adopt almost identical
measures in the colonies.   More serious than these, however,

was a fresh cleavage in the cabinet. During the first part of 1848, Russell appears to have fallen under the influence of a group consisting of Lansdowne, Monteagle and Clarendon. Unlike Grey, these men were interested in emigration primarily as a measure to relieve distress in Ireland, and set the country on its feet again ; and they had more or less converted Russell to this point of view.[67] But it was the direction in which he himself had been moving since 1847. Even in July of that year, he had observed : ' Emigration : It is evident that the draining away of part of the population in the West would be one of the most certain ways of freeing capital to be employed in the cultivation of land '.[68] Then he had studied the evidence delivered before the select committee ; and, finally, come to the conclusion that state-assisted emigration might have, upon a grand scale, all the beneficial effects which landlord-assisted emigration appeared to have had, upon a small.

When, therefore, the autumn session of 1848 came to an end, Russell went at once to Ireland to consult with the lord lieutenant.[69] The arguments for a vast emigration had just then been rendered all the more powerful by the fourth successive potato failure ; and Clarendon and Russell rapidly came to the conclusion that it must take a central place in their proposals for recovery. Apparently believing, like Disraeli, that the Irish question was ' the pope one day and potatoes the next ', they were anxious to work in, as well, a partial establishment of the Catholic clergy. Accordingly, a scheme was drawn up to embrace both purposes : the money for the undertakings was to be raised by an Irish land and house tax ; and an emigration fund of £5,000,000 was to be administered by a commission set up for that purpose, and spent through the agency of the poor law unions.[70] The cabinet, however, objected that Ireland was in no condition to bear a further tax, and that state payment of the clergy would never be accepted by the Irish church ; and with ominous mutterings already in Ulster, that Protestant loyalty might be tried too high, and with the pope himself flying from the year of revolutions, Clarendon and Russell finally decided to go all out for large scale emigration by itself.[71]

For the reasons we have discussed above, it was most unlikely that anything would have come of this second project. No attempt had been made to work it out in detail, or to face the many practical difficulties which it involved ; and, with passions inflamed by 1848, a considerable body of Irish opinion would certainly have construed it as a depopulation engineered by Britain. But, in any event, the proposal was defeated by two ' preliminary forces ' which had operated against assisted emigration throughout our period : parsimony and divisions within the cabinet. For the Greyites in the ministry combined to defeat Russell once again. Grey himself was still backing his Halifax-Quebec railroad plan, and Wood, according to Monteagle, was quite determined that no money should be spent at all.[72] Russell could not overcome such opposition, and took his failure very much to heart.[73] It is true that Clarendon (supported, of course, by the indefatigable Monteagle)[74] continued to press for emigration for several months.[75] But when his demands came up officially in the following year, Wood refused point blank to entertain them.[76] Nor was Grey himself any more fortunate in his endeavours. When his railroad project came to be discussed in 1849, it met such heavy criticisms upon every side that he was forced to abandon it in despair.[77]

These were the last of the serious attempts to solve Irish difficulties by state-assisted emigration. As early as March 1849, a member of the government struck a note of alarm at the vast extent and steadiness of the current movement ;[78] and this cry was taken up increasingly as the year progressed. Two seasons later, even the emigration commissioners were profoundly disturbed by the loss of population. Emigration, they said, was exceeding the natural increase by, at the very least, four to one, and it included a disproportionately high number from the child bearing age groups : unless it ' be soon arrested, the country will be deserted by its original population '.[79] And, in solemn terms, the lord lieutenant directed the attention of the census commissioners to the same problem.[80] All this marked a sharp change in the general attitude. On the whole, the public opinion of the late 1840's desired the state's intervention to increase the Irish exodus ;[81] if anything, the public opinion of the 1850's desired the state's intervention to reduce it. Similarly, many, like Grey, who had worked for systematic colonisation during the famine years, now felt only relief that nothing of the sort was ever carried through.[82] In the new era of *laissez faire,* the colonial reformers seemed as much out of place as the protectionists ; the prolonged Irish crisis

had been, at most, their Indian summer. 'Indeed', writes
Hitchens, 'the whole topic of emigration which had been so
prominent for a generation was now beginning to pass into the
background. . . . The colonial reformers passed off the scene ;
the Manchester school and " separatism " were supreme '.[83] Until
the first brassy noises of the new imperialism were heard three
decades later, state assisted emigration was left aside to gather
dust. Meanwhile, the great flood, which the famine had released,
swept on silently year by year, scarcely noticed by the imperial
government[84] until the dragon's teeth sown by want and misery
in Ireland had sprung up armed men in a new land.

## IV.   ASSISTED EMIGRATION TO AUSTRALIA

Some few of the emigrants to North America may have intended
to return, but scarcely any of those to the southern colonies could
have hoped to do so. The voyage itself was difficult and long,
and after a passage of three months or more Ireland must have
seemed as remote as another planet. Yet this fact did not in itself
greatly discourage emigration to Australia. The original decision
to emigrate at all was much more critical than that which fixed
upon a destination. Once he had embarked, almost every famine
emigrant felt that he had burnt his boats behind him, and neither
contemplated, nor worked for, a return to his old society.[1] The
famine emigration to Australia was small, not because Australia
was so distant, but because Australian passages were so much
more expensive than American,[2] and because there had been so
little Irish emigration to the southern colonies before 1845.[3]
And these factors explain, as well, why the voluntary emigration
during our period should have been almost negligible, so small,[4]
in fact, that we may concentrate exclusively upon that assisted
and managed by the government. This last was in no sense
novel. It had been long established, and long applied to Ireland ;
and during the famine years, as before, it was financed by individual colonies eager to recruit a labour force, from monies
raised by the sale of colonial land. There is no need here to
disentangle the complicated story of the earlier undertakings.[5]
It is enough to observe that the years which immediately preceded
the famine were marked by a change from the 'old bounty
system' to the new, from a system of 'private enterprise, open to

all who might wish to enter it ' to a system of contracts regulated
by the imperial government ;[6]   and to note that the main
tendencies to be seen in our period are, first, the strengthening
of home control over the conduct of the emigration,[7] and,
second, the total loss of colonial control over the selection of the
emigrants.

The significance of these developments was at once apparent
in the first two projects which concern us.  Both were launched
in 1847, under Grey's direction, and involved the sending out
from Ireland of the wives and children of former settlers, pardoned
convicts and ticket-of-leave men.[8]  Since they were on a very
minor scale, Grey argued that they were in the clear interest
of everyone concerned, and that the economy which had hitherto
prevented them was ' false and inhuman '.[9]  But he was rudely
awakened by the colonial reaction, for the colonists keenly resented
the fact that women and children of this sort were being sent
out at a time when no money was available to pay the passages
of ' free ' adult emigrants ;[10] and the subsequent dispute aptly
illustrates the difference in approach between the colonial office
and the colonies, which lay at the bottom of the perennial
Australian dissatisfaction.  In either case, Grey could plead
humanity, and the necessity for establishing secure family life
in the new colonies.  But the colonists were paying for his
philanthropy ;   and they demanded, instead, men and women
who could play a part in opening up a virgin country, pastoral
and agricultural labourers, rural tradesmen, female domestic
servants and suitable wives for the pioneering farmers.  It could
not be denied that many of those whom Grey sent out, now and
later, did not fit into any of these categories.  He might reply
that ' suitable ' emigrants did not offer themselves in anything
like sufficient numbers, and that he was, in fact, selecting the
best that were available.[11]  But his arguments fell on deaf ears.
The colonists took account only of the deficiencies in the emigration, and ignored the difficulties of the commissioners.
These facts must be borne in mind, when we consider later
the complaints which greeted some portions of the Irish emigration.

All this was in the future.  At the beginning of our period,
there had been no assisted emigration for two years, and labour
had become extremely scarce.  New South Wales and Western

Australia were begging for settlers,[12] promising them the highest
wages, and a rapid expansion in agriculture, industry and mining.[13]
An Australian newspaper even proposed a public subscription to
relieve the distress in Ireland by providing passages for thousands
of Irish paupers ;[14] and a group of Irish Australians urged those
at home to form emigration societies for this purpose.[15]  When
the mounting pressure from Australia coincided with the potato
blights in Ireland, and with the disappointment of so many hopes
of state-assisted emigration, the imperial government was persuaded to take action once again.   £100,000 was advanced to
New South Wales, and a fresh emigration to that colony began
almost at once.   By the end of 1847, four vessels had already set
sail ; and it was planned to send out another eighty ships with
20,000 emigrants before the close of 1849.[16]   This first group
was predominantly Irish—almost all were drawn from Munster
and Connacht, where there was, of course, no difficulty in recruiting people for Australia[17]—and the commissioners did not
hide their dissatisfaction with the fact :  it was virtually impossible,
they pleaded, to secure British labourers or artisans.[18]   And there
was a further ground for complaint.   The colonies (in Grey's
opinion, at any rate) badly needed women to remedy the dis-
proportion between the sexes ;[19] and most of the Irish emigrants
were males.   This was an old difficulty ;  it had never been easy
to recruit respectable women for Australia.   But it appeared
more acute than usual at this moment, because Grey, who had
always been a fervent advocate of female emigration, was now
in office.   Consequently, when Nassau Senior suggested that the
scheme be extended to Irish orphan girls, with an ' industrial
and domestic education suitable to colonial life ',[20] Grey seized
upon the notion as a solution to his difficulty.   So also did the
Irish boards of guardians ;[21] for they had found it impossible
to place the hordes of homeless children whom the famine had
left upon their hands.   Only the colonists were dissatisfied with
the proposal.   They had always opposed pauper emigration ;
in fact, they had an understanding with the colonial office that
no paupers should be included in the 1847 undertakings.   But
the selection now rested with the imperial government alone ;
and the commissioners and Grey forthwith decided to send some
2,000 Irish orphans, between the ages of fourteen and eighteen
years.   To justify their action, they pointed out that this was

the best female emigration that could be hoped for in the circumstances, and promised that the girls would be of good character, and well trained for domestic service.[22]

The children set sail from Plymouth, where a depot had been long established. It was unfair to suggest, as some did,[23] that they were treated as mere chattels, as economic commodities to be shipped as expeditiously as possible. On the contrary, the commissioners' precautions seem reasonably conscientious. The girls were lectured on the passage at the depot and given medical examinations and inoculations before they were embarked.[24] Both diet and accommodation at sea were said to have been vastly superior to those on ordinary vessels.[25] A matron was appointed to look after the orphans, and teach them reading and writing during the voyage ;[26] and their moral well being was 'secured' by cutting their quarters off completely from the crew's.[27] Some of the regulations were paper measures only ; and one or two, like the monitorial system to maintain discipline,[28] were obviously unworkable. But, generally speaking, the commissioners had done their best with the material at their disposal. And they had insisted that the orphans were under the governor's protection from the moment they landed in Australia, and that they were to be placed only in good and respectable employment, under bond.[29] Nor can it be doubted that the girls themselves were anxious to be off.[30] Most expected to get husbands as soon as they were landed, and all appear to have been adequately fitted out. And, of course, the unions were even more pleased with the arrangement. They were required only to provide the girls with clothes, and pay for their transportation to Plymouth depot.[31] Since the Australian contribution was three times as great as theirs, they felt, no doubt, that they had got the better of the bargain.

The project was put into operation almost as soon as it was devised ; in fact, the first vessel managed to get away by May 1848.[32] It had been left to the Irish poor law inspectors to explain the scheme to the various boards of guardians ; and many misunderstandings followed. Nenagh believed that every orphan over the age of eighteen was being sent out ;[33] Limerick, Sligo and Killarney thought that the emigration included boys ;[34] and many other unions sent in their lists of candidates too late.[35] Similarly, most were dissatisfied with the quotas they had been

allowed, and Cork and Limerick vainly petitioned the lord
lieutenant to have theirs increased.[36]   Needless to say, there
was no difficulty in making up the numbers.   Edward Senior,
who was in charge of the selections from the northern unions,
reported that he had found an abundance of suitable girls in
those he visited ;[37] and on the whole, this claim of 'suitability'
was not unjustified.   It is true that the commissioners could
not keep their promise that the orphans would be well grounded
in domestic work ; but, otherwise, the great majority seemed
satisfactory.   When Divett, a member of the commons, complained of the appearence of a party awaiting embarkation at
Plymouth, the commissioners themselves inspected the depot
and reported that, while the girls were not as neat as English
orphans, they appeared clean, 'good-humoured and well
disposed'.   Again, the chaplain found them strong and impulsive
'but with kind words, very tractable' ; and the emigration
officer believed that a few months of healthy life would correct
their years of underdevelopment and hunger.[38]   These good
accounts were borne out, substantially, by later reports from the
colonies.   With the exception of a single group, scarcely any
Irish girls were accused of vicious habits.[39]   In this, they compared
most favourably with the current English orphans, and even with
the general body of assisted female emigration.[40]

Nevertheless, the first to land in South Australia were badly
received, for there was a rooted prejudice against Irish immigration amongst the colonists.[41]   Before any vessel arrived, the
reception committee began to press the home government for
Scots and English orphans to offset the Irish.[42]   But the initial
coldness was dissipated by the good conduct of  the first few
girls to be employed ; and, in the end, every orphan was provided
for within a fortnight of her landing.   Indeed, South Australia
immediately petitioned Grey to send out several hundred more ;[43]
and, in the following year, the emigration officer at Adelaide
reported that the Irish girls were giving satisfaction everywhere,
and that the colony would welcome up to 1,000 of them
annually.[44]   In New South Wales, the emigrants made an equally
good first impression.   The Sydney agent wrote that they were
well conducted ; that the reception depot was running smoothly ;
and that employers could find nothing to complain of in the
girls but ignorance.[45]   But all had not gone well with the

emigration to New South Wales; and, eventually, a grave scandal came to light. It concerned the vessel ' Earl Grey '. Its arrival at Sydney had aroused no comment; there had been only two deaths at sea; and, in spite of the rumours which had preceded them, more than half the orphans were immediately employed.[46] Nevertheless, the surgeon superintendent had made complaints which could not be ignored; and Fitzroy, the governor general, appointed a committee to investigate them. This committee reported that fifty-six of the orphans, the ' Belfast girls ', were ' abandoned profligates ', some of them even professed prostitutes. Fitzroy instantly segregated them from the other girls, whose conduct had been irreproachable, and demanded a home inquiry which Grey was forced to institute.[47] In their turn, the emigration and Irish poor law commissioners reported that, after ' a most searching investigation ', the utmost substantiation of the Australian charges to be found was that two girls had been improperly substituted for others selected by Senior, and that the matron of Belfast union suspected that two of her charges had been seduced already. Senior, who was himself responsible for the selection of the ' Belfast girls ', virtually ignored the colonial complaints, and, instead, accused the surgeon superintendent of inefficiency and prejudice. Grey and the commissioners adopted much the same attitude as Senior;[48] and it was the surgeon, therefore, who became the whipping boy for everyone, while the long and specific report from the Sydney committee was conveniently left aside. Not merely was the affair shabbily hushed up; but a man, who had taken his responsibilities seriously, was dismissed as a busy-body and a prude, without any reason whatsoever.

As we have said, this was an isolated scandal. On the whole, the first pauper emigration was tolerably successful from the standpoint of the colonies and from that of the girls themselves.[49] And, for the Irish boards of guardians, the success was quite unqualified. When the scheme came to an end in July 1849, they had been relieved of more than 2,000 orphans who could not have been provided for at home. Indeed, the unions which had sent girls out were now complaining that their quotas had been insufficient, while the unions which had sent none protested against the discrimination exercised against them. This feeling soon became so powerful that the poor law commissioners asked the lord lieutenant to extend the undertaking.[50] The government yielded immediately, and authorised the selection of a further 2,000 orphans. This second emigration followed closely the pattern of the first; but there was now a growing feeling against the Irish children in the colonies. It was first expressed just after the second project had got under way; it gained rapidly in force; and, by mid-1850, it was irresistible. The main cause of this dissatisfaction appears to have been the increasing difficulty of finding work for girls who were quite untrained as domestic servants; but there was, besides, an undertone of anti-Catholic and anti-Irish sentiment. At any rate, it soon reached such a pitch that the commissioners had no alternative but to abandon the scheme entirely.[51]

Meanwhile, the ordinary assisted emigration had proceeded steadily since 1847; and despite the early predominance of Irish, they were quickly outnumbered. Of the 18,000 persons sent out during 1847 and 1848, only 3,500 were Irish. This violated the commissioners' undertaking to allot the places in proportion to the population of each country in the United Kingdom, whereby Ireland was entitled to a third. In their own defence, they had pleaded that most of the existing population in Australia was of British origin.[52] But, by 1849, such a position was becoming increasingly difficult to maintain.[53] Public opinion in Ireland was restive; Mrs Chisholm had taken up the cudgels once again;[54] and Irish societies in Australia were campaigning hotly.[55] The upshot was that the inequality in the Irish emigration was fully remedied during 1850. Indeed, the pendulum soon moved in the opposite direction; and, in 1851, New South Wales was forced to accept double its due quota of Irish immigrants.[56] In its turn, this increase brought many protests from the Australian settlers, who asserted that Irish landlords were seizing the opportunity to rid themselves of their most wretched tenants.[57] This was untrue; landlords had no part to play in the selections. But there was certainly reason for believing that the emigration was not attracting the better sort of smallholder.[58] When a recruiting agent visited Cavan in 1849, it was, he said, the poor and destitute of the neighbourhood who crowded round him;[59] and a surgeon, with much experience of the Australian trade, reported that Irish emigrants were often so badly clothed that he had had to cut up blankets to cover them during the voyage.[60]

Yet the difficulty of obtaining any alternative emigration was never really overcome ; and right down to 1856, the poor Irish element remained disproportionately large, despite all colonial protests, and every exertion of the commissioners.[61]

This famine emigration was managed from Plymouth more or less upon the accepted lines. Though the system was extravagant,[62] and the prospective settlers far from the colonial ideal, it was difficult to envisage anything better at the time ; and, at very least, it proved a *deus ex machina* for 14,000 Irish people, who could not otherwise have reached the south.[63] No doubt, it was negligible in comparison with the great exodus to North America ; and, within a few years, the assistance from Australia was to cease completely. Moreover, the high rates of passage, the undeveloped condition of the colonies, and the virtual absence of a remittance system,[64] meant that it could not beget further emigration as the North American had done. The large Irish emigration to Australia, which took place later in the century, was due to a variety of other causes, amongst them, the rise in the standard of living at home, the discovery of gold in the colonies, the civil war and periodic depressions in the United States, and the improvements which steam brought about in the passenger trade. But, for all that, the famine emigration to Australia was superior to its voluntary counterpart in almost every respect, from the conditions prevailing at sea to the prospects of the immigrants in their new environment.

## V. SHIPPING AND THE VOYAGE

Fares were by no means constant during the famine years : they rose and fell with the demand on shipping, and varied from port to port, and from season to season.[1] In settling them, the shipping agent had to take many factors into account, from the current price of foodstuffs to the immigrant legislation of North America. He did not, however, send his vessels to those ports which were closest to the watersheds of emigration ; instead, emigrants went to the great ports, with the largest traffic, to embark. Perhaps this seemed to bring the mountain to Mahomet, but the truth was that the passenger trade was not of first importance to owners and charterers in 1845. Freights were often too high, and speed too important, for them to undergo

AN EMIGRATION AGENT'S OFFICE.

*Illustrated London News*, 1851.

the delays and restrictions which carrying emigrants involved. Indeed, we might say that passengers were taken only on sufferance and as a necessary evil. All the Irish Atlantic vessels were primarily engaged in the timber or foodstuffs trades ; similarly, the Liverpool vessels depended principally upon American timber, grain or cotton.[2] In each case, for want of other cargoes, they had come gradually to rely upon emigrants for the outward voyage. However tiresome passengers might be, owners were glad enough to get them when the alternative was to sail in ballast, and at a total loss.[3]

The haphazard nature of such a traffic meant that prices were continually fluctuating. Brokers never kept strictly to the rates they advertised ; and they had no hesitation in breaking contracts, if they could secure a higher fare.[4] Similarly, the emigrants would haggle and make bargains for themselves, in peasant fashion, whenever the opportunity arose.[5] Nevertheless, it is possible to trace roughly the rise and fall in prices throughout our period. According to official estimates for 1846, passages to British North America cost 50s. to 60s. everywhere, and passages to the United States varied between 70s. and £5 according to the port.[6] In the following season, the fluctuations were much more marked. The number seeking passages in February and March was quite unprecedented, and the shortage in shipping universal and acute.[7] The brokers in Dublin declared that a hundred vessels would not satisfy the demand ;[8] and at Cork, it was said, more than half the intending emigrants were being turned away.[9] To make matters still worse, many British vessels, normally employed in the passenger trade, were now tempted to sail for the United States in ballast by the high freights which followed the repeal of the corn laws.[10] Accordingly, fares rose suddenly and sharply.[11] At many Irish ports, they were almost doubled, and at Liverpool, they hovered for a time between six and seven pounds.[12] But the boom was short lived. By mid-April, the emigration had fallen off appreciably ; and, in the long run, the repeal of the corn laws worked to the advantage of the emigrants, for the American ships, which had landed maize at various points along the Irish coast during the first months of the year, had to accept passengers for their return voyages.[13] The remainder of the Irish demand was satisfied from the pool of vessels lying idle in the spring. It was satisfied almost as soon as its extent was realised, because it had now become profitable to charter vessels for the emigrant trade alone.[14]  As early as April 22, the emigration commissioners reported that there was no longer any shortage of shipping in Cork, so many London craft had been diverted there ;[15] and by the summer the situation had righted itself completely.  Everywhere fares had fallen to the levels of the preceding season.

The variations in the rates of passage were never afterwards so remarkable, for the great season of 1847 set the trade upon a regular and permanent basis.  An altogether unprecedented demand for shipping had quickly been supplied ; and owners and brokers took the lesson of the year so much to heart that in only one subsequent season, 1851, was there any comparable scarcity of vessels.[16]  The passenger trade was now a rising business, well worth concentrating on alone ; and as Carter, the great London shipper, had prophesied, once the traffic became fixed and certain, fares were inclined to fall and shipping facilities to improve.[17]  Admittedly, this tendency towards cheaper rates, which competition bred, was offset by the passenger acts of 1847–55. Each new requirement placed fresh expenses on the shipper, and, therefore, ultimately, upon the emigrant himself.  Consequently, fares were, if anything, rather higher at the close of the famine period than they had been in the early 1840's.  The cheapest steerage passage to New York cost 75s. as a rule, and St Lawrence rates were only 10s. under this, at best.[18]  Nevertheless, the increase was more than compensated for by the new dietary scale,[19] which saved the emigrant a pound or more, and by the new speed and comfort which the more modern vessels had to offer. Indeed, we can see in the 1850's the beginnings of a total revolution in the trade.  Already, smart new ' liners ' of a thousand tons or more, which could advertise such luxuries as ventilated quarters and flush decks fore and aft, were being built especially to carry passengers from Liverpool ; already, the average passage had dropped by a week in length.  It is true that the select committee on emigrant ships in 1854 revealed a state of things which almost passed belief,[20] and that general improvements were very slow in coming, down to 1860.  But even in 1854 we can find abundant signs that the ' bad old days ' were numbered, and that the age of steel and iron was at hand.[21]

In 1845, however, the emigrant trade was still a mere

subordinate interest of the Atlantic merchantmen. Few of the British vessels drew over 400 tons, though they commonly carried more than 200 people ;[22] and the emigration officer at Cork reported that even the American ships, engaged in the foodstuffs trade with that city, were nothing larger.[23] As the Atlantic crossing averaged some forty days,[24] it was, therefore, a period of the utmost misery for steerage passengers, who had to spend the weeks in wretched, stifling quarters, battened under hatches in stormy weather.[25] Melville did not exaggerate in the slightest in describing the 'Highlander' in *Redburn*.

> How, then, with the friendless emigrants, stowed away like bales of cotton, and packed like slaves in a slave ship ; confined in a place that, during storm time, must be closed against both light and air, who can do no cooking, nor warm so much as a cup of water ? . . . Nor is this all . . . passengers are cut off from the most indispensable conveniences of a civilised dwelling. . . . We had not been at sea one week, when to hold your head down the fore-hatchway was like holding it down a suddenly opened cess pool.

Even the best cargo ships, the 'Highlanders', then, were thoroughly unsuitable for emigrants ; and matters were a great deal worse whenever the demand for passages was keen, and anything from coasting schooners to Tyneside 'Noah's Arks' might be pressed into service.[26] Some of the vessels used were quite disgraceful. One ship regularly employed in the New Brunswick run was officially described as 'a mere tub, altogether unfit for the passenger trade' ;[27] and when another, the 'Vesta', put into Berehaven in distress in 1847, her rigging was found to have been rotted through, her hull leaking, and her steerage quarters in a shambles.[28] It is true that the timber vessels, which were commonly used for emigrants, had the advantage of relatively spacious holds ;[29] but these holds made them heavy rolling 'sailers',[30] and precluded them from using permanent upper decks. The substitute or 'temporary' decks were nothing more than bare planks laid uncaulked upon the ship's beams, which could never be cleansed because the cargo was stowed immediately beneath.[31]

On the whole, American vessels enjoyed the better reputation. For one thing, they were less crowded ;[32] congress demanded more superficial deck space for each passenger than parliament. For another, they were greatly superior in speed, accommodation and design.[33]   Steam was soon to bring the golden age of the New England merchantmen to a sudden end ;[34] but throughout our period American ships were still most eagerly sought after, despite the higher rates which they demanded.   For in these years British oaken vessels, and British crews and seamanship, had few defenders.[35]   The scornful remark which greeted the arrival of the ' Emigrant ' at New York, ' a British ship of course—no others come in such condition ',[36] expressed a general Yankee feeling of disdain, which the public opinion of the time endorsed. Yet the superiority was by no means so overwhelming as the Americans believed.   As early as 1848, the New York commissioners for emigration had to grant that, though their own tramps and packet ships still had the edge, British vessels were improving to a remarkable degree ;[37] and six years later, two experienced government officers remarked on the great advances which Liverpool had made : now her ships were ' as fine as any in the world '.[38]

To the famine emigrants, at any rate, the distinction was marginal—a barely perceptible difference in the degree of discomfort and misery to be endured.   The overcrowding in the steerage, the airless quarters and the seemingly interminable passage were common to vessels of all sorts.   These were the forces that brought about the fatal apathy in passengers, which so many observers emphasised.[39]   It was important because it led them to sink without resistance into disease, and to disregard the simplest precautions against infection.[40]   When Stephen de Vere sailed in the steerage in 1847, he found hundreds of people lying there like sacks together, quite motionless, with neither light nor air ;  many, struck down with fever, had ' no food or medicine other than casual charity ', and could scarcely turn in their narrow berths.[41]   This was the state of things on ordinary vessels ;  and many were a great deal worse.   The ' Sarah and Elizabeth ', for instance, cleared from Killala a month after her appointed sailing date, by which time a number of the passengers had exhausted their little sea stock.   But their miseries were only beginning when they sailed.   Thirty-six berths had been provided for 260 persons.   The master was a drunken brute, who issued no provisions whatsoever, and only a little putrid water.

Conditions in the hold, wrote the emigration officer at Quebec, 'fully realised the worst state of a slaver'.[42] When want led to fever, the master, too, fell a victim, and his body and the bodies of the many passengers who had died already were left to putrify on board. Again, even the emigration officers at New Orleans were scandalised by the appearance of the 'Blanche' in 1851. They found pigs and people lying together on the deck in 'filth and feculent matter'. The master and crew were down with fever, almost to a man; and two of the passengers committed suicide, even as the ship came up the river. The whole spectacle was 'such as humanity shudders to contemplate'.[43]

Passengers, of course, brought much of their misery upon themselves by their own ignorance and uncleanly habits. No vessel had anything like effective sanitation, but, even had the privies been secure and satisfactory, the emigrants would scarcely have known how to use them properly.[44] Moreover, it was impossible to air or scrub out the steerage quarters, and most passengers refused point blank to leave them and go up on deck.[45] Instead, they were 'content' to live 'like pigs' between decks,[46] without order of any sort imposed upon them. Now and then, the master of a first rate Liverpool vessel might appoint a handful of the more respectable passengers to act as monitors.[47] But, in most cases, there was no one whatsoever to enforce discipline or even the most elementary rules of cleanliness.[48] Yet, whatever the faults of emigrants, they were not entirely without excuse. Much of the apathy and irresponsibility can be attributed, fairly enough, to that sense of impending disaster which seemed to hang over everyone at sea. Once an infectious disease broke out, there was no knowing how it might be arrested, and no available remedy in which anyone could place much faith. Medicines were crude and scanty; and not one vessel in fifty carried a medical officer on board. When an emigrant succumbed to fever, his companions could do nothing for him. One man recalled that, during his passage, he had once felt so ill and hopeless that he bade farewell to all his friends, put on his surplice and burial habit, and then laid down to die;[49] and this sort of resignation appears to have been common right through the famine period.

For an explanation of such fatalism, and an understanding of the nature of disease at sea, we must turn to 1847. The mortality and sickness of that season were unprecedented and unparalleled ;[50] in a most dramatic way, it shows the effect of the forces we have just considered in bringing about calamities on ship. Some bare figures will speak for themselves : during 1847, one passenger in forty died on vessels bound for Canada from Limerick, Killala and New Ross ; on Liverpool and Sligo vessels, one in fourteen ; on Cork vessels, one in nine.[51] In all, about 5% of those who took ship perished at sea in one way or another, apart from the fresh calamities which altogether overwhelmed the remainder once they landed in the new world.[52] Now it was generally agreed that this mortality was caused either by ship fever, a form of typhus spread by lice, or by dysentery, which flourished when people were debilitated. But it was another matter to locate and deal with the sources of infection. Here there was the widest disagreement. Many believed, of course, that the bad living conditions which prevailed at sea lay at the bottom of the evil. The New Brunswick board of physicians blamed the dirt and foulness of the holds, and the impure water and provisions ;[53] Minturn, an experienced New York shipper, the lack of ventilation ;[54] some, the deplorable cooking arrangements ;[55] others, the fact that peasants, accustomed all their lives to oatmeal and potatoes, were forced to eat an entirely different diet aboard ship.[56] Obviously, this kind of explanation had much validity : unhealthy conditions in the steerage quarters inevitably spread and hastened the infection. But it did not meet the facts completely. Ship fever ravaged vessels with ' good ' living conditions quite as severely as those with ' bad '. The mortality rate on two government transports, which sailed from Cork in the spring of 1847, was much higher than that on many of the lumbering timber hulks, although the transports were excellently disciplined and provisioned ;[57] and, conversely, the German vessels, which were commonly more overcrowded than the Irish, suffered little from dysentery or typhus during the season.[58] Clearly then, the distress in Ireland and the cumulative effects of undernourishment at home must have been contributory factors. But still less did they afford a *total* explanation of infection. Many of the emigrants were cottiers of the same social standing, who had undergone much the same hardship and privation before their embarkation ; yet typhus by no means attacked particular groups with equal force. Two large parties of Wandesforde's tenants, for example, sailed at the same time, under almost identical circumstances, but the death rate on one vessel was three times higher than the other ;[59] and there were very many cases of this kind.

One factor, however, seemed constant throughout the season, the high mortality on vessels sailing from the larger city ports. Douglas, the Canadian quarantine surgeon, made this the starting point of his research. He knew that typhus was generally contracted in dirty and overpopulated surroundings, and discovered that, wherever ship fever had broken out, the infection had been carried from the shore. The first victim was found, almost invariably, to have been suffering from the disease when he came aboard. Douglas thereupon concluded that the true seed beds of infection were the slums and alleys where the emigrants had lodged before their embarkation.[60] This diagnosis was, to some extent, corroborated in later seasons, when outbreaks of cholera and typhus were often traced back to lodging houses in Cork or Liverpool,[61] but it no more encompassed all the facts than did the other explanations. The town of Sligo had as black a record as Liverpool in 1847 ; and the year itself was not repeated, though the docklands of the city ports were as foul in 1860 as in 1845. All that contemporary inquiries can tell us is that these docklands were the immediate sources of infection, but that its effect would not have been at all so devastating had not the emigrants of 1847 come to them in a weakened state, and left them to spend a month or more in confined, unhealthy quarters ; in short, that it was the coincidence of the three factors we have considered which brought about the great disaster.

Certainly, it was not possible to speak with more exactness at the time. Neither the necessary evidence nor a scientific method of weighing it was available. When the emigration commissioners attempted to draw conclusions from statistics they had gathered in 1853, they found that the extraordinary differences in the mortality rates of individual Liverpool vessels could not be accounted for at all by looking to the times of sailings, or the conditions between decks, or the numbers aboard ship, or even the emigrants' places of origin.[62] Yet, a mere five years before, they had not hesitated to attribute some improvement which they had noticed in the health of emigrants to the compulsory employment of physicians upon the larger vessels.[63] In this, they were most certainly mistaken. The respectable houses did try to secure competent ship doctors,[64] and a few of these may have enforced cleanliness and discipline, and taken intelligent precautions against disease. But, generally speaking, the terms which owners offered were so bad that only the younger surgeons, without experience, or the men who had already failed at home, were tempted to accept.[65] Vere Foster described the physician of the ' Washington ' as a foul mouthed bully, who touted for money amongst the steerage passengers, and charged exorbitant prices for his medicines ;[66] and there were even cases of men appointed without any medical knowledge whatsoever.[67] But the fact that medical officers were required at all was, at least, an indication that the age of regulative reform had come. Still more so was the commissioners' abandonment of the facile *post hoc ergo propter hoc* type of explanation, which had been so common in the 1840's, and their setting about a still more minute investigation, when they found that fuller data would yield no easy answer to the problem.[68] For all this was a confession of faith in the basic method of nineteenth century social reform, ' statistical inquiry ', and an acceptance of a new sort of responsibility by the state.[69]

### VI.   THE IRISH IN BRITISH NORTH AMERICA

The state's responsibility for immigrants in the colonies was as ill-defined as the whole relationship of Westminster and the provinces in the affair. Roughly, we can say that it felt it had a duty to assist the destitute ; but that, down to 1847, this feeling was almost nullified by its fear of being imposed on by the Irish. Similarly, the machinery of relief had been set up with misgivings ;[1] and its scope remained undefined. The keystone of whatever protective system there existed was a rigorous quarantine for every vessel. No immigrant might leave his quarantine station (Grosse Island at Quebec or Partridge Island at St John), until he had been passed as fit by the government physician ; and there was at least one lazaretto, capable of holding a hundred people, on each quarantine ground. To make these measures effective, emigration officers were placed at the ports of disembarkation, and at strategic points along the St Lawrence valley. In theory, their duties were regulatory and advisory ; but, in fact, most of their work consisted of relieving the destitute as best they could, and sending them up country on the steamers, to avoid any unhealthy concentration of labourers in a single place. These meagre services were paid for by a grant from the imperial treasury,[2] and a provincial tax of five shillings for each adult immigrant, which the shipping agents included in the fares. As the emigration commissioners believed that immigrants took advantage of the relief afforded, and were encouraged by their friends or landlords to ' practise deception and thus be conveyed west at the expense of the Government ',[3] the imperial grant was restricted to £1,500 in most seasons. But, since passages on the St Lawrence steamers were cheap, and emigrants usually in good health, even this sum was adequate in the years immediately before the famine.[4] After a fashion, the relief machinery could cope with perhaps 30,000 people in a healthy year. But it had grave limitations, which remained concealed during the early 1840's, and even during the season of 1846.

Most of the emigrants of 1846 were classed as clean and industrious, if poor. As was customary, about a third of them left for the United States as soon as they disembarked. Others joined friends in Upper Canada, or in the Ottawa or Niagara districts, and the remainder got work readily on railroads or in the harvest fields.[5] It is true that those who arrived in October were in poor shape, for they had been driven out by the second blight at the very end of the season.[6] But even they had no difficulty in finding work ; labour was still so scarce that employers were offering up to four shillings a day.[7] In all, an Irish emigration of 25,000, the largest since 1842, was absorbed quite smoothly by the Canadas ; and in New Brunswick the season passed off equally happily.[8] In one respect, this was unfortunate, for it engendered a false sense of security ; and people continued to speak as if Canada could comfortably accept a very large new labour force every year.[9] It is true that some observed that the emigrants of 1846 were unusually destitute and sickly, and that the margin of safety had been narrow. In fact, it was their representations which induced the imperial government to raise its grant at all.[10] But, if 1846 had not fallen out so well, it would have been seen more clearly that the existing machinery was not geared to meet the emergency which threatened ; that the only defences against typhus were old and rotting lazarettos, mere relics of the disastrous season of

1832 ;[11] and that many abuses in the protective system, which had been denounced for years,[12] still remained unreformed.

As things were, the facilities at Quebec were altogether overtaxed from the moment the first vessels of 1847 entered quarantine. Each had lost passengers and landed the survivors in varying degress of misery and disease. Within a week, the hospitals were filled ; and, by the end of May, more than 12,000 people were living on Grosse Island. Few had any shelter whatsoever ; food stocks were running low ; and the dreaded warm season was at hand.[13] From this time until the end of August, when the new hospital was at last completed,[14] the situation was almost continuously beyond the control of the authorities.[15] A. C. Buchanan, the chief emigration officer stationed at Grosse Island, had succeeded in getting army tents from the ordnance,[16] but they gave little comfort, either in wet weather or in hot. Thousands had still to lie on damp and open spaces,[17] dying ‘ like fish out of water ’, among the stones and mud flats of the beaches.[18] Some of this fatal congestion arose from the unprecedented numbers who kept arriving, either infected with typhus or too debilitated to be moved ; and some of it from the reluctance of the healthy members of a family to desert the others, a practice which naturally spread the disease still further.[19] But the overcrowding had an even more disastrous consequence. It left Buchanan with no alternative but to pack off to the interior several thousand people, who were likely to fall ill at once.[20] Neither he nor the other officers can be blamed for this : they were trapped in a house of cards, and every move they made seemed to bring still more tumbling down. But sending convalescents up-river, packed ‘ like pigs on the deck of a Cork and Bristol ’ steamer, so that many died even while they were on board, merely spread typhus to every town from Quebec to Montreal and farther west.[21] These places, in their turn, could not improvise the necessary machinery of relief, and fell into a panic lest the inhabitants should be infected. When the Irish arrived, people fled from Toronto and Kingston into the countryside ; and what the feeling was in Montreal may be conjectured from a great mound preserved there to this day, bearing the legend, ‘ The remains of six thousand immigrants who died of ship fever ’.[22] The executive council at once demanded that each town be given food and medical assistance, if the towns, for their part, would set up boards of health to administer relief; and with the Canadians by now in a very ugly mood,[23] Elgin had no choice but to accept the proposal.[24]

Only long after the season had ended, could the colonists estimate the disorganisation of their society. At least 20,000 immigrants, some 30% of the entire Irish emigration, had perished by the close of 1847. Another 30,000, including almost all the able bodied and desirable settlers, had crossed to the United States, in spite of the barriers which the Americans had raised against them. Consequently, Canada found herself with only the helpless and the destitute.[25] Winter relief depots had to be maintained throughout the provinces,[26] and every orphanage was filled, though many French Canadians had already adopted Irish children.[27] Immigrants still thronged the hospitals of the inland cities; and the lazarettos at Quebec and Montreal, which could hold only a thousand people when the season opened, were housing fourteen times that number in December. The only relief in the whole sombre picture was the humanity and courage of those who attended the sick. Twenty-three of the twenty-six doctors on Grosse Island had contracted fever; almost forty of the staff had died; nineteen priests went down with typhus; and Buchanan himself was at death's door.[28] Indeed, every responsible observer paid tribute to the generosity and promptness of the Canadians, once the blow had fallen on them.[29] The only substantial criticism which was made was that they had ignored the warnings of the provincial officers, and the experience of former seasons, and were, to that extent, responsible for the total lack of preparation. For, as we have said, every report for 1846 had looked forward with the deepest apprehension.[30] Buchanan had complained that he held only a miserable balance of relief money to deal with what threatened to be an emigration of 'unequalled destitution';[31] his fellow officer in Upper Canada had warned the commissioners that he would need a larger grant if he were to distribute the wretched Irish quickly, and prevent their concentrating in the cities;[32] and Dr Douglas, the chief medical officer at Grosse Island, had reported, 'The . . . almost total failure this year . . . will have the effect of pouring on our shores thousands of debilitated and sickly emigrants'.[33] Nor could it be pleaded that the happenings of 1847 were unprecedented. Though on a much smaller scale, the cholera outbreak of 1832 was marked by very many of the characteristics of 1847, from the overwhelming of the protective system to the fear and resentment of the colonists.[34]   It is true that the Canadians might have replied that they could not have known the Irish situation ;   that, since emigration was not a steady factor to be relied upon, it would have been unreasonable to expect them to reorganise their whole protective system for an uncertain contingency ;   and that, in any event, the rather academic recommendations of 1846 were poles apart from the fearful reality of Grosse Island.   Even so, they cannot be absolved entirely from responsibility.   Such serious and specific warnings should never have been disregarded.

It was only natural, however, that Canadian attention should have been directed, not to their own want of preparation, but to the unjust burden which had been cast upon them ;   and, at one juncture, their feeling against the emigration ran high indeed.[35]   Elgin, who was no alarmist, was greatly disturbed by his tour of the provinces in the autumn.[36]   He told Grey bluntly, ' that section of the French who dislike British emigration at all times find, as might be expected, in the circumstances of this year, a theme for copious declamation.   Persons who cherish republican sympathies ascribe these evils to our dependent condition as colonists '.[37]   It was all very well for Englishmen to suggest that the famine was a judgment on the whole world, which Canada could not fairly have been spared,[38] or that the Canadians should take the rough with the smooth in emigration.   These suggestions merely reminded colonists that the Americans had been largely spared the judgment, and that it was the American refusal to accept immigrants with ship fever, which had cast so much of the rough upon their shores.[39]   The plain fact was that Canada had spent five times as much upon relief as the United States,[40] and was now determined to be reimbursed.   Earlier in the season, Grey had demanded the strictest care in the administration of relief, lest immigrants ' relax their exertion to provide for themselves ' ;   and he had refused to discuss the total debt at all, until an exact account of the expenditure was rendered.[41]   But Elgin had merely to point out the fearful suffering which cheese-paring would cause, and the dangerous temper of the colonists, to silence his admonitions ;[42] and in the end even Charles Wood submitted.   ' I have read ', he said,

'Elgin's letter on the disease of the Canadian immigration, and I really think that *we* ought to pay the bill for the effects '.[43] Thus, the government was forced to defray the outstanding relief expenses, £80,000, and to refund the provincial parliament more than £70,000, which had been spent on the immigrants.[44] But it was determined that 1847 should not be repeated. A condition precedent of the indemnity was that the provinces would assume complete responsibility for all future emigration : the treasury would grant £1,500 a year, and not a penny more.[45] To enable the colonies to shoulder the new burden, Grey suggested that they raise the immigrant tax ; this would at once procure more money for relief, and diminish the necessity for spending it.[46] They, of course, seized upon this opportunity to discourage emigration. The tax was doubled, and masters were henceforth required to enter heavy bonds for every passenger who seemed likely to become a public charge.[47] Grey considered that, in this, the Canadians had gone too far ; and he condemned the measures as crude and indiscriminate.[48] But the burnt child feared the fire : as Elgin put it, public opinion in the provinces had to be nursed back into confidence.[49] Meanwhile, the shock it had received was not without its good effects. The whole quarantine system was set on a new basis for 1848. The stations were enlarged ; the commissariat and island generally put under military control ; and the inland transportation completely overhauled.[50]

The 1847 emigration to New Brunswick need not be described in detail. Though it followed much the same calamitous course as Canada's, it was on a very much smaller scale, and, therefore, brought more readily under control. Indeed, so prompt were the measures, which Perley took on Partridge Island, that the quarantine surgeon could write by mid-July, ' I trust the worst is over '.[51] His expectation was fulfilled so far as the quarantine itself was concerned. Though immigrants suffered the same discomforts as their fellows on Grosse Island,[52] a more or less steady progress was maintained all through the autumn. But their fate was less happy in St John, and towns in the interior where they were dispersed. As they congregated in city slums or makeshift hospitals, debility and malnutrition took their toll ; and this, in turn, spread typhus to the colonists.[53] Thereafter, things fell out almost exactly as in Canada. The healthy and the able-bodied left at once for the United States ; the fear and anger of the New Brunswickers increased ; their pressure on the governor general, Colebrooke, forced Grey to assume complete responsibility for the expenses ; and, finally, there came stringent immigrant legislation for 1848, and a thorough reorganisation of the protective system. Though the season was by no means as disastrous as the Canadian, Perley's report made melancholy reading. One-seventh of the 16,000 Irish immigrants had died before the year was out ; one half of the remainder had crossed to the United States ; many more were being kept in almshouses and orphanages ;[54] and there was so much vagrancy amongst the rest that Grey himself suggested it be put down by the harsh measures then in force in Ireland,[55] and Colebrooke toyed with the idea of returning some of them to their homes.[56]

. Both Canada and New Brunswick awaited the first vessels of 1848 with much anxiety. But when they arrived, it was at once apparent that the emigration would be small, and the death rate low. The mortality at sea had averaged only one death for each vessel ; and, up to midsummer, less than fifty people had died upon Grosse Island.[57] Altogether, some 25,000 Irish emigrated to Canada during 1848. Eight thousand of them, it was estimated, re-emigrated to the United States ; only 10% remained in the eastern townships, where trade was very slack ; and the rest moved north or west of the Great Lakes to join friends or relatives. It is true that they were, as ever, very poor ; but, with a strict economy in the administration of relief, the whole season cost Canada only £12,500, a sum which the new tax covered fully.[58] Moreover, there was a mere 150 deaths amongst the Irish in the provinces, so that, all in all, Canadians had good reason to feel satisfied with the year. New Brunswick's experience was not quite so happy.[59] Those of the Irish who did not cross to the United States found it very difficult to get employment,[60] for a severe, though temporary, depression in the lumber trade had shaken the colonial economy to its roots ; and, as we have seen already, the ambitious scheme to settle Fitzwilliam's tenants by labour upon public works fell through dismally.[61] On the whole, however, the season compared very favourably with 1847.

The only reason to regret it was the sharp decline in the volume of emigration, for this was causing a distinct financial, and possibly a general economic, loss to every colony. The timber vessels had yielded their margin of advantage over the American, when the new acts so inflated fares to the St Lawrence that it was cheaper, in most cases, to embark directly for the United States.[62] Masters and owners joined in condemning the provincial measures ; some, in fact, withdrew completely from the trade.[63] More than fifty vessels clearing for Quebec in the spring of 1848 changed their destinations to New York or Boston, when the news reached Europe ;[64] and shipping agents rejected many passengers who might have been considered public charges by the provinces.[65] In short, Canada and New Brunswick appeared to have thrown away whatever gain they might have had from the extraordinary increase in Irish emigration. Such, at any rate, was the dominant opinion in the colonies by the end of 1848 ; and no voices were raised in protest when, before the new season opened, the barriers, which had been built up so eagerly a year before, were totally dismantled.[66] But the lost St Lawrence trade was not recovered. Although the Canadian immigrants of 1849 (unlike those to the United States) were healthy, the volume of emigration was very small, and the continuing depression in the lumber trade drove most of the Irish across the border before long. Similarly, only 10% of those who landed at St John settled permanently in New Brunswick.[67]

The disappointment of 1849, together with some encouragement from Elgin,[68] induced the provinces to take more positive steps to win back the valuable traffic. The St Lawrence was now linked with Chicago by canal, and the Canadians promised to return half the provincial tax to each immigrant who passed directly to the middle west through Quebec.[69] But this concession was as ineffective as their other action ; and the permanent immigration was equally discouraging. Though 10,000 of the Irish settled down in Upper Canada during 1850, the remainder re-emigrated, as usual, to the Atlantic or New England states.[70] A still further reduction in the tax was made in 1851 ; and this, in fact, turned out to be the most successful season since 1845. Almost 18,000 of the Irish moved to the western districts, and many others got employment on farms or public works along the St Lawrence valley.[71] But this was not enough. Colonial trade had left the doldrums of the 1840's, and the provinces had begun to ride a long wave of prosperity. No doubt, the steady Irish emigration of the decade, averaging between fifteen and twenty thousand permanent settlers every year, was a useful addition for public works, railroads and agriculture. But the provinces needed very many more ; and wages were high, and labour was short, for season after season down to 1860. Consequently, it was argued that Canada and New Brunswick had, in effect, cut off their nose to spite their face ; that they had been caught napping when the distress in Ireland was at its worst, and then permanently discouraged emigration when the crisis was already passed. It could not be denied that the 1848 legislation had diverted much of the Irish emigration to the United States ; and it seemed significant that a very high proportion of those, who settled permanently in British North America after 1847, were joining friends or relatives. ' Latterly ', wrote the commissioners, ' the course of emigration has very much depended on the direction taken by the friends of emigrants who have preceded them '.[72]   So the argument ran as follows : if the Canadians had seized the opportunity of 1847–8, won a larger body of Irish immigrants, and, perhaps, opened up the farther west with their labour, this would have had an important cumulative, as well as an immediate, effect. It was certainly true that Irish emigration followed in the wake of former emigration ; but it seems most improbable that British North America could have attracted permanently a much higher proportion of the voluntary movement during the critical years, 1847–50, when the pattern was being established. The continuous re-emigration is sufficient proof of this. And further, Canada could never have competed seriously for Irish labour with its economically mature and industrialised neighbour without adopting some form of systematic colonisation; and, so far as the provinces were concerned, systematic colonisation was out of the question during those years in which it might have been acceptable in Ireland.

### VII.   THE IRISH IN THE UNITED STATES OF AMERICA

The evidence on the famine emigration to the United States is neither full nor precise, but we can safely say that 75% of Irish emigrants to the new world settled there. As we have seen, the passenger trade tended to follow the commercial sea lanes, and some 50% of this number landed at New York, the most important of the Atlantic ports.[1]   Yet, in 1846, New York's immigrant

legislation was at once more severe and less effective than that
of Canada. A quarantine hospital was maintained from the
proceeds of a landing tax, but masters were compelled to enter
bonds indemnifying the city against further expenses in main--
taining immigrants. These bonds were generally regarded as
irksome, and were of no real value to the immigrants themselves ;
for the masters invariably transferred their liability to shipping
brokers, who had small means and few scruples ; and, in
consequence, sick or distressed immigrants were badly treated.[2]
Moreover, the system of frauds obtaining in the city at that time
exceeded even Liverpool's in both efficiency and extent ; the
inland transportation was riddled with abuse ;[3] and the for-
warding houses grossly overcharged for rail and canal fares,
often issuing bogus tickets into the bargain.[4] 'I and others
engaged in the business', confessed one agent, 'get all we can
from the passengers, except that I never shave a lady when
travelling alone . . . I have all I get over a certain amount which
is paid to the transportation companies'.[5] It is true that the
Irish emigration society of New York, like those in Boston and
New Orleans, did what it could to mitigate the evils by setting
immigrants upon their guard ; but, obviously, its scope was
very limited.[6]

It was not surprising, therefore, that New York was more
alive than British North America to the probable effects of famine
upon emigration ; and, early in 1846, the state legislature hurried
through a bill to make the bond requirements still more stringent.
As things turned out, it was not immediately needed, for there
was no serious epidemic in the season. But there was still much
reason for disquiet. The death rate on vessels arriving at New
York, Boston and Philadelphia during the summer had been
unusually high ;[7] and the last emigrants to arrive were very
destitute.[8] Consequently, the Americans, who were well informed
of the progress of distress in Ireland, took alarm at these early
symptoms, and adopted firm measures in the spring of 1847.
First the federal legislation was tightened up. The act of 1819,[9]
which had never been particularly effective, and was now completely out of date, was repealed ; and a new statute brought
radical changes. Henceforth, every passenger, regardless of his
age, was to be allowed fourteen feet of superficial space, and the
penalties for overcrowding were extraordinarily severe : masters

might be fined $150 for each passenger they carried over the statutory number.[10] On paper, this was an advance, albeit a temporary advance, upon the British code. But, in fact, there was no adequate federal machinery to enforce it ; and American masters had always spoken the rebel language of private enterprise,[11] and were to do so successfully for years to come.[12] Nevertheless, the new act achieved something of its object indirectly, for the harsh penalties it imposed frightened shipping agents into raising the United States passages considerably, and thus diverted most of the poorest and most destitute passengers of 1847 to British North America.[13] The states themselves formed the second line of defence. Under pressure from the emigration societies and some of the wealthier merchants,[14] the New York legislature, in May, 1847, reconstructed the entire quarantine system, and placed it in the hands of ten commissioners, most of whom had experience of the trade. From monies to be raised by a head tax of $1.50 on each emigrant, these commissioners were to provide a quarantine hospital, an emigration staff and transportation assistance for the distressed.[15] The reform turned out to be a prodigious undertaking. Many years later, the commissioners reported, ' The work never ceases, new schemes of fraud spring up whenever the occasion offers ' ;[16] and, in 1847, they were beginning almost from nothing. The first difficulty was to arrange that emigrants be conveyed from quarantine to the city without falling into the hands of ' runners '. This they attempted to overcome by compelling passengers to disembark on to licensed lighters, which were under the surveillance of their officers.[17] Next, they set up a central relief office, which was to serve also as an employment bureau ;[18] and, finally, an emigrant hospital. The hospital proved satisfactory from the start,[19] and, on the whole, the commissioners were pleased with their achievements in the year of difficulties.[20] The death rate amongst immigrants, they reported, was relatively low ;[21] their stop-gap measures had roused few complaints ;[22] and they had overcome the natural prejudices of the permanent emigration staff whom they had inherited.[23]

Nevertheless, neither New York nor the other Atlantic ports escaped completely from the effects of 1847. During the spring, emergency lazarettos had to be set up on Long and Staten Islands,[24] and there were outbreaks of typhus at Philadelphia and Baltimore.[25]

Several of the river towns, like Albany, refused to allow immigrants on their way westwards to leave their steamers ; and in some New England cities there were scenes of popular hysteria reminiscent of Kingston or Toronto. Boston was worst hit of all by the early epidemics, and the Massachusetts state assembly rushed through a bill requiring all masters to enter bonds of $1,000, indemnifying the state against all expenses incurred on the head of any of their passengers.[26] This outrageous demand virtually prohibited emigration to Boston during the second half of 1847. Many vessels, learning of the new legislation when they arrived there, were forced to turn north to New Brunswick, thereby adding greatly to the miseries of that colony.[27] Eventually, this state enactment was held by the supreme court, in the celebrated 'passenger cases', to have been unconstitutional, on the grounds that it interfered with foreign commerce, which was the province of the federal government.[28] But by the time the judgment had been given, the damage was done, so far as British North America was concerned. The cumulative effect of federal and state legislation during the spring of 1847 had been to turn the worst of the emigration firmly northwards ; and although the season was still amongst the worst that the United States was to experience, New York and Boston were spared the disastrous and universal epidemics of Quebec and Montreal.

In almost every season in the famine and immediate post-famine years, there were occasional outbreaks of cholera and typhus in American ports. The spring emigration of 1848 brought much ship fever with it, for it was now the turn of the British provinces to divert the most destitute of the emigrants by adopting restrictive legislation.[29] Similarly, in both 1849 and 1851, there were serious cholera epidemics in almost all the places of disembarkation ; and, in 1849, these were aggravated by a harsh winter and a severe depression in trade. The New York commissioners were hard pressed to maintain their quarantine and relief, and, much to the indignation of the nativists, were forced to spend over $380,000 in assisting immigrants throughout the year.[30] 'We are obliged', wrote one, 'to keep supplies of provision in our office in the city to give to those who come in famishing. . . . The women and children we cannot thrust aside'.[31] Again, the winter and spring of 1853–4 brought another devastating epidemic.[32] Yet matters never reached such a pitch in the United

States as they had in British North America in 1847 ; and for this,
we can find four main reasons.  First, the conditions in Ireland
which had contributed to the disasters of that year were not
repeated.  Second, the constant mass migration which 1847
initiated gradually secured the regularisation of the trade.  Third,
the Atlantic states, unlike either British North America or the
United Kingdom ports, could rely sufficiently upon a great and
steady volume of emigration every year to warrant improvements on a grand scale in their protective systems.[33]  And lastly,
and perhaps most important of all, the American economy, for
all its sharp and sudden periods of distress, showed astonishing
recuperative powers and a remarkable over-all expansion during
these years.  At this stage in its industrial and agrarian revolutions,
America had an almost insatiable appetite for cheap labour.

   The great bulk of the famine emigrants chose the United States
as a settling ground for family, traditional or economic reasons.
But there was, besides, a general, if naive, belief amongst them
that it was ' the home of liberty ', a country in which a degraded
people might regain its dignity.  It was ironical, therefore, that
Irishmen should have encountered a more bitter and coherent
prejudice against them in America than in any British colony,
or, indeed, in any part of Britain itself, except perhaps in Scotland.[34]
Native Americanism, which formed the hard core of the opposition,
merely expressed in a violent and ugly form a resentment against
the Irish influx which was very generally felt.  Behind the militant
nativism of orangemen and fanatics, there lay a widespread
distrust of ' Romanism ',[35] a persistent fear that cheap Irish labour
might drag down the general level of wages, and a certain yankee
disdain for the ignorant, shiftless and priestridden Irish peasant.
In this sense, it is true to say that the movement was ' the climax
of a long slumbering . . . national hatred of foreign immigration '.[36]
It appears to have originated in the southern states, and first came
to a head in the anti-Catholic riots in Philadelphia, Richmond and
Charleston during 1844–5, when many convents and churches
were burnt and looted, and a number of people killed in the
street fighting which ensued.[37]  A similar outbreak in New York
was prevented only by Bishop Hughes' endeavours : he organised
his congregations into a fighting force to protect their churches,
and to win state assistance for denominational schools.[38]  Such
retaliations may have been necessary to save Catholics from unjust

discrimination, but they were not, as we shall see, without their unfortunate consequences.

The great majority of Americans could not give countenance to these disturbances. The report of a committee of the New York state assembly, which investigated the subject in 1848, and dismissed the riots as so many storms in teacups, represented the attitude of good sense and moderation which in normal times should have prevailed. It pointed out that immigrants lost their peculiarly national characteristics very quickly, if they were given rights instead of grievances, and that 'there are no truer American citizens than the children of those who came among us aliens '.[39] But in spite of the force of these observations and of the many other public professions of toleration, the prejudices we have already mentioned could not lightly be overcome. It was, after all, difficult to reconcile the *Weltanschauung* and ethics of ' the cold, shrewd, frugal, correct, meeting going Yankees '[40] with those of the immigrants who had just arrived. Americans were genuinely appalled by the destitute condition of the Irish ;[41] and their pride was stung by what they imagined Britain's policy to be, namely, to use the United States as a ' refuse dump ' for criminals and paupers.[42] Moreover, the fear that cheap Irish labour would eventually throw Americans out of their employment was naturally accentuated by the famine emigrations, and it appears to have reached a climax during the depression of 1849. On this last point, however, there was some disagreement. Many believed that the Irish were indispensable as the rude labouring force which made possible the golden expansion in the national economy : why should American razors be wasted in chopping blocks ?[43] But even moderates who accepted this point of view might reply, like Jesse Chickering, that there were ' things more precious than physical aggrandisement ' ; the Irish were not ' fit for liberty '.[44] And this feeling was reinforced by all those who were convinced that, whatever their immediate usefulness, the new Irish proletariat must, in the long run, lower the standard of living of the native workers, ' the greatest calamity which the folly of man could bring upon the land '.[45]

Much more important, however, than any of these considerations in fomenting the anti-Irish sentiment was the ' divided allegiance ' of the immigrants themselves. There was, in the first place, a certain danger (or so it was supposed) that Irish nationalist activities

might involve the United States in the dreaded 'foreign entangle-
ments in Europe'.[46] This fear was not completely groundless.
Some Irishmen, even before they emigrated, appear to have
regarded America primarily as a base for revolutionary movements.
When Henry Grattan's tenants were leaving for the new world,
they told him that they would return with 'rifles on their
shoulders'.[47] And the language of Irish-American periodicals
only too often provided nativists with ammunition for their
contention that the Irish immigration would eventually prove
to be the Trojan horse of the republic. For the line which these
papers generally took was that Ireland's political relief from
'the vampire oppressor' by the United States was justifiable as
'the soundest American national policy' and the 'holiest sentiment
of humanity'.[48] It was only to be expected that such arguments
should cause general alarm. Even the federal authorities felt
them to be a real danger. As the matter was put by the president
of the supreme court, passing judgment in the case of twelve
naturalised Irishmen, who had founded a revolutionary club in
Cincinnati to achieve Irish independence,

> I censure no Irishman for sympathising with his native land,
> and ardently desiring the restoration of the rights of its people ;
> but . . . these feelings ought not to be indulged in at the hazard
> of the interests and peace of the country of his adoption. . . .
> There can be no such thing as a divided natural allegiance.
> The obligations of citizenship cannot exist in favour of diff-
> erent nationalities at the same time.[49]

It is impossible to deny the justice of such a judgment. If
Americans are here to be blamed at all, it can only be for ex-
aggerating the seriousness of this danger to their neutrality, and
for the extravagance of their reaction to the provocation.

The 'Irish vote' was regarded as an equally grave and more
immediate threat to the American system. The 'threat' had
sprung from the great increase in the proportion of foreign born
voters. Even in the period 1830 to 1845, the ratio had risen
from one in forty to one in seven,[50] and the wave of famine
emigrations completed the profound and disturbing changes
in the existing political settlement. These were first apparent
in the narrower field of party support. It seems scarcely too much
to say that, in the years which immediately followed the famine

emigration, the Irish electors held the balance of power between the major parties. In practice, of course, they voted almost as a bloc, and stuck by the democrats through thick and thin. All efforts to swing the Irish vote away from Tammany, or from the equivalent machines in other cities, were ultimately unsuccessful.[51] There were Irish whigs and, later, Irish republicans, but they were few in number, and generally regarded as ' quislings ' by their fellow countrymen. Such a mode of mass and sectional voting struck hard at the ideal of ' Jeffersonian ' democracy, and in its scale, at least, introduced a new element into the arrangements. Many educated Irishmen, therefore, accepted the American view that it amounted to an abuse of the electoral system.[52] But they could reasonably add that there was no easy solution to the problem. Their want of education, their economic dependence on the political machines, and the delicacy of their situation as new and poor arrivals, all compelled the immigrants to adopt some form of block voting. Unity of action was essential in the face of nativism and the general hostility, and it secured rights and protection for the Irish which would otherwise have been completely out of reach. It is, in fact, impossible to distinguish here between cause and effect. The prejudice against the Irish forced them to hold together, and the mechanical majorities they gave their venal politicians deepened the prejudice against them.[53]

It is scarcely too much to find the ultimate cause of the American hostility in the tendency of Irish immigrants to settle in compact groups in urban areas, for this tendency was responsible for most of their crime, poverty, disease, clannishness and political behaviour. By 1867, for example, almost half a million people of Irish origin were living in the thirteen principal cities of the United States, over 200,000 of them in New York, some 100,000 in Philadelphia, and nearly 50,000 in Boston.[54] This fact raises one of the central problems of Irish emigration : why was it that, although 80% of the Irish emigrants were of rural origin,[55] only some 6% in all settled permanently on the land in the United States ?[56] Why was this so in spite of the ceaseless warnings of Irish priests, political leaders and newspapers that city life exposed them to grave dangers and miseries ; in spite of the existence of cheap transport to the interior ;[57] and in spite of the comparative success of the few who finally settled there ? The paradox cannot be explained completely, but several factors may be mentioned which take us some distance on that road. First, it must be remembered that, although the famine emigrants were generally countrymen, a very high proportion of these had been cottiers or squatters, and, therefore, scarcely belonged to an agricultural class, in the true sense of the words. Their farming experience had been more or less confined to the primitive raising of potatoes and root crops ; and the conacre system of land tenure meant that they were accustomed to live in close communities, rather than in rural isolation. And not only were they unfitted for a frontier life by temperament and training : they also lacked the capital needed to buy out, and settle on, holdings in the western states,[58] and their whole experience of agriculture at home must have disenchanted many with such projects. Then, we must take into account the strange manner in which so many of the immigrants who had any savings frittered them away in a sort of aimless micawberism, until finally they had sunk to the general level of their countrymen.[59] It was often pointed out that an immigrant's whole future in America might depend on his exertions in the first weeks after his arrival, and Irish immigrants were generally content to drift along, where fate had cast them, until it seemed too late to strike out once again. The original decision might have been brought about by any of a dozen causes : the reaction against their former life or passage ; sickness after they had disembarked ; the fraud of runners or lodging keepers ;[60] the presence of friends or relatives ; and so on. But once the decision (if the word itself is not too strong a term) had been taken, the fascination of urban life, with ready money and the sort of companionship to which they were accustomed, was usually irresistible.[61] There were, of course, two further influences at work, one, the drawing together in self defence—this we have already considered ; the other, the church's desire to keep its forces closely knit, in order to make easy the organisation of Catholicism upon a new soil.[62]

At any rate, for whatever reason, the Irish were concentrated in the coastal belt running south from Maine to Long Island, in the Rochester-Buffalo area of upper New York state, south and west of the Great Lakes, and in the industrial regions of Pennsylvania.[63] Some moved west with the gold and silver rushes of the ' fifties ' ;[64] and many others settled permanently in California, where there were Catholic traditions of long standing, and where the discovery of gold had coincided with the great wave of famine emigration.[65]  But the vast majority had chosen, or were forced, to make their homes in the larger urban areas, where living conditions were deplorable.  Wages were, perhaps, five times as high as those in Ireland, but the standards and cost of living had risen almost in proportion.[66]  Moreover, the immigrants were now subject to the effects of frequent and devastating depressions. Rents were exorbitant, particularly in the overcrowded Irish wards in New York, where insanitary and sordid surroundings often led to disease and vice.[67]  All over the United States, in fact, mortality rates were highest amongst the Irish, who were particularly prone to the diseases occasioned by dirt, over-crowding or alcohol,[68] and to pauperdom or lunacy.[69]  This was due, in part, to the type of employment in which they were usually engaged, as well as to their habits and environment. They worked in the heavy industries, in mining, or in railroad or canal construction, with all the common features of the labour camps, grinding toil, cheap whiskey, and the truck system.[70] Whether in Scotland, New England or Australia, the Irish formed the main army of the unskilled labour which built the cities and communications, and everywhere they paid a cruel price for their employment.

But the prejudice against them was slowly worn down, if not away.  There was, it is true, a revival of nativist feeling in the 'know-nothing' movement of 1854-5.  The usual pattern of riots and convent burnings followed, and Irish immigrants in Massachusetts and Connecticut were deprived of their right to serve in the militia.[71]  But 'know-nothingism' was almost immediately swallowed up in the excitement caused by the slavery issue and the formation of the new republican party, and many Americans were shamed by the hooliganism and recrudescence of bigotry displayed in 1854-5, when the 'worst' of the Irish emigration was already past.[72]  The civil war appears to have dissipated still more of the hostility.  Whether or not the Irish had been opposed to slavery,[73] an extraordinarily high proportion of them joined the union forces for economic or other reasons. Meagher's genuine knight errantry sprang to the liberation of the oppressed.  'Never ', he told his fellow countrymen, 'was there a cause more sacred, nor one more just, nor one more urgent ',[74] and incidents like the massacre of his regiment, the famous 69th New York, at Antietam, together with the exploits of other Irish regiments at the Bull Run, Fredericksburg and Chancellorsville, were widely publicised throughout the north.[75]  Many Irish fought, too, upon the confederate side, though relatively few had settled in the southern states.[76]  More important than any Irish feats of arms, however, was the fact that the war had enlarged the concept of nationality, and that a large number of Americans, who had never before met Irish immigrants upon an equal footing, now worked with them in a common cause.  The charitable activities of the nursing orders may also have done much to undermine the native hostility to Catholicism.

Finally, we must consider the problem of assimilation in a more general way.  Paradoxically enough (for their crimes were, in many eyes, those of clannishness and divided loyalty), the Irish possessed in a high degree the supreme immigrant virtue of adaptability to their surroundings, and almost without exception they spoke English.  Where they did not congregate together, therefore, they should have been readily 'assimilated' to the norm.  But four-fifths of them, at least, were Catholics, and most contemporary Americans considered that Catholicism was *per se* an insurmountable barrier to complete absorption.  It was indeed asserted that 'breathing the free air' of the United States a very high proportion of the Irish threw over their religion.[77]  Such an assertion cannot be dealt with certainly at this distance of time.  Outside the Irish quarters, doubtless, many cast aside, or scarcely attended to the disintegration of their faith.  The high intellectual tide in the United States was turning against organised belief ; the church visible scarcely existed outside the urban areas ; mixed marriages were common, and Catholicism often a bar to professional advancement.  But it must be remembered that, relatively, very few Irish settled or moved far away from the main concentrations of their group ; and even of those who did it seems safe to say that, compared with other immigrants in a corresponding situation, it was the Irish who were most distinguished for their adherence to their Church.  Thus, from circumstance, loyalty or whatever cause, the great bulk of the famine immigrants and of their immediate descendants and successors remained religiously, and (most Americans would have said) *ex post facto* racially and in ideology an 'alien body'.  But here contemporary Americans begged the question. To the nativist, the American way of life appeared an absolute and a constant. But the nineteenth-century historian finds it ever-variable. To him, the Americanism of, say, 1900 was at least partially the product of the very pace, scale and variety of the nineteenth-century immigrations[78] and of the almost ceaseless impact of the exotic upon the existing inhabitants and institutions. Not only does this view bring the famine emigration into new perspective ; it also illuminates the fact that that emigration was peculiarly telling. As (together with the German) the first of the mass migrations, it would in any event have brought great innovations in its train. But three of its characteristics, its intractable religion, its urban concentration and the extraordinary political capacity of so many of its members, greatly augmented its explosive force ; and its consequences did not diminish but increased in time, as new and still vaster and more exotic immigrations both strengthened the hand of the politically dominant Irish and pressed them steadily upwards in the social scale.[79] In short, the American system, political or ideological, cannot be regarded as the exclusive property or artefact of any single element within the whole ; indeed, it would be more accurate (though not, of course, the whole truth) to characterise it as the product of the relationships and tensions between the elements. If these simple facts are recognised, the Irish will surely be allotted some significant place in the nineteenth-century development of the American. None would suggest that an Irishless United States in 1900 would have been a Hamlet without the prince. But few would dispute that it would have been a very different and a poorer play.

APPENDIX I.   THE VOLUME OF OVERSEAS EMIGRATION

| Year | Irish Emigration to United States (1,000's) | % of Annual Emigration | Irish Emigration to British North America (1,000's) | % of Annual Emigration | Irish Emigration to Australia (1,000's) | % of Annual Emigration | % of Annual Emigration directed to other places | Annual Totals (1,000's) |
|---|---|---|---|---|---|---|---|---|
| 1841* | 12 | 70·4 | 2 | 10·7 | 3 | 18·8 | 0·1 | 16 |
| 1842 | 49 | 55·9 | 39 | 44·0 | 1 | 1·1 | | 90 |
| 1843 | 23 | 62·4 | 14 | 36·2 | ·5 | 1·4 | | 38 |
| 1844 | 37 | 68·6 | 16 | 30·4 | ·5 | 1·0 | | 54 |
| 1845 | 50 | 66·9 | 25 | 23·0 | | | 0·1 | 75 |
| 1846 | 68 | 64·2 | 38 | 35·8 | | | | 106 |
| 1847 | 117 | 54·3 | 97 | 45·2 | 1 | ·5 | | 215 |
| 1848 | 154 | 86·2 | 23 | 13·8 | 2 | 1·0 | | 178 |
| 1849 | 177 | 82·4 | 31 | 14·3 | 7 | 3·3 | | 214 |
| 1850 | 181 | 86·4 | 24 | 11·7 | 4 | 1·9 | | 209 |
| 1851 | 216 | 86·3 | 29 | 11·8 | 5 | 1·9 | | 250 |
| 1852 | 193 | 81·4 | 22 | 9·8 | 6 | 2·8 | | 220 |
| 1853 | 157 | 81·5 | 22 | 11·6 | 13 | 6·6 | 0·3 | 193 |
| 1854 | 111 | 73·9 | 23 | 15·3 | 16 | 10·8 | | 150 |
| 1855 | 57 | 72·4 | 6 | 7·9 | 16 | 19·6 | 0·1 | 79 |

Totals (1,000's)
and
averages : 1,601   76·7     412     19·7     75     3·6           2,088

* From June 30th of that year only.

NOTE—These statistics are taken from *Census of Ireland, 1851*, part vi, p. iv. They almost certainly fall short of the true totals, though the margin of error may not be very great. No allowance was made for stowaways, illegal embarkations or illegal sailings, although there are many references to these practices. Moreover, the returns assume that only 90% of the emigration from Liverpool (by far the most important of the embarkation ports) was Irish in origin. This was a distinct underestimate for the years 1845–50,† though it may have been an overestimate for the years 1852–5, when the German emigration from Liverpool appears to have been considerable. We should note, too, that no account was taken of Irish emigration from the Clyde until 1850, despite the practice of Ulster and north Connacht emigrants of embarking at Glasgow or Greenock. To allow for these omissions we should perhaps add something like 5% to the annual totals.

† *10th rep. C.L.E.C.*, 5, [1204], H.C. 1850, xxiii ; *11th rep. C.L.E.C.*, 1, [1383], H.C. 1851, xxii.

# THE FAMINE IN IRISH ORAL TRADITION
## By ROGER J. McHugh.

A FAMINE SCENE.

*Illustrated London News,* 1847.

# CHAPTER VII

# The Famine in Irish oral tradition

## I. INTRODUCTION

IN this chapter an attempt is made to present the picture of the famine retained in Irish oral tradition, as far as it can be pieced together from the tradition of hundreds of our people who still discuss the experiences of their ancestors in famine times. During the past century such experiences have been told and retold around the firesides of the farming and fishing communities of the districts which bore the brunt of the famine ; they have been firmly linked to associations of place, of family and of language ; in many places they are as real to the inhabitants today as are the events of last year.

The task of making them real to the world at large could not have been undertaken without the co-operation of the Irish Folklore Commission, its officials, collectors and informants. Their work was not without grave handicaps, for it was undertaken at a time when, owing to the inadequate endowment of the Commission, much valuable material seemed to have been lost forever. Thirty or forty years ago many old people who remembered the famine were still alive ; but few of their recollections were recorded and only accounts at second and third hand are now available. With the passage of time, oral tradition tends to become blurred and its flavour of personality and of place to become weaker. Could anything of value result from a survey of oral tradition ? Had oral tradition anything to add to the newspaper reports, the travellers' accounts, the official documents of the period ? Or could it supply anything more than a vague and distorted outline to place beside the clear picture presented by the historian ?

Such were inevitable questions for the writer of this chapter
before the collection and examination of available Irish oral
tradition about the famine had been undertaken. The reader
of it can answer them to his own satisfaction only when he has
come to the end of it ; for the answers depend upon whether
or not oral tradition can be shown to harmonise with or to
render more vivid and graphic the picture of the famine as
experienced by its sufferers, and upon whether or not oral
tradition brings new facts to light.

The survey has been divided into six parts which deal respectively with the potato and the blight ; food during the
famine ; relief ; disease ; death and burial ; social changes.
Numerical references indicate the county and volume of the
collectors' records ; alphabetical, the questionnaire replies.
These are in the archives of the Irish Folklore Commission.

## II.   THE BLIGHT

The dependence of the vast majority of our people upon the
potato is underlined by Irish oral tradition about pre-famine
times. ' They knew how many basketfuls of spuds they'd dig in
each day ', says a co. Cork account of two brothers who lived on
a small holding then : ' They knew how many baskets of potatoes
went to the pit.  They knew how many potfuls went to each basket
and at three potfuls a day they knew the day they would have no
more potatoes.'[1]  Boiled potatoes, placed in a basket made of
unpeeled rods and allowed to ' teem ' or drain on the doorstep,
then peeled with the thumbnail, which was kept at a certain length
for the purpose, formed the staple diet of people in the poorer
areas.  Meat was rarely eaten except at Christmas or Easter.
If fish was served with potatoes it was placed on top of the basket
and was eaten with the fingers, but the usual ' kitchen ' (garnish)
was simply salt and water or milk, placed on a saucer which rested
on a stool near the dinner-table and into which the potatoes
would be dipped.  Such a meal was sometimes called ' dab at
the stool ' or ' dip at the stool ' ; it was also called ironically
by such names as *scadán caoch* (blind herring) or ' scudum up the

road ', since the presence of a *scadán* (herring) had to be imagined. Any potatoes left over from a meal would be used for potato-cake, slim cake or *fleatair* or might be put into the embers for any hungry person who might call. Children going to school would carry with them cold potatoes for lunch and would sometimes give their largest lunch-potato to their schoolmaster. Fishermen would carry quantities of cooked potatoes with them on their trips— the fishermen of Teelin, co. Donegal, had specially made woollen stocking-bags in which they carried mashed potatoes[2]—or would bring ' live ' turf in their boats and cook them with fish at sea. On the land, labourers employed in digging potatoes would be allowed a ' cast ' of potatoes, as many large potatoes as they could roast on an open fire and eat at one sitting.[3] If in addition to this we consider other purposes, such as the feeding of livestock, or the making of starch, for which the potato was used, the important part which it played in the family and social life of the people needs no further emphasis.

On the subject of the types and varieties of potatoes used immediately before the famine, oral tradition has much to say ; the use of certain types which it mentions, such as Rocks, Cups, Lumpers, Pink Eyes, Leathercoats and Skerry Blues has been formally authenticated. The use of other kinds, such as Codders, Minions, Thistlewhippers, Weavers, is not easy to check ; new varieties of seed were introduced during the famine years and their use may have been attributed to pre-famine times : also, the same variety is often known by different names in different parts ; Rocks are known in some areas as ' Protestants ', because they were first imported and used by Protestants ; other districts refer to them as Scotch Downs and Green Tops, while names such as ' Bulls ' and ' Bucks ' are probably local names for the Cluster potato. Of all these types and varieties mentioned, Cups, Scotch Downs and Lumpers are usually those said to have failed during the famine . . .

' The first downfall that Ireland got, the lumpers they were black
When I hired with Captain Murphy to work my passage to New York.'

begins one old ballad,[4] while another gives a rhyming dialogue

between the Scotch Down potato and the Champion, the best
seed-potato imported after the failure :

> ' You dirty clown ', says the Scotsdown,
> ' How dare you me oppose !
> ' Twas I supported Ireland
> When you darent show your nose.'
> Outspoke the noble Champion
> With courage stout and brave :
> ' Only I happened to sail over here
> There'd be thousands in their grave.'[5]

The methods of cultivation then in use are often recalled as
contributing powerfully to the potato failure. Potatoes were
planted year after year in the same field, with no change of seed,
and thus crops and land were both weakened. Since poorer
people had only small haggards or ' gardens ', they were most
affected by the lack of crop rotation. Those who got plots from
farmers on conacre usually got the same plot year after year—
one still finds fields called by such names as ' the men's field ',
' the potato field ', though they are no longer let in conacre
strips.[6] Manure was rarely obtainable by such cultivators, who
seldom had livestock of their own and often grew their ' grass
potatoes ' in ridges or ' lazy beds ' without manure. In some
districts where dung was obtainable its value was weakened
by mixture with peat instead of with straw, which was needed
for thatching, and this mixture tended to produce an overgrowth
of weeds. Tillage land was also weakened by the widespread
custom of burning ' scraw ' or upper sod for manure ; it was
hacked in March, raked up dry in May and burned, the ashes
being spread on the ground before the potato ridges were made.
This practice, which was called *béiteail,* survives in the saying,
*Tá deireadh le béiteáil anois* (There is an end to *béiteáil* now),
still used in rural Ireland when a shower comes. It was a practice
upon which some landlords frowned and which they punished
by eviction. Furze and lime were also used as substitutes for dung,
while in coastal districts *leas fairrge,* seaweed or manure obtained
from fishguts and shell fish was used and is still thought to have
damaged the land.[7]

This impoverishment of the land and the need for proper crop-rotation and other safeguards was realised generally only after the famine.  In the years immediately before it the potatoes flourished despite the crude method of their cultivation.  At that time they were usually sown in wide ' rigs ', ' lands ' or ridges about twelve feet wide with a furrow at each side, the land being prepared with spades or wooden ploughs and the potatoes being ' dibbled in ' or broadcast and then covered over with spades or shovels.  They were usually planted in April or May and were dug in six weeks, a second crop being set in July in some districts, where it was common for people to be eating new potatoes while they were sowing the seed for a second crop.  In the fertile midlands ' laggards ' might delay setting their one crop until July, while in others the tradition is that during those years potatoes grew irrespective of what time of year they were planted.[8]

It is ironical that probably the most widespread tradition about the potatoes during these pre-famine years concerns their profusion.  So abundant was their growth, it is said, that people did not know what to do with their surplus potatoes ;  they left them stacked in heaps at the backs of ditches, piled them in the gaps of fences, used them as top-dressing, buried them or stacked them in the fields and burned them.  Anecdotes are still told of how men brought loads of potatoes to market and had to heel them into ditches because they were left unsold, and of how such waste aroused in others a feeling of foreboding that the day would come when it would be regretted.  Hence, though to-day the potato failure is usually attributed to natural causes, and though a few people adhere to the belief expressed in a popular ballad—

> The pledge we've violated
> Blest Father Mathew gave us
> And that brought desolation
> To our poor country—[9]

a great many of the old people believed and some still believe that the famine was a punishment for waste, a scourge sent from God because of the abuse of plenty.

The circumstances under which the blight struck and withered this profusion left an awful impression upon the minds of those who witnessed it, and are reflected in the tradition which has

come down from them : a tradition of an ominous season of
mist, of storms of rain and wind alternating with periods of
vast and terrible stillness ; of the names of fields where the blight
first appeared and of men who first noticed the heavy smell
of decay or saw the brown spots spreading on the leaves, the
blackened stalks slowly leaning over, the potato-pits ominously
sagging.  Sometimes there was but slight alarm at first, for
potato disease in a less virulent form was no stranger.  In other
districts panic spread quickly as whole fields were laid waste
in a few hours : people who had gone to bed, leaving fields
green as holly, awoke to find them black as soot or to see a brown
swath of decay spreading rapidly over a whole field and from
field to field.  Accounts differ from district to district, for there
were local variations of time and of effect ;  moory or boggy
land escaped wholly or partly in some districts ;  sandy soil
escaped in others, while bogs were smitten ;  generally, low-lying
ground was less immune than mountain land, which was stronger,
and mossy soil less immune than clay ;  some coastal districts,
notably islands, were unaffected, others were blasted while
inland districts near them were untouched.  It is not unusual to
find that in the same townland crops within a few hundred yards
of each other would meet different fates, while one townland
might escape completely and no crops whatever remain unaffected in the next.

Such variations do not affect the main outlines of the picture
registered in the traditions of the north-west, west and south-
west, a picture of the Irish peasant clinging to a ramshackle
social structure whose main prop was snapping while he was
bewildered, frightened and totally unequipped with any means
of diverting disaster.  Various remedies were tried ;  some planted
seed-potatoes earlier in the hope that a recurrence of the blight
would find the tubers strong enough to resist it ;  others worked
frantically, cutting affected stalks to arrest the spread of the blight,
burning fires to purify the air, changing potatoes to better-
ventilated pits, piling mounds of turf, stones or clay over them,
sprinkling the fields with holy water, as if to check some hunger-
demon who was devouring the land.  In a few instances lime
and guano appear to have been used with some success, but these
were rarely obtainable by the majority of people in the affected
areas ;  for these, early planting was the only remedy which met

with any success. In the main, the blight continued, affecting alike growing potatoes, pitted potatoes or those which had been stored in barns or in houses.

So at a stroke the potato, whose surplus a short time before men had despised, became a prized possession for which multitudes followed the ploughs of strong farmers or rooted through ridges over and over again. Oral tradition has many anecdotes which help to make vivid the change ; of men who dug all day, often in vain, to find enough potatoes for one meal ; of farmers of formerly fertile acres who now starved ; of the high prices paid for seed-potatoes and the zeal with which they were hidden, guarded and husbanded against the next planting. To stretch out the seed, the ' eye ' of the potato with a minute part of the ' flesh ' adhering to it, would be picked out with a goose quill or a nail ; this would be planted, the rest eaten ; the most minute *póiríní,* potatoes so small that they ' could be riddled in a sieve ', *bachlógaí* (potato-buds) and even the stalks themselves would be kept and planted, sometimes very successfully. Yet the persistence of the blight until 1847 finally discouraged many of those who still had some precious seed left and caused them to abandon their holdings.

In many parts of Ireland the lesson of thrift which this great reversal—' the time of the scarcity '—taught to our forefathers is still remembered a century later. ' I remember that my grandfather would become furious with us when we were young if he saw any of us wasting food ', wrote one informant ; ' he would refer to the famine. And when he was ploughing he would not leave a potato, however small, that the plough would turn up, without picking it up '.[10] Other informants recalled similar rebukes by old people who would always pick up a stray potato or who were known long after the famine to burst into tears at the sight of a good dish of floury potatoes, as they remembered the bad times.

III. FOOD DURING THE FAMINE

A large body of oral tradition of the famine times relates to the food eaten during those years and it is interesting to see what alternatives were resorted to, now that the staple food of many areas was gone. Old people to-day can still talk of a ' feast ' of that time, which they had heard their fathers talk about—a meal of boiled turnips and fish or of boiled cabbage, oatmeal and cream—and so light up the background of scarcity, but the bulk of tradition furnishes more direct and fuller information.

Even blighted potatoes were still sought after ; they could be grated, soaked in water and (when the bad matter had been skimmed off) could be made into 'boxty' bread ; or the good parts could be cut out of them and used for food.  Grain was now grown by many people for the first time and in some districts mills were erected to meet the increased demand for milling ; in others people relied on hand-querns as they had done before the famine.  Generally, oats was the chief grain crop which the people turned to—in some districts wheat was grown mainly for thatching-straw—and the farmer who was lucky enough to have a surplus after his grain had been sold to pay his rent could feed his family upon a variety of oaten foods ; oatmeal porridge, oatcakes, oatmeal dumplings ('water whelps') ; crushed oats steeped in water and known as 'sowans' (sounds), or 'cheerins' ; 'brawlum', 'broes' and other oatmeal foods ; while the meal itself was sometimes simply damped and eaten raw.  Other simple dishes made from grain included *gráinseachán* or *grán-bhruith* (grain boiled in water), *prásán seagail* (rye boiled with milk), 'flummery' (boiled chaff-juice) and various types of porridge. For the majority even such simple fare would be out of the question, and the farmers who could provide barley boiled with meat, or the fishermen who could rely upon the fish which they had hitherto sold were greatly envied.

The fatal dependence of people upon the potato is manifest also in the lack of vegetable substitutes in many parts. Turnips, for example, were unknown in many districts before the famine. Mayo tradition records that when the people of Ballycroy were given turnip-seed they tried to sow it as potatoes were sown.[1] In several areas the distribution of turnip-seed by individuals or committees spread the popularity of the vegetable rapidly. *Thionntuigh a gcroiceánn buidhe ó bheith ag ithe na swedes* ('their skin turned yellow from eating swedes'), says an account from Barnesmore, co. Donegal,[2] and there is no doubt that the turnip was a great mainstay for those who could get it, but through the lethargy of custom, the inaccessibility of remote districts and the lack of distributing centres and supplies, this was not always possible. Kilkenny farmers who had formerly lived in plenty would close their doors at meal-time through shame at having nothing but turnips to eat,[3] but in Sligo crowds of starving men and women would gather in the turnip fields and scramble for the turnip-cuttings left by the harvesters.[4] The better-off people would boil them with meat or fish or make them into 'skoddy' (boiled turnips and oatmeal), 'turnip bóxty' or 'champ' (mashed turnips); the poor would be glad to eat them slice by slice roasted on the tongs. Cabbage appears to have been extensively used as a substitute food, but, although other foods such as peas, beans and vetches are sometimes mentioned in traditional accounts, they were not cultivated to any considerable extent in the areas most affected. It is of interest that substitute foods have given rise to local names for famine times; in one co. Cork district, for example, one of the famine years was known as *blian na dturnaipí*[5] (the year of the turnips), while in Castleisland, co. Kerry, a particularly hard month was remembered as 'July of the cabbage'.[6]

Many curious substitutes for the potato were eagerly sought. People followed the plough or rooted in the ground for the *práta clúracán* (pignut) or for roots of fern or dandelion, which they would boil, roast or crush with meal to make bread. Children searched the woods for nuts, the bogs and mountains for berries; the fruit of holly, beech, crab-apple and laurel trees and the leaves and barks of certain trees were also devoured; in some parts cresses were gathered until the ditches and streams were cleared completely of them, while the leaves of the dock, the sorrel and the dandelion were widely used.

> *Praiseach bhuidhe na ngort*
> *biadh na ndaoine mbocht* [7]
> 'Charlock of the fields
> Food of poor people.'

is a saying still quoted in relation to that time, as during the famine this yellow-flowered weed was a common food. 'It is recorded that some people came from the neighbouring parish of Cratloe to eat the wonderful crop of *praiseach bhuidhe* growing in Frost's field at Punchbowl Cross', says an account from Cratloe, co. Clare,[8] while the tradition of other districts tells of people thronging into the fields for the same purpose and of families who lived for months upon a patch of this weed. Borage (*bráiste*, *borráiste*), which normally is pullled out of corn and discarded, and all kinds of wild vegetables were also eaten. So were nettles, which according to a Kerry tradition were used before the famine and when boiled were considered a cure for blood disorders.[9] Now they were eagerly sought by hungry people, who might travel miles for them : ' I heard my own mother to say she saw the people travelling miles to the graveyards to gather the nettles that grew there ', said an old man of Enniskean, co. Cork : ' They grew higher and better in graveyards than any other where.'[10] When gathered they would be chopped finely and boiled with oatmeal or made into soup. It is natural that the indiscriminate use of nettles and of berries is sometimes recalled as having caused disease and death.

For those who kept a little livestock the situation was made desperate by the loss of the potato and of feeding-stuff. There are widespread memories of the diminution during these years of livestock, which was sometimes slaughtered for food, sometimes because it could be fed no longer. Pigs, upon which so many of the conacre farmers depended to pay their rents, were particularly susceptible to cholera, and their dwindling numbers meant that the way was prepared for widespread evictions. Many farmers who hesitated to kill their cattle were forced to extract blood from them regularly. The blood was usually extracted by skilled men, although several accounts tell of cattle and even horses dying from unskilled or excessive bleeding. ' A man named Curnane brought seven or eight cows to my father's father to draw blood for his starving family, about a quart from each cow', said one informant,[11] and this amount was quite usual. Generally young animals were bled ; the blood-letter would cut a vein in the neck, would extract the blood and stop the bleeding by putting a pin through the skin across the incision in the vein and would secure it in position by lapping a few hairs from the animal's tail around it. The blood so obtained would be carried home in jars or buckets ; it would be salted and fried, or boiled with milk, meal, vegetables or herbs, or made into such food as ' relish cakes ', which were obtained by mixing and baking it with mushrooms and cabbage. It was generally estimated to be a good strong nourishing food. It is also noteworthy that the practice of blood-letting survives in certain place-names ; it was usual to assemble the cattle of a district for bleeding at specific points, and some of these are still called by associative names, for example, *lag na fola* (the hollow of the blood), *bogach na fola* (the moor of the blood) and *Cnoc a' Daimh* (the hill of the ox), all of which are in co. Mayo, are thought to have been so named ;[12] though one cannot say with certainty that all such names date from famine times, it is probable that many of them do.

In the coastal areas of the western seaboard people lived mainly by fishing and were not so dependent upon the potato, which was not cultivated to the same extent as in inland parts and in some places was not cultivated at all ; Teelin, co. Donegal, for example, used to import potatoes from Connacht and now had to depend entirely upon fish.[13]    But even such districts could still carry on by selling their surplus fish and living on the remainder, part of which would be salted and dried against a season of scarcity.    Poteen was made in many of these places and recollections of people who lived almost entirely upon fish and poteen during the famine years are not infrequent.    Crowds would travel from far inland to ' tramp ' for fluke in the shallow coastal waters or to gather the *cnuasach trágha,* shore-food which kept many alive, edible seaweeds and shell-fish.    Shore-food had been used before the famine by poor people—' *Seachain tigh an tábhairne nó is báirnigh is beatha dhuit* ' (' avoid the tavern or you'll live on limpets '), says the proverb—but now it was sought by unprecedented numbers, sometimes with fatal consequences. The sea-dwellers themselves, who often dealt in edible seaweeds, would know that dilisk eaten cold is dangerous, that *dúlamán* is not usually eaten until after the first severe frost in winter, and that certain shell-fish must be boiled and are fatal if eaten raw after a long fast ; the migrants often contracted disease for lack of such knowledge and many such victims are recalled, sometimes by association with huge piles of shells found in caves or laid bare through tillage operations or coastal erosion.[14]

Rivers and lakes were of course intensively fished—Wicklow tradition records that so many came groping for eels and trout that some rivers were entirely cleared of them[15]—but in many cases the fishing was preserved by the landlords who punished poachers by imprisonment.    Animal food of every kind was used ; horses and asses, dried snails, frogs and hedgehogs baked in clay.    Crows were eaten, sea-birds were brought down with loaded sticks skilfully thrown, men clambered trees, mountains and cliffs searching for eggs. The frantic search for food of any kind has left its strong imprint upon local tradition which still recalls fights over the bodies of foxes, people who made soup from dogs, the eating of rats and of diseased animals, hungry children begging for pig-food, or starving women delightedly carrying home the entrails of fish or of cattle to their families.

Strong, too, is the memory of food-stealing during the famine years. Potato and turnip crops were often raided by night; the ridges would be opened and the growing tubers extracted by hand, as spades would make too much noise, the stalks being left untouched so that the loss would remain undiscovered for some time; the bolder raiders would cram clusters of potatoes hastily into a sack and make a dash for it. Potatoes stored in barns or kept in dwellinghouses were not always safe, as they were often 'speared' with a long pointed rod inserted through a hole in the thatch. Some farmers used to bury their seed-potatoes in the floors of their houses; others sat up at night in the fields in specially built *botháin* or watch-houses before which huge watch-fires burned. Most of them would deal roughly with trespassers and would jail or beat them, or would tie them to posts or cartwheels as a warning to others, and would sometimes shoot to kill.[16] Others were slow to punish, would fire warning shots or sound horns at night to notify their presence, and would sometimes deal leniently with first offenders.[17] The names of both types have passed into many local traditions, which also recall the kinds of mantraps used at this time; deep pits covered with bracken in which people sometimes died, or traps with spikes which pierced the feet of the raiders. There are also many traditional stories which centre around the stealing of sheep, which was widespread despite the use of sheep-bells, the sleeping out of herds and the severe penalties, of which the most common was transportation. Donegal tradition, for example, records the exploits of *Domhnall na Molt* (Donal of the wethers) who used to bury the sheep-skins in a bog where they were found years afterwards by turf-cutters,[18] while the shanachies of Kerry can still tell about *na mná bána,* the fair women who worked with a man at this practice,[19] and those of Westmeath about the sheep-stealers who skinned their sheep at night on the long flat tombstones of local graveyards.[20] Such sheep-stealers are sometimes remembered by name because they gave part of their spoils to destitute people, because they never stole from their neighbours but travelled farther afield, or because they were considerate enough to leave the sheepsheads behind them as a sign that the sheep had not strayed. Others are re-collected because they were transported or by association with certain feuds or reprisals which their work caused. The latter is not surprising, for a family's few sheep might represent its only hope of survival.

Though sheep-stealing is still remembered with censure, tradition generally recognises the stark necessity which often drove people to steal at the time and records with approval the names of farmers who dealt leniently with sheep-stealers or of people who refused to give information about them. Sometimes reticence was enforced by the stealers themselves upon people who had witnessed their actions, but more often it seems to have resulted from recognition of the essential injustice of the social system at that time. It is interesting to note in this connection that in isolated parts of Mayo, Clare, Galway and Donegal where a strong communal feeling caused people to share their food— ' Níor itheadar i gcóir é gan na cómharsana bheith buidheach' (' they did not eat aright unless the neighbours were thankful ')— there is a comparative lack of traditional accounts of stealing.

Organised robbery of food-supplies appears to have been sporadic and comparatively rare. This is perhaps surprising if one considers only traditional recollections of the export of food from Ireland during the famine ; how the corn of east Clare was stored in the big stores at Tuaimgréine from whence it went to other countries ;[21] how in 1847 fourteen schooners of about two hundred tons each left Westport, a badly stricken area, laden with wheat and oats ;[22] or how the double rows of grain-carts passed day after day from west to east across Meath.[23] But reasons are not hard to find and are provided better by other sources than by folk tradition which, being close to the realities of dislocation and starvation, rarely assesses the political and social causes. As far as it does assess them, it emphasises the lack of leaders after O'Connell, the general helplessness and bewilderment of the people, and the force which ordained that the small farmer should starve while in his garden his stock of oats, marked with the landlord's mark, awaited the cart which would take it away

for export.    Some local attacks on meal-depots or food-wagons
are recalled in detail but add little to the information obtainable
in printed sources or in the ' outrage papers '.    A typical account,
which a co. Meath informant had heard from his father and
mother, may be mentioned.    It describes an attack on meal-carts
proceeding through Meath by a number of men armed with
scythe-blades and pitchforks.    The carts were guarded by two
soldiers who ordered them to halt.    One soldier deliberately
fired above the attackers, the other shot one of them.    The raiders
secured possession of the meal, cut the bags in two to make their
transport easy and cleared away, carrying the wounded man with
them.    He died later and his funeral party was held up and questioned
by a force which was combing the locality for the culprits.    The
coffin would have been opened and its victim identified but for
fear of fever, and the attackers remained undiscovered.[24]    Such
attacks are thought to have led to the erection of police-barracks
in some lonely places.

Many stories still told in rural Ireland about that time centre
around the miraculous appearance of food.    Of these the most
widespread and the most popular is that of the ' charitable woman ',
which occurs with local variations in widely separated districts
throughout Ireland.    The following version of it was recorded
by a native of co. Cork, where the tradition is perhaps strongest,
and is typical.

> I often heard of Mrs. Ned Fitzgerald, Mountinfant, two
> miles north of our village.    She was grandmother to the
> present owners and always helped the poor and never left a
> hungry man, woman or child go unfed from her door.    One
> day, as I heard, a poor woman with two starving children came
> to her house.    She gave them milk to drink and bread to eat.
> The poor woman was eating nothing herself but attending to
> the children.    When Mrs. Fitzgerald saw this she said to the
> poor woman : ' Now take and eat yourself first and eat enough
> and keep yourself as strong as you can, so that you may be
> able to provide for your children ; for what could they do if
> you allowed yourself to starve, and who would look after
> them ? '    This good woman never refused to give her skim
> milk to the poor and often her husband used to blame her
> for giving away the milk and letting the calves go hungry.

It was told how one day he was ploughing near the house and he saw so many poor people leaving the house with ' gallons ' of milk on their heads that he got vexed and made for the house to scold his wife for giving away so much milk. He said to her : ' You are giving away all my milk and starving my calves and not caring a bit what price they'd be making '. She said the calves had grass and water and wouldn't starve, and that she couldn't refuse poor neighbours a drop of milk for starving children. ' There's milk going all day ', he said, ' and come now and show me what you have for the calves in the evening '. He ran out to the dairy himself and she thought : ' Tis unknown what he'll do when he finds all the pans empty '. But when he went into the place, lo and behold, all the pans were full of milk as if she had given nothing away ; full of milk and cream they were, though he had seen milk being taken away all day. He got an awful surprise and went away back to his plough ; and 'twas said he never again interfered with his good wife about what milk she'd give away to the poor ; and his calves grew and thrived and he never had better calves than he had that very year when his wife had all the milk given away to the children of her poor neighbours.[25]

The details of this story vary with regard to the identity and locality of the ' charitable woman ' and the nature of the food given by her. The *dénouement* also varies ; stored potatoes increase until the door of the barn in which they are kept cannot be opened, or the meal-chest is found to be full instead of empty ; but in essence the story is the same in Galway as in Cork, in Mayo as in Wexford. Next in frequency is the story of the visitor who is hospitably treated by poor people and who rewards them by causing food to appear. Sometimes he is a holy man, sometimes an unnamed visitor, who changes a potful of boiling water into one of meat and soup, or causes the empty meal-chest to become full to the brim. Stories of food appearing in answer to prayer are also frequent ; a miraculous growth of mushrooms answers a poor widow's prayer ; a ploughman prays for the starving people who watch him and the plough turns up potatoes where there were none before ; or small potatoes become large after the priest's help has been sought. In other cases food appears to the necessitous without supplication ; a poor woman boils stones in a pot to quieten her crying children and the contents turn to soup ; another fills a bag with sand which turns to meal ; others find their wells full of milk or are fed by the fairies. Occasionally one can perceive a rational explanation of such stories : for example, food thought to have appeared miraculously was sometimes found in the morning on village greens ; from other accounts it seems certain that charitable people sometimes left food in such places by night to avoid the danger of infection from crowds of starving people by day. Similarly the growing of potatoes from stalk-buds is thought to have been miraculous in some districts, while the inhabitants of others regard it as natural, though unusual. But the story of the 'charitable woman' and similar stories appear to be based on the firm belief that God increases the store of charitable people—

> Má táim-se fial agus mo lámh a' síne
> Beidh líon an fhollamhuithe 'g cóir na h-oidhche[26]
> 'If I am lavish and my hand outstretched
> The void will be filled by nightfall—'

the reputed saying of a charitable woman, expresses this belief directly.

Linked with such stories are many memories of genuine acts of charity during the famine which are still retained in many parts of Ireland. 'Clann Pháidín na bláithche buige, an aráin eorna ⁊ an bhrachdin seagail'[27] ('the family of Paudeen of the yellow buttermilk, the barley bread and rye porridge ') is a saying about one Donegal family which fed the poor during famine times ; others are remembered for particular acts of kindness, sometimes because when their members died, many decades after the famine, their coffins were followed to the grave by crowds of people whom they had helped. Individual priests and parsons who showed kindness then are similarly recalled. The general re-collection of the state of the former at that time is that they were almost on the same level of poverty as the people and that their sparse dues were affected by the decline of the marriage and birth rates and by the fear of disease, which diminished their congregations and often led to the abandonment of 'stations'. Several of them are remembered for their efforts on relief committees, or for sharing their food with the poor ; others because they died from fever contracted while anointing the dying—a number of these are still commemorated by plaques in Irish Catholic churches—or for co-operating with the parsons in relief-work. In general they lacked the influence which the parsons could command among the landlords and government officials, and those of them who became 'landlord priests' to enrich themselves are still spoken of with dislike. One curious tradition, widespread in Mayo and sometimes met outside it, concerns a priest or priests who warned people against planting seed-potatoes in 1847, when the general belief was that the blight would continue.[28] Those who disregarded this advice are said to have had a good crop and this is advanced as one reason why people turned Protestant, but it is notable that the tradition occurs most frequently in Mayo, which contained a noted proselytising centre at Achill.

The vividness with which individual acts of charity are remembered still is some indication of the grim setting in which they were performed. The attitude of the people towards official charity, whether in the form of food or of relief work, is very different.

#### IV. RELIEF: FOOD AND WORK

Indian meal, the chief food distributed by way of relief during the famine, is remembered by a variety of names—'yellow Indian', 'yellow buck', 'India buck', etc.—and the circumstances of its distribution, its price and rationing are often recalled with great accuracy. Old people in most parts of the country rated it highly as a strong nutritive food, superior to oatmeal in many respects. Yet in several districts it earned a bad reputation, probably because when first imported it was distributed in coarse lumps which had to be boiled for a comparatively long time ; it spat much while boiling and children had to be put out of the room for fear of their being scalded. Many people died from dysentery through eating it without cooking it sufficiently, and government pamphlets were issued to warn about this. To-day one finds a lasting prejudice against it in some places, but this does not appear to be general. What is general, however, is a lasting dislike of the manner in which it was distributed. An account from co. Donegal helps towards an understanding of this. It tells of the meal-centre at Falcarragh, co. Donegal, a big store run by local Protestant landlords who sold meal there at a half-crown per stone, the ration being one stone per person. Nobody was allowed to enter the store and the people crowded outside it. There was a door in the gable ; the man who wished to buy meal would tie his half-crown in the corner of his meal-bag and would throw it up to the man in charge of distribution. The latter had a long stick with an iron crook ; when the meal had been put into the bag he would let it down to the buyer by means of this. If there was any crushing or scuffling below, as there often was, people being so afraid of not getting a ration that they were ready to kill each other for it, the man would descend and would belabour them with his stick until they became orderly again.[1] It is still recalled by the people of Teelin, co. Donegal, that the window of one such store was broken and that the price of meal was immediately raised until the damage had been paid for.[2]

Anecdotes about the evasion of rationing are still told in many places : an old woman gets three separate rations by disguising herself ;[3] an old man christens his cat Seán in order to procure an extra ration for himself ;[4] people bury their dead at night to prevent the loss of their rations.[5] In places, only the head of a house would be allowed to take food away from the centres, and it is indicative of the strain which hunger placed upon family ties that the whole family would sometimes accompany him.

Many traditional accounts of food-distribution centre around the large boilers used in the preparation of porridge and of soup. Several of these are still extant and though now used to store oats, and as drinking-troughs, dye-vats and cisterns, can serve to remind people of famine times. These boilers were sometimes set up in buildings with special chimneys, sometimes in the open. Huge fires would be lighted under them and their smoke would be the signal for hungry crowds to assemble, their noggins in their hands, as they waited until their names or numbers were called. Often hunger could be too strong for them and the strong would shove aside the weak, or turn upon someone from another district who had taken a place in their queue, or rush frantically at the boiler and get badly scalded by plunging their noggins into it or by having soup thrown in their faces by the men in charge of it. Once served with their pint of free soup or stirabout, people would hurry off to hold their noggins or cans in running water, to cool it quickly, or, if they were too weak to carry home their share, would stretch themselves on the ground and lap it up. The wisest would hang back in the queue, hoping to get the better soup from the bottom of the boiler, or the 'screb' (crust) of burnt stirabout, which they would eat like bread out of their hands.

Food thus distributed is widely recalled as being poor in quality. Although through the kindness of local landlords or the integrity of local committees good food was sometimes provided, the general picture is otherwise. A sack of Indian meal might be all that went into the boiler, producing a thin watery 'prawpeen' or 'poorhouse porridge' which is still described in a variety of graphic ways : 'It wouldn't firm' ;[6] *bhíodh sé lom i gceart*[7] (it was properly thin) ; 'a mule couldn't leave the trace of her hoof on it' ;[8] 'it would run a mile on a plank and scald a man at the end of it'.[9] Sometimes soup would be made from old or diseased animals, or 'porridge' would consist of a handful of meal thrown into cold water. The reason why relief-food was often of such poor quality is in many accounts attributed to the diversion of supplies of food by local committees or powerful individuals or their agents, who are said to have sold it to friends and relations or to have used it to feed their own livestock :

'Our committee the wicked thieving schemers
Kept it to feed their own parents at home'

says one local ballad,[10] while several accounts tell how the livestock of local landlords grew fat on relief-food intended for the starving poor, whose meal had been doctored by being damped or by being mixed with chaff. The men in charge of boilers or meal centres are often blamed for their dishonesty, in local anecdotes and verses ; some verses of fulsome praise survive in which the distributor, pencil in hand, is hailed as the morning star, the blossom of youth, or as a deity presiding over the hungry crowds, but these were invariably written by hungry poets who thought to obtain his favour ; verses about such men are usually bitingly satirical, while anecdotes describe the ill-luck which followed them, how their lines died out or how they ended their days in beggary.

Such traditional memories help to explain why today people in rural Ireland, while appreciating that relief-food kept many

alive who otherwise would have starved, often speak of it with
bitterness.   There was also the humiliation which many felt at
existing on relief-food, where they had previously been comparatively independent as long as the potato continued to grow.
Another strong reason for the bitterness is the association of
any form of food-distribution with proselytising work, which
had been carried on for many years before the famine and which
increased in certain districts during it.   This varied with the
outlook, strength and influence of local Protestant landlords,
the existence of organised bible-reading societies and schools,
and the strength of Catholic opposition in such districts.   Where
such circumstances were favourable, offers of food now became
a strong inducement to adults to attend bible-reading classes or
to send their children to local Protestant schools.   Meat soup
would be offered on Fridays to starving people whose resistance
might be worn thin by hunger,[11] and the strong influence which
local Protestants could exert in providing money, in securing
better allocations of food or of contracts for relief-works, or in
providing people with land or labour upon their own estates,
was often exerted to the full in the distressed areas, Catholics
who ' turned ' being especially favoured and those of them who
were well educated being sometimes appointed as proselytisers.[12]
The tests imposed on people who sought relief in such areas
were often extremely drastic, ranging from their attendance at
Protestant churches, schools and lectures to enforced denial of the
main tenets of Catholicism and active insults to statues of the
Blessed Virgin.[13]   Local conflicts between Protestant and Catholic
clergymen now increased and local traditions recall many of their
circumstances ;   sermons against and curses laid upon ' soupers '
and their adherents by local priests ;   how one priest wrote a
satire against them which brought so much derision upon them
that they abandoned their work[14] or how another excommunicated
a man who had the misfortune to drop a Protestant bible while in
a Catholic church ;[15] the routing of the soupers by mass-attacks
of Catholic congregations,[16] and how well-meaning Protestants
who opened relief-depots in which no tests were imposed found
themselves assaulted in the same way.[17]   Some counter-measures
to proselytism took the form of religious tests imposed at Catholic
relief-centres.   Elsewhere Catholic schools were erected in
opposition to Protestant schools, which were often barred to

Catholics by the local priest. Emigrants often lamented the bitter circumstances which forced them to remain illiterate in their youth, a sore handicap to them when they went abroad.

The people's attitude to those who changed their religion at that time varies from a recognition that necessity forced them to it to contemptuous attacks on all 'jumpers', 'turners' and 'soupers', as both they and the proselytisers are called, and by association to an active dislike of relief-food, whether properly linked with proselytising or not. In some districts people may joke about 'soupers' without sting ; in others, taunts that the ancestors of such a one drank the landlord's soup or ate his 'hairy bacon' are considered as deadly insults, as is the nickname *cat breac* (speckled cat) which referred to the picture on the covers of Protestant school-books. In other districts again, references to people whose forefathers 'took the soup' or received 'charity meal' are not intended to convey any hint of proselytism but are a way of saying that their stock was once reduced to beggary. In many districts anecdotes about temporary 'turning' are frequent ; a woman answers a proselytiser's question as to why she had come for relief with the words *le grádh dom' bholg* (for my belly's sake) ;[18] '*Mícheál a' ghabhair*' is allowed to graze his cow on a minister's land but is caught going to Mass and answers that he goes west for the cow and east for his soul, or engages in a rhyming dialogue to the same effect :

'*A Mhichíl a' ghabhair, cad a shéol thú san am san eadrainn ?*
*An saol a bheith gann ⁊ is cuma liom teampuill nó Aifreann.*
*Ar airighis teagasg Naómh Pól is gach caibidiol cóir a leanas é ?*
*D'airíos ⁊ d'éistíos-sa leo ach 's an mhin eorna leanfad-sa.*'[19]
'Michael of the goat, what sailed you at this time among us ?
The time to be scarce and church and Mass are all one to me.
Did you hear St. Paul's teaching and follow each chapter aright ?
I heeded and heard, but it's barley meal that I'll follow.'

On the whole, such temporary turning is regarded charitably as the result of hunger ; '*An uair a bhog an saoghal, agus gur thug Dia aon ghreim dóibh féin d'fhágadar annsan iad*', says *Tomás Ó Criomhthainn* of the few poor people on the Blasket Island who sent their children to souphouse and school ; 'when the times softened and God gave them a bit for themselves they abandoned them'.[20] Those who remained Protestant were comparatively

few and in some districts are still remembered as 'turners' and are
not usually classed with Protestants.[21]

Much published information about the relief-schemes of the
famine times is available and oral tradition has not a great deal
to add to it, except in so far as personal accounts or local landmarks
which are remembered, help to light the picture from within.
One informant in co. Leitrim, for example, knew an old man who
had worked on a famine roadmaking scheme ; he said that he
got two meals of stirabout a day, and was paid twopence a day in
addition, women who worked on the same scheme being paid
threehalfpence ; he saw women fall exhausted while wheeling
barrows ; the 'gaffer' (ganger) would allow his workers to lend
a hand with passing funerals.[22]    An old man from co. Donegal
who was ninety-six years old in 1925 recollected working as a
youth on a similar road-scheme ; he used to walk five miles to
work each day, carrying for his lunch a small amount of yellow-
meal bread which he often ate before reaching the scheme, and he
would get nothing else until he returned home that evening.[23]
In the parish of Inistioge, co. Kilkenny, people were employed by
local landlords in clearing old fences, 'squaring' and enlarging
fields, and road-making.    People travelled miles to work and
women handled shovels beside men at drain-making.    At lunch
hour the labourers would clean their shovels, place their wetted
rations of yellow meal on them and eat their lunch.    Some labourers
who came very long distances lived in a loft and used to pool
their rations.    English and Scotch engineers were employed at
good salaries, but the workers received only fourpence a day.[24]
Other accounts describe the making of drains, boundary-walls
and roads, how hills were levelled, rivers deepened and canals cut,
and how in coastal areas quays, sea-walls and piers were erected.
The names of people who worked on such schemes, of the local
landlords who set them on foot and of the engineers and overseers
in charge of them are often given in great detail ; some informants describe the long distances travelled to them and how
many people died on the way ; how sand and stones for roads
were carried in baskets or wheeled in barrows and how hungry
people sat around hoping that some of the labourers would be
forced to drop out and leave places for them ; and they mention
by name overseers who used the whip on the workers and others
who were lenient.    On the whole stewards in charge of these

schemes are recalled with dislike ; they were usually appointed
from among fairly well-off people, demesne stewards, bailiffs,
policemen and the like ; many were callous and drove their
workers hard ; anecdotes about them tell how such a one
would discharge a man if he raised his head from work,[25] how
another would ask whether the barrow was broken when the
man wheeling it collapsed from hunger,[26] or how a third
would use his iron measuring rod to belabour his workers.[27]

Many of these relief-works are recalled as having been of
permanent use, resulting in improved communications between
towns and in better land, but a widespread recollection of useless
works prevails.  Side-roads which were to connect main roads
were made through waste lands into bogs and mountains, and
were never finished, or when finished proved unusable ; tons
of stones were broken for road-making and were then abandoned ;
boundary walls were built around barren land, acres of mountain
land being ' walled in for hares alone '.  The useless nature of
such works, together with the circumstances of labour upon
them, *ó dhubh dubh ┐ obair chruaidh ┐ ualaí troma* [28] (from dark to
dark with hard work and heavy loads) helps to explain the general
dislike of them which exists ; as does the frequent opinion that
the landlords and their sycophants ' got the fat of the money '
and used the schemes to benefit their own holdings.  At the same
time it is recognised that the relief-schemes provided a means of
existence, however precarious ; *do b'ionann an obair ┐ min bhuidhe*
(work meant yellow meal) and any means of obtaining food was
welcome.

Relief, whether given through food distribution or relief schemes
has left its stamp upon the local place-names of many parts.  For
example, Stirabout Lane in *Lios a Londúin,* co. Galway,[29] and
*Páirc an tSúip* (Soup Park) in *Gurran na Fola,* West Kerry,[30]
are named after food-centres, and places similarly named are to
be found in many Irish counties.  Still more derive their names
from association with relief-schemes ; Brochan Road,[31] *Bealach
an Breachain* (Porridge Way), *Droichead na Mine* (Meal Bridge),[32]
Stirabout Quay,[33] Stirabout Drain,[34] the Meal Road ; whatever
names may appear on maps, local people often use those dating
from the famine.  Often such names arise from the association
of individuals with famine relief-schemes ; thus *Bealach Mór
Cheallaigh* (Kelly's big road)[35] in north-west Donegal has been

christened after the engineer in charge of its making ; *Bealach an athar Domhnall* (Father Donal's Road)[36] in Rannafast, co. Donegal, after the priest who sponsored it ; a road into a bog in co. Leitrim is called ' Barton's Line ' after a local landlord.[37] One of the most interesting of such names is that used by old people in Carrick-on-Suir when referring to the local fair-green. It is called ' the Calcut ' and the origin of the name is given as follows : during the famine a sum subscribed at Calcutta was applied to employing people at the work of diverting the Suir to its present course. The old river bed was made into a fair-green, and since the money had been subscribed at Calcutta the green was so named.[38]

### V.   DISEASE

The traces which the ravages of disease left upon the memory of our people are evident in many ways. Although to-day some traditional accounts distinguish between the different kinds of disease which were widespread during the famine, most of them do not, but refer simply to *an droch-thinneas* (' the bad sickness '), ' the disease ', ' the fever ', and so on, and the informant will usually add ' God bless and protect us ! ', ' *Go dtárrthuighidh Dia sinn !* ' or some such pious ejaculation, the meticulous use of which is indicative of the lasting fear of disease. The insanitary conditions under which people lived then are often recalled : the dunghills piled close beside the house, the stagnant pools about it, the frightful overcrowding. Fever was no stranger to most districts before the famine ; ' *Ní raibh suim aca i bhfiabhras ins an am sin ach oiread ┑ atá ag na daoinibh i slaghdán anois* '[1] (' they put no more heed on fever then than people now put on a cold ') but the famine brought bad food, black potatoes, infected livestock, yellow meal insufficiently cooked, and the spread of disease through the weakened people was rapid.

In many of the areas through which it swept there were no facilities for the treatment of infected people. There was no hospital, for example, on Clear Island, co. Cork, and people relied on the skill of old people who had some traditional herbal knowledge ;[2] Cloghanealy and Rannafast in co. Donegal had neither hospital nor doctor.[3] Other districts had doctors but the area which they had to cover was so large that infected people would die while awaiting them. Existing hospitals were filled beyond capacity in many areas. Bailieboro' workhouse, for example, was built to accommodate about 700 people ; according to local tradition famine years saw over 1,000 inmates distributed between its fever hospital and the workhouse proper, and the guardians had to rent two auxiliary houses in the town.[4]   The census of 1851 bears out this appalling jump in numbers ; receptions in 1847 were 429, in 1849 they numbered 1,517.   Other accounts paint a similar picture, telling of poorhouses and hospitals crowded to the doors with sick and dying, of people dying in streets, laneways and sheds near them, because unable to obtain admission.   ' One poor man took his mother in [to Bandon poorhouse] on a donkey-cart ', says one account,   ' on his way home he found two poor creatures by the roadside ;  he turned and took them in also.   Three journeys he made on that day and the last time he went the place was so overcrowded that they were lying near the laneway leading to it '.[5]   Another describes a hospital built during the famine, a long low building with a tarred roof, full to the doors of patients old and young, with corpses lying stark naked outside it.[6]   A third describes the erection of a temporary shelter for patients outside Shillelagh poorhouse— ' they put up poles outside and put litter on top of them and patients who were not too bad were placed under these shelters in the open '.[7]

It is unnecessary to extend these accounts, which are paralleled by many printed descriptions.   What one finds in traditional accounts more than in printed sources is the attitude of the people towards workhouses and fever-hospitals.   Their dread of them seems to have been general and it was only as a last resort that they would go, while many preferred to die among their relatives than to go there for treatment, and to this day it is sometimes ' drawn down ' to people that their ancestors were ' paupers '— inmates of the workhouse.

Another matter upon which tradition casts some light is the treatment of fever in certain areas by the people themselves. ' Some old women were able to cure it ', says one account ; ' as they knew when to give the food after the whey '.[8]   An old man of Kilcoleman, co. Cork, gave one collector a detailed account which he had from his mother, of how she and her brother were cured of fever by her own mother's use of such treatment : ' Her mother knew what she had as soon as she got sick, as good

as any doctor could tell it ', he said. ' She knew it was the bad
sickness from the colour of the urine.' She removed the two
patients from the rest of the family of seven to a deserted house :
' There was no doctor called in, nor was there any medicine given ;
the old woman was nurse and doctor herself. They did not get
a mouthful to eat, but plenty of drinks of two-milk whey, the
lightest and most sustaining drink going at the time. . . . She
knew again, from the colour of the urine, when it had cleared
away, and the first bite they got to eat when they got well was
a toasted potato, only one, although, she said, they would eat
a dozen '.[9]

The necessity for the isolation of the patients appears to have
been recognised generally. They would be moved to barns
or sheds ; the door would be built up with turf and the patient
and nurse would be thus shut off from other people ; food would
be passed in through the window, often on a shovel, by relatives
or friends who would be careful not to handle vessels used by the
infected person.[10] Sometimes patients would be left in special
hut-shelters built against sheltered ditches by placing a thatch of
brambles, briers and rushes over poles and sod-walls ; many such
' scailps ' were to be seen along the roadsides or in stray places
where they had been hastily erected over fever-stricken people
who had collapsed there.[11] Other victims would be dragged into
some convenient place of shelter, the arch of a bridge or the
ruins of an old house or monastery.

In some districts widely separated from each other some
information survives about the tending of sick people by certain
' nurses *Gaelacha* ' (Irish nurses), local women who had some
medical knowledge and who devoted themselves to this task.
Several accounts describe how patients were put into *brácaí*
(sheds) of the type indicated previously—a field where such
a hut once stood is still known locally as *pairc an bhráca* (the
fever-hut field) ; there they would be tended by an ' Irish nurse ',
a strong healthy woman who knew the traditional remedies. The
patient would be fed on two-milk whey, obtained by boiling new
milk and adding skim milk to it ; he would drink this and would
eat the curd as well. The nurses washed their faces and hands
in urine, as a safeguard against infection.[12] These accounts are
from co. Tipperary and co. Kerry. A Galway tradition recalls
similar nurses,[13] while a Donegal informant was able to name two

such women who used to treat their patients with herb-juice.[14] Other diets for fever patients were cress and wild garlic, milk and water boiled with salt, sheep's blood. Poteen was widely used as a safeguard against infection ; it was sometimes given to patients, while those who had to bury fever-victims would use it, sometimes receiving a bottle as part of their wages.[15] Abstention from food, which was forced upon so many at this time, was practised voluntarily by others as a precaution ; in one part of Westmeath it is thought to have given rise to a custom still observed by a few local families, that of abstention from meat on days when no fast is ordained.[16]

In districts ravaged by fever during the famine a graphic tradition remains which can still show by its revealing flashes what havoc it wrought in many places. ' I heard from my parents that you couldn't count all the houses across the bog from Coolatore Cross to Ballinlug. A great many died of the sickness ' :[17] *Chualaidh mise mo mháthair a' rádh go raibh baile talamh thíos ins an áit ar tógadh í ar an Ardaidh Mhóir ┐ gur ghlan ┐ gur scuab sé an baile*[18] (I heard my mother saying that there was a townland where she was raised in Ardamore and that it [fever] cleaned and swept the townland) ; ' It is estimated that about three people in every house in the Inistioge district of this period died either of fever or of cholera during those years ' ;[19] ' Coolgarra was wiped out at that time with scarlet fever. There were forty houses in it and there is only one there now.'[20] Such typical accounts are sometimes given with a terrible clarity, which needs neither comment nor embellishment. An old woman of *Doire na Mainsear, Anagaire,* co. Donegal, for example, gave such an account, here presented in a close translation from her native Irish :

There were houses in this district in which all died of fever and none were buried. Things were so bad at that time that no one cared how the other was. Every household was left to itself and no one would come in or out to it. Families began to die and the rest were so weak and far spent that they could do nothing for them but leave them until the last one in the house died. All in the house died and the bodies lay here and there through it. They were never moved from it. There were many hungry dogs going about ; and they say, God save us, that they were going into these houses and eating the bodies.

When the fever went by and those who were left after it came to themselves a little, they went to those houses. The door-leaves had dropped from the doors ; when they went in there was nothing to be seen but people's bones lying about the house. They gathered the bones and buried them together in one grave. Then they burned the house to the ground.[21]

The burning of infected houses by the neighbours appears to have been widespread ; the ruin of one such house in Rannafast, co. Donegal, is still known locally as *An Teach Dóighte* (The Burnt House),[22] and several accounts of similar places recall how informants were told in their youth by parents to avoid them. Sometimes fear of infection was so great that the houses would not be entered at all, but would be fired, or their roofs and walls broken in, the bodies of fever-victims being left inside. 'There is an old ruin there across the river where a whole family died of fever', an old farmer who lived near Sneem, co. Kerry, told a collector ; 'They had to knock the house down on them and the dogs drew away their bodies. The old ruin is there in Johnny Denis's land, across the river from the graveyard '.[23] The location of such ruins is often pointed out.

Sometimes the fate of individual families who were struck by fever is recalled in detail. An old woman of Kilcoleman, co. Cork, for example, remembered hearing from her mother about a neighbouring family, a mother and her two grown sons ;

> They were very badly off, for the men couldn't get work anywhere around them. The hunger brought on the sickness— the fever, God bless us— and the two sons were buried. The neighbours went in and got some sort of a coffin and buried them. The couple of men that would go into a house where death from the dread sickness was would not enter without first having a meal, a good, full meal ; they said there was more danger of contagion if they were hungry or weak. They buried them anyway and the poor mother was not able to go to the graveyard with them. Some time after . . . when some neighbour went to see the old woman, she was found dead and her body almost eaten away with the rats.[24]

This is but one of many accounts which tell with the same clarity and detail of similar families. ' *Níor fhág sin coirnéal ar bith 'na dhiaidh nach dtáinig sé isteach ann, ⁊ ba bheag muirghineacha*

*nár sciob sé leis duine ⁊ beirt as*',[25] said an old woman of Teelin,
co. Donegal, of the ravages of fever in her native district : 'It
didn't leave any corner after it that it didn't enter and few were
the families it didn't sweep one or two from', and as much might
be said for many and many a part of Ireland.

Not only did disease take its toll of the population but it helped
to disrupt the people's social life and to destroy their customs
and observances. Victims would be left unburied or would be
buried where they fell and relatives would sometimes deny the
identity of their dead brethren for fear of having to bury them.
Neighbours shunned each other's houses even in districts where
communal help and sharing was traditional. Against tradition
too, the 'wandering man' was often turned from the door or
was shunned ; '*Síntí an déirc chúcha ach ní fhéachadh aoinne ortha
díreach san aghaidh ar eagla a n-anála is an galar uathbhásach a bhí á
iomchar aca*'[26] one informant said graphically ; 'The alms would
be stretched towards them, but nobody would look them straight
in the face, for fear of their breaths and of the terrible disease they
carried'. For the first time in many districts, the doors were
locked to keep out strangers. Many years after the famine was
spent, fever persisted ; it is said that it stayed in the walls and
thatch of houses and in the dungheaps, and would recur year after
year when the piled nets of the fishermen were brought out from
their corner or when the farmer drew manure to plant his crops.
And the fear lasted and can be felt to-day in the hushed voice,
the pious ejaculation or the grim tones of those who can still
recall it from the past.

### VI. DEATH AND BURIAL

Memories of famine deaths are often very vivid and their
nature is best conveyed by selection : 'Murty Larry O'Sullivan,
the poet, told Johnny Batt that one morning when he was going
to Kenmare he saw thirty dead bodies lying on the road at the
edge of the town between Dr Maybury's house and the Bell
Height' ;[1] 'I heard my grandmother saying—she was from the
Kenmare side—that the worst sight she ever saw was a woman
laid out on the street [in Kenmare] and the baby at her breast.
She died of famine fever—nobody would take the child, and in
the evening the child was eating the Mother's breast' ;[2] 'My
mother remembered the famine of '48. She remembered finding

a mother and daughter on the path, locked in each other's arms, within a few yards of *Rin an Daimh* ; on the *casán* (path) going across to Claedach above the *Gleann a' Phréacháin* lake. She was sent on a message with another little girl. The night was snowy— there was a little snow on their clothes '.[3] These extracts are taken from accounts given by various informants in one county and were paralleled repeatedly throughout the country by men and women who could still name local families who went to bed to await death, people who gave food to starving strangers only to see them swell and die before their eyes, men and women who found corpses by the roadside or in lonely places, and the location of stray famine graves.

Sometimes such stories seem to owe their survival partly to a dramatic quality which caused their retention ; a starving man eats pig-food and is found dead afterwards, with money in his pocket ;[4] a man who is accustomed to kill speckled birds on a certain island is trapped there by continuous storms and dies ' *agus éanlaithe an aeir a' teacht ┐ a' piocadh a chuid cnámha* '[5] ('and the birds of the air coming and picking his bones'). Sometimes the sight would be so pathetic in itself that its witness never forgot it ; one old man used to tell how he went from Rannafast to Sligo and called at a house in which lived a woman and her child ; he found them starving to death and called to them on his way from Sligo with food ; ' *Níl aon lá go dteachaidh Ned i dtalamh nach mbíodh sé ag cainnt ar sin agus a' rádh gur sin an radharc a ba mhó a chuaidh fríd a chroidhe dá bhfaca sé ariamh ; an bhean 'na luighe marbh ┐ a' leanbh beag a diúl uirthi ┐ é a' caoineadh leis an ocras* '[6] ('there was no day until Ned died but he'd be talking about that and saying that of all sights that pierced his heart that was the worst he saw ; the woman lying dead and the little child sucking at her and he wailing with hunger '). A woman in Sneem parish, co. Kerry, remembered her uncle's account of a family named Casey which lived at the foot of a nearby mountain :

There were seven or eight of them, a neat little family ; they had white heads. My uncle Mick used to cry when he used be telling the story. The oldest girl went the six days of the week to Sneem for soup and came empty. On the seventh day five of them died. I remembered one of them [a survivor]— she was a withered old little woman. . . . The *ologón* they ruz [raised] the sixth day, when she came without any food was something dreadful. Years after, my father was ditching near the ruin and he found the bones of an old man and a child ; the arm of the old man was around the child.'[7]

Often the horror of these scenes leaps out at one by reason of such simple telling : ' One day Stephen Regan met a dog dragging a child's head along. He took the head from the dog and buried it and set a tree over it. The family to whom the child belonged were getting relief for the child and for that reason did not report its death.'[8]

The deaths of people who died rather than seek relief, of fathers who starved to death rather than deprive their children of the little food that remained are often described with the same graphic realism. To recount further is unnecessary. ' *Bhídis 'á gcailliúint ar nós na siocán, fé mar bheadh siocain in ndiaidh a t-seaca* ',[9] said an old man who was recording his information on the ediphone ; ' people were fading like frost after frosty weather '. As widespread as frost, but not as transient, is the memory of their passing.

It has been indicated already that corpses were often left unburied, through fear of fever. There were other reasons as well ; the overcrowding of graveyards, for example ; the scarcity of gravediggers, who could not keep pace with their work, so that bodies awaiting burial would be devoured by pigs or other animals ; physical weakness and mental apathy from hunger. ' The living were out of their feeling and besides were unable to carry a corpse to the graveyard.'[10]

Burial in coffins became exceptional. In those districts where wood was obtainable carpenters worked day and night. A Rossport coffin-maker, Andrew Gannon, used to tell of making six coffins in one day ;[11] coffins would consist of a few boards hammered together and tarred on the inside. Wood might be brought by the purchaser ; all kinds of wood were requisitioned—dressers, tables, boats, old coffin-boards taken from graveyards. One informant's grandfather used to go from house to house making coffins at a half-crown apiece ;[12] the grandfather of another recalled making a coffin for a young man who brought a log of bogwood ; the price tendered was one shilling ; but as the young man had not eaten for two days he gave him the coffin for nothing.[13] There is some recollection of ' committee coffins ' or ' poorhouse coffins ', which could be purchased cheaply but burial in such coffins was sometimes regarded as a slur on

the friends and relatives of the dead person, who would collect/
enough to buy boards, paint and mounting and would have a
coffin made by some local handyman.  This custom of collecting a
' burial charge ' or ' offering ' is dated from the famine in some
parts.  Money so subscribed was intended specifically for burial
expenses.  A story is still told in co. Clare of a woman who was
rebuked for spending it on food for her surviving children and
who replied with grim logic : ' *Ní chothuigheann an marbh an beo* '
(' the dead do not feed the living ').[14]  In Clare also a verse attributed to a local poet of that time is quoted :

> *Is dána an rud domh-sa a bheith a' súil le cómhra*
> *Is maith an rud domh-sa má dh'fhuighim bairlín*
> *Is a Rí na glóire, tabhair fuascailt domh-sa*
> *Go dteigh mé im chómhnuidhe san gcill úd*
> It's a bold thing for me to expect a coffin
> It's a good thing for me if I get a sheet
> And, King of Glory, relieve me
> That I may dwell in the churchyard beyond.[15]

A great number of traditional accounts endorse his words.
People buried their relatives in sheets when they could obtain
them ;  others wrapped corpses in sacking, in straw mats, in
barrel-staves wrapped about with *súgán* ropes (straw ropes) and,
in places where the art of basket-making was practised, in basket-
coffins.  Where possible, the dead were given Christian burial.
' *Ní' mha' leobhtha an corp a chur san uaigh gan rud éicint a chur
timpeall air* ', said one informant, and he adds, as if to confirm
the verse quoted above : ' *Ba mha' leó iad a thóirt go dti an roilic
nó comh gar do ┐ b'fhéidir leobhtha.  Thart annseo i nAna' Chuain
tá roint mha' crámhaí amach i bhfad ins na goirt ó bhallaí an teampuill* '[16]
(' They didn't like to bury the corpse without putting something
around it : they liked to take it to the churchyard or as close
to it as possible.  Over here in *Anach Cuain* there are a good
many bones far out in the fields from the church walls ').
Many were buried far from the vicinity of any graveyard, their
resting places perhaps forgotten until turned up years later by
the plough or by the road-worker's spade.

The use of communal coffins is widely recollected.  Sometimes
these were ordinary coffins which were carried to the graveyard
and when the corpses were emptied out of them were left by

the graveside for the next people who needed them. Coffins with hinged or detachable bottoms were also used : ' they opened it the same way as you'd open the bottom of " bawrthogs " when putting out dung '[17]; ' they were on sort of hinges or something and when you'd take a corp to Creggan burying-ground, you'd let the corp out of the coffin and use it again'.[18] In Donegal such coffins are called *comhunracha measóige*, coffins with movable bottoms like panniers, and are described as having one side fastened by a couple of loops of rope with a bolt across underneath secured by another rope-loop which could be untied easily.[19] In the parish of Drumholme in the same county they are said to have been used during the cholera epidemic of 1832 (*bliain na Cholera*, the year of the Cholera, as it is still called), but curiously are not remembered during the famine years.[20] In Inistioge, co. Kilkenny, an eighty-year-old farmer recounted descriptions, of how corpses brought from the local poorhouse were buried ; the coffins had handles front and rear and were carried like hand-barrows to the burial-pit ; by pulling a trigger the bottom of the coffin was released and the corpse was allowed to fall into the pit ; it was buried without a habit, and any available covering over it would be removed and would be used again to cover another victim ; some clay and lime would be thrown into the pit.[21] Such communal coffins appear to have been let for hire in some parts. They were used more widely by workhouse burial-contractors.

These contractors, their methods of transport—ass-cart, dray, handbarrow—their personal habits, and their names and nick-names are often described ; ' *Peadar beag a' gangman* ', who buried the dead from Galway poorhouse ;[22] Jackeen Ó *Sioda* who was hired to collect and bury stray corpses ;[23] Higgins of Kilkeel who used to say that only drink enabled him to survive his work;[24] ' Paddy the Puncher ' who was said to have finished off many a dying man because he was paid so much per corpse ;[25] ' Yellow George ' who carried corpses from Tullamore workhouse on a dray.[26] The last of these is said to have replied to the protests of a man whom he was trying to bury that the doctor knew best ; an anecdote which is told about other contractors in several parts of the country. Similar stories are frequent ; a ' corpse ' protests from a hinged coffin and the contractor replies that the drop will kill him anyway ;[27] another refuses to be buried, lives for many years and never again speaks to the man who tried to bury him.[28]  Behind such humorous stories a grim truth often seems to lurk.  It is still said in Monaghan that people were heard to cry out from their coffins on the way to burial,[29] and Galway tradition records that many people were buried alive at Cearnagcapall.[30]  Two independent accounts from different parts of co. Cork[31] tell how a certain child was brought for dead with a number of corpses to be buried in a grave-pit in the Abbey graveyard near Skibbereen.  Both his legs were broken by the gravedigger's spade before he was found to be alive.  He survived the famine and was known to many people of west Cork, who still relate the history of his knock-knees and attribute to him a verse beginning

'I arose from the dead in the year '48
Though a grave in the Abbey had near been my fate . . .'

The graveyard itself now contains a memorial to the many famine victims buried there.

The burial of the dead was greatly handicapped by lack of transport as the death-roll swelled.  In the towns carts would carry fever-victims to the hospitals and would find coffins ready to be transported for burial.  Sometimes the problem was solved by digging huge pits near hospitals and poorhouses.  People dying in Castlerea workhouse were put into a room along whose sloping floor-boards they could be slid into a grave-pit outside the gable ;  the gable grew black from the lime used and was called the Black Gable.[32]  The terror which such places inspired was one reason for people's hatred of the workhouse.  These huge pits would hold upwards of fifty bodies which would be cast in on sods, sprinkled with lime and hastily filled in.  Their sites are still remembered in many parts of Ireland and are sometimes shunned.  *Poll an Churtha* (the Burial Hole) in the parish of Kilcummin, for example, is still avoided at night,[33] while up to sixty years ago old people near Ennistymon were terrified that they might be buried in *Poll na ndob* (Mud Hole) another site of communal burials during the famine.[34]  In some districts the landlord's cart would be sent around to collect unburied bodies, but there were many isolated districts of the south and west where roads were bad or did not exist at all.  The desire for burial in consecrated ground was so strong that dying people

would be seen dragging themselves towards the local graveyards.
Friends and relatives would resort to every means to lay the dead
with their ancestors. Sometimes corpses would be transported
in relays from one district to another until the graveyard was
reached, and the shoulders of men would grow sore from carrying
coffins. Workers on one relief-scheme sometimes would be
allowed to pass on coffins to the next. Too often the relatives
would be forced to travel long distances carrying their dead as
best they could ; on the backs of horses or asses, or in sheets or
creels secured with ropes upon their own backs. Descriptions
of such grim journeys are widespread :

'My father told me that he saw a man carrying his brother's
corpse on his back from Bailieboro' to Moybologue graveyard.
He had no one to help him and he had to dig the grave and bury
the corpse himself . . . people didn't like to attend the funeral
because the man died of fever. My father said it was the
saddest sight he had ever seen '.[35]

'Do chonnaic sé Tadhg bocht Labhráis ⁊ ciseán mór ar a dhruim
aige ⁊ corp a dhriféar marbh istigh ann. Do bhí, adubhairt sé, an
ceann ar sileadh síos lasmuigh de bhuinne bhéil an chiseáin ⁊ as an
gceann san do bhí caise de ghruaig bhreágh bhuidhe óir ar sileadh
síos ⁊ é ag scuabadh an bhóthair.' ('He saw poor Tadhg Labhráis
with a basket on his back and the corpse of his dead sister inside
it. The head, he said, was drooping down over the edge of the
basket and from it a twist of bright yellow hair hung down,
sweeping the road.')[36]

'One of these men [i.e. strangers who died in the locality]
had brought the corpses of his two children in a bag to be
buried in the churchyard of Nohoval, an Irish mile and a half
from Knocknagree and six miles from his home. The children
had died of want and he brought them all the way on
his back to Nohoval and going back he died of hunger and
exhaustion.'[37]

There are many accounts which are equally harrowing ; stories
of mothers carrying children's corpses in sacks or sheets, of boys
wheeling their dead parents in barrows, of old men lamenting as
they brought their dead children for burial, that there would be no
one to do the same for them on the morrow.
Many sites of graveyards used at that time are still remembered,

though long since disused. Some of these were auxiliary graveyards, some were specially reserved for fever victims, others
were Protestant graveyards in which Catholics were interred.
A number of graveyards which formerly were used only for
children seem to have been first used for the burial of adults then.
An account from co. Donegal describes one of these : ' *Tá oileán
amuigh de chósta na Rosann annseo a dtugtar Oileán na Marbh air . . .
ba ghnáth páistí a gheobhadh bás gan bhaisteadh a chur ar an oileán seo ;
nuair a tháinig an fiabhras ⁊ líonadh suas Roilig na Cruite, chuadhthas
a' cur daoine ar an oileán seo fosta ⁊ tá áit na n-uaigheann le feiceáil
go fóill* '[38]* ('There is an island off the coast of the Rosses here,
which they call the Island of the Dead . . . it was customary to
bury unbaptised children on it ; when the fever came and Cruit
churchyard was filled up people were buried on this island and
their burial-places are to be seen still '). Accounts from co.
Galway and co. Mayo mention similar graveyards.[39]

Even scattered burial places of stray victims of hunger and
of fever who were buried in fields, sandpits, ruins and raths are
remembered ; sometimes because they were local people who asked
to be buried on their own land or who could not be carried to
the graveyard, sometimes because they were strangers to the
locality. Many instances are given of corpses being buried in
sod fences, the breastwork of sods being removed for the purpose
and a few stones left marking the rebuilt fence. Tradition about
such stray places is sometimes very general ; it is said, for example,
that in a certain part of *Anach Cuain,* co. Galway, there is no
field in which people were not buried then,[40] or that every few
yards of the road between Attymass and Bonnifanaghy contains a
grave.[41] But it is often specific, recording the name, native
district and what is known about the person so buried, together
with the exact location of the grave. Such graves were sometimes
marked by stones placed singly or in cairns, by crosses, by saplings
or by large stone flags. Few of these flags were inscribed, but
one of them is still to be seen in Tuosist, co. Kerry. It bears
the simple inscription '1847. Let none meddle here '.[42]

For years after the famine these graves would be treated with
respect by the old people, who would not plough over them in
fields but would raise the plough and avoid them ; they would cut
the grass on them and spread it over them, not giving it to stock
or making any use of it. This may have been partly due to

reverence, partly as a precaution against recurrent fever. If people new to the district disturbed the bones of the dead they would be condemned for going against tradition.

Famine burials also have left their mark upon place-names in Ireland ; the sites of such burials are sometimes called by the name of the person buried there, or by some name such as ' the old woman's grave ', ' the starving man's grave '. In the eastern part of the Joyce country are three places, within a few miles of each other, which are all said to have been named for such reasons ; *Cros Ruaidhrí, Meall Nóirín Ruadh* and *Sruthán an Bhaicín* (Rory's Cross, Red Noreen's Knoll, the Baceen's Stream). The first got its name in the following way : a man from *Bealach a' Measg* on the shores of Lough Mask died at Croagh Patrick, where he had gone either begging or on pilgrimage. His son and two other male relatives travelled thirty miles to find the body. They carried it back with only two halts, the first of which was on a hilltop between co. Galway and co. Mayo. Here they raised a small cross and a small cairn which was added to by anyone who passed that way. The gap on the hilltop was thenceforth known as *Bealach na Croise* or *Cros Ruaidhrí*. *Nóirín Ruadh* was the sister of this man ; she died of fever about this time ; her nephew crossed Lough Mask to fetch the body home for burial ; he was forced by storms to leave her body on a knoll while sheltering and the knoll was named after her. The third place commemorates a travelling man, *an baicín*, who was found dead and was buried on the bank of a stream.[43] Through similar associations, places where many funerals met or passed are known by such names as *bearna na gcorp, bóithrín na gcorp*, etc.,[44] though the reasons for such names are now fading from popular recollection as the old people whose fathers and mothers remembered them fade slowly from life.

## VII.   CHANGES IN THE IRISH COUNTRYSIDE

Where history views the disruptive changes which the famine caused in the family and social life of the people in general terms, oral tradition centres around individual families, people and places, and its generalisations usually extend no farther than the townland or the parish. Its information, being concrete and particular, contributes something to the general picture. Nowhere is this more evident than in the study of that permanent nexus of change, the land. How necessity and force, the Gregory quarter-acre clause and the evicting landlord wrested the land from so many during that time is a matter of history. How that history lives in the minds of people who are still on the land can be gleaned only from the scattered material of tradition ; from comments of the old people, when farms are sold, upon how the same farms changed hands for a bag of meal during the bad times ; from their knowledge of why certain farm-lands are indented by the lands of neighbours whose ancestors secured fields on promise of restoration after the famine, or of how certain demesne walls are built not with 'courses', continuous lengths of stone, but with round stones taken from the dwelling-houses of evicted tenants, some of whom laboured at this very work ; from graphic stories of evictions and of how the evicted people cursed landlord and bailiff, whose families were followed by misfortune from that out.

Many of their recollections centre around the landlords of that time. Those of them who were kind are remembered because they did their best to relieve the necessitous, because they stinted themselves or reduced their rents or worked honestly on relief-committees. Others are remembered for negative reasons, because they did not evict, raise rents or proselytise. The general impression of the landlord is bad. His 'rent-warners' or spies were always on the alert for any excuse to raise the rent, so that meat would be hastily hidden if one of them approached the house while a family was enjoying this rarity. Seasonal migration, the sale of crops, livestock, kelp or knitted goods might provide enough money to pay the rent, but claims for duty work or for 'presents' would add another load to the bent back of the peasant farmer. *Cíos an tailimh nó biadh an leinbh* ('the rent or the child's food') ; the old saying conveys that sense of desperation with which so many laboured and clung to the land, their one hope of survival. Anecdotes about evicting landlords still keep their memories alive ; one used to exclaim with satisfaction at the rising death-rate ;[1] another said 'that he would not leave a Catholic tenant from the bridge of Newport to the bridge of Knockaboley' ;[2] a third used to shout 'get away to hell !' to people who sought relief, until the poorhouse was built, when he substituted 'get away to the poorhouse !' to which an old woman replied that the poorhouse had proved a great

saviour of souls.[3]  Similar anecdotes centre about the agents and
bailiffs ;  where landlords are sometimes praised or are thought
culpable mainly because they left everything to their agents,
these are remembered almost invariably as having been merciless
and hard, grinding for arrears of rent, evicting, levying fines for
improvements or without cause, and using the people's need to
become rich by securing for themselves good holdings from
which the tenants had been driven.  Their characteristics or
typical remarks are recounted ;  Foster, who used to turn away
his head when speaking to a Catholic ;[4]  Chambree, who said
' that he'd leave the race of a horse between the houses here ' ;[5]
Jellicoe, who used to make people surrender the few potatoes
they would find while weeding and who once gave his workmen a half-holiday to witness a hanging, in order to teach them
to obey the law.[6]   Others are still referred to by contemptuous
nicknames, usually an indication that they had sprung from the
very people whom they were oppressing ;  ' the crony Byrne ',[7]
' Condy Nanny ' whom the sheriff restrained from evicting a
sick woman ;[8]  ' Peadar na splainnce ' who always brought a
splannc (spark) to fire the roofs of the evicted.[9]  In many places
throughout Ireland the lives of such men are traced to the present
day and it is still held against people that their ancestors once
acted as agents or bailiffs at the time of the famine.  So too with
' grabbers ', who took up the farms of evicted people or who
caused them to be evicted by offering increased rents for their
holdings.  ' Grabbers ' were sometimes agents who knew the
best farms and the means of the tenants to a penny and so could
time their coups to a nicety.  Sometimes they were shopkeepers ;
though in many districts these were unknown until after the famine,
the hardpressed farmer in other districts would borrow on credit
from them to pay his rent ;  often ' beidh an gamhain ithte i mbolg
na bó ' (' the calf would be eaten while unborn '), through arrears
mounting and extravagant interest for ' trust meal ' and other goods,
and the farm would have to be mortgaged to the shopkeeper,
who would foreclose when necessity was greatest.  The bitter
memory of such ' grabbing ', whether by shopkeepers, agents
or strong farmers, was lasting ;  like other bitter memories it is
often the cause of reticence among people to-day, sometimes
because their own ancestors were involved, but more often because
of a charitable wish to avoid hurting the feelings of neighbours.

' *Bhí cuid aca san a chuidigh le n-a gcómhursannaí an uair sin* ', says one account which gives a list, compiled from the old people of the district, of farmers who were ' strong ' during the famine, ' *agus bhí cuid eile acu a raibh lúthghair ortha gur bánuigheadh a raibh fá dtaobh daobhtha, gur thuit siad isteach ina gcuid áiteacha go bog. Tá siad thart fá dtaobh dúinn annseo, daoine a dteárn an mhuinntir a tháinic rómpa sin—ach caithfimíd sin a fhágáil mar sin ┐ ár gcos a bhrúghadh air* ',[10] (' There were some of those who shared with their neighbours then and others who rejoiced that all around them were evicted so that they fell in nicely for their places. We have them around here since, people whose ancestors did that—but we must leave it so and press it underfoot '). With which charitable sentiment it is probably best to concur.

Where history follows the mass of evictions to the poorhouses and the ports, local tradition preserves many memories of those who settled elsewhere. Some settled in their own neighbourhood, on poor mountain or bogland, where they were offered holdings by the evicting landlord or where common land existed. The Knockananna district of Wicklow, for example, was the scene of such settling on a commons called ' the black bawns ' where families which ' the Crony Byrne ' had evicted huddled their cabins so closely that two doors would be put on the one jamb. Here it is also recalled how evictees would sometimes build new cabins on the boundary line of two estates, so that joint action by two landlords would be necessary to evict them again.[11] Memories of similar settlements, of wretched sod-cabins hastily built into fences or erected in bare lonely places, even in grave-yards, are widespread. Widespread also are recollections of migrants from other districts ; they are particularly strong where the district into which these migrants came was comparatively stable during the famine. For example, old people in the Ards district of co. Down or in the more prosperous parts of Cavan, Tipperary and Wicklow can still recall the names of such migrants, where they came from, where they settled and whether their family-lines died out or are still to be found in the locality. They tell many anecdotes of such migrants ; how no migrant was left without food or lodging in Meelick, co. Galway ;[12] how the death of Kildare people who settled in Knocknaskeagh, co. Wicklow, would be heralded by a phantom funeral going towards Kildare ;[13] how a co. Down farmer succoured the migrants and how his fields escaped the blight which struck his district later ;[14] how the descendants of famine migrants who settled in Sligo, Roscommon and Galway are still known locally as ' siar againnes' from the phrase ' siar againne' ('back west with us') which their ancestors would use.[15]

Oral tradition has much to say about emigration during the famine. Many of its details are already known, though it is interesting to note the accuracy with which the names of ports and of destinations, the duration of the voyage, and the cost of passage are usually recalled. Such memories are often strongest in those parts which had little or no experience of emigration before the famine and from which for the first time whole families then went ' body and sleeves' from the land which they had held for generations ; and to this is probably due the detail with which it will be recollected how families got their passage money by borrowing, by working on relief-schemes, or by surrendering their land and ' taking the emigration'. The phrase has its tinge of bitterness that land had to be surrendered in this way ; yet while the utilising of emigration schemes by landlords wishing to clear their estates is generally endorsed, it is clear that the common belief that the blight would persist often caused people to press their holdings upon those who were later accused of ' grabbing' them, while others were forced by the threat of eviction to take up deserted holdings which they did not want.

Preparations for emigrating would often occupy whole communities for a considerable period. Where it could be managed, supplies of potatoes or of meal would be accumulated. Oatcake was the usual food taken ; a week would be spent by neighbours and friends of the emigrating families in making it ; it would be baked three times, until it was of a slate-like hardness. Emigrants would also take bedding, where possible, and many would carry a sod of turf. The scenes at their departure would be heart-rending. One old man in the district of the Rosses, co. Donegal, gave a typical account which he had heard in his youth. He told how before the famine people of this district were able to make a living on their poor holdings, but how the famine first uprooted them. Emigration being a new experience, people felt it more keenly. On the night before the departure, people would crowd into the house of the emigrating family and would try to cheer

them by making forced merriment until morning ; but for all
that the house would be ' *comh brónach le teach faire* ' (as sad
as a wake-house). When the time for departure came, the emigrants
would make ready and would bid farewell to the company, which
would accompany them to where the car for Derry was waiting :
' *Bhéadh cuid de na mná a thuiteadh i laige nuair a tcídhfeadh siad a
nduine ag imtheacht. Cuid eile a chrochfadh iad féin as a' charr leis
an té a bhi ag imtheacht a choinneail. Ach nuair a d'imtheochadh sé
thógfadh an t-iomlán eadar mhná ⁊ fir, uallán caointe a bhainfeadh
macall' as na beanna* ' (' Some of the women would fall fainting
when they saw any person going, others would hang out of
the car to keep back the departing one ; but when it would go,
the whole lot, men and women, would raise a cry of grief that
would wrest an echo from the peaks ').[16]  Sometimes contingents
of friends and relatives would walk from Tipperary to Cobh,[17]
or from Cratloe, co. Clare, a distance of forty miles to Kilrush ;
' the banks of the Shannon used to be lined with people and the
sights witnessed would break your heart '.[18]  And even when the
port was reached, emigrants might have to wait over a week for
a ship or for favourable weather, and further supplies of food
might have to be despatched to them.[19]

The worst had yet to be faced. People who left home ' *comh láidir
le binn don sliabh* ', ' as strong as the mountain-peak ', succumbed
in large numbers to the fever engendered by bad food, insanitary
conditions, overcrowding. The story of the ' coffin-ships '
needs no retelling here, but a few revealing memories may be
quoted. Thus oral tradition in south Kerry recalls the deaths
of many emigrants from the Lansdowne estate, co. Kerry, in the
' Lansdowne ward ' of a New York fever-hospital, and the burial of
their bodies on the banks of the Hudson ;[20] an account from
Cratloe, co. Clare, tells of the foundering of an emigrant ship off
Newfoundland, on whose coast a memorial is said to have been
erected.[21] The noted *seanchaidhe*, Peig Sayers, spoke of a woman
emigrant of that time who during a storm spent long hours under
hatches with the corpse of a girl who had died at sea.

' *Deireadh sí gurbh shin é an greim is mó rug riamh uirthe ; do
cailleadh an cailín ⁊ ó lár a' lae go dtí na sé a chlog lár na mháireach
sara bhféud an captaen na haistí d'oscailt do bhí sí féin ⁊ an cailín
marbh ansan ⁊ nuair a luaisceadh an t-árthach tuigtí dhí go n-oscaluíodh
an corp a súile ⁊ an beul. . . .* '.[22] (' She used to say that that was

the worst thing she ever suffered ; the girl died and from the middle of one day until six o'clock the next, before the captain could open the hatches, she and the dead girl were there ; and when the vessel would lurch, it seemed to her that the corpse would open its eyes and mouth ').

The memory of the destination and subsequent fate of these emigrants has been largely lost, although in places it is still very vivid and in general it can still light up the history of our scattered race with recollections of the hiring-fairs at Quebec, of emigrants buried on the banks of the St Lawrence river, of how the child who was later known as Fighting Phil Sheridan left Beagh in an emigrant cart, of Irish-speaking districts in Australia and America. Such fragments often clearly relate to emigration during the famine times, but a number of them inevitably have become confused with emigration of a later date.

The upheaval which the famine caused in the family and social life of the people is best seen in the traditions of parts of Ireland where there was much communal life in pre-famine days, notably in parts of Donegal, Mayo, Sligo, Galway, Cork and Kerry which were remote from towns, had few roads and preserved a way of life which, though not exempt from the limitations imposed by the land system upon the country at large, was more traditional and less subject to change. In such districts communal sharing of work was general ; men would work together in *meitheal* or *cómhar* in harvesting, turf-cutting, fishing, boatmaking, drawing lime, building, while the women would co-operate in weaving, knitting, dyeing, or in helping the men. There was much sharing of food ; if a farmer slaughtered a beast his family would share the meat with others—' *Níor itheadar i gcoír é gan na cómharsana a bheith buidheach* ', ' they did not eat it aright without the neighbours being thankful ' ; if a member of a boat's crew died, a share would be set aside for his widow. People would co-operate in building houses for the homeless and in housing them while the building was in progress. This communal spirit pervaded their entertainment ; they would go ' rambling ' or on *céilidhe* to each other's houses, where they would dance and dispute, discuss the news of some wandering ballad-maker, or listen to traditional songs, poems and stories ; and such activities continued side by side with those manifest at fairs and patterns, at wakes and at the many weddings which throve on the conacre system. Such communities were often almost completely self-contained ; wheat would be grown to pay the landlord, flax to make clothes and linen, while sheep would provide frieze and thread ; shops were rare and were relied upon mainly for tobacco, snuff, dye and tea ; each district had its spinners and weavers, its thatchers, carpenters, blacksmiths, shoemakers and nailers.

The famine blasted many of these communities out of existence.

'*Cha rabh ceird ar a t-saoghal nach rabh fear ar a' Bheáltaine an uair sin a bhí ábalta boc a bhuaileadh uirthe—bhí na figheadóirí a b'fhearr sa tír ann ; bhí saoir cloiche, saoir adhmaid, cúipéaraí, tuigheadóirí ┐ achan seort fear céirde a dtiocfadh a ainmniú ar an bhaile seo, ┐ indiaidh bhliadhanta na gorta, cha rabh fios tuairisc a dtrian le fághail. D'imthigh siad uilig leo ins na cianta coimhthigheacha ┐ char fhill siad ariamh ó shoin. Bhí ballógaí a gcuid toighthe ann gur rannadh na talta, ┐ scriosadh amach iad annsin ┐ rinneadh claidheacha leis na clocha ┐ níl lorg ar bith le feiceál ortha anois*'.[23] ('There was no trade in the world then but some man of Beltany could try it—the best weavers in the country were there ; there were masons, carpenters, coopers, thatchers and every kind of tradesman you could name in this townland ; and after the famine years neither tale nor tidings of them was to be found. They all went into strange and distant lands and never returned since : the ruins of their houses were there until the land was divided and they were cleared and fences made of the stones, leaving no trace of them to be seen now ').

So runs a typical account, which comes from the townland of Beltany in Gortahork, co. Donegal. Another, from the Rosses, co. Donegal, illustrates the psychological changes which attended such ruin, as they were recalled by an eighty-year-old woman ; she said that hardship and hunger broke the communal spirit of the people, who became preoccupied with the struggle to survive and lost their sympathy for each other.

'*Ba chuma cé a bhí gaolmhar duit, ba é do charaid an t-é a bhéarfadh greim duit le cur in do bhéal. D'imthigh an spórt ┐ an caitheamh aimsire. Stad an fhilidheacht ┐ a' ceol ┐ damhsa. Chaill siad agus rinne siad dearmad de iomlán ┐ nuair a bhisigh an saoghal ar dhoigheannaí eile ni tháinig na rudaí seo ariamh arais mar bhi siad. Mharbh an gorta achan rud.*'[24] ('It didn't matter who was related to you, your friend was whoever would give you a bite to put in your mouth. Sport and pastimes disappeared. Poetry, music and dancing stopped. They lost and forgot them all and when the times improved in other respects, these things never returned as they had been. The famine killed everything '.)

It is not surprising to find that many old people dated a decline in Christian charity from that time.

Multitudes of the wandering people of the famine, uprooted and set drifting by such changes, have not even a place in the memory now, nor does any landmark exist to tell of their passing. ' *Do luigh an droch-shaoghal ortha* ', said one Kerry *seanchaidhe,* ' *chimil sé sop is uisge do'n áit.* '[25]  (' The famine lay upon them and it rubbed a wet wisp across the place.')   In many districts nothing is left but a vague recollection by old people that their fathers had told them how a dozen chimneys smoked where none is to-day, that whole villages once stood and people clustered ' as thick as stares ' where nothing but a slight unevenness in the fields and a forlorn *sceach* or two is to be seen.   But in other town-lands, traces of various kinds exist.   These are sometimes names of places—*Baile an Tobair, Loch lár an bhaile, Sean-bhaile*—where no village now exists but where tradition records that villages stood in the famine times.   Sometimes they are names of fields and houses—*Páircín Hector, Garraí Mhíchíl, Máire Bhuidhe's* old house— which are said to bear the names of tenants of a century ago. Sometimes they are the ruins of old cabins, the remains of ditches, gate-pillars and fences—' *Maireann na cuaillí críona ach ní mhaireann an lámh a shín iad* ' (' the old posts remain but not the hand that set them ')—sometimes old potato-ridges overgrown with grass and barely discernible on the slopes which no man tills to-day.   Where tradition is strongest, principally in the scattered Gaelic-speaking districts of the west and south, one may still hear the full names of their former tenants, their subsequent fate and the gradations by which their land descended to its present owners.

### VIII.   CONCLUSION

This survey of traditional recollections of the famine must now end. I believe that its contents justify an affirmative answer to the questions which I have posed at the start ; for it seems clear that oral tradition, by the way in which it relates experience to daily life, can play its part in adding something human and vivid to our understanding of the past and can also bring new information to light. It would be easy to over-estimate the value of oral tradition, which is not always subject to the exact checks required by the historian ; but one cannot ignore the contribution, both factual and psychological, which it has to offer.

The 'Great Hunger' caused the most sweeping changes in Ireland's social and economic structure. For the relevant facts one goes to contemporary newspapers, to the tables of the Census of 1851, to the report of the Society of Friends, to Father O'Rourke's history. How these facts and their implications, grasped by individual minds and leading to decisions, in turn were translated into action may be read in the pages of Lalor, of Mitchel or of O'Donovan Rossa. In literature proper the grim shadow of that event reaches from its century to ours ; from the pages of Carleton's novel, *The black prophet,* written at the height of the famine and gathering what strength it has from its author's recollections of earlier famines, to the more controlled prose of Liam O'Flaherty's more recent novel, *Famine,* which has something of the simple and forceful quality of these oral accounts ; or from many of the poems of Mangan, who died of famine fever, to Gerald Healy's play, *The black stranger,* or the ironic title of Patrick Kavanagh's poem, *The great hunger.*

'Fiction', wrote Carleton in his preface, 'is frequently transcended by the terrible realities of truth.' The truth which I have tried to piece together from scattered oral accounts is not essentially different from the truth derivable from the materials which I have mentioned. If more amorphous, its peculiar personal and local flavour communicates its own especial reality and it has an objectivity and a detachment which perhaps seems strange, until one reflects that the history of the famine was indelibly printed upon the lives of our forefathers, that to them it was an accepted fact and might be recalled as a great and ruinous storm might be recalled. The perspective of the famine will be found in the other chapters of this book. The truth of this chapter, as far as I have succeeded in conveying it, is the truth, heard from afar, of the men and women who were caught up, uncomprehending and frantic, in that disaster.

# Notes

CHAPTER I

## IRELAND ON THE EVE OF THE FAMINE

### i. POPULATION AND RURAL LIFE

[1] T. R. Malthus, *An essay on the principle of population as it affects the future improvement of society* (London, 1798).

[2] K. H. Connell, *The population of Ireland, 1750–1854* (Oxford, 1950).

[3] *Poor inquiry (Ireland) : Report on the state of the Irish poor in Great Britain*, p. iii, H.C. 1836 (40), xxxiv. 429.

[4] R. B. Madgwick, *Emigration into eastern Australia* (London, 1937) ; N. MacDonald, *Canada 1763–1841 : Immigration and settlement* (London, 1939) ; A. Redford, *Labour migration in England 1800–1850* (Manchester, 1950) ; D. P. MacDonald, *Scotland's shifting population* (Glasgow, 1937), and W. F. Adams, *Ireland and the Irish emigration to the new world* (Yale, 1932). The appendix to this last mentioned work gives estimates of the numbers of emigrants during the first half of the century.

[5] *The state of Ireland* (Carlow, 1820).

[6] T. Newenham, *A statistical and historical inquiry into the progress and magnitude of the population of Ireland* (London, 1805) and see also *Report of H.M. commissioners of inquiry . . . in respect to the occupation of land in Ireland*, pt. ii, p. 972, H.C. 1845 (616), xx. 978. *Evidence taken before H.M. commissioners of inquiry . . . in respect to the occupation of land in Ireland*, pt. ii, p. 437, H.C. 1845 (616), xx. 443.

[7] *Evidence taken before H.M. commissioners of inquiry . . . in respect to the occupation of land in Ireland*, pt. ii, p. 437, H.C. 1845 (616), xx. 443.

[8] *Evidence taken before H.M. commissioners of inquiry . . . in respect to the occupation of land in Ireland*, pt. ii, p. 98, H.C. 1845 (616), xx. 104.

[9] A. Flood, *Poor laws* (Dublin, 1830), p. 14.

[10] *Evidence taken before H.M. commissioners of inquiry . . . in respect to the occupation of land in Ireland*, pt. i, pp. 148–50, 157, H.C. 1845 (606), xix. 210–14, 219. Pt. ii, pp. 895–6, H.C. 1845 (616), xx. 903–4, ibid. pt. iii, p. 174, H.C. 1845 (657), xxi. 180.

[11] *Report . . . on the state of the poor in Ireland*, p. 398, H.C. 1830 (667), vii. 572.

[12] *Incumbered estates inquiry commission, Ireland . . . appendix*, pp. 82–133, H.C. 1854–5, xix. 632–83.

[13] John Hancock an experienced and intelligent Ulster land agent defined tenant-right as a) the claim of the tenant or his heir to remain in possession as long as the rent was paid and b) the sum which, in the event of a change of occupancy either at the wish of the landlord or the tenant, the new occupant must pay to the old one for the peaceable enjoyment of his holding. (W. N. Hancock, *The tenant-right of Ulster . . .* (Dublin, 1845), p. 7.)

[14] *Report from H.M. commissioners of inquiry . . . in respect to the occupation of land in Ireland*, p. 484, H.C. 1845 (605), xix. 546.

[15] *Report from H.M. commissioners of inquiry . . . in respect to the occupation of land in Ireland*, p. 386, H.C. 1845 (616), xx. 392.

437

## ii.  INDUSTRIES AND COMMUNICATIONS

[1] C. Gill, *The rise of the Irish linen industry* (Oxford, 1925), pp. 130–7 ; J. J. Monaghan, ' The rise and fall of the Belfast cotton industry,' in *IHS.* iii. 1–17 ; *Reports from the assistant handloom weavers' commissioners*, pt. iii, p. 591 ff, H.C. 1840 (43), xxiii. 435 ff.

[2] E. Wakefield, *An account of Ireland* (London, 1812), i. 723.

[3] *Second report of the commissioners appointed to consider and recommend a general system of railways for Ireland, appendix I*, pp. 15–23, H.C. 1837–8 (145), xxxv. 599–621 ; S. Lewis, *Topographical dictionary of Ireland* (London, 1839) ; Fraser, *Gleanings in Ireland* (London, 1802), p. 12.

[4] *Reports from the assistant handloom weavers' commissioners*, pt. ii, pp. 601–14, H.C. 1840 (43), xxiii. 445–58.

[5] *Second report of the commissioners appointed to consider . . . a general system of railways for Ireland*, p. 8, H.C. 1837–8 (145), xxxv.; *Reports from the assistant handloom weavers' commissioners*, p. 598, H.C. 1840 (43), xxiii. 442.

[6] *Second report of the commissioners appointed to consider . . . a general system of railways for Ireland*, p. 14, appendix, p. 75, H.C. 1837–8 (145), xxxv.; *Reports from the assistant handloom weavers' commissioners*, pt. ii, pp. 660–1, H.C. 1840 (43), xxiii. 504–5.

[7] See *The Parliamentary gazetteer of Ireland*, 3 vols. (London, 1844–6) ; S. Lewis, *Topographical dictionary of Ireland*, 2 vols. (London, 1839) and *Reports of the assistant handloom weavers' commissioners*, pp. 659–69, H.C. 1840 (43), xxiii. 505–13.

[8] J. J. Monaghan, ' The rise of the cotton industry ', in *IHS*, iii. 1–17.

[9] *Reports of the inspectors of factories . . . for the half year ending 31 Dec. 1842*, pp. 13–14, H.C. 1843 (429), xxvii. 297–8.

[10] *Parliamentary gazetteer*, iii. 289.

[11] *Reports from the assistant handloom weavers' commissioners*, p. 655, H.C. 1840 (43), xxiii. 499.

[12] *The parliamentary gazetteer of Ireland*; S. Lewis, *Topographical dictionary of Ireland*; *Reports from the assistant handloom weavers' commissioners*, pp. 655–9, 773–800, H.C. 1840 (43), xxiii. 499–503, 617–44.

[13] *Reports from the assistant handloom weavers' commissioners*, pp. 627–31, H.C. 1840 (43), xxiii. 471–5.

[14] *Reports from the assistant handloom weavers' commissioners*, pp. 711, 634, H.C. 1840 (43), xxiii. 555, 478. For the cotton and linen industries in Ulster see E. R. R. Green, *The Lagan valley 1800–1850* (London, 1949).

[15] *Belfast and its environs* (Dublin, 1842), p. 2.

[16] D. J. Owen, *History of Belfast* (Belfast, 1921), pp. 217–35 ; G. Benn, *History of the town of Belfast* (London, 1880), ii. 124 ; Ball & Miller, *Belfast harbour : report upon the harbour and dock accommodation* (Glasgow, 1862).

[17] For Irish roads in this period see I. J. Herring, ' Ulster roads on the eve of the railway age ', in *IHS*, ii. 160–88, ' The " bians " ', in *UJA*, ii. 130–7, 115–22, and ' Travelling conditions in the early nineteenth century ', in *UJA*, iv. 2–11.

[18] For the early history of Irish railways see J. C. Conroy, *History of railways in Ireland* (London, 1928) ; K. Murray, *The Great Northern railway (Ireland)* (Dublin, 1935).

[19] Spring-Rice to Morpeth, 26 Sept. 1838 ; Spring-Rice to Normanby, 23 Nov. 1838, 2 Jan. 1839 (Monteagle papers).

[20] *Hansard*, 3 series, xlv. 1060 ff.

[21] Spring-Rice to T. Drummond, 2 Dec. 1838 (Monteagle papers) ; *Railways (Ireland) commission . . .  appendix, pt. ii*, p. 36, H.C. 1867–8 (4018), xxxii. 504.

### iii. CENTRAL AND LOCAL GOVERNMENT

[1] 44 Geo. III c. 105.

[2] 57 Geo. III c. 5, 5 Geo. IV. c. 23.

[3] 56 Geo. III c. 98.

[4] 4 Geo. IV c. 23 ; 7 & 8 Geo. IV c. 55 ; 2 & 3 Will. IV c. 99 ; I Will. IV c. 8.

[5] The best available guide to the Irish civil service in the early forties is *Thom' Irish almanac and official directory for the year 1845* (Dublin, 1845).

[6] 6 & 7 Will. IV c. 83. *Report of select committee on miscellaneous expenditure . . . evidence*, pp. 121–2, 994–5, H.C. 1847–8 (543), xviii. 185–6, 358–9 ; 5 & 6 Vict. c. 89 ; 5 & 6 Will. IV c. 67.

[7] 7 & 8 Geo. IV c. 60.

[8] *D.N.B.*

[9] W. M. Torrens, *Memoirs of the Rt. Hon. William Viscount Melbourne* (London, 1878), i. 259.

[10] Relations between De Grey and Eliot are discussed at considerable length in letters printed in C. S. Parker, *Sir Robert Peel* (London, 1891–9), iii. 34–68, 111–13 and C. S. Parker, *Life and letters of Sir James Graham* (London, 1907), i. 348–58.

[11] *Hansard*, new series, ix. 1212 ff., xxiv. 555 ff.

[12] For Irish county government during the early nineteenth century see *Report of the select committee on county cess (Ireland), with the minutes of evidences, appendices and index*, H.C. 1836 (527), xii ; *Report of the commissioners appointed to revise the several laws under or by virtue of which moneys are now raised by grand jury presentments in Ireland*, H.C. 1842 (386), xxiv ; *Report of the select committee on grand jury presentments (Ireland)*, H.C. 1867–8 (382), *Hansard*, xxxvi. 115, 3 series, ix. 135–6, i. 914–31, xv. 961–4, xviiii. 562–3 ; T. Rice, *An inquiry into the effect of the Irish grand iury laws* (London, 1815) ; H. Lindsay, *The present state of the Irish grand jury law* (Armagh, 1837).

[13] The Irish municipal corporations are fully described in the report of the commissioners appointed to inquire into them in 1834: *First report of the commissioners appointed to inquire into the municipal corporations in Ireland*, H.C. 1835 (23), xxvii, *Supplement to the first report*, H.C. 1835 (24, 27, 28), 1836 (29), xxiv.

[14] This figure includes Trim where the corporation's sole function was the division of the corporate estates among its members.

[15] 24 Geo. III c. 40.

[16] 3 Geo. IV c. 103.

[17] 54 Geo. III c. 131.

[18] H. R. Addison, *Recollections of an Irish police magistrate*, London (n.d.), p. 77.

[19] *A return of the constabulary force of Ireland*, H.C. 1833 (518), xxxii and *A return of the peace preservation force in Ireland . . .*, H.C. 1834 (201), xlvii.

[20] *Report from the select committee of the house of lords appointed to consider . . . extending the functions of the constabulary in Ireland*, pp. 4–6, H.C. 1854 (53), x. 10–11.

[21] *Minutes of evidence taken before the select committee appointed to inquire into the state of Ireland*, pt. III, p. 1001, H.C. 1839 (468), xii. 139.

[22] 6 & 7 Will. IV c. 13 ; 2 & 3 Vict. c. 75. *Report of the Lords' select committee appointed to inquire into the state of Ireland*, H.C. 1839 (468), xii ; *Report from the select committee of the house of Lords appointed to consider the consequences of extending the functions of the constabulary in Ireland*, H.C. 1854 (53), x.

[23] *A return of the number of the Irish police*, H.C. 1844 (189), xxxix.

[24] This remark was made by a witness before a parliamentary committee. (*Report from the select committee of the house of lords . . . appointed to consider extending the functions of the constabulary in Ireland*, p. 148, H.C. 1854 (53), x. 154.

iv.  SICKNESS AND POVERTY

[1] 11 & 12 Geo. III c. 30.

[2] These institutions are described in *Report . . . on the state of the poor in Ireland,* 1830, H.C. pp. 24–34, 1830, vii ; *Poor inquiry (Ireland)* appendix B and appendix C, H.C. 1835 (369), xxxii. 1836, xxx.

[3] For the Irish dispensaries see First report of *H.M. commission of inquiry into the condition of the poorer classes in Ireland,* App. B. C. 1835 (369), xxxii ; *Report from the select committee of the house of lords on the laws relating to the relief of the destitute poor and the operation of medical charities in Ireland,* H.C. 1846 (694), xi ; and *Report from the select committee on medical charities together with the minutes of evidence,* pp. 167, 369, H.C. 1843 (412), x. 181, 383.

[4] First report *from the commissioners for inquiry into the condition of the poorer classes in Ireland, appendix,* p. 345, H.C. 1835 (369), xxxii. 361.

[5] *Report . . . medical charities . . . ,* pp. 104–6, H.C. 1843 (412), x. 118–120.

[6] *Report . . . on the state of the poor in Ireland,* pp. 25, 168, 235, H.C. 1830 (667), vii. 25, 340, 407.

[7] *Report from the select committee of the house of lords on the state of the lunatic poor in Ireland,* H.C. 1843 (625), x.

[8] C. A. Cameron, *History of the royal college of surgeons in Ireland and of the Irish schools of medicine . . .* (Dublin, 1916).

[9] T. C. P. Kirkpatrick, *History of medical teaching in Trinity College, Dublin* (Dublin, 1912) ; A. Macalister, *James Macartney . . . a memoir* (London, 1900).

[10] R. J. Graves, *Studies in physiology and medicine* (London, 1863), pp. xxi–xxiv ; W. Stokes, *William Stokes, his life and work 1804–1878* (London, 1898) ; T. G. Moorhead, *A short history of Sir Patrick Dun's Hospital* (Dublin, 1942) ; R. J. Rowlette, *The Medical press and circular, 1839–1939* (London, 1939).

[11] *Poor Inquiry (Ireland), appendix C,* pp. 7–9, H.C. 1836 (35), xxx. 43–5 ; Appendix B, p. 22, H.C. 1836 (369), xxxii. pt. ii ; *Report on the state of the poor,* p. 30, H.C. 1830 (667), vii.

[12] The loans were generally repaid, see *An account (since the union) of all sums of money advanced on loan for public works or other purposes in Ireland,* H.C. 1850 (718), liv. 91–239.

[13] *Thirteenth annual report from the board of public works in Ireland,* H.C. 1845 (640), xxvi.

[14] *Thirteenth annual report from the board of public works in Ireland,* H.C. 1845, (640), xxvi. The proceedings of the board of public works between its foundation and 1845 can be studied in its annual reports, H.C. 1833 (75), xvii ; 1834 (240), xl ; 1835 (76), xxxvi ; 1836 (314), xxxvi ; 1837 (483), xxxiii ; 1837–8 (433), xxxv ; 1839 (129), xx ; 1840 (327), xxviii ; 1841 (252), xii ; 1842 (384), xxiv ; 1843 (467), xxviii ; 1844 (555), xxx ; 1845 (640), xxvi ; 1847 (762), xvii.

[15] *Poor inquiry (Ireland)* appendix C, Pt. 1, pp. 11–14, H.C. 1836 (35), xxx. 47–51 ; Pt. II, pp. 30–46, H.C. 1836 (35), xxx. 254–68.

[16] *Hansard,* ix. 1196.

[17] First report *from H.M. commissioners of inquiry into the condition of the poorer classes in Ireland,* p. vii, H.C. 1835 (369), xxxii. 7.

[18] *Report from the lords' select committee appointed to inquire into the state of Ireland,* p. 3, H.C. 1826 (40), v. 661 ; *Report from the select committee appointed to take into consideration the state of the poorer classes in Ireland,* p. 55, H.C. 1830 (667), vii ; *First report from the select committee on the state of disease and condition of the labouring poor in Ireland,* p. 5, H.C. 1819 (314), viii.

[19] *Hansard,* 3 series, v. 1112.

**20** *Edinburgh Review*, lix. 227–61.

**21** *Hansard*, 3 series, xxxi. 227.

**22** *Quarterly Review*, xliv. 511–54.

**23** *Westminster Review*, xxv. 332–65.

**24** *Third report of the commissioners for inquiry into the state of the poorer classes in Ireland*, H.C. 1836 (35), xxx.

**25** R. Whately, *Introductory lectures on political economy*, 4th ed. (London, 1855), p. 204.

**26** G. C. Lewis, *Remarks on the third report of the commissioners*, H.C. 1837 (91), li ; *Letter from N. W. Senior on the third report of the commission of inquiry into the condition of the poor in Ireland*, H.C. 1837 (26), li.

**27** G. F. Lewis, *Letters of The Rt. Hon. Sir George Cornewall Lewis* (London, 1870), i. 54.

**28** See G. Nicholls, *Report . . . on poor laws, Ireland*, H.C. 1837 (69), 1837 li ; *second report*, H.C. 1837 (104), xxxviii, and G. Nicholls, *A history of the English poor law*, new ed. containing a biography by H. G. Willick. 2 vols. (London, 1878).

**29** *Hansard*, 3 series, xl. 774–89, 947–91, 1007–27, 1229–46, xli. 61–81, 374–85, 732–41, 974–1002, 1179–99, xlii. 675–717, xliii. 1–71.

**30** The working of the Irish poor law in the period under consideration is dealt with in great detail in the reports of the poor law commissioners for 1839–45, H.C. 1840 (253), xvii ; 1841 (327), xi ; 1842 (389) (399), xix ; 1843 (468) (491), xxi ; 1844 (560) (589), xix ; 1846 (704) (745), xix, and *Report from the committee on union workhouses in Ireland*, H.C. 1844 (441), xiv, and *Report of the commissioner of inquiry into contracts for certain union workhouses in Ireland*, 1844 (362), xxx.

**31** *Eighth annual report of the poor law commissioners*, p. 29, H.C. 1842 (389), xix. 35, and Wilkinson's reports printed as appendices to the seventh, eighth and ninth reports of the poor law commissioners.

**32** *Report : commission for inquiring into the execution of the contracts for certain union workhouses in Ireland*, and appendix, H.C. 1844 (562, 568), xxx ; G. Nicholls, *A history of the English poor law* (new ed. London, 1898) i. pp. lxi–lxiv.

**33** *Eleventh annual report of the poor law commissioners*, p. 23, H.C. 1845 (624), xxvii. 273.

**34** *Tenth annual report of the poor law commissioners*, pp. 34, H.C. 1844 (560), xix. 46–7.

**35** *Eighth annual report of the poor law commissioners*, appendix, pp. 154–6, H.C. 1842 (389), xix ; *Report of the select committee of the house of lords on the laws relating to the relief of the destitute poor . . . in Ireland*, p. 170, H.C. 1846 (694), xi.

**36** *Sixth annual report of the poor law commissioners*, p. 30, H.C. 1840 (245), xvii. 430 ; *Seventh annual report of the poor law commissioners*, pp. 56–8, H.C. 1841 (327). xi. 354–6.

**37** *Fifth annual report of the poor law commissioners*, p. 28, H.C. 1839 (239), xx. 32.

**38** The regulations are given in the appendix to the *Sixth annual report of the poor law commissioners*, pp. 133–44, H.C. 1840 (253), xvii. 539–50.

**39** *Eighth annual report of the poor law commissioners*, appendix C, pp. 152–3, H.C. 1842 (399), xix. 164–5.

**40** *Sixth annual report of the poor law commissioners*, p. 39, H.C. 1840 (245), xvii. 439.

**41** *Seventh annual report of the poor law commissioners*, p. 47, H.C. 1841 (327), xi. 345.

**42** Appendix to the *Seventh annual report of the poor law commissioners*, pp. 196–9, H.C. 1841 (327), xi. 494–9 ; *Ninth annual report of the poor law commissioners*, pp. 37–8, 1843 (468), xxi. 32–3.

**43** *Northern Whig*, 30 July 1842.

### V.  THE STATE AND EDUCATION

[1] *Report of the census commissioners, Ireland,* H.C. 1843 (504), pp. 33, 438–9, xxvi. 33, 546–7.

[2] *The fourteenth report of the commissioners of the board of education in Ireland* and *First report of the commissioners on education in Ireland,* H.C. 1825 (400), xii.

[3] For the grammar schools see in particular *Report from the select committee on foundation schools and education in Ireland,* H.C. 1837–8 (701), vii.

### vi.  THE CHURCHES

[1] *Report of the select committee . . . appointed to inquire into the state of Ireland,* pt. i, p. 436, H.C. 1839 (486), xi. 439 ; *Report from the select committee on laws relating to the relief of the destitute poor . . . in Ireland,* p. xii, appendix, pp. 115–26, H.C. 1846 (694), xi. 14, xi, pt. ii, 119–30 ; *Report from the select committee on medical charities (Ireland),* 198–206, 288–92, H.C. 1843 (412), x. 214–20, 302–8.

[2] An imperfect guide to the distribution of religious bodies in Ireland is provided by the figures contained in the *First report of the commissioners of public instruction in Ireland,* H.C. 1835 (45), xxxiii.

[3] W. D. Killen, *A history of the presbyterian church in Ireland,* ed. T. S. Reid (Belfast, 1867), iii. 432.

[4] For Maynooth at this period see Most Rev. J. J. Healy, *Maynooth College centenary history 1795–1895* (Dublin, 1895) ; Rev. G. Crolly, *The life of the Most Rev. R. Crolly* (Dublin, 1851), pp. xxxiii–xxxvii ; *Report of H.M. commissioners appointed to inquire into the management and government of the college of Maynooth,* H.C. 1854–5 (1896), xxii.

[5] H.O. 100/246.

[6] 1 & 2 Vict. c. 109.

[7] *Diocesan returns, 1833 . . .* H.C. 1835 (81), xlvii ; *Thom's Irish almanac . . . for the year 1845.*

[8] This view was clearly expressed in Stanley's celebrated speech on the Irish Establishment in 1824.  (*Hansard,* new series, ix. 562 ff.)

[9] *Report from the select committee on tithes, Ireland,* p. 355, H.C. 1831–2 (177), xxi.

[10] The sources for clerical incomes in the different Irish denominations are—the Reports of the commissioners of ecclesiastical inquiry (Ireland), H.C. 1833 (762), xxi, 1834 (589), xxiii, 1836 (264), xxv, 1837 (570), xxi ; Bishop Doyle's evidence before two parliamentary committees: *Report of the select committee on the state of Ireland,* p. 185, H.C. 1825 (129), viii and *Second report from the select committee of the house of Lords . . . to inquire into tithes,* p. 97, H.C. 1831–2 (271), xxii ; W. D. Killen, *A history of the presbyterian church in Ireland,* iii, p. 407 ; C. Porter, *Irish presbyterian biographical sketches* (Belfast, 1883), 21.

[11] The outlook of the Irish evangelicals can best be gathered from the biographies of several of the leading members of the movement, S. Madden, *Memoir of the life of the Rev. Peter Roe* (Dublin, 1842), J. Walker, *Essays and Correspondence,* 2 vols. (London, 1838) and *Brief memorials of the life of Benjamin Mathias* (Dublin, 1842).

[12] See J. L. Porter, *Life and times of Henry Cooke,* 1871, and J. A. Crozier, *Life of Henry Montgomery,* i. 1875.

### vii.  THE POLITICAL SCENE

[1] For O'Connell's intellectual background and outlook see W. J. Fitzpatrick, *Correspondence of Daniel O'Connell,* 2 vols. (London, 1888) ; R. Dudley Edwards, ' The contribution of Young Ireland to the development of the Irish national idea ', in *Feilscribhinn Torna* (Cork, 1947).

[2] W. J. Fitzpatrick, *Correspondence of Daniel O'Connell*, ii. 34.

[3] R. B. O'Brien, *Thomas Drummond . . . life and letters* (London, 1889), pp. 273–87.

[4] W. J. Fitzpatrick, *Correspondence of Daniel O'Connell*, ii. 104–5.

[5] W. J. Fitzpatrick, *Correspondence of Daniel O'Connell*, ii. pp. 149–50.

[6] W. E. Hudson, *A treatise on the elective franchise and the registration of electors in Ireland under the reform act of 1832* (Dublin, 1832).

[7] *Electors (Ireland) . . .* H.C. 1846 (469), xlii. 215–47.

[8] *Dublin Evening Mail*, 7, 17, 19, 22 July 1841.

[9] C. G. Duffy has described, with remarkable objectivity considering his own vigorous participation, Irish politics during the early *forties in Young Ireland: a fragment of Irish history 1840–50* (London, 1880), *Thomas Davis: the memoirs of an Irish patriot 1840–46* (London, 1890) and *My life in two hemispheres* (London, 1898). The recent literature on the period is surveyed by K. B. Nowlan in ' Writings in connection with Thomas Davis and the Young Ireland centenary, 1945 ', in *IHS*, v. 265–72.

[10] For an exposition of this programme see O'Connell's speech at Mullingar (*Nation*, 20 May 1843).

[11] C. S. Parker, *Sir Robert Peel from his private papers* (London, 1891–9), iii. 46–9.

[12] C. S. Parker, *The life and letters of Sir James Graham . . . 1792–1861*. 2 vols. (London, 1907), i. 355–7 ; C. S. Parker, *Sir Robert Peel*, iii. 51–2.

[13] C. S. Parker, *The life and letters of Sir James Graham*, i. 408–9.

[14] C. S. Parker, *Sir Robert Peel*, iii. 56–60.

[15] C. S. Parker, *Sir Robert Peel*, iii. 105–7, 113–4, 116–7.

[16] Graham to De Grey, 1 Mar. 1844, Parker, *Life and letters of Sir J. Graham*, i. 405–6 ; Graham to Peel, 20 and 25 Oct. 1843, Parker, *Sir Robert Peel*, iii. 65–7.

[17] Stanley to Peel, 21 Oct. 1843 and 18 Feb. 1844. Parker, *Sir Robert Peel*, iii. 66–7.

[18] Memorandum 1 Feb. 1844, Parker, *Sir Robert Peel*, iii. 101–2.

[19] *Hansard*, 3 series, lxxxi. 211 ff, 1116 ff.

[20] For the discussions on the act and its working see Most Rev. William Walsh, ' The board of charitable donations and bequests ' (pts. ix, xi, xii of ' The law in its relation to religious interests ', in *Irish Ecclesiastical Record*, xvi. 875–94, 971–96).

[21] C. S. Parker, *Sir Robert Peel*, iii. 126–31, *Life and letters of Sir James Graham*, i. 418–22.

[22] C. S. Parker, *Sir Robert Peel*, iii. 176.

[23] *Nation*, 23 Aug. 1845.

[24] G. Duffy, *Thomas Davis*, p. 329 ; T. Davis, *Literary and historical essays* (Dublin, 1846), p. 52. For a consideration of Davis's outlook see T. W. Moody, *Thomas Davis 1814–45* (Dublin, 1845).

[25] *Nation*, 12 July 1844.

[26] C. G. Duffy, *Young Ireland* (London, 1880), p. 287.

[27] C. G. Duffy, *Thomas Davis*, p. 107 ; *Nation*, 24 June 1843 ; R. Clarke ' The relations between O'Connell and the Young Irelanders ', in *IHS*, iii. 17–30.

[28] *Nation*, Oct. 1844, G. Duffy, *Thomas Davis*, p. 262 ; *Young Ireland*, pp. 575–609.

[29] *Nation*, 17, 24, 31 May, 28 June 1845.

[30] *Pilot*, 12 Sept. 1845.

CHAPTER II

# AGRICULTURE

## i. INTRODUCTION

[1] *Report of the commissioners appointed to take the census of Ireland for the year 1841*, parl. papers, pp. xi, xii, and xxxiii, H.C. 1843 (504), xxiv. Hereafter cited as *1841 census*.

[2] *Thom's Irish almanac and official directory for the year 1845* (Dublin, 1845), p. 163.

[3] Léonce de Lavergne, *Essai sur l'économie rurale de l'Angleterre de l'Écosse et de l'Irlande* (3 ed., Paris, 1858), pp. 380–1.

[4] K. H. Connell, *The population of Ireland 1750–1845* (Oxford, 1950), p. 113.

[5] Nassau William Senior, *Journals, conversations and essays relating to Ireland* (London, 1868), i. 298.

[6] *Commissioners of inquiry into the state of the law and practice in respect of the occupation of land in Ireland, evidence,* ii. parl. papers, 922–3 [C. 606], H.C. 1845, xix. Hereafter cited as *Devon commission*.

[7] J. P. Kennedy, *Digest of evidence taken before Her Majesty's commissioners of inquiry into the state of the law and practice in respect to the occupation of land in Ireland* (Dublin, 1847), p. 14.

[8] J. S. Mill in *Principles of political economy* (London, 1848), i. 368 defined the term cottier as covering ' all peasant farmers whose rents are determined by competition '. J. E. Cairnes in *Political essays* (London, 1873), p. 164, similarly held ' the determination of his rent by competition ' to be ' the essential characteristic of the cottier tenant'.
The normal Irish usage is shown by the witnesses examined by the poor commissioners, who regarded a cottier as primarily the tenant of a cabin and a small portion of land, holding at will and bound to labour for his landlord whenever required. See *First report of inquiry into the condition of the poorer classes in Ireland*, appendix D, parl. papers, pp. 75–83 [C. 36], H.C. 1836, xxxi. Hereafter cited as *Poor inquiry*. Thomas Larcom too, in the agricultural statistics, uses the term cottier only for holdings which do not exceed one acre.

[9] *Poor inquiry*, appendix D, answers to questions 18 and 20 of supplement.

[10] The fullest details on conacre are to be found in the *Poor inquiry*, appendix F, pp. 1–34, and the answers to questions 21–3 in the supplement, containing information on the subject from most Irish parishes. The meaning of the word ' conacre ' has never been satisfactorily explained. The practice had other names—' rood land ' in Ulster, ' quarter ground ' in Limerick, ' stang ' in Wexford, ' dairy ground ' in Waterford, and ' score ground ' in Kerry.

[11] *Poor inquiry*, appendix D, answers to question 4 of supplement.

[12] *Poor inquiry*, appendix D, pp. 93–113, and the answers to questions 8–10 in the supplement.

[13] *Poor inquiry*, appendix D, pp. 15, 39, 49, 53, 55 and 57.

[14] *Poor inquiry*, appendix E, p. 74.

[15] Isaac Weld, *Statistical survey of the county of Roscommon* (Dublin, 1832), pp. 463–4.

[16] *Report from the select committee on agriculture,* p. 510, parl. papers, H.C. 1836 (79), viii.

## ii. TILLAGE

[1] Ibid., p. 422 and *Third report from the select committee appointed to inquire into the state of agriculture,* p. 259, parl. papers, H.C. 1836 (465), viii.

[2] *Returns of agricultural produce in Ireland in the year 1847*, p. vi, parl. papers, H.C. 1847–8 (923), lvii.

[3] Thomas Newenham, *A view of the natural, political, and commercial circumstances of Ireland* (London, 1809), pp. 136–7. He states that 248 mills were built between 1759 and 1790.

[4] H. Townsend, *Statistical survey of the county of Cork* (Dublin, 1810), p. 451.

[5] Arthur Young, *A tour in Ireland* (London, 1780), i. 128.

[6] T. Radcliff, *A report on the agriculture and live stock of the county of Kerry* (Dublin, 1814), pp. 106–9.

[7] J. C. Curwen, *Observations on the state of Ireland* (1818), i. 222.

[8] Hely Dutton, *A statistical and agricultural survey of the county of Galway* (Dublin, 1824), pp. 12 and 432–3.

[9] H. D. Inglis, *A journey throughout Ireland, during the spring, summer, and autumn of 1834* (4 ed., London, 1836), p. 74. For details of wheat growing in Tipperary at this time, see R. C. Simington (ed.), ' Tithe Applotment books of 1834 : agricultural returns, produce and prices ', in *Dept. of Agric. Jn.*, xxxviii. 239–343.

[10] Lewis, *Topog. dict. Ire.*, i. 243 and 500 ; ii. 644.

[11] *Rep. from s. c. on agriculture*, pp. 198–9.

[12] *Returns relating to the importation and exportation of corn, foreign and colonial ; annual and weekly average price of wheat and other grain ; quantities imported ; amount of duty received, etc.*, p. 70, parl. papers, H.C. 1843 (177), liii.

[13] There are numerous descriptions of the old Irish ploughs. One of the fullest is in W. Tighe, *Statistical observations relative to the county of Kilkenny, made in the years 1800 and 1801* (Dublin, 1802), pp. 293–6.

[14] Martin Doyle, *A cyclopaedia of practical husbandry* (Dublin, 1839), pp. 167, 170, 403, and 501–2.

[15] *Poor inquiry*, appendix F, pp. 384–5.

[16] Martin Doyle, op. cit., pp. 318–19.

[17] Sir Charles Coote, *Statistical survey of the county of Armagh* (Dublin, 1804), pp. 189–90, and *Rep. from s. c. on agriculture*, p. 198.

[18] *Returns relating to the importation and exportation of corn*, p. 70.

[19] *Second report of the commissioners appointed to consider and recommend a general system of railways for Ireland*, pp. 75, 80, 82, and 87, parl. papers, H.C. 1837–8 (145), xxxv.

[20] Martin Doyle, op. cit., p. 367, and Curwen, op. cit., i. 108.

[21] *Rep. from the s. c. on agric.*, p. 332.

[22] Dutton, op. cit., pp. 34–41, and *Poor inquiry*, appendix F, pp. 390–1.

[23] Radcliff, *Kerry*, pp. 31–7, and *Poor inquiry*, appendix F, pp. 393 and 396.

[24] Doyle, op. cit., p. 367, and *Poor inquiry*, appendix F, p. 412.

[25] Tighe, op. cit., p. 221 ; *3rd rep. from the s. c. on agric.*, p. 268 ; T. Radcliff, *Report on the agriculture and live stock of the county of Wicklow* (Dublin, 1812), pp. 6 and 368–9, and *Rep. from the s.c. on agric.*, p. 497.

[26] Dutton, op. cit., p. 35 ; Doyle, op. cit., pp. 366–7, and W. D. Davidson, 'History of potato varieties ', in *Dept. Agric. Jn.*, xxxiii. 59–64.

[27] P. W. Joyce (ed.), *Old Irish folk music and songs* (1909), p. 218.

[28] Curwen, op. cit., i. 251.

[29] Radcliff, *Kerry*, p. 21, and *Poor inquiry*, appendix F, pp. 393, 396, 400 and 404. For further details of reclamation see K. H. Connell,' The colonisation of waste land in Ireland, 1780–1845 ', in *Economic History Review*, ser. 2, iii. 44–61.

### iii. GRAZING AND DAIRY-FARMING

[1] *3rd rep. from the s. c. on agric.*, p. 258.

[2] Dutton, op. cit., pp. 105–7.

[3] *Devon commission*, i. 946 ; ii. 70, 78, 313, and 371.

[4] Weld, op. cit., pp. 374–5 and 667.

[5] Dutton, op. cit., pp. 141–2.

[6] *Rep. from the s. c. on agric.*, p. 335.

[7] For descriptions of Ballinasloe market, see Dutton op. cit., pp. 118–19 and 144–5, and Weld, op. cit., pp. 570–1.

[8] Doyle, op. cit., p. 333.

[9] David Low, *The breeds of the domestic animals of the British Islands* (London, 1842), i. 45, and *Poor inquiry*, appendix F, pp. 406 and 413.

[10] [W. Youatt] *Cattle* (London, 1834), p. 186 ; Curwen, op. cit., ii. 138, and *Poor inquiry*, appendix F, p. 389.

[11] George Garrard, *A description of the different varieties of oxen common in the British Isles* (London, 1800), no. ii, p. 2 and Youatt, op. cit., pp. 179–80.

[12] *Rep. from the s. c. on agric.*, pp. 384–5.

[13] Radcliff, *Kerry*, pp. 61 and 118–24.

[14] Edward Wakefield, *An account of Ireland statistical and political* (London, 1812), i. 323–5 and *Poor inquiry*, appendix F, pp. 392, 398, 405, and 414–15.

[15] There is an authoritative account of the Cork butter market in W. O'Sullivan, *The economic history of Cork city* (1937), but it goes no further than 1800. A mass of information on the dairying industry is to be found in *Report from the select committee appointed to inquire into the butter trade of Ireland*, parl. papers, H.C. 1826 (406), v.

[16] Butter exported from each port of Ireland, 1823 : Belfast 41,451 cwts ; Cork 126,015 cwts ; Dublin 31,352 cwts ; Limerick 41,404 cwts ; Newry 58,590 cwts ; Waterford 138,899 cwts. *An account of the quantity of butter exported from Ireland, or the last twenty years : distinguishing the ports from which, and the countries to which, exported*, pp. 5–7, parl. papers, H.C. 1826 (338), xxiii.

[17] *Rep. from the s. c. on agric.*, pp. 407 and 630, and *Railway commission*, appendix B, p. 91.

[18] Tighe, op. cit., pp. 319–21.

[19] Curwen, op. cit., i. 290, and Radcliff, *Wicklow*, pp. 120 and 142.

[20] Low, op. cit., ii. 13–16.

[21] Weld, op. cit., p. 666.

[22] W. Youatt, *The pig* (London, 1847), p. 65, and *Poor inquiry*, appendix F, p. 385.

[23] H. D. Richardson, *Domestic pigs* (London, 1873), p. 48, and Youatt, *The pig*, p. 65.

[24] *Railway commission*, appendix B, pp. 73, 75, and 87.

[25] John O'Donovan, *The economic history of live stock in Ireland* (1940), p. 273, and Richardson, op. cit., p. 143.

[26] *Railway commission*, appendix B, p. 91, and *Report from the select committee of the house of lords appointed to inquire into the state of agriculture in England and Wales*, p. 406, parl. papers, H.C. 1837 (464), v.

## iv.  THE WESTERN SEABOARD

[1] See pp. 89–90.

[2] *Devon commission,* iv. 280–9.    On the system generally, see E. Estyn Evans, *Irish heritage* (1942), pp. 47–52.

[3] P. Knight, *Erris in the Irish highlands and the Atlantic railway* (Dublin, 1836), pp. 46–7.

[4] [John Wiggins] *South of Ireland : rints to Irish landlords* (London, 1824), p. 13.

[5] John McEvoy, *Statistical survey of the county of Tyrone* (Dublin, 1802), p. 88 ; Senior, op. cit., ii. 41, and *3rd rep. from the s. c. on agric.*, p. 280.

[6] For definitions of 'sums' in different parts of the country, see Wakefield, op. cit., i. 309, 316, and 349 ; Sir Charles Coote, *Statistical survey of the county of Monaghan* (Dublin, 1801), p. 165 ; McEvoy, *Tyrone,* p. 8, and Knight, op. cit., p. 46.

[7] *Devon commission,* ii. 415 and 441, and iv. 280–9.

[8] Coote, *Monaghan,* pp. 142–4.

[9] T. C. Foster, *Letters on the condition of the people of Ireland* (2 ed., London, 1847), pp. 110–11.

[10] Lord George Hill, *Facts from Gweedore* (Dublin, 1845), pp. 13–16.   There is a series of articles on buailteachas, including a bibliography by Professor J. H. Delargy, in *Béaloideas,* xiii. 130–72.

[11] Hill, op. cit., pp. 13–14 ;  Weld, op. cit., p. 475, and Dutton, op. cit., p. 518.

[12] *Poor inquiry,* appendix F, p. 351, and *Devon commission,* ii. 24–5 ;   iii. 799–800 ; iv. 171–2, 336–7.

[13] *1841 census,* pp. xxvi–vii ;   *Devon commission,* ii. 383 and 815, and iii. 207 and 850.   See also, Barbara M. Kerr, ' Irish seasonal migration to Great Britain, 1800–38 ', in *IHS,* iii. 365–80.

[14] *Devon commission,* i. 37 and ii. 213, 375 and 383.


## v.  SUGGESTED REMEDIES

[1] Kennedy, op. cit., pp. 399, 565 and 569.  He gives an outline of his schemes in his pamphlet *Instruct, employ ; don't hang them* (London, 1835).   See also, David Kennedy, ' Captain Pitt Kennedy's plan for Irish agriculture, 1835–45 ', in *Ir. Comm. Hist. Sc. Bull.,* no. 32.

[2] For a more optimistic view of the possibilities of reclamation, see K. H. Connell in *Economic History Review,* ser. 2, iii. 44–71.

[3] William Blacker, *Prize essay, addressed to the agricultural committee of the Royal Dublin Society :  on the management of landed property in Ireland* (Dublin, 1834), p. 16.

[4] *Devon commission,* i. 317–18 and *Lords' s. c. on agric.,* p. 358.

[5] G. H. Kinahan, *A handy book on the reclamation of waste lands, Ireland* (Dublin, 1882), pp. viii–xii.

[6] *First report of the select committee appointed to inquire into the amount of advances made by the commissioners of public works in Ireland,* pp. 3–4, parl. papers, H.C. 1835 (329), xx.

[7] *S. c. on public works, second report,* pp. 24–6, H.C. 1835 (573), xx.

[8] *Devon commission,* iv. 338–41 and James Caird, *The plantation scheme* (Edinburgh, 1850), pp. 106–8.

[9] W. P. Coyne (ed.), *Ireland : industrial and agricultura l* (Dublin, 1901), pp. 90–1

[10] H. F. Berry, *A history of the Royal Dublin Society* (1915), pp. 222–3, 247–8 and 277.

[11] Coyne, op. cit., pp. 181–96 and *Thom's almanac, 1846*, p. 287 and ibid., 1851, 354.

[12] J. S. Mill, *Principles of political economy* (London, 1848), i. 369 and 381.

[13] *Devon commission*, i. 197.

[14] Opinon varies about the contribution of Ulster tenant right to the relative prosperity of the north. The essential feature of the custom was that it assured compensation for improvements by securing the tenant the right to sell his interest in his holding. It was also customary in Ulster to determine rents by impartial valuation at regular intervals. Against this must be placed the competitive price paid for the tenant right on entering a farm. The most telling criticism of the Ulster custom is that it existed equally in Down and in Donegal, the latter a county whose poverty equalled that of the worst parts of Connacht.

[15] *Report from the select committee on the employment of the poor in Ireland*, pp. 4–5, parl. papers, H.C. 1823 (561), vi.

## vi. THE FAMINE AND AFTER

[1] Quoted in W. P. O'Brien, *The great famine in Ireland* (1896), pp. 70–1.

[2] *Returns of agricultural produce in Ireland, in the year 1847*, p. vi, parl. papers, [C. 923], H.C. 1847, lvii.

[3] Quoted from articles in the Dublin *Herald* by Francis Dowdall in *Thom's almanac, 1848*, pp. 165–7.

[4] *Returns of agricultural produce in Ireland, in the year 1847 : part 2, stock*, pp. iii–iv, parl. papers, [C. 1000], H.C. 1847–8, lvii.

[5] *An account of the number of live cattle exported from Ireland to Great Britain, in each year from 1846 to 1849, both inclusive*, p. 1, parl. papers, H.C. 1850 (423), lii.

[6] *Returns of agr. prod., 1847, pt. 2*, p. iv.

[7] *Live cattle exported, 1846–9*, p. 1.

[8] *First annual report of the commissioners for administering the laws for relief of the poor in Ireland*, appendix A, no. viii, ' Inquiry and reports as to the prospects in regard to the agricultural crops in Ireland in the ensuing harvest (1848) ', p. 116, parl. papers, [C. 963], H.C. 1847–8, xxxiii.

[9] *Returns of agricultural produce in Ireland in the year 1848*, p. v [C. 1116], parl. papers, H.C. 1849, xlix.

[10] Ibid., p. vii.

[11] *Returns of agricultural produce in Ireland, in the year 1849*, pp. iv–v and vii, parl. papers, [C. 1245], H.C. 1850, li.

[12] *Returns of agricultural produce in Ireland, in the year 1850*, pp. iii, v, and viii, parl. papers, [C. 1404], H.C. 1851, l.

[13] *The census of Ireland for the year 1851, part 2 : returns of agricultural produce in 1851*, pp. vi and xiii–xiv, parl. papers, [C. 1589], H.C. 1852–3, xciii. The table is from Coyne, op. cit., p. 318. The figures of holdings for 1841 and 1847 showed discrepancies, officially explained by the confusing element of Irish acres. As a result, both Hancock, Thom's statistician, and the later figures in Coyne differ from the 1847 returns. The differences are not big enough to affect percentages.

[14] *Returns of agricultural produce in Ireland, in the year 1852*, pp. vi–vii, parl. papers, [C. 1714], H.C. 1854, lvii ; *Agricultural statistics, 1847–1926*, pp. xxxii–iv.

[15] *Returns of agr. prod., 1851*, p. vi, and *1st ann. rep. poor law commsnrs.*, appendix A, p. 116.

[16] *Thom's almanac, 1852*, p. 240.

[17] James A. Lawson, ' On the agricultural statistics of Ireland ', in *Stat. Soc. Ire. Jn.*, iii. 6–8.

CHAPTER III

# THE POLITICAL BACKGROUND

## ii. THE COMING OF THE BLIGHT

[1] *Dublin Evening Post*, 7, 23 Sept. 1845 ; Sir J. Graham to Sir R. Peel, 18 Sept., 28 Sept. 1845, Peel papers, Add. MS 40 451, ff. 286–7, 318–9 ; C. E. Trevelyan, *The Irish crisis*, pp. 38–9.

[2] P.R.O.I., Relief Commission papers (constabulary reports), 20–5, 28 Oct. 1845.

[3] Ibid., 2, 4 Jan. 1846.

[4] Peel to Lord Heytesbury (lord lieutenant of Ireland), 15 Oct. 1845, Peel papers, Add. MS 40 479, ff. 499–506 ; W. C. Taylor, *Life and times of Sir Robert Peel*, iii. 238 ; H. Goulburn to Peel, 27 Nov. 1845, Peel papers, Add. MS 40 445, ff. 276–9.

[5] Graham to Peel, 18 Sept. 1845, Peel papers, Add. MS 40 451, ff. 286–7 ; Relief commission papers (constabulary office), 16 Sept. 1845 ; Graham to Peel, 20 Oct. 1845, Peel papers, Add. MS 40 451, ff. 410–3 ; Heytesbury to Peel, 24 Oct. 1845, *Memoirs by Sir Robert Peel*, ii. 133–4.

[6] Ibid., 141–8.

[7] Peel to Lord Stanley, 5 Nov. 1845, ibid., 162–3 ; Peel to Queen Victoria, 8 Dec. 1845, ibid., 223–6 ; Lord John Russell to Queen Victoria, 16 Dec. 1845, ibid., 238–40 ; Peel to Queen Victoria, 17 Dec. 1845, ibid., 240–1 ; Lord Grey to Russell, 19 Dec. 1845, Russell papers, P.R.O. 30/22/4 ; *The Greville memoirs* (2nd part), ii. 393–4 ; Daniel O'Connell to William Smith O'Brien, 20 Dec. 1845, Smith O'Brien papers, vol. 435, no. 1445.

[8] *Nation*, 25 Oct. 1845.

[9] Graham to Heytesbury, 31 Oct. 1845, Graham papers.

[10] *Dublin Evening Post*, 4 Nov. 1845 ; *Nation*, 8 Nov. 1845.

[11] Ibid.

[12] Ibid.

[13] Ibid., 10 Jan. 1846.

[14] Repeal Assoc. meeting, 15 Dec., *Nation*, 20 Dec. 1845.

[15] R. B. McDowell, *Public opinion and government policy in Ireland, 1801–1846*, p. 158 ; B. O'Reilly, *John MacHale, archbishop of Tuam, his life, times and correspondence*, i. 499–500.

[16] *Nation*, 29 Nov., 6, 20 Dec. 1845.

[17] Repeal Assoc. meeting, 8 Dec., *Nation*, 13 Dec. 1845.

[18] C. Gavan Duffy, *Four years of Irish history*, pp. 43–4.

[19] Duffy, op. cit. p. 17 ; *Freeman's Journal*, 16 Dec. 1845 ; *Nation*, 6 Dec. 1845.

[20] *The Times*, 19 Feb., 2 April 1846.

[21] *Dublin Evening Mail*, 2 March 1846 ; *Dublin Evening Post*, 24 Aug. 1847.

[22] Peel to Graham, 28 Dec. 1845, Peel papers, Add. MS 40 452, ff. 83–4 ; C. S. Parker, *The life and letters of Sir James Graham*, ii. 29–30.

[23] *Hansard*, lxxxiii. 1–5, 81.

[24] *Memoirs . . . by Peel*, ii. 302–5 ; *Hansard*, lxxxv. 333–60.

[25] Morley, *Life of Richard Cobden*, i. 379.

[26] *Nation*, 28 March 1846 ; *Dublin Evening Post*, 28 March, 1846.

[27] *Dublin Evening Post*, 4 April 1846.

[28] Smith O'Brien to Lord George Bentinck, 19 April 1846, Smith O'Brien papers, vol. 436, no. 1551.

[29] *Greville memoirs* (2nd pt.), ii. 384–5.

[30] *Hansard*, lxxxv. 980–90.

[31] Ibid., 1014–5.

[32] Ibid., lxxxvi. 1201.

[33] Ibid., lxxxvii. 29–37.

[34] Ibid., 959–61.

[35] C. E. Trevelyan to Sir R. Routh, 22 Jan. 1846, *Corresp. explan. of the measures adopted*, parl. papers, H.C. 1846 (735), xxxvii. 14–8 ; *Hansard*, lxxxiv. 780–4.

[36] Under the public works act (9 Vic. c. 1), provision was made for a maximum free grant of £50,000, though ultimately some £366,000 was advanced under this act. *Hansard*, xciv. 49–72.

[37] *Nation*, 7 Feb. 1846.

[38] *Hansard*, lxxxiii. 1050–68 ; lxxxiv. 987–8.

[39] Ibid., lxxxviii. 283–4.

[40] Ibid., lxxxvi. 1196–7 ; lxxxvii. 279–94.

[41] Ibid., lxxxviii. 283–4.

[42] Lord John Russell to the Duke of Leinster, 17 Oct. 1846, Russell papers, P.R.O. 30/22/5. See also, G. P. Gooch, *The later correspondence of Lord John Russell*, i. 155–8.

[43] *Corresp. explan. of the measures adopted*, pp. 148–9.

[44] *Nation*, 18 April 1846 ; Lt.-Gen. Blackeney (Commander-in-Chief, Ireland) to Lord Somerset, 4 June, 9 July, 5 Sept. 1846, Kilmainham papers, vol. 238, pp. 23, 28, 33.

[45] *Nation*, 15 Aug. 1846.

### iii.   THE SEASON OF CRISIS

[1] Thomas Davis to Smith O'Brien, 27 Oct. 1844, Smith O'Brien papers, vol. 434, no. 1296 ; Thomas Davis to Smith O'Brien, 3 Nov. 1844, ibid., vol. 434, no. 1282.

[2] D. O'Connell to J. MacHale, 19 Feb. 1845, B. O'Reilly, *John MacHale, archbishop of Tuam, his life, times and correspondence*, i. 573.

[3] D. O'Connell to Smith O'Brien, 30 June 1846, Smith O'Brien papers, vol. 437, no. 1648.

[4] D. O'Connell to D. R. Pigot, 8 July 1846, Fitzpatrick, *Correspondence of Daniel O'Connell*, ii. 379.

[5] M. Crean to Smith O'Brien, 9 July 1846, Smith O'Brien papers, vol. 437, no. 1653.

[6] *Nation*, 18 July 1846.

[7] D. O'Connell to Smith O'Brien, 18 July 1846, Smith O'Brien papers, vol. 437, no. 1663 ; Smith O'Brien to C. Gavan Duffy, 12 Oct. 1846, N. Lib. Ir. MS 2642, no. 3444.

[8] *The Times*, 13 Aug. 1846 ; *Pilot*, 5 Aug. 1846 ; *Nation*, 8, 15 Aug. 1846.

[9] Ibid., 12 Dec. 1846.

[10] Ibid., 31 Oct. 1846.

[11] Smith O'Brien to Gavan Duffy, 12 Oct. 1846, N. Lib. Ir. MS 2642, no. 3444.

[12] *Freeman's Journal*, 23 Sept. 1846.

[13] *Nation*, 7 Nov. 1846.

[14] ' I do not consider the present as a favourable moment for inviting the public at large to co-operate with us. The public mind is not yet prepared for such an effort. . . .' Smith O'Brien to Gavan Duffy, 11 Nov. 1846, N. Lib. Ir. MS 2642, no. 3451 ; R. O'Gorman to Smith O'Brien, 27 Nov. 1846, Smith O'Brien papers, vo.1 437, no. 1710

[15] Ibid.

[16] *Nation*, 5 Dec. 1846.

[17] Ibid., 12 Dec. 1846.

[18] Smith O'Brien to Gavan Duffy, 15 Dec. 1846, N. Lib. Ir. MS 2642, no. 3464.

[19] J. B. Dillon to Smith O'Brien, (Dec. 1846), Smith O'Brien papers, vol. 434, no. 1299 ; Smith O'Brien to Gavan Duffy, 13 Dec. 1846, N. Lib. Ir. MS 2642, no. 3463.

[20] *Nation*, 15 Dec. 1846.

[21] Smith O'Brien to Gavan Duffy, 24 Dec. 1846, N. Lib. Ir. MS 2642, no. 3468.

[22] J. B. Dillon to Smith O'Brien, 19 Dec. (1846), Smith O'Brien papers, vol. 434, no. 1301 ; Smith O'Brien to Gavan Duffy, 24 Dec. 1846, N. Lib. Ir. MS 2642, no. 3468 ; *Nation*, 2 Jan. 1847.

[23] Gavan Duffy, *Four years of Irish history*, p. 129.

[24] Repeal Assoc. meeting, 6 July, *Nation*, 11 July 1846 ; *Freeman's Journal*, 17 July 1846 ; *Pilot*, 29 June 1846 ; *Dublin Evening Post*, 7 July 1846.

[25] E. Halévy, *The age of Peel and Cobden*, pp. 133–5.

[26] *Hansard*, lxxxviii. 283–4.

[27] Ibid.

[28] *Dublin Evening Post*, 5 May 1846 ; *Corresp. explan. of the measures adopted*, p. 208.

[29] Ibid., pp. 109–10.

[30] P.R.O.I., Relief commission papers (constabulary reports), 20 May 1846.

[31] *Hansard*, lxxxviii. 766–78.

[32] Sir R. Routh to Lord Monteagle, 22 Oct. 1846, Monteagle papers ; Peel to Graham, 30 Dec. 1846, Graham papers.

[33] D. O'Connell to T. Ray (Sec. Repeal Assoc.), 17 Sept. 1846, Repeal Association papers ; *Freeman's Journal*, 20 Aug. 1846.

[34] *Hansard*, lxxxviii. 953.

[35] 9 and 10 Vic. c. 107 ; *Nation*, 26 Sept. 1846.

[36] *Dublin Evening Mail*, 21 Sept. 1846.

[37] *Dublin Evening Post*, 3 Oct. 1846 ; *Nation*, 3 Oct. 1846.

[38] Lord John Russell to earl of Devon, 24 Aug. 1846, Monteagle papers ; Sir Charles Wood to Monteagle, Sept. 1846, ibid.

[39] Trevelyan to Labouchere (copy), 5 Sept. 1846, ibid. See also *Economist* (30 Jan. 1847), v. 113–17 . . . ' under such a calamity what can a government do to alleviate it ? Extremely little. A government may remove all impediments which interfere to prevent the people from providing for themselves, but beyond that they can do little '.

[40] Russell to the duke of Leinster, 17 Oct. 1846, Russell papers, P.R.O. 30/22/5 ; G. P. Gooch, op. cit., i. 155–8 ; Sir C. Wood to Russell, 2 Dec. 1846, Russell papers, P.R.O. 30/22/5.

[41] Russell to Bessborough, 4 Oct. 1846, Russell papers, P.R.O. 30/22/5.

[42] Bessborough to Russell, 30 Sept. 1846, Russell papers, P.R.O. 30/22/5.

[43] Wood to Russell, 14 Oct. 1846 ; Russell to Bessborough, 4 Oct. 1846, Russell papers, P.R.O. 30/22/5. *Final report from the board of public works, Ireland, relating to measures adopted for the relief of distress in July and August 1847*, parl. papers, 1849 (1047), xxiii. 725–36.

[44] Monteagle to Russell, 4 Oct. 1846 ; Wood to Russell, 14 Oct. 1846, Russell papers, P.R.O. 30/22/5. *Infra* p. 157.

[45] Russell to Bessborough, 6 Nov. 1846, Russell papers, P.R.O. 30/22/5.

[46] Russell to Wood, 15 Oct. 1846, G. P. Gooch, op. cit., i. 154.

[47] Lansdowne to Russell, 30 Nov. 1846, Russell papers, P.R.O. 30/22/5 ; Russell to Lansdowne, 2 Dec. 1846, Gooch op. cit., i. 162–3 ; Bessborough to Russell, 29 Dec. 1846 ; Bessborough to Russell, 19 Jan. 1847 ; Marquis of Clanricarde to Russell, 8 Jan. 1847, Russell papers, P.R.O. 30/22/5.

[48] Russell to Lord Clarendon, 10 Nov. 1847, Russell papers, P.R.O. 30/22/6.

[49] ' I cannot make my own mind up entirely about the merchants—I know all the difficulties that arise when you begin to interfere with trade, but it is difficult to persuade a starving population that one class should be permitted to make 50 per cent by the sale of provisions, while they are dying in want of them.' Bessborough to Russell, 23 Jan. 1847, Russell papers, P.R.O. 30/22/6 ; *Economist* (2 Jan. 1847), v. 3–4.

[50] Trevelyan to Monteagle (Oct. 1846), Monteagle papers ; *Economist* (23 Jan. 1847), v. 85–6.

[51] Ibid. (14 Nov. 1846), iv. 1481–2.

[52] Ibid. (1 Aug. 1846), iv. 998 ; (6 Feb. 1847), v. 159.

[53] Labouchere to Russell, 8 Jan. 1847, Russell papers, P.R.O. 30/22/6.

[54] *A return showing the average daily number of persons employed on relief works in Ireland, during the week ending the 6 March 1847*, parl. papers, H.C. 1847 (185), liv. 23–4.

[55] *Economist* (30 Jan. 1847), v. 113–7 ; *Hansard*, lxxxix. 76–84.

[56] Bessborough to Russell, 8 Jan. 1847 ; Labouchere to Russell, 8 Jan. 1847, Russell papers, P.R.O. 30/22/6.

[57] *Freeman's Journal*, 6 Nov., 28 Dec. 1846, 11 Feb. 1847 ; *Dublin Evening Post*, 20 Oct., 10 Dec. 1846, 9 Jan. 1847.

[58] *First annual report of the commissioners for administering the laws for relief of the poor in Ireland*, parl. papers, 1847–8, (943) xxxiii. 377–580.

[59] *Hansard*, lxxxix. 76–84 ; Bessborough to Russell, 23 Jan. 1847, Russell papers, P.R.O. 30/22/6.

[60] *Fifth, sixth and seventh reports of the relief commissioners constituted under the act 10 Vict. c. 7, and correspondence connected therewith ; with appendix*, parl. papers, 1847–8 (876) xxix. 27–206.

iv.  THE IRISH PARTY

[1] *Nation*, 26 Sept. 1846.

[2] *Dublin Evening Post*, 26 Sept. 1846 ; *Nation*, 3 Oct. 1846.

[3] Ibid., 14 Nov., 26 Dec. 1846.

[4] John Mitchel to Smith O'Brien, 30 Dec. 1846, Smith O'Brien papers, vol. 437, no. 1747.

[5] Repeal Assoc. meeting, 7 Dec., *Nation*, 12 Dec. 1846

[6] *Dublin Evening Post*, 26 Sept. 1846 ; *Nation*, 10 Oct. 1846.

[7] *Dublin Evening Mail*, 16 Dec. 1846.

[8] Vesey Foster to Smith O'Brien, 14 Dec. 1846, Smith O'Brien papers, vol. 437, no. 1733.

[9] *Nation*, 19 Dec. 1846 ; Labouchere to Russell, 8 Jan. 1847, Russell papers, P.R.O. 30/22/6.

[10] *Nation*, 16 Jan. 1847.

[11] Ibid.

[12] *Freeman's Journal*, 1 May 1847 ; Bessborough to Russell, 16 Jan. 1847, Russell papers, P.R.O. 30/22/6.

[13] Gavan Duffy, *My life in two hemispheres*, i. 239 ; D. O'Connell to T. Ray, 13 Feb. 1847, Fitzpatrick, *Correspondence of Daniel O'Connell*, ii. 405–7.

[14] *Nation*, 16 Jan. 1847.

[15] Ibid. ; John Mitchel to Smith O'Brien, 30 Dec. 1846, Smith O'Brien papers, vol. 437, no. 1747.

[16] Russell to Bessborough, 29 Sept. 1846, Russell papers, P.R.O. 30/22/5.

[17] Russell to Bessborough, 30 Sept. 1846, Russell papers, P.R.O. 30/22/5.

[18] Labouchere to Russell, 25 Nov. 1846, Russell papers, P.R.O. 30/22/5.

[19] Bessborough to Russell, 3 Oct. 1846 ; Lansdowne to Russell, 15 Oct. 1846 ; Russell to Bessborough, 6 Nov. 1846, Russell papers, P.R.O. 30/22/5.

[20] Russell to Bessborough, 18, 27 Jan. 1847, Russell papers, P.R.O. 30/22/6 ; Russell to Bessborough, 11 Oct. 1846, Russell papers, P.R.O. 30/22/5.

[21] Infra p. 164 ; Russell to Bessborough, 11 Oct. 1846, Russell papers, P.R.O. 30/22/5.

[22] *Hansard*, lxxxix. 76–84. (The scheme to distribute food) '. . . is the least objectionable mode of relief which has been suggested. . . .' *Economist* (30 Jan. 1847), v. 113–17.

[23] *Return of all sums granted or advanced on account of the distress and famine . . . during the years 1846, 1847, 1848, and 1849, with amount of repayments*, parl. papers, H.C. 1849 (325), xlviii. 5–6.

[24] *Hansard*, lxxxix. 426–54.

[25] *Freeman's Journal*, 22 Jan. 1847 ; *Nation*, 30 Jan. 1847.

[26] *Hansard*, lxxxix. 101–9, 773–802.

[27] *Nation*, 13 Feb. 1847.

[28] *Dublin Evening Mail*, 8 Feb. 1847 ; *Nation*, 13 Feb. 1847.

[29] P. Smyth to Smith O'Brien, 11 Feb. 1847, Smith O'Brien papers, vol. 438, no. 1791 ; *Dublin Evening Mail*, 5 Feb. 1847.

[30] *Hansard*, xc.

[31] *Nation*, 13 Feb. 1847.

[32] *Hansard*, xc. 86–116.

[33] Ibid. lxxxix. 1216–8 ; 1211–3 ; 1220.

[34] Peel to Graham, 30 Dec. 1846, Graham papers ; Graham to Peel, 3 Jan. 1847, Peel papers, Add. MS 40 452, ff. 199–204 ; *Hansard*, lxxxix. 157–64 ; xc. 65–86.

[35] Ibid., xc. 123–6.

[36] *Nation*, 27 Feb. 1847.

[37] Ibid.

[38] *Dublin Evening Mail*, 1 Feb. 1847 ; *Hansard*, lxxxix. 631.

[39] *Nation*, 20 Feb. 1847 ; *Dublin Evening Mail*, 10 Feb. 1847.

[40] *Hansard*, lxxix. 631.

[41] Daniel O'Connell to T. Ray, 6 Feb. 1847, Fitzpatrick, *Corresp. of Daniel O'Connell*, ii. 401–2.

[42] *Nation*, 13 March 1847.

43 *Hansard*, xc. 1397–99 ; Irish Confed. meeting, 7 April, *Nation*, 10 April 1847 ; *Freeman's Journal*, 1 May 1847.

44 *Hansard*, lxxxix. 109–22, 473–5 ; xci. 171–5.

45 Ibid., 583–93.

46 For example see, D. Gwynn, *Young Ireland and 1848*, pp. 105–6.

47 *Freeman's Journal*, 1 May 1847 ; *Hansard*, xciii. 636–8, 632–3.

48 Ibid., xci. 1420–4 ; xcii. 213–98 ; xciii. 1019–44.

49 D. O'Connell to T. Ray, 6 Feb. 1847, Fitzpatrick, *Correspondence of Daniel O'Connell*, ii. 401–2 ; Bessborough to Russell, 24 Feb. 1847, Russell papers, P.R.O. 30/22/6.

50 *Nation*, 13 March 1847.

51 Labouchere to Russell, 13 Nov. 1846 ; Russell to Labouchere, 24 Nov. 1846, Russell papers, P.R.O. 30/22/5.

52 Russell to Bessborough, 26 Feb. 1847, ibid., 30/22/6.

53 *Nation*, 16 Jan. 1847.

54 Gavan Duffy, *Four years of Irish history*, p. 140.

55 *First annual report of the commissioners for administering the laws for relief of the poor in Ireland*, parl. papers, 1847–8 (963), xxxiii. 377–580.

56 *Returns of agricultural produce in Ireland in the year 1847 : part 11, stock*, parl. papers, 1847–8 (1000), lvii. 109–30.

57 *Nation*, 10 April 1847 ; Gavan Duffy, *Four Years of Irish history*, p. 137.

58 *Nation*, 17, 24 April 1847.

59 Ibid., 8 May 1847 ; *Freeman's Journal*, 5 May 1847.

60 *Nation*, 8 May, 24 April 1847.

61 Infra p. 173.

62 H. Goulburn to Peel, 24 Aug. 1847, Peel papers, Add. MS 40 445, ff. 404–6.

63 Halévy, *The age of Peel and Cobden*, pp. 155–61.

64 Richard O'Gorman to Smith O'Brien, 14 July 1847, Smith O'Brien papers, vol. 438, no. 1932 ; Goulburn to Peel, 24 Aug. 1847, Peel papers, Add. MS 40 445, ff. 404–6.

65 *Freeman's Journal*, 1 June 1847 ; *Nation*, 12 June 1847.

66 Ibid., 14, 28 Aug. 1847.

67 Repeal Assoc. meetings, 7, 21 June, *Nation*, 12, 26 June 1847

68 *Dublin Evening Mail*, 9 Aug. 1847 ; *Nation*, 4 Sept. 1847.

69 Ibid.

70 Gavan Duffy, *Four years of Irish history*, p. 148.

71 *Nation*, 4 Sept. 1847 ; McGee to Smith O'Brien, 1 Sept. 1847, Smith O'Brien papers, vol. 439, no. 1974.

72 *Freeman's Journal*, 1 June 1847.

### V.  TENANT-RIGHT AND REPEAL

1 *Hansard*, xciii. 632–3.

2 Ibid., lxxxv. 492–527.

3 Repeal Association meetings, 15, 22 June, *Nation*, 20, 27 June 1846 ; *Evidence taken before H.M.'s commissioners of inquiry into the state of the law and practice in respect to the occupation of land in Ireland, part III*, parl. papers, 1845 (657), xxi. 939–48.

[4] *Nation*, 14 Nov., 26 Dec. 1846.

[5] John Mitchel to Smith O'Brien, 30 Dec. 1846, Smith O'Brien papers, vol. 437, no. 1747.

[6] T. W. Rolleston, *Prose writings of Thomas Davis*, pp. 73–5 ; *Nation*, 25 April 1846, 6 March 1847.

[7] *Freeman's Journal*, 22 July 1847 ; *Hansard*, xciii. 632–3.

[8] *Northern Whig*, 2 March, 1847 ; *Hansard*, xcix. 974–6 ; *Evidence . . . part 1* (Devon commission), parl. papers, 1845 (606), xix. pp. 735–6, 738–9, 889.

[9] *Nation*, 6, 27 Feb. 1847, Trenwith to J. Fintan Lalor, 5 May 1847, Lalor papers, N. Lib. Ir. MS 340.

[10] *Northern Whig*, 2 March 1847 ; *Nation*, 10 April 1847 ; Gavan Duffy, *My life in two hemispheres*, i. 203.

[11] *Nation*, 31 July, 20 Aug. 1847.

[12] Ibid., 12 June 1847 ; *Abstract of all notices served upon relieving officers of poor law districts in Ireland by landowners and others under the act 11 & 12 Vict.,* parl. papers, H.C. 1849 (517), xlix. 279–314.

[13] Lalor papers, N. Lib. Ir. MS 340.

[14] Gavan Duffy, *Four years of Irish history*, p. 167.

[15] Ibid., pp. 167–8.

[16] Gavan Duffy to Fintan Lalor (Jan. 1847), Lalor papers, N. Lib. Ir. MS 340 ; Gavan Duffy to Fintan Lalor, 24 Feb. (1847), ibid.

[17] McGee to Fintan Lalor, 20 March 1847, ibid.

[18] Fogarty, *James Fintan Lalor*, pp. 7–25 (texts of the *Nation* letters).

[19] Ibid.

[20] D'Arcy McGee to Fintan Lalor, 20 March 1847, Lalor papers, N. Lib. Ir. MS 340 ; Fintan Lalor to Gavan Duffy, 11 Jan. 1847, ibid ; Fintan Lalor to John Mitchel, 21 June 1847, Fogarty, *James Fintan Lalor*, pp. 1–6, 42–6.

[21] John Mitchel to Smith O'Brien, 8 Sept. 1847, Smith O'Brien papers, vol. 439, no. 1893 ; Michael Doheny to Smith O'Brien, 7 Sept. 1847, ibid., no. 1980.

[22] *Nation*, 30 Oct. 1847.

[23] Ibid., 20 Nov. 1847.

[24] Ibid., 11, 16 Sept. 1847.

[25] *Freeman's Journal*, 2 June 1847.

[26] Infra, p. 174.

[27] Goulburn to Peel, 24 Aug. 1847, Peel papers, Add. MS 40 445, ff. 404–6.

[28] *Dublin Evening Post*, 9 Nov. 1847.

[29] *The Times*, 15 Oct. 1847 ; Memorial of the Catholic hierarchy to the lord lieutenant, 21 Oct. 1847, *Nation*, 30 Oct. 1847.

[30] Lalor to Mitchel, 21 June 1847, Fogarty, *James Fintan Lalor*, pp. 42–6 ; Mitchel to Smith O'Brien, 8 Aug. 1847, Smith O'Brien papers, vol. 439, no. 1956.

[31] Mitchel to Smith O'Brien, 8 Aug. 1847, Smith O'Brien papers, vol. 439, no. 1956.

[32] Gavan Duffy to Smith O'Brien (Sept. 1847), ibid., vol. 439, no. 2232.

[33] *Nation*, 30 Oct. 1847.

[34] O'Connell's 'national council' met on 2 November, the other sponsored by the Irish council, on 4 November, *Freeman's Journal*, 6, 18 Nov. 1847.

[35] Henry Grattan to Smith O'Brien, 16 Sept. 1847, Smith O'Brien papers, vol. 439, no. 1994 ; William Fagan, M.P., to John O'Connell, 8 Sept. 1847, *Nation*, 18 Sept. 1847.

[36] *Nation,* 6 Nov. 1847.

[37] *Freeman's Journal,* 4 Nov. 1847.

[38] *Nation,* 6 Nov. 1847.

[39] Ibid.

[40] Ibid.

[41] Gavan Duffy, *Four years of Irish history,* p. 153 ; John Mitchel to Gavan Duffy, 7 Jan. 1848, *Nation,* 8 Jan. 1848.

[42] Ibid., 20 Nov. 1847.

[43] McGee to Smith O'Brien, 7 Sept. 1847, Smith O'Brien papers, vol. 439, no 1985 ; J. Mitchel to Smith O'Brien, 30 Sept. 1847, Gavan Duffy, *Four years of Irish history,* p. 173.

[44] *Nation,* 13 Nov. 1847 ; Gavan Duffy, *My life in two hemispheres,* i. 240–1.

[45] *Nation,* 13 Nov. 1847.

[46] Mitchel to Smith O'Brien, 30 Sept. 1847, Gavan Duffy, *Four years of Irish history,* p. 173.

[47] McGee to Smith O'Brien, 1 Sept. 1847, Smith O'Brien papers, vol. 439, no. 1974 ; Gavan Duffy to Smith O'Brien, (late 1847), ibid., vol. 441, no. 2244.

[48] Doheny, *The felon's track,* pp. 120–6 ; R.I.A. MS 23 H 44 (Minute book of the Irish Confederation).

[49] Gavan Duffy, *Four years of Irish history,* p. 175.

## vi.  KINDNESS AND COERCION

[1] *Account of public monies expended or advanced by way of loan in the years 1845, 1846, 1847 and 1848 for the relief of distress in Ireland,* parl. papers, H.C. 1847–8 (723), liv. 5–26 ; *Return of all sums of money granted or advanced on account of the distress and famine, or in aid of the administration of the poor law in Ireland during the years 1846, 1847, 1848 and 1849 with amount of repayments,* parl. papers, H.C. 1849 (352), xlviii. 5–6.

[2] *Dublin Evening Post,* 18 Sept. 1847.

[3] *Tables showing the number of criminal offenders committed for trial or bailed . . . in the year 1848, and the result of the proceedings,* parl. papers, 1848 (1067), xliv. 129–228.

[4] Returns of military parties furnished in aid of the civil power, Kilmainham papers, vol. 226.

[5] W. Stanley (Sec. Poor Law Commissioners) to Rev. T. Costello (of Castlebar), 18 Dec. 1847, *Dublin Evening Post,* 6 Jan. 1848.

[6] *Abstract of all notices served upon relieving officers of poor law districts in Ireland by landowners and others . . . ,* parl. papers, H.C. 1849 (517), xlix. 279–314 ; Bernard O'Reilly, *John MacHale, archbishop of Tuam, his life, times and correspondence,* ii. 26.

[7] Irish Council, 28 Sept., *Nation,* 2 Oct. 1847 ; *The Times,* 11 Oct. 1847 ; Irish Confed., 20 Oct., *Nation,* 23 Oct. 1847.

[8] Irish Confed., 26 Aug., *Nation,* 28 Aug. 1847.

[9] Irish Confed., 16 Sept., *Nation,* 18 Sept. 1847.

[10] Ibid., 8 Jan. 1848.

[11] Ibid., 9 Oct. 1847.

[12] John Mitchel, *An apology for the British government in Ireland.*

[13] Repeal Assoc. meeting, 27 Sept., *Freeman's Journal,* 28 Sept. 1847.

[14] Memorial of the Catholic hierarchy to the lord lieutenant of Ireland, 21 Oct. 1847, *Nation*, 30 Oct. 1847.

[15] *The Times*, 15 Oct. 1847 ; *Hansard*, xcv. 279–312.

[16] *Evidence . . . part I* (Devon commission), parl. papers, 1845 (606), xix.

[17] Russell to Clarendon, 10 Nov. 1847, Russell papers, P.R.O. 30/22/6. See also, Walpole, *The life of Lord John Russell*, i. 462–4.

[18] *Freeman's Journal*, 22, 24 Nov. 1847 ; *Evidence . . . part I* (Devon commission), parl. papers, 1845 (606), xix.

[19] *Hansard*, xcvi. 673–700.

[20] Clarendon to Henry Reeve, 18 Sept. 1847, Clarendon papers, letter-book II, See also H. E. Maxwell, *The life and letters of George William, fourth earl of Clarendon*, i. 280.

[21] C. Wood to Clarendon, 23 July 1847, Clarendon papers, box 9, bundle 42 ; Clarendon to Russell, 10 Aug, 1847, ibid., letter-book I.

[22] Clarendon to Russell, 10 Aug. 1847, ibid., letter-book I.

[23] Clarendon to Russell, 1 Oct. 1847, ibid., letter-book I ; Clarendon to Russell, 13 Oct. 1847, ibid., letter-book I ; MacHale to Clarendon, 9 Dec. 1847, B. O'Reilly, op. cit., ii. 34–6.

[24] Clarendon to Russell, 12 Nov. 1847, Clarendon papers, letter-book I.

[25] Clarendon to Russell, 10 Nov. 1847, ibid., letter-book I.

[26] Clarendon to Russell, 12 Nov. 1847, ibid., letter-book I.

[27] Russell to Clarendon, 10 Nov. 1847, Russell papers, P.R.O. 30/22/6 ; Clarendon to Russell, 18 Nov. 1847, ibid.

[28] *Hansard*, xiv. 270–312.

[29] Ibid., xcv. 342–3, 347–55 ; *The Times*, 1 Dec. 1847 ; Clarendon to Russell, 30 Nov. 1847, Clarendon papers, letter-book I.

[30] *Hansard*, xcv. 11–4.

[31] Sir John Clapham, *The bank of England, a history*, ii. 197–9 ; Redcliffe N. Salaman, *The history and social influence of the potato*, pp. 298–9 ; Halévy, *The age of Peel and Cobden*, pp. 170–82.

[32] *Hansard*, xcv. 312–7, 701–13, 328–34, 341–2, 976–9.

[33] *Nation*, 4 Sept. 1847.

[34] *Hansard*, xcv. 355–6.

[35] Ibid., 976–9.

[36] Mark Hovell, *The chartist movement*, pp. 95, 163.

[37] *Hansard*, xcv. 317–21.

[38] Hovell, op. cit., p. 283.

[39] *Hansard*, xcv. 317–21, 728–38.

[40] Ibid., 752–65.

[41] *Nation*, 11 Dec. 1847 ; *Hansard*, xcv. 769–774.

[42] Ibid., 752–65, 766–8, 769–74.

[43] Ibid., 797–8.

[44] *Nation*, 8 Jan. 1848.

[45] Doheny, *The felon's track*, pp. 120–6 ; McGee to Smith O'Brien, 30 Dec. 1847, Smith O'Brien papers, vol. 439, no. 2040.

[46] *Nation*, 4 Dec. 1847, 8 Jan. 1848.

[47] R. O'Gorman to Smith O'Brien, 14 Dec. 1847, Smith O'Brien papers, vol. 439, no. 2033 ; Minute book of the Irish Confederation, R.I.A. MS 23 H 44.

[48] R. O'Gorman to Smith O'Brien, 3 Dec. 1847, Smith O'Brien papers, vol. 439, no. 2030 ; Gavan Duffy to Smith O'Brien, (late 1847), ibid., vol. 441, no. 2232 ; T. F. Meagher to Smith O'Brien, (late 1847), ibid., no. 2298.

[49] R. O'Gorman to Smith O'Brien, 14 Dec. 1847, ibid., vol. 439, no. 2033 ; McGee to Smith O'Brien, 30 Dec. 1847, ibid., no. 2040.

[50] *Nation,* 5 Feb. 1848.

[51] *Nation,* 5 Feb. 1848.

[52] McGee to Smith O'Brien, 30 Dec. 1847, Smith O'Brien papers, vol. 439, no. 2040 ; Mitchel to Fintan Lalor, 4 Jan. 1848, Fogarty, *James Fintan Lalor,* pp. 120–2.

[53] Irish Confed., 12 Jan., *Nation,* 15 Jan. 1848.

[54] Ibid., 8 Jan. 1848.

[55] Ibid., 8 Jan. 1848 ; Gavan Duffy, *Four years of Irish history,* p. 175 ; Irish Confed., 2 Feb., *Nation,* 5 Feb. 1848.

[56] Irish Confed., 4 Feb. 1848, *Nation,* 12 Feb. 1848 ; B. O'Reilly, *John MacHale, archbishop of Tuam, his life, times and corresp.,* ii. 26.

[57] *Account of the quantities of wheat, barley, oats, etc., imported into Great Britain from Ireland, in each month of the year 1846,* parl. papers, H.C. 1847 (32), lix. 493–4. See also H.C. 1847 (727), lix. 25–6.

## vii. THE MONTHS OF REVOLUTION

[1] Mitchel to Acting Sec., Irish Confederation, 7 Feb. 1848, *United Irishman,* 12 Feb. 1848.

[2] W. J. O'Neill Daunt to Smith O'Brien, 5 Jan. 1848, Smith O'Brien papers, vol. 441, no. 2348.

[3] John F. Broderick, *The Holy See and the Irish movement for the repeal of the union with England, 1829–1847,* passim.

[4] Halévy, *The age of Peel and Cobden,* pp. 194–6 ; *supra* p. 179 ; Clarendon to Russell, 1 Oct. 1847, Clarendon papers, letter-book I.

[5] *The Times,* 9 Dec. 1847 ; *Hansard,* xcv. 675–96 ; Clarendon to Russell, 17 Nov. 1847, Russell papers, P.R.O. 30/22/6.

[6] Clarendon to Russell, 25 Nov. 1847, Clarendon papers, letter-book I, also in Russell papers, P.R.O. 30/22/6.

[7] *Dublin Evening Post,* 5 Feb. 1848.

[8] B. O'Reilly, op. cit., 109–15.

[9] *Freeman's Journal,* 3 Jan. 1848.

[10] Petre to Palmerston, 5 Dec. 1847, F.O. papers, 43/40 ; Minto to Russell, 2 Jan. 1848, Russell papers, P.R.O. 30/22/7.

[11] Clarendon to Palmerston, 23 Jan. 1848, Clarendon papers, letter-book II.

[12] Clarendon to Minto, 9 Feb. 1848, ibid., letter-book II.

[13] Sir G. Grey to Clarendon, 23 Nov. 1847, ibid., Ireland, box 4, bundle 21 ; Clarendon to Russell, 30 Nov. 1847, ibid., letter-book I.

[14] Repeal Assoc. meeting, 17 Jan., *Freeman's Journal,* 18 Jan. 1848.

[15] O'Neill Daunt to Smith O'Brien, 14 Jan. 1848, Smith O'Brien papers, vol. 441, no. 2352 ; *Nation,* 22 Jan. 1848.

[16] John B. Dillon to Smith O'Brien, 3 Jan. 1848, Smith O'Brien papers, vol. 441, no. 2347.

[17] John O'Connell to the people of Ireland, 21 Jan. 1848, *Dublin Evening Post*, 27 Jan. 1848.

[18] *Freeman's Journal*, 10 Jan. 1848 ; Repeal Assoc. meeting, 17 Jan., *Freeman's Journal*, 18 Jan. 1848.

[19] Pouthas, *Democraties et capitalisme*, pp. 69–79 ; Seignobos, *La revolution de 1848, le second empire, 1848–1859*, pp. 285–6.

[20] *Nation*, 4 March 1848 ; *Freeman's Journal*, 11 March 1848.

[21] Halévy, op. cit., pp. 2–6.

[22] Seignobos, op. cit., p. 282 ; Lord Palmerston to earl of Clarendon, 9 March 1848, Ashley, *The life and correspondence of Henry John Temple, Viscount Palmerston*, ii. 74–5.

[23] J. O'Connell to Ledru Rollin, 29 Feb. 1848, *Freeman's Journal*, 7 March 1848.

[24] Smith O'Brien to Cloncurry, 29 Feb. 1848, *Nation*, 11 March 1848.

[25] Ibid., 4, 11 March 1848.

[26] *Pilot*, 1 March 1848 ; *Nation*, 4 March 1848.

[27] *Freeman's Journal*, 1 March 1848 ; *Nation*, 11 March 1848 ; Lord Normanby, *A year of revolution*, i. 171.

[28] *Freeman's Journal*, 8 March 1848.

[29] Ibid.

[30] Michael Doheny, *The felon's track*, p. 127.

[31] *Nation*, 25 March 1848.

[32] *Dublin EveningMail*, 8 March 1848 ; Clarendon to Sir G. Grey, 20 March 1848, Clarendon papers, letter-book II.

[33] *Nation*, 25 March 1848.

[34] Ibid., 11, 18 March 1848.

[35] Ibid., 25 March 1848.

[36] Gavan Duffy to Smith O'Brien, (March 1848), Smith O'Brien papers, vol. 441, no. 2255.

[37] *Nation*, 25 March 1848 ; Smith O'Brien to Gavan Duffy, 24 March 1848, Gavan Duffy, *Four years of Irish history*, p. 202.

[38] *Nation*, 25 March 1848.

[39] Memorandum by Sir Charles Wood, 31 March 1848, Gooch, *Later corresp. of Lord John Russell*, i. 225–6. See also, Russell papers, P.R.O. 30/22/7.

[40] Military reports, 4 March, 5 April 1848, Kilmainham papers, vol. 238, pp. 133, 140.

[41] Seignobos, op. cit., p. 282 ; Halévy, *The age of Peel and Cobden*, pp. 182–98.

[42] Palmerston to Lord Normanby (British ambassador, Paris), 26 Feb. 1848, Ashley, *The life and correspondence of Henry John Temple, Viscount Palmerston*, ii. 71. Normanby to Palmerston, 2 March 1848, F.O. papers, 27/804.

[43] Normanby, *A year of revolution*, i. 226 ; ' Identified ' instead of ' identical ' in Normanby to Palmerston, 18 March 1848, F.O. papers 27/805.

[44] *Moniteur Universel*, 18 March 1848 ; *The Times*, 20 March 1848.

[45] Normanby, op. cit., i. 243–6.

[46] *Moniteur Universel*, 19 March 1848.

[47] Palmerston to Normanby, 21 March 1848, Correspondence, Archives des Affairs Etrangers (Paris), vol. 669, no. 116.

[48] Normanby, op. cit., i. 250–4, 272–4 ; Normanby to Palmerston, 23 March 1848, F.O. papers 27/805.

[49] Normanby, op. cit., i. 276–7.

[50] *Moniteur Universel,* 4 April 1848.

[51] Palmerston to Normanby, 6 April 1848, F.O. papers 27/806.

[52] Gavan Duffy, *Young Ireland,* i. 148–54 ; Ledru Rollin to Smith O'Brien, 30 March 1848, Smith O'Brien papers, vol. 442, no 2406 ; Normanby, op. cit., i. 286.

[53] *Freeman's Journal,* 8 April 1848.

[54] Irish Confed. meeting, 5 April, *Nation,* 8 April 1848.

[55] *United Irishman,* 8 April 1848.

[56] *Hansard,* xcvii. 1205–7.

[57] Repeal Assoc. meeting, 10 April, *Freeman's Journal,* 11 April 1848 ; *Nation,* 22 April 1848.

[58] Ibid., 29 April 1848.

[59] Mitchel to Smith O'Brien, 5 May 1848, Smith O'Brien papers, vol. 442, no. 2445 ; *Nation,* 8, 22 April 1848.

[60] Gavan Duffy, *Four years of Irish history,* pp. 208–9.

[61] Clarendon to Henry Reeve, 21 Jan. 1848, Laughton, *Memoirs of the life and correspondence of Henry Reeve,* i. 192–5.

[62] Clarendon to Russell, 2 March 1848, Clarendon papers, letter-book II.

[63] Grey to Clarendon, 8 March 1848, ibid., box 5, bundle 21.

[64] Clarendon to Grey, 12 March 1848, ibid., letter-book II.

[65] Grey to Clarendon, 18 March 1848, ibid., box 5, bundle 1 ; Clarendon to Grey, 20 March 1848, ibid., letter-book II.

[66] Clarendon to Russell, 25 March 1848, ibid.

[67] Clarendon to Russell, 30 March 1848, Russell papers, P.R.O. 30/22/7.

[68] Clarendon to Russell, 31 March 1848, Clarendon papers, letter-book II.

[69] Grey to Clarendon, 27 March 1848, ibid., box 5, bundle 21.

[70] Clarendon to Russell, 31 March 1848, ibid., letter-book II ; Grey to Clarendon, 3 April 1848, ibid., box 5, bundle 21.

[71] Memorandum, 30 March 1848, Russell papers, P.R.O. 30/22/7 ; Walpole, *Life of Lord John Russell,* ii. 64–5.

[72] Memorandum by Earl Grey, 30 March 1848, Russell papers, P.R.O. 30/22/7 ; Memorandum by Sir Charles Wood, 31 March 1848, Gooch, *Later correspondence of Lord John Russell,* i. 225–6, Russell papers, P.R.O. 30/22/7 ; Memorandum by Lord Palmerston, 31 March 1848, Gooch, op. cit., 223–5, Russell papers, P.R.O. 30/22/7 ; Memorandum by Lord Lansdowne, 30 March 1848, Gooch, op. cit., 223, Russell papers, P.R.O. 30/22/7.

[73] *Hansard,* xcvii. 1205–7 ; Lord John Campbell to Russell, (April 1848), Russell papers, P.R.O. 30/22/7 ; Gooch, op. cit., i. 227–8.

[74] *Hansard,* xcviii. 20–34.

[75] Clarendon to Russell, 8 April 1848, Clarendon papers, letter-book II.

[76] Clarendon to Grey, (12) April 1848, ibid., letter-book II ; Grey to Clarendon, 17 April 1848, ibid., box 5, bundle 21.

[77] *Hansard,* xcviii. 73–80.

[78] Ibid., 34–7, 119, 92–6, 383–5, 463–70.

[79] Ibid., 537.

[80] *Freeman's Journal,* 13 April 1848 ; *Nation,* 29 April 1848 ; Clarendon to Grey, 28 April 1848, Clarendon papers, letter-book II.

[81] J. O'Connell to Russell, 4 April 1848, Russell papers, P.R.O. 30/22/7 ; *Nation*, 15 April 1848.

[82] *United Irishman*, 6 May 1848 ; Gavan Duffy, *Four years of Irish history*, p. 211.

[83] *Nation*, 6 May 1848 ; *United Irishman*, 6 May 1848.

[84] Clarendon to Russell, 2 May 1848, Clarendon papers, letter-book II ; Clarendon to Henry Reeve, 10 May 1848, Laughton, *Memoirs of the life and correspondence of Henry Reeve*, i. 200–1.

[85] Clarendon to Grey, (10–11) May 1848, Clarendon papers, letter-book II.

[86] Grey to Clarendon, 16 May 1848, ibid., box 5, bundle 21 ; Clarendon to Russell, 23 May 1848, ibid., letter-book II.

[87] *United Irishman*, 29 April, 6 May 1848.

[88] *Nation*, 27 May 1848.

[89] Gavan Duffy, *Four years of Irish history*, pp. 212–3.

[90] John Mitchel, *Jail journal, or five years in British prisons*.

[91] *United Irishman*, 11 March, 8 April 1848.

[92] Repeal Assoc., 29 May, *Freeman's Journal*, 30 May 1848.

[93] Sir Colman O'Loghlen to Smith O'Brien, 4 June 1848, Smith O'Brien papers, vol. 442, no. 2465.

[94] Irish Confederation, 6 June, *Nation*, 10 June 1848.

[95] *Freeman's Journal*, 12 June 1848.

[96] John O'Connell to the people of Ireland, 23 June 1848, *Nation*, 24 June 1848.

[97] Sir Colman O'Loghlen to Smith O'Brien, 11 June 1848, Smith O'Brien papers, vol. 442, no. 2472.

[98] *Freeman's Journal*, 13 June 1848.

[99] Sir Colman O'Loghlen to Smith O'Brien, 11 June 1848, Smith O'Brien papers, vol. 442, no. 2472 ; *Nation*, 24 June, 1848.

[100] John O'Connell to the people of Ireland, 23 June 1848, *Nation*, 24 June 1848.

[101] *Irish Felon*, 24 June 1848 ; *Nation*, 8, 15 July 1848.

[102] Gavan Duffy, *Four years of Irish history*, pp. 217–8.

[103] Doheny, *The felon's track*, p. 152 ; Fogarty, *James Fintan Lalor*, pp. 92–6.

[104] Grey to Clarendon, 1 June 1848, Clarendon papers, box 5, bundle 21.

[105] Clarendon to Russell, 4 June 1848, ibid., letter-book II ; Clarendon to Russell, 15 June 1848, ibid., letter-book III.

[106] Clarendon to Grey, 18 July 1848, ibid., letter-book III.

[107] Grey to Clarendon, 6 July 1848 ; Grey to Clarendon, 21 July 1848, ibid., box 5, bundle 21.

[108] S.P.O. Ir., Outrage papers, cartons 1514, 6/947 ; 1514, 6/961 ; Grey to Clarendon, 17 July 1848, Clarendon papers, box 5, bundle 21.

[109] *Hansard*, c. 696–713.

[110] Ibid., c. 743.

[111] *Nation*, 29 July 1848.

[112] Gavan Duffy, *Four years of Irish history*, pp. 229–30.

CHAPTER IV

# THE ORGANISATION AND ADMINISTRATION OF RELIEF, 1845–52

## i. INTRODUCTION

[1] *Hansard*, 3 series, lxxxiii. 1070.  The fact that more than 3,000,000 persons received rations from local committees in the summer of 1847 is evidence of the numbers depending on the potato crop.

[2] See my article, ' The scientific investigation of the failure of the potato crop in Ireland, 1845–6 ', in *Ir. Hist. St.*, v. 123–38 (Sept. 1946).

[3] J. O'Rourke, *History of the great Irish famine*, pp. 53–9.

[4] *Freeman's Journal*, 4 Nov. 1845.

[5] C. S. Parker, *Sir Robert Peel*, iii. 223.

[6]*Memoirs by . . . Peel*, ii. 188 ;  *Dublin Evening Post*, 16 Sept. 1845.

[7] Ibid., 4 Nov. 1845 ; *Freeman's Journal*, 31 Oct. 1845 ; *Nenagh Guardian*, 29 Oct. 1845 ; P.R.O.I., Relief Commission papers, C.S.O. papers, 1845, passim (1A.50.77).

[8] *Dublin Evening Post*, 1 Nov. 1845.

[9]*Memoirs by . . . Peel*, ii. 134.

[10] *Dublin Evening Post*, 8 Nov. 1845.

## ii. SIR ROBERT PEEL'S RELIEF SCHEME, 1845–6

[1] State Paper Office, Dublin Castle (hereafter S.P.O.), Reg. paper 1846, Z8804 ; *Hansard*, 3 series, lxxxiii. 727.

[2] *Correspondence explanatory of the measures adopted for the relief of distress*, p. 16 (H.C. 1846 (735), xxxvii (hereafter *Corr. explan. of measures adopted*)).

[3] B.M., Add. MS 40452 f. 9, Peel to Graham (Nov. 1845).

[4] Trevelyan, *Irish crisis*, p. 104 ;  *Corr. explan. of measures adopted*, pp. 131, 218 ; P.R.O.I., 1A.50.86, Relief commission papers.

[5] *Corr. explan. of measures adopted*, p. 2 ; Parker, *Life and Letters of Sir James Graham*, ii. 26.

[6] *Cork Constitution*, 5 Feb. 1846 ; Trevelyan, *Irish crisis*, p. 46 ;  *Corr. explan. of measures adopted*, pp. 1–3, 7, 20–21.

[7] Ibid., pp. 1, 15.

[8] *The Times*, 23 Jan. 1846.

[9] *Corr. explan. of measures adopted*, p. 14.

[10] Parker, *Correspondence of Sir Robert Peel*, iii. 469.

[11] Parker, *Life and Letters of Sir James Graham*, ii. 38–9.

[12] P.R.O.I., Relief commission papers, minutes, 1846.

[13] *Corr. explan. of measures adopted*, pp. 100, 103 ; *Dublin Evening Post*, 5 Mar. 1846.

[14] *Hansard*, 3 series, lxxxv. 713.

[15] *Dublin Evening Post*, 31 Mar. 1846 ; *Illustrated London News*, 4 Apr. 1846 ; *Corr. explan. of measures adopted*, p. 219.

[16] Ibid., pp. 233–4.

[17] Ibid., pp. 118–9, 221.

[18] Ibid., pp. 30, 54, 72, 86 ; *Limerick Chronicle*, 22 July 1846.

[19] S.P.O., C.S.O. 2nd division, minutes, Nov. 1845, pp. 37–8.

[20] Trevelyan, *Irish crisis*, p. 24.

[21] S.P.O., Reg. papers, 1846, Z19420, Report on relief schemes in Munster by John Ball, pp. 5–8.

[22] *Corr. explan. of measures adopted*, p. 230 ; S.P.O., Reg. papers, 1846, Z19420, pp. 8–11 ; *Dublin Evening Post*, 4 Apr. 1846.

[23] *Corr. explan. of measures adopted*, pp. 40–1, 235–47 ; S.P.O., Reg. papers, 1846, Z14142.

[24] *Corr. explan. of measures adopted*, pp. 16, 17, 231 ; S.P.O., Reg. papers, 1846, Z19420, pp. 57, 58, 63.

[25] Ibid., p. 65–6 ; *Nenagh Guardian*, 2 May, 11 July 1846 ; *Cork Constitution*, 23 May 1846.

[26] *Corr. explan. of measures adopted*, p. 100.

[27] Ibid., pp. 4, 291 ; ' Eight Seven ', *The evils of monopoly and its remedy*, p. 3 ; *Nenagh Guardian*, 19 Nov. 1845 ; *Dublin Evening Post*, 29 Aug. 1846 ; W. N. Hancock, *Three lectures*, pp. 26–7.

[28] 9 Vic. c. 1–4.

[29] S.P.O., Reg. papers, 1846, W9014 ; P.R.O.I. IA.50.82 ; *County of Cork, extraordinary presentment sessions . . .* (1846), p. 7 ; *Corr. explan. of measures adopted*, p. 41.

[30] Ibid., pp. 4, 291 ; S.P.O., Reg. papers, 1846, Z19420, pp. 20–22, and Z14412 ; P.R.O.I., 1A.50.84, Extracts from minutes, 11–12.

[31] S.P.O., Reg. papers, 1846, W11041 (enclosure), W13664, and W13942 ; *Connaught Ranger*, 12 Aug. 1846 ; W. H. Smith, *A twelve months residence in Ireland*, p. 62 ; *Corr. explan. of measures adopted*, p. 360.

[32] Ibid., p. 344 ; *Board of Works corr.*, i. 76, 79 (H.C. 1847 (764) l).

[33] *Corr. explan. of measures adopted*, p. 342.

[34] Ibid., pp. 270, 340 ; *Board of Works corr.*, i. 62, 74 ; N.L.I., MSS, Monteagle correspondence, Wood to Monteagle, 10 and C.30, Sept. 1846, Monteagle to Wood, 14 Sept. 1846.

[35] *Corr. explan. of measures adopted*, p. 249.

[36] *Dublin University Magazine*, xxix. 503 (Apr. 1847).

[37] Trevelyan, *Irish crisis*, p. 49 ; *The Times*, 7 Jan. 1847 ; *Cork Constitution*, 16 July 1846 ; *Dublin Evening Mail*, 26 Mar. 1847 ; *Nation*, 15 Aug. 1846.

[38] 5 Apr. 1847.

## iii. RELIEF BY PUBLIC WORKS, 1846–7

[1] *Corr. explan. of measures adopted*, p. 208.

[2] *Hansard*, 3 series, lxxxviii. 773.

[3] N.L.I., MSS, Monteagle correspondence, Memorandum of C. E. Trevelyan, 1 Aug. 1846.

[4] *Hansard*, 3 series, lxxxviii. 766–78.

[5] *Hansard*, 3 series, lxxxviii. 776.

[6] Ibid., cols. 778–9.

[7] *Freeman's Journal*, 22 Sept. 1846 ; N.L.I., MS 3143, Repeal Association papers, O'Connell to Ray, 17 Sept. 1846.

[8] *Hansard*, 3 series, lxxxviii. 776 ; Trevelyan memorandum, pp. 11–12.

[9] *Commissariat corr.* i. 208, 403, 430.

[10] Ibid., pp. 408–9.

[11] Ibid., p. 381.

[12] *Corr. explan. of measures adopted,* p. 215.

[13] *Commissariat corr.* i. 104.

[14] Ibid., 97.

[15] Ibid., 106.

[16] Ibid., 10–11.

[17] Ibid., 108.

[18] Ibid., p. 420.

[19] Ibid., p. 337.

[20] Ibid., p. 425.

[21] Ibid., pp. 37, 41, 50, 472.

[22] Ibid., pp. 481, 506–7.

[23] Ibid., pp. 247–9.

[24] Gooch, *Later correspondence of Lord John Russell,* i. 147.

[25] *Commissariat corr.* i. 490–2.

[26] *Cork Constitution,* 13, 17 Oct. 1846.

[27] N.L.I., MSS, Monteagle correspondence, Monteagle to Bessborough, 1 Oct. 1846 ; *Freeman's Journal,* 19 Oct. 1846.

[28] *Commissariat corr.* i. 378, 393, 450, 492.

[29] Ibid., ii. 225.

[30] Ibid., i. 247–8, 492.

[31] Ibid., pp. 247–8.

[32] Ibid. pp. 482–90 ; ii. 2–5, 14.

[33] N.L.I., MSS, Monteagle correspondence, Memorandum of C. E. Trevelyan, 1 Aug. 1846.

[34] *Board of Works corr.* i. 9 (H.C. 1847 (764), l.).

[35] *Board of Works corr.* i. 7–9 ; S.P.O., Distress papers, 1846, D5455.

[36] Ibid., D5552, D7032 ; ibid., Reg. papers, 1846, W16266 ; P.R.O.I., Relief commission papers, inspecting officers' reports, 1A.50.64 ; *Transactions of the Central Relief Committee of the Society of Friends,* pp. 154, 180 ; *Board of Works corr.,* ii. 24.

[37] Ibid., i. 219–21, 269, ii. 2 ; S.P.O., Reg. papers, 1846, W19092 ; ibid., 1847, H1198 ; ibid., Distress papers, 1846, D8482 ; *Transactions of the Central Relief Committee of the Society of Friends,* p. 154 ; *Freeman's Journal,* 27 Oct. 1846 ; *Cork Examiner,* 20 Nov. 1846.

[38] *Freeman's Journal,* 21 Nov. 1846 ; *Nation,* 30 Jan. 1847 ; *Board of Works corr.,* i. 268–9.

[39] Ibid., i. 74, 88, ii. 25, 189 ; John Hamilton, *A word from an Irish landowner,* p. 14 ; P.R.O.I., Relief commission papers, inspecting officers' reports (Douglas), 11 Dec. 1846, 8 Feb. 1847, 1A.50.64 ; *Transactions of the Central Relief Committee of the Society of Friends,* p. 161 ; *Cork Constitution,* 17 Dec. 1846 ; *Freeman's Journal,* 21 Jan. 1847.

[40] *Board of Works corr.,* i. 85 ; N.L.I., MSS, Monteagle correspondence, Devon to S. E. Spring Rice, Sept. 1846 ; Trevelyan to same, 9 Sept. 1846 ; Bessborough to Monteagle, 25, 30 Sept. 1846.

[41] *Board of Works corr.,* i. 101, 189–90, 370–3, 506–12 ; *Freeman's Journal,* 7 Oct. 1846 ; S.P.O., Reg. papers, 1846, W17246 ; ibid., Distress papers, 1846, D8647, D9301.

[42] N.L.I., MSS, Monteagle correspondence, Charles Wood to Monteagle, 10, 19 Oct. 1846 ; Bessborough to same, 19 Oct. 1846.

[43] *Board of Works corr.,* i. 27–47, 163–4 ; S.P.O., Distress papers, 1846, D6759 ; ibid., 1847, D2714 ; ibid., Reg. papers, 1846, W18312 ; *Hansard,* 3 series, lxxxix. 773 *et seq.,* xc. 122 ; 16 Rept. Board of Works, p. 25 ; P.R.O.I., Relief commission papers, No. 11997, 1A.50.71.

[44] Trevelyan, *Irish crisis*, pp. 58–65 ; S.P.O., Reg. papers, 1846, W19824, W21018, W21246, W23278 ; N.L.I., MS 5533, National Board minutes, 7 Jan., 6, 28 May 1847 (I am indebted to Mr. T. Ó Raifeartaigh, M.A., for this information).

[45] Dec. 1846, Jan. 1847.

[46] *Central Relief Committee of the Society of Friends, Extracts from correspondence*, i. 21.

[47] Ibid., ii. 7.

[48] Ibid., ii. 11.

[49] *Transaction of the Central Relief Committee of the Society of Friends*, p. 153 ; *Commissariat corr.*, i. 504 ; *Freeman's Journal*, 18, 21, 23 Jan., 16 Feb. 1847 ; *Warder*, 23 Jan. 1847 ; *Nation*, 13 Feb. 1847.

[50] *Rept. of the Board of Works . . . for March, April and May* 1847, pp. 4, 7 ; 16 *Rept. of the Board of Works*, p. 152.

## iv. THE SOUP-KITCHENS, 1847

[1] N.L.I., MS 7745, Larcom papers, Trevelyan to Jones, 14 Jan. 1847.

[2] *Transactions of the Central Relief Committee of the Society of Friends*, p. 136.

[3] *Commissariat corr.* i. 333.

[4] Ibid., pp. 427, 437.

[5] *Hansard*, 3 series, lxxxix. 444.

[6] 10 Vic. c. 7.

[7] *Commissariat corr.* ii. 55–7.

[8] Ibid., p. 107.

[9] Ibid., pp. 108–9 ; Trevelyan, *Irish crisis*, p. 85.

[10] *Commissariat corr.* ii. 168, 170–1.

[11] *Freeman's Journal*, 21 Apr. 1847.

[12] Trevelyan, *Irish crisis*, p. 42.

[13] *Relief commission*, 10 Vic. cap. 7, p. 24.

[14] Ibid., pp. 4–5, 11, 20, 24–8 ; *Hansard*, 3 series, lxxxix. 426–36 ; xc. 506.

[15] *Freeman's Journal*, 11 June 1847 ; S.P.O., Distress papers, 1847, D4339–48, D5255, D5264, D5404, D5406, D5586, D7155 ; Ibid., Reg. papers, 1847, H7419.

[16] *2 Rept. relief commissioners*, p. (3) ; *4 Rept. relief commissioners*, p. 3 ; *5 Rept. relief commissioners*, pp. 3, 5.

[17] *1 Rept. relief commissioners*, p. 55 ; *Supplementary appendix to 7 rept. relief commissioners*, pp. 5–6, and appendix, p. 31 ; *Cork Constitution*, 17 July 1847 ; *Freeman's Journal*, 27 Apr. 1847.

[18] *Cork Constitution*, 17 July, 1847 ; *Freeman's Journal*, 21, 25, 31 May 1847 ; S.P.O., Distress papers, 1847, D7037, D7994 ; *Supplementary appendix to 7 rept. relief commissioners*, pp. 4–5.

[19] S.P.O., Distress papers, 1847, D7301.

[20] Ibid., D7018 ; *Supplementary appendix to 7 rept. relief commissioners*, pp. 6–7.

[21] Ibid., *Commissariat corr.*, ii. 93, 137, 148–9 ; S.P.O., Reg. papers, 1847, H6127.

[22] See my article ' The Society of Friends and the great famine ', in *Studies*, xxxix. 203–13 (June 1950) ; *British Association for the relief of extreme distress in Ireland and Scotland, Report . . .*, pp. 27, 100–3 ; N.L.I., MSS, Monteagle correspondence, C. E. Trevelyan to Sir John Burgoyne, 1 May 1847.

[23] *2 Rept. relief commissioners*, appendix, pp. 24–6; *3 Rept.* ditto, p. 3; *4 Rept.* ditto, p. 3; *5 Rept.* ditto, p. 3.

[24] S.P.O., Distress papers, 1847, D7016 ; *Report on the consolidated annuities*, p. 3, H.C. 1852 (1463), xlvii. ; *Supplementary appendix to 7 rept. relief commissioners*, p. 9.

[25] *Transactions of the Central Relief Committee of the Society of Friends*, pp. 200–1.

[26] See my article, ' Food problems during the great Irish famine ', in *R.S.A.I. Jn.*, lxxxii. 99–108.

## V.   POOR LAW RELIEF, 1847–52

[1] G. P. Gooch, ed., *Later correspondence of Lord John Russell*, i. 146.

[2] P.R.O.I., Relief commission papers, No. 11603, 1A.50.71.

[3] *Correspondence relating to state of the workhouses*, i. 54.

[4] S.P.O., Distress papers, 1847, D143.

[5] *Correspondence relating to state of the workhouses*, i. 13–14, 44.

[6] *Society of Friends : extracts from correspondence*, i. 5–6.

[7] *A copy of reports made to the Board of Health . . . workhouses in Cork, Bantry and Lurgan*, pp. 13–14 (H.C. 1847 (257) liv.

[8] 10 Vic. c. 31.

[9] *Dublin Gazette*, 22 Aug. 1847 ; *1 Rept. poor law commissioners*, p. 6 ; *Papers relating to state of workhouses*, iv. 22.

[10] *2 Rept. poor law commissioners*, p. 19.

[11] A. Moore, *The poor law unions . . . of Ireland*, p. 43 ; *Transactions of the Central Relief Committee of the Society of Friends*, p. 43 ; *5 Rept. poor law commissioners*, pp. 16–17.

[12] *3 Rept. commons committee on poor law*, pp. 1–2, qq. 710–14.

[13] *Papers relating to state of workhouses*, vi. 13 ; viii. 109.

[14] *2 Rept. poor law commissioners*, p. 7 ; *Report of the British Association for . . . Relief*, pp. 40–1.

[15] *3 Rept. commons committee on poor law*, p. 1, q. 710.

[16] Ibid., p. 14, qq. 886, 889 ; R. Barry O'Brien, *Fifty years of concessions to Ireland*, i. 568.

[17] *3 Rept. commons committee on poor law*, p. 111, q. 2301 ; *8 Rept. of same*, p. 76, q. 7025.

[18] *4 Rept. lords committee on poor law*, p. 848, qq. 8518, 8520.

[19] *Supplementary compendium of Irish poor law*, pp. 593–4, 625 ; *Papers relating to state of the workhouses*, iii. 208–10.

[20] Ibid., iv. 40.

[21] *1 Rept. poor law commissioners*, pp. 11–12 ; *2 Rept. of same*, p. 15.

[22] *1 Rept. lords committee on poor law*, p. 179, q. 1983 ; *Freeman's Journal*, 10 Mar. 1848.

[23] *Collector's manual*, pp. 1–10.

[24] *Papers relating to state of workhouses*, iv. 44–6, 103.

[25] *Freeman's Journal*, 31 Dec. 1847, 11 Feb., 15 Dec. 1848.

[26] Ibid., 11 May 1848 ; *Papers relating to state of workhouses*, v. 270 ; J. P. Kennedy, *Correspondence on . . . the failure of the potato crop*, p. 34.

[27] S.P.O., Reg. papers, 1847, O1607, O1667.

[28] Ibid., H11829 ; *2 Rept. poor law commissioners*, p. 7.

[29] 2 and 3 Vic. c. 24 ; *2 Rept. poor law commissioners*, p. 11.

[30] *Papers relating to the state of workhouses*, iv. 32 ; *Supplementary compendium o Irish poor law*, pp. 648–9.

[31] Ibid., pp. 659–61 ; 10 Vic. c. 31.

[32] *Freeman's Journal*, 2 June 1848.

[33] *5 Rept. poor law commissioners*, p. 4.

[34] *Compendium of Irish poor law*, pp. 299, 301 ; *Papers relating to the state of workhouses*, vii. 169.

[35] *Returns from . . . county gaols . . . and . . . workhouses of the daily diet* (H.C. 1847–8 (486), liii.) ; *Freeman's Journal*, 2, 10, 19 Feb. 1848 ; *Papers relating to the state of workhouses*, v. 455–6, vi. 140.

[36] Minutes of Kilrush board of guardians, 22 Dec. 1847, p. 231 ; *Papers relating to state of workhouses*, v. 257–8, vi. 870, viii. 206.

[37] J. Forbes, *Memorandums made in Ireland*, ii. 257 ; Minutes of Rathdrum board of guardians, 25 Oct. 1850.

[38] 11 and 12 Vic. c. 25 ; *5 Rept. poor law commissioners*, pp. 125–42.

[39] *Society of Friends : Extracts from correspondence*, i. 6 ; *Papers relating to the state of workhouses*, iv. 111.

[40] *Correspondence relating to state of workhouses*, iii. 210–11.

[41] *Papers relating to state of workhouses*, vii. 98 ; *Freeman's Journal*, 15 Dec. 1847 ; Minutes of Sligo board of guardians, 15 June 1850, p. 355.

[42] *Compendium of Irish poor law*, p. 300.

[43] *Papers relating to state of workhouses*, v. 234.

[44] S.P.O., Government correspondence book, 75, p. 411.

[45] *1 Rept. poor law commissioners*, p. 21.

[46] *Freeman's Journal*, 12 June 1848.

[47] *5 Rept. poor law commissioners*, p. 6.

[48] W. N. Hancock, *Report on the supposed progressive decline of Irish prosperity*, p. 65 ; *Supplementary compendium of Irish poor law*, pp. 674–9.

[49] Ibid., p. 680 ; *Papers relating to state of workhouses*, v. 23.

[50] Ibid., vi. 34.

[51] Ibid., v. 25, vii. 111 ; *Supplementary compendium of Irish poor law*, p. 679.

[52] *Papers relating to state of workhouses*, v. 2.

[53] Ibid., vii. 181.

[54] Ibid., v. 337, vii. 181.

[55] 10 Vic. c. 31, sect. 2.

[56] *Papers relating to the state of workhouses*, v. 213 ; *Supplementary compendium of Irish poor law*, p. 678 ; *9 Rept. commons committee on Irish poor law*, p. 30, q. 7623 ; *5 Rept. lords committee on Irish poor law*, p. 945.

[57] *1 Rept. poor law commissioners*, pp. 15–16.

[58] *Papers relating to state of workhouses*, vii. 13 ; *14 Rept. commons committee on poor law*, pp. 77, 141 (qq. 12441, 13159).

[59] Ibid., pp. 77, 92 (qq. 12444–9, 12647–8) ; *Freeman's Journal*, 19 Feb. 1848, 8 May 1849.

[60] *Freeman's Journal*, 27 June 1849.

[61] Ibid., 26 Dec. 1848.

[62] Ibid., 17 Dec. 1847, 27, 28 Jan., 30 Dec. 1848, 8 May 1849.

[63] Ibid., 15, 19 Feb. 1848.

[64] Ibid., 11, 19 Feb. 1848.

[65] Ibid., 19 May 1848.

[66] *Transactions of the Central Relief Committee of the Society of Friends*, p. 200 ; Society of Friends Historical Library, MSS, R. D. Webb's Visit to counties Mayo and Galway, p. 4.

[67] *Freeman's Journal*, 22 Apr. 1848 ; *Census*, 1851, pt. v, vol. i. p. 310.

[68] *14 Rept. commons committee on poor law*, p. 75, qq. 12412–8 ; *Freeman's Journal*, 2 Jan. 1849.

[69] 1 Mar. 1847.

[70] *Morning Chronicle*, 31 Mar. 1847 ; Ward, *Remedies for Ireland*, p. 22.

[71] *Papers relating to state of workhouses*, vi. 807 ; *Freeman's Journal*, 26 Jan. 1848.

[72] Ibid., 2, 9 Feb., 15 June 1848 ; *Papers relating to state of workhouses*, vii. 105.

[73] Ibid., vi. 504, vii. 9–10 ; *Freeman's Journal*, 28 Mar. 1848.

[74] *Papers relating to state of workhouses*, vii. 11–12 ; *Freeman's Journal*, 15, 20 June 1848.

[75] *7 Rept. commons committee on poor law*, p. 120, q. 5820.

[76] *Freeman's Journal*, 5 May 1848, 2 Jan. 1849 ; *Papers relating to state of workhouses*, vii. 188.

[77] *6 Rept. lords committee on poor law*, pp. (5)–(6).

[78] *Appendix to 14 Rept. commons committee on poor law*, p. 304.

[79] 25 and 26 Vic. c. 83, sect. 2.

[80] *3 Rept. poor law commissioners*, p. 3 ; *4 Rept.* of the same, pp. 3–4 ; *5 Rept.* of the same, pp. 3–5.

[81] *Census*, 1851, pt. ii. pp. iii–vi.

## vi.   CONCLUSION

[1] *Census*, 1851, pt. v, vol. i. pp. 243, 245, 253.

[2] N.L.I., MSS, Monteagle correspondence, Trevelyan to S. E. Spring Rice, 2 Sept. 1846.

[3] G. P. Gooch, ed., *Later correspondence of Lord John Russell*, i. 172–3.

[4] 10 and 11 Vic. c. 87.

[5] *Report on the consolidated annuities*, p. 4.

[6] 15 and 16 Vic. c. 16.

[7] *Hansard*, 3 series, cxxv. 1402–3.

[8] *Nation*, 23 Apr. 1853 ; *Dublin Evening Mail*, 20, 22, 25 Apr. 1853 ; *Dublin Evening Post*, 21 Apr. 1853.

[9] Parker, *Correspondence of Sir Robert Peel*, iii. 462–5.

[10] Gooch, *Later correspondence of Lord John Russell*, i. 156.

[11] Woodward, *The age of reform*, p. 15.

[12] N.L.I., MSS, Monteagle correspondence, Trevelyan to Monteagle, 9 Oct. 1846.

[13] *Irish crisis*, pp. 147–8.

[14] See my article, ' The Society of Friends and the great famine ', in *Studies*, xxxi. 203–13 (June 1950).

[15] O'Neill, ' Sidelights on souperism ', in *Ir. Eccles. Rec.*, lxxi. 50–64 (Jan. 1949).

[16] *The works of Edmund Burke* (ed. Henry Rogers), ii. 250–1 ; G. Trulock, *Remedies suggested to meet the present state of Ireland*, p. 19.

[17] *Irish crisis*, p. 183.

[18] Ibid., p. 185.

[19] *Report of the Indian famine relief commission* (1880), pt. i. pp. 10–16, 57 ; *Report of the Indian famine commission* (1901), p. 36.

CHAPTER V

# MEDICAL HISTORY OF THE FAMINE

## i. INTRODUCTION

[1] See ' The identification of some pestilences recorded in the Irish Annals ' in *Irish Historical Studies*, vi. 169–88 (Mar. 1949).

## iii. CHARACTERS OF THE EPIDEMIC DISEASES

[2] A form of contagious septic ophthalmia attacked many of those reduced by hunger ; 380 persons are recorded to have been totally blinded and 972 to have lost one eye.

[3] In contemporary reports, this rector's name appears both as ' Traill ' and 'Traill Hall '.

## iv. MEDICAL ORGANISATION AND ARRANGEMENTS

[4] Senior commissariat officer in the Waterloo campaign. His text-book on commissariat services in peace and war was long a standard work. From Nov. 1845 to Oct. 1848 was employed in superintending the distribution of famine relief in Ireland.

[5] Originally professor of chemistry, Apothecaries' Hall, Dublin. An advocate of applying scientific principles to farming. Fellow of the Royal Society, and of the Royal College of Physicians, Ireland. Later, president, Queen's College, Cork.

[6] Experienced in poor-law administration in England and Scotland. From Nov. 1845, chief commissioner of the poor laws in Ireland. He ' probably served on more commissions than any other man of his time'.

[7] Surgeon to the Meath Hospital, Dublin ; president, Royal College of Surgeons, Ireland.

[8] The eminent physician ; described ' Corrigan's pulse'. Five times president, Royal College of Physicians, Ireland ; created a baronet in 1866.

## vi. FEVER ACTS, AND TEMPORARY FEVER HOSPITALS

[9] The Fever Act, 11 and 12 Vic., empowered the board of health to make orders for the management of temporary fever hospitals. Those issued included : (1) that there shall be a separate bedstead for every patient ; (2) that every patient, on admission, shall be provided with a straw bed in sacking, two sheets, two blankets, a rug, pillow, and night-shirt ; (3) that the night-shirt, and sheets, and the straw, shall be changed on every Thursday in each week, and oftener if soiled ; (4) that the straw shall be changed for each patient. Directions were also given regarding the cleaning and ventilation of the wards.

## viii. ATTEMPTS TO LIMIT THE SPREAD OF INFECTION

[10] A ' fairy doctor ' (*liaigh sídhe*), made use of incantations (*orthannaí*) which varied with the condition to be treated.

CHAPTER VI

# IRISH EMIGRATION TO THE UNITED STATES OF AMERICA AND THE BRITISH COLONIES DURING THE FAMINE

### i. INTRODUCTION

[1] *Pilot,* 16 and 30 Mar. and 8 Apr. 1846 ; *Tipperary Vindicator,* 10 Mar. and 4, 8 and 25 Apr. 1846 ; *Kerry Evening Post,* 31 Mar. 1846 ; *Dublin Evening Post,* 12 May 1846 ; etc.

[2] On the whole, the spring emigration to British North America followed the pattern of former years, *Elgin : Grey papers,* iii, pp. 1090–1 ; and, despite the increased numbers, the emigration generally passed off very well, C.O. 384/79, 88 Emigration, report of Lt Hodder, 5 Jan. 1847. Indeed, the only substantial effect of the first potato failure upon emigration was the agitation to allow Indian meal to be substituted for potatoes in the official food allowance. After much hesitation, an order in council was passed permitting it, C.O. 384/80, 61 Emigration, commissioners : Stephen, 14 Jan. 1847 ; C.O. 386/39, pp. 148–9, 363–4, 13 Feb. and 31 Mar. 1846.

[3] *Pilot,* 16 Nov. 1846 ; *Dublin Evening Post,* 17 Nov. 1846 ; *Tipperary Vindicator,* 3 Oct. 1846. The heavy emigration was maintained right through the winter, R. Murray, *Ireland in its present condition,* p. 10.

[4] Cf. C.O. 384/80, 1069 Emigration, commissioners : Stephen, 19 June 1847. ' Sea stock ' was the passenger's personal store of provisions for the voyage.

[5] *Papers rel. emigration B.N.A.,* 28, [777], H.C. 1847, xxxix ; *Elgin : Grey papers,* iii, p. 1093.

[6] Russell papers, P.R.O. 30/22 (referred to below as Russell Papers), box 7, Clanricarde : Russell, 8 Jan. 1847. See also ibid., 5, Clanricarde : Russell, 17 Dec. 1846.

[7] Monteagle MSS, N.L.I., Monteagle : Grey, 9 Oct. 1846.

[8] *Rep. select comm. colonisation Ire.,* 111, 198, 206–7, 248, 307, 332–4, Q. 1103–5, 2160, 2407–16, 2984, 3212–31, [737], H.C. 1847, vi (evidence of Rev. Mr Montgomery, W. Monsell and Fr Mathew). Petitions for state aided emigration soon began to pour into parliament, *Hansard,* 3 series, lxxxix, 923, 5 Feb. 1847 ; xc, 1326, 1334–7, 15 Mar. 1847 ; xci, 200–3, 18 Mar. 1847 ; etc. It is interesting to note that, during the distress of 1831–2, only two petitions of this nature were sent to parliament.

[9] C.O. 384/80, 198 Emigration, commissioners : Stephen, 10 Feb. 1847. See also *Northern Whig,* 6 Feb. 1847 ; *Tipperary Vindicator,* 27 Jan. and 10 Feb. 1847.

[10] ' Gladly leaving their wretched country,' *Morning Chronicle,* 20 Jan. 1847 ; *Cork Constitution,* 13 Feb. 1847.

[11] Whether for house property in Waterford, or farms in the Golden Vale, it was a buyer's market everywhere in Munster. Ennis fair was the best for years, due, it was said, to the ' spirit of emigration abroad ', and Limerick cattle sales were flooded with the livestock of ' warm ' men who were leaving, *Kerry Evening Post,* 12 and 27 Feb. 1847 ; *Waterford Mail,* 13 Mar. 1847 ; *Tipperary Vindicator,* 13 and 17 Mar. 1847 ; *Nation,* 17 Apr. 1847, p. 443 ; *Limerick Chronicle,* 10 May 1847 ; etc.

[12] *Freeman's Journal,* 23 Mar. 1847 ; *Ballinasloe Star,* quoted by *Cork Constitution,* 27 Mar. 1847. See also C. E. Trevelyan, *The Irish crisis,* pp. 134–5 ; *Waterford Mail,* 13 Mar. 1847. Mayo and north Roscommon emigrants generally used Sligo as an embarkation port, *Nation,* 27 Mar. 1847, p. 389.

13 *Cork Constitution*, 5, 13 and 18 Mar. 1847.

14 *Rep. select comm. colonisation Ire.*, 243, Q. 2359–61, [737], H.C. 1847, vi. See also *1st rep. select comm. colonisation Ire.*, 181, Q. 1934–9, H.C. 1847–8, (415), xvii (evidence of J. Besnard) ; 11*th rep. C.L.E.C.*, 2–3, [1383], H.C. 1851, xxii. (C.L.E.C. is the abbreviation I use for the colonial land and emigration commissioners).

15 E.g., *Limerick Chronicle*, 6, 13 and 27 Jan. 1847 ; *Nation*, 27 Mar. 1847, p. 389.

16 E.g., *Morning Chronicle*, 2 Apr. 1847, p. 2 ; *Tipperary Vindicator*, 14 Apr. 1847 ; *Galway Vindicator*, quoted by *Nation*, 24 Apr. 1847, p. 460.

17 *Southern Reporter*, quoted by *Kerry Evening Post*, 5 May 1847.

18 *Hansard*, 3 series, xcv, 98–105, 23 Nov. 1847 (J. O'Connell). The death census of the loyal repeal association throws much light on parish emigration during the period, 1 Oct. 1846 to 31 Mar. 1847, see *Nation*, 15 May 1847, p. 511 ; 5 June 1847, p. 558 ; 19 June 1847, p. 570.

19 *Galway Mercury*, quoted by *Morning Chronicle*, 2 Apr. 1847, p. 2. See also *Kerry Evening Post*, 13 and 24 Mar. 1847 ; *Freeman's Journal*, 16 Mar. 1847 ; *Waterford Mail*, 13 Mar. 1847 ; *Limerick Chronicle*, 13 Mar. 1847 ; etc.

20 Cf. D. A. E. Harkness, ' Irish emigration ', in *International migrations*, ii, p. 276.

21 *Rep. select comm. colonisation Ire.*, 174, 212, 255–6, Q. 1676, 2070–2, 2480–5, [737], H.C. 1847, vi. J. Walsh, a Kilkenny land agent, estimated the average capital loss to Ireland by the emigration of each family as £50, at least, ibid., 190–1, Q. 1873–80. John O'Donovan, the antiquarian, noted that some of the middle classes had been brought almost to despair, O'Donovan papers, N.L.I., O'Donovan : D. MacCarthy, 12 Jan. and 14 Feb. 1848.

22 Especially in the later spring, e.g., *Limerick Chronicle*, 24 Mar., 17 Apr. and 8, 19 and 26 May 1847 ; *Farmer's Gazette*, 22 May 1847, p. 61 ; *Morning Chronicle*, 20 May 1847, p. 3 ; *Waterford Mail*, 12 May 1847 ; *Kerry Evening Post*, 20 Mar. 1847.

23 E.g., *Kerry Evening Post*, 14 Apr. 1847.

24 *Morning Chronicle*, 3 Mar. 1847, p. 7. Some of the bourgeoisie were going, not because bankruptcy hung over them immediately, but in the expectation, as Mr Gillespie of Newport put it, of ' that competency which my family demands, but which my country refuses her industrious sons ', *Nation*, 9 Oct. 1847, p. 845. John Egan, a Limerick manufacturer, whose business had collapsed in the general distress, used almost the same words before he sailed, *Limerick Chronicle*, 1 Sept. 1847.

25 E.g., *Cork Constitution*, 27 Apr. 1847 ; *Nation*, 3 Apr. 1847 ; p. 413.

26 For the Irish emigration to Scotland during 1847 see J. E. Handley, *The Irish in modern Scotland*, pp. 20–30.

27 The chief emigration officer's annual report from Canada said that, in the Irish immigration of 1847, the proportion of children had risen from the usual 25% to 33%, *Further papers rel. emigration B.N.A.*, 12–21, [964], H.C. 1847–8, xlvii.

28 *Hansard*, 3 series, xcvii, 6 Apr. 1848 (French).

29 Russell papers, 6, Clarendon : Russell, 28 Aug. 1847. T. F. Elliot of the colonial office believed that such reports greatly discouraged Irish emigration because of the extraordinary rapidity with which they were spread and appreciated at home, *Rep. select comm. colonisation Ire.*, 468, Q. 4433, [737], H.C. 1847, vi.

30 This does not mean, of course, that matters were any better at this stage ; on the contrary, after the third successive season of failure, they were worse, see Russell papers, 7, Lansdowne : Russell, 9 Feb. 1848. The question here is whether there were any grounds for hope of an ultimate recovery.

31 *Limerick Chronicle*, 19 and 26 Feb. 1848 ; *Kerry Evening Post*, 23 Feb. 1848 ; *Sligo Journal*, quoted by *Freeman's Journal*, 22 Feb. 1848.

32 The sailing in ballast of the *Triumph* (for many years engaged in the Limerick emigrant–timber trade), was a straw that showed how the wind was blowing, *Limerick Chronicle*, 12 Apr. 1848.

[33] See Mrs Smith's diary, 2 July 1848.

[34] *2nd rep. select comm. colonisation Ire.,* 291, Q. 2742, H.C. 1847–8, (593), xvii. See also C.O. 384/80, 1649 Emigration, 2 Oct. 1847 ; *Papers rel. emigration B.N.A.,* 39–40, [932], H.C. 1847–8, xlvii.

[35] *Hansard,* 3 series, civ, 3 Apr. 1849 (W. Monsell).

[36] *Cork Examiner,* 7 Nov. 1848 ; *Cork Constitution,* 1 Feb. 1849 ; *Tipperary Vindicator,* 6 and 16 Dec. 1848 ; *Limerick Chronicle,* 8, 18 and 29 Nov. 1848 ; etc. There were, of course, similar reports from other parts of Ireland, e.g., the midlands, *Advocate,* 28 Oct. 1848, p. 13. Urban emigration may have been heavy, too, for trade had collapsed completely. Dublin shopkeepers and artisans were said to have been leaving in great numbers, *Limerick Chronicle,* 15 Nov. 1848.

[37] *Limerick Chronicle,* 18 Nov. 1848.

[38] *3rd rep. select comm. poor laws Ire.,* 25, Q. 1039–40, H.C. 1849, (137), xv, part i ; *Hansard,* 3 series, ciii, 77, 1 Mar. 1849 (Sir H. Barron) ; *Freeman's Journal,* 27 Feb. and 6 and 9 Mar. 1849 ; *Waterford Mail,* 28 and 31 Mar. 1849. Despite heavy seas and wretched weather, there were January sailings from Irish ports for the first time on record, *Advocate,* 20 Jan. 1849, p. 193 ; *Waterford Mail,* 24 Jan. and 3 Feb. 1849.

[39] *Hansard,* 3 series, civ, 479–80, and 19 Apr. 1849 (Herbert).

[40] *Morning Herald,* 27 Jan. 1849 ; *Freeman's Journal,* 20 and 23 May 1849.

[41] *Freeman's Journal,* 30 Apr. 1849. Several girls refused to plead guilty lest it should prejudice their chances of transportation, *Mayo Telegraph,* quoted by ibid., 28 Apr. 1849. The house of commons, and particularly John Bright, were horrified to learn from Sharman Crawford that young men on trial often begged the courts to pass sentences of transportation on them, *Hansard,* 3 series, civ, 1109, 2 May 1849.

[42] *3rd rep. select comm. poor laws Ire.,* 176, Q. 3196–7, H.C. 1849, (137), xv, part i ; *Freeman's Journal,* 6 Apr. 1849.

[43] *Hansard,* 3 series, civ, 240, 3 Apr. 1849 ; ibid., civ, 102–3, 30 Mar. 1849 (Sir R. Peel). See also *Tipperary Vindicator,* 11 Apr. 1849 ; *Freeman's Journal,* 17 Apr. 1849.

[44] E.g. *4th rep. select comm. poor laws Ire.,* 9, Q. 3608–13, H.C. 1849, (170), xv, part i. See also *9th rep. select comm. poor laws Ire.,* 53–4, Q. 7926–33, (301), H.C. 1849, xv, part i.

[45] E.g. *8th rep. select comm. poor laws Ire.,* 73–4, Q. 6975–86, H.C. 1849, (259), xv, part i. For the 'quality' of Munster emigrants, see also Monteagle MSS, N.L.I., 1848, 582 ; *9th rep. select comm. poor laws Ire.,* 135–6, Q. 9172–8, H.C. 1849, (301), xv, part i.

[46] *7th rep. select comm. poor laws Ire.,* 14, Q. 5209–11, H.C. 1849, (237), xv, part i.

[47] C.O. 384/84, 2888 Emigration, commissioners : Merivale, 4 Apr. 1849.

[48] *4th rep. select comm. poor laws Ire.,* 29, Q. 3884–90, H.C. 1849, (170), xv, part i ; *Hansard,* 3 series, cii, 299, 5 Feb. 1849 ; cii, 507, 9 Feb. 1849 ; ciii, 278, 6 Mar. 1849 ; civ, 893, 26 Apr. 1849 ; etc.

[49] *Hansard,* 3 series, cii, 288–9, 493–4, 538, 5 and 9 Feb. 1849.

[50] Ibid., cii, 613, 21 Feb. 1849. For an impression of the country at this time, Carlyle's *Reminiscences of my Irish journey in 1849,* which is written with characteristic bile and penetration, is excellent. See also *7th rep. select comm. poor laws Ire.,* 95, Q. 5703, H.C. 1849, (237), xv, part i ; *Elgin : Grey papers,* iii, p. 1102.

[51] *Hansard,* 3 series, cv, 8 June 1849 (H. Grattan).

[52] Ibid., cvi, 542, 550, 20 Apr. 1849.

[53] Sir T. Martin, *Life of the prince consort,* ii, pp. 136–7. See also Mrs Smith's diary, 8 Apr. 1847 ; *Further papers rel. emigration B.N.A.,* 18, [971], H.C. 1847–8, xlvii ; *Morning Chronicle,* 23 Mar. 1847, p. 7 ; *Limerick Chronicle,* 14 Nov. 1848 ; *Tipperary Vindicator,* 13 Dec. 1848.

[54] Monteagle MSS, N.L.I., Roche : Monteagle, 14 Dec. 1849.

[55] For an impression of the vast autumn and winter emigration from the southern ports, see, e.g., *Nation,* 29 Sept. and 6 and 20 Oct. 1849, pp. 69, 84 and 116 ; *Waterford Mail,* 3 Oct. 1849. For the emigration from Dublin, Sligo and Belfast, see *Freeman's Journal* for the first fortnight in October.

[56] E.g., *Nation,* 6 Oct. and 15 Dec. 1849, pp. 85 and 244.

[57] *14th rep. select comm. poor laws Ire.,* 17, 42–6, Q. 11691, 11996–12049, H.C. 1849, (572), xv, part ii.

[58] *7th rep. select comm. poor laws Ire.,* 89–90, Q. 5682–3, H.C. 1849, (237), xv, part i (A. de Vere). See also *Morning Chronicle,* 15 July, 1850, p. 5 ; *Kerry Evening Post,* 16 Dec. 1848. Stewart, a northern landlord, provides us with a typical instance of the procedure. He knew a widow with six helpless children who had persuaded some one to pay the fare of her eldest boy. His remittances kept the family alive during the prolonged distress of 1846–7 ; and by 1848 he had saved sufficient money to provide passages for all the others, *7th rep. select comm. poor laws Ire.,* 31, H.C. 1849, (237), xv, part i.

[59] E.g. *Papers rel. emigration B.N.A.,* 57–61, H.C. 1849, (593. II), xxxviii ; *Papers rel. emigration B.N.A.,* 46, H.C. 1851, (384), xl.

[60] I have covered the sort of material I have been using down to 1855, at least, except for Irish newspaper and periodical material, which I have covered only in ' sample ' lots for the years 1852–5.

[61] *Sligo Journal,* quoted by *The Times,* 14 Oct. 1851, p. 8.

[62] *Census of Ireland,* 1851, general report, vi, p. lxxxi.

[63] The fear that Irish emigration would have this effect was expressed as early as 1851, *The Times,* 6 Oct. 1851, p. 5.

[64] *13th rep. C.L.E.C.,* 10–12, [1647], H.C. 1852–3, xl.

[65] The census of 1861 shows all these trends confirmed.

[66] They were as follows : between the ages of one year and ten years, 11% of the total emigration ; between ten and twenty, 25% ; between twenty and thirty, 40% ; between thirty and forty, 11% ; between forty and fifty, 7% ; over fifty, 4%, *Census of Ireland,* 1851, general report, vi, p. 55. 2% were infants. There are no statistics for the years before 1851, but it seems likely that the emigration of 1846–50 contained a higher proportion of young people. Until 1847, the volume of remittances was small ; it grew immensely thereafter, and many of these remittances would have paid the passages of children and elderly people.

[67] For some contemporary comment on the census of 1851 as relating to Irish emigration, see *Economist,* 13 Sept. 1856 ; *Saturday Review,* 13 Sept. 1856, pp. 434–5.

[68] For the pre-famine emigration, see W. F. Adams, *Ireland and Irish emigration to the new world from 1815 to the famine.*

## ii. LANDLORD–ASSISTED EMIGRATION

[1] The evidence before the Devon commission suggests that landlord-assisted emigration was known in most counties. Adams, op. cit., shows that it was an established practice in some areas, e.g., Kilkenny.

[2] For a discussion of the trend towards consolidation, see K. H. Connell, *The population of Ireland, 1750–1845,* pp. 171–83.

[3] *Rep. select comm. colonisation Ire.,* 193, [737], H.C. 1847, vi. Several other Kilkenny landlords, like Lords Darnley and Bessborough, had also sent tenants out from their estates, ibid., 189, Q. 1855–9 (evidence of J. Walsh). Miley, a Dublin shipping agent, said in 1847 that he ' was engaged for several years ' in clearing estates by emigration, *Papers rel. emigration B.N.A.,* 44–6, H.C. 1847–8, (50), xlvii. See also *Rep. select comm. colonisation Ire.,* 538–9, Q. 4866–72, 4882, [737], H.C. 1847, vi (evidence of A. de Vere) ; *Pilot,* 29 May 1847.

[4] *2nd rep. select comm. colonisation Ire.*, 258–60, H.C. 1847–8, (593), xvii.

[5] *Devon commission*, i, 153–4 (evidence of J. Lynch).

[6] Limerick and Clare were old centres of landlord-assisted emigration.

[7] *Papers rel. emigration B.N.A.*, 10–11, [777], H.C. 1847, xxxix.

[8] F. Morehouse, 'Irish emigration during the forties', in *American Historical Review*, xxxiii, pp. 584–5. He paid about £40,000 for the estate.

[9] *Rep. select comm. colonisation Ire.*, 335–6, Q. 3241–55, [737], H.C. 1847, vi (evidence of F. Spaight). He said that, for a cost of 70s. for each emigrant, he had practically wiped out crime and distress on his estate, and that the tenants had gone gladly, without ill feeling, ibid., 338–42, Q. 3274–97. The O'Connellite press, however, told a different story, when some of those 'who escaped from America' returned to their hovels at Derry Castle, *Tipperary Vindicator*, 2 June 1847.

[10] *Papers rel. emigration B.N.A.*, 10–11, [777], H.C. 1847, xxxix.

[11] Many pleaded (with some truth, no doubt) that they were too poor to do anything themselves, e.g., C.O. 38/80, 304 Miscellaneous, 26 Feb. 1847.

[12] Every man of common sense, wrote Clanricarde to Russell, is convinced of the necessity of emigration, but cottiers and landlords alike are bankrupt ; 'are we, the Government, to interfere, or to stand by and see them [the people] die ?', Russell papers, 5, Clanricarde : Russell, 8 Jan. 1847.

[13] Cf. *Morning Chronicle*, 11 March 1847, p. 2. Hitherto, landlords had been eager to meet the government halfway in this matter, and common action in a common cause was often urged, e.g., *Hansard*, 3 series, lxxxix, 901, 937, 4 and 8 Feb. 1847.

[14] *Morning Chronicle*, 23 Mar. 1847, p. 7. No doubt, this figure was an exaggeration but the total must have been very large.

[15] *Tipperary Vindicator*, 10 Mar. 1847.

[16] *Nation*, 10 Apr. 1847, p. 428.

[17] E.g., Mrs Finch of Nenagh, *Cork Constitution*, 27 Apr. 1847 ; Warren of Ballingarry, *Waterford Mail*, 1 May 1847 ; Clarke of Bishopswood, *Nation*, 27 Mar. 1847 ; Wingfield in Sligo, ibid., 12 June 1847, p. 566 ; Guiness in Wexford, *Limerick Chronicle*, 10 Mar. 1847.

[18] For a lively account of the difficulties of a landlord contemplating assisted emigration, see a letter from E. B. Roche, a M.P. for Cork, to the emigration commissioners, which begins, 'I am like a man in a Garrison infested by the Enemy', C.O. 384/80, 344 Miscellaneous, 6 Mar. 1847.

[19] *Further papers rel. emigration B.N.A.*, 23–5, [964], H.C. 1847–8, xlvii.

[20] This last may have been due to the fact that few assisted emigrants were sent from Liverpool, because Liverpool fares were rather higher than the Irish.

[21] *Further papers rel. emigration B.N.A.*, 16, [964], H.C. 1847–8, xlvii.

[22] Ibid., 52, [932], H.C. 1847–8, xlvii.

[23] *Papers rel. emigration B.N.A.*, 20, H.C. 1847–8, (50), xlvii. The Canadians believed that landlords, especially those in distressed areas, had been driven by the poor law to rid their estates only of those people who were a public burden. *Further papers rel. emigration B.N.A.*, 5, H.C. 1847–8, [985], H.C. 1847–8, xlvii. But, in fact, unless a property were virtually coextensive with an electoral district, or the other estates in the division were without paupers, the landowner was, at his own expense, relieving others of their share in the common burden of pauperdom.

[24] *Hansard*, 3 series, xcvi, 682–3, 15 Feb. 1848 (Sharman Crawford).

[25] It was very difficult to discover whether or not tenants had been given landing money ; they went to great pains to conceal what they had, *Papers rel. emigration B.N.A.*, 28, [1025], H.C. 1849, xxxiii.

²⁶ Wyndham complained bitterly to the government of the increases in the Canadian immigrant tax, which greatly raised the cost of his assisted emigration, C.O. 384/81, Wyndham : Grey, 820 Emigration, 20 Apr. 1848. For the dreadful condition of Wyndham's emigrants when they landed at Quebec, see *Further papers rel. emigration B.N.A.*, 1–6, [971], H.C. 1847–8, xlvii.

²⁷ One of the most important undertakings in 1848 was the clearing of the crown lands at Irvilloughter and Boughill in co. Galway. P.R.O.I. Quit Rent Office collection, Office of Woods Land Revenue letter and report entry books, No. 9. pp. 232–40. The project appears to have turned out reasonably well.

²⁸ For Wyndham's activity during 1849, see *Further papers rel. emigration B.N.A.*, 38, [1025], H.C. 1849, xxxiii ; for Spaight's, see *Tipperary Vindicator*, 11 Apr. 1849. See also *Freeman's Journal*, 25 May 1849.

²⁹ *Hansard*, 3 series, cii, 458, 9 Feb. 1849 ; cvii, 371, 16 July 1849 ; cv, 1292, 8 June 1849 (Stanley). Stanley himself had experimented with assisted emigration before the famine.

³⁰ *Hansard*, 3 series, cii, 797–9, 16 Feb. 1849.

³¹ Ibid., civ, 870, 26 Apr. 1849.

³² I have found no instance of assisted emigration arising from a transfer of property under the Encumbered Estates Act, 1849.

³³ J. R. Stuart Trench, *The realities of Irish life*, pp. 121–5.

³⁴ *Papers rel. emigration B.N.A.*, 16, H.C. 1851, (348), xl ; *Papers rel. emigration B.N.A.*, 20, 30–1, [1474], H.C. 1852, xxxiii ; *Papers rel. emigration North American colonies*, 9, [1650], H.C. 1852–3, lxviii ; *Papers rel. emigration North American colonies*, 19, [1763], H.C. 1854, lxvi ; *Copies rel. emigration North American colonies*, 7, H.C. 1857, (14), x ; etc.

³⁵ This is my own estimate, based on British North American statistics. It is put forward most tentatively. There are no figures for the American ports, and even those for Canada and New Brunswick cannot be relied upon completely (see C.O. 384/78, 1352 Canada, 17 Dec. 1845). These returns depended on the replies of emigrants, who might have read some sinister purpose into the questioning, and answered incorrectly (*Papers rel. emigration B.N.A.*, 10–11, 20, [777], H.C. 1847, xxxix). Very probably, the amount of landlord emigration directed towards the United States was disproportionately small. Proprietors preferred to settle their people in a colony rather than a hostile republic ; and St Lawrence and New Brunswick fares were lower than American, because the immigrant legislation of congress and the states was more stringent than the colonial. Finally, it must be remembered how difficult it was to decide exactly what amounted to ' assistance '.

³⁶ E.g., Palmerston's assisted emigration, see *Hansard*, 3 series, cv, 300–12, 15 May 1849 (W. Monsell) ; *Papers rel. emigration B.N.A.*, 40, [932], H.C. 1847–8, xlvii.

³⁷ *Freeman's Journal*, 15 July 1850. Of the nationalist newspapers, the *Nation* was much the most steadfast in its opposition, see my article ' The Irish catholic clergy and emigration during the great famine ', in *Irish Historical Studies*, v, no. 20, p. 290. See also *Rep. select comm. colonisation Ire.*, 250–1, Q. 2433–42, [737], H.C. 1847, vi (evidence of Fr Mathew).

³⁸ C.O. 384/80, 300 Emigration, 23 Feb. 1847. See also H.O. 381/19, p. 299, 23 Mar. 1847.

³⁹ E.g., families on one Roscommon estate were given only 65s. each ; of course, few of them could get beyond Liverpool, *Rep. select comm. colonisation Ire.*, 123, 154–5, Q. 1191, 1497–507, [737], H.C. 1847, vi.

⁴⁰ Monteagle MSS, N.L.I., Peel : Monteagle, 14 Sept. 1849.

⁴¹ Stuart Trench, op. cit., pp. 124–6.

⁴² *Cork Examiner*, 3 May 1848.

⁴³ Cf. W. F. Burn, ' Free trade in land : an aspect of the Irish question ', in *T.R.H.S.* 4th, xviii, pp. 64–71.

[44] S. Walpole, *The life of Lord John Russell*, ii, p. 463.  Professor Burn uses this illustration.

[45] *1st rep. select comm. colonisation Ire.*, 202, H.C. 1847–8, (415), xvii.

[46] According to the agent, most of the cottiers were quite content to accept the offer, ibid., 203.  See also *Limerick Chronicle*, 26 May 1847.

[47] The amounts entered were so absurdly large as to throw doubt upon the agent's testimony.  He may, however, have made a clerical mistake.

[48] He might have added that many another proprietor in his situation would simply have thrown his cottiers upon the roadside.  As one landlord reasoned, emigration would have cost him 12d. in the shilling, but to put his tenants on the rates cost him only 4d., since there were two other landed men in his electoral district who would have to share the expense of maintaining them, *Hansard*, 3 series, civ, 870, 26 Apr. 1849.  For an alleged case of similar ' economy ' on the part of the ecclesiastical commissioners, see ibid., cii, 507, 9 Feb. 1849 (J. Sadlier).  See also C.O. 384/80, 1313 Miscellaneous, petition from W. Lucas's former tenants, 31 July 1847.

[49] *1st rep. select comm. colonisation Ire.*, 201, H.C. 1847–8, (415), xvii.  Gore Booth, a ' good ' landlord, justified his action in this way : since his land was greatly over-populated, and since he had ' no right to turn these people out in the world ', emigration was the only course open to him, *Rep. select comm. colonisation Ire.*, 157–8, Q. 1530–9, [737], H.C. 1847, vi.  He had to eat into his English capital to pay for the removals, and all he expected in return was more regular rents for larger holdings, *2nd rep. select comm. colonisation Ire.*, 267–73, Q. 2684–789, H.C. 1847–8, (593), xvii.

[50] *Further papers rel. emigration B.N.A.*, 5, [985], H.C. 1847–8, xlvii.

[51] It was suggested that Mahon's assisted emigration was the reason for his murder, *Hansard*, 3 series, xcv, 82–3, (H. Grattan), though this was subsequently denied, ibid., 911 (M. O'Connell).  A Roscommon fund for shooting ' oppressors ', however, appears to have received support from the new world, ibid., 297–302 (Earl Grey). See also Russell papers, G.D. 22/6, Clarendon : Russell, 17 and 30 Nov. 1847, and Sir H. Maxwell, *Life and letters of . . . Clarendon*, pp. 280–4.  Apart from this disputed case, I have come across only one other instance of a landlord being attacked for any cause connected with assisted emigration, during these years.  He was Ussher of Lismore, *Limerick Chronicle*, 22 May 1847.

[52] Russell papers, 7, Clarendon : Russell, 30 Nov. 1847.

[53] P.R.O.I. Quit Rent Office collection, Office of Woods Land Revenue letter and report entry books, no. 9, pp. 10, 45.

[54] Ibid., pp. 49–50.  Those who had actually been evicted had been sent off to the United States already *pour encourager les autres*, ibid., p. 48.

[55] Ibid., pp. 121, 141.

[56] Ibid., pp. 121, 132.  Already, the vultures were hovering about the cleared lands ; one applicant for 300 acres, a bankrupt butcher, had been turned down curtly.

[57] Ibid., pp. 152, 171, 190, 195.

[58] The commissioners pronounced the emigration a complete success, although its cost was almost double the original estimate, ibid, no. 10, pp. 85–6.  De Vere believed that such efforts were ' far beyond the means of mere individuals ', *7th rep. select comm. poor laws Ire.*, 87–8, Q. 8661–72, H.C. 1849, (231), xv, part i ; and this line was taken, too, by some people who used Ballykilcline as an argument for state aided emigration, e.g., *Edinburgh Review*, xci, p. 29.

[59] During 1847, many landlords were accused of ' brutal extermination ', amongst them, Lords de Vesci, Midleton and Darnley, the bishop of Ripon, Wyndham, Wandesforde, Hamilton and Dr Collins.  In most cases, the colonial accusations were met with blank denials.  The first case concerned Collins' cottiers, *Papers rel. emigration B.N.A.*, 21–6, 32, H.C. 1847–8, (50), xlvii.  Collins was a persistent advocate of emigration, and produced many pamphlets in its favour (see bibliography).  He was most distinguished in his own profession, O'D. Browne, *The Rotunda hospital*, 1745–1945, p. 109.

[60] He said that he had proposed to the lord lieutenant in 1846 that his tenants form a colony in Canada, the capital to be raised on the security of the cleared estate, *2nd rep. select comm. colonisation Ire.*, 272, Q. 2756-7, H.C. 1847-8, (593), xvii. There was, however, no record of such an application at the colonial office, C.O. 384/81, 736 Emigration, 13 Apr. 1848.

[61] *2nd rep. select comm. colonisation Ire.*, 261, 275, Q. 2353-4, 2786, H.C. 1847-8, (593), xvii.

[62] Ibid., 260-1, Q. 2612. Gore Booth had his passengers mustered at his own house, and again upon embarkation, for medical examinations.

[63] Some 1,500 at a cost of roughly £4 each.

[64] It was difficult to find work for them, because they demanded the highest rate of wages, although they were unskilled, ibid., 265, Q. 2612.

[65] Sir Robert's emigrants, wrote the master of his first vessel, 'could not be classed as common advintururs . . . or his Brothers ship Classed among the dirty, old Emigrant hired Vessels', *3rd rep. select comm. colonisation Ire.*, 122-3, H.C. 1849, (86), xi ; *2nd rep. select comm. colonisation Ire.*, 265, Q. 2678, H.C. 1847-8, (593), xvi.

[66] *9th rep. select comm. poor laws Ire.*, 40-1, Q. 7727-40, H.C. 1849, (301), xv, part i. See also *Morning Chronicle*, 31 Mar. 1847, p. 6.

[67] *Papers rel. emigration B.N.A.*, 61-2, 89-90, H.C. 1847-8, (50), xlvii.

[68] Ibid., 100 ; *2nd rep. select comm. colonisation Ire.*, 264, H.C. 1847-8, (593), xvii.

[69] *Papers rel. emigration B.N.A.*, 100-1, H.C. 1847-8, (50), xlvii.

[70] His public position was, of course, partly responsible for these outbursts, T. Walrond, *Letters and journals of . . . Elgin*, pp. 45-6 ; *Papers rel. emigration B.N.A.*, 158, H.C. 1847-8, (50), xlvii ; F. Morehouse, op. cit. in *A.H.R.*, xxxiii, pp. 583-4.

[71] Some of the passengers on Gore Booth's vessels belonged to Palmerston's estate ; this was not generally known, *Papers rel. emigration B.N.A.*, 163, H.C. 1847-8, (50), xlvii.

[72] Ibid., 113-14.

[73] *Further papers rel. emigration B.N.A.*, 157-8, [932], H.C. 1847-8, xlvii.

[74] *Further papers rel. emigration B.N.A.*, 47-8, [932], H.C. 1847-8, xlvii.

[75] A. Ferrie, *Letter to . . . Lord Grey . . . in relation to emigration to Canada during the summer of 1847* ; see also, *Further papers rel. emigration B.N.A.*, 36-42, [932], H.C. 1847-8, xlvii ; C.O. 384/79, 34 Canada. With his tongue in his cheek, no doubt, Ferrie ostentatiously exempted Palmerston from personal responsibility.

[76] *2nd rep. select comm. colonisation Ire.*, 266-7, Q. 2682-92, H.C. 1847-8, (593), xvii.

[77] *Rep. select comm. colonisation Ire.*, 151-2, [737], H.C. 1847, vi. Kincaid took it for granted that they should have been near-paupers ; otherwise, he said, they would not have accepted emigration, *Papers rel. emigration B.N.A.*, 162-4, H.C. 1847-8, (50), xlvii.

[78] *Further papers rel. emigration B.N.A.*, 38-40, [932], H.C. 1847-8, xlvii. T. F. Elliot believed that Kincaid could have rebutted all Ferrie's charges, C.O. 384/81, 469 Canada, 7 Mar. 1848. This was clearly wrong.

[79] E.g., one of Perley's complaints was that many of Palmerston's emigrants were dressed in the foulest rags, and that some of the children were stark naked, *Papers rel. emigration B.N.A.*, 150, H.C. 1847-8, (50), xlvii. Kincaid's reply was that they had put on their worst clothes to arouse compassion, *2nd rep. select comm. colonisation Ire.*, 275, Q. 2784-5, H.C. 1847-8, (593), xvii. Nor had End any difficulty in dealing with the foolish counter charges which Kincaid had made against him, *Further papers rel. emigration B.N.A.*, 54-5, [932], H.C. 1847-8, xlvii.

[80] It was more or less on these grounds that Gore Booth defended his emigration, *2nd rep. select comm. colonisation Ire.*, 267-74, Q. 2693-780, H.C. 1847-8, (593), xvii.

[81] *Papers rel. emigration B.N.A.*, 158, 163, H.C. 1847–8, (50), xlvii.  For the effect of Palmerston's emigration upon his own estate, see *9th rep. select comm. poor laws Ire.*, 36–7, Q. 7682–700, H.C. 1849, (301), xv, part i.

[82] For further evidence that landlords' prime object was to remove the worst, and retain the best, of their cottiers, see C.O. 384/28, 20 Mar. 1831, unclassified ; C.O. 384/69, 1648 Emigration, commissioners : Stephen, 8 Nov. 1842.

### iii.  GOVERNMENT POLICY AND STATE AID FOR EMIGRATION

[1] For a typical contemporary exposition of the advantages of systematic emigration, see *Westminster Review*, lviii, pp. 398–452.

[2] Almost every parliamentary committee on Irish affairs since 1820 had recommended the adoption of some measure of the kind.

[3] C.O. 384/81, 1075 Canada, 12 June 1848.  See also C.O. 384/88, 158 Canada, 9 Jan. 1850 ;  C.O. 384/90, 453 Australia, 17 Jan. 1853.  No less a true believer in colonial reform than Buller came to oppose state aided emigration upon these grounds, Howick papers, quoted by W. P. Morrell, *British colonial policy in the age of Peel and Russell*, p. 433.

[4] According to Morrell, he had no interest in colonial problems or needs, his nature demanding grandeur of conception and the flashing glory of debate, and his office no more than obscure and painful labour, Morrell, op. cit., pp. 32–6.

[5] *Hansard*, 3 series, lxxxi, 212 ;  Adams, op. cit., p. 328.

[6] Cf. E. Halevy, *The Age of Peel and Cobden*, p. 14.  Gladstone may have approached the whole question of emigration rather cautiously, see C.O. 384/78, 290 Canada, 23 Mar. 1846.

[7] Peel remained sceptical of the undertaking.  On 15 July 1826, Horton wrote to him, ' With respect to emigration I do not feel at all less sanguine that you will change your opinion . . . I *pledge* myself to effect your ultimate conversion ', C.O. 324/96, pp. 165–6.  The dismal fate of the projects was scarcely likely to bring this about, C.O. 384/52, 266 Canada, Feb. 1839.

[8] *Hansard*, 3 series, lxxxix, 163.

[9] Russell papers, 5, 16 Nov. 1846.

[10] Halevy, op. cit., p. 256.

[11] A memorandum of Prince Albert's, dated 6 July 1846, runs : ' There is the *Grey Party*, consisting of Lord Grey, Lord Clarendon, Sir George Grey and Mr Wood ; they are against Lord Lansdowne, Lord Minto, Lord Auckland and Sir John Hobhouse, stigmatising them as old women.  Lord John leans entirely to the last-named gentlemen ', *Letters of Queen Victoria*, ii, p. 102.

[12] Morrell, op. cit., p. 202.

[13] E. M. Wrong, *Charles Buller and responsible government*, pp. 56–8.

[14] Cf. Earl Grey, *The colonial policy of Lord John Russell's administration*, i, pp. vii–viii.

[15] W. P. Moneypenny and G. E. Buckle, *The Life of Benjamin Disraeli*, i, p. 1052, Disraeli : Stanley, 28 Dec. 1849.  By the time he left office, Grey had abandoned these principles and joined in the chorus of congratulation upon the state's wisdom in doing nothing during the famine years, Grey, op. cit., pp. 240–5.  See also *Edinburgh Review*, xcviii, p. 88.

[16] E.g., Morrell, op. cit., pp. 201–3 ; K. N. Bell and W. P. Morrell, *Select documents on British colonial policy, 1830–1860*, p. xxxiii ; R. B. Madgwick, *Immigration into Eastern Australia, 1788–1851*, pp. 196–7.

[17] He had served as chancellor of the exchequer under Melbourne.

[18] Monteagle MSS, N.L.I., Monteagle : Grey, 9 Oct. 1846.

[19] *Rep. select comm. colonisation Ire.*, 26–7, appendix 3, [737], H.C. 1847, vi.

[20] Russell papers, 5, Grey : Russell, 16 Oct. 1846.

[21] Grey never lost this fear. Two years later, he wrote to Russell, ' the best safe-guard [for Canada] would be a large military and *English* emigration—unfortunately if we adopt any measure for increasing emigration we could not help sending out a large proportion of Irish and adding to the Irish inhabitants of Canada is adding to our worst enemies ', ibid., 7, Grey: Russell, 6 Sept. 1848. See also C.O. 384/88, 1799 Emigration, 17 Jan. 1851.

[22] Russell papers, 5, Grey : Russell, 16 Oct. 1846.

[23] His scheme was remarkably similar to one put forward by J. R. Godley in March, 1847, which Grey rejected out of hand, though it was, if anything, more practicable than his own, see my article, op. cit., pp. 291–3. Grey's conception of a ' community ' was based on the English village, not on its Irish counterpart, a confusion which might have proved fatal, had his scheme been put into action. Cf. ' Grey's tone of thought and speech had always the cold impartial ring of an aristocratic statesman passing judgment on things in which he would feel little direct concern ', *Economist*, 13 Nov. 1858 ; see also C.O. 384/82, 1312 Emigration, 23 June 1848.

[24] Monteagle MSS, N.L.I., Grey : Monteagle, 14 Oct. 1846.

[25] Ibid., Monteagle : Grey, 22 Oct. 1846.

[26] G. P. Gooch, *The Later Correspondence of Lord John Russell*, i, pp. 168–9. For Grey's opinions at this time, see C.O. 384/78, 1661 Canada, Grey's minute, 19 Dec. 1846.

[27] Russell papers, 5, Russell : Bessborough, 8 Dec. 1846.

[28] Ibid., 5, correspondence between Bessborough and Russell, 8 to 29 Dec. 1846. Bessborough himself was attracted by Bentinck's Irish policy, which was more positive and ambitious than Russell's, Moneypenny and Buckle, op. cit., i, pp. 790–1.

[29] Russell papers, 5, Russell : Bessborough, 16 Dec. 1846.

[30] He told the Irish in October, 1846 that ' the interference of the state deadens private energy . . . and after superseding all other exertion finds itself unequal to the gigantic task it has undertaken ', Russell papers, 5, Russell : Bessborough, 17 Oct. 1846.

[31] *Hansard,* 3 series, xxxix, 485–6, 1 Dec. 1837.

[32] Russell papers, 5, Russell : Bessborough, 29 Dec. 1846.

[33] *Papers rel. emigration B.N.A.,* 3–6, [777], H.C. 1847, xxxix.

[34] For Draper himself, see *Letters from Lord Sydenham to Lord John Russell,* edit. P. Knaplund, p. 47 ; J. L. Morison, *British supremacy and Canadian self government, 1839–1854,* p. 194.

[35] *Further papers rel. emigration B.N.A.,* 6–8, [824], H.C. 1847, xxxix.

[36] Ibid., 6–9 ; C.O. 384/79, 499 Canada, commissioners : J. Stephen, 27 Mar. 1847.

[37] Grey told Russell that the estimates given him (£48,000 for settling 500 families) were so enormous that ' it would be practically impossible to attempt it,' Russell papers, 6, Grey : Russell, 26 Jan. 1847.

[38] *Further papers rel. emigration B.N.A.,* 34–5, [824], H.C. 1847, xxxix ; *7th rep. C.L.E.C.,* 17, [809], H.C. 1847, xxxiii ; *Papers rel. emigration B.N.A.,* 15, H.C. 1847–8, (50), xlvii.

[39] They had opposed his recent project firmly, C.O. 384/79, 128 North America, 28 Jan. 1847. Stephen, in fact, believed that it was the commissioners who had induced Grey to abandon his village scheme, C.O. 384/80, 1317 Emigration, minute of J. Stephen, 31 July 1847.

[40] Apart from all other considerations, the cost of passages to Australia put any large scale emigration to the southern colonies out of the question.

[41] Outside his own particular field and interests, Grey appears to have shared this conception.

[42] Howick papers, quoted by Morrell, op. cit., pp. 472–3.

[43] See *7th rep. C.L.E.C.*, 3, [809], H.C. 1847, xxxiii ; *8th rep. C.L.E.C.*, 14, [961], H.C. 1847–8, xxvi.

[44] *7th rep. C.L.E.C.*, 20, [809], H.C. 1847, xxxiii ; *Hansard*, 3 series, xcii, 1165, 20 May 1847 (B. Hawes). Stephen agreed with Grey that ' the months ahead will have so many sources of panic that nothing new should be added ', C.O. 384/80, Miscellaneous, 15 Jan. 1847. The emigration commissioners were in great confusion for the first two months of the year. Cf. A year later, Stephen wrote to Aubrey de Vere, ' I have passed my life in a chaos of colonial controversies. I would not return to them for the wealth of the Rothschilds. But Irish controversies are . . . much the worst ', W. Ward, *Aubrey de Vere : a memoir*, pp. 134–6.

[45] *Papers rel. emigration B.N.A.*, 35, [777], H.C. 1847, xxxiii.

[46] Ibid., 35–7 ; *Papers rel. emigration B.N.A.*, 15, H.C. 1847–8, (50), xlvii.

[47] *7th rep. C.L.E.C.*, 21, [809], H.C. 1847, xxxiii.

[48] *8th rep. C.L.E.C.*, 14, [961], H.C. 1847–8, xxii.

[49] *Hansard*, 3 series, xc, 1330–1, 15 Mar. 1847. Russell, however, had adopted a more cautious attitude in the commons, ibid., lxxxix, 447–50, 25 Jan. 1847 ; xc, 1244–5, 12 Mar. 1847.

[50] C.O. 384/79, 588 Emigration, H.O. : Stephen, 12 Apr. 1847 ; 709 Emigration, commissioners : Stephen, 28 Apr. 1847 ; etc.

[51] *Papers rel. emigration B.N.A.*, 168, H.C. 1847–8, (50), xlvii.

[52] *Further papers rel. emigration B.N.A.*, 32–4, 65–6, [932], H.C. 1847–8, xlvii. Before the close of 1848, however, this decision appears to have been forgotten.

[53] *Papers rel. emigration B.N.A.*, 27–8, H.C. 1847–8, (50), xlvii.

[54] *Papers rel. emigration B.N.A.*, 36, H.C. 1847–8, (50), xlvii.

[55] Still less is it to excuse Grey's line of conduct, for this had the additional demerit of resting upon incorrect and foolish calculations.

[56] An increase in the staff of officers and the use of hulks would have made it possible to prevent many of those who were infected with typhus from embarking. This would have reduced the death rate at sea and in the provinces considerably ; and, very probably, the consequent saving in colonial relief measures would have compensated for the fresh expenditure at home.

[57] *Hansard*, 3 series, lxxxix, 891–9, 5 Feb. 1847.

[58] Ibid., xcii, 899, 1 June 1847.

[59] *Hansard*, 3 series, xciii, 108–17, 4 June 1847. Such arrogance was, of course, hotly resented in Ireland, and the *Northern Whig* spoke of his ' imperious presumption ' in refusing all assistance, *Northern Whig*, 8 June 1847.

[60] *Rep. select comm. colonisation Ire.*, xi–xii, [737], H.C. 1847, vi.

[61] *Rep. select comm. colonisation Ire.*, xi–xii, [737], H.C. 1847, i–iv. Morrell puts the matter a shade too strongly, ' The Report . . . discountenanced the belief that colonisation could by itself remedy Irish distress, and instead of enlarging upon the advantages of any specific plan, pointed out the limitations of them all ', Morrell, op. cit., p. 432. No one ever supposed that emigration could *per se* remedy Irish distress ; and the impression which the report, as a whole, leaves is that of a natural distaste for conclusions, rather than any conscious purpose of deflating.

[62] *Hansard*, 3 series, ci, 23–36, 10 Aug. 1847.

[63] Ibid., ci, 39–50, 10 Aug. 1847.

[64] C. Greville, *Journals,* ii, p. 77, 28 Nov. 1830.

[65] Russell papers, 6, Clarendon : Russell, 27 Dec. 1847.

[66] *3rd rep. select comm. colonisation Ire.,* 78–81, H.C. 1849, (86), xi.

[67] Russell papers, 7, the correspondence which Russell conducted with each, during the period, May to August 1848.

[68] Russell papers, 6, memorandum dated July, 1847 ; see also, ibid., 7, memorandum dated June, 1848, and Gooch, op. cit., i, p. 225.

[69] Compare this with Russell's flying visit to Ireland in 1833, which had not dissimilar consequences, H. W. Carless Davies, *The age of Grey and Peel,* pp. 251–3.

[70] Russell papers, 7, Russell : T. Reddington, 6 Sept. 1848. See also, S. Walpole, *Lord John Russell,* ii, pp. 75–6 ; Reid, *Lord John Russell,* p. 158.

[71] Walpole, op. cit., ii, p. 78.

[72] Monteagle MSS, N.L.I., Clarendon : Monteagle, 28 Jan. 1849. Grey replied non-committally, when he was first asked for his views on Russell's scheme. He said that so large scale a project would require a great deal of preparation, but that this was not necessarily a disadvantage, Russell papers, 7, Grey : Russell, 14 Sept. 1848.

[73] For a time he considered resignation, Monteagle MSS, N.L.I., Clarendon : Monteagle, 1 Jan. 1849 ; Walpole, op. cit., ii, pp. 80–1.

[74] *Hansard,* 3 series, cii, 460–1, 9 Feb. 1849.

[75] Monteagle MSS, N.L.I., Clarendon : Monteagle, 28 Jan. 1849. Clarendon blamed Wood's niggardliness and the invincible stupidity of Irish landlords for his repeated failures.

[76] Russell papers, G.D. 7, Wood : Russell, 1 June 1849.

[77] Monteagle MSS, N.L.I., Clarendon : Monteagle, 28 Jan. 1849.

[78] *Hansard,* 3 series, ciii, 151–3, 2 Mar. 1849 (Charles Wood).

[79] *12th rep. C.L.E.C.,* 10–11, [1499], H.C. 1852, xviii.

[80] *Census of Ireland, 1851,* general report, vi, pp. 53–4.

[81] Very probably, this chapter has dealt with Grey's and Russell's main projects at disproportionate length. This was necessary to give the episodes in sufficient detail, and both are fairly representative—one, of schemes with colonial ends in view ; the other, of schemes with Irish ends in view. But it must not be forgotten that they were merely *primus inter pares* ; and that there was much discussion, both in and out of parliament, which we have not had space to describe.

[82] On the other hand, Grey still wanted the continuation of Irish emigration until the ' natural balance ' between capital and labour was established, Grey, op. cit., i, p. 243.

[83] F. H. Hitchens, *The Colonial Land and Emigration Commission,* p. 292. See also Morrell, op. cit., p. 446.

[84] During and immediately after the famine, periodic emigration returns were circulated monthly in the cabinet ; later, this was reduced to a quarterly circulation ; and in 1854 it was dropped completely, C.O. 384/92, 678 Emigration North America, minute of T. F. Elliot, 20 Jan. 1854.

### iv. ASSISTED EMIGRATION TO AUSTRALIA

[1] This was less true of Irish emigrants in the latter half of the nineteenth century.

[2] A steerage passage to Australia cost about £20, or roughly five times as much as one to the United States.

[3] See *Rep. select comm. colonisation Ire.*, 111–21, 176, Q. 1106–74, 1708–10, [737], H.C. 1847, vi ; *2nd rep. select comm. colonisation Ire.*, 271, Q. 2744–8, H.C. 1847–8, (593), xvii ; C.O. 384/80, 1649 and 1683 Emigration, 2 Oct. 1847.

[4] Before the 1850's, it never exceeded 1,000 annually.

[5] Such an emigration was always difficult to carry out, because of the dangers of the passage and the extravagant demands of the colonists ; and many experiments in its execution were made during the first forty years of the nineteenth century. For these experiments, see Madgwick, op. cit.

[6] Ibid., pp. 189–91.

[7] As early as 1840, Russell had written, ' the Emigration Commissioners should not be made responsible for such parts of the system as they cannot control ', C.O. 384/59, 2,500 Emigration, minute of Russell, undated, December, 1840.

[8] *Papers rel. emigration Australia*, 10–12, H.C. 1847–8, (50. II), xlvii. See also Madgwick, op. cit., pp. 191–2. The campaign which culminated in these projects was initiated by Mrs Chisholm, a social reformer, who worked on behalf of Irish immigrants in Australia. Cf. C. Chisholm, *Emigration and transportation relatively considered.*

[9] *Papers rel. emigration Australia*, 22, H.C. 1847–8, (50. II), xlvii.

[10] The colonial funds had run out by 1844, and there had been no assisted emigration since that year, ibid., 7–9.

[11] Cf. Madgwick, op. cit., p. 217.

[12] C.O. 384/78, 1181 Canada, 6 Oct. 1846.

[13] *3rd rep. select comm. colonisation Ire.*, 4–55 H.C. 1849, (86), xi

[14] *Geelong Advertiser*, quoted by *Tipperary Vindicator*, 2 Oct. 184'

[15] *1st rep. select comm. colonisation Ire.*, 175, H.C. 1847–8, (415), xvii. This last proposal was acted on at a Cavan county meeting ; and the society which was formed appears to have come to some understanding with the Australian committees, *Nation*, 8 Sept. 1847, p. 22. But nothing came of it in the end.

[16] *2nd rep. select comm. colonisation Ire.*, 295, Q. 2871–6, H.C. 1847–8, (593), xvii (evidence of T. Murdoch).

[17] Most of them were relatives of earlier Irish emigrants. Previously, Fr Mathew had said that, although these emigrants had done well in Australia, they had not encouraged others to join them, because of the backward conditions in the settlements, *Rep. select comm. colonisation Ire.*, 251–2 Q. 2443–50, [737], H.C. 1847, vi.

[18] *Papers rel. emigration Australia*, 83–4, [968], H.C. 1847–8, xlvii. There was group emigration of another kind during 1847. Sir Montague Chapman, exercising tardily a right he had earned under the nomination system in 1840, sent out 200 of his Westmeath tenants in the spring, *Rep. select comm. colonisation Ire.*, 456–8, [737], H.C. 1847, vi.

[19] There were at that time roughly seven males to every female.

[20] *3rd rep. select comm. poor laws Ire.*, 133, Q. 2331–4, H.C. 1849, (137), xv, part i.

[21] *2nd rep. select comm. colonisation Ire.*, 295–6, Q. 2878, H.C. 1847–8, (415), xvii.

[22] *Papers rel. emigration Australia*, 110–12, [986], H.C. 1847–8, xlvii ; *1st rep. select comm. colonisation Ire.*, 59, Q. 540–2, H.C. 1847–8, (415), xvii. It must be remembered that communication between the home country and the colonies usually took about six months at this time, a fact which accounts for several of the peculiarities of the assisted emigration.

[23] E.g., *Hansard*, 3 series, xcvi, 968, 2 Feb. 1848.

[24] *1st rep. poor law commissioners Ire.*, 99, [963], H.C. 1847–8, xxxiii. See also *Cork Constitution*, 7 Nov. 1848 and 23 Jan. 1849.

[25] *1st rep. poor law commissioners Ire.*, 155, and appendix A, v, [963], H.C. 1847–8, xxxiii. Attempts were made to secure satisfactory lighting and ventilation between decks ; and space was screened off for a hospital.

[26] *National board of education minutes*, 6 and 22 Apr. 1849. See also C.O. 384/86, 9129 Emigration, commissioners : Merivale, 31 Oct. 1851.

[27] *1st rep. poor law commissioners Ire.*, 96–7, [963], H.C. 1847–8, xxxiii.

[28] *The Times*, 24 Jan. 1849.

[29] On Grey's suggestion, committees were formed in Australia, under the patronage of Catholic and anglican bishops, to look after the girls' religion, *Papers rel. emigration Australia*, 88–91, [968], H.C. 1847–8, xlvii.

[30] Apparently, the method of selection was this : all girls in the workhouse sat in the refectory, some reading, some writing, while the emigration officer walked up and down, making his choice, *Dublin Evening Post*, 21 Aug. 1849. Most accounts of the departure of a group of orphans pictured them as being healthy, neatly dressed, and in the highest spirits at the prospects before them, e.g., *Freeman's Journal*, 19 Apr. 1849 ; *Tipperary Vindicator*, 13 Jan. and 29 Aug. 1849 ; etc.

[31] *2nd rep. select comm. colonisation Ire.*, 296, Q. 2880–4, H.C. 1847–8, (593), xvii. The cost to the unions was less than £5 per capita.

[32] Ibid., 296, Q. 2878–9.

[33] *Tipperary Vindicator*, 22 Mar. 1848. See also *1st rep. poor law commissioners Ire.*, 96, [963], H.C. 1847–8, xxxiii.

[34] *2nd rep. select comm. colonisation Ire.*, 271, Q. 2734–8, H.C. 1847–8, (593), xvii ; *Limerick Chronicle*, 29 Apr. and 3 June 1848.

[35] *3rd rep. select comm. poor laws Ire.*, 81, Q. 1809, H.C. 1849, (137), xv, part i.

[36] *Limerick Chronicle*, 11 Oct. and 18 and 25 Nov. 1848.

[37] *3rd rep. select comm. poor laws Ire.*, 114, Q. 2350–7, H.C. 1849, (137), xv, part i. In Senior's case, this report seems ironical in the light of later developments. The selections from other parts of the country were made by emigration officers, Friend of Cork covering the west and south west, and Henry of Dublin, the remaining counties.

[38] *Papers rel. emigration Australia*, 29–30, H.C. 1849, (593), xxxiii.

[39] Madgwick, op. cit., pp. 210–11.

[40] Ibid., pp. 199–202.

[41] We may conjecture that some of the antipathy to the girls had a religious and racial basis ; and that some merely manifested the old feeling against pauper immigration.

[42] *Papers rel. emigration Australia*, 178–9, H.C. 1849, (593), xxxiii. Young, the governor general, does not seem to have been well disposed towards the emigrants, cf., ibid., 208–9.

[43] *Papers rel. emigration Australia*, 217, H.C. 1849, (593), xxxiii.

[44] Ibid., 221 ; *9th rep. C.L.E.C.*, 13, [1082], H.C. 1849, xxii.

[45] *Papers rel. emigration Australia*, 59–60, [1163], H.C. 1850, xl.

[46] *9th rep. C.L.E.C.*, 8, [1082], H.C. 1849, xxii.

[47] *10th rep. C.L.E.C.*, 10, [1024], H.C. 1850, xxiii.

[48] *Papers rel. emigration Australia*, 94–8, 106–26, [1163], 1850, xl.

[49] *11th rep. C.L.E.C.*, 4, 14, [1383], H.C. 1851, xxii. See also *Freeman's Journal*, 14 Oct. 1850 ; *Advocate*, 3 Oct. 1849, p. 165.

[50] *2nd rep. poor law commissioners Ire.*, 9–10, [1119], H.C. 1849, xxv.

[51] In the three years of its operation, more than 4,000 Irish orphans reached Australia. The bulk of them landed in New South Wales, Madgwick, op. cit., pp. 211–12.

[52] *Papers rel. emigration Australia,* 215–16, [1163], H.C. 1850, xl.

[53] *10th rep. C.L.E.C.,* 18–19, [1024], H.C. 1851, xxiii.

[54] Monteagle MSS, N.L.I., Mrs Chisholm : Monteagle, 9 Feb. 1849.

[55] *Papers rel. emigration Australia,* 199–201, [1163], H.C. 1850, xl. See also *Nation,* 23 Mar. 1850, p. 477 ; *Hansard,* 3 series, cii, 1217, 26 Feb. 1849.

[56] *11th rep. C.L.E.C.,* 5, [1383], H.C. 1851, xxii ; *12th rep. C.L.E.C.,* 23–6, [1499], H.C. 1852, xvii.

[57] *Papers rel. emigration Australia,* 79–81, [1489], H.C. 1852, xxxiv. The commissioners' apology was not flattering to Ireland, see ibid., 108–9.

[58] *1st rep. select comm. colonisation Ire.,* 53–4, Q. 484–93, H.C. 1847–8, (415), xvii. Aubrey de Vere made some suggestions for recruiting a better type of emigrant, *7th rep. select comm. poor laws Ire.,* 92, Q. 5689–93, H.C. 1849, (237), xv, part i ; and the commissioners sent an agent to Ulster in 1852 to promote emigration from the province, C.O. 384/98, 5063 Australian Emigration, 30 May 1857.

[59] *Nation,* 6 Oct. 1849, p. 85.

[60] *Papers rel. emigration Australia,* 84–5, [1489], H.C. 1852, xxxiv.

[61] C.O. 384/92, 6410 Emigration, 26 July 1854 ; C.O. 384/97, 7618 South Australia Emigration, 22 Aug. 1856 ; C.O. 384/98, 5063 Australia Emigration, 30 May 1857 ; *Adelaide Observer,* quoted by *The Times,* 16 Aug. 1856 ; *The Times,* 22 Aug. 1856.

[62] *Hansard,* 3 series, civ, 332, 347, 16 Apr. 1849 ; *7th rep. select comm. poor laws Ire.,* 92, Q. 5689–93, H.C. 1849, (237), xv, part i.

[63] Most of them came from Cork or Tipperary, the main centres of the pre-famine movement, or from the north eastern parts of Ulster.

[64] Monteagle MSS, N.L.I., letters from assisted emigrants to Monteagle or Lady Monteagle, during the period, 12 Jan. 1849 to 13 Apr. 1857.


## V. SHIPPING AND THE VOYAGE

[1] C.O. 384/80, 1333 Emigration North America. Even from day to day, at times, *2nd rep. select comm. emigrant ships,* 45–6, Q. 3820, H.C. 1854, (349), xiii.

[2] By 1848, a three cornered traffic, New Orleans or some other southern port to Liverpool with cotton, Liverpool to the Atlantic states with emigrants, and New York to the south with manufactured goods, coals or hard cargoes, was an established pattern, *Liverpool Mercury,* quoted by *Freeman's Journal,* 4 Apr. 1849.

[3] *Rep. select comm. colonisation Ire.,* 479–80, Q. 4474–87, [737], H.C. 1847, vi (evidence of R. Carter). See also C.O. 384/73, 324 Emigration, 25 Feb. 1842.

[4] C.O. 384/79, 660 Emigration, 22 Apr. 1847 ; *Papers rel. emigration B.N.A.,* 170, 178, H.C. 1847–8, (50), xlvii.

[5] The case of the ' Faithful ' shows how this traffic was carried on. The master, hoping to avoid the passenger acts by embarking and landing his passengers where no emigration officers were stationed, agreed to take seventeen of them for 40s. each, and two others for 10s. each. One man was to work his passage out ; another was to pay for his sister's passage by labour in Canada ; and so on, *12th rep. C.L.E.C.,* 84, [1499], H.C. 1852, xviii. This case came to light accidently, *Papers rel. emigration B.N.A.,* 1–2, H.C. 1851, (348), xl. A good deal of this sort of private bargaining must have taken place unnoticed.

[6] *Rep. select comm. colonisation Ire.,* 446, Q. 4427, [737], H.C. 1847, vi.

[7] *Papers rel. emigration B.N.A.,* 170, H.C. 1847–8, (50), xlvii.

[8] *Freeman's Journal,* 25 Mar. and 2 Apr. 1847.

[9] C.O. 384/80, 344 Miscellaneous Emigration, 6 Mar. 1847.

[10] *Rep. select comm. colonisation Ire.,* 482–3, Q. 4507–18, [737], H.C. 1847, vi. More than half a million tons of British shipping cleared for North America in ballast during 1847, ibid., 16, appendix iii. Sailing in ballast enabled vessels to secure a second cargo of foodstuffs in the season.

[11] Other factors exaggerated this tendency, as well, e.g., the increase in the price of bread, and the stringency of the new state immigrant legislation in the United States, *Morning Chronicle,* 3 May 1847, p. 6.

[12] C.O. 384/79, 660 Emigration, commissioners : J. Stephen, 22 Apr. 1847 ; *Rep. select comm. colonisation Ire.,* 210, 249, 446, Q. 2045, 2419, 4427, [737], H.C. 1847, vi.

[13] *9th rep. select comm. poor laws Ire.,* 24–5, Q. 7504–10, H.C. 1849, (301), xv, part i ; *Rep. select comm. colonisation Ire.,* 634–5, Q. 3232–41, [737], H.C. 1847, vi (evidence of W. Monsell).

[14] *Rep. select comm. colonisation Ire.,* 481–3, Q. 4498–518, [737], H.C. 1847, vi.

[15] They had always maintained, the report continued, that ' when the Season arrived, the ordinary course of Trade would supply vessels,' C.O. 384/79, 660 Emigration, commissioners : J. Stephen, 22 Apr. 1847.

[16] E.g., *The Times,* 24 June 1851 ; *Nation,* 5 Apr. 1851, p. 501.

[17] *Rep. select comm. colonisation Ire.,* 482–3, Q. 4507–18, [737], H.C. 1847, vi.

[18] This represented a great levelling up in the fares, although United States rates had once sunk below Canadian during 1848, C.O. 384/84, 361 Miscellaneous, 13 Jan. 1849 ; C.O. 384/81, 820 Emigration, 20 Apr. 1848. For the 1850 rates, see C.O. 384/88, 158 Canada, 8 Jan. 1850 ; for the 1854 rates see *1st rep. select comm. emigrant ships,* 78, Q. 1292, H.C. 1854, (163), xiii.

[19] To appreciate the prodigious advances which had been made since the 1830's see C.O. 384/30, 1333 Emigration, customs : T. F. Elliot, 28 Jan. 1832.

[20] See especially *2nd rep. select comm. emigrant ships,* iii–xii, H.C. 1854, (349), xiii.

[21] Cf. R. L. Schuyler *The fall of the old colonial system,* pp. 171–2. In 1851, the commissioners, anticipating a complete revolution in the trade within a decade, rushed through legislation to meet it, C.O. 384/86, 815 Emigration, 25 Jan. 1851 ; *11th rep. C.L.E.C.,* 2–3, [1383], H.C. 1851, xxii.

[22] E.g., for 1846, *Papers rel. emigration B.N.A.,* 8, [777], H.C. 1847, xxxix ; *7th rep. C.L.E.C.,* 63, [899], H.C. 1847, xxxiii.

[23] *Rep. select comm. passenger acts,* 494–5, Q. 4372, H.C. 1851, (632), xix.

[24] Passages from Irish Atlantic ports were usually some four days shorter than those from Liverpool, *Rep. select comm. colonisation Ire.,* 342–4, Q. 3302–13, [737], H.C. 1847, vi (evidence of F. Spaight).

[25] Hatches were placed over the ventilation shafts during bad weather, *2nd rep. select comm. colonisation Ire.,* 344–5, Q. 3300–13, H.C. 1847–8, (593), xvii. This was done at night, as well. According to one witness, the resultant filth and stench was ' indescribable,' *1st rep. select comm. emigrant ships,* 83–4, Q. 1400–42, H.C. 1854, (163), xiii (evidence of S. Redmond).

[26] E.g., *Freeman's Journal,* 2 and 7 Apr. 1849 ; *Nation,* 5 Apr. 1851, p. 501.

[27] *Papers rel. emigration B.N.A.,* 53, 58, [1474], H.C. 1852, xxxiii.

[28] *Cork Constitution,* 8 May 1847.

[29] *7th rep. C.L.E.C.,* 2, [809], H.C. 1847, xxxiii ; *1st rep. select comm. emigrant ships,* 156, Q. 2874, 2882–4, H.C. 1854, (163), xiii.

[30] They were sometimes known as ' kettle bottoms ' in the trade, *Papers rel. emigration B.N.A.,* 34, H.C. 1851, (348), xl. See also *Further papers rel. emigration B.N.A.,* 8–17, 42–50, [964], H.C. 1847–8, xlvii.

[31] *2nd rep. select comm. colonisation Ire.,* 345, Q. 3306, H.C. 1847–8, (593), xvi. Heavy freight was usually stowed in the orlop.

[32] *Rep. select comm. colonisation Ire.,* 16–17, 58–9, [737], H.C. 1847, vi.

[33] C.O. 384/82, 1768 Emigration, 9 Sept. 1848 ; C.O. 384/88, 158 Canada, 8 Jan. 1850. In one respect, American vessels were inferior to British. Since their decks were permanent and carried much superstructure, passengers found it difficult to take exercise, *Rep. select comm. passenger acts,* 485–6, Q. 4288–93, H.C. 1851, (632), xix.

[34] Schuyler, op. cit., pp. 174–5.

[35] E.g., *Hansard,* 3 series, xcii, 1237–40, 21 May 1847 (R. V. Smith) ; xcviii, 1019–20, 15 May 1848 (H. Labouchere) ; xcix, 528, 9 June 1848 (Sir George Clark). See also R. G. Albion, *The rise of New York port,* pp. 330–40.

[36] *Freeman's Journal,* 28 Mar. 1848.

[37] J. F. Maguire, *The Irish in America,* p. 181.

[38] *1st rep. select comm. emigrant ships,* 175, Q. 3194, H.C. 1854, (163), xiii (evidence of Capt. Schomberg) ; ibid., 156, Q. 2870 (evidence of Capt. Walker).

[39] *Papers rel. emigration B.N.A.,* 13–14, H.C. 1847–8, (50), xlvii. This indifference may have been caused, in part, by malnutrition, and, in part, by that sort of quietism which so many contemporaries observed in the Irish character. Cf. ' Through all, the forbearance of the Irish peasantry and the calm submission with which they bore the deadliest ills that can fall on man can scarcely be paralleled in the history of any people ,' *Census of Ireland, 1851,* general report, part v, p. 243.

[40] *Further papers rel. emigration B.N.A.,* 17, [964], H.C. 1847–8, xlvii.

[41] C.O. 384/79, 535 Canada, S. de Vere : Monteagle. De Vere was a humanitarian who sailed to Canada as a steerage passenger in 1847 so ' that he might speak as a witness respecting the sufferings of Emigrants ', and do something to improve their lot, W. Ward, *Aubrey de Vere, a memoir,* p. 184.

[42] *Papers rel. emigration B.N.A.,* 9–10, 26–7, [777], H.C. 1847, xxxix. The vessel, which had been built in 1763, was quite unfit for emigrants. See also C.O. 384/78, 1181 Canada, 3 Oct. 1846 ; C.O. 384/79, 211 Canada, 13 Feb. 1847 ; *7th rep. C.L.E.C.,* 19, [809], H.C. 1847, xxxiii ; *Nation,* 5 Sept. 1846, p. 741.

[43] C.O. 384/88, 4018 North America, 29 Mar. and 5 Apr. 1851. The ' Bache M'Ever ' had arrived in New Orleans in much the same state in 1850, C.O. 384/88, 3531 Emigration, 27 Apr. 1850 ; 2338 Emigration, 27 Mar. 1850. See also *1st rep. select comm. emigrant ships,* 118–22, Q. 2070–195, H.C. 1854, (163), xiii.

[44] *Further papers rel. emigration B.N.A.,* 14, [932], H.C. 1847–8, xlvii. What closets there were were so unsubstantial that the first heavy sea would break them up completely, and complaints about sanitation were universal, C.O. 384/89, 3365 Emigration, 14 Apr. 1852 ; C.O. 384/73, 767 Emigration, 7 Apr. 1842. But the problems in marine engineering which they posed seemed insoluble at the time, *1st rep. select comm. emigrant ships,* 25, 114, Q. 290–7, 2009–11, H.C. 1854, (163), xiii.

[45] *Rep. select comm. passenger acts,* 486, Q. 4294–7, H.C. 1851, (632), xix.

[46] *Rep. select comm. passenger acts,* 416–30, 491–2, Q. 3788–851, 4341–50.

[47] *Morning Chronicle,* 15 July 1850, p. 5.

[48] Though the 1852 act required the employment of stewards on large vessels to maintain order, decency and cleanliness, the regulation was avoided, in spirit, at least, by appointing one of the passengers themselves ; it was pleaded that qualified men could not be obtained, *1st rep. select comm. emigrant ships,* 87, Q. 1494–505, H.C. 1854, (163), xiii ; *2nd rep. select comm. emigrant ships,* 152–3, Q. 5789–91, H.C. 1854, (349), xiii.

[49] *3rd rep. select comm. colonisation Ire.,* appendix x, 125–32, H.C. 1849, (86), xi.

[50] Of course, many of the dangers and evils it lights up were present potentially in every other season.

[51] *Further papers rel. emigration B.N.A.*, 23–31, [964], H.C. 1847–8, xlvii. The death rate was highest during the spring and summer, *Papers rel. emigration B.N.A.*, 22–3, [777], H.C. 1847, xxxix ; *Papers rel. emigration B.N.A.*, 11, 87–92, 105–6, 128, 144, H.C. 1847–8, (50), xlvii.

[52] According to United States statistics, 17% of the total 1847 emigration perished during the year, *1st rep. select comm. emigrant ships*, 100, Q. 1736–40, H.C. 1854, (163), xiii. This must have included deaths after disembarkation.

[53] *Papers rel. emigration B.N.A.*, 108–9, 122, H.C. 1847–8, (50), xlvii. This opinion appears to have been shared by the colonial officials, ibid., 55–61, 103–4.

[54] *1st rep. select comm. emigrant ships*, 124, 158, Q. 2250–4, 2921–32, H.C. 1854, (163), xiii.

[55] *2nd rep. select comm. colonisation Ire.*, 344–5, Q. 3302–13, H.C. 1847–8, (593), xvii.

[56] *Papers rel. emigration B.N.A.*, 33, H.C. 1847–8, (50), xlvii. Other suggested causes were the long passages, the smallness of vessels, and the fact that so many of them carried freight, ibid., 179 ; *Further papers rel. emigration B.N.A.*, 13, [964], H.C. 1847–8, xlvii. According to Melville, it was ' noisome confinement in so close, unventilated and crowded a den,' together with hunger and personal un-cleanliness, which brought on fever.

[57] *Further papers rel. emigration B.N.A.*, 8, [985], H.C. 1847–8, xlvii. See also *Papers rel. emigration B.N.A.*, 138–40, 147, H.C. 1847–8, (50), xlvii.

[58] *Papers rel. emigration B.N.A.*, 31–9, H.C. 1847–8, (50), xlvii.

[59] *Further papers rel. emigration B.N.A.*, 5, [985], H.C. 1847–8, xlvii.

[60] *Further papers rel. emigration B.N.A.*, 8, [985], H.C. 1847–8, xlvii. The emigration commissioners appear to have shared this view, C.O. 384/81, 1649 Emigration, 30 Aug. 1848 ; *1st rep. select comm. colonisation Ire.*, 43–4, Q. 451, H.C. 1847–8, (419), xvii (evidence of T. F. Elliot). See also *Daily News*, quoted by *Waterford Mail*, 30 Jan. 1847. Passengers sometimes complained of feeling bilious and depressed after leaving their lodging houses, *Papers rel. emigration B.N.A.*, 138, H.C. 1847–8, (50), xlvii.

[61] E.g., *Papers rel. emigration North American colonies*, 38, 57–61, H.C. 1849, (593.II), xxxviii ; *Despatches rel. emigration North American colonies*, 4, 12, 30–5, H.C. 1851, (348), xl.

[62] These statistics were based on the brokers' returns for vessels sailing from Liverpool to New York between 8 Aug. and 3 Nov. 1853, C.O. 384/92, 3414 North America Emigration, 20 Apr. 1854.

[63] *Further papers rel. emigration B.N.A.*, 16, [985], H.C. 1847–8, xlvii ; *Papers rel. emigration B.N.A.*, 25–6, [1025], H.C. 1849, xxxviii. They often found other causes, such as increases in food or space allowances, for similar ' improvements,' C.O. 384/81, 749 North America, 5 Apr. 1848.

[64] E.g., Mulligan MSS, Dr Urquhart : Dr Mulligan, 17 Oct. 1851 ; *Further papers rel. emigration B.N.A.*, 12–13, [964], H.C. 1847–8, xlvii.

[65] *1st rep. select comm. emigrant ships*, 28 115, Q. 432–45, 2016–20, H.C. 1854, (163), xiii. The emigrant ships committee found the general standard of competence very low, *2nd rep. select comm. emigrant ships*, v, H.C. 1854, (349), xiii.

[66] *Treatment of passengers on board ' Washington,'* 3–6, H.C. 1851, (198), xl.

[67] *1st rep. select comm. emigrant ships*, 86–8, 121, Q. 1506–14, 2141–68, H.C. 1854, (163), xiii. See also *1st rep. select comm. colonisation Ire.*, 50–1, H.C. 1847–8, (415), xvii.

[68] *1st rep. select comm. emigrant ships*, 9, 19, 21, Q. 105–15, 290–3, 325, H.C. 1854, (163), xiii.

[69] In the long run, Irish emigration profited greatly from both, but many seasons were to pass before it did so fully ; and, during those years, cholera and typhus epidemics still swept the vessels now and then. For 1853, the worst season since

1847, see C.O. 384/90, 10939 Emigration, 10 Nov. 1853 ; C.O. 384/92, 449 North
America Emigration, 10 Jan. 1854 ; *The Times*, 27 Dec. 1853 ; for the cholera
outbreak of 1849, see C.O. 384/83, 8397 Canada Emigration, 2 Oct. 1849.

## vi. THE IRISH IN BRITISH NORTH AMERICA

[1] See C.O. 384/69, 118 Canada, commissioners : Stephen, 2 Feb. 1842 ; ibid.,
unmarked, commissioners : Stephen, 9 May 1842 ; C.O. 384/74, 246 Canada,
8 Mar. 1843.

[2] *Rep. select comm. colonisation Ire.*, 10, 13–15, Q. 57–68, 88–101 [737], H.C. 1847,
vi (evidence of T. F. Elliot). The treasury believed that relief was primarily a
colonial affair, and that the United Kingdom should be charged with none of the
expense, C.O. 384/43, 1066 Lower Canada, Treasury : Stephen, 29 June 1837.
But its efforts to avoid paying part of the cost ultimately failed.

[3] C.O. 384/75, 315 Canada, 21 Mar. 1844. The commissioners were at pains
to conceal even the existence of the fund, C.O. 384/78, 61 Canada, 24 Jan. 1846 ;
ibid., 290 Canada, 23 Mar. 1846.

[4] *2nd rep. select comm. colonisation Ire.*, 287, Q. 2830, H.C. 1847–8, (593), xvii.
New Brunswick appropriated some of the immigrant tax each year for its own
purposes, in spite of annual remonstrances, ibid., 283–4, Q. 2796–801 ; *Rep. select
comm. colonisation Ire.*, 19–20, Q. 159–62, [737], H.C. 1847, vi.

[5] *Papers rel. emigration B.N.A.*, 90, H.C. 1847–8, (50), xlvii.

[6] *Elgin : Grey papers*, iii, p. 1093.

[7] *Papers rel. emigration B.N.A.*, 26–8, [777], H.C. 1847, xxxix.

[8] About one half of the 9,000 Irish emigrants to New Brunswick crossed the border
to the United States, and the remainder got good employment, as there was a boom
in shipbuilding and public works, ibid., 39. But the death rate in quarantine at
St John was 5%, *Papers rel. emigration B.N.A.*, 90, H.C. 1847–8, (50), xlvii.

[9] The commissioners were always loath to publish encouraging accounts of this
nature. ' Such publications,' they told Stephen, ' are calculated to raise undue
expectations among intending Emigrants,' C.O. 384/78, 1209 Canada, 10 Nov. 1845.

[10] *Papers rel. emigration B.N.A.*, 14–41, [777], H.C. 1847, xxxix. The New Brunswick assembly had placed £3,000 at Perley's disposal, *Further papers rel. emigration
B.N.A.*, 20, [824], H.C. 1847, xxxix.

[11] *Morning Chronicle*, 17 May 1847, p. 3.

[12] E.g., the provisioning system at Quebec, *Annual rep. Canadian agent general
emigration*, 5, 10, H.C. 1837, (132), xlii ; C.O. 384/35, 1823 Lower Canada, 30 May
1834 ; C.O. 384/38, 845 Emigration, 29 Aug. 1835 ; or the overcrowding on the
river steamers, C.O. 384/69, 580 Emigration Canada, commissioners : Stephen,
12 Apr. 1842.

[13] *Papers rel. emigration B.N.A.*, 3–4, H.C. 1847–8, (50), xlvii.

[14] C.O. 384/81, 1518 Canada, commissioners : Merivale, 4 Aug. 1848.

[15] It was, in fact, the Irish famine being reenacted upon the other side of the
Atlantic ; and the colonial officials, like those at home, were forced to spend money
and assume powers quite recklessly, simply because no other course seemed possible.
From the outset, for example, Buchanan went so far as to compel all servants to
remain upon the stricken island, unless they could provide substitutes for themselves,
C.O. 384/81, 1518 Canada, commissioners : Merivale, 4 Aug. 1848.

[16] *Papers rel. emigration B.N.A.*, 3–4, H.C. 1847–8, (50), xlvii.

[17] *Morning Chronicle*, 24 July 1847, p. 7.

[18] Maguire, op. cit., pp. 136–7. A midshipman who visited the island in July
said that his blood ran cold when he first saw the bodies heaped together by the
shallow graves, and the sick almost naked on the earth, *Cork Constitution*, 5 Aug. 1847.

[19] *3rd rep. select comm. colonisation Ire.*, 123–4, H.C. 1849, (86), xi.

[20] *Papers rel. emigration B.N.A.*, 3–4, 8–9, H.C. 1847–8, (50), xlvii.

[21] The phrase was Stephen de Vere's, *Further papers rel. emigration B.N.A.*, 15, [932], H.C. 1847–8, xlvii. A little later, the Canadian local authorities limited very strictly the numbers who might be carried, *Further papers rel. emigration B.N.A.*, 20, [964], H.C. 1847–8, xlvii.

[22] For the relief measures taken in Montreal, see G. R. C. Keep, ʻThe Irish Congregations in nineteenth century Montreal,' in *Irish Ecclesiastical Record*, Dec. 1950, pp 503–6. For a description of the Montreal hospital arrangements, see *Ami de la religion*, quoted by *Tipperary Vindicator*, 25 Aug. 1847. See also Maguire, op. cit., pp. 145–8, 152–4.

[23] *Montreal Herald*, quoted by *Northern Whig*, 13 July 1847.

[24] *Papers rel. emigration B.N.A.*, 5–8, H.C. 1847–8, (50), xlvii.

[25] Ibid., 20–1 ; *Further papers rel. emigration B.N.A.*, 1–5, 22–31, [932], H.C. 1847–8, xlvii ; *Further papers rel. emigration B.N.A.*, 17–23, [964], H.C. 1847–8, xlvii ; etc.

[26] *Papers rel. emigration B.N.A.*, 20, H.C. 1847–8, (50), xlvii.

[27] *Further papers rel. emigration B.N.A.*, 18, [932], H.C. 1847–8, xlvii ; Keep, op. cit., p. 503 ; Maguire, op. cit., pp. 138–50.

[28] Scarcely anyone on the island escaped infection for longer than three weeks, *Further papers rel. emigration B.N.A.*, 7–11, [985], H.C. 1847–8, xlvii ; C.O. 384/81, 1518 Canada commissioners : Merivale, 4 Aug. 1848. In the interior the story was the same. At Montreal, a whole congregation of nursing nuns succumbed to fever ; at Point St Charles, the bishop himself fell a victim, Maguire, op. cit., pp. 136–7, 145–8.

[29] See *8th rep. C.L.E.C.*, 14–15, [961], H.C. 1847–8, xxvi.

[30] *Papers rel. emigration B.N.A.*, 30–1, [777], H.C. 1847, xxxix.

[31] Ibid., 14–16.

[32] Ibid., 29.

[33] Ibid., 30–1 ; *Further papers rel. emigration B.N.A.*, 5, [985], H.C. 1847–8, xlvii. This uneasiness appears to have been shared by many provident Canadians, *Morning Chronicle*, 19 Apr. 1847, p. 2. See also C. Gavan Duffy, *Four years of Irish history*, p. 532 ; *Rep. select comm. colonisation Ire.*, appendix 5, 33–4, [737], H.C. 1847, vi (evidence of A. C. Buchanan).

[34] *Durham report*, p. 83, Q. 576, Appendix (B), H.C. 1839, (3.III), xvii. See also C.O. 384/35, 4138 Lower Canada, Buchanan : Hay, 23 Sept. 1834.

[35] *Papers rel. emigration B.N.A.*, 5–8, H.C. 1847–8, (50), xlvii ; Ferrie, op. cit., pp. 1–10 ; *Further papers rel. emigration B.N.A.*, 35–42, [932], H.C. 1847–8, xlvii.

[36] *Papers rel. emigration B.N.A.*, 26, 31, H.C. 1847–8, (50), xlvii. Canadian newspapers were denouncing Britain in terms reminiscent of more dangerous days, W. P. M. Kennedy, *Lord Elgin*, pp. 60–1.

[37] Walrond, op. cit., pp. 43–5.

[38] *Papers rel. emigration B.N.A.*, 13, H.C. 1847–8, (50), xlvii. The inhabitants of Toronto declared that, if the emigration were a chastening from God, it would have been borne meekly, but that it had sprung instead from slovenly neglect, *Further papers rel. emigration B.N.A.*, 21–2, [932], H.C. 1847–8, xlvii.

[39] *Papers rel. emigration B.N.A.*, 61–2, 85, H.C. 1847–8, (50), xlvii. See also N. F. Davin, *The Irishman in Canada*, p. 541. The new federal and state restrictive immigrant legislation of 1847 increased the fares to the United States considerably, and thus diverted much of the emigration to British North America.

[40] *Further papers rel. emigration B.N.A.*, 6, [932], H.C. 1847–8, xlvii.

⁴¹ *Papers rel. emigration B.N.A.,* 6, H.C. 1847–8, (50), xlvii.

⁴² Ibid., 14–16. Grey appears to have accepted Elgin's judgment almost at once *Further papers rel. emigration B.N.A.,* 32–3, [932], H.C. 1847–8, xlvii.

⁴³ Russell papers, 6, Wood : Russell, 5 Sept. 1847.

⁴⁴ There was protracted bickering between the treasury and the provinces about the details of the accounts. The treasury regarded the Canadian claims as ' unsatisfactory and insufficient,' *Copies . . . of despatches rel. emigration B.N.A.,* 35–8, H.C. 1851, (348), xl. It is rather surprising that the question of this indemnity was never raised in parliament.

⁴⁵ *Further papers rel. emigration B.N.A.,* 32–4, 65–6, [932], H.C. 1847–8, xlvii ; *Further papers rel. emigration B.N.A.,* 33, [964], H.C. 1847–8, xlvii.

⁴⁶ *Papers rel. emigration B.N.A.,* 27–31, 38–9, 159–60, H.C. 1847–8, (50), xlvii.

⁴⁷ *Further papers rel. emigration B.N.A.,* 35–40, 52–3, [964], H.C. 1847–8, xlvii. The minor provisions of the new statutes were equally severe.

⁴⁸ *Further papers rel. emigration B.N.A.,* 27–9, [932], H.C. 1847–8, xlvii.

⁴⁹ *Papers rel. emigration B.N.A.,* 38–41, 165–6, H.C. 1847–8, (50), xlvii.

⁵⁰ *1st rep. select comm. colonisation Ire.,* 51–2, Q. 478–80, H.C. 1847–8, (415), xvii ; *Further papers rel. emigration B.N.A.,* 1–9, [985], H.C. 1847–8, xlvii. See also *Cork Examiner,* 8 May 1848.

⁵¹ *Papers rel. emigration B.N.A.,* 63–9, 71, 90, 120–9, H.C. 1847–8, (50), xlvii.

⁵² Ibid., 122–6.

⁵³ Ibid., 87–104.

⁵⁴ *Further papers rel. emigration B.N.A.,* 45–6, 50–8, 64–5, [932], H.C. 1847–8, xlvii.

⁵⁵ *Papers rel. emigration B.N.A.,* 159, H.C. 1847–8, (50), xlvii.

⁵⁶ Ibid., 150. There were precedents for such action. In 1843, Canada assisted several immigrants out of public funds to return to Ireland, C.O. 384/74, 667 Canada, commissioners : Hope, 28 June 1843. And by sec. 17, c. 46, of the revised state laws of Massachusetts in 1850, a similar power was given to any justice of the peace in the state. But the imperial government always strongly opposed the use of colonial funds for such a purpose.

⁵⁷ *Papers rel. emigration B.N.A.,* 3–6, 38–9, [1025], H.C. 1849, xxxviii. In the later part of the season, the health of the immigrants was, if anything, even better.

⁵⁸ *Papers rel. emigration B.N.A.,* 14, 25–30, 37–41, [1025], H.C. 1849, xxxviii. See also *Limerick Chronicle,* 2 Sept. and 1 Nov. 1848.

⁵⁹ *Further papers rel. emigration B.N.A.,* 8–18, [971], H.C. 1847–8, xlvii.

⁶⁰ *Further papers rel. emigration B.N.A.,* 41–50, [964], H.C. 1847–8, xlvii ; *Further papers rel. emigration B.N.A.,* 13–19, [985], H.C. 1847–8, xlvii.

⁶¹ To some extent, the consequences of this failure reawakened the colonial resentment, *Papers rel. emigration North American colonies,* 47–8, 57–63, H.C. 1849, (593.II), xxxviii.

⁶² C.O. 384/84, 361 Miscellaneous, commissioners : Merivale, 13 Jan. 1849 ; C.O. 384/81, 820 Emigration North America, 20 Apr. 1848.

⁶³ *2nd rep. select comm. colonisation Ire.,* 271, 285–94, Q. 2740, 2811–62, H.C. 1847–8, (593), xvii.

⁶⁴ *Papers rel. emigration B.N.A.,* 26–7, [1025], H.C. 1849, xxxviii. See also C.O. 384/81, 734 Canada, 7 Apr. 1848.

⁶⁵ C.O. 384/81, 820 Emigration North America, F. Spaight : Col. Wyndham, 10 Apr. 1848 ; C.O. 384/81, 421 Emigration, printed circular issued by J. & W. Robertson, 25 Feb. 1848.

⁶⁶ *Papers rel. emigration North American colonies,* 1, 74, H.C. 1849, (593.II), xxxviii ; *Papers rel. emigration B.N.A.,* 18, [1025], H.C. 1849, xxxviii.

[67] *10th rep. C.L.E.C.*, 1–3, [1024], H.C. 1850, xxiii ; *Papers rel. emigration North American colonies*, 49–62, H.C. 1849, (593.II), xxxviii ; *Copies . . . of despatches rel. emigration North American colonies*, 40, H.C. 1851, (348), xl.

[68] *Reports . . . on past and present state of H.M. colonial possessions*, 4, [1919], H.C. 1854–5, xxxvi, report of Elgin.

[69] *Copies . . . of despatches rel. emigration North American colonies*, 5–14, 66–7, H.C. 1851, (348), xl.

[70] Ibid., 16–22, 30–5, 47–8. This was so in spite of a particularly keen demand for labour on the Montreal : Portland railroad.

[71] *Papers rel. emigration North American colonies*, 23–6, 34–5, 43–9, [1474], H.C. 1852, xxxiii. Timber merchants were offering as much as 3s. 4d. a day for labourers, ibid., 54 ; *12th rep. C.L.E.C.*, 10–11, [1499], H.C. 1852, xviii.

[72] *Copies . . . of despatches rel. emigration North American colonies*, 33–6, H.C. 1857, (125), xxviii. Many vain efforts were made to persuade the imperial authorities to do something to divert the stream of Irish emigration to the provinces, C.O. 384/88, 158 Canada Emigration, commissioners : Merivale, 8 Jan. 1850.

## vii. THE IRISH IN THE UNITED STATES OF AMERICA

[1] This number includes some who had re-emigrated from British North America on coastal vessels.

[2] Maguire, op. cit., pp. 184–6, 208.

[3] Cf. *3rd rep. select comm. colonisation Ire.*, 85, appendix Q, H.C. 1849, (86), xi. See also *Nation*, 4 Sept. 1847, p. 775.

[4] *State of New York in assembly, document no. 46, 1848*, evidence of C. Webb.

[5] Ibid., evidence of H. Vail. See also *Tipperary Vindicator*, 29 Apr. 1848.

[6] See R. J. Purcell, ' The Irish emigration society of New York ', in *Studies*, xxvii, pp. 583–99 ; Peyton, op. cit., p. 75 ; *Nation*, 21 and 29 Aug. 1847, pp. 729, 731 ; my article, op. cit., in *I.H.S.*, v, pp. 300–2.

[7] E.g., *Boston Pilot*, quoted by *Pilot*, 24 June 1846 ; *Freeman's Journal*, 18 July 1846.

[8] *2nd rep. select comm. colonisation Ire.*, 333, Q. 3188–92, H.C. 1847–8, (593), xvii (evidence of R. B. Minturn).

[9] Entitled *An act, regulating passenger ships and vessels, 2nd March 1819.*

[10] *Rep. select comm. colonisation Ire.*, 261–2, appendix 28, 17371, H.C. 1847, vi. See also *2nd rep. select comm. colonisation Ire.*, 286, Q. 2820, H.C. 1847–8, (593), xvii ; *Papers rel. emigration B.N.A.*, 37, H.C. 1847–8, (50), xlvii.

[11] Like the captain who wrote, ' if I am not capable of judging what is proper for the stowage and management of any ship after 21 years, masters of American ships may hereafter know that the confidence hitherto reposed in them has been misplaced ', C.O. 384/88, 7161 Emigration, 20 Aug. 1851.

[12] E.g., C.O. 384/88, 9669 and 10116 North America, 15 and 20 Nov. 1851.

[13] *Further papers rel. emigration B.N.A.*, 5, 19851, H.C. 1847–8, xlvii.

[14] *First report commissioners of emigration, New York, 1847*, quoted by Maguire, op. cit., p. 187.

[15] The text of the New York state legislation is contained in *Papers rel. emigration North American colonies*, 78–81, H.C. 1849, (593), xxxviii.

[16] *Twentieth report commissioners of emigration, New York, 1866*, quoted by Maguire, op. cit., pp. 211–12.

[17] *3rd rep. select comm. colonisation Ire.*, 86–8, appendix Q, H.C. 1849, (86), xi,

[18] This secondary purpose was never satisfactorily fulfilled.

[19] *3rd rep. select comm. colonisation Ire.*, 333–8, H.C. 1849, (86), xi.

[20] Ibid., 87, appendix Q.

[21] Only 850 of the 7,000 patients who entered the emigrant hospital died during 1847.

[22] *3rd rep. select comm. colonisation Ire.*, 86–7, appendix Q, H.C. 1849, (86), xi.

[23] *State of New York in assembly, document no. 46, 1848*, pp. 81–2. See also *2nd rep. select comm. colonisation Ire.*, 342–4, Q. 3287–301, H.C. 1847–8, (593), xvii.

[24] *Morning Chronicle*, 15 and 29 June 1847, pp. 4 and 6 respectively.

[25] Ibid., 15 May 1847, p. 6. See also *Limerick Chronicle*, 17 and 27 July 1847 ; *Waterford Mail*, 26 May 1847 ; etc.

[26] *2nd rep. select comm. colonisation Ire.*, 286, Q. 2820–2, H.C. 1847–8, (593), xvii ; Russell papers, 6, Russell's letter of 20 Apr. 1847 ; M. L. Hansen, *The Atlantic migration*, pp. 256–7.

[27] C.O. 384/79, 1407 Emigration, commissioners : J. Stephen, 16 Aug. 1847 ; *Further papers rel. emigration B.N.A.*, 13–15, [971], H.C. 1847–8, xlvii.

[28] Hansen, op. cit., pp. 259–60.

[29] *Second report commissioners of emigration, New York, 1848*, quoted by *Freeman's Journal*, 22 Feb. 1849. See also *Tipperary Vindicator*, 2 Aug. 1848. These outbreaks were quickly mastered everywhere except, perhaps, at New Orleans.

[30] *Nation*, 23 Feb. and 2 Mar. 1850, pp. 404 and 424.

[31] C.O. 384/83, extract from D. Colden's letter, 17 Feb. 1849. Cf. C.O. 384/88, 9004 Emigration, notice of New York emigration commissioners, 25 Sept. 1851.

[32] C.O. 384/90, 10939 Emigration, 10 Nov. 1853 ; C.O. 384/92, 449 North America, 10 Jan. 1854 ; C.O. 384/93, 4295 North America, undated, April, 1854 ; etc.

[33] See *Papers rel. emigration North American colonies*, 81–90, H.C. 1849, (593.II), xxxviii ; Maguire, op. cit., pp. 187–98.

[34] Handley, op. cit., pp. 93–121.

[35] The German Catholics, who settled in the agricultural parts of the middle west, do not seem to have encountered a similar hostility, T. Maynard, *The story of American Catholicism*, p. 277.

[36] P. H. D. Bagenal, *The American Irish and their influence on Irish politics*, pp. 37–41.

[37] There were large ' Scots–Irish ' populations in all these towns.

[38] Maguire, op. cit., pp. 424–5, 430–7. It is interesting to note that Hughes' move was opposed by many New York Catholics, as being impolitic, and to compare this division of opinion with similar manifestations in English Catholicism at this time.

[39] *New York Assembly document no. 168*, (1848), 1–5, quoted by E. Abbott, *Historical aspects of the immigration problem*, pp. 1–5.

[40] R. Ogden, *Life and letters of Edwin Lawrence Godkin*, quoted by Abbott, op. cit., pp. 515–17.

[41] The New York civic authorities reported that the Irish were much the most destitute of the immigrant groups, *New York State Assembly document no. 216*, (1845), 1–5, quoted by Abbott, op. cit., pp. 580–3.

[42] *Massachusetts Senate document no. 46*, (1848), quoted by Abbott, op. cit., pp. 584–93 ; *Congressional Globe*, 33rd congress, 2nd session, pp. 389–91, quoted by Abbott, op. cit., p. 602.

[43] In ' The Irish in New York in the early eighteen-sixties,' in *Irish Historical Studies*, vii, pp. 87–108, A. P. Man, Jr., stresses the fact that in New York the Irish immigrants had to compete with the negro workers for the more menial sorts of employment. But the projects which I am discussing here, road and canal building,

and similar public works, were largely dependent upon a supply of cheap Irish labour.

[44] J. Chickering, *Immigration into the United States,* pp. 1–2, 52–65, quoted by Abbott, op. cit., pp. 760–3.

[45] *North American Review,* lxxiv, pp. 221–32, quoted by Abbott, op. cit., pp. 288–92.

[46] T. R. Whitney, *A defence of American policy . . .* , pp. 161–85, quoted by Abbott, op. cit., pp. 819–24.

[47] *Hansard,* 3 series, c, 761–2, 24 July 1848.

[48] The actual quotations are from *Citizen* (New York), II, 5 Aug. 1855, p. 536, and 9 Feb. 1856, p. 89, quoted by Abbott, op. cit., pp. 475–7.

[49] United States v. Samuel Lumsden et al., *Bond's Reports,* I, pp. 9–27, quoted by Abbott, op. cit., p. 483. Fenianism may have brought about some interesting developments in this doctrine.

[50] *Address to the delegates of the native American convention . . . July 4th, 1845,* quoted by Abbott, op. cit., pp. 744–9.

[51] D. W. Brogan, *The American political system,* pp. 56–7.

[52] Even some 'liberals' believed that the sacred franchise should be withheld from 'this living mass of moral putrescence and pitiable ignorance', *Congressional Globe,* 29th congress, 2nd session, pp. 386–7, quoted by Abbott, op. cit., pp. 755–7.

[53] Needless to say, the fact that the political activities of Irish bosses and their underlings led them into corruption, disorders and gang warfare was, for many Americans, a further ground for condemning the Irish immigration as a whole.

[54] *24th annual report of the New York association for the improvement of the condition of the poor,* quoted by Abbott, op, cit., p. 652.

[55] *U.S. census, 1870,* quoted by Bagenal, op. cit., pp. 34–6.

[56] *U.S. statistics, etc.,* quoted by Abbott, op. cit., pp. 333–5.

[57] See Albion, op. cit., appendix xxvi.

[58] *2nd annual report of the state commissioners of emigration in Wisconsin, 1854,* quoted by Abbott, op. cit., p. 130.

[59] E.g. *Boston Evening Museum* and *Boston Pilot,* quoted by *Tipperary Vindicator,* 25 Aug. 1849.

[60] E.g. *Treatment of passengers on board 'Washington',* 6–7, H.C. 1851, (168), xl

[61] Maguire, op. cit., pp. 5–6, 214–16.

[62] This last was undoubtedly a very powerful factor, but its influence may have been exaggerated. So far as I know, the subject has never been sufficiently examined.

[63] *U.S. census,* 1860, pp. xxviii–xxxii, quoted by Abbott, op. cit., pp. 328–32.

[64] For an account of the part which the Irish played in the Comstock and Bonanza workings, see E. F. Roberts, *Ireland in America,* p. 161.

[65] Cf. J. O'Donovan, *A brief account of his countrymen.*

[66] W. N. Hancock, *Report on the supposed progressive decline of Irish prosperity,* p. 10.

[67] Maguire, op. cit., pp. 189, 217–36. See also *Boston city document, no. 66, 1849,* pp. 9–15, quoted by Abbott, op. cit., pp. 593–6.

[68] *The sanitary condition of Boston: a report from a medical commission,* pp. 63–78, 150–2, quoted by Abbott, op. cit., pp. 664–71.

[69] *New York state assembly document, no. 34, 1848,* pp. 91, 218–19, quoted by Abbott, op. cit., pp. 607–17 ; *Nation,* 6 Apr. 1850, p. 502.

[70] *2nd rep. select comm. colonisation Ire.,* 338–40, Q. 3238–65, H.C. 1847–8, (593), xvii ; Peyton, op. cit., pp. 17–23 ; *Annual report of the New York association for improving the condition of the poor,* pp. 25–33, quoted by Abbott, op. cit., pp. 17–23.

[71] Bagenal, op. cit., pp. 37–41, 56–9 ; *Citizen*, II, 27 Jan. 1855, p. 56, quoted by Abbott, op. cit., pp. 467–70.

[72] Cf. R. H. Lord, J. E. Sexton and E. T. Harrington, *History of the archdiocese of Boston*, ii, pp. 679–80.

[73] For conflicting views, see Man, op. cit. ; Maguire, op. cit., pp. 253–9 ; and *North Star* (a negro newspaper), quoted by *Tipperary Vindicator*, 17 June 1848.

[74] W. F. Lyons, *Meagher*, pp. 46–7.

[75] Ibid., pp. 42–50, 66, 68–9 ; Maguire, op. cit., pp. 545–84, 642–53.

[76] Apart from economic reasons, the anti-Catholic sentiment of the south may have played some part in this.

[77] Rev. W. C. Plunket, *The church and the census, 1865*, p. 28. For the opposite point of view, see Rev. G. Shaughnessy, *Has the immigrant kept the faith ?* Over 80% of the famine emigrants were Roman Catholics, *Statistical review of immigration, 1820–1910*, iii, p. 416, quoted by Shaughnessy, op. cit., p. 131.

[78] Cf. F. Thistletwaite, *The Great Experiment*.

[79] B. Thomas, *Migration and Economic Growth*, chap. ix.

CHAPTER VII

# THE FAMINE IN IRISH ORAL TRADITION

## ii. THE BLIGHT

[1] Cork, i. 38.

[2] Donegal, ii. 21.

[3] Leitrim, i. 30. Mayo, iv. 13.

[4] Wexford, i. 53.

[5] Westmeath, ii. 34.

[6] E.g. Meath, i. 12. Kerry, i. 31.

[7] Cork, iii. 7, 42. Donegal, vi. 3. Down, iii. 3. Kerry, ii. 41.

[8] Cork, iii. 7, 42. Kerry, i. 51. Kilkenny, i. 7–11. Meath, i. 12. Sligo, i. 20.

[9] Kerry, i. 191–2.

[10] Tipperary, p. 13

## iii. FOOD DURING THE FAMINE

[1] Mayo, ii. 41.

[2] Donegal, iv. 28.

[3] Kilkenny, i. 47.

[4] Sligo, i. 49.

[5] Cork, J.

[6] Kerry, E.

[7] Kerry, ii. 19.

[8] Clare, F.

[9] Kerry, ii. 71.

[10] Cork, ii. 10.

[11] Cork, J.

[12] Mayo, iii. 73. Mayo, H, N.

[13] Donegal, ii. 57.

[14] Donegal, iv. 21. Kerry, i. 65. Kerry, A. Mayo, ii. various.

[15] Wicklow, i. 16, 57, 69.

[16] Kerry, i. 101–2. Cork, A. Westmeath, A.

[17] Cavan, i. 7, 81. Kerry, ii. 69.

[18] Donegal, i. 22–3.

[19] Kerry, i. 182.

[20] Westmeath, i. 33.

[21] Clare, I.

[22] Mayo, D.

[23] Meath, i. 25.

[24] Meath, i. 26.

[25] Cork, i. 16–17.

[26] Kerry, ii. 98.

[27] Donegal, i. 43.

[28] Mayo, H, J, K, M, N. Tipperary, H, I.

## iv. RELIEF : FOOD AND WORK

[1] Donegal, i. 38–9.

[2] Donegal, ii. 76.

[3] Donegal, i. 39.

[4] Kerry, i. 179.

[5] Mayo, J.

[6] Galway, iii. 44.

[7] Donegal, iv. 11.

[8] Kerry, i. 150.

[9] Cork, ii. 68.

[10] Kerry, G.

[11] Armagh, i. 42. Cavan, i. 14, 95. Down, B. Leix, A. Tipperary, i. 32.

[12] Mayo, ii. 37. Mayo, iii. 84, 94.

[13] Armagh, i. 20. Clare, A. Donegal, F. Galway, v. 13–16. Kerry, ii. 57. Kildare, B. Mayo, N. Tipperary, i. 15. Wexford, i. 77.

[14] Cork, E.

[15] Mayo, N.

[16] Cavan, i. 34. Galway, v. 92. Mayo, ii. 10, 26. Westmeath, i. 40.

[17] Clare, G.
[18] Kerry, ii. 57.
[19] Kerry, ii. 92.
[20] *Dinnsheanchas na mBlascaodai.*
[21] Kerry, A. Cork, B. Cork, K.
[22] Leitrim, i. 44.
[23] Donegal, v. 35–6.
[24] Kilkenny, i. 52.
[25] Wicklow, i. 85.
[26] Donegal, i. 65.
[27] Mayo, ii. 44.
[28] Kerry, ii. 32.
[29] Galway, ii. 62.
[30] Kerry, i. 29.
[31] Donegal, A.
[32] Cork, J.
[33] Galway, iv. 43.
[34] Armagh, A.
[35] Donegal, iv. 31. Donegal, v. 26.
[36] Donegal, vi. 38.
[37] Leitrim, i. 44.
[38] Kilkenny, B.

## V. DISEASE

[1] Donegal, ii. 68.
[2] Cork, iv. 39.
[3] Donegal, i. 28, 37.
[4] Cavan, i. 25.
[5] Cork, ii. 21.
[6] Donegal, v. 15.
[7] Wicklow, i. 76.
[8] Kilkenny, B.
[9] Cork, ii. 43.
[10] Cork, i. 72. Donegal, i. 25. Leix, A.
[11] Cork, i. 72. Donegal, i. 25. Wicklow, i. 24, 25.
[12] Tipperary, i. 5, 11, 27. Kerry, i. 57.
[13] Galway, iv. 28.
[14] Donegal, vi. 13.
[15] Donegal, i. 8, 28.
[16] Westmeath, i. 79.
[17] Westmeath, i. 61.
[18] Donegal, i. 25.

[19] Kilkenny, i. 19.
[20] Wicklow, i. 76.
[21] Donegal, vi. 78.
[22] Donegal, vi. 21.
[23] Kerry, i. 106.
[24] Cork, ii. 57.
[25] Donegal, ii. 67.
[26] Tipperary, i. 24.

## vi.  DEATH AND BURIAL

[1] Kerry, G.
[2] Kerry, i. 105.
[3] Kerry, i. 161.
[4] Cavan, i. 23.
[5] Donegal, ii. 61.
[6] Donegal, vi. 23.
[7] Kerry, i. 112.
[8] Kerry, G.
[9] Kerry, i. 165.
[10] Mayo, ii. 42.
[11] Mayo, iii. 64.
[12] Cork, iv. 61.
[13] Sligo, i. 26.
[14] Clare, i. 37.
[15] Clare, i. 35.
[16] Galway, v. 7.
[17] Cavan, i. 54.
[18] Armagh, i. 3.
[19] Donegal, i. 27.
[20] Donegal, iii. 32.
[21] Kilkenny, i. 18.
[22] Galway, v. 9.
[23] Galway, v. 34.
[24] Down, i. 40.
[25] Tipperary, E.
[26] Offaly, A.
[27] Wicklow, i. 39, 64.
[28] Kerry, i. 109.
[29] Monaghan, B.
[30] Galway, A.
[31] Cork, F, K.
[32] Galway, C.

[33] Kerry, F, C.
[34] Clare, i. 39.
[35] Cavan, i. 30.
[36] Cork, iv. 41.
[37] Cork, i.
[38] Donegal, vi. 76.
[39] Galway, v. 22, 54. Mayo, ii. 65.
[40] Galway, v. 45.
[41] Mayo, iv. 4.
[42] Kerry, G.
[43] Mayo, i. 3.
[44] Mayo, iii. 63, iv. 4. Cork A.

### vii.   CHANGES IN THE IRISH COUNTRYSIDE

[1] Wexford, i. 78.
[2] Mayo, ii. 30.
[3] Cork, ii. 22.
[4] Donegal, v. 39.
[5] Armagh, i. 25.
[6] Tipperary, E.
[7] Wicklow, i. 23.
[8] Donegal, v. 41.
[9] Galway, v. 36.
[10] Donegal, i. 17.
[11] Wicklow, i. 28.
[12] Galway, ii. 15.
[13] Wicklow, i. 44.
[14] Down, C.
[15] Mayo, K.
[16] Donegal, vi. 52.
[17] Tipperary, A.
[18] Clare, Q.
[19] Donegal, iv. 9. Sligo, i. 31.
[20] Kerry, B.
[21] Clare, G.
[22] Kerry, ii. 21.
[23] Donegal, i. 16.
[24] Ibid, vi. 9.
[25] Kerry, ii. 6.

# Select Bibliography

## SYNOPSIS

## I.—MANUSCRIPTS

Dublin.

*National Library of Ireland :*

    Gavan Duffy papers.

    Fintan Lalor papers.

    Larcom papers.

    Monteagle papers.

    Smith O'Brien papers.

    O'Connell papers.

    John O'Donovan papers.

    Repeal Association papers.

*Public Record Office :*

    Board of works papers.

    Relief commission papers 1845–7.

    Society of Friends relief of distress papers.

*Irish State Paper Office :*
  Distress papers 1846–7.
  Fever hospital returns 1845–6.
  Outrage papers 1848–9.
  Government correspondence books.
  Registered papers 1845–51.

*Royal Irish Academy :*
  Correspondence book of the Irish Confederation (MS 23 H 41).
  Gavan Duffy papers (MS 12 P. 15).

London.
*British Museum :*
  Aberdeen papers (Add. MS 43151).
  Peel papers (Add. MS 40445–40540).

*Public Record Office :*
  Colonial Office papers.
  Foreign Office papers (F.O. 27/804–6, 43/38–42, 44/1–2).
  Minute book of the colonial and emigration commissioners (H.O. 122).
  Russell papers.

Paris.
*Ministry of Foreign Affairs :*
  Correspondance commerciale 1845–8.
  Correspondance 1847–8.

Oxford.
*Bodleian Library :*
  Clarendon papers.

*Manuscripts in private ownership :*
  Graham papers at Netherby, Longtown, Cumberland. [Microfilm
    of papers in the National Library of Ireland.]

## II.—PARLIAMENTARY PAPERS

*Report on the state of the poor in Ireland.* H.C. 1830 (667), vii.

*First report of the commissioners of public instruction in Ireland.* H.C. 1835
(45), xxxiii.

*First report of H.M. commission of inquiry into the condition of the poorer classes in Ireland.* App. B.C. 1835 (369), xxxii.

*Poor inquiry (Ireland) : Report on the state of the Irish poor in Great Britain.* H.C. 1836 (40), xxxiv.

*Third report from the select committee appointed to inquire into the state of agriculture.* H.C. 1836 (465), viii.

*Poor Inquiry (Ireland).* H.C. 1836 (35), xxx ; H.C. 1836 (369), xxxii.

*Report of the select committee on county cess (Ireland), with the minutes of evidences, appendices and index.* H.C. 1836 (527), xii.

*Letter from N. W. Senior on the third report of the commission of inquiry into the condition of the poor in Ireland.* H.C. 1837 (26), li.

Nicholls, G., *Report . . . on poor laws, Ireland.* H.C. 1837 (69), 1837, li. Second report H.C. 1837 (104), xxxviii.

*Annual report of the Canadian agent general for emigration.* H.C. 1837 (132), xlii.

*Second report of the commissioners appointed to consider and recommend a general system of railways for Ireland.* H.C. 1837–8 (145), xxxv.

*Report from the select committee on foundation schools and education in Ireland.* H.C. 1837–8 (701), vii.

*Report of the Lords' select committee appointed to inquire into the state of Ireland.* H.C. 1839 (468), xii.

*Minutes of evidence taken before the select committee appointed to inquire into the state of Ireland.* Pt. III. H.C. 1839 (468), xii.

*Reports of the poor law commissioners.* H.C. 1840 (253), xvii.

*Reports of the poor law commissioners.* H.C. 1841 (327), xi.

*Reports of the poor law commissioners.* H.C. 1842 (389), (399), xix.

*Returns relating to the importation and exportation of corn, foreign and colonial ; annual and weekly average price of wheat and other grain ; quantities imported ; amount of duty received, etc.* H.C. 1843 (177), liii.

*Reports of the poor law commissioners.* H.C. 1843 (468), (491), xxi.

*Report of the commissioners appointed to take the census of Ireland for the year 1841.* H.C. 1843 (504), xxiv.

*Report from the select committee of the house of lords on the state of the lunatic poor in Ireland.* H.C. 1843 (625), x.

*Reports of the poor law commissioners.* H.C. 1844 (560), (589), xix.

*Report from Her Majesty's commissioners of inquiry into the state of the law and practice in respect to the occupation of land in Ireland.* H.C. 1845 (605), xix.

*Evidence taken before Her Majesty's commissioners of inquiry into the state of the law and practice in respect to the occupation of land in Ireland ; together with appendix and plans.* Pts. i–iii. H.C. 1845 (606), (616), (657), xix, xx, xxi.

*Copy of the report of Dr. Playfair and Mr. Lindley on the present state of the Irish potato crop, and on the prospect of approaching scarcity.* H.C. 1846 (28), xxvii.

*Report from the select committee of the house of lords on the laws relating to the destitute poor and the operation of medical charities in Ireland.* H.C. 1846, (694), xi.

*Reports of the poor law commissioners.* H.C. 1846 (704), (745), xix.

*General reports from the colonial land and emigration commissioners.* H.C. 1846 (706), xxiv.

*Correspondence explanatory of the measures adopted by Her Majesty's government for the relief of distress arising from the failure of the potato crop in Ireland.* H.C. 1846 (735), xxxvii.

*Correspondence from July 1846 to January 1847, relating to the measures adopted for the relief of distress in Ireland.* H.C. 1847 (761), li.

*Report from the lords select committee on colonization from Ireland.* H.C. 1847 (737), vi ; (737 II), vi.

*Correspondence from July 1846 to January 1847, relating to the relief of distress in Ireland.* Board of works series. H.C. 1847 (764), i.

*Papers relative to emigration to the British colonies in North America.* H.C. 1847 (771), xxxix.

*Correspondence from January to March 1847, relating to the measures adopted for the relief of distress in Ireland.* Board of works series (part II). H.C. 1847 (797), lii.

*Papers relative to emigration—part I, British provinces in North America.* H.C. 1847–8 (50), xlvii.

*Reports from the commissioners to the colonial office respecting emigration to the British North American colonies.* H.C. 1847–8 (in 50), xlvii.

*Papers relative to emigration to the Australian colonies.* H.C. 1847–8 (50, II), xlvii.

*Returns of agricultural produce in Ireland, in the year 1847.* H.C. 1847–8 (923), lvii.

*Returns of agricultural produce in Ireland, in the year 1847 : part 2, stock.* H.C. 1847–8 (1000), lvii.

*Returns of agricultural produce in Ireland in the year 1847.* H.C. 1847–8 (923), vii.

*First report from the lords select committee on colonization from Ireland.* H.C. 1847–8 (415), xvii.

*First report from the select committee on poor laws (Ireland).* H.C. 1849 (58), xv.

*An account of the number of live cattle exported from Ireland to Great Britain, in each year from 1846 to 1849, both inclusive.* H.C. 1850 (423), lii.

*Receipts and expenditure of county infirmaries in Ireland for the years 1847, 1848 and 1849 ; also the number of cases relieved in each of the same years.* H.C. 1850 (497), li.

*An account (since the union) of all sums of money advanced on loan for public works or other purposes in Ireland.* H.C. 1850 (718), liv.

*Copies or extracts of despatches relative to emigration to the North American colonies.* H.C. 1851 (348), xl.

*Report from the select committee on the passenger acts.* H.C. 1851 (632), xix.

*Abstract of the census of Ireland, taken in 1841 and 1851, arranged according to the counties . . .* H.C. 1851 (673), l.

*The census of Ireland for the year 1851, part 2: returns of agricultural produce in 1851.* H.C. 1852–3 (15–89), xciii.

*First report from the select committee on emigrant ships.* H.C. 1854 (163), xiii.


III.—PARLIAMENTARY DEBATES

*Hansard,* third series.


IV.—NEWSPAPERS AND PERIODICALS

*Advocate* (Dublin).
*Cork Constitution.*
*Cork Examiner.*
*Dublin Evening Mail.*
*Dublin Evening Post.*
*Dublin Quarterly Journal of Medical Science.*
*Economist.*
*Edinburgh Review.*
*Evening Packet* (Dublin).
*Freeman's Journal* (Dublin).
*Illustrated London News.*
*Limerick Chronicle.*
*Moniteur Universel.*
*Morning Herald* (London).
*Nation* (Dublin).
*Northern Whig* (Belfast).
*Pilot* (Dublin).
*The Times* (London).
*Tipperary Vindicator.*
*Tribune* (Dublin).
*United Irishman* (Dublin).
*Waterford Mail.*

## V.—PUBLISHED MEMOIRS, DOCUMENTS AND CORRESPONDENCE

Ashley, Evelyn. — *The life and correspondence of Henry John Temple, Viscount Palmerston.* 2 vols. London 1879.

British Association. — *British Association for the relief of the extreme distress in Ireland and Scotland: Report with correspondence of the agents, tables, etc. and a list of subscribers.* London 1849.

Dasent, Arthur Irwin. — *John Thadeus Delane, editor of ' The Times,' his life and correspondence.* 2 vols. London 1908

Daunt, W. J. O'Neill — *A life spent for Ireland; being selections from the journals of the late W. J. O'Neill Daunt, edited by his daughter.* London 1896.

Davis, Thomas. — *Essays, literary and historical.* Ed. D. J. O'Donoghue. Dundalk 1914.

Doheny, Michael. — *The felon's track, or history of the attempted outbreaks in Ireland embracing the leading events in the Irish struggle from the year 1843 to the close of 1848.* Dublin 1914.

Duffy, Sir Charles Gavan. — *My life in two hemispheres.* 2 vols. London 1898.

Doughty, Sir Arthur J. (ed.) — *The Elgin–Grey papers 1846–52.* 4 vols. Ottawa 1937.

Fitzpatrick, W. J. (ed.) — *Correspondence of Daniel O'Connell, the Liberator.* 2 vols. London 1888.

Fogarty, L. (ed.) — *James Fintan Lalor, patriot and political essayist.* Dublin 1947.

Gooch, G. P. (ed.). — *The later correspondence of Lord John Russell, 1840–1878.* 2 vols. London 1925.

Greville, Charles Cavendish Fulke. — *The Greville memoirs (second part). A journal of the reign of Queen Victoria from 1837 to 1852.* 3 vols. London 1885.

Knaplund, P. — *Letters from Lord Sydenham to Lord John Russell.* London 1931.

Laughton, John Knox. — *Memoirs of the life and correspondence of Henry Reeve, C.B., D.C.I.* 2 vols. London 1898.

Lucas, Sir C. (ed.) — *Lord Durham's report on the affairs of British North America.* 3 vols. Oxford 1912.

Maxwell, Sir Herbert E. — *The life and letters of George William, fourth earl of Clarendon.* 2 vols. London 1913.

Mitchel, John.

*Jail journal, or five years in British prisons.*
ed. Arthur Griffith. Dublin 1913.

Moran, P. F.

*Reverend James Maher : letters with a memoir.*
Dublin 1877.

Normanby, Constantine
Henry, Marquis of

*A year of revolution, from a journal kept in
Paris in 1848.* 2 vols. London 1857.

O'Brien, R. Barry.

*Thomas Drummond . . . life and letters.*
London 1889.

O'Reilly, Bernard.

*John MacHale, archbishop of Tuam, his life,
times and correspondence.* 2 vols. New York
1890.

Parker, Charles Stuart.

*Life and letters of Sir James Graham, second
baronet of Netherby.* 2 vols. London 1907.
*Sir Robert Peel from his private correspondence*
(vol. i), *from his private papers* (vols. ii, iii).
London (i) 1891, (ii, iii) 1899.

Society of Friends.

*Transactions of the central relief committee of
the Society of Friends during the famine in
Ireland in 1846 and 1847.* Dublin 1852.

State of New York.

*State of New York in assembly : report of
the assembly of 1847 to investigate frauds upon
emigrants.* New York 1848.

Torrens, W. M.

*Memoirs of the Rt. Hon. William 2nd Viscount
Melbourne.* 2 vols. London 1878.

Walrond, T.

*Letters and journals of James Bruce, eighth earl
of Elgin.* London 1872.

Ward, W.

*Aubrey de Vere : a memoir.* London 1904.

## VI.—OTHER CONTEMPORARY PRINTED SOURCES

Butt, Isaac.

*A voice for Ireland : the famine in the land.*
Dublin 1847.

Caird, James.

*The plantation scheme.* Edinburgh 1850.

Flood, A.

*Poor laws.* Dublin 1830.

Foster, T. C.

*Letters on the condition of the people of Ireland.*
London 1847.

Godley, J. R.

*Letters from America.* Dublin 1844.
*Observations on an Irish poor law.* Dublin
1847.

Grey, Henry George,
3rd Earl.

*The colonial policy of Lord John Russell's
administration.* 2 vols. London 1853.

| Hancock, W. N. | *The tenant-right of Ulster . . .* Dublin 1845. *On the condition of the Irish labourer.* Dublin 1848. |
| Kennedy, J. Pitt. | *Digest of evidence taken before Her Majesty's commissioners of inquiry into the state of the law and practice in respect to the occupation of land in Ireland.* Dublin 1847. |
| Lindsay, H. | *The present state of the Irish Grand jury law.* Armagh 1837. |
| McGee, T. D'Arcy. | *A history of the Irish settlers in North America . . .* Boston 1852. |
| Murray, R. | *Ireland, its present condition and future prospects.* Dublin 1847. |
| O'Brien, W. Smith. | *Reproductive employment : a series of letters to the landed proprietors of Ireland.* Dublin 1847. |
| Senior, N. W. | *Journals, essays and conversations relating to Ireland.* London 1868. |
| Trevelyan, C. E. | *The Irish crisis.* London 1848. |
| Whately, R. | *Introductory lectures on political economy.* London 1855. |

## VII.—Secondary authorities

| Adams, W. F. | *Ireland and Irish emigration to the new world from 1815 to the famine.* London 1932. Yale 1932. |
| Bell, Herbert C. F. | *Lord Palmerston.* 2 vols. London 1936. |
| Broderick, John F. | *The Holy See and the Irish movement for the repeal of the union with England 1829–1847.* Rome 1951. |
| Burn, W. F. | ' Free trade in land : an aspect of the Irish question '. In *Transactions of the Royal Historical Society.* 4th, xviii. |
| Cameron, C. A. | *History of the Royal College of Surgeons in Ireland and of the Irish schools of medicine. . . .* Dublin 1916. |
| Clark, George Kitson. | ' The repeal of the corn laws and the politics of the forties '. In *Economic History Review,* second series, iv. |
| Clarke, R. | ' The relations between O'Connell and the Young Irelanders '. In *Irish Historical Studies,* iii. |

Connell, K. H.      *The population of Ireland 1750–1845.* Oxford 1950.
'The colonisation of waste land in Ireland, 1780–1845'. In *Economic History Review*, second series, iii.

Connolly, James.      *Labour in Irish history.* Dublin 1910.

Crolly, Rev. G.      *The life of the Most Rev. Dr. Crolly, Archbishop of Armagh. . . .* Dublin 1851.

Davin, N. F.      *The Irishmen in Canada.* Toronto 1877.

Davidson, W. D.      'The history of the potato and its progress in Ireland'. In *Department of Agriculture Journal*, xxxiv.

Dalargy, J. H.      'Buailteachas'. In *Bealoideas*, xiii.

De Courcy, H., and
  Shea, J. G.      *A history of the catholic church in the United States.* New York 1896.

De Vere, Aubrey.      *Recollections.* London 1897.

Duffy, Sir Charles Gavan.      *Young Ireland, a fragment of Irish history 1840–1845.* Dublin 1884 (Irish people's edition).
*The league of north and south. An episode in Irish history, 1830–1854.* London 1886.
*Young Ireland. Part 2 of four years of Irish history, 1845–1849.* Dublin 1887 (Irish people's edition).
*Thomas Davis: the memoirs of an Irish patriot 1840–46.* London 1890.

Edwards, R. Dudley.      'The contribution of Young Ireland to the development of the Irish national idea'. In *Féilscríbhín Tórna.* Cork 1947.

Erickson, Arvel B.      *The public career of Sir James Graham.* Oxford 1952.

Evans, E. Estyn.      *Irish heritage.* Dundalk 1942.

Gill, C.      *The rise of the Irish linen industry.* Oxford 1925.

Green, E. R. R.      *The Lagan valley 1800–1850.* London 1949.

Gwynn, Denis.      *Young Ireland and 1848.* Cork 1949.

Handley, J. E.      *The Irish in Scotland, 1790–1845.* Cork 1943.
*The Irish in modern Scotland.* Cork 1947.

Hansen, M. L.      *The Atlantic migration, 1607–1860.* Harvard 1940.

Herring, I. J.      'Ulster roads on the eve of the railway age'. In *Irish Historical Studies*, ii.

Hitchens, F. H.      *The colonial land and emigration commission.* Philadelphia 1931.

Hogan, J. F.      *The Irish in Australia.* London 1887.

Hovell, Mark.      *The chartist movement.* Manchester 1918.

Kennedy, David.      'Captain Pitt Kennedy's plan for Irish agriculture, 1835–45'. In *Bulletin of the Irish Committee of Historical Sciences.* No. 32.

Kerr, Barbara M.      'Irish seasonal migration to Great Britain, 1800–38'. In *Irish Historical Studies,* iii.

Lawson, James A.      'On the agricultural statistics of Ireland'. In *Journal of the Statistical Society of Ireland,* iii.

MacDonagh, Oliver.      'Emigration and the state, 1833–55 : an essay in administrative history'. In *Transactions of the Royal Historical Society,* 5th, v.

     'The Irish catholic clergy and emigration during the great famine'. In *Irish Historical Studies,* v.

     'The regulation of the emigrant traffic from the United Kingdom, 1842–55'. In *Irish Historical Studies,* ix.

McDowell, R. B.      *Public opinion and government policy in Ireland, 1801–1846.* London 1952.

Madgwick, R. B.      *Immigration into Eastern Australia, 1788–1851.* London 1937.

Maguire, John Francis.      *The Irish in America.* London 1868.

Monaghan, J. J.      'The rise and fall of the Belfast cotton industry'. In *Irish Historical Studies,* iii.

Moody, T. W.      *Thomas Davis, 1814–45.* Dublin 1945.

Morehouse, F.      'The Irish migration of the "forties"'. In *American Historical Review,* xxxiii.

Morley, John.      *Life of Richard Cobden.* 2 vols. London 1881.

Morrell, W. P.      *British colonial policy in the age of Peel and Russell.* Oxford 1930.

Nowlan, K. B.      'Writings in connection with Thomas Davis and the Young Ireland centenary, 1945'. In *Irish Historical Studies,* v.

O'Brien, W. P.      *The great famine in Ireland and a retrospect of the fifty years, 1845–95.* London 1896.

O'Donovan, John.      *The economic history of live stock in Ireland.* Cork 1940.

O'Neill, T. P.
'The scientific investigation of the failure of the potato crop in Ireland, 1845–6'. In *Irish Historical Studies*, v.
'Food problems during the great Irish famine'. In *Journal of the Royal Society of Antiquaries of Ireland*, lxxxii.
'The Society of Friends and the Great Famine'. In *Studies*, xxxix.

O'Rourke, J.
*The history of the great Irish famine of 1847, with notices of earlier famines.* Dublin 1875.

O'Sullivan, T. F.
*The Young Irelanders.* Tralee 1945.

O'Sullivan, W.
*The economic history of Cork city.* Cork 1937.

Salaman, Redcliffe N.
*The history and social influence of the potato.* Cambridge 1949.

Simington, R. C.
'Tithe applotment books of 1834 : agricultural returns, produce and prices'. In *Department of Agriculture Journal*, xxxviii.

Taylor, William Cooke.
*Life and times of Sir Robert Peel.* 4 vols. London 1846–51.

Thistletwaite, F.
*The great experiment.* Cambridge 1956.

Thomas, B.
*Migration and economic growth : a study of Great Britain and the Atlantic economy.* Cambridge 1954.

Walsh, William J.
'The board of charitable donations and bequests'. In *Irish Ecclesiastical Record*, xvi.

## VIII.—Works of reference

*Dictionary of national biography.* London 1908–

Lewis, S. *A topographical dictionary of Ireland.* 2 vols. London 1839.

*Thom's Irish almanac and official directory,* 1844–

# Bibliography to the New Edition

What follows is a selection of work on the Great Famine and on its economic and social context, mainly published since the mid-1950s. For further bibliographies see Mokyr (1983b), Ó Gráda (1989), and Bourke (1993). I have also appended a list of unpublished dissertations containing famine-related material.

Akenson, Donald H. (1993). *The Irish Diaspora*, Belfast: Institute of Irish Studies.

Black, R.D.C. (1957). 'Irish History and the Great Famine', *Threshold*, 1(2), 51–9.

Black, R.D.C. (1960). *Economic Thought & the Irish Question, 1817–1870*, Cambridge: Cambridge University Press.

Bourke, P.M.A. (1965). 'The Agricultural Statistics of the 1841 Census of Ireland: a Critical Review', *Economic History Review*, 18(2), 376–91.

Bourke, Austin (1993). *The Visitation of God ? The Potato and the Irish Famine*, Dublin: Lilliput.

Boyle, Phelim P. and C. Ó Gráda (1986). 'Fertility Trends, Excess Mortality, and the Great Irish Famine', *Demography*, 23, 543–62.

Campbell, Stephen J. (1994). *The Great Irish Famine: Words and Images from the Famine Museum, Strokestown Park, County Roscommon*, Strokestown: Famine Museum.

Clarkson, L.A. and E. Margaret Crawford (1988). 'Dietary Directions: A Topographical Survey of Irish Diet, 1836' in P. Roebuck & R. Mitchison (eds.), *Economy & Society in Scotland and Ireland 1500–1939*, Edinburgh: John Donald, 171–92.

Connell, Kenneth (1967). *Irish Peasant Society*, Oxford: Oxford University Press.

Cousens, S.H. (1963). 'The Regional Variation in Mortality During the Great Irish Famine', *Proceedings of the Royal Irish Academy*, 63C, 127–49.

Crawford, E.M. (1981). 'Indian Meal and Pellagra in Nineteenth-century Ireland', in J.M. Goldstrom and L.A. Clarkson (eds.), *Irish Population, Economy and Society*, Oxford: Oxford University Press, 113–33.

Crawford, E.M. (1984). 'Dearth, Diet and Disease in Ireland: A Case Study of Nutritional Deficiency', *Medical History*, 28, 151–61.

Crawford, E.M. (ed.) (1989). *Famine, The Irish Experience, 900–1900: Subsistence Crises & Famine in Ireland*, Edinburgh: Donald.

Crotty, Raymond D. (1966). *Irish Agricultural Production*, Cork: Cork UP.

Cullen, L.M. (1968b). 'Irish History Without the Potato', *Past and Present*, no. 40, 72–83.

Cullen, L.M. (1981). *The Emergence of Modern Ireland*, London: Batsford.

Culloty, A.T. (1986). *Ballydesmond/Baile Deasmhumhan: A Rural Parish in its Historical Setting*, Dublin: Elo Press, 129–51.

Daly M.E. (1986). *The Great Famine in Ireland*, Dundalk: Dublin Historical Association.

Devine, T.M. (1988). *The Great Highland Famine*, Edinburgh: John Donald.

Devine, T.M. (1994). 'Why Scotland Did Not Starve', in Connolly, Houston, and Morris, *Conflict, Identity and Economic Development*.

Dickson, David (1989). 'The Gap in Famines: A Useful Myth?' in Crawford, *Famine*, 96–111.

Donnelly, J.S. (1975). *The Land & the People of Nineteenth-Century Cork*, London: Routledge & Kegan Paul.

Donnelly, J.S. (1988). 'The Great Famine, 1845–52', in Vaughan, *A New History of Ireland*, vol. 5, 272–371.

Donnelly, J.S. (1993). 'The Famine and its Interpreters, Old and New', *History Ireland*, vol. 1(3).

Dwyer, Gerard and C. Lindsay (1984). 'Robert Giffen and the Irish Potato', *American Economic Review*, 74, 188–92.

Fitzpatrick, David (1984). *Irish Emigration 1820–1914*, Dublin: Irish Economic and Social History Society.

Fitzpatrick, D. (1986). 'Marriage since the Famine', in Art Cosgrove (ed.), *Marriage in Ireland*, Dublin: College Press.

Fitzpatrick, D. (1992). 'Famine, Entitlements and Seduction in Ireland, 1846–1851', mimeo.

Freeman, T.W. (1956). *Pre-Famine Ireland: A Study in Human Geography*, Manchester University Press.

Froggatt, Peter (1989). 'The Response of the Medical Profession to the Great famine', in Crawford, *Famine*, 134–56.

Garner, Edward (1986). *To Die by Inches: The Famine in North-East Cork*, Fermoy: Éigse Books.

Goldstrom, Max & L.A. Clarkson (eds.) (1981). *Irish Population, Economy and Society: Essays in Memory of K.H. Connell*, Oxford: Oxford University Press.

Grant, James (1990). 'The Great Famine and the Poor Law in the Province of Ulster: the Rate-in-Aid Issue of 1849', *Irish Historical Studies*, vol. XXVII, 30–47.

Gray, Peter (1994). 'Potatoes and Providence: British Government Responses to the Great Famine', *Bullán*, vol. 1(1), 75–90.

Gray, Peter (1993). '*Punch* and the Famine', *History Ireland*, vol. 1(2) (1993).

Hannigan, Ken (1991). 'Wicklow in the Famine Years', *Wicklow Historical Society*, vol. 1(5), 37–56.

Hannigan, Ken (1993). 'Eye-witness Accounts of the Famine in Wicklow', *Wicklow Historical Society*, vol. 1(6), 11–26.

Hayes, Samuel (1797). *Essays in Answer to All the Queries on the Culture of Potatoes*, Dublin: Sleator.

Hernon, J.M. (1987). 'A Victorian Cromwell: Sir Charles Trevelyan, the Famine and the Age of Improvement', *Éire-Ireland*, vol. XXII, 15–29.

Hickey, Patrick (1993). 'Famine, Mortality, and Emigration: A Profile of Six Parishes in the Poor Law Union of Skibbereen, 1846–7', in P. O'Flanagan and C. Buttimer (eds). *Cork: History and Society*, Dublin: Geography Publications, 873–918.

Hoffman, Elizabeth and Joel Mokyr (1983). 'Peasants, Poverty, and Potatoes: Transactions Costs in Prefamine Ireland', in G. Saxonhouse and G. Wright (eds), *Technique, Spirit & Form in the Making of the Modern Economy: Essays in Honour of William N. Parker*, Greenwich, Connecticut: Greenwood Press.

Hoppen, K.T. (1989). *Ireland Since 1800: Conflict & Conformity*, London: Longman.

Hynes, E. (1978). 'The Great Hunger and Irish Catholicism', *Societas*, vol. VIII, 137–56.

Irish University Press, British Parliamentary Papers, 'Famine' Series (eight volumes), Shannon, Ireland: Irish University Press.

Johnson, James H. (1988). 'The Distribution of Irish Emigration in the Decades Before the Great Famine', *Irish Geography*, vol. 21, 78–87.

Kennedy, Liam (1983). 'Studies in Irish Econometric History', *Irish Historical Studies*, vol. XXIII, no. 91, 193–213.

Kierse, Seán (1984). *The Famine Years in the Parish of Killaloe 1845–1851*, Killaloe: Boru Books.

Kinealy, Christine (1989). 'The Poor Law during the Great Famine: an Administration in Crisis', in Crawford, *Famine*, 157–75.

Kinealy, Christine (1994). *This Great Calamity: the Great Irish Famine, 1845–52*, Gill & Macmillan.

López Linage, Javier (1991). *De Papa a Patata: La diffusión espanola del tubérculo andino*, Madrid: Ministerio de Agricultura, Pesca y Alimentacion.

Lynch, Patrick and John Vaizey (1960). *Guinness's Brewery in the Irish Economy, 1759–1876*, Cambridge: Cambridge University Press.

McArthur, W.A. (1944). 'Famines in Britain and Ireland', *Journal of the British Archaeological Association*, 3rd ser., vol. 9, 66–71.

McGregor, Patrick (1984). 'The Impact of the Blight on the Pre-Famine Rural Economy of Ireland', *Economic and Social Review*, vol. 15(4), 289–303.

McGregor, Patrick (1989). 'Demographic Pressure and the Irish Famine: Malthus After Mokyr', *Land Economics*, vol. 65, 228–38.

McKay, Robert (1961). *An Anthology of the Potato*, Dublin: Figgis.

Mackay, W. Donald (1990). *Flight from Famine: The Coming of the Irish to Toronto*, London and Toronto: McClelland & Stewart.

Mac Síthigh, Tomás (1984). *Paróiste an Fheirtéaraigh: Stairsheanchas an Cheantair i dTréimhse an Ghorta Mhóir*, Dublin: Coiscéim.

Martineau, Harriet (1854). *Letters from Ireland*, London: Chapman.

Mokyr, Joel (1980a). 'The Deadly Fungus: An Econometric Examination of the Short-term Demographic Impact of the Irish Famine', *Research in Population Economics*, vol. 2, 237–77.

Mokyr, J. (1980b). 'Industrialization and Poverty in Ireland and the Netherlands: Some Notes Toward a Comparative Case Study', *Journal of Interdisciplinary History*, vol. X(3), 429–59.

Mokyr, J. (1983a). 'Uncertainty and the Pre-famine Economy', in Devine and Dickson, *Ireland and Scotland*, 89–101.

Mokyr, J. (1983b, rev. edition 1985). *Why Ireland Starved: A Quantitative and Analytical History of the Irish Economy, 1800–1850*, London: Allen & Unwin.

Mokyr, J. and C. Ó Gráda (1982). 'Emigration and Poverty in Prefamine Ireland', *Explorations in Economic History*, vol. 19, 360–84.

Mokyr, J. and C. Ó Gráda (1988). 'Poor and Getting Poorer ? Irish Living Standards Before the Famine', *Economic History Review*, vol. XLI, 209–35.

Morash, Chris (1989). *The Hungry Voice: The Poetry of the Irish Famine*, Dublin: Irish Academic Press.

Nicholson, Asenath (1851). *Annals of the Famine in Ireland in 1847, 1848, and 1849*, New York: E. French.

O'Brien, Gerard (1986). 'Workhouse Management in Pre-famine Ireland', *Proceedings of the Royal Irish Academy*, vol. 86C, 113–34.

O'Brien, W.P. (1896). *The Great Famine in Ireland*, London: Downey.

Ó Ciosáin, Micheál (1988). *Cnoc an Fhómhair*, Maynooth: An Sagart.

Ó Cróinín, Donncha A. (1982–3). 'Eachtra ar an nDroch-Shaol', *Éigse*, vol. 19, p. 173.

Ó Duigneáin, P. (1984). *North Leitrim in Famine Times*, Manorhamilton: Drumlin Distributors.

O'Gallagher, Marianne (1984). *Grosse Ile: Gateway to Canada, 1832–1937*, Ste Foy, Québec.

Ó Gráda, C. (1984). 'Malthus and the Pre-Famine Economy', in A.E. Murphy (ed.), *Economists and the Irish Economy From the Eighteenth Century To the Present Day*, Dublin: IAP, 75–95.

Ó Gráda, C. (1988). *Ireland Before and After the Famine: Explorations in Economic History 1800–1930*, Manchester: Manchester University Press [rev. edition 1993].

Ó Gráda, C. (1989). *The Great Irish Famine*, London: Macmillan.

Ó Gráda, C. (1991a). 'The Heights of Clonmel Prisoners, 1845–9: Some Dietary Implications', *Irish Economic and Social History*, vol. 19, 24–33.

Ó Gráda, C. (1991b). 'An Early Irish Reaction to Malthus', *History of Political Economy*, vol. 23(1), 93–4.

Ó Gráda, C. (1992). '"Making History" in Ireland in the 1940s and 1950s: The Saga of *The Great Famine*', *The Irish Review*, no. 12, 87–107.

Ó Gráda, C. (1994). *Ireland: A New Economic History, 1780–1939*, Oxford: OUP.

Ó Mainín, Micheál (1971). 'Amhrán an Ghorta', in Micheál Ó Ciosáin (ed.), *Céad Bliain*, Baile an Fhirtéaraigh: Muintir Phiarais, 190–3.

O'Neill, Áine (1990). 'Peig Sayers and Need Foods: a Note on the Famine Food Referred to in the Peig Sayers Material in the Archives of the Department of Irish Folklore', *Sinsear: the Folklore Journal*, No. 6, 75–82.

O'Neill, Thomas P. (1950). 'The Society of Friends and the Great Famine', *Studies*, vol. 39, 203–13.

O'Neill, Timothy P. (1973). 'Fever & Public Health in Pre-Famine Ireland', *Royal Society of Antiquaries of Ireland Journal*, vol. 103, 1–34.

O'Rourke, Kevin (1991). 'Did the Great Famine Matter?', *Journal of Economic History*, vol. 51, 1–22.

Rees, Jim (1994). *A Farewell to Famine*, Arklow: Arklow Enterprise Centre.

Scrope, George Poulett (1847). *Reply to a Speech of the Archbishop of Dublin*, London: Ridgeway.

Senior, Nassau W. (1868). *Journals, Essays and Conversations Relating to Ireland*, London: Longmans, Green.

Solar, Peter M. (1979). 'The Agricultural Trade Statistics in the Irish Railway Commissioners' Report', *Irish Economic and Social History*, vol. VI, 24–40.

Solar, P.M. (1984). 'Why Ireland Starved: A Critical Review of the Econometric Results', *Irish Economic and Social History*, vol. 10, 107–15.

Solar, P.M. (1989). 'The Singularity of the Great Irish Famine', in Crawford, *Famine*, 112–31.

Solar, P.M. and M. Goossens (1991). 'Belgian and Irish Agriculture in 1840–5', in B.M.S. Campbell & M. Overton (eds), *Land, Labour & Livestock: Historical Studies in European Agricultural Productivity*, Manchester: Manchester University Press, 364–84.

Staehle, Hans (1950–1). 'Statistical Notes on the Economic History of Irish Agriculture, 1847–1913', *Journal of the Statistical and Social Inquiry Society of Ireland*, vol. 18, 444–71.

Trollope, Anthony (1849–50). 'Six Letters to the Examiner', reprinted as Lance O. Tingay (ed.) (1987). *The Irish Famine*, London: Silverbridge Press.

Vaughan, W.E. (1988). *A New History of Ireland: Ireland Under the Union, 1801–70*, Oxford: Oxford University Press.

Vincent, Joan (1992). 'A Political Orchestration of the Irish Famine: County Fermanagh, May 1847', in Marilyn Silverman and P.H. Gulliver (eds), *Approaching the Past: Historical Anthropology through Irish Case Studies*, New York: Columbia University Press, 75–98.

Vincent, Joan (forthcoming). *The Culture and Politics of the Irish Famine: Fermanagh, 1836–1856.*

Walker, Linus H. (1978). *One Man's Famine: One Man's Tribute to Bro. Paul James O'Connor*, Galway: Host Litho Printers.

Watkins, Susan C. and Jane Mencken (1985). 'Famines in Historical Perspective', *Population & Development Review*, vol. 11, 647–75.

Woodham-Smith, Cecil (1962). *The Great Hunger*, London: Hamilton.

Woods, C.J. (1987). 'American Travellers in Ireland Before and During the Great Famine: A Case of Culture-Shock', in Wolfgang Zach and Heinz Kosok (eds). *Literary Interrelations: Ireland, England and the New World*, Tubingen: Narr.


UNPUBLISHED DISSERTATIONS

Bourke, P.M.A. (1965). 'The Potato, Blight, Weather and the Irish Famine' (Ph.D. NUI/UCC).

Eiricksson, Andres (1992). 'Crime and Popular Protest in Co. Clare, 1815–1852' (Ph.D. TCD).

Foley, Kieran (1987). 'The Killarney Poor Law Guardians and the Famine, 1845–52' (M.A. NUI/UCD).

Grant, James (1986). 'The Great Famine in the Province of Ulster – The Mechanism of Relief' (Ph.D. QUB).

Gray, Peter H. (1992). 'British Politics and the Irish Land Question, 1843–1850', Cambridge.

Hickey, Patrick (1980). 'A Study of Four Peninsular Parishes in Cork, 1796–1855' (Ph.D. NUI/UCC).

Holt, Jon H. (1967). 'The Quakers in the Great Irish Famine' (M.Litt., TCD).

Kinealy, Christine (1984). 'The Administration of the Poor Law in Ireland, 1838–62' (Ph.D., TCD).

Lee, J.J. (1965). 'An Economic History of Irish Railways, 1836–1853' (M.A. NUI/UCD).

McCabe, Desmond (1991). 'Law, Conflict and Social Change: County Mayo 1820–1845' (Ph.D. NUI/UCD).

McCarthy, R.B. (1982). 'The Estates of Trinity College, Dublin, in the Nineteenth Century' (Ph.D. TCD).

Montague, R.J. (1976). 'Relief and Reconstruction: Public Policy in Ireland, 1845–9' (D.Phil. Oxford).

O'Dwyer, Peter (1968), 'John Spratt O. Carm., 1796–1871' (Ph.D. Pontifical University, Rome).

O'Neill, Timothy P. (1965). 'The Famine of 1822' (M.A. NUI/UCD).

O'Neill, Timothy P. (1971). 'The State, Poverty and Distress in Ireland, 1815–45' (Ph.D. NUI/UCD).

O'Neill, Tomas P. (1946). 'The Organisation and Administration of Relief During the Great Famine' (M.A. NUI/UCD).

O'Rourke, Kevin (1989). 'Agricultural Change and Rural Depopulation: Ireland, 1845–1876' (Ph.D. Harvard University).

Solar, Peter M. (1987). 'Growth and Distribution in Irish Agriculture Before the Famine' (Ph.D. Stanford University).

# Index of Names